Essentials of Specific Learning Disability Identification

Essentials of Psychological Assessment Series
Series Editors, Alan S. Kaufman and Nadeen L. Kaufman

Essentials

of Specific Learning

Disability Identification

Second Edition

Edited by

Vincent C. Alfonso

Dawn P. Flanagan

WILEY

This edition first published 2018
© 2018 John Wiley and Sons, Inc.

Edition History
John Wiley and Sons, Inc. (1e, 2010)

Registered Office
John Wiley & Sons, Inc., 111 River Street, Hoboken, NJ 07030, USA

Editorial Office
111 River Street, Hoboken, NJ 07030, USA

For details of our global editorial offices, customer services, and more information about Wiley products visit us at www.wiley.com.

Wiley also publishes its books in a variety of electronic formats and by print-on-demand. Some content that appears in standard print versions of this book may not be available in other formats.

Library of Congress Cataloging-in-Publication Data

Names: Alfonso, Vincent C., editor. | Flanagan, Dawn P., editor.
Title: Essentials of specific learning disability identification / edited by
  Vincent C. Alfonso, Dawn P. Flanagan.
Description: Second edition. | Hoboken, NJ : John Wiley & Sons, 2018. |
  Includes index. |
Identifiers: LCCN 2017053859 (print) | LCCN 2017061536 (ebook) | ISBN
  9781119313854 (pdf) | ISBN 9781119313861 (epub) | ISBN 9781119313847 (pbk.)
Subjects: LCSH: Learning disabilities. | Learning disabled children.
Classification: LCC LC4704 (ebook) | LCC LC4704 .E77 2018 (print) | DDC
  371.9/043–dc23
LC record available at https://lccn.loc.gov/2017053859

Cover image: © Greg Kuchik/Getty Images

Cover design by Wiley

Set in 10.5/13 pt AGaramondPro-Regular by Thomson Digital, Noida, India

Printed in the United States of America

SKY10024346_012121

CONTENTS

FOREWORD

According to the calculations of the National Center for Educational Statistics at the US Department of Education (USDOE), and as it has been for decades, the most frequently occurring disability among school-age individuals in the United States is a specific learning disability (SLD). In fact, it accounts for nearly half of all disabilities in the school-age population. It may well then come as a surprise to those who do not work in the field that in spite of the presence of a common definition of SLD, one that has essentially remained unchanged since written into federal law in 1975, there remains very little agreement about the best model or method of identifying students with SLD. Beginning with the first version of the federal law requiring the public schools of the United States to provide a free and appropriate public education to students with disabilities (P.L. 94-142, the Education for All Handicapped Children Act), the disagreements over the best approach to identification of an SLD have grown. Prior to 2004, the federal regulations for implementation of the various versions of Individuals with Disabilities Education Act (IDEA) required, as a necessary but insufficient condition (except in special circumstances), the presence of a severe discrepancy between aptitude and achievement for a diagnosis of SLD. The 2004 Individuals with Disabilities Education Improvement Act's (IDEIA) accompanying regulations (all 307 small-print *Federal Register* pages of them), which retained the definition of SLD essentially as written in the 1975 law, dropped this requirement, and instead allows schools to use one or a combination of three basic approaches to SLD identification: the severe discrepancy criteria of prior regulations, a process based on the response of a student to evidence-based (aka science) interventions for learning problems (known popularly as the RTI approach), or any other approach the state or local education agency determines to be a scientifically or research-based approach to determination of an SLD.

The vagaries and ambiguities of the federal regulations and the pressure on schools to do what is new, and to do so quickly, led to chaos in the field and fed considerably to a polemic debate about how to determine best an SLD. As if this were not enough controversy, note that the regulations concerning the determination of SLD in school-age individuals (basically K–12) apply only to public schools and private schools that receive federal monies. Colleges and universities, the Social Security Administration, state departments of rehabilitation, the medical community, the courts, and other agencies that are involved in SLD identification and the provision of services and funding for these individuals can, and most do, apply different methods and have different rules for identification of an SLD. What is adopted then as the best method of diagnosis in the K–12 school systems often will be found unacceptable to other agencies, frustrating individuals who carry out such a diagnosis, the students' parents, and the agencies themselves. This has led to considerable litigation over who is eligible for which services and where as well as who is best to provide them. The vagaries of the federal regulations and the potential for extensive litigation in the absence of clear guidance from the USDOE are the primary reasons I so often refer to IDEIA as the "education lawyers' welfare act of 2004."

The issues of accurate and appropriate models from which to identify individuals with SLD sorely need attention from the academic community of scholars in a format that enables academics and practitioners to understand the many and diverse models being promoted as best practice. The first edition of *Essentials of Specific Learning Disability Identification* made a practical foray into this arena, and it did so succinctly, without sacrifice of a clear understanding of each model, and represented educational, medical, psychometric, and neuropsychological models in its various chapters. The second edition continues in this vein, following the successful blueprint of the first edition and bringing back leaders in research and in practice to update their works and add information about special considerations in this field.

The opening chapters focus on descriptive efforts of the manifestations of SLD in the academically critical areas of reading, writing, math, oral expression, and listening, though some of the authors emphasize identification and some intervention in these chapters as well. Some argue differences in neuropsychological organization of the brain, others argue specific deficits, and still others continue to call on developmental delay as the essence of an SLD. There is less recognition in certain chapters than one might suppose that SLD is a very heterogeneous group of disorders and that the underlying mechanism is not at all likely to be the same for everyone, although clearly most authors recognize this reality. Nonverbal learning disabilities, a concept rejected in the official diagnostic nomenclature of psychiatry and little recognized in federal legislation but heavily researched, is also covered and covered well by a leading scholar in school and child neuropsychology.

The second part of the work emphasizes models and methods of SLD identification, and herein we also find divergent views. After reading the volume, it is nothing less than striking the number of seemingly sound but incompatible models that are presented, especially knowing how many other models are in existence across the various state education agencies—not to mention the many other governmental agencies and programs using wholly different approaches. Every model presented in the latter half of this work has strengths in the approaches recommended for SLD identification, and each set of authors presents its case well. Nevertheless, the approaches, several of which are highly similar, will identify different children. Some are also just fundamentally incompatible; for example, although most emphasize the absolute necessity for a disorder in one or more of the basic processes underlying learning, at least one dismisses this aspect of the SLD definition as unnecessary even to assess or consider.

As in the first edition, Fletcher and Miciak lead off the chapters focused on diagnostic methods and models with a clear presentation of the RTI model as he and his colleagues perceive of it as best implemented. His well-reasoned approach has much to recommend it, but unfortunately many states have adopted a far more radical RTI-only approach, which, as Fletcher laudably notes, is not just poor practice but inconsistent with the federal regulations. Burns and colleagues follow up on RTI approaches in another coherent presentation of a controversial area. Subsequently, other extensively researched models described in the first edition are presented again here but are updated to reflect a decade of research and are presented generally in clearer terms. For example, Naglieri and Feifer give us a very different model from RTI, one that is more theory-driven than any of the other models but that provides good empirical support for the approach and practical advice on its implementation. Alston-Abel and her colleague treat us to a very accomplished work that takes on the complex issues of diagnosis and treatment of several types of SLD in the face of comorbidities, an issue dealt with poorly by most existing models, particularly RTI-only models. Their case for evidence-based models and ones that emphasize early identification and intervention is well made, along with their case for educating all children better. Flanagan and her colleagues attempt, and accomplish well, an integration of methods that also requires an integration of conflicting theories as well as practice models that may seem incompatible on the surface. Cheramie and colleagues provide a case study illustration of their preferred method, which appears in several prior chapters.

The final part of the second edition deals with special issues encountered by all who engage in the evaluation of students suspected as having an SLD. For example, differentiating cultural and linguistic differences from disabilities in the context of SLD determination is directly addressed with examples. Although this is often talked about, few give us this kind of concrete guidance to avoiding such diagnostic mistakes based on culture and language. We could all benefit still from reading the works of E. Paul Torrance from the 1970s on "differences not deficits" in such a context. Differential diagnosis, as in differentiating SLD from other disorders that may look like SLD in the absence of a comprehensive assessment, is addressed in a highly welcomed addition to the work.

This work presents a strong reflection of the state of the field, updated and with some entirely new views compared to the first edition, and it does a great service by putting theories of the development and etiology of SLD, commentary on interventions, and the dominant models of SLD identification between common covers. The editors have once again done a superb job in selecting authors to represent the viewpoints given and to elaborate with sufficient specificity the identification models, in most cases to the point at which they can be put into place after reading this book carefully. The greatest problem readers will face will be one of deciding which model(s) to follow, because all are appealing. There are authors of chapters in this work with whom I have had scholarly exchanges, and with whom I vehemently disagree on some issues but with whom I find myself in agreement on others. So I must count myself among those who will experience great dissonance in adopting and recommending a specific model of diagnosis for all children suspected of SLD to others based on the models proffered herein. We have much to learn from the disagreements in this work, and it is indeed such disagreements and lack of compatibility of models and methods on which science thrives. I suspect that as our science moves forward, we will continue to find, as we have since the mid-2000s, that all of these models have merit and utility for accurate and appropriate identification of individuals with SLD but not for the same individuals. Individuals with SLD make up a heterogeneous group, and we truly need different models for their accurate identification (aka different strokes for different folks) that are objective and evidence-based, such as provided in this work. Now, if we can just make them all part of a common, coherent system and stop the search for the one answer to the diagnosis of SLD for all students and the one teaching model that educates them all effectively—that will be our greatest progress!

Cecil R. Reynolds
Austin, Texas

SERIES PREFACE

I n the Essentials of Psychological Assessment series, we have attempted to provide the reader with books that will deliver key practical information in the most efficient and accessible style. The series features instruments in a variety of domains, such as cognition, personality, education, and neuropsychology, as well as special topics, such as identification of SLD. Wherever feasible, visual shortcuts to highlight key points are used, alongside systematic, step-by-step guidelines. Theory and research are continually woven into the fabric of each book, but always to enhance clinical inference, never to sidetrack or overwhelm. This latest volume to the Essentials series covers a wide range of topics related to SLD identification in a manner that is readily accessible to practitioners.

IDEA 2004 and its attendant regulations provided our field with an opportunity to focus on the academic progress of all students, including those with SLD. The last decade was marked by a departure from a wait-to-fail ability-achievement discrepancy model to a response to intervention (RTI) model for SLD identification. In adopting the latter method, the field was encouraged by RTI proponents to give up cognitive and neuropsychological tests and, thus, ignore more than 30 years of empirical research that has culminated in substantial evidence for the biological bases of learning disorders in reading, math, written language, and oral language. When RTI is applied in isolation, it fails to identify individual differences in cognitive abilities and neuropsychological processes and ignores the fact that students with SLD have different needs and learning profiles than students with undifferentiated low achievement. In recognition of this fact, an alternative research approach to SLD identification, known as the pattern of strengths and weakness (PSW) approach, is being used with greater frequency. The PSW approach considers the relations among cognitive abilities, neuropsychological processes, and academic performance in SLD identification. Most (but not all) of the distinguished contributors to this edited book believe that without cognitive and neuropsychological testing, little can be known about the cognitive capabilities, processing strengths and weaknesses, nature of responses, and neurobiological correlates of students who fail to respond to evidence-based instruction and intervention.

This second edition, edited by the esteemed Vincent C. Alfonso and Dawn P. Flanagan, once again offers practitioners state-of-the-art information on SLDs. Part I of this book includes definitions and manifestations of SLD in reading, math, writing, and oral language. A new chapter was added in Part I that covers the latest research on nonverbal learning disabilities. Part II provides practitioners with a variety of research-based methods and models for identifying SLD in the schools and in the private sector. This edition was expanded to include more information on RTI and PSW methods as well as neuropsychological approaches to SLD identification. The overarching theme of this edition of *Essentials of Specific Learning Disabilities Identification* is that PSW and neuropsychological approaches may be used within the context of an RTI service delivery model, with the goal of expanding (rather than limiting) the methods and data sources that are available to practitioners. Part III of this book focuses on special considerations in SLD identification. New content in this section includes a chapter on differential diagnosis of SLD versus other difficulties as well as a chapter that enhances our knowledge of word reading skills based on the latest reading research. It is our belief, and the belief of the editors of this book, that when practitioners use the approaches described here in an informed and systematic way, they will yield information about a student's learning difficulties and educational needs that will be of value to all, but most especially, to the student with SLD.

Alan S. Kaufman, PhD, and Nadeen L. Kaufman, EdD,
Series Editors
Yale University School of Medicine

ACKNOWLEDGMENTS

We thank Tisha Rossi, executive editor, Purvi Patel, project editor, Susan Geraghty, copyeditor, and Audrey Koh, production editor from John Wiley & Sons, for their encouragement and support of this book and for their assistance throughout the many phases of production. We acknowledge Katherine Palmer and Virginia Cooper for assisting us through every phase of this book and for often dropping everything to respond to our requests in a timely and complete manner. We also extend a heartfelt thank-you to the contributing authors for their professionalism, scholarship, and pleasant and cooperative working style. It was a great pleasure to work with such an esteemed group of researchers and scholars! Finally, we wish to thank Alan and Nadeen Kaufman for their support, guidance, and friendship. They are not only the editors of the Essentials of Psychological Assessment series, but also true leaders in the field.

Part One

DEFINITIONS AND MANIFESTATIONS OF SPECIFIC LEARNING DISABILITIES

One

OVERVIEW OF SPECIFIC LEARNING DISABILITIES

Marlene Sotelo-Dynega
Dawn P. Flanagan
Vincent C. Alfonso

T he purpose of this chapter is to provide a brief overview of the definitions and classification systems of and methods for identification of specific learning disabilities (SLDs). Historically, children who did not perform as expected academically were evaluated and often identified as having a learning disability (LD) (Kavale & Forness, 2006). The number of children in the United States identified as having LD has "increased by more than 300 percent" since the enactment of the Education for All Handicapped Children Act of 1975 (P.L. 94-142; Cortiella & Horowitz, 2014). This landmark legislation included criteria for the identification of exceptional learners, including children with LD, and mandated that they receive a free and appropriate public education (FAPE). Each reauthorization of P.L. 94-142 maintained its original intent, including the most recent reauthorization, the Individuals with Disabilities Education Improvement Act of 2004 (P.L. 108-446; hereafter referred to as *IDEA 2004*). Rapid Reference 1.1 highlights the most salient changes to this legislation through the present day.

The US Department of Education (USDOE) has collected data on students who have qualified for special education services since 1975. The most current data show that over 2.3 million school-age children are classified as SLD. This figure represents nearly 5% of the approximate 50 million students currently

Essentials of Specific Learning Disability Identification, Second Edition.
Edited by Vincent C. Alfonso and Dawn P. Flanagan
© 2018 John Wiley & Sons, Inc. Published 2018 by John Wiley & Sons, Inc.

≡ Rapid Reference 1.1

Salient Changes in Special Education Law from 1975 to 2004

1975	Education for All Handicapped Children Act (EHA) P.L. 94-142	Guaranteed school-age (5–21 years) children with disabilities the right to a FAPE.
1986	EHA P.L. 99-457	Extended the purpose of EHA to include children from birth to 5 years: • FAPE was mandated for children ages 3–21 years. • States were encouraged to develop early-intervention programs for children with disabilities from birth to 2 years.
1990	EHA renamed the Individuals with Disabilities Education Act (IDEA) P.L. 101-476	The term *handicapped child* was replaced with *child with a disability*. Autism and traumatic brain injury classifications were added. Transition services for children with disabilities were mandated by age 16 years. It defined assistive technology devices and services. It required that the child with a disability be included in the general education environment to the maximum extent possible.
1997	IDEA P.L. 105-17	Extended the least-restrictive environment (LRE) to ensure that *all* students would have access to the general curriculum. Schools are required to consider the inclusion of assistive technology devices and services in the individualized education plans of all students. Orientation and mobility services were added to the list of related services for children who need instruction in navigating within and to and from their school environment.
2004	IDEA renamed the Individuals with Disabilities Education Improvement Act (IDEIA)[1] P.L. 108-446	Statute is aligned with the No Child Left Behind Act (NCLB) of 2001. Focus of statute is on doing what works and increasing achievement expectations for children with disabilities. Changes are made to the evaluation procedures used to identify specific LDs.

[1] *IDEA* (rather than *IDEIA*) is used most often to refer to the 2004 reauthorization and, therefore, will be used throughout this book.

≡ Rapid Reference 1.2

....

Students Ages 6–21 Years Served Under IDEA 2004

IDEA Disability Category	Percentage of All Disabilities[1]	Percentage of Total School Enrollment[2]
Specific Learning Disability	38.82	3.50
Speech or Language Impairment	17.26	1.56
Other Health Impairments	14.99	1.35
Autism	9.10	.82
Intellectual Disability	6.92	0.62
Emotional Disturbance	5.73	0.52
Developmental Delay (Ages 3–9 years only)	2.47	0.22
Multiple Disabilities	2.07	0.19
Hearing Impairments	1.11	0.10
Orthopedic Impairments	.68	0.06
Traumatic Brain Injury	0.42	0.04
Visual Impairments	0.41	0.04
Deaf-Blindness	0.02	0.00

[1] US Department of Education (2016a).
[2] US Department of Education (2016b).

enrolled in the nation's schools (Kena et al., 2015). Furthermore, of all school-age students who have been classified with an educationally disabling condition, 39% are classified as SLD (USDOE, 2016a). Rapid Reference 1.2 shows that none of the other 12 IDEA 2004 disability categories approximates the prevalence rate of SLD in the population, a trend that has been consistent since 1980 (USDOE, 2016b).

A BRIEF HISTORY OF THE DEFINITION OF LEARNING DISABILITY

Definitions of LD date back to the mid- to late 1800s within the fields of neurology, psychology, and education (Mather & Goldstein, 2008). The earliest recorded definitions of LD were developed by clinicians based on their observations of individuals who experienced considerable difficulties with the acquisition of basic academic skills, despite their average or above-average general intelligence, or those who lost their ability to perform specific tasks after a brain injury that resulted from either a head trauma or stroke (Kaufman, 2008). Given that clinicians at that time did not have the necessary technology or psychometrically defensible instrumentation to test their hypotheses about brain-based LD, the medically focused study of LD stagnated, leading to the development of socially constructed, educationally focused definitions that *presumed* an underlying neurological etiology (Hale & Fiorello, 2004; Kaufman, 2008; Lyon et al., 2001).

In 1963, Samuel Kirk addressed a group of educators and parents at the Exploration Into the Problems of the Perceptually Handicapped Child conference in Chicago, Illinois. The purposes of the conference were to (1) gather information from leading professionals from diverse fields about the problems of children who had perceptually based learning difficulties and (2) develop a national organization that would lobby to secure services for these children. At this conference, Kirk presented a paper entitled "Learning Disabilities" that was based on his recently published book, *Educating Exceptional Children* (Kirk, 1962). In this paper, Kirk defined LD as

> a retardation, disorder, or delayed development in one or more of the processes of speech, language, reading, writing, arithmetic, or other school subjects resulting from a psychological handicap caused by a possible cerebral dysfunction and/or emotional or behavioral disturbances. It is not the result of mental retardation, sensory deprivation, or cultural and instructional factors. (p. 263)

Not only did the conference participants accept Kirk's term *LD* and corresponding definition but also they formed an organization that is now known as the Learning Disabilities Association of America (LDA). The LDA continues to influence the "frameworks for legislation, theories, diagnostic procedures, educational practices, research and training models" as they pertain to identifying and educating individuals with LD (LDA, n.d.a, ¶ 2).

Kirk's conceptualization of LD influenced other organizations' definitions of LD, including the Council for Exceptional Children (CEC), as well as federal legislation (e.g., P.L. 94-142). In addition, 11 different definitions of LD in use between 1982 and 1989 contained aspects of Kirk's 1962 definition. Therefore, it is not surprising that a comprehensive review of these definitions revealed more agreement than disagreement about the construct of LD (Hammill, 1990). Interestingly, none of the definitions strongly influenced developments in LD identification, mainly because they tended to focus on conceptual rather than operational elements and focused more on exclusionary rather than inclusionary criteria. Rapid Reference 1.3 illustrates the salient features of the most common definitions of LD that were proposed by national and international organizations and LD researchers, beginning with Kirk's 1962 definition. The majority of definitions depict LD as a neurologically based disorder or a disorder in psychological processing that causes learning problems and manifests as academic skill weaknesses. In addition, most definitions indicate that LD may co-occur with other disabilities.

Although the definitions of LD included in Rapid Reference 1.3 vary in terms of their inclusion of certain features (e.g., average or better intelligence, evident across the life span), the most widely used definition is the one included in IDEA 2004 (Cortiella, 2009). Unlike other definitions, the IDEA 2004 definition refers to a *specific* LD, implying that the disability or disorder affects specific academic skills or domains. According to IDEA 2004, SLD is defined as follows:

> The term "specific learning disability" means a disorder in one or more of the basic psychological processes involved in understanding or in using language, spoken or written, which may manifest itself in the imperfect ability to listen, think, speak, read, spell, or do mathematical calculations. Such a term includes such conditions as perceptual disabilities, brain injury, minimal brain dysfunction, dyslexia, and developmental aphasia. Such a term does not include a learning problem that is primarily the result of visual, hearing, or motor disabilities; of mental retardation; of emotional disturbance; or of environmental, cultural, or economic disadvantage. (IDEA 2004, §602.30, Definitions)

Because definitions of LD do not explicitly guide how a condition is identified or diagnosed, classification systems of LD were developed. Three of the most frequently used classification systems for LD are described next.

CLASSIFICATION SYSTEMS FOR LD

"Classification criteria are the rules that are applied to determine if individuals are eligible for a particular diagnosis" (Reschly, Hosp, & Schmied, 2003, p. 2). Although the evaluation of LD in school-age children is guided by the mandate of IDEA 2004 and its attendant regulations, diagnostic criteria for LD are also included in the *Diagnostic and Statistical Manual of Mental Disorders* (5th ed.) (*DSM-5*; American Psychiatric Association, 2013), and the *International Classification of Diseases* (*ICD-10*; World Health Organization, 2016). Rapid Reference 1.4 includes the type of LDs

C A U T I O N

Because the three major classification systems use somewhat vague and ambiguous terms, it is difficult to identify SLD reliably and validly. Thus, multiple data sources and data-gathering methods must be used to ensure that children are diagnosed accurately.

Salient Features of Learning Disability Definitions

Source	Ability-Achievement Discrepancy	Average or Above-Average Intelligence	Neurological Basis	Disorder in a Psychological Process	Evident Across the Life Span	Listening and Speaking	Academic Problems	Conceptual Problems	Nonacademic, Language, or Conceptual Disorders as LD	Potential for Multiple Disabilities
Samuel Kirk (1962)	—	✓	✓	✓	✓	✓	✓	—	✓	✓
Barbara Bateman (1965)	✓	—	✓	✓	—	—	✓	—	—	✓
National Advisory Committee on Handicapped Children (1968)	—	—	✓	✓	—	✓	✓	✓	—	✓
Northwestern University (Kass & Myklebust, 1969)	✓	—	—	✓	✓	✓	✓	—	✓	✓
Council for Exceptional Children, Division for Children with Learning Disabilities (1967)	—	✓	✓	✓	—	✓	—	—	—	—
Joseph Wepman and colleagues (1975)	—	—	—	✓	—		✓	—	—	—
Education for All Handicapped Children Act (1975)	✓	—	—	✓	—	✓	✓	—	—	✓

Source								
US Office of Education (1977)	—	—	—	√	√	√	√	√
National Joint Committee on Learning Disabilities (1981, 1982, 1991, 1998)	—	—	√	√	√	√	√	√
Learning Disabilities Association of America (n.d.b)	√	√	—	√	√	√	√	—
Interagency Committee on Learning Disabilities (1987)	—	—	√	√	√	√	√	√
Individuals with Disabilities Education Act (1986, 1990, 1997, 2004)	—	√	√	√	√	√	√	√
Kavale, Spaulding, and Beam (2009)	√	√	—	√	√	√	—	√
Flanagan and colleagues (2002, 2006, 2007, 2011, 2013)	√	√	√	√	√	√	—	√

Note: This table was adapted from Hammill (1990). A recent review of these definitions has shown that none of the definitions that were originally presented have been updated. Currently, although the NCLD continues to use the definition that was published in 1990, they recently published a 52-page document titled "The State of Learning Disabilities" (Cortiella & Horowitz, 2014) summarizing the current research available regarding the nature of LD across the life span. Furthermore, some additional definitions that were published after the Hammill article was published were added to this table.

Rapid Reference 1.4

Three Frequently Used Diagnostic Classification Systems for Learning Disability

Classification System	Types of Learning Disorder	Examples of Classification Criteria[1]

Diagnostic and Statistical Manual of Mental Disorders (5th ed.) (DSM-5, 2013)	Specific learning disorder:
	• With impairment in reading
	• With impairment in written expression
	• With impairment in mathematics
		Specific learning disorder:
		
		A. Difficulties learning and using academic skills, as indicated by the presence of at least one of the following … that have persisted for at least 6 months, despite the provision of interventions that target those difficulties:
		
		  1. Inaccurate or slow and effortful word reading
		  2. Difficulty understanding the meaning of what is read
		  3. Difficulties with spelling
		  4. Difficulties with written expression
		  5. Difficulties mastering number sense, number facts, or calculation
		  6. Difficulties with mathematical reasoning
		
		B. The affected academic skills are substantially and quantifiably below those expected for the individual's chronological age and cause significant interference with academic or occupational performance … as confirmed by individually administered standardized achievement measures and comprehensive clinical assessment.

C. The learning difficulties begin during school-age years but may not become fully manifest until the demands for those affected academic skills exceed the individual's limited capacities.

D. The learning difficulties are not better accounted for by intellectual disabilities, uncorrected visual or auditory acuity, other mental or neurological disorders, psychosocial adversity, lack of proficiency in the language of academic instruction, or inadequate educational instruction.

International Classification of Diseases (ICD-10, 2016)	Specific reading disorder: • Specific spelling disorder • Specific disorder of arithmetical skills • Mixed disorder of scholastic skills • Other developmental disorders of scholastic skills • Developmental disorder of scholastic skills, unspecified	Specific reading disorder: • Specific reading disorder is a specific and significant impairment in the development of reading skills that is not solely accounted for by mental age, visual acuity problems, or inadequate schooling. • Reading comprehension skill, reading word recognition, oral reading skill, and performance of tasks requiring reading may all be affected. • Spelling difficulties are frequently associated with specific reading disorder and commonly remain into adolescence even after some progress in reading has been made. • Specific developmental disorders of reading are commonly preceded by a history of disorders in speech or language development. • Associated emotional and behavioral disturbances are common during the school-age period. • This diagnosis includes backward reading, developmental dyslexia, and specific reading retardation. • This diagnosis excludes alexia, dyslexia NOS, and reading difficulties secondary to emotional distress.

Classification System	Types of Learning Disorder	Examples of Classification Criteria[1]
Individuals with Disabilities Education Improvement Act (IDEA 2004)	Specific learning disability in: • Oral expression • Listening comprehension • Written expression • Basic reading skill • Reading fluency • Reading comprehension • Mathematics calculation • Mathematics problem-solving	Specific learning disability: 1. A disorder in one or more of the basic psychological processes. 2. Includes conditions such as perceptual disabilities, brain injury, minimal brain dysfunction, dyslexia, and developmental aphasia. 3. Learning difficulties must not be primarily the result of • A visual, hearing, or motor disability • Mental retardation • Emotional disturbance • Cultural factors • Environmental or economic disadvantage • Limited English proficiency

[1] For the *ICD-10* diagnostic classification system, there are specific criteria for each disorder that are listed in the second column of this Rapid Reference. Criteria for only one of these disorders are included in the third column to serve as an example.

and classification criteria for LD in each system. Noteworthy is the fact that all three systems use somewhat vague and ambiguous terms, which interfere significantly with the efforts of practitioners to identify LD reliably and validly (Kavale & Forness, 2000, 2006).

Despite the existence of various classification systems, students ages 3 to 21 years who experience learning difficulties in school are most typically evaluated according to IDEA 2004 specifications (IDEA 2004, §614) to determine if they qualify for special education services. Because the classification category of SLD as described in the IDEA statute includes imprecise terms, the USDOE published the federal regulations (34 CFR, Part 300) with the intent of clarifying the statute and providing guidance to state educational agencies (SEAs) as they worked to develop their own regulations. The guidelines provided by the 2006 federal regulations were more detailed in their specifications of *how* an SLD should be identified.

METHODS OF SLD IDENTIFICATION AND THE 2006 FEDERAL REGULATIONS

Although the definition of SLD has remained virtually the same for the past 30 years, the methodology used to identify SLD changed with the last revision of IDEA 2004. According to the 2006 federal regulations (34 CFR §300.307–309), a state must adopt criteria for determining that a child has SLD; the criteria (1) must not require the use of a severe discrepancy between intellectual ability and achievement; (2) must permit the use of a process based on a child's response to scientific, research-based interventions; and (3) may permit the use of other alternative research-based procedures for determining whether a child has SLD. Many controversies have ensued since the publication of the three options for SLD identification. The controversies have been written about extensively because they pertain to the exact meaning of the guidelines, the specifications of a comprehensive evaluation, the implications of using Response to Intervention (RTI) as the sole method for SLD identification, and the lack of legal knowledge among decision makers and, therefore, will not be repeated here (see Chapters 7 and 8 in this book and refer to Gresham, Restori, & Cook, 2008; Kavale, Kauffman, Bachmeier, & LeFever, 2008; Reschly et al., 2003; Reynolds & Shaywitz, 2009a, 2009b; Zirkel & Thomas, 2010, for a summary). The remainder of this chapter focuses on clarifying the three options for SLD identification, because these three options are currently being implemented across states (see Rapid Reference 1.5).

≋ Rapid Reference 1.5

Methods for Identifying SLD Across States

- Coomer (2015) surveyed the 50 state education agencies to determine which of the three options included in the 2006 federal regulations was selected for SLD identification.
- All 50 states have adopted the federal definition of SLD.
- All 50 states "allow" RTI as a method to identify SLD.
- Eleven states solely use RTI to identify SLD.
- Thirty-nine states also allow the discrepancy model or PSW approach.

Note: For state-by-state details regarding SLD eligibility determination, see Coomer (2015; Table 3, pp. 30–31).
Source: Coomer (2015).

Ability-Achievement Discrepancy

A discrepancy between intellectual ability and academic achievement continues, in one form or another, to be central to many SLD identification approaches because it assists in operationally defining *unexpected underachievement* (e.g., Kavale & Flanagan, 2007; Kavale & Forness, 1995; Lyon et al., 2001; Wiederholt, 1974; Zirkel & Thomas, 2010). Despite being a laudable attempt at an empirically based method of SLD identification, the traditional ability-achievement (or IQ-achievement) discrepancy method was fraught with problems (e.g., Aaron, 1997; Ceci, 1990, 1996; Siegel, 1999; Stanovich, 1988; Sternberg & Grigorenko, 2002; Stuebing et al., 2002), many of which are identified in Rapid Reference 1.6. The failure of the ability-achievement discrepancy method to identify SLD reliably and validly was summarized well by Ysseldyke (2005), who stated,

> Professional associations, advocacy groups, and government agencies have formed task forces and task forces on the task forces to study identification of students with LD. We have had mega-analyses of meta-analyses and syntheses of syntheses. Nearly all groups have reached the same conclusion: There is little empirical support for test-based discrepancy models in identification of students as LD. (p. 125)

Thus, the fact that states could no longer require the use of a severe discrepancy between intellectual ability and achievement (IDEA 2004) was viewed by many as a welcomed change to the law. The void left by the elimination of the discrepancy

≡ Rapid Reference 1.6

Salient Problems with the Ability-Achievement Discrepancy Method

- Fails to adequately differentiate between students with LD from students who are low achievers
- Based on the erroneous assumption that IQ is a near-perfect predictor of achievement and is synonymous with an individual's potential
- Applied inconsistently across states, districts, and schools, rendering the diagnosis arbitrary and capricious
- A discrepancy between ability and achievement may be statistically significant but not clinically relevant.
- Is a wait-to-fail method because discrepancies between ability and achievement typically are not evident until the child has reached the third or fourth grade
- Does not identify the area of processing deficit
- Leads to overidentification of minority students
- Does not inform intervention

mandate was filled by a method that allowed states to use a process based on a child's RTI to assist in SLD identification.

Response to Intervention (RTI)

The concept of RTI grew out of concerns about how SLD is identified. For example, traditional methods of SLD identification, mainly ability-achievement discrepancy, were applied inconsistently across states and often led to misidentification of students as well as overidentification of minority students (e.g., Bradley, Danielson, & Hallahan, 2002; Learning Disabilities Roundtable, 2005; President's Commission on Excellence in Special Education, 2002). Such difficulties with traditional methods led to a "paradigm shift" (Reschly, 2004) that was based on the concept of *treatment validity*, "whereby it is possible 'to simultaneously inform, foster, and document

DON'T FORGET

Although RTI may be permitted under IDEA 2004, the driving force behind promoting RTI was found in the No Child Left Behind (NCLB; P.L. 107-110, 2001) legislation. In December 2015, the Every Student Succeeds Act (ESSA) replaced NCLB and removed all mention of RTI.

the necessity for and effectiveness of special treatment'" (Fuchs & Fuchs, 1998, p. 207).

At the most general level, RTI is part of a multitiered system of support (MTSS) approach to the early identification of students with academic or behavioral difficulties. For the purpose of this chapter, we will focus on RTI for academic difficulties only. The RTI process begins with the provision of quality instruction for all students in the general education classroom, along with universal screening to identify students who are at risk for academic failure, primarily in the area of reading (Tier 1). Students who are at risk for reading failure—that is, those who have not benefitted from the instruction provided to all students in the classroom—are then given scientifically based interventions, usually following a standard treatment protocol (Tier 2). If a student does not respond as expected to the intervention provided at Tier 2, he or she may be identified as a *nonresponder* and selected to receive additional and more-intensive interventions in an attempt to increase his or her rate of learning. When one type of intervention does not appear to result in gains for the student, a new intervention is provided until the desired response is achieved.

The inclusion of RTI in the law as an allowable option for SLD identification has created perhaps the most controversy since IDEA was reauthorized in 2004. This is because, in districts that follow an RTI-*only* approach, students who repeatedly fail to demonstrate an adequate response to increasingly intensive interventions are deemed to have SLD *by default*. Such an approach does not appear to be in compliance with the regulations. For example, according to the regulations, states must (1) use a variety of assessment tools and strategies to gather relevant functional, developmental, and academic information (34 CFR §300.304 (b)(1)); (2) not use any single measure or assessment as the sole criterion for determining whether a child has a disability (34 CFR §300.304(b)(2)); (3) use technically sound instruments that may assess the relative contribution of cognitive and behavioral factors, in addition to physical or developmental factors (34 CFR §300.304(b)(3)); (4) assess the child in all areas related to the suspected disability (34 CFR §300.304(c)(4)); (5) ensure that the evaluation is sufficiently comprehensive to identify all of the child's special education and related service needs (34 CFR §300.304(c)(6)); and (6) ensure that assessment tools and strategies provide relevant information that directly assists persons in determining the needs of the child (34 CFR §300.304(c)(7)).

Although the use of RTI as a stand-alone method for SLD identification is inconsistent with the intent of the law, this type of service delivery model has been an influential force in the schools in recent years, particularly with respect to shaping Tier 1 and Tier 2 assessments for intervention in the general education setting. The emphasis in an RTI model on ensuring that students are benefitting from empirically based instruction and verifying their response to instruction, via a systematic collection of data, has elevated screening and progress monitoring procedures to new heights and has led many to embrace this type of service delivery model for the purposes of prevention and remediation.

In a landmark study, Balu and colleagues (2015) studied the impact of RTI across 13 states and 20,000 students. Considering that one of the main purposes of RTI is prevent reading issues for students who are at risk, the study found that in a sample of first-graders who were selected to receive interventions at Tiers 2 and 3 had negative results on a grade-level comprehensive measure of reading. Furthermore, second- and third-graders who were slotted to receive Tier 2 interventions did not show progress that was significant either. The results of this study have raised much concern among school personnel given the amount of time and funding necessary to implement an RTI process (Sparks, 2015). Additionally, these results also allude to the potential effect of individual differences among the students who are in need of further intervention. It is challenging to understand why a student is not responding to scientifically based instruction or interventions without investigating their profile of cognitive strengths and weaknesses. Regardless, RTI can be helpful in determining why a student is not responding. Rapid Reference 1.7 highlights some of the most salient strengths and weaknesses of the RTI service delivery model regarding its use in the SLD identification process.

Alternative Research-Based Procedures for SLD Identification

The third option included in the 2006 regulations allows "the use of other alternative research-based procedures" for determining SLD (§300.307[a]). Although vague, this option has been interpreted by some as involving the evaluation of a pattern of strengths and weaknesses in the identification of SLD via tests of academic achievement, cognitive abilities, and neuropsychological processes (Hale et al., 2008, 2010; Zirkel & Thomas, 2010). Several empirically based methods of SLD identification that are consistent with the third option are presented in this book, such as Alston-Abel and Berninger's "Integrating Instructionally Relevant Specific LD Diagnoses, Patterns of Strengths and Weaknesses, and Positive Home-School Partnerships: Free and Appropriate Public Education for *All*" (Chapter 10); Flanagan and colleagues' "Dual Discrepancy/Consistence Operational Definition of SLD: Integrating Multiple Data Sources and Multiple Data-Gathering Methods" (Chapter 11); and Naglieri and Feifer's "Pattern of Strengths and Weaknesses Made Easy: The Discrepancy/Consistency Model" (Chapter 12). Readers may also be interested in a comparison of Schultz and

≡ Rapid Reference 1.7

Strengths and Weaknesses of RTI

Salient Weaknesses of RTI as a Stand-Alone Method of SLD Identification	Salient Strengths of an RTI Service Delivery Model
• Lack of research regarding which RTI model works best, standard treatment protocol, or problem-solving model, or under what circumstances each model should be used	• Focus is on the provision of more effective instruction
• Lack of agreement on which curricula, instructional methods, or measurement tools should be used	• Allows schools to intervene early to meet the needs of struggling learners
• Confusion surrounding what constitutes an empirically based approach	• Collected data better inform instruction than data generated by traditional ability-achievement discrepancy method
• Lack of agreement on which methods work across grades and academic content areas	• Helps ensure that the student's poor academic performance is not due to poor instruction
• Different methods of response-nonresponse, leading to different children being labeled as responders-nonresponders	• Holds educators accountable for documenting repeated assessments of students' achievement and progress during instruction
• No consensus on how to ensure treatment integrity	
• No indication of a true positive (SLD identification) in an RTI model	

Source: Data from Learning Disabilities Association of America, White Paper (Hale et al., 2010).

Stephens's (2015) core-selective evaluation process and the Flanagan and colleagues DD/C model (Chapter 13).

Figure 1.1 provides an illustration of the three common components of third-method approaches to SLD identification (Flanagan, Fiorello, & Ortiz, 2010; Hale et al., 2008). The two bottom ovals depict academic and cognitive weaknesses, and their horizontal alignment indicates that the level of performance in both domains (academic and cognitive) is expected to be similar or consistent.

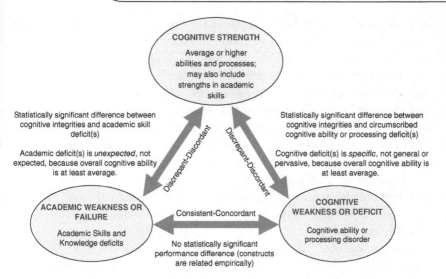

Figure 1.1. Common Components of Third-Method Approaches to SLD Identification

Source: Flanagan et al. (2010); Hale, Flanagan, and Naglieri (2008).

The double-headed arrow between the bottom two ovals indicates that the difference between measured performances in the weak academic area(s) is not significantly different from performance in the weak cognitive area(s). Again, in children with SLD there exists an empirical or otherwise clearly observable and meaningful relationship between the academic and cognitive deficits, because the cognitive deficit is the presumed cause of the academic deficit. The oval depicted at the top of Figure 1.1 represents generally average (or better) cognitive or intellectual ability. The double-headed arrows between the top oval and the two bottom ovals in the figure indicate the presence of a statistically significant or clinically meaningful difference in measured performance between general cognitive ability and the areas of academic and cognitive weakness. The pattern of cognitive and academic strengths and weaknesses represented in Figure 1.1 retains and reflects the concept of unexpected underachievement that has historically been synonymous with the SLD construct (Kavale & Forness, 2000).

CONCLUSION

In this chapter we reviewed briefly the prevailing definitions, diagnostic classification systems, and methods of identifying LD. The federal definition of SLD has remained virtually the same for the past 30 years, and SLD remains the most frequently diagnosed educationally disabling condition in our nation's schools. Despite no change in the definition of SLD in the most recent reauthorization of IDEA, the methods for identifying SLD, as per the 2006 federal regulations, have changed. For example, ability-achievement discrepancy can no longer be mandated, although it remains a viable option in the majority of states. RTI has been adopted by several states as the required approach for SLD identification, despite the fact that using this method alone is inconsistent with the federal law. Third-option or research-based alternatives to SLD identification are permitted in more than 20 states throughout the country and hold promise for identifying SLD in more reliable and valid ways than was achieved via previous methods (e.g., the traditional ability-achievement discrepancy method).

The remainder of this book addresses in greater detail the topics discussed briefly in this chapter. For example, Chapters 2 through 6 provide in-depth coverage of how SLD manifests in reading, math, writing, oral language, and nonverbal learning disabilities. Chapters 7 through 13 include discussions of RTI and several third-method approaches for SLD identification. Chapter 14 describes how practitioners can distinguish cultural and linguistic differences from SLD in the evaluation of English language learners. Finally, Chapter 15 covers the differential diagnosis of SLD, and other issues related to the acquisition of academic skills and the identification of nonverbal learning disability. The confusion that has surrounded methods of SLD identification for many years, along with the obvious disconnect between the definition of SLD and the most typical methods of identifying it, continue to spark controversy. The chapters that follow, written by leading experts in the field, have the potential to shape future reauthorizations of IDEA and bring greater clarity to the definition of and methods for identifying SLD.

RESOURCES

Center on Response to Intervention: www.rti4success.org. The center provides technical assistance to states and districts and builds the capacity of states to assist districts in implementing proven models for RTI/EIS.

Child Mind Institute: https://childmind.org/. This website provides resources for the families and educators of children with mental health and learning disorders.

Council for Exceptional Children: www.cec.sped.org. This website provides professional development resources, including a blog on RTI and a side-by-side comparison of the IDEA regulations and information about how the changes will affect students and teachers.

Early Childhood Technical Assistance Center: http://ectacenter.org/sec619/stateregs.asp. This page provides links to state regulations and other policy documents (statutes, procedures, and guidance materials) for implementing Part B of IDEA.

IDEA 2004: https://sites.ed.gov/idea/. Statutes, regulations, and other documents related to IDEA 2004 are found here.

IDEA Partnership: www.ideapartnership.org. This website offers resources developed by the IDEA Partnership (a collaboration of more than 55 national organizations, technical assistance providers, and organizations and agencies at state and local levels) and the Office of Special Education Programs (OSEP).

LD Online: www.ldonline.org. This website provides comprehensive information about learning disabilities and ADHD, with valuable resources for parents, educators, and students.

Learning Disabilities Association of America: https://ldaamerica.org/. The LDA is an organization that has provided support for people with LD and their families since the 1960s.

National Association of School Psychologists (NASP): www.nasponline.org/research-and-policy/professional-positions/position-statements. This is a position statement on the identification of students with SLDs (adopted in July 2011).

National Association of State Directors of Special Education (NASDSE): www.nasdse.org. This is the official website of the NASDSE, with up-to-date information about projects and initiatives related to RTI, charter schools, and the IDEA Partnership.

National Center for Learning Disabilities: www.ld.org. The NCLD works to ensure that the nation's 15 million children, adolescents, and adults with LDs have every opportunity to succeed in school, work, and life.

National Committee on Learning Disabilities (NJCLD): www.ldonline.org/about/partners/njcld. This website describes the mission of the NCLD and its member organizations. It provides research articles and contact information for associations that offer assistance to individuals with SLD.

National Resource Center on Learning Disabilities (NRCLD): www.nrcld.org. This website provides resources for educators and parents, including a toolkit on using RTI in SLD determination.

RTI Action Network: www.rtinetwork.org. This is a website dedicated to the effective implementation of RTI in districts nationwide.

Understood: www.understood.org/en. This is an organization that is dedicated to helping the parents of children who are struggling to learn.

What Works Clearinghouse, Institute of Education Sciences: https://ies .ed.gov/ncee/wwc/. This website offers scientific evidence about best practices in education.

Each state has a special education advisory panel that provides the state's Department of Education with guidance about special education and related services for children with disabilities. Check your own state's Department of Education website for specific information about your area.

US Department of Education (USDOE): www.ed.gov. This is the home page of the USDOE, which provides current information about education policies and initiatives in the United States.

🐟 TEST YOURSELF 🐟

1. **The number of children identified with SLD has remained relatively consistent since the enactment of P.L. 94-142 in 1975. True or false?**

2. **Historically, definitions of LD have strongly influenced how we have identified LD. True or false?**

3. **In the public schools, SLD is identified primarily by the following:**
   (a) *DSM-5* criteria
   (b) IDEA and its attendant regulations
   (c) *ICD-10*
   (d) All of the above

4. **According to the 2006 federal regulations, a district *must not require* use of the following procedure to identify SLD:**
   (a) Response to intervention (RTI) process
   (b) Ability-achievement discrepancy model
   (c) Alternative research-based procedures
   (d) Psychoeducational assessments

5. **RTI has not been validated as a method for SLD identification. True or false?**

6. **Which of the following is not a salient strength of RTI?**
   (a) Focus is on the provision of more effective instruction.
   (b) It allows schools to intervene early to meet the needs of struggling learners.
   (c) It collects data that better inform instruction than data generated by traditional ability-achievement discrepancy method.
   (d) A true positive (SLD identification) is evident in an RTI model.

7. **More than half of the states allow the use of the discrepancy model or a research-based alternative to SLD identification (PSW). True or false?**

8. **SLD has an underlying neurological etiology. True or false?**

9. **According to IDEA 2004, a child may have SLD in any of the following except:**

    (a) Written expression

    (b) Reading fluency skills

    (c) Mathematics calculation

    (d) Spelling

10. **A child can have an SLD in only one academic area. True or false?**

Answers: 1. False; 2. False; 3. b; 4. b; 5. True; 6. d; 7. True; 8. True; 9. d; 10. False.

REFERENCES

Aaron P. G. (1997). The impending demise of the discrepancy formula. *Review of Educational Research, 67,* 461–50.

American Psychiatric Association. (2013). *Diagnostic and statistical manual of mental disorders* (5th ed.). Washington, DC: Author.

Balu, R., Zhu, P., Doolittle, F., Schiller, E., Jenkins, J., & Gersten, R. (2015). *Evaluation of response to intervention practices for elementary school reading* (NCEE 2016–4000). Washington, DC: National Center for Education Evaluation and Regional Assistance, Institute of Education Sciences, US Department of Education.

Bateman, B. (1965). An educational view of a diagnostic approach to learning disorders. In J. Hellmuth (Ed.), *Learning disorders* (Vol. 1, pp. 219–239). Seattle, WA: Special Child Publications.

Bradley, R., Danielson, L. C., & Hallahan, D. P. (2002). *Identification of learning disabilities: Research to practice.* Mahwah, NJ: Erlbaum.

Ceci, S. J. (1990). *On intelligence—more or less: A bio-ecological treatise on intellectual development.* Englewood Cliffs, NJ: Prentice Hall.

Ceci, S. J. (1996). *On intelligence: A biological treatise on intellectual development* (expanded ed.). Cambridge, MA: Harvard University Press.

Coomer, L. F. (2015). *Definitions and criteria used by state education departments for identifying specific learning disabilities* (Unpublished master's thesis). Western Kentucky University, Bowling Green, Kentucky.

Cortiella, C. (2009). *The state of learning disabilities 2009.* New York, NY: National Center for Learning Disabilities.

Cortiella, C., & Horowitz, S. H. (2014). *The state of learning disabilities: Facts, trends and emerging issues.* New York, NY: National Center for Learning Disabilities.

Council for Exceptional Children. Division for Children with Learning Disabilities. (1967). Working definition of learning disabilities. Unpublished manuscript. Arlington, VA: Author.

Flanagan, D. P., & Alfonso, V. C. (2011). *Essentials of specific learning disability identification.* Hoboken, NJ: Wiley.

Flanagan, D. P., Fiorello, C. A., & Ortiz, S. O. (2010). Enhancing practice through application of Cattell-Horn-Carroll theory and research: A "third method" approach to specific learning disability identification. *Psychology in the Schools, 47*(7), 739–760.

Flanagan, D. P., Ortiz, S. O., & Alfonso, V. C. (2007). *Essentials of Cross-Battery Assessment* (2nd ed.). New York, NY: Wiley.

Flanagan, D. P., Ortiz, S. O., & Alfonso, V. C. (2013). *Essentials of Cross-Battery Assessment* (3rd ed.). Hoboken, NJ: Wiley.

Flanagan, D. P., Ortiz, S. O., Alfonso, V. C., & Mascolo, J. T. (2002). *The achievement test desk reference (ATDR): Comprehensive assessment and learning disabilities.* Boston, MA: Allyn & Bacon.

Flanagan, D. P., Ortiz, S. O., Alfonso, V. C., & Mascolo, J. T. (2006). *The achievement test desk reference* (2nd ed.). New York, NY: Wiley.

Fuchs, L. S., & Fuchs, D. (1998). Treatment validity: A unifying concept for reconceptualizing the identification of learning disabilities. *Learning Disabilities Research and Practice, 13,* 204–219.

Gresham, F. M., Restori, A. F., & Cook, C. R. (2008). To test or not to test: Issues pertaining to response to intervention and cognitive testing. *NASP Communiqué, 37*(1), 5–7.

Hale, J., Alfonso, V., Berninger, V., Bracken, B., Christo, C., Clark, E., . . . Yalof, J. (2010). Critical issues in response-to-intervention, comprehensive evaluation, and specific learning disabilities identification and intervention: An expert white paper consensus. *Learning Disability Quarterly, 33*(3), 223–236.

Hale, J. B., & Fiorello, C. A. (2004). *School neuropsychology: A practitioner's handbook.* New York, NY: Guilford.

Hale, J. B., Fiorello, C. A., Dumont, R., Willis, J. O., Rackley, C., & Elliott, C. (2008). Differential Ability Scales—second edition (neuro)psychological predictors of math performance for typical children and children with math disabilities. *Psychology in the Schools, 45,* 838–858.

Hale, J. B., Flanagan, D. P., & Naglieri, J. A. (2008). Alternative research-based methods for IDEA (2004) identification of children with specific learning disabilities. *Communique, 36*(8), 1, 14–17.

Hammill, D. D. (1990). On defining learning disabilities: An emerging consensus. *Journal of Learning Disabilities, 23,* 74–84.

Interagency Committee on Learning Disabilities. (1987). *Learning disabilities: A report to the U.S. Congress.* Bethesda, MD: National Institutes of Health.

Kass, C., & Myklebust, H. (1969). Learning disability: An educational definition. *Journal of Learning Disabilities, 2,* 377–379.

Kaufman, A. S. (2008). Neuropsychology and specific learning disabilities: Lessons from the past, as a guide to present controversies and future clinical practice. In E. Fletcher-Janzen & C. R. Reynolds (Eds.), *Neuropsychological perspectives on learning disabilities in the era of RTI: Recommendations for diagnosis and intervention* (pp. 1–13). Hoboken, NJ: Wiley.

Kavale, K. A., & Flanagan, D. P. (2007). Ability-achievement discrepancy, RTI, and assessment of cognitive abilities/processes in SLD identification: Toward a contemporary operational definition. In S. Jimerson, M. Burns, & A. Van Der Heyden (Eds.), *Handbook* of response to intervention: The science and practice of assessment and intervention (pp. 130–147). New York, NY: Springer Science.

Kavale, K. A., & Forness, S. R. (1995). Social skill deficits and training: A meta-analysis. In T. E. Scruggs & M. A. Mastropieri (Eds.), *Advances in learning and behavioral disabilities* (Vol. 9, pp. 119–160). Greenwich, CT: JAI Press.

Kavale, K. A., & Forness, S. R. (2000). What definitions of learning disability say and don't say: A critical analysis. *Journal of Learning Disabilities, 33*(3), 239–256.

Kavale, K. A., & Forness, S. R. (2006). Learning disability as a discipline. In H. L. Swanson, K. R. Harris, & S. Graham (Eds.), *Handbook of learning disabilities* (pp. 76–93). New York, NY: Guilford.

Kavale, K. A., Kauffman, J. M., Bachmeier, R. J., & LeFever, G. B. (2008). Response-to-intervention: Separating the rhetoric of self-congratulation from the reality of specific learning disability identification. *Learning Disability Quarterly, 31*, 135–150.

Kavale, K. A., Spaulding, L. S., & Beam, A. P. (2009). A time to define: Making the specific learning disability definition prescribe specific learning disability. *Learning Disability Quarterly, 31*, 39–48.

Kena, G., Musu-Gillette, L., Robinson, J., Wang, X., Rathbun, A., Zhang, J., Wilkinson-Flicker, S., Barmer, A., & Dunlop Velez, E. (2015). *The condition of education 2015* (NCES 2015-144). US Department of Education, National Center for Education Statistics. Washington, DC. Retrieved November 22, 2017, from http://nces.ed.gov/pubsearch

Kirk, S. A. (1962). *Educating exceptional children.* Boston, MA: Houghton Mifflin.

Learning Disability Association of America. (n.d.a). *History of LDA.* Retrieved from www.ldanatl.org/about/print_history.asp

Learning Disability Association of America. (n.d.b). *Types of learning disabilities.* Retrieved from https://ldaamerica.org/types-of-learning-disabilities/

Learning Disabilities Roundtable. (2005). *2004 learning disabilities roundtable: Comments and recommendations on regulatory issues under the Individuals Education Improvement Act of 2004, Public Law 108–446.* Retrieved from www.nasponline.org/advocacy/2004LDRoundtableRecsTransmittal.pdf

Lyon, G. R., Fletcher, J. M., Shaywitz, S. E., Shaywitz, B. A., Torgesen, J. K., Wood, F. B., Schulte, A., & Olson, R. (2001). *Rethinking learning disabilities.* Washington, DC: Thomas Fordham Foundation. Retrieved from www.ppionline.org/documents/SpecialEd_ch12.pdf

Mather, N., & Goldstein, S. (2008). *Learning disabilities and challenging behaviors: A guide to intervention and classroom management* (2nd ed.). Baltimore, MD: Brookes.

National Advisory Committee on Handicapped Children. (1968). *Special education for handicapped children* (first annual report). Washington, DC: Department of Health, Education, & Welfare.

National Joint Committee on Learning Disabilities. (1981). Learning disabilities: Issues on definition. Unpublished manuscript. (Available from The Orton Dyslexia Society, 724 York Road, Baltimore, MD 21204).

National Joint Committee on Learning Disabilities. (1982). Learning disabilities: Issues on definition. *Asha, 24*(11), 945–947.

National Joint Committee on Learning Disabilities. (1991). Learning disabilities: Issues on definition. *Asha, 33*(5), 18–20.

National Joint Committee on Learning Disabilities. (1998). Operationalizing the NJCLD definition of learning disabilities for ongoing assessment in schools. *Asha, 40*(18), 258a–g. Retrieved from www.asha.org/policy/RP1998-00130/

President's Commission on Excellence in Special Education Report. (2002). *A new era: Revitalizing special education for children and their families.* Jessup, MD: Education Publications Center, US Department of Education. Retrieved from www2.ed.gov/inits/commissionsboards/whspecialeducation/reports/info.html

Reschly, D. J. (2004). Paradigm shift, outcomes criteria, and behavioral interventions: Foundations for the future of school psychology. *School Psychology Review, 33,* 408–416.

Reschly, D. J., Hosp, J. L., & Schmied, C. M. (2003). *And miles to go . . . : State SLD requirements and authoritative recommendations.* Nashville, TN: National Research Center on Learning Disabilities. Retrieved from www.nrcld.org/about/research/states/

Reynolds, C. R., & Shaywitz, S. E. (2009a). Response to intervention: Prevention and remediation, perhaps. Diagnosis, no. *Child Development Perspectives, 3*(1), 44–47.

Reynolds, C. R., & Shaywitz, S. E. (2009b). Response to intervention: Ready or not? Or, from wait-to-fail to watch-them-fail. *School Psychology Quarterly, 24*(2), 130–145.

Schultz, E., & Stephens, T. (2015). Core-selective evaluation process: An efficient and comprehensive approach to identify SLD using the WJ IV. *The Journal of the Texas Educational Diagnostician Association, 44*(2), 5–12.

Siegel, L. S. (1999). Issues in the definition and diagnosis of learning disabilities: A perspective on *Guckenberger v. Boston University. Journal of Learning Disabilities, 32* (4), 304–319.

Sparks, S. D. (2015). RTI practice falls short of promise, research finds. *Education Week, 35* (12), 1.

Stanovich, K. E. (1988). Explaining the differences between the dyslexic and the garden-variety poor reader: The phonological-core variable-difference model. *Journal of Experimental Child Psychology, 38,* 175–190.

Sternberg, R. J., & Grigorenko, E. L. (2002). *Our labeled children: What every parent and teacher needs to know about learning disabilities.* Cambridge, MA: Perseus.

Stuebing, K. K., Fletcher, J. M., LeDoux, J. M., Lyon, G. R., Shaywitz, S. E., & Shaywitz, B. A. (2002). Validity of IQ-discrepancy classifications of reading disabilities: A meta-analysis. *American Educational Research Journal, 39,* 469–518.

US Department of Education. (2016a). Number of students ages 6 through 21 served under IDEA, Part B, by disability and state: 2015–16. IDEA section 618 data products: Static tables. Retrieved November 22, 1017, from www2.ed.gov/programs/osepidea/618-data/static-tables/index.html

US Department of Education. (2016b). Students ages 6 through 21 served under IDEA, Part B, as a percentage of population, by disability category and state: 2015–16. IDEA section 618 data products: Static tables. Retrieved November 22, 1017, from www2.ed.gov/programs/osepidea/618-data/static-tables/index.html

U. S. Office of Education. (1977). Definition and criteria for defining students as learning disabled. *Federal Register, 42*(250), 65083.

Wepman, J., Cruickshank, W., Deutsch, C., Morency, A., & Strother, C. (1975). Learning disabilities. In N. Hobbs (Ed.), *Issues in the classification of children* (Vol. 1, pp. 300–317). San Francisco, CA: Jossey-Bass.

Wiederholt, J. L. (1974). Historical perspectives on the education of the learning disabled. In L. Mann & D. Sabatino (Eds.), *The second review of special education* (pp. 103–152). Philadelphia, PA: JSE Press.

World Health Organization. (2016). *International classification of diseases* (10th rev.). Geneva, Switzerland: Author.

Ysseldyke, J. E. (2005). Assessment and decision making for students with learning disabilities: What if this is as good as it gets? *Learning Disability Quarterly, 28,* 125–128.

Zirkel, P. A., & Thomas, L. B. (2010). State laws for RTI: An updated snapshot. *Teaching Exceptional Children, 42*(3), 56–63.

Two

THE NEUROPSYCHOLOGY OF READING DISORDERS

How SLD Manifests in Reading

Steven G. Feifer

The pulse of America's educational system is frequently measured by the rhythmic and often palpable beat of one particular statistical metric: US literacy rates. However, if literacy were indeed an actual patient, the US educational system would be on life support. According to the National Center for Education Statistics (NCES; 2015), literacy rates have remained relatively stagnant over the past 25 years. The National Assessment of Educational Progress (NAEP) is commissioned by the NCES to provide group-level data on student achievement in various subjects, including literacy. Every two years, the NAEP uses a carefully designed sampling procedure that best represents the geographical, racial, ethnic, and socioeconomic diversity of the schools in the United States. Hundreds of thousands of students in public and private schools participate in the study. As can be readily observed in Figures 2.1 and 2.2, there has been relatively little academic growth in the number of students considered to be *proficient* readers in Grades 4 and 8. In fact, among the nationally representative samples from public and private schools, only 36% of fourth-grade students and 34% of eighth-grade students are reading at, or above, a proficient level.

The NAEP reading assessments are designed to measure reading competency in areas such as literary texts, informational texts, persuasive texts, poetry, and

Essentials of Specific Learning Disability Identification, Second Edition.
Edited by Vincent C. Alfonso and Dawn P. Flanagan.
© 2018 John Wiley & Sons, Inc. Published 2018 by John Wiley & Sons, Inc.

Trend in fourth-grade NAEP reading average scores

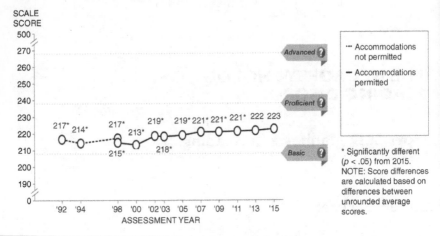

Figure 2.1. US Literacy Rates Among Fourth-Grade Students

Source: NAEP (2015).

Trend in eighth-grade NAEP reading average scores

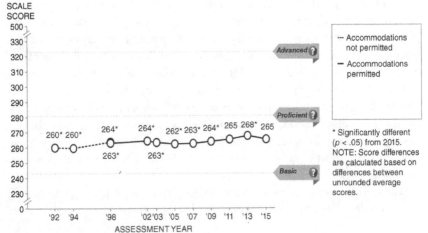

Figure 2.2. US Literacy Rates Among Eighth-Grade Students

Source: NAEP (2015).

≡ Rapid Reference 2.1

Variety of Reading-Related Tasks

Locate and recall: When locating or recalling information from what they have read, students need to identify main ideas or focus on specific elements of a story.

Integrate and interpret: When integrating and interpreting what they have read, students need to make comparisons, explain character motivation, or examine relations of ideas across the text.

Critique and evaluate: When critiquing or evaluating what they have read, students need to view the text critically by examining it from numerous perspectives, as well as evaluate the text quality or the effectiveness of particular aspects of the text.

procedural-based texts. Students in Grades 4, 8, and 12 are expected to demonstrate vocabulary knowledge in addition to literary reasoning skills by responding to a variety of reading-related tasks including those listed in Rapid Reference 2.1.

Perhaps what makes the NAEP reading data so disconcerting is the fact that stagnant literacy trends have followed in the wake of No Child Left Behind (NCLB; Klein, 2015). In January 2002, NCLB was enacted to ensure that all students, not just a high percentage of students, reach a proficient reading and math level by 2014. As the decade-long journey embarked, schools were required to demonstrate adequate yearly progress toward reaching 100% student proficiency by publicly reporting student test scores in Grades 3 through 8 inclusive of all student subgroups including low-income students, students with disabilities, English language learners, as well as racial and ethnic groups. Failure to make adequate yearly progress toward reading and math proficiency was grounds for being labeled a *failing school* and being subjected to mandatory interventions. By 2010, nearly 40% of America's schools had failed to make adequate yearly progress. By 2014, 43 states had been granted waivers to opt out of the mandatory interventions. Political pundits have surely criticized the effectiveness of this legislation, though the law's original intent, which was to improve educational equity for students from lower-income families and increase federal spending to districts serving lower-income students, was often

DON'T FORGET

Literacy remains a significant problem in the United States, with nearly two-thirds of all fourth- through eighth-grade students not on a proficient level in their reading skills.

≡ Rapid Reference 2.2

Challenges Faced by Students with Learning Disabilities

- Students with LDs earn lower grades and experience higher rates of course failure.
- More than one-third of students with LDs have been retained at least once.
- The national high school graduation rate stands at 82%, but only 68% of students with an SLD leave high school with a regular diploma.
- Young adults with LDs attend 4-year colleges at half the rate of the general population.
- College-completion rate of young adults with an LD is a meager 41%.
- Only 17% of young adults with an LD receive supports and accommodations in college.

overlooked. What clearly remains is a national problem in literacy. According to the National Center for Learning Disabilities (NCLD, 2014), students with specific learning disabilities (SLDs), many of which are reading disabilities, face the educational challenges listed in Rapid Reference 2.2

THE IDENTIFICATION QUANDARY

For decades, one of the most rigorously debated topics in school psychology has centered on best practices toward identifying, classifying, and remediating children with reading disabilities. Subsequent to the 2004 reauthorization of the Individuals with Disabilities Education Improvement Act (IDEIA; P.L. 108-446, but referred to as IDEA 2004), states can no longer require school districts to use a discrepancy between intelligence quotient (IQ) and achievement as being a necessary condition to identify students as having a reading disability. There have been numerous shortcomings inherent with the *discrepancy model* including the overreliance on a Full Scale IQ to capture the dynamic properties of learning, a lack of agreement on the magnitude of the discrepancy at various ages and grades, the statistical impreciseness of the method, and the inability to identify young learners (Feifer & Della Toffalo, 2007; Hale & Fiorello, 2004).

From a neuroscientific perspective, Tanaka and colleagues (2011) demonstrated that the discrepancy model was also at odds with how reading is truly represented in the brain. Using functional magnetic resonance imaging (fMRI) analysis, students between the ages of 7 and 16 years were divided between those who had a significant discrepancy between their cognitive ability and academic achievement in reading (*discrepant group*) and those who had below-average intellectual abilities and demonstrated no discrepancy between their lower cognitive ability and lower reading achievement (*non-discrepant group*). It should be noted that the discrepant and non-discrepant groups had similar reading scores; hence, the only significant difference between the groups was the discrepant children had higher cognitive ability scores. The results of the fMRI analysis were rather revealing; namely, there were no neuropsychological differences between the groups. In essence, both sets of children had underactive areas in the left parietal lobe and visual-word form association areas responsible for independent reading skills (Tanaka et al., 2011). These researchers concluded that IQ was not a mitigating factor in the determination of SLD from a brain-based perspective.

IDEA (2004) paved the way for a paradigm shift in the identification of an SLD, because schools were finally able to discard the mechanistic and conceptually flawed approaches inherent within the discrepancy model. Instead, the Response to Intervention (RTI) model was ushered in as a more viable alternative. RTI emphasized evidence-based approaches to instruction, progress monitoring, early screening, and intervention for struggling readers (Fletcher & Vaughn, 2009; Torgesen, 2009). In this respect, RTI has been extremely useful for providing early intervention for children at risk for a reading disorder; however, as an assessment methodology, RTI fails to explain adequately *why* a child may be faltering with reading (Feifer & Della Toffalo, 2007). Furthermore, RTI remains incapable of differential diagnosis and is dependent on a subjective and contextual definition of what constitutes an SLD (Reynolds & Shaywitz, 2009). In summary, without additional assessments it remains unclear as to which cognitive constructs directly contribute to a child's core reading deficit (i.e., phonological awareness, retrieval fluency, orthographic processing, working memory, vocabulary development, etc.) and, most important, which inherent strengths can assist in remediation (Semrud-Clikeman, Fine, & Harder, 2005). Without a clear delineation of specific cognitive strengths and weaknesses, individualized instruction becomes highly problematic and a one-size-fits-all intervention approach is often assumed for most children. The problem with a one-size-fits-all approach is not all students with reading disorders profit equally from the exact same remediation techniques (Heim et al., 2008).

So the question remains: Based on current neuroscientific research, what is the best approach to SLD identification and remediation? A third option, defined as an *alternative research-based approach,* emerged in the IDEA federal regulations (US Department of Education, Office of Special Education and Rehabilitative Services, 2006), which allows for the examination of a pattern of strengths and weaknesses (PSW) toward SLD identification (Hale, Flanagan, & Naglieri, 2008). The PSW approach has been advocated by eminent researchers within the field (Hale et al., 2010) and is consistent with cognitive neuropsychology that defines an SLD as a disorder of a basic psychological process. Furthermore, it is explicitly stated in federal statutes (IDEA 2004) that a learning disorder should be defined in the following manner:

> Specific learning disability means a disorder in one or more of the basic psychological processes involved in understanding or in using language, spoken or written, that may manifest itself in the imperfect ability to listen, think, speak, read, write, spell, or to do mathematical calculations. (CFR 300.8(c)(10))

It stands to reason that before adopting a PSW model to identify reading disorders in children, there must be a coordinated effort to delineate which psychological processes are directly related to reading in order to achieve some consensus with respect to diagnosis. Furthermore, the identification of reading-related processes must be evaluated in a developmental manner, meaning that certain processes, such as phonological awareness, may be more crucial during the initial stages of reading, whereas other processes, such as fluency, may be more influential later in the reading process (Frijters et al., 2011). Finally, an effective PSW model must be sensitive to time-lag differences in the acquisition of important psychological processes necessary for reading to emerge.

For instance, Kuppen and Goswami (2016) examined the developmental trajectory for children with dyslexia compared to garden-variety poor readers with lower global IQ scores. The children with dyslexia tended to have rather atypical development in phonological awareness, whereas students with lower cognitive abilities showed more of a developmental delay or time-lag difference compared to peers, though they were not necessarily atypical. There were also differences with respect to other psychological processes including short-term memory, rapid and automatic naming skills, and auditory-processing skills between children with lower cognitive abilities and children with dyslexia. Notwithstanding, the National Association of School Psychologists (NASP; 2011) issued a position paper on SLDs in order to begin conceptualizing learning challenges from a processing strengths and weaknesses approach. (See Rapid Reference 2.3 for excerpts from this positon paper.)

DEFINING READING DISORDERS

Developmental dyslexia has traditionally been defined as a neurodevelopmental disorder hindering the acquisition of reading abilities that cannot otherwise be explained by deficits in general intelligence, academic learning opportunities, general motivation, or specific sensory acuity (World Health Organization, 2008). Most school systems abide by the IDEA (2004), which subsumes dyslexia

⟹ Rapid Reference 2.3

Excerpts from the NASP (2011) Position Statement on Learning Disabilities

- Specific learning disabilities are endogenous in nature and are characterized by *neurologically* based deficits in cognitive processes.
- These deficits are specific; that is, they impact on particular cognitive processes that interfere with the acquisition of academic skills.
- Specific learning disabilities are *heterogeneous*—there are various types of learning disabilities, and there is no single defining academic or cognitive deficit or characteristic common to all types of specific learning disabilities.
- Relying on an ability-achievement discrepancy as the sole means of identifying children with SLDs is at odds with scientific research and with best practice.

under the general category of *learning disabled.* For those practitioners in private settings who comply with the nomenclature in the *Diagnostic and Statistical Manual of Mental Disorders* (5th ed.) (*DSM-5;* American Psychiatric Association, 2013), the term *specific learning disorder* is used instead, with dyslexia simply being referenced as an alternative term to denote a persistent pattern of learning difficulties. Therefore, it has been extremely difficult to pin down the exact prevalence rates of dyslexia because of the varying definitions of this most elusive term. Rapid Reference 2.4 presents a glimpse at some of the definitional confusion surrounding the term *dyslexia* by various credentialing organizations.

C A U T I O N

Developmental dyslexia is not a visual-spatial processing deficit, but instead a linguistic disorder disrupting the brain's phonological and decoding pathways resulting in inaccurate oral reading and poor spelling skills.

Despite the differences in nomenclature, the phonological deficit model has consistently been used to explain learning challenges associated with developmental dyslexia. This model posits that basic reading skills fail to develop because of an inability to identify, classify, organize, and manipulate properly the 44 units of sounds (phonemes) in the English language (Crews & D'Amato, 2009). The phonological deficit model has been criticized for numerous reasons, including its assumption that dyslexia is a homogeneous condition stemming only from an inability to process the distinctive sound units of the language and the model's failure to account for the developmental trajectory of phonological awareness on reading (Araújo, Pacheco, Faísca, Petersson, & Reiss, 2010; Frijters et al., 2011).

≡ *Rapid Reference 2.4*

Defining Dyslexia

IDA: Deficits in accurate and fluent word recognition, decoding, and spelling, with secondary effects on reading comprehension

ICD-10: Marked by reading achievement that falls substantially below that expected given the individual's chronological age, measured intelligence, and age-appropriate education

WHO: A neurodevelopmental disorder hindering the acquisition of reading that cannot otherwise be explained by IQ, academic opportunities, motivation, or specific sensory acuity

IDEIA: A learning disability that is a basic disorder of a psychological process used in understanding oral, spoken, or written language, and may manifest in the imperfect ability to listen, think, speak, read, write, spell, or do math; it may include conditions such as dyslexia

DSM-5: Dropped the term as a stand-alone condition and classifies reading issues under the generic term of *specific learning disorder*; however, *dyslexia* is an alternative term used to refer to a pattern of learning difficulties characterized by problems with accurate or fluent word recognition, poor decoding, and poor spelling abilities

Note: IDA = International Dyslexia Association; ICD-10 = *International Classification of Diseases* (10th ed.); WHO = World Health Organization; IDEIA = Individuals with Disabilities Education Improvement Act; DSM-5 = *Diagnostic and Statistical Manual of Mental Disorders* (5th ed.).

Finally, the model fails to account for why numerous phonological-processing skills tend to be preserved in some disabled readers (Shany & Share, 2011). The fact remains that phonological processing simply cannot account for every variance among readers. Furthermore, according to Hulme and Snowling (2015), reducing dyslexia to a deficit solely in phonological awareness suggests that phonological training will be the key to remediate this condition. In summary, there is a need to recognize that dyslexia is a more complex and nuanced condition involving more than just phonological deficits.

Cognitive neuroscience has explored the notion that reading disorders are multifocal in origin and therefore consist of different phenotypes (Peterson, Pennington, & Olson, 2013). Clearly, students with reading disorders manifest a vast array of learning needs and often vary in their response to targeted intervention strategies as well. Perhaps there is a need to view reading disorders as being a much broader neurodevelopmental syndrome, especially because cross-cultural research has demonstrated that reading pathways in the brain vary depending on the alphabetic writing system of the language spoken by the individual (Hadzibeganovic et al., 2010). For instance, transparent orthographies such as Italian, Greek, and Finnish have very few phonologically inconsistent words, whereas English and French contain a large number of phonologically irregular words (i.e., *yacht, debt, onion*) as well as homophones (i.e., *maid* and *made*) (Spinelli et al., 2009). Interestingly, readers with dyslexia often show more pronounced deficits on tasks involving naming speed and not necessarily on tasks involving phonological processing in transparent languages because these languages demand far less phonological analysis (O'Brien, Wolf, & Lovett, 2012). Every language has a unique alphabetic principle requiring various linguistic processing demands, and this argues against a universal pathophysiological basis of reading in the brain (Hadzibeganovic et al., 2010). Instead, there must be different subtypes of reading disorders manifested by different neural mechanisms in the brain.

READING AND THE BRAIN

Recent neuropsychological research has focused much of its acumen in determining which specific psychological processing deficits are correlated with reading impairments (Benjamin & Gaab, 2012; Gooch, Snowling, & Hulme, 2011; Horowitz-Kraus et al., 2014; Shaywitz & Shaywitz, 2005). For instance, most reading difficulties stem from the inability to integrate orthography (alphabet system) with phonology (sound units), with weaknesses due in part to structural deficits or micro-lesions in the left inferior parietal lobe (Cao, Bitan, & Booth, 2008; Heim et al., 2008).

According to Norton, Beach, and Gabrielli (2015), a complex linguistic skill, such as reading, involves not only multiple brain regions and numerous pathways but also precise neural timing or functional connectivity between these neural systems in order for fluent reading to emerge. In fact, under-activation (hypo-activation) in posterior regions of the brain inclusive of the left fusiform gyrus and visual word-form association areas are often seen among children with dyslexia. The notion of under-activation implies that reading disorders manifest, in part, from poor timing or functioning coherence between dedicated brain regions involved with automatic word-recognition skills. Perhaps an appropriate analogy is that reading is likened to a cerebral orchestra and therefore requires each individual musician, or psychological process, to play in the right tone, key, and, most important, timed in a manner to properly harmonize the sound.

Similarly, developmental dyslexia is primarily associated with the rhythm and timing involved in the temporal perception and sequencing of sounds in order to develop automatic word-recognition skills. Therefore, syllable timing deficits in the acoustical pathways of the brain may be leading to atypical development of phonological representations for spoken words, the central cognitive characteristic of developmental dyslexia across most languages (Leong & Goswami, 2014). In

≡ Rapid Reference 2.5

Key Psychological Processes Involved in the Timing of Reading

Process	Reading Function
Phonemic awareness	Identifying, recognizing, categorizing, and manipulating the 44 sounds of the English language
Phonological processing	Connecting the alphabetic code or letter symbol system with its corresponding phonemic code
Decoding	The application of phonological processing to accurately sound out the printed word form
Orthographic perception	The ability to detect and recognize accurately the alphabetic code
Orthographic processing	The ability to recognize the printed word form as a visual gestalt, or unique whole, in order to develop more-fluent text-recognition skills
Morphological processing	The ability to recognize the printed word form using morphological or semantic cues to facility word recognition
Fluency	The rapid and automatic recognition of the printed word form in isolation or in context
Prosody	The emotional tone or tenor the author intended for a passage to be read
Retrieval fluency	The speed at which a letter or sound cue can trigger a lexical representation
Vocabulary	The child's semantic knowledge or general fund of language development skills
Working memory	The ability to suspend temporarily previously read information with newly acquired information in conscious awareness
Executive functioning	The ability to self-organize and retrieve archived verbal information to facilitate text comprehension

summary, if one of the core musicians is off-key, then inefficient timing or poor functional coherence between specific neural correlates may be contributing to faulty reading. Rapid Reference 2.5 provides an overview of the cerebral orchestra of psychological processes involved with reading.

As neuropsychological research continues to reconceptualize dyslexia as manifesting from a variety of neurocognitive pathologies, genetic studies have also bolstered the credibility of a multiple model of dyslexia consisting of specific subtypes of reading disorders (Pernet, Poline, Demonet, & Rousselet, 2009). Furthermore, Cao et al. (2008) suggested that reading disorders may stem from faulty genetic transcriptions that primarily interfere with the functional connectivity or timing mechanisms in the brain within various regions that support key linguistic processes. This, in fact, raises a fascinating question for most psychologists and educators. Can targeted intervention approaches actually change brain chemistry and improve the timing of learning? The answer to this provocative question appears to be "yes."

Studies are beginning to show that targeted interventions often lead to metabolic changes in the brain of learners with SLDs. For instance, Hoeft et al. (2011) revealed that greater right prefrontal activation during a reading task for students with SLDs was not only indicative of the brain being able to recruit additional neural pathways to support the reading process but also was a better predictor of reading gains than standardized reading or behavioral tests. Horowitz-Kraus and colleagues (2014) used a fluency-based training method called Reading Acceleration Program (RAP) for 20 minutes per day over a 4-week trial period for children ages 8–12 years with reading disorders. As can be seen from Figure 2.3, there was clear shift of metabolic activity from the right hemisphere to the left hemisphere, the dominant hemisphere for reading and linguistic-related tasks, following just 4 weeks of training.

These types of metabolic changes in brain chemistry stemming from targeted interventions are consistent with Barquero, Davis, and Cutting's (2014) position documenting similar cerebral changes in children with dyslexia. In some cases, there is hemispheric *normalization,* in which the left hemisphere begins to assert its dominance in the reading process. In other cases, there is hemispheric *compensation,* in which novel brain structures, often in more frontal regions of the brain, become activated during the reading process. In summary, cognitive neuroscience is beginning to

DON'T FORGET

Cognitive neuroscience is beginning to document clear changes in brain metabolism as a result of specific reading interventions, though it remains unclear as to whether children with dyslexia normalize or compensate in the metabolic changes that occur.

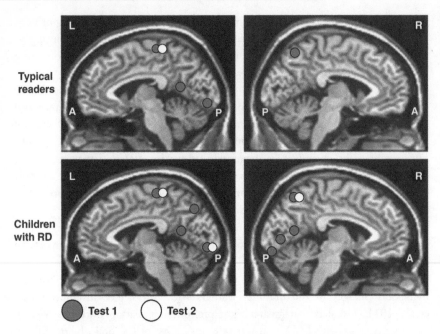

Figure 2.3. Typical Readers (Top Row) Typically Have More Metabolic Activity in the Left Hemisphere While Reading (Grey Dots). However, this pattern is reversed among students with Reading Disorders (RD). After 4 Weeks of Training (White Dots), the Metabolic Activity Switched to the Dominant Left Hemisphere for Students With Reading Disorders.

Source: Horowitz-Kraus et al. (2014).

document clear changes in the brain as a result of specific reading interventions, though it remains unclear as to whether a particular child will normalize or compensate in the metabolic changes that occur. Future research on the direct impact of targeted interventions at specific developmental ages with all different kinds of reading disorders is needed.

SUBTYPES OF READING DISORDERS

The cognitive neuropsychological literature is rife with classification schemes purported to subdivide readers into distinct categories, and opinions vary as to the most efficacious manner to catalog reading deficits. For instance, Ho, Chan, Lee, Tsang, and Luan (2004) noted deficiencies based on a combination of phonological memory skills, rapid naming skills, orthographic processing skills, or global deficiencies in all skill-related areas. King, Giess, and Lombardino (2007) found four specific subgroups of dyslexia based again on a combination of rapid naming tasks and phonological awareness, whereas Lachmann, Berti, Kujala, and Schröger (2005) divided reading deficits into two subtypes: accurate word reading skills and nonword reading skills.

Heim and colleagues (2008) proposed three distinct subgroups of reading disorders, with one subtype mainly consisting of phonological awareness deficits, a second subtype consisting of visual attention deficits, and a third subtype involving multiple cognitive deficits with phonological awareness and visual perceptual skills. This multiple-route model was founded on the notion that phonological dyslexia was characterized by poor reading accuracy at the sublexical level. However, surface dyslexia was associated with impairment at the whole-word, or lexical, level primarily because of poor orthographical processing deficits hindering the ability to take in the entire visual word form (Peterson et al., 2013). Feifer (2011) and Feifer and Della Toffalo (2007) summarized four general subtypes of reading disorders: dysphonetic dyslexia, surface dyslexia, mixed dyslexia, and reading comprehension deficits.

Dysphonetic Dyslexia

The first reading disorder subtype is termed *dysphonetic dyslexia* and is characterized by the reader's inability to use a phonological route to bridge letters and sounds successfully. Instead, the reader tends to rely too much on visual and orthographic cues to identify words in print. Because these readers rarely rely on letter-to-sound conversions, they frequently guess on words based on the initial letter. For instance, the word *cat* may be read as *couch* or *corn*. These students have tremendous difficulty incorporating strategies that would enable them to read words rapidly in a sound-based manner, and they tend to approach reading by simply memorizing whole words. According to Noble and McCandliss (2005), poor phonological processing in the early years leads to inefficient neural mappings between letters and sounds in the later years. Furthermore, because these children do not perceive sounds as discrete entities, overlapping bursts of sounds must now be painstakingly deciphered at the metacognitive level, causing confusion (Grizzle & Simms, 2009). From a neuropsychological standpoint, the supramarginal gyrus (see Figure 2.4), located at the juncture of the temporal and parietal lobes, is a key brain region responsible for the temporal ordering of phonological information (McCandliss & Noble, 2003; Sandak et al., 2004; Shaywitz, 2003). Therefore, early intervention emphasizing the development of phonemic awareness and phonological processing is vital to remediating this type of reading deficiency.

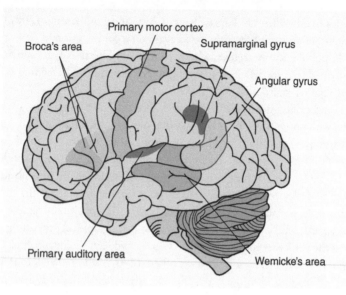

Figure 2.4 Reading Brain Circuitry

The primary auditory area helps modulate phonemic awareness and processing of phonemes. Higher-level phonological processing is modulated by the supramarginal gyrus, which facilitates decoding skills. Deficits in these pathways may lead to *dysphonetic dyslexia*. Conversely, the angular gyrus helps modulate symbolic information stored in a language dependent code and facilitates orthographic processing. Deficits in this region may lead to *surface dyslexia*.

Surface Dyslexia

The second reading disorder subtype is termed *surface dyslexia*, and in many respects is the sheer opposite of the dysphonetic dyslexia subtype. Students with this subtype of dyslexia are readily able to sound out words, but they lack the ability to recognize words automatically and effortlessly in print. Consequently, they tend to be letter-by-letter and sound-by-sound readers, because these students rely too heavily on the phonological properties of the word and underappreciate the orthographical or spatial properties of the visual word form. Most words are painstakingly broken down to individual phonemes and read slowly and laboriously. Fluency tends to suffer the most, though phonological processing skills remain relatively intact.

According to Friedmann and Lukov (2008), surface dyslexia can be further subdivided based on specific deficits within text orthography. For instance, some students may have more difficulty with *orthographical input* or letter-recognition skills. Consequently, deficits with orthographical input can result in letter transpositions or letter reversals. This can be differentiated from deficits with higher levels of *orthographical processing* and the ability to recognize rapidly the printed word form as a whole. Furthermore, deficits in orthographical processing can lead to difficulty determining whether a letter string is a word or a nonword, thereby compromising the reader's text-comprehension skills. Last, students with deficits in *orthographical output* struggle to read out loud because oral reading forces them to match orthography to a phonological lexicon. There is often great difficulty reading phonologically irregular words that do not follow a consistent grapheme to phoneme conversion (e.g., *yacht, debt*). This often results in dysfluent and labored oral reading skills.

The neural circuitry involved with surface dyslexia includes the left angular gyrus (see Figure 2.4), an important brain region that plays a role in the orthographic assembly of the visual word form (Sakurai, Asami, & Mannen, 2010). Because this particular brain region is sensitive to the visual word form, children with surface dyslexia tend to struggle with automatic letter- or word-recognition skills, and overall reading fluency skills (Cao et al., 2008). It is interesting to note that the left angular gyrus is also one of the key areas of the brain responsible for math fact retrieval (Ansari, 2008; Butterworth & Varma, 2014). Perhaps this is why children who have difficulty with reading fluency and automatically recognizing words in print also have difficulty with speeded math drills, because of a shared inability to recall and retrieve symbolic information stored in a language-dependent code. After all, nearly two-thirds of children with a math learning disability also have a reading disability (Ashkenazi, Black, Abrams, Hoeft, & Menon, 2013). Specific interventions for readers with surface dyslexia should focus on enhancing automaticity, pacing, and fluency skills with practice on contextual-based reading, and less emphasis on isolated and discrete skills used in more of a phonological approach.

Mixed Dyslexia

The third reading disorder subtype is *mixed dyslexia* and constitutes the most severe type of reading disability for students. Generally, these readers have difficulty across the language spectrum and are characterized by a combination of poor phonological-processing skills, slower rapid and automatic word-recognition skills, inconsistent language-comprehension skills, and bizarre error patterns in their reading. The "double-deficit" breakdown in reading often applies here, because mixed dyslexia is associated with numerous deficits that can disrupt the natural flow of automatically recognizing words in print. According to Cao et al. (2008), children with severe reading difficulties often have weaker modulatory effects from the left fusiform gyrus to the left inferior parietal lobes, suggesting deficits integrating phonological representations *and* orthographical representations into reading. In other words, there is no usable key to unlock successfully the reading code. Hence, most interventions should focus on a balanced literacy approach, which targets multiple aspects of the reading process to yield the best opportunity for success.

Reading Comprehension Deficits

The final reading disorder subtype involves deficits in *reading comprehension skills*. In essence, these readers struggle to derive meaning from print despite good reading mechanics. To help determine the underlying causes for reading comprehension deficits, a thorough assessment of reading should focus on the following three processes. First, there should be an emphasis on examining executive functioning skills, which refer to the strategies students use to self-organize incoming information with previously read material. Second, working memory, or the amount of memory needed to hold and manipulate information while engaged in a particular cognitive task, should be assessed. Last, language foundation skills, which refers to the breadth and depth of vocabulary words with which a student is familiar, should be measured as well (Feifer & Della Toffalo, 2007).

Children with reading comprehension difficulties often display marked deficits on certain executive functioning skills, especially working memory skills (Reiter, Tucha, & Lange, 2005; Willcutt et al., 2001). Simply put, the longer information is available in our working memory, the greater our mental flexibility to manipulate and store this information in a manner that facilitates retrieval. Working memory also aids in the ability to transfer isolated and discrete learning skills to a classroom reading situation (Crews & D'Amato, 2009). According to Cutting, Materek, Cole, Levine, and Mahone (2009), executive functioning includes the capacity to plan, organize, and self-monitor

C A U T I O N

Schools should not attempt to use just one intervention strategy and simply change the intensity of the strategy to meet the needs of the student. Instead, there should be multiple interventions used to address each of the aforementioned reading disorders' subtypes.

incoming information to facilitate text comprehension. Therefore, targeted interventions should assist children to better self-organize and summarize information more effectively as well as to teach children to read with a specific plan in order to determine the more-salient aspects of the text.

USING PSW TO ASSESS READING DISORDERS: AN INTRODUCTION TO THE FEIFER ASSESSMENT OF READING

The Feifer Assessment of Reading, or FAR (Feifer & Gerhardstein-Nader, 2015), is a comprehensive reading test designed to examine the underlying cognitive and linguistic processes that support proficient reading skills. The FAR was designed to examine reading disorders from a brain-based educational model of learning. The test is composed of 15 individual subtests measuring various aspects of phonological development, orthographical processing, decoding skills, morphological awareness, reading fluency, and comprehension skills. The FAR is unique for three primary reasons. First, the instrument is designed to assist users in determining the presence of a reading disorder using a PSW model. Second, the FAR is constructed to determine which of the four reading disorder subtypes a student exhibits. For instance, lower scores on the Phonological Index is suggestive of dysphonetic dyslexia, whereas lower scores on the Fluency Index is suggestive of surface dyslexia. If a student obtains lower scores on the Phonological Index and Fluency Index, it is suggestive of mixed dyslexia. Finally, lower scores on the Comprehension Index is suggestive of a reading comprehension disorder.

Perhaps what makes the FAR unique is that it is not a traditional academic achievement test, but rather represents a diagnostic educational assessment with targeted areas of psychological processing built directly into the test. Therefore, the test is ideally constructed for practitioners to use within a PSW model, because the primary psychological processing components of reading are embedded within the instrument. Most academic achievement tests measure global attributes of a skill (e.g., reading) and yield information detailing where a student is functioning on that particular skill. The FAR is a diagnostic achievement test designed to assist practitioners in determining why an individual student is struggling in reading and to inform intervention selection based on a neuroscientific learning paradigm. Specifically, the test is based on a gradiental model of brain functioning, which takes a hierarchical approach to cortical organization and cognitive processing (Goldberg, 1989). The gradiental model implies that various components of reading are organized along different neurodevelopmental pathways in the brain and that each pathway or axis consists of primary, secondary, and tertiary areas of processing information. For instance, within the Phonological Index, the primary psychological process is phonemic awareness, or the ability to decipher sounds in words. The secondary process is decoding, or the ability to apply these sounds toward the identification of words that are phonetically consistent. The tertiary process is the ability to apply phonics in a manner that enables the student to accurately read targeted words embedded within a particular context.

For examinees in prekindergarten, the full FAR battery consists of eight subtests and takes approximately 35 minutes to administer. For examinees in kindergarten to Grade 1, the full FAR battery consists of 11 subtests and takes approximately 60 minutes to administer. For examinees in Grade 2 to college, the full FAR battery consists of 14 subtests and takes approximately 1 hour and 15 minutes to administer. Examiners can choose to administer the full battery or, for a shorter administration

Table 2.1 FAR Indexes and Subtests

Index	Subtest	Grade Range	Administration Time (minutes)
Phonological Index (PI)	Phonemic Awareness (PA)	PK to college	5 to 10
	Nonsense Word Decoding (NWD)	Grade 2 to college	2
	Isolated Word Reading fluency (ISO)	K to college	1
	Oral Reading Fluency (ORF)	K to college	2 to 3
	Positioning Sounds (PS)	PK to college	3 to 4
Fluency Index (FI)	Rapid Automatic Naming (RAN)	PK to college	2
	Verbal Fluency (VF)	PK to college	2
	Visual Perception (VP)	PK to college	1
	Orthographical Processing (OP)	K to college	8
	Irregular Word Reading Fluency (IRR)	Grade 2 to college	1
Comprehension Index (CI)	Semantic Concepts (SC)	PK to college	5 to 8
	Word Recall (WR)	PK to college	4
	Print Knowledge (PK)	PK to Grade 1	4
	Morphological Processing (MP)	Grade 2 to college	7
	Silent Reading Fluency (SRF)	Grade 2 to college	8

time, only the subtests associated with an individual reading index (i.e., Phonological Index, Fluency Index, Comprehension Index, and Mixed Index) or individual subtests. In addition, the FAR screening battery is ideal for progress monitoring, and consists of three subtest measures inclusive of phonemic awareness, rapid automatic naming, and semantic concepts. The screener requires approximately 15–20 minutes to administer. Table 2.1 provides an overview of the subtest structure of the FAR.

DON'T FORGET

The FAR is a diagnostic educational assessment designed to examine the underlying cognitive and linguistic processes that support proficient reading skills. The FAR was designed to examine reading disorders from a brain-based educational model of learning. The test is ideal for a PSW model, because the primary psychological processing components of reading are embedded within the instrument.

CASE STUDY

Rick is a 6-year-old student currently in the first grade at Shookstown Elementary School. He was referred for a comprehensive psychological assessment due to continued concerns acquiring basic reading readiness skills as well as his inconsistent attention span. According to his teacher, Rick appeared to be regressing with his overall reading skills and struggled to consistently identify letters and sound out words. Of particular concern was Rick's low frustration tolerance when reading and tendency to shut down when confused. He had been receiving reading intervention services approximately twice a week for 30 minutes per day.

Test Results

Rick was administered the FAR, and the following scores were obtained in which the mean equals 100 (see Table 2.2).

FAR Total Index

Rick obtained a FAR Total Index standard score of 82 +/−4, which is in the below-average range of functioning and at the 12th percentile compared to peers. This score was considered an absolute weakness because his developmental reading skills were more than one standard deviation below grade-level peers. The following reading index scores were obtained in which the mean equals 100.

Table 2.2 Rick's Index Scores

FAR Index	Standard Score (95% CI)	Percentile Rank	Qualitative Descriptor
Phonological Index	79 (+/−3)	8	Moderately below average
Fluency Index	87 (+/−8)	19	Below average
Mixed Index	80 (+/−4)	9	Below average
Comprehension Index	92 (+/−10)	30	Average
FAR Total Index	**82 (+/−4)**	**12**	**Below average**

Phonological Index

Rick's Phonological Index standard score was 79 +/−3, which was in the moderately below-average range and at the 8th percentile compared to peers (see Table 2.3). He had extreme difficulty on most tasks measuring basic

Table 2.3 Rick's Phonological Subtest and Index Scores

Phonological Subtest	Standard Score	Percentile Rank	Qualitative Descriptor
Phonemic Awareness: A series of four tasks arranged in a hierarchy of increasing difficulty measuring rhyming, blending, segmenting, and manipulating sounds.	76	5	Moderately below average
Positioning Sounds: A phonemic localization task requiring the student to determine the missing sound located either in the beginning, middle, or ending position of a word using a visual cue.	88	21	Below average
Isolated Word Reading Fluency: The student reads a list of words of increasing difficulty in 60 seconds.	66	1	Significantly below average
Oral Reading Fluency: The student reads a passage composed of the same words as the isolated word reading fluency task in 60 seconds.	68	1	Significantly below average
Phonological Index	**79 (+/−3)**	**8**	**Moderately below average**

phonemic awareness (*phonemic awareness*) skills. For instance, Rick was inconsistent with core rhyming skills and struggled to blend and segment sounds in words as well. He performed much better when isolating sounds in words using a picture cue (*positioning sounds*) than when having to blend or manipulate sounds in words. This suggested he benefitted from visual cueing and external structure to identify sounds in words. A significant weakness was noted in his ability to apply decoding skills to words in print (*isolated word reading fluency*). He recognized a few more words when presented in context (*oral reading fluency*) than in isolation, suggesting he benefits from using semantic cues to help with word identification.

Fluency Index

Rick's Fluency Index standard score was 90 +/−8, which was in the lower end of the average range and at the 25th percentile compared to peers (see Table 2.4). He performed adequately when rapidly identifying a series of objects, though was inconsistent when rapidly identifying letters (*rapid naming*). Rick often had difficulty distinguishing between a *p* and *d* in print. There were noted inconsistencies on verbal retrieval tasks as well, because he performed much better when retrieving words from a semantic category (i.e., *animals*) rather than retrieving

Table 2.4 Rick's Fluency Subtest and Index Scores

Fluency Subtest	Standard Score	Percentile Rank	Qualitative Descriptor
Rapid Automatic Naming: A series of timed tasks requiring the student to name as many objects, letters, or stencils in 30 seconds.	90	25	Average
Verbal Fluency: Requires the student to name as many items that start with a particular category or items that start with a particular letter in 60 seconds.	95	37	Average
Visual Perception: The student must identify letters printed backward from an array of letters or words in 30 seconds.	92	30	Average
Orthographic Processing: The student is required to recall a letter, or group of letters, from a previously seen target word.	90	25	Average
Fluency Index	**(90 +/−8)**	**25**	**Average**

words that started with a particular letter (*verbal fluency*). This suggested that Rick had much better access to his lexicon of words using semantic cues rather than phonological ones. Last, Rick performed adequately when distinguishing between letters printed backward from actual letters (*visual perception*), though at times, he was confused by *d*, *g*, and *q*. His orthographic perception of whole words still appeared to be emerging (*orthographic processing*).

Comprehension Index

Rick's Comprehension Index standard score was 92 +/−5, which was in the average range and at the 30th percentile compared to peers (see Table 2.5). His overall vocabulary skills and core language development appeared sound (*semantic concepts*). Rick also had little difficulty with working memory for verbal information, though he struggled during the free recall trial and performed best when the examiner presented him with specific categories to retrieve the information (i.e., "Tell me all the fruits you remember."). His profile of scores suggested that despite Rick's strong vocabulary knowledge, he needs to learn how to self-organize verbal

Table 2.5 Rick's Comprehension Subtest and Index Scores

Comprehension Subtest	Standard Score	Percentile Rank	Qualitative Descriptor
Print Knowledge: Requires the student to answer a series of preliteracy questions about various parts of a story book.	90	25	Average
Semantic Concepts: A multiple-choice test requiring the student to select the correct antonym or synonym of a target word.	102	55	Average
Word Recall: Requires the student to repeat back a list of words over a series of two trials; the second trial requires the student to recall a word from a selected list.	94	34	Average
Silent Reading Fluency: The student reads a passage silently, and then the passage is removed. The student is required to answer eight comprehension questions—four literal and four inferential—from the story.			Too young to administer this test
Comprehension Index	92 (+/−5)	30	**Average**

information better to facilitate text recall. His preliteracy skills were still emerging (*print knowledge*), because Rick struggled at times to identify various punctuation marks in print.

FAR Summary

Rick presented the profile of a student with dysphonetic dyslexia due to significant difficulty with basic phonemic awareness skills and an inability to apply decoding skills to identify words in print. His overall vocabulary knowledge was a relative strength, though he tends to over-rely on visual and semantic cues when identifying words due to an inability to sound them out. Rick would benefit from an explicit phonics training program administered on a daily basis.

Home and School Recommendations

1. Rick would benefit from an explicit phonological instructional method for reading (i.e., Fundations, Alphabetic Phonics, etc.). Students with emerging phonics skills benefit from small-group interventions (up to four children) and interventions consistently implemented every day for a minimum of 30–40 minutes. His progress should be frequently monitored using curriculum-based measurement in conjunction with the school's reading specialist.

2. Rick's phonological processing skills need to be strengthened. Specific activities such as reading Dr. Seuss books to foster rhyming skills and learn vowel patterns as well as activities requiring him to identify which of three sight words is spelled correctly (i.e., *wuz, whas,* or *was*) may help to develop automaticity recognizing vowel patterns in words.

3. Rick needs further practice understanding the positioning of sounds in words in order to foster more-accurate reading skills. He should practice identifying and writing isolated sounds in words to learn consonant and vowel boundaries. For instance, show him a picture of a birthday cake with the letters **C-** ___ **-KE** spelled underneath. When he can consistently identify and write the missing letter, change the positioning of the missing sound. Rick should begin by isolating initial sound positions, then ending sound positions, and finally medial vowel blends and vowel digraphs.

4. Rick may benefit from working at home with computer programs aimed at enhancing phonological development (i.e., Earobics I, Earobics II, Lexia, etc.).

5. Rick would benefit from working with a tutor after school to assist with his reading, writing, and spelling skills.

6. Rick's overall orthographic processing skills were inconsistent, which is why he makes frequent reversals. Perhaps color-coding individual letters and letter stems along with using colored letter tiles will help him develop more-consistent letter-recognition skills and assist in his spelling as well.

7. Rick may benefit from a specific reading intervention program focusing on developing fluency and speed (i.e., Read Naturally, Fluency Formula, Great Leaps, etc.). It should be noted his fluency issues are primarily related to poor automaticity of sounds, hence, the need for addressing phonological development as well.

8. Rick's mother should continue to practice reading high-interest materials with him at home for 20 minutes each evening as well as ask him questions about the story in order to foster literacy skills.

9. Rick needs to develop more confidence as a reader. His mother may want to set up a behavioral incentive plan at home, rewarding him for each minute he attempts to read independently, with minutes playing his favorite video game.

10. Classroom modifications such as preferential seating to minimize distractions, modifying or chunking assignments, and providing him with word bank words to assist with spelling and word-recognition skills may be helpful as well.

CONCLUSION

This chapter attempted to highlight one of the most crucial educational issues facing our nation today: stagnant literacy rates. Literacy remains a significant problem in the United States with nearly two-thirds of all fourth- through eighth-grade students not reading at a proficient level. As school psychologists and other practitioners have grappled and, at times, bickered over best practices in assessing reading disorders in children, cognitive neuroscience has provided wonderful insights into how all children learn. In fact, recent advances in neuropsychology have enabled educators to bear witness to actual metabolic changes in the brain based on targeted intervention approaches. Therefore, using a PSW model to identify specific subtypes of reading disorders in children is not only more aligned with current knowledge about the brain but also enables PSW assessment techniques to more readily and directly inform intervention approaches as well.

The FAR represents a new genre of testing: a diagnostic educational assessment instrument. The FAR is ideally constructed for practitioners to use within a PSW model, because the primary psychological processing components of reading are embedded within the assessment and therefore are more capable of directly informing intervention decision making by specifying the subtype of reading disorder. In summary, perhaps education, psychology, and neuroscience need to converge on a more-interdisciplinary trajectory and work together in helping all children improve their literacy skills by further developing more-effective assessment tools and interventions strategies to help struggling learners of all ages.

🐟 TEST YOURSELF 🐟

1. **According to the National Center for Learning Disabilities (2014), which of the following statements are true?**

   (a) Student with learning disabilities earn lower grades and experience higher rates of course failure.

   (b) The high school graduation rate of students with learning disabilities is lower than nondisabled peers.

   (c) More than one-third of students with learning disabilities have been retained at least once.

   (d) All of the above are true.

2. *Developmental dyslexia* **is a term that can be defined as:**

   (a) Pronounced visual-spatial and memory deficits causing students to perceive words in an inverted or backward manner

   (b) A neurodevelopmental disorder hindering the ability to acquire basic phonemic awareness or decoding skills that hinders accurate word recognition and spelling skills, with secondary effects on reading comprehension

   (c) A significant discrepancy between global cognitive ability scores and global reading scores

   (d) A term that is synonymous with learning disabled

3. **According to the National Association of School Psychologists, learning disorders are neurologically based deficits, heterogeneous in nature, consist of multiple subtypes, differ in degree, and require evidence-based multitiered service delivery systems. True or false?**

4. **The type of reading disability characterized by poor fluency and speed, deficits in orthographic processing, and difficulty reading phonologically irregular words is:**

   (a) Mixed dyslexia

   (b) Surface dyslexia

   (c) Phonological dyslexia

   (d) Comprehension dyslexia

5. **Targeted reading interventions can actually change brain chemistry by creating alternative pathways to help assist the reading process. True or false?**

6. **The type of reading disability characterized by deficits in acquiring basic sound-symbol relationships necessary to decode words accurately is:**
   (a) Mixed dyslexia
   (b) Surface dyslexia
   (c) Phonological dyslexia
   (d) Deep dyslexia

7. **Which of the following statements is true about the Feifer Assessment of Reading?**
   (a) It is based on a gradiental model of brain functioning.
   (b) It is designed to tease out four subtypes of reading disorders.
   (c) It can be used to diagnose developmental dyslexia in children.
   (d) All of the above are true.

8. **Developmental dyslexia is the direct result of a cerebral insult or a specific lesion in the brain occurring after the age of 12 years resulting in difficulty deriving meaning from the printed word form. True or false?**

9. **The type of reading disability characterized by phonological and orthographic deficits and usually results in students being significantly below grade level is:**
   (a) Mixed dyslexia
   (b) Surface dyslexia
   (c) Phonological dyslexia
   (d) Comprehension dyslexia

10. **According to the National Assessment of Educational Progress (2015), the No Child Left Behind Act has resulted in significant reading gains for fourth- and eighth-grade US students. True or false?**

Answers: 1. d; 2. b; 3. True; 4. b; 5. True; 6. c; 7. d; 8. False; 9. a; 10. False.

REFERENCES

American Psychiatric Association. (2013). *Diagnostic and statistical manual of mental disorders* (5th ed.). Arlington, VA: Author.

Ansari, D. (2008). Effects of development and enculturation on number representation in the brain. *Nature Review Neuroscience, 9*, 278–291.

Araújo, S., Pacheco, A., Faísca, L., Petersson, K. M., & Reis, A. (2010). Visual rapid naming and phonological abilities: Different subtypes in dyslexic children. *International Journal of Psychology, 45*, 443–452.

Ashkenazi, S., Black, J. M., Abrams, D. A., Hoeft, F., & Menon, V. (2013). Neurobiological underpinnings of math and reading learning disabilities. *Journal of Learning Disabilities, 46*, 549–569.

Barquero, L. A., Davis, N., & Cutting, L. E. (2014). Neuroimaging of reading intervention and activation likelihood estimate meta-analysis. *PLOS ONE*, *9*(1), 1–16.

Benjamin, C.F.A., & Gaab, N. (2012). What's the story? The tale of reading fluency told at speed. *Human Brain Mapping*, *33*(11), 2572–2585.

Butterworth, B., & Varma, S. (2014). Mathematical development. In D. Mareschal, B. Butterworth, A. Tolmie, D. Mareschal, B. Butterworth, & A. Tolmie (Eds.), *Educational neuroscience* (pp. 201–236). Hoboken, NJ: Wiley-Blackwell.

Cao, F., Bitan, T., & Booth, J. R. (2008). Effective brain connectivity in children with reading difficulties during phonological processing. *Brain and Language*, *107*, 91–101.

Crews, K. J., & D'Amato, R. C. (2009). Subtyping children's reading disabilities using a comprehensive neuropsychological measure. *International Journal of Neuroscience*, *119*, 1615–1639.

Cutting, L. E., Materek, A., Cole, C.A.S., Levine, T. M., & Mahone, E. M. (2009). Effects of fluency, oral language, and executive function on reading comprehension performance. *Annals of Dyslexia*, *59*, 34–54.

Feifer, S. G. (2011). How SLD manifests in reading. In D. P. Flanagan & V. C. Alfonso (Eds.), *Essentials of specific learning disability identification* (pp. 21–42). Hoboken, NJ: Wiley.

Feifer, S. G., & Della Toffalo, D. A. (2007). *Integrating RTI with cognitive neuropsychology: A scientific approach to reading.* Middletown, MD: School Neuropsych Press.

Feifer, S. G., & Gerhardstein-Nader, R. (2015). *Feifer Assessment of Reading: Professional manual.* Lutz, FL: PAR.

Fletcher, J. M., & Vaughn, S. (2009). Response to intervention: Preventing and remediating academic difficulties. *Child Development Perspectives*, *3*, 30–37.

Friedmann, N., & Lukov, L. (2008). Developmental surface dyslexias. *Cortex*, *44*, 1146–1160.

Frijters, J. C., Lovett, M. W., Steinbach, K. A., Wolf, M., Sevcik, R. A., & Morris, R. D. (2011). Neurocognitive predictors of reading outcomes for children with reading disabilities. *Journal of Learning Disabilities*, *44*, 150–166.

Goldberg, E. (1989). Gradiental approach to neocortical functional organization. *Journal of Clinical and Experimental Neuropsychology*, *11*, 489–517.

Gooch, D., Snowling, M., & Hulme, C. (2011). Time perception, phonological skills and executive function in children with dyslexia and/or ADHD symptoms. *The Journal of Child Psychology and Psychiatry*, *52*(2), 195–203.

Grizzle, K. L., & Simms, M. D. (2009). Language and learning: A discussion of typical and disordered development. *Current Problems in Pediatric Adolescent Health Care*, *39*, 168–189.

Hadzibeganovic, T., van den Noort, M., Bosch, P., Perc, M., van Kralingen, R., Mondt, K., & Coltheart, M. (2010). Cross-linguistic neuroimaging and dyslexia: A critical view. *Cortex*, *46*, 1312–1316.

Hale, J., Alfonso, V., Berninger, V., Bracken, B., Christo, C., Clark, E., . . . & Yalof, J. (2010). Critical issues in response-to-intervention, comprehensive evaluation, and specific learning disabilities identification and intervention: An expert white paper consensus. *Learning Disability Quarterly*, *33*(3), 223–236.

Hale, J. B., & Fiorello, C. A. (2004). *School neuropsychology: A practitioner's handbook.* New York, NY: Guilford.

Hale, J. B., Flanagan, D. P., & Naglieri, J. A. (2008). Alternative research-based methods for IDEA (2004) identification of children with specific learning disabilities. *Communique*, *36*(8), 14–17.

Heim, S., Tschierse, J., Amunts, K., Wilms, M., Vossel, S., Willmes, K., . . . & Huber, W. (2008). Cognitive subtypes of dyslexia. *Acta Neurobiologiae Experimentalis*, *68*, 73–82.

Ho, C.S.H., Chan, D.W.O., Lee, S. H., Tsang, S. M., & Luan, V. H. (2004). Cognitive profiling and preliminary subtyping in Chinese developmental dyslexia. *Cognition*, *91*, 43–75.

Hoeft, F., McCandliss, B. D., Black, J. M., Gantman, A., Zakerani, N., Hulme, C., . . . & Gabrieli, J.D.E. (2011). Neural systems predicting long-term outcome in dyslexia. *Proceedings of the National Academy of Sciences of the United States of America*, *108*(1), 361–366.

Horowitz-Kraus, T., Vannest, J. J., Kadis, D., Cicchino, N., Wang, Y.Y., & Holland, S. K. (2014). Reading acceleration training changes brain circuitry in children with reading difficulties. *Brain and Behavior*, *4*(6), 886–902.

Hulme, C., & Snowling, M. J. (2015). Learning to read: What we know and what we need to understand better. *Child Developmental Perspectives*, *7*(1), 1–5.

King, W. M., Giess, S. A., & Lombardino, L. J. (2007). Subtyping of children with developmental dyslexia via bootstrap aggregated clustering and the gap statistic: Comparison with the double-deficit hypothesis. *International Journal of Language and Communication Disorders*, *42*, 77–95.

Klein, A. (2015, April 10). No Child Left Behind overview: Definitions, requirements, criticisms, and more. *Education Week*.

Kuppen, S. E., & Goswami, U. (2016). Developmental trajectories for children with dyslexia and low IQ poor readers. *Developmental Psychology*, *52*(5), 717–734.

Lachmann, T., Berti, S., Kujala, T., & Schröger, E. (2005). Diagnostic subgroups of developmental dyslexia have different deficits in neural processing of tones and phonemes. *International Journal of Psychophysiology*, *56*, 105–120.

Leong, V., & Goswami, U. (2014). Assessment of rhythmic entrainment at multiple timescales in dyslexia: Evidence for disruption to syllable timing. *Hearing Research*, *308*, 141–161.

McCandliss, B. D., & Noble, K. G. (2003). The development of reading impairment: A cognitive neuroscience model. *Mental Retardation and Developmental Disabilities Research Reviews*, *9*, 196–205.

National Assessment of Educational Progress (NAEP). (2015). *The nation's report card*. Retrieved from http://nces.ed.gov/nationsreportcard/

National Association of School Psychologists (NASP). (2011). *Identification of students with specific learning disabilities*. Retrieved from www.nasponline.org/about_nasp/positionpapers/Identification_of_SLD.pdf

National Center for Education Statistics. (2015). *The nation's report card: NAEP reading 2015*. Washington, DC: Institute of Education Sciences, US Department of Education.

National Center for Learning Disabilities. (2014). *The state of learning disabilities* (3rd ed.). New York, NY: NCLD Publications.

Noble, K. G., & McCandliss, B. D. (2005). Reading development and impairment: Behavioral, social, and neurobiological factors. *Developmental and Behavioral Pediatrics, 26*(5), 370–376.

Norton, E. S., Beach, S. D., & Gabrielli, J.D.E. (2015). Neurobiology of dyslexia. *Current Opinion in Neurobiology, 30*, 73–78.

O'Brien, B. A., Wolf, M., & Lovett, M. W. (2012). A taxometric investigation of developmental dyslexia subtypes. *Dyslexia, 18*, 16–39.

Pernet, C. R., Poline, J. B., Demonet, J. F., & Rousselet, G. A. (2009). Brain classification reveals the right cerebellum as the best biomarker of dyslexia. *BMC Neuroscience, 10*, 67.

Peterson, R. L., Pennington, B. F., & Olson, R. K. (2013). Subtypes of developmental dyslexia: Testing the predictions of the dual-route and connectionist frameworks. *Cognition, 126*, 20–38.

Reiter, A., Tucha, O., & Lange, K. W. (2005). Executive functions in children with dyslexia. *Dyslexia, 11*, 116–131.

Reynolds, C. R., & Shaywitz, S. E. (2009). Response to intervention: Prevention and remediation, perhaps. Diagnosis, no. *Child Development Perspectives, 3*(1) 44–47.

Sakurai, Y., Asami, M., & Mannen, T. (2010). Alexia and agraphia with lesions of the angular and supramarginal gyri: Evidence for the disruption of sequential processing. *Journal of the Neurological Sciences, 288*, 25–33.

Sandak, R., Mencl, W. E., Frost, S., Rueckl, J. G., Katz, L., Moore, D. L., . . . & Pugh, K. R. (2004). The neurobiology of adaptive learning in reading: A contrast of different training conditions. *Cognitive, Affective, & Behavioral Neuroscience, 4*, 67–88.

Semrud-Clikeman, M., Fine, J., & Harder, L. (2005). Providing neuropsychological services to students with learning disabilities. In R. K. D'Amato, E. Fletcher-Janzen, & C. R. Reynolds (Eds.), *Handbook of school neuropsychology* (pp. 403–424). New York, NY: Wiley.

Shany, M., & Share, D. L. (2011). Subtypes of reading disability in a shallow orthography: A double dissociation between accuracy-disabled and rate-disabled readers of Hebrew. *Annals of Dyslexia, 61*, 64–84.

Shaywitz, S. (2003). *Overcoming dyslexia: A new and complete science-based program for reading problems at any level.* New York, NY: Random House.

Shaywitz, S. E., & Shaywitz, B. A. (2005). Dyslexia (specific reading disability). *Biological Psychiatry, 57*(11), 1301–1309.

Spinelli, D., Brizzolara, D., De Luca, M., Gasperini, F., Martelli, M., & Zoccolotti, P. (2009). Subtypes of developmental dyslexia in transparent orthographies: A comment on Lachmann and Van Leewen. *Cognitive Neuropsychology, 26*(8), 752–758.

Tanaka, H., Black, J. M., Hulme, C., Stanley, L. M., Kesler, S. R., Whitfield-Gabrieli, S., . . . & Hoeft, F. (2011). The brain basis of the phonological deficit in dyslexia is independent of IQ. *Psychological Sciences, 22*(11), 1442–1451.

Torgesen, J. K. (2009). The response to intervention instructional model: Some outcomes from a large-scale implementation in reading first schools. *Child Development Perspectives, 3*(1), 38–40.

US Department of Education, Office of Special Education and Rehabilitative Services. (2006). *Twenty-sixth annual report to Congress on the implementation of the Individuals with Disabilities Education Act.* Washington, DC: Author.

Willcutt, E. G., Olson, R. K., Pennington, B. F., Boada, R., Ogline, J. S., Tunick, R. A., & Chabildas, N. A. (2001). Comparison of the cognitive deficits in reading disability and attention deficit hyperactivity disorder. *Journal of Abnormal Psychology, 110*, 157–172.

World Health Organization. (2008). *International statistical classification of diseases and related health problems* (2nd ed., 10th rev.). Geneva, Switzerland: Author.

Three

HOW SLD MANIFESTS IN MATHEMATICS

Michèle M. M. Mazzocco
Rose Vukovic

There are many reasons why mathematics may be difficult for some students, and the presence of specific mathematics learning disabilities (MLDs) is only one such reason. As we emphasize throughout this chapter, the nature of mathematics difficulties varies across students and across development. Since the reported incidence of mathematics difficulties (e.g., National Assessment of Educational Process [NAEP], 2015) far exceeds the estimated cumulative incidence of MLD, most students who experience difficulty with mathematics at some point during their school-age years do not have MLD. This means that school psychologists and other practitioners in the schools (e.g., LD specialists, special education teachers) should be able to recognize when MLD *is* indicated and when MLD is *not* indicated. Knowledge of this distinction does not serve to identify *who* needs educational services; instead, it serves to inform *what* services may be needed by a given student struggling with mathematics, because instruction, remediation, or intervention plans depend on the nature of a student's mathematics difficulties (e.g., number, fluency, or reasoning difficulties). Unfortunately, differentiating between MLD and other mathematics difficulties is not always straightforward. Thus, in addition to understanding what indicates the presence or absence of MLD, school psychologists and other practitioners benefit from an awareness of the controversies surrounding definitions of MLD. This knowledge can guide interpretation of conflicting research findings

Essentials of Specific Learning Disability Identification, Second Edition.
Edited by Vincent C. Alfonso and Dawn P. Flanagan
© 2018 John Wiley & Sons, Inc. Published 2018 by John Wiley & Sons, Inc.

or recommendations and may inform assessment planning and instructional recommendations.

This chapter includes a brief summary of key research on how students with MLD differ from students with other mathematics difficulties, an overview of the implications of this knowledge for assessment and intervention, and acknowledgment of unanswered research questions about MLD. Included is a resource list of materials designed to enhance an understanding of MLD and tools to help identify individual differences in foundational mathematics skills.

DEFINITION, ETIOLOGY, AND INCIDENCE OF MATHEMATICS LEARNING DISABILITY

Not all students who have difficulty learning mathematics have MLD, including some students with persistent low achievement (LA) in mathematics. The differences between MLD and LA reveal that there are many potential reasons why students may have mathematics difficulties. For this reason, it is useful to be aware of the defining features of MLD.

Defining MLD

One of the challenges faced by researchers of MLD—and by anyone synthesizing MLD research findings—is the inconsistency with which MLD has been defined across studies, an issue that has persisted for many years (Lewis & Fisher, 2016; Mazzocco, 2007). This inconsistency is a natural consequence of the lack of a universally agreed-on definition of MLD, the lack of a single universally accepted measure of mathematics achievement, the failure to identify one or more specific cognitive skills or deficits as a cause of MLD, and the many related but etiologically distinct skills that comprise the repertoire of "mathematics skills" (e.g., Petrill et al., 2012). Of the approaches historically used to identify LD in general, there is no evidence to support the use of an achievement and IQ score discrepancy (Stuebing et al., 2002) for MLD (Mazzocco, 2007), so this approach is rarely adopted in current research and should be avoided in practice (Fletcher, Lyon, Fuchs, & Barnes, 2007). An achievement score-cutoff approach predominates in the research, but its use varies, and it is not (by itself) recommended for determining MLD (or LD in general; e.g., Stuebing, Fletcher, Branum-Martin, & Francis, 2012). Some researchers' cutoffs are set so high (i.e., at the 25th or 35th percentile) that they overidentify MLD. Motivated by a concern that this high cutoff leads to combining children with very different sorts of mathematics difficulties into one classified group, researchers began to differentiate students with more severe (e.g., below the 11th percentile) versus more moderate LA in mathematics (e.g., 11th to 25th percentile as per Murphy, Mazzocco, Hanich, & Early, 2007; Stock, Desoete, & Roeyers, 2010), and these researchers showed that some of the cognitive correlates of mathematics difficulties and the nature of mathematics difficulties sometimes differ across such subgroups (Geary, Hoard, Byrd-Craven, Nugent, & Numtee, 2007; Murphy et al., 2007; Stock et al., 2010). Importantly, the similarities that exist between individuals on either side of this low threshold cutoff support the notion that skills linked to MLD (and to LD in general) are dimensional rather than categorical (e.g., Petrill & Kovas, 2015). However, key differences in cognitive skills or correlates do emerge across MLD and LA groups and implicate that these groups may be considered separately in research and, potentially, in practice. Throughout this chapter, key similarities and differences are highlighted so that the groups are not merely defined by an arbitrary cutoff point or score.

The cutoff approach used to differentiate MLD and LA from each other (and from typically achieving students) does not, by itself, identify which core skills underlye MLD. The approach is, however, aligned with the three following principles relevant to defining MLD. First, many students who experience persistent mathematics difficulties do not meet the aforementioned MLD criteria (e.g., students with LA). Therefore, poor math achievement per se does not definitively reflect MLD. (The lack of MLD does not, however, negate the need to provide instructional support for students with moderate or mild mathematics difficulties.) Second, an important feature of MLD and LA is that they persist over time (e.g., Geary et al., 2007). Therefore, any definition of MLD should reflect poor performance at more than one point in time, provided that the intervals between time points are sufficient for learning to occur—which may depend on the skill assessed or measure used. Such persistence is not absolute but it contrasts with short-lived mathematics difficulties. The limitations of this persistence are worth considering because mathematics performance fluctuations are expected and may vary with skills tested and measures used (e.g., Martin et al., 2012). Third, regarding difficulties that surface but do not persist, short-lived difficulties with mathematics may reflect the complexity or novelty of specific mathematics principles or procedures, the effort required to learn or master new mathematics content, motivational and social influences including math anxiety, or the lack of opportunity for sound mathematics instruction. These underpinnings are neither causes nor defining characteristics of MLD, but they do contribute to why mathematics may challenge many students at some points in time but not others. It stands to reason that these factors may exacerbate manifestation of MLD or LA.

DON'T FORGET

···

There is no widely accepted definition of MLD, no widely accepted skills test of MLD, and no standard cutoff score used to differentiate MLD and LA. There is no support for the use of discrepancy scores to diagnose MLD. Instead, diagnosis should involve attention to the many subskills that support mathematics learning.

Why do researchers still use mathematics achievement cutoff scores to classify students as having or not having MLD if the cutoff approach is imperfect for identifying LD (e.g., Martin et al., 2012)? This practice persists because the subskills that underlie MLD have not been definitively isolated. Otherwise, a skills-based test would be a more-informative, more-direct indicator of MLD than an achievement cutoff, as is the case with measures of phonological awareness or decoding to identify an SLD in reading. Thus, the cutoff scores currently applied to broad measures of mathematics achievement are proxies for these not-yet-identified core deficits of MLD. Until such core skills are identified, researchers and practitioners rely on achievement scores and other behavioral criteria (as illustrated by the *Diagnostic and Statistical Manual of Mental Disorders* (5th ed.) [*DSM-5*] definition, American Psychiatric Association [APA], 2013) to identify MLD.

Fortunately, in the last decade, some robust cognitive characteristics of MLD and LA have emerged from the research. As discussed further on in the chapter (see "Domain-Specific Skills Related to MLD: Number Sense" and "Domain General Cognitive Abilities: Cognitive Correlates of MLD"), numerical underpinnings of MLD are gaining research support as potential core MLD deficits (e.g., Vanbinst, Ansari, Ghesquière, & De Smedt, 2016) and are thus surfacing in more assessment measures (including informal assessments described further on in this chapter). Evolving definitions of MLD are increasingly based on these numerical skills and also attend to distinct components of mathematics, leading to the use of more-specific terms such as *arithmetic disorder, arithmetic fluency disorder,* and *dyscalculia,* as reflected in the *DSM-5.* These refer to specific difficulties with arithmetic procedures, number combination fluency (such as speed of math fact retrieval or mental computation), or processing single numbers or quantities, respectively, all of which are far more narrowly defined than is difficulty with the whole of mathematics. The use of different terms may add confusion about how to define MLD, but considered together it reflects the range of skills that comprise mathematical thinking. In the *DSM-5,* specific learning difficulties in mathematics include, but are not limited to, dyscalculia. Therefore, in this chapter, the term *dyscalculia* is interpreted as one type of MLD. Regardless of the degree to which they do or do not overlap, each of these terms refers to individual differences in cognitive skills that contribute to students' mathematics achievement and that are influenced by cognitive and environmental factors, as elaborated in the following section.

Etiology of MLD

There is converging evidence that genetic and environmental factors influence variation in mathematics achievement among individuals with or without MLD. Mathematics achievement is a multifaceted construct rather than a single cognitive process, so we would expect it to be affected by a range of factors. Moreover, behaviors that indicate mathematics achievement vary with age, so the relative contribution of factors that influence mathematics achievement may also vary with age. Thus, genetic and environmental contributions to mathematics are not viewed as causes of MLD but as influences on the likelihood that individuals will manifest MLD. Environmental factors are varied and include physical influences, such as prenatal environments or environmental stressors, and social influences, such as socioeconomic status (SES) and the types of learning opportunities individuals encounter. These factors interact with each other in determining the developmental course of mathematical cognition, learning, and achievement.

Much of the evidence on genetic and environmental contributions is drawn from large-scale studies of identical and fraternal twins (e.g., Petrill & Kovas, 2015). Through these studies, researchers can estimate the influence of genetics, shared environments, and non-shared environments on achievement, including mathematics and reading. In general, heritability of mathematics—the variation in mathematics attributed to genetic influences—increases with age, but it never reaches 100%. *This means that there is nearly always a potential for some environmental factors to make a difference.* From several US- and UK-based studies, estimates of mathematics achievement heritability range from .34 to .73 (Petrill & Kovas, 2015). Moreover, the stability in mathematics achievement level itself also appears highly heritable, but more longitudinal studies are needed to confirm this association. Note that these heritability figures are not specific to MLD, but rather to mathematics achievement. Twin researchers have shown that heritability of mathematics achievement is relatively constant at all levels of mathematics ability; that is, among individuals with MLD, typical achievement, or high ability. They have also shown that heritability differs for different types of mathematics skills, supporting the notion that skills such as mathematics fluency and mathematics calculation are independent of each other even if both are heritable (e.g., Petrill et al., 2012).

Studies of specific populations with a known increased risk for MLD, such as persons with Williams or Turner syndrome, provide additional evidence of

DON'T FORGET

Genetic and environmental factors account for variation in students' mathematics performance, which means there is nearly always a potential for some environmental factors to make a difference.

genetic, biologically based etiologies of a risk for MLD, as do findings of different manifestations of MLD across syndromes (Mazzocco, Quintero, Murphy, & McCloskey, 2015). It is worth noting that variation in mathematics achievement profiles is evident even within these populations, which is not surprising given that individuals with the same syndrome have unshared genes and environments. Considered together, these findings indicate that school psychologists and other practitioners should not expect all MLDs to manifest in the same way, because students will have had unique environmental and genetic influences on the development of their mathematical thinking and mathematics achievement.

Incidence of MLD

Mirroring the variation in definitions of MLD, prevalence rates of MLD vary based on classification criteria. This variation illustrates the lack of specificity associated with most classification schemes for SLD. It is remarkable, therefore, that the rates of MLD are fairly similar across studies. (Note that similar rates do not guarantee that the same combination of individuals is identified by different classification methods.) In her review of studies conducted in the United States, Europe, Israel, and India, Shalev (2007) reported prevalence rates of approximately 7% on average, ranging from approximately 3% to 14% across these nations. The cumulative incidence of MLD by the end of high school years, based on an epidemiological cohort study in the Midwestern United States, was 6% to 14% of all students (Barberesi, Katusic, Colligan, Weaver, & Jacobsen, 2005). This means that 6% to 14% of all students will meet MLD criteria at some point before the end of their high school years. However MLD is defined, the incidence rate stabilizes at age 13 years, indicating that most students are identified by about eighth grade.

The low cumulative incidence rates reported during primary school (2.1%) highlights the need for early screening of MLD as a critical first step to help set children's mathematics achievement development on a more favorable course (whether their challenges are MLD, delays, or other sources of mathematics difficulties). With greater knowledge of the primary correlates and early predictors of mathematics achievement described in the following section, early identification of MLD (or at least of MLD at-risk status) is possible. Moreover, slow growth in mathematics-related skills during primary school (before Grade 3) accounts for much of the significant differences seen in students with versus without MLD all the way through Grade 5 (e.g., Geary, Hoard, Nugent, & Bailey, 2013; Murphy et al., 2007). In a sense, this means that failure to identify and respond to math difficulties in the early school years may increase cumulative incidence rates.

These prevalence and incidence rates apply only to MLD. Another 10% or so of all students will have persistent LA. Others still will have occasional difficulty in mathematics. When policy reports indicate alarmingly high rates of poor achievement, such as 50% or higher rates of failure to achieve basic mastery on areas of the NAEP annual mathematics assessments, these reflect the combination of MLD, LA, and other contributions to poor mathematics achievement.

MANIFESTATION OF MLD: SUBGROUPS, SUBTYPES, AND COGNITIVE CORRELATES

MLD and LA are heterogeneous classifications. This means that there are several manifestations of mathematics difficulties and several mathematics skills with which students in these groups may have difficulty. (This is exacerbated by the fact that many students with MLD also have reading disability [RD]). There are several possible approaches to differentiating subgroups of individuals with MLD from each other and from individuals with LA. In this section, we draw from three such approaches. Our primary approach pertains to identifying "domain-specific" and "domain-general" cognitive correlates of mathematics ability and disability, recognizing that some individuals experience difficulties in only some of these cognitive domains. That is, some students' mathematics difficulties may be specific to foundational mathematics skills (such as number processing), whereas other students may have intact numerical skills but have difficulty with general cognitive skills (that is, skills that are not specific to mathematics). Many students with MLD or LA may have one or more areas of cognitive difficulty. A related approach pertains to three potential domain-general subtypes of MLD for which there is currently some evidence base. These are the semantic memory, procedural, and visuospatial-based mathematics difficulties initially proposed by Geary (1993) that have since been somewhat refined (Geary, 2011). These are referred to within the context of domain-general cognitive correlates. The third approach attends to the mathematical impairments identified in the *DSM-5*, which focus on different domains of mathematics, such as number, math facts, fact fluency, and math reasoning, but which in turn are related to the skills on which the first two approaches are based. These three approaches are, therefore, not mutually exclusive or completely overlapping. Each has important implications for MLD or LA subgroups.

Domain-Specific Skills Related to MLD: Number Sense

Domain-specific skills related to MLD include those skills that involve perceiving and processing numerical or quantitative information, either through informal non-symbolic quantitative processes that do not depend on instruction and are not specific to humans or through precise mathematical procedures and knowledge acquired through formal instruction in school and other settings. Although we refer to these as domain specific, we caution readers that they are, nevertheless, associated with domain-general skills such as attention, which are described in the section "Domain General Cognitive Abilities: Cognitive Correlates of MLD."

As is noted for definitions of MLD, there is no single definition of *number sense* (Berch, 2005; Reynvoet, Smets, & Sasanguie, 2016). Mathematics educators and policy makers typically use the term *number sense* broadly by referring to a range of skills, knowledge, or functions related to number (National Mathematics Advisory Panel, 2008, p. 27). By contrast, cognitive scientists typically limit use of the term *number sense* to a specific, intuitive, nonverbal ability to identify approximate quantities, an ability sometimes referred to as a *gut sense* of number. As elaborated in the following section, this intuitive ability differs from the formal number skills learned in or out of school. It is useful for school psychologists and other practitioners to recognize that each of these distinct numerical skills may contribute to students' mathematics learning difficulties.

Nonsymbolic Number Skills

Cognitive scientists have proposed that two systems support intuitive number sense (Feigenson, Dehaene, & Spelke, 2004). *Subitizing* is the ability to identify rapidly and accurately small sets (up to three or four items) without counting. This ability is supported by the *object tracking system*, a construct relevant to recognizing only small exact quantities. To recognize the two-ness or three-ness of a set, a student need not have corresponding set size labels (i.e., number words) or knowledge of Arabic digits. Indeed, young infants, nonhuman primates, and fish are all capable of subitizing. (There is emerging evidence that pattern recognition supports subitizing-like behaviors for sets larger than three, particularly if those sets appear as a pattern of subsets that can each be subitized, such as recognizing two rows of three dots on a die as six [Krajcsi, Szabó, & Mórocz, 2013]). Thus some pattern recognition may benefit from the ability to subitize. By contrast, recognizing sets larger than four is supported by the *approximate number system,* which is characterized by rapid and accurate assessment of larger approximate quantities. As is true for subitizing, determining which of two sets is "more" does not require knowledge of number symbols or labels. Infants, nonhuman primates, and birds are all capable of approximate quantity discrimination.

Subitizing and approximate quantity discrimination are considered *intuitive* because neither depends on formal instruction or formal number knowledge. They are considered *nonverbal* and *nonsymbolic* because they do not require verbal processing or responses, and they do not rely on symbols such as numerals or number words. These skills are often measured via implicit tasks. Once we begin to use words or symbols to represent these quantities, we engage symbolic number processes. (To appreciate the nature of these nonsymbolic skills and how they differ from counting or other formal *symbolic* skills, complete the simulation on the Panamath website included in the "Assessment Resources" section at the end of this chapter.) Explicit tasks are typically used to measure these symbolic skills (e.g., Reynvoet et al., 2016).

On average, individuals with MLD count rather than subitize very small sets of items (Koontz & Berch, 1996) or have smaller subitizing ranges (Kucian & von Aster, 2015), and they have significantly more immature approximate number skills than their LA or typically developing peers (Bugden & Ansari, 2015; Mazzocco, Feigenson, & Halberda, 2011; Piazza et al., 2010; Stock et al., 2010), especially in kindergarten (Stock et al., 2010). These do not appear to be short-lived differences, because they are evident even in high school students (Mazzocco et al., 2011). Some researchers argue that these nonsymbolic skills are necessary, but not sufficient, for mathematics achievement (Mazzocco et al., 2011) and that nonsymbolic number abilities are subject to very large individual differences throughout the life span (Halberda, Ly, Willmer, Naiman, & Germine, 2012). Although deficits in this basic level of numerical processing differentiate some students with MLD from other students, a relatively small portion of individuals who struggle with school mathematics show weak nonsymbolic number skills. School psychologists and other practitioners should benefit from the awareness of these skills, because it strengthens their understanding and recognition of the challenges faced by some students with MLD.

> **DON'T FORGET**
> ....
> Psychologists and other practitioners should not expect all MLDs to manifest in the same way, because students will have had unique environmental and genetic influences on the development of their mathematical thinking and mathematics achievement.

Symbolic Number Skills: Costs and Benefits
Regardless of the role of nonsymbolic skills, consensus is emerging that *symbolic* number skills play a more significant role in mathematics development and possibly in MLD. It is difficult, if not impossible, to avoid the use of symbols when

discussing or even thinking about mathematics. Arithmetic and higher mathematics are built on the use of symbols, which include numerals and number words early in development and fractions, variables, and complex notations in later school years. These symbols are used to refer to quantities or to relations between quantities, but not all children automatically equate each symbol (such as the Arabic numeral *2* or the word *two*) with its corresponding quantity, at least not early in development. For most typically developing children, the link between whole number symbols and nonsymbolic quantities becomes automatized sometime between kindergarten and Grade 3 (Girelli, Lucangeli, & Butterworth, 2000). A major benefit to mastering these symbolic skills is that doing so allows us to think about numbers and operations well beyond those that can be directly viewed. This supports more complex arithmetic and mathematics.

The timing and extent to which symbolic skills are automatized varies with development, and they might never become *completely* automatic even in adulthood (Lyons, Ansari, & Beilock, 2012). In other words, there is a cost (in terms of mental effort and response time) to linking symbols to quantities (just as there is a cost to decoding written words). Usually that cost is trivial or becomes relatively trivial with development. For instance, it may be *easier* to recognize visually that the solution to $10 + 4$ is larger than the solution to $8 + 3$ when this problem is depicted nonsymbolically (i.e., with pictures item sets) versus with arithmetic statements (as done in this sentence), but in adults the relative difficulty imposed by symbolic arithmetic might be detectable only when reaction time is measured at the level of milliseconds. Among young children, the time delay is more evident. The cost may be greater, slowing performance considerably, for students of all ages if they have less automatized symbolic number skills.

When symbolic numerical processing is compromised, this performance cost is not limited to early childhood. Price, Mazzocco, and Ansari (2013) provided evidence that even in high school, some students rely on very deliberate versus automatic retrieval to evaluate whether simple arithmetic statements are true (e.g., $4 + 3 = 7$) or false (e.g., $4 + 3 = 9$), suggesting that less automatic symbolic mapping skills affect processing speed. Accuracy may also be affected, depending on task complexity. Early symbolic number skills such as numeral identification and counting sets (at Grades K or 1) predict later mathematics achievement, even as late as high school, and weak symbolic number skills appear to be a core deficit of MLD (Olsson, Östergren, & Träff, 2016; Vanbinst et al., 2016). Although current debates center on the relative contribution of symbolic and nonsymbolic skills to MLD (and to mathematics achievement), measures of these allegedly simple numerical skills may be informative and appear to differentiate children with MLD from children with LA (Bugden & Ansari, 2015; Mazzocco et al., 2011; Olsson et al., 2016).

It is worth noting that, thus far, we have focused on number skills that pertain to numerical magnitude (how many), but numbers are also used to represent ordinal positions relative to a range of attributes such as size (e.g., the second largest bowl) or to serial position in space (e.g., second in line) or time (e.g., second inning), and so forth. Magnitude and ordinal number skills independently influence arithmetic performance (Goffin & Ansari, 2016), and there is emerging evidence that separate cognitive systems are responsible for processing magnitude and ordinal information. Children (Kaufman, Vogel, Starke, & Schocke, 2009) and adults (De Visscher, Szmalec, Van Der Linden, & Noël, 2015; Rubinsten & Sury, 2011) with MLD may have deficits in ordinal information processing, and these may be involved in the manifestation of weak nonsymbolic magnitude skills. These findings serve to remind us that although informal measures of symbolic or nonsymbolic skills are potentially informative supplements to a traditional assessment, they are not widely accepted as diagnostic of MLD on their own.

Number tasks may suggest risk status for MLD or the nature of mathematical difficulties as a complement to standardized assessment. Of course, *performance on these tasks should be evaluated relative to students' home- and school-based opportunities to learn or practice the skills being evaluated,* because variation in even intuitive number skills is accounted for by genetic *and* environmental factors (Tosto et al., 2014). In the United States, young children from low socioeconomic backgrounds are at significantly higher risk of poor symbolic numerical skills compared to their more socioeconomically advantaged peers (Jordan & Levine, 2009), but there is no evidence to implicate that this is due to higher rates of MLD. See Rapid Reference 3.1.

Several formal mathematics achievement or ability assessments include a measure of symbolic number knowledge. Informal measures are also available. Reviewing these informal, experimental symbolic measures (noted in the "Assessment Resources" section) may shed light on the nature of symbolic skills in comparison to the previously discussed nonsymbolic skills.

DON'T FORGET

Nonsymbolic numerical skills are informative, but they are not widely accepted as diagnostic of MLD on their own. Number skills may suggest risk status for MLD or other mathematical difficulties, but performance on these tasks should be evaluated relative to students' opportunities to learn or practice number skills.

Number Knowledge, Counting, and Arithmetic

Symbolic number skills include a wide range of formal mathematics skills that children learn from parents, teachers, and their environment. The procedural

≡ *Rapid Reference 3.1*

Contrasting Two Types of Numerical Abilities

Category of Skill	Key Characteristics of These Types of Skills and Tasks	Examples from the Resource Section
Nonsymbolic	• Intuitive (i.e., these skills are universal; they develop without instruction, even if instruction leads to improvement). • Nonsymbolic (i.e., based on actual sets of visual, auditory, or kinesthetic stimuli, not symbols that represent them). • Nonverbal (do not require a verbal response or mediation—instead, it is a gut sense of quantity). • Accuracy: Exact (for arrays < 4) or approximate (for larger arrays).	Simulation: The Panamath demo on the Panamath.org website provides an example of a visual, approximate, nonsymbolic task.
Symbolic	• Formal (i.e., these skills develop as a result of instruction, at home or school or in society; and the specific symbols to be learned vary across cultures). • Symbols (e.g., Arabic digits, number words, tallies, or other notations) are used to *represent* quantities. • Accuracy: May be exact or estimations, depending on the task. • Automatization: One aspect of the development of symbolic skills is that they gradually become automatized, such as in terms of automatic knowledge of single digits, fraction values, and number combinations.	Simulation: "Exact change" simulation on Misunderstood Minds website emphasizes the challenges faced when symbolic skills are not automatic.

and conceptual aspects of symbolic skills support each other. For example, through learning and carrying out counting procedures that they initially copy, children learn *how* to count, but they also begin to learn what the number words *mean*. In this way, counting procedures support developing number knowledge. Enhanced number knowledge then refines counting procedures and strengthens their efficiency, especially for more complex counting such as skip counting by twos or fives. This dynamic relation between counting procedures and knowledge parallels the relation between other levels of procedural and conceptual mathematics, including learning to solve and retrieve number combinations. In the latter case, practice with number combination fluency helps build knowledge of number combinations and vice versa (e.g., Rittle-Johnson & Alibali, 1999). This principle also supports learning of whole number and fraction concepts, as mentioned in item C in the "Implications for Instruction and Intervention" section of this chapter.

The typical trajectory of some number knowledge and skills is well described, and it differs from the trajectory observed in students with MLD. Typically developing preschoolers learn the number word–counting sequence (rote counting) well before they understand the meaning of counting (Gelman & Gallistel, 1978; Sarnecka, 2015), but this should not be confused with meaningful counting. These typical precursors to enumeration are normal, but they are not evidence of mathematical processing. Once young children begin to understand the *meaning* of number words and of the counting process, they do so gradually, understanding the meaning of *one* before *two,* and so forth, through the preschool years. On average, typically developing kindergarteners recognize essential counting principles, such as one-to-one correspondence, that the number of items in a set remains the same even if the set is rearranged (number constancy), and that counting out a set determines how many are in the set (cardinality) (see Rapid Reference 3.2). Typically developing children and, later, young children with MLD may make errors that reflect incomplete mastery of these counting principles (Mazzocco & Thompson, 2005), but many students with MLD (and most with LA) do not. Difficulties related to MLD are more evident when counting principles are tested using unfamiliar procedures—that are less reliant on rote procedures—such as asking student to evaluate the accuracy of others' counting instead of counting sets on their own (Geary, Hoard, Byrd-Craven, & DeSoto, 2004). For instance, even kindergarteners or first-graders with MLD are likely to use one-to-one correspondence correctly when asked to count a set of objects *on their own,* but when watching a puppet or other person count items, children with MLD are less likely to detect counting principle violations, such as double counting (Geary et al., 2004) or inappropriate use of skip counting word sequences (e.g., saying, *2, 4, 6, 8* when pointing to one dot at a time). By kindergarten, failing the basic counting principles listed in Rapid Reference 3.2 is an indicator of risk for poor mathematics outcomes. Important, intact counting procedures are not an indicator that a child does *not* have MLD (Murphy & Mazzocco, 2008). Other symbolic skills also need to be evaluated.

≡ *Rapid Reference 3.2*

Implicit Counting Behaviors and Principles

Type of Behavior or Principle	Description
Early Childhood Precursors	
Recites number words	Child recites a number (e.g., *1, 3*) without necessarily understanding the quantity associated with it.
Recites count word sequence ("Counts aloud")	Child recites number words in sequence, initially incorrectly, and gradually more correctly, independent of enumerating. This is not true "counting."
Recites count words related to objects	The child uses number words when pointing to objects but does not conform to the following essential principles.
Essential Implicit Counting Principles	
One-to-one correspondence	One and only one word tag (e.g., *1, 2*) is assigned to each counted object.
Stable order	Order of the word tags must be invariant across counted sets.
Cardinality	The value of the final word tag represents the quantity of items in the counted set.
Abstraction	Objects of any kind can be collected and counted together.
Order irrelevance	Items within a given set can be tagged in any sequence (as long as one-to-one correspondence is maintained).
Unessential Features (not a principle of counting, not predictive of later mathematics, and unnecessary teaching points unless used to support tracking or other organizational strategy)	
Standard direction	Counting proceeds from left to right.
Adjacency	Consecutive count of contiguous objects
Pointing	Counted objects are typically pointed at once.
Start at an end	Counting starts at one of the end points of an array of objects.

Source: Adapted with permission from Rapid Reference 3.1 by Geary (2011).

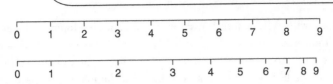

Figure 3.1. Linear versus Logarithmic.

Note: The top number line is the mathematic representation where the distance between successive whole numbers is equal. The bottom number line shows how children represent numbers before learning the mathematical number line. For them, the difference between 1 and 2 seems larger than that between 2 and 3. As numerals get larger, they seem less and less different from one another.

Counting skills involve mapping number words onto quantities, but symbols such as Arabic digits are also linked to corresponding quantities. By kindergarten, typically developing children and children with LA are readily able to name most one-digit and many two-digit numbers, but primary schoolchildren with MLD may make more errors naming digits (Mazzocco & Thompson, 2005) and take longer to write numbers to dictation (van Loosbroek, Dirkx, Hulstijn, & Janssen, 2009).

Number lines are yet another way to represent single numbers and their relation to one another. Number line skills have been extensively studied in typical development and in persons with MLD and are believed to reflect how formal instruction affects thinking about numbers and number relations. Standard number line tasks typically involve showing a number line with designated end points (as in Figure 3.1) and asking children to place specific numbers individually at correct positions on the line. Initially, even typically developing children make characteristic errors in their number line responses, such that regardless of the order in which numbers are placed, children's placements are more compressed for larger number values than for smaller numbers (conforming to a logarithmic pattern; see Figure 3.1). Gradually, their responses shift toward a more representative, evenly spaced, linear depiction of sequential numbers, which is viewed as a response to schooling on number skills specifically (Siegler & Robinson, 1982). Not surprisingly, this shift occurs at different developmental time points depending on the familiarity of numbers used, beginning at about first grade (for the numbers 1 to 10) and later for larger numbers (1 to 100 and so forth; Siegler & Opfer, 2003).

These shifts in number line task responses have been interpreted as reflecting how instruction alters the mental representation children have of numbers and their relative properties, but some researchers argue that these shifts reflect different strategies toward using end points to guide those response patterns (Sasanguie, Verschaffel, Reynvoet, & Luwel, 2016).

Children with MLD and LA show a different developmental pattern on number line tasks. First, children with MLD or LA have an early disadvantage and are less likely to manifest this shift toward linear number line responses early on (in early Grade 1, when both groups have had limited schooling on number lines); but by Grade 2, children with LA are as likely as their typically developing peers to conform to linear number line responses, whereas children with MLD continue to respond consistent with a logarithmic versus linear distribution (Geary, Hoard, Nugent, & Byrd-Craven, 2008). These researchers interpret this finding as indicating that children with LA are likely to reap gains on number line representations through the regular schooling they have received by Grade 2 and that children with MLD are not (Geary et al., 2008). The reasons for these differential outcomes is not known, but this pattern supports the persistence of MLD and LA levels of performance, as discussed previously in the "Defining MLD" section.

From primary school onward, MLD may also manifest in estimation errors and place value errors (Mazzocco, Murphy, Brown, Rinne, & Herold, 2013) when working with whole numbers and either slowed or inaccurate arithmetic. These difficulties persist into adulthood, with individuals with MLD being more prone to estimation, place value, transcoding, and arithmetic errors, or at least to very slow performance on these tasks (McCloskey, 2007) compared to persons without MLD. (More information about arithmetic fluency is discussed in the section entitled "Processing Speed and Problem-Solving.") These difficulties also parallel errors seen in fractions, such that between Grades 4 to 8, students with MLD are not making gains in their understanding of fraction concepts and procedures that would be expected with advancing grades, whereas students with LA do show such gains, albeit more slowly than children with typical mathematics achievement (Mazzocco, Myers, Lewis, Hanich, & Murphy, 2013).

There are several important caveats to this description of numerical difficulties. First, they may be logical manifestations of the nonsymbolic or symbolic numerical difficulties that characterize MLD, as described in the previous section. Second, these manifestations reflect group averages, but not all students with MLD will manifest all these characteristics. Third, these behaviors also have organizational, procedural, and visual-spatial components, and thus in some children these behaviors may actually reflect the role of domain general skills involved in MLD either in addition to or instead of numerical deficits. These domain general skills are considered next.

CAUTION

There are many definitions and components of "number sense," so not all measures of number sense are necessarily measuring the same skills.

Domain General Cognitive Abilities: Cognitive Correlates of MLD

The numerical skills described in the previous section do not occur in isolation from other cognitive skills. Attending to or comparing quantities may involve visual-spatial abilities. Attending to sets, comparing quantities, and completing arithmetic problems all involve selective attention and working memory. Counting items in a set involves visual tracking, updating, self-monitoring, and other executive function skills. Carrying out procedures and retrieving facts are influenced by general processing speed. Each of these skills may also involve language and may be subject to intrapersonal and cultural social influences. These are all considerations for assessment and educational planning for children who struggle with mathematics. But how are these skills manifested in students with MLD?

Memory and Semantic Memory

Memory is integral to learning, but it is not a domain-specific aspect of mathematics because it supports learning across all subjects. Students whose MLD is predominantly rooted in numerical processing difficulties do not necessarily differ from their peers in all memory abilities. When students with MLD have strong overall verbal or nonverbal memory skills, they may be so proficient at remembering what steps to execute during familiar procedures (e.g., how to count, the sequence used when regrouping, when commutativity applies to problem-solving), or they may be able to recall overlearned math facts so well that their successful reliance on memory masks an underlying MLD (Murphy & Mazzocco, 2008). Thus school psychologists and other practitioners should attend to whether a given student's mathematics difficulty is due to memory difficulties per se, whether students are having difficulty remembering mathematics procedures and math facts suggestive of specific semantic memory difficulties (Geary, 1993, 2011), or whether strong memory skills are helping a student overcome mathematics difficulties in the early school years. The degree to which strong memory can help students with MLD has its limits, because as students progress through higher grades, the memory loads required to keep up with their peers will be unmanageable in a way similar to the limits of sight word reading as a strategy to overcome dyslexia (Juel, 1988; Stanovich & Siegel, 1994). Yet, it is much more common for students with MLD to have difficulty with arithmetic facts than to excel on them. In some instances, this seems related to specific difficulty in long-term semantic memory.

One area in which memory difficulties are apparent in many students with MLD is in their inconsistent retrieval of answers to "math facts" they have been exposed to repeatedly and that are thus overlearned by most grade-level peers (e.g.,

Jordan, Hanich, & Kaplan, 2003). Evidence suggests that the difficulty is not tied to difficulties with overall long-term memory per se, because students with MLD do retrieve these facts accurately, but not consistently. This inconsistency may be related to difficulty either retrieving verbal information from long-term memory (i.e., *semantic memory;* Geary, 1993) or difficulty ignoring irrelevant associated solutions (such as difficulty ignoring 25 when faced with the problem, 5 × 4). Although students should be permitted to use finger counting if doing so is necessary for their success, it is useful to assess students' math fact retrieval directly, asking them to solve without calculating during assessment. Using this approach, Geary and colleagues have found that retrieval errors in students with MLD and in some children with LA emerge early (by second grade) remain stable through at least Grade 4 and include a much higher rate of associated solution errors compared to typically achieving students. Interestingly, a subgroup of students with LA showed no decline in their high rate of associated solution errors over time, even though students with MLD did. This suggests that a subgroup of students with math LA have a particular difficulty with math fact retrieval, and they may represent a semantic memory subgroup of mathematics learning difficulties (Geary, 1993, 2011).

Geary's findings are consistent with those from earlier longitudinal studies demonstrating the stability of arithmetic fluency difficulties in students with MLD and LA, from Grades 2 to 3 (Jordan et al., 2003) and from Grades 2 to 5 (Chong & Siegel, 2008). This is in contrast to procedural deficits (such as in correctly carrying out multistep arithmetic) that are more likely to diminish over time (Chong & Siegel, 2008). There are mixed findings regarding whether the fact retrieval deficits are associated with comorbid reading disability (Geary, 1993) or not (Jordan et al., 2003).

Even among eighth-graders, students with MLD or LA complete overlearned arithmetic problems more slowly than their typically achieving peers (Mazzocco, Devlin, & McKenney, 2008). In a study of these skills, typically achieving eighth-graders completed a problem set in 2 minutes on average, whereas students in the LA group took 2½ minutes and students with MLD took nearly 3½ minutes. (This can make quite a difference on a classroom quiz designed to take 10 minutes!) Despite slower performance, students with MLD made more errors than did students with LA, whose performance level approached ceiling levels (as did the typically achieving students'). Hence, there is a difference between slow and accurate, versus slow and inaccurate, performance.

What about the types of errors made by students with MLD or LA? Mazzocco and colleagues (2008) showed that students with LA made more of the types of errors typically observed in arithmetic problem-solving, such as being off by one (e.g., $5 + 3 = 9$) or coming up with a solution that is incorrect but associated with the right answer (e.g., $5 \times 4 = 25$). These *associated solution errors* are common even among arithmetically competent adults, wherein a solution given for a problem (such as 5×4) is a valid solution for an associated problem ($5 \times 5 = 25$). Most individuals (including the students in the LA or typically achieving groups in this study) who make associated solution errors tend to make errors that are consistent with the "decade" of the correct solution. That is, it is more likely that an error to 5×4 will be another response in the 20s (such as 25) than a response not in the 20s (such as 15, 35, or 65). In this study, the rate of these decade consistent errors was high (60% on average) among the associated solution errors made by students in the LA or typically achieving groups, as anticipated, with no difference between the groups. Although students with MLD also made some associated solution errors, theirs were less likely to be decade consistent. Moreover, students with MLD also made errors that were difficult to classify and grossly inaccurate (e.g., $18 + 8 = 13$) or revealed place value confusion. These kinds of errors were rarely seen in the LA and typically achieving groups.

Considered together, fact-retrieval errors are common among students with MLD or LA, and are likely to persist throughout the school years for many of these students. The simulation on "using basic math facts" listed in the "Background Resources" section (PBS Misunderstood Minds) demonstrates how frustrating this can be for students and how it impedes their performance. This has the added effect of turning a "simple" problem into a difficult one for students who have semantic fluency difficulties or other obstacles to fact retrieval. It is important to recognize that this fact retrieval may not reflect slower information processing of all kinds, as elaborated in the next section.

Processing Speed and Problem-Solving

Processing speed, or the general speed with which individuals complete relatively easy automated tasks, is often measured in studies of MLD. Across many studies comparing students with MLD versus LA, students in both groups take longer to name digits, compare quantities, rank order fractions, or finish word problems, on average, compared to typically developing students (e.g., Geary et al., 2013; Mazzocco & Grimm, 2013), in addition to math fact problems, noted in the previous section. These findings are observed through most of the primary and middle school years and in the few studies of high school performance as well. School psychologists should attend to *whether* a given student consistently takes longer to complete specific mathematics assignments or tasks relative to grade-level peers, on *what kinds* of mathematics problems, and what may account for the slower performance (as briefly detailed previously for math facts).

Because students with MLD, on average, process numerical information less automatically than their typically achieving or LA peers, the more effortful number processing may impede overall speed of problem-solving. This explanation suggests that slower numerical processing speed underlies the slower problem-solving observed among students with MLD. An alternative explanation is that the lack of (or impaired) automatic numerical processing leads students with MLD to abandon numerical procedures altogether and to rely on different (and less-efficient) strategies to solve problems. There is some support for this notion. For instance, most students rely on finger counting when first learning number combinations (Jordan, Kaplan, Ramineni & Locuniak, 2008), gradually abandoning it by about Grade 2 when their number-combination skills become more accurate. But students with MLD are more likely than their peers to rely on finger counting into third grade (Geary, 1993) and even into sixth grade (Mazzocco et al., 2008), and they may rely on other overlearned laborious procedures that typically developing children abandon for more-efficient shortcuts (Geary et al., 2004). Immature numerical behaviors are observed in practical problem-solving as well, such as clock reading. At approximately Grades 3 to 6, children with MLD make age-*in*appropriate clock reading errors on analog and digital clocks that are not seen in their typically developing peers (Burny, Valcke, & Deseote, 2012). General processing speed measures are included in many standardized cognitive assessments, but these are not necessarily reflective of the numerical processing that is slowed in some students with MLD. Moreover, these standardized cognitive tests are not effective for differentiating among different types of processing difficulties and related executive function skills such as working memory (Raghubar, Barnes, & Hecht, 2010).

Executive Function Skills

Processing speed is often discussed in terms of automatized behaviors, but much of mathematics problem-solving is more deliberate. Moreover, if students do not succeed on retrieving math facts or executing well-mastered procedures, even simple problems may be difficult. (The simulation on *multistep problems,* listed as a "Background Resources" on Misunderstood Minds website at the end of this chapter, exemplifies this point.) On unfamiliar or difficult problems, executive function skills support learning and doing mathematics. These executive function skills are collectively considered deliberate, goal-oriented cognitive processes required to succeed on effortful tasks. They include the ability to maintain attention during a task (sustained attention), the ability to consider and shift between multiple perspectives or strategies (cognitive flexibility), the ability to inhibit making an automatic, overlearned response (inhibitory control), and the ability to mentally hold on to information while manipulating it (e.g., adding or multiplying), updating it (e.g., holding on to partial sums or products during arithmetic or long division), evaluating it (e.g., deciding if the solution you arrived at is correct), and keeping track of steps required (whether in counting, addition, division, or geometry, for example). It is not surprising, therefore, that there is a well-established association between mathematics achievement and executive function skills (e.g., Bull, Espy, & Wiebe, 2008; Clements & Sarama, 2014; Fuchs et al., 2006), and that this association is observed among students of all ages. Difficulties in these executive, working memory skills are implicated in the *procedural MLD subtype* first described by Geary in 1993. Since then, research has demonstrated that students whose MLD seems most closely rooted in procedural difficulties make larger gains over time than children with semantic memory–based MLD or dyscalculia (i.e., deficiency in nonsymbolic number skills).

Although the nature and direction of that association may vary with age and across types of mathematics tasks, it is clear that working memory skills are particularly relevant to new and difficult problems (e.g., Herold, Bock, Murphy, & Mazzocco, work in preparation). Teachers may, in an effort to scaffold difficult problems or make problems "easier," provide additional examples, explanations, or instructions, which might have the opposite effect of overloading working memory demands even more. Students with low working memory are at higher risk for poor mathematics achievement (Alloway & Alloway, 2010), and students with MLD have working memory difficulties (Geary et al., 2007; Siegel & Ryan, 1989). This does not mean that the two populations are identical, however, and the exact amount of overlap between the two is unknown. It is worth noting that the "easy" problems that pose challenges to students with MLD or LA demand more of their working memory resources compared to the demands that these easy problems impose on typically achieving students. This has the effect of limiting the available resources because working memory is so taxed.

It may be difficult to ascertain whether a student's difficulty with a mathematics problem reflects difficulty with executive function skills, mathematical skills, or both. For instance, if a student's MLD (e.g., numerical processing difficulties) poses a greater need for working memory resources during one-digit number combination problems, for this student, this task is essentially a working memory task, but the task is not a working memory task for students who can readily retrieve number combination responses (e.g., Mazzocco & Hanich, 2010). This means that a student with MLD who has strong working memory would be more likely to meet the demands of this task than a student with MLD who has low or average working memory skills. Reducing working memory demands will assist the student who has the requisite mathematics skills but insufficient working memory resources to complete the task (or to advance those skills). If mathematics skills themselves are deficient, decreasing the working memory demands may be helpful but insufficient.

Even math anxiety, the tension that interferes with solving mathematics problems in everyday life and school settings, may operate by overloading the working memory system. That is, when mental effort is occupied by ruminating thoughts (such as, "I am no good at these types of problems"), it interferes with the effort required to solve the problem at hand (Johns, Schmader, & Martens, 2005). This association demonstrates the intricate links between cognition and psychosocial factors in MLD, which informs interventions that may diminish math anxiety or its effects.

> **DON'T FORGET**
> ....
> Not all children manifest MLD in the same way.

PSYCHOSOCIAL CORRELATES: MATH MOTIVATION AND MATH ANXIETY

Imagine having just one or a few of the difficulties that manifest as MLD and how these difficulties might influence your motivation to succeed at mathematics, your anxiety about doing mathematics, or both. *Math motivation* involves a sense that mathematics is valuable, a desire to succeed at mathematics, and the willingness to exert effort to succeed on mathematics problems and assignments (Gottfried, Marcoulides, Gottfried, Oliver, & Guerin, 2007). *Mathematics anxiety* is defined as "feelings of tension and anxiety that interfere with the manipulation of numbers and the solving of mathematical problems in a wide variety of ordinary life and academic situations" (Richardson & Suinn, 1972, p. 551). Math motivation and math anxiety interact with each other in a complex manner (Wang et al., 2015). In a recent study of adolescents and adults with different mathematics performance levels, whether math anxiety was associated with poorer mathematics performance depended, in part, on math motivation levels. Among individuals demonstrating a positive motivation toward mathematics, persons with moderate levels of math anxiety had *better* mathematics performance (on four measures of mathematics) than did persons with either very low or very high levels of math anxiety. This pattern parallels the classic psychological findings on arousal, motivation, and performance (Yerkes & Dodson, 1908) and suggests that moderate anxiety may enhance attention or working memory. By contrast, among persons with low math motivation, math anxiety and mathematics performance had a negative linear relation with each other, such that higher math anxiety predicted lower mathematics scores. Despite these different patterns of math anxiety effects, high levels of math anxiety led to relatively lower mathematics performance (compared to low or moderate math anxiety), regardless of math motivation level, for all but the least demanding of the four math tasks studied by Wang et al. (2015).

The roots of math motivation and math anxiety are not known, but intrinsic and extrinsic factors seem to play a role in math motivation. In a large international twin study, 9- to 16-year-olds' enjoyment of mathematics and their self-rated mathematics ability were highly heritable. Remarkably, shared environment (such as being in the same home or classroom) accounted for limited variation in math motivation or self-perceived ability, whereas about 60% of the variance was explained by non-shared (i.e., individual specific) environmental factors (Kovas et al., 2015). It is unclear exactly what those factors are, but it is clear that home, classroom, and genetics are not the sole influences on the development of math motivation and math anxiety. For instance, students' perceptions of their classroom environment are related to their mathematics performance, but this relation is mediated by students' self-perceived mathematics ability and their interest in mathematics (Tosto, Asbury, Mazzocco, Petrill, & Kovas, 2016).

Math motivation and math anxiety are not causes of MLD, but they are discussed here because they may influence mathematics achievement and play a role in some students' mathematics difficulties. There is some evidence that students with MLD or LA report higher levels of math anxiety than their typically developing peers (Wu, Willcutt, Escovar, & Menon, 2014). This means that school psychologists and other practitioners should consider self-perceived mathematics ability, sentiments about mathematics, and math anxiety in evaluations of students with suspected MLD. At the same time, however, it is important to remember that indicators of low mathematics motivation or of high mathematics anxiety do not, by themselves, indicate MLD (because most students refer to negative experience with mathematics at least once during their school years; Furner & Duffy, 2002), but they may indicate higher risk for later poor mathematics achievement. It is also important to recognize that these factors are relevant at all grade levels and that information of this nature may surface during informal, flexible interviews with students.

Another factor relevant to psychosocial influences on mathematics are sex differences in mathematics, which are also described as having biological and psychosocial roots. With respect to MLD, the research base is mixed, with no

CAUTION

Math motivation and math anxiety are not causes of MLD, but they may influence mathematics achievement and play a role in some students' mathematics difficulties.

overall consistent report of higher rates of MLD in girls or boys. Assessment and intervention of MLD should not be determined based on students' sex, but there is some evidence that girls are more likely to experience stereotype threat that interferes with their mathematics in childhood (Beilock, Gunderson, Ramirez, & Levine, 2010) and adulthood (Johns et al., 2005), but this again is not linked to MLD. For instance, students' mathematics achievement gains are associated with their teachers' mathematics anxiety levels, but only among girls who endorse the belief that girls are bad at mathematics (Beilock et al., 2010). In this case, it seems that the experiences affecting girls' own self-perception of their mathematics ability (thus leading to gender stereotypes) influenced whether a teacher with high math anxiety affected their mathematics learning. The precise mechanism of this teacher effect is not clear. Fortunately, math anxiety seems to diminish with individualized tutoring, even among students with MLD (Iuculano et al., 2015).

IMPLICATIONS FOR ASSESSMENT

There is no single widely accepted definition of MLD, but guiding principles for MLD assessment and instruction have a solid basis in research, as briefly summarized in this chapter. From this research, it is clear that there are many possible obstacles to mathematics achievement difficulties; therefore, assessment of possible MLD requires attending to a range of skills assessments and informal out-of-range testing in addition to standardized achievement and cognitive tests. Based on the evidence presented in this chapter, the principal manifestations of MLD include persistently poor number skills, slow or inaccurate arithmetic fluency observed across the school years, inefficient strategy use during problem-solving, and atypical math errors. This calls for assessments that include behavioral observations of students' number knowledge and other symbolic number skills, an evaluation of the strategies students use when doing mathematics, observations of the amount of effort students must exert when completing grade-level "easy" calculations, and an evaluation of the types of errors students make.

Assessments of number skills are useful screens for risk for later mathematics difficulties, whether those difficulties are tied to MLD, LA, or other risk factors for poor mathematics achievement that are linked to reduced learning opportunities, such as SES. Number skills that are particularly informative of later mathematics achievement include nonsymbolic magnitude judgments, symbolic magnitude judgments, counting skills (in particular, cardinality), digit naming (recognizing Arabic digits), and small-number addition or decomposition (with or without manipulatives). These skills represent a subset of the full range of early number skills that support counting, number knowledge (i.e., awareness of the meaning of numbers), and number relations (including operations).

Stock et al. (2010) included a range of mathematical tasks in their kindergarten battery, and at that age they found that a nonsymbolic magnitude comparison task was the most successful single-measure screen for MLD. Nosworthy, Bugden, Archibald, Evans, and Ansari (2013) developed a paper-and-pencil screener that involved nonsymbolic and symbolic magnitude comparison that was found it to be predictive of Grades 1 to 3 concurrent mathematics achievement, but they found that the symbolic items were more predictive than the nonsymbolic ones. Thus, a current research question concerns whether and when nonsymbolic versus symbolic screens are most predictive. Given the short time required to do so, including both types of items in an informal screen is appropriate (Desoete, Ceulemans, de Weerdt, & Pieters, 2012), as was done in the following studies (see Rapid Reference 3.3).

By measuring a subset of number skills (number identification, comparison, conceptual counting, cardinality, and addition; see Rapid Reference 3.3) in 224 kindergartners, Mazzocco and Thompson (2005) correctly classified 87% of students as likely or unlikely to meet MLD criteria by the end of Grade 3. Remarkably, Stock et al. (2010) had similar results, correctly identifying 87.5% of 7- to 8-year-olds with MLD based on kindergarten counting (procedural and conceptual) and magnitude comparison tasks. Geary, Bailey, and Hoard (2009) developed the number sets screening tool, a group-administered pencil-and-paper measure used to assess the speed and accuracy with which children identify numbers and the quantity of object arrays and how quickly they compose and decompose these arrays. Performance on this combination of number skills measured at Grade 1 was predictive of Grade 3 mathematics achievement scores and correctly identified 67% of children with MLD and 90% of children without MLD in Grade 3. There is some indication that these screens have long-term value: More recently, Geary and colleagues (2013) reported that the number sets (in addition to other measures) given in Grade 1 predicted Grade 8 numeracy ability. Clearly, early number skills are important, even if their precise mechanisms on mathematics learning and achievement are unclear. Note, however, that these measures are screens for risk status, but none are diagnostic tools.

Math motivation and math anxiety are also worth exploring, through informal interviews or classroom observation, and should be considered in the context of a student's prior experiences, if those are known. Practitioners should consider the

⇛ Rapid Reference 3.3

Samples of a Wide Range of Number Skills Items

All but the first are symbolic number skills.

Skill	Sample Item	Key Feature (and Reference Provided in Resources List)
Nonsymbolic magnitude comparison	★★★ ★★ ★★ ★ "Which is more?" (cross out larger)	Responses are rapid and involve no counting or clumping; captures "gut sense" of quantity (Nosworthy et al., 2013). Note that if this task is completed by actually *counting* the sets of stars it is not a nonsymbolic task. Also see Panamath in Assessment Resources.
Numeral identification	7 3 5 2 1 6 "Read these numbers."	Responses indicate automatic mapping of number word to symbol. Subtests focused on these skills appear in many formal mathematics assessments.
Symbolic magnitude comparison	5 3 "Which is more?" (cross out larger)	This taps recognition of symbolic representations, or what numbers mean (Nosworthy et al., 2013).
Cardinality	"Give me 5 stars." (child is given 10 stars, must give examiner exactly 5)	If a child can accurately "give" the correct number of items, consistently, this is partial evidence of cardinality. (Also see Rapid Reference 3.2.)
Decomposition	3 2 4 3 "Which pair equals 5?"	Responses involve composing and decomposing one value into subsets of smaller, combined values (Geary et al., 2009; Mazzocco & Hanich, 2010).
Ordinality	3 4 2 7 3 8 6 2 1 "Re-arrange these numbers in order."	This taps ordinality (Lyons & Ansari, 2015).

persistence of mathematics difficulties over time, because these contribute to the prediction of at-risk status (Morgan, Farkas, & Wu, 2009).

In the presence or absence of a historical record, it is essential to make educated decisions about instructional planning and to recognize that occasional success may reflect successful compensatory strategies. It is also essential to remember that MLD, although it often co-occurs with reading disability, can also be independent of reading disabilities. It is certainly possible for children who have high intelligence to have an MLD—including gifted "twice exceptional" students.

> **DON'T FORGET**
> ....
> Note whether the difficulties observed are limited to new mathematics topics or to overlearned skills, and document observations and outcomes to help establish a historical record.

Finally, the evidence for familial and environmental influences on MLD is noteworthy. This does not imply that family histories must be positive for MLD but that siblings of children with MLD will be at higher risk than siblings of children without MLD (e.g., Desoete, Praet, Titeca, & Ceulemans, 2013). Likewise, shared environments may include low-SES status, another risk factor for poor mathematics achievement (Jordan & Levine, 2009), but not a risk factor for MLD (e.g., Wu, Morgan, & Farkas, 2014).

IMPLICATIONS FOR INSTRUCTION AND INTERVENTION

Implications for instructional planning can also be drawn from the research base, including many studies on mathematics intervention for students with or without MLD. Current initiatives focused on instruction and intervention for students with MLD, similar to other types of LDs (as detailed in Chapters 7 and 8), follow a three-tiered public health model focused on primary prevention (general education and universal design), secondary intervention (pre-referral interventions), and tertiary intervention (special education). Research-based practices and progress monitoring are fundamental pillars at each tier.

At the most basic level of numerical skills studied in MLD, the early nonsymbolic skills have not been studied in an RTI framework. This may be because they are not the skills targeted by formal mathematics instruction. There is, however, emerging evidence that practice on nonsymbolic skills improves mathematics performance in primary school-age students (Käser et al., 2013) and adults (Park & Brannon, 2013). Some successful applications of this practice occur with direct mathematics skills support (Kucian & von Aster, 2015). Yet in some studies of nonsymbolic skill interventions among students with MLD, transfer to arithmetic or other school mathematics skills is not observed (e.g., Wilson,

Revkin, Cohen, Cohen, & Dehaene, 2006). This is an area in which much more research is needed. In the meantime, if the goal is to improve students' school mathematics skills, a logical resource is recent studies on instructional and interventions focused on those skills.

Likewise, early symbolic number skills interventions may diminish the severity or persistence of early mathematics difficulties in students at risk for MLD. In typically achieving students, number learning is subject to learning trajectories emerging from number knowledge, to understanding relations between numbers, and later to operating on numbers (Clements & Sarama, 2009). Dyson, Jordan, Beliakoff, and Hassinger-Das (2015) have shown that early number skills can be improved; their kindergarten intervention based on this learning trajectory was effective among at-risk learners. It is unclear, however, if students with MLD will show comparable gains. Regardless, this study and others suggest that building number skills is important for Tier 1 instruction and, when indicated, for Tier 2 intervention.

In general, effective mathematics instruction at Tier 1 (Fuchs & Fuchs, 2001) includes the following characteristics:

- Actively engages learners and provides many opportunities for students to respond
- Holds students and teachers accountable for student learning
- Employs cognitive strategies instruction to teach steps explicitly, for identifying problem types and problem-solving solutions
- Builds students' conceptual understanding in conjunction with procedural understanding (which aligns with Common Core)

There are several whole-class research-based programs that can be used to supplement mathematics instruction at Tier 1. Two particularly useful resources for identifying such programs are listed in the resource section at the end of this chapter: The *Best Evidence Encyclopedia* and the *National Center on Intensive Intervention.*

When students do not respond to effective Tier 1 instruction, more intensive small-group interventions are prescribed. At Tier 2, interventions can be delivered according to a standard protocol (i.e., everyone receives the same intervention) or a problem-solving protocol (i.e., interventions are selected based on the student's particular profile). There are pros and cons to each model (e.g., see Fuchs, Fuchs, & Stecker, 2010), and various practitioners play an important role in deciding which approach best fits the students' needs and capacity of the school. These decisions can be informed by the seven guiding principles of effective instruction at Tier 2 for struggling mathematics learners developed by Fuchs and colleagues (2008) and listed in Rapid Reference 3.4. Also, it is important to attend to the domain-general cognitive skills that support mathematical learning and performance.

≡ *Rapid Reference 3.4*

Principles of Effective Tier 2 Instruction

- Instruction is explicit, systematic, and didactic (versus discovery-oriented). Explicit, systematic instruction is a hallmark of Tier 2 interventions and has been validated for teaching word problems (Fuchs et al., 2008), number combinations (Fuchs et al., 2009), and fractions (Fuchs, Malone, Shumacher, Namkung, & Wang, 2017).

- Learning challenges are minimized through carefully sequenced instruction that builds on students' knowledge. For example, one way for students to consolidate learning is through explaining their thinking as they talk through problem solution. However, students struggling with mathematics may find it extremely difficult to explain their thinking, which limits opportunities to learn using this approach. Fuchs and colleagues (2017) find that within the context of an intervention explicitly targeting fractions, children with MLD or LA learn more about fractions when they are *provided* with high-quality explanations as opposed to when expected to *generate* their own explanations. Providing struggling learners high-quality explanations may minimize potential learning roadblocks, undo or prevent misconceptions, and give students a chance to integrate their existing knowledge with high-quality explanations.

- Instruction includes a strong conceptual basis (versus a sole focus on procedures). For example, Fuchs et al. (2017) find that teaching fraction concepts produces larger gains in conceptual and procedural understanding of fractions than does teaching fraction procedures without concepts.

- Instruction includes ample opportunities for skill mastery through drill and practice. For example, Fuchs and colleagues (2017) find that just 5–7 minutes of either conceptual practice (i.e., practice explaining fraction concepts) or fluency practice (i.e., practice automatizing steps for deriving accurate solutions to fraction problems) produces gains in fraction outcomes in children with MLD or LA.

- The learning sequence builds on a cumulative review of newly and previously learned material. For example, Fuchs and colleagues (2017) find that interventions for struggling mathematics learners that are focused and targeted in scope produce greater gains in learning for children with MLD or LA than are interventions that cover greater breadth of topics but with less depth. This structure provides struggling learners with opportunities to consolidate their learning and provides a solid foundation for new learning to occur.

- Given that students requiring Tier 2 supports have a demonstrated history of repeated failure in mathematics, effective Tier 2 instruction incorporates motivators—from behavioral ("beat your score") to tangible (e.g., stickers) to help students stay engaged in learning.

- Effectiveness and responsiveness are determined by ongoing progress monitoring.

Empirically validated programs that are designed to be used at Tier 2 appear in the *Best Evidence Encyclopedia* and the *National Center on Intensive Intervention* links in the "Instructional Resources" section at the end of this chapter. Note that although several of these interventions target different aspects of mathematics (e.g., number-fact fluency, arithmetic calculations, word problem-solving), they are primarily designed to be delivered according to standard protocol. In the absence of evidence-based interventions targeting particular skills, the principles previously identified should guide the evaluation of potential programs to be implemented in schools.

Finally, at tertiary intervention—or special education—instruction is most intensive. In special education, "intensity" can vary along several dimensions: frequency (e.g., five times per week versus three times per week), dosage (e.g., 45 minutes per session versus 20 minutes per session), rate (e.g., slower versus faster pace characteristic of Tier 1), pupil-teacher ratio (i.e., individualized versus small groups), curriculum (e.g., scripted programs versus experimental teaching), and progress monitoring (e.g., daily versus weekly).

As of yet, there is no "cure" for MLD and no one magic intervention that is effective for all students. Best practice for students who require supports beyond Tier 2 is to deliver research-based interventions that show evidence of effectiveness for the student and to do so more intensely (e.g., deliver the same intervention more frequently and at a higher dosage) compared to students without MLD. However, a hallmark of special education is individualized instruction, which means that students with MLD who require Tier 3 supports will likely require individualized programming. The best methodology for delivering individualized instruction is what Fuchs et al. (2010) refer to as *experimental teaching* and, in early childhood, may be supported by what Ginsburg (1981, 1997) refers to as *clinical* or *flexible interviewing*. Experimental teaching is an iterative, data-driven process whereby hypotheses for a student's learning challenges are generated based on a student's errors or gaps in mathematical understanding—identified through formal and informal assessments, classroom permanent products, and clinical interviews—systematic and explicit instruction is provided based on hypotheses, and data are collected to confirm or revise hypotheses. Others have found that such instructional decision making can be delivered class-wide to enhance gains from more individualized mathematics instruction (Connor et al., 2017).

In addition to the principles for secondary intervention just described, the following are guiding principles of tertiary intervention (Fuchs & Fuchs, 2001; Fuchs et al., 2008, 2010):

- Focus on the individual student and unique learning profile
- Intensive delivery of instruction (either Tier 2 intervention or content identified through experimental teaching), including continuously monitoring student's response
- Skills-based instruction that explicitly teaches skills in authentic, contextualized applications

CONCLUSION

There is no consensus definition of MLD, but there is widespread consensus that there are multiple roots to mathematics difficulties. These roots are aligned with a wide range of numerical skills and domain-general skills in memory, language, and executive functions, all of which are subject to biological and environmental influences. Some of the domain-general contributions to MLD are also linked to reading disability and may explain the high rate of comorbidity in these distinct manifestations of SLD (Vukovic, 2012; Willcut et al., 2013). Regarding domain-specific skills linked to MLD, some researchers argue that nonsymbolic numerical skills are necessary, but not sufficient, for mathematics achievement (Mazzocco et al., 2011), and that marked deficiencies of non-symbolic skills are the hallmark of dyscalculia (Butterworth, Varma, & Laurillard, 2011). This notion is consistent with one specific aspect of the *DSM-5* criteria for SLD in mathematics. Alternative explanations for MLD apply to large numbers of students with consistent, lifelong challenges in number combinations (semantic memory MLD)—aligned with the *DSM-5* focus on poor arithmetic fluency—and those with procedural deficits linked to poor executive function and processing skills—aligned with the *DSM-5* emphasis on mathematics reasoning. Many students with MLD or LA have difficulties in more than one aspect of mathematics achievement.

These distinctions among skills are somewhat false dichotomies, as implicated by the importance of relations between nonsymbolic and symbolic domain-specific skills, the connections between procedural and conceptual domain general skills, and the interplay between domain-specific and domain-general skills. Moreover, the relative importance of each type of skill, and of its relation to each other, will vary across developmental periods (Ansari, 2010; Chu, vanMarle, & Geary, 2016), meaning that characteristics of MLD may manifest differently at different ages. Additional correlates of MLD, such as visuospatial and visual motor skills, have as yet a smaller evidence base than the correlates described in this chapter and are thus less explicitly implicated in the *DSM-5*. Nevertheless, these skills have been linked to numeric and executive function skills. More research on these roles has begun to emerge in the last 10 years, supporting subtype profiles including in spatial-related MLD (e.g., Bartelet, Ansari, Vaessen, & Blomert, 2014).

What these manifestations of MLD have in common is the robust and debilitating effect each has on students' mathematical learning, performance, achievement, and disposition and the persistence of MLD even if its manifestation changes. Fortunately, promising instructional approaches are making a positive difference for many of these students. Therefore, the objective of this chapter was to provide information that supports the role of school psychologists in working to identify students with MLD, to identify them early, identify the mathematics skills in most need for support among children with MLD and other mathematics difficulties, and exploit available resources—including those in the next section— to develop effective educational plans.

BACKGROUND RESOURCES

Berch and Mazzocco (2007). This edited book—*Why Is Math So Hard for Children?*—provides an authoritative review of the nature and origins of mathematics learning difficulties and disabilities. It is an appropriate reference book for researchers, educators, clinicians, and students.

Dehaene (2011). This revised and updated book—*The Number Sense: How the Mind Creates Mathematics*—explores the mathematical mind, including understanding the numerical competencies not unique to humans, how the human brain creates numbers, and how rudimentary numerical competencies form the foundation for mathematics. It is an appropriate reference for researchers, educators, and clinicians interested in learning about how our brains are wired to process numbers and mathematics.

Multiple websites intended for parents and teachers are also useful for a variety of practitioners. The following websites focus on learning disability in general, but they also include information specific to mathematics learning difficulties. Across the websites, the terms used to refer to these challenges include *math difficulties, math disabilities,* or *dyscalculia,* which is related to our discussion of MLD definitions at the beginning of the chapter.

- www.understood.org, an online program of the National Center for Learning Disabilities (NCLD), includes a section called "Through your child's eyes" that provides simulations, guidelines, and information specific to mathematics learning difficulties from the perspective of children of different age groups at this website: www. understood.org/en/tools/through-your-childs-eyes/personalize. The simulations illustrate aspects of "number sense" and working memory discussed in this chapter. In particular, the simulations activity called "Exact Change" helps illustrate the importance of automaticity in symbolic number skills and describes the challenges faced when those skills are not automatic. The child interviews also relate to our discussion of the role of mathematics attitudes, dispositions, and mathematics anxiety.

- www.pbs.org/wgbh/misunderstoodminds/math.html has simulations that help support understanding how math fluency, attentional, and visual spatial difficulties interfere with mathematics learning. This is related to the multiple sources of mathematics difficulty discussed in the "Memory and Semantic Memory" and "Executive Function" sections of this chapter.
- www.ldonline.org/indepth/math provides numerous articles related to specific aspects of mathematics instruction for children with MLD.

ASSESSMENT RESOURCES

Several informal assessments referred to in this chapter are available online, at no cost. Note that these are not standardized norm-referenced clinical measures but are intended for researcher use or to supplement informal observations of individuals. We list three of them here:

- Panamath is a quick informal assessment of the nonverbal, nonsymbolic number sense described in the "Nonsymbolic Skills" section of the chapter. The demo can be completed in less than 2 minutes, and it demonstrates the signature characteristics of this aspect of number sense—an intuitive "gut" sense of number that does not involve counting. Visit Panamath.org.
- Two measures of symbolic number skills are described in the "Implications for Assessment" section.
  - Dr. Geary's Number Sets Screening Tool, published in 2009, is available from the study authors.
  - Dr. Ansari's numeracy screener is available online (www .numeracyscreener.org).

- Information on a dyscalculia screener aligned for individuals from the United Kingdom appears on Dr. Brian Butterworth's website at www.mathematicalbrain.com.

INSTRUCTIONAL RESOURCES

The What Works Clearinghouse (WWC), a resource available on the Institute of Education Sciences website and overseen by the US Department of Education, lists evidence-based resources for parents, educators, school administrators, and policy makers (http://ies.ed.gov/ncee/wwc). These resources include reviews of mathematics curricula and instructional practice guides. As of 2017, one of several math practice guides focuses specifically on students who struggle with mathematics, and these can be downloaded at no cost (https://ies.ed.gov/ncee/wwc/PracticeGuides). The remaining practice guides are not specific to MLDs but may support teachers' instructional efforts in teaching fractions, supporting math problem-solving, word problems, and early mathematics. The practice guide on encouraging girls to pursue mathematics is relevant to the discussion of mathematics motivation and math anxiety that appears in the chapter.

Another WWC site (http://ies.ed.gov/ncee/wwc/mathhome.aspx) provides links to evidence-based practice for students from early childhood to high school and interventions that are relevant for practitioners. Note that when the "evidence" listed on this site is reported as "minimal," this is a reflection of the fact that there is relatively little research on mathematics learning disabilities. "Minimal" does not mean "weak" evidence, but the website does disclose whether the intervention has been studied by few or several researchers.

Similar to the WWC, two other sites that provide reviews of interventions, including mathematics interventions, are Best Evidence Encyclopedia (www.bestevidence.org/math/elem/top.htm) and National Center on Intensive Intervention (www.intensiveintervention.org/chart/instructional-intervention-tools).

The Center on Instruction website (www.centeroninstruction.org) provides links to a range of resources on special education screening instruction, professional development, and Common Core Standards for Mathematics, including online courses and webinars that can be completed at no cost.

This Iris Center website specific to mathematics (http://iris.peabody.vanderbilt.edu/iris-resource-locator/?term=math) provides teaching modules, briefs, and other user-friendly resources related to high-quality mathematics instruction, including for students with MLD.

🐟 TEST YOURSELF 🐟

1. **Which one of the following statements is true about the definition of specific learning disability in mathematics (MLD)?**

   (a) Defining MLD is complicated by the many skills that comprise mathematics achievement.

   (b) There is no single, widely accepted definition of MLD.

   (c) Defining MLD is complicated by the fact that its manifestation varies across individuals and across development.

   (d) All three of the above statements are true.

2. **Which of the following statements is true regarding using different mathematics achievement measures to identify students with specific learning disability in mathematics (MLD)?**

   (a) Across all measures used, the same children will be identified.

   (b) If different measures are used, different children may be identified.

   (c) Regardless of which measure is used, it is best to rely on an ability-achievement discrepancy to identify MLD.

   (d) Regardless of the measure used, there are clear cut-off points for determining MLD.

3. **Some researchers distinguish between children with MLD and children with low achievement (LA) in mathematics. Which of the following is *not* a characteristic of these two groups?**

   (a) In both groups, mathematics difficulties are likely to persist.

   (b) Children with MLD have more severe mathematics difficulties than children with LA.

   (c) LA is a homogeneous classification whereas MLD is a heterogeneous classification.

   (d) Children with MLD are more likely than children with LA to have difficulties in more basic numerical processing.

4. **Which of the following is true about the incidence of MLD?**

   (a) MLD is rare and occurs in less than 2% of the population.

   (b) MLD affects approximately 7% to 10% of the general population.

   (c) MLD affects over 50% of the population.

   (d) MLD affects 25% of children and 10% of adults.

5. **Research on the contribution of genetics to MLD reveals that:**

   (a) There are genetic contributions to mathematics achievement levels overall; these are not specific to MLD.

   (b) The genetic contributions to mathematics achievement differ for fluency versus calculation skills, but both are heritable.

   (c) The genetic contributions to MLD are so high that environmental effects are unlikely.

   (d) A and b are true.

6. **Which of the following is true about tasks used to measure nonsymbolic number skills?**

    (a) If a child is asked to count dots or other pictures that appear in a task, then the task is not measuring nonsymbolic skills.

    (b) If a numerical task involves dots or other objects instead of words or digits, it must be a measure of nonsymbolic skills.

    (c) If a numerical task is completed quickly, it is a measure of nonsymbolic skills.

    (d) A task cannot depend on nonsymbolic and symbolic skills; only one can be used at a time.

7. **When assessing for difficulties in executive function skills or processing speed that may contribute to MLD:**

    (a) Results from cognitive assessments can be reliably used to isolate specific difficulties related to MLD.

    (b) Results from cognitive assessments should be supplemented with formal and informal assessments of mathematics skills to isolate difficulties related to MLD.

    (c) Results from informal assessments can be reliably used to isolate difficulties related to MLD.

    (d) None of the above is true.

8. **Which of the following statements is true for intervention planning?**

    (a) Children with MLD or LA are likely to benefit from the same mathematics interventions for number combination skills.

    (b) Children with MLD or LA are likely to have number combination difficulties, so intervention should be provided to both groups. Some children with LA and some with MLD may have very persistent math-retrieval deficits, so their intervention needs may differ.

    (c) Only children with MLD require intervention. Children with LA tend to grow out of their math difficulties.

    (d) Only children with LA require intervention, because children with MLD will not respond to intervention.

9. **Which of the following statements is true about mathematics motivation and math anxiety?**

    (a) Environment, motivation, and math anxiety all contribute to MLD manifestation, but none of these causes MLD.

    (b) Environment and motivation contribute to MLD manifestation, but math anxiety causes MLD.

    (c) Mathematics motivation and math anxiety contribute to MLD manifestation, but only environmental factors cause MLD.

    (d) Math anxiety always has a negative impact on mathematics performance.

    Consider this scenario for question 10. A Grade 2 student presents with the following broad mathematics achievement score history: fall kindergarten, 5th percentile; spring kindergarten, 16th percentile; spring first grade, 8th percentile; spring second grade 10th percentile.

10. **Which of the following is true about determining if this profile is a manifestation of MLD?**

   (a) Because some scores are above the 15th percentile, the child cannot have MLD.

   (b) Because most of the scores are below the 15th percentile, the child must have MLD.

   (c) Because all of the scores are below average, the student may need educational support regardless of whether MLD is implicated.

   (d) Because all of the scores are broad measures, they are not informative of MLD.

Answers: 1. d; 2. b; 3. c; 4. b; 5. d; 6. a; 7. b; 8. b; 9. a; 10. c.

REFERENCES

Alloway, T. P., & Alloway, R. G. (2010). Investigating the predictive roles of working memory and IQ in academic attainment. *Journal of Experimental Child Psychology, 106*(1), 20–29. doi: 10.1016/j.jecp.2009.11.003

American Psychiatric Association. (2013). *Diagnostic and statistical manual of mental disorders* (5th ed.). Washington, DC: Author.

Ansari, D. (2010). Neurocognitive approaches to developmental disorders of numerical and mathematical cognition: The perils of neglecting the role of development. *Learning and Individual Differences, 20*(2), 123–129. doi: 10.1016/j.lindif.2009.06.001

Barberesi, M. J., Katusic, S. K., Colligan, R. C., Weaver, A. L., & Jacobsen, S. J. (2005). Math learning disorder: Incidence in a population-based birth cohort. *Ambulatory Pediatrics, 5*(5), 281–289. doi: 10.1367/A04-209R.1

Bartelet, D., Ansari, D., Vaessen, A., & Blomert, L. (2014). Cognitive subtypes of mathematics learning difficulties in primary education. *Research in Developmental Disabilities, 35*(3), 657–670. doi: 10.1016/j.ridd.2013.12.010

Beilock, S. L., Gunderson, E. A., Ramirez, G., & Levine, S. C. (2010). Female teachers' math anxiety affects girls' math achievement. *Proceedings of the National Academy of Sciences, 107*(5), 1860–1863. doi: 10.1073/pnas.0910967107

Berch, D. B. (2005). Making sense of number sense. *Journal of Learning Disabilities, 38*(4), 333–339.

Berch, D. B., & Mazzocco, M.M.M. (2007). *Why is math hard for some children: The nature and origins of mathematics learning difficulties and disabilities.* Baltimore, MD: Brookes.

Bugden, S., & Ansari, D. (2015). How can cognitive developmental neuroscience constrain our understanding of developmental dyscalculia? In S. Chinn (Ed.), *The Routledge International handbook of dyscalculia and mathematical learning difficulties* (pp. 18–43). New York, NY: Routledge.

Bull, R., Espy, K. A., & Wiebe, S. A. (2008). Short-term memory, working memory, and executive functions in preschoolers: Longitudinal predictors of mathematical achievement at age 7 years. *Developmental Neuropsychology, 33*(3), 205–228. doi: 10.1080/87565640801982312

Burny, E., Valcke, M., & Desoete, A. (2012). Clock reading: An underestimated topic in children with mathematics difficulties. *Journal of Learning Disabilities, 45*(4), 351–360. doi: 10.1177/0022219411407773

Butterworth, B., Varma, S., & Laurillard, D. (2011). Dyscalculia: From brain to education. *Science, 332*(6033), 1049–1053.

Chong, S. L., & Siegel, L. S. (2008). Stability of computational deficits in math learning disability from second through fifth grades. *Developmental Neuropsychology, 33*(3), 300–317. doi: 10.1080/87565640801982387

Chu, F. W., vanMarle, K., & Geary, D. C. (2016). Predicting children's reading and mathematics achievement from early quantitative knowledge and domain-general cognitive abilities. *Frontiers in Psychology, 7.* doi: 10.3389/fpsyg.2016.00775

Clements, D. H., & Sarama, J. (2009). *Learning and teaching early math: The learning trajectories approach.* New York, NY: Routledge.

Clements, D., & Sarama, J. (2014). *The importance of the early years. Science, technology, & mathematics (STEM).* Thousand Oaks, CA: Corwin.

Connor, C. M., Mazzocco, M.M.M., Kurz, T., Tighe, E. L., Crowe, E. C., & Morrison, F. (2017). Using assessment to individualize early mathematics instruction. *Journal of School Psychology.* Retrieved from https://doi.org/10.1016/j.jsp.2017.04.005

Dehaene, S. (2011). *The number sense: How the mind creates mathematics.* New York, NY: Oxford University Press.

Desoete, A., Ceulemans, A., De Weerdt, F., & Pieters, S. (2012). Can we predict mathematical learning disabilities from symbolic and non-symbolic comparison tasks in kindergarten? Findings from a longitudinal study. *British Journal of Educational Psychology, 82*(1), 64–81. doi: 10.1348/2044-8279.002002

Desoete, A., Praet, M., Titeca, D., & Ceulemans, A. (2013). Cognitive phenotype of mathematical learning disabilities: What can we learn from siblings? *Research in Developmental Disabilities, 34*(1), 404–412. doi: 10.1016/j.ridd.2012.08.022

De Visscher, A., Szmalec, A., Van Der Linden, L., & Noël, M. P. (2015). Serial-order learning impairment and hypersensitivity-to-interference in dyscalculia. *Cognition, 144,* 38–48. doi: 10.1016/j.cognition.2015.07.007

Dyson, N., Jordan, N. C., Beliakoff, A., & Hassinger-Das, B. (2015). A kindergarten number sense intervention with contrasting practice conditions for low-achieving children. *Journal of Research in Mathematics Education, 46,* 331–370.

Feigenson, L., Dehaene, S., & Spelke, E. S. (2004). Core systems of number. *Trends in Cognitive Sciences, 8*(7), 307–314. doi: 10.1016/j.tics.2004.05.002

Fletcher, J. M., Lyon, G. R., Fuchs, L. S., & Barnes, M. A. (2007). *Learning disabilities: From identification to intervention.* New York, NY: Guilford.

Fuchs, L., & Fuchs, D. (2001). Principles for the prevention and intervention of mathematics difficulties. *Learning Disabilities Research and Practice, 16*(2), 85–95. doi: 10.1111/0938-8982.00010

Fuchs, L. S., Fuchs, D., Compton, D. L., Powell, S. R., Seethaler, P. M., Capizzi, A. M., & Fletcher, J. M. (2006). The cognitive correlates of third grade skill in arithmetic, algorithmic computation, and arithmetic word problems. *Journal of Educational Psychology, 98*(1), 29–43. doi: 10.1037/0022-0663.98.1.29.

Fuchs, L., Fuchs, D., Powell, S. R., Seethaler, P. M., Cirino, P. T., & Fletcher, J. M. (2008). Intensive intervention for students with mathematics disabilities: Seven principles of effective practice. *Learning Disability Quarterly, 31*(2), 79–92.

Fuchs, D., Fuchs, L., & Stecker, P. M. (2010). The "blurring" of special education in a new continuum of general education placements and services. *Exceptional Children, 76*(3), 301–323. doi: 10.1177/001440291007600304

Fuchs, L., Malone, A. S., Shumacher, R. F., Namkung, J., & Wang, A. (2017). Fraction intervention for students with mathematics difficulties: Lessons learned from five randomized control trials. *Journal of Learning Disabilities, 50*(6), 631–639. doi: 10.1177/0022219416677249

Fuchs, L. S., Powell, S. R., Seethaler, P. M., Cirino, P. T., Fletcher, J. M., Fuchs, D., Hamlett, C. L., & Zumeta, R. O. (2009). Remediating number combination and word problem deficits among students with mathematics difficulties: A randomized control trial. *Journal of Educational Psychology, 101*(3), 561–576. doi: 10.1037/a0014701

Furner, J. M., & Duffy, M. L. (2002). Equity for all students in the new millennium: Disabling math anxiety. *Intervention in School and Clinic, 38*(2), 67–74. doi: 10.1177/10534512020380020101

Geary, D. C. (1993). Mathematical disabilities: Cognitive, neuropsychological, and genetic components. *Psychological Bulletin, 114*(2), 345–362. doi: 10.1037/0033-2909.114.2.345

Geary, D. C. (2011). Cognitive predictors of individual differences in achievement growth in mathematics: A five-year longitudinal study. *Developmental Psychology, 47*(6), 1539–1552. doi: 10.1037/a0025510

Geary, D. C., Bailey, D. H., & Hoard, M. K. (2009). Predicting mathematical achievement and mathematical learning disability with a simple screening tool the number sets test. *Journal of Psychoeducational Assessment, 27*(3), 265–279. doi: 10.1177/0734282908330592

Geary, D. C., Hoard, M. K., Byrd-Craven, J., & DeSoto, M. C. (2004). Strategy choices in simple and complex addition: Contributions of working memory and counting knowledge for children with mathematical disability. *Journal of Experimental Child Psychology, 88*(2), 121–151. doi: 10.1016/j.jecp.2004.03.002

Geary, D. C., Hoard, M. K., Byrd-Craven, J., Nugent, L., & Numtee, C. (2007). Cognitive mechanisms underlying achievement deficits in children with mathematical learning disability. *Child Development, 78*(4), 1343–1359. doi: 10.1111/j.1467-8624.2007.01069.x

Geary, D. C., Hoard, M. K., Nugent, L., & Bailey, H. D. (2013). Adolescents' functional numeracy is predicted by their school entry number system knowledge. *PLOS ONE, 8*(1), e54651. doi: 10.1371/journal.pone.0054651

Geary, D. C., Hoard, M. K., Nugent, L., & Byrd-Craven, J. (2008). Development of number line representations in children with mathematical learning disability. *Developmental Neuropsychology, 33*(3), 277–299. doi: 10.1080/87565640801982361

Gelman, R., & Gallistel, C. (1978). *The child's understanding of number.* Cambridge, MA: Harvard University Press.

Ginsburg, H. (1981). The clinical interview in psychological research on mathematical thinking: Aims, rationales, techniques. *For the Learning of Mathematics, 1*(3), 4–11.

Ginsburg, H. (1997). *Entering the child's mind: The clinical interview in psychological research and practice.* Cambridge, UK: Cambridge University Press.

Girelli, L., Lucangeli, D., & Butterworth, B. (2000). The development of automaticity in accessing number magnitude. *Journal of Experimental Child Psychology, 76*(2), 104–122. doi: 10.1006/jecp.2000.2564

Goffin, C., & Ansari, D. (2016). Beyond magnitude: Judging ordinality of symbolic number is unrelated to magnitude comparison and independently relates to individual differences in arithmetic. *Cognition, 150,* 68–76. doi: 10.1016/j.cognition.2016.01.018

Gottfried, A., Marcoulides, G., Gottfried, A., Oliver, P., & Guerin, D. (2007). Multivariate latent change modeling of developmental decline in academic intrinsic math motivation and achievement: Childhood through adolescence. *International Journal of Behavioral Development, 31*(4), 317–327. doi: 10.1177/0165025407077752

Halberda, J., Ly, R., Willmer, J., Naiman, D., & Germine, L. (2012). Number sense across the life span as revealed by a massive Internet-based sample. *Proceedings of the National Academy of Sciences, 109*(28), 11116–11120. doi: 10.1073/pnas.1200196109

Iuculano, T., Rosenberg-Lee, M., Richardson, J., Tenison, C., Fuchs, L., Supekar, K., & Menon, V. (2015). Cognitive tutoring induces widespread neuroplasticity and remediates brain function in children with mathematical learning disabilities. *Nature Communications, 6.* doi: 10.1038/ncomms9453

Johns, M., Schmader, T., & Martens, A. (2005). Knowing is half the battle teaching stereotype threat as a means of improving women's math performance. *Psychological Science, 16*(3), 175–179. doi: 10.1111/j.0956-7976.2005.00799.x

Jordan, N. C., Hanich, L. B., & Kaplan, D. (2003). A longitudinal study of mathematical competencies in children with specific mathematics difficulties versus children with comorbid mathematics and reading difficulties. *Child Development, 74*(3), 834–850. doi: 10.1111/1467-8624.00571

Jordan, N. C., Kaplan, D., Ramineni, C., & Locuniak, M. N. (2008). Development of number combination skill in the early school years: When do fingers help? *Developmental Science, 11*(5), 662–668. doi: 10.1111/j.1467-7687.2008.00715.x

Jordan, N. C., & Levine, S. C. (2009). Socioeconomic variation, number competence, and mathematics learning difficulties in young children. *Developmental Disabilities Research Reviews, 15,* 60–68. doi: 10.1002/ddrr.46

Juel, C. (1988). Learning to read and write: A longitudinal study of fifty-four children from first through fourth grade. *Journal of Educational Psychology, 80*(4), 437–447.

Käser, T., Baschera, G. M., Kohn, J., Kucian, K., Richtmann, V., Grond, U., Gross, M,. & von Aster, M. (2013). Design and evaluation of the computer-based training program Calcularis for enhancing numerical cognition. *Frontiers in Psychology, 4.* doi: 10.3389/fpsyg.2013.00489

Kaufmann, L., Vogel, S. E., Starke, M., & Schocke, M. (2009). Numerical and nonnumerical ordinality processing in children with and without developmental dyscalculia: Evidence from fMRI. *Cognitive Development, 24*(4), 486–494. doi: 10.1016/j.cogdev.2009.09.001

Koontz, K. L., & Berch, D. B. (1996). Identifying simple numerical stimuli: Processing inefficiencies exhibited by arithmetic learning disabled children. *Mathematical Cognition, 2,* 1–23. doi: 10.1080/135467996387525

Kovas, Y., Garon-Carrier, G., Boivin, M., Petrill, S. A., Plomin, R., Malykh, S. B., & Brendgen, M. (2015). Why children differ in motivation to learn: Insights from over 13,000 twins from 6 countries. *Personality and Individual Differences, 80*, 51–63.

Krajcsi, A., Szabó, E., & Mórocz, I. Á. (2013). Subitizing is sensitive to the arrangement of objects. *Experimental Psychology, 60*(4), 227–234. doi: 10.1027/1618-3169/a000191

Kucian, K., & von Aster, M. (2015). Developmental dyscalculia. *European Journal of Pediatrics, 174*(1), 1–13. doi: 10.1007/s00431-014-2455-7

Lewis, K. E., & Fisher, M. B. (2016). Taking stock of 40 years of research on mathematical learning disability: Methodological issues and future directions. *Journal for Research in Mathematics Education, 47*(4), 338–371.

Lyons, I. M., & Ansari, D. (2015). Numerical order processing in children: From reversing the distance-effect to predicting arithmetic. *Mind, Brain, and Education, 9*, 207–221. doi: 10.1111/mbe.12094

Lyons, I. M., Ansari, D., & Beilock, S. L. (2012). Symbolic estrangement: Evidence against a strong association between numerical symbols and the quantities they represent. *Journal of Experimental Psychology: General, 141*(4), 635–641. doi: 10.1037/a0027248

Martin, R. B., Cirino, P. T., Barnes, M. A., Ewing-Cobbs, L., Fuchs, L. S., Stuebing, K. K., & Fletcher, J. M. (2012). Prediction and stability of mathematics skill and difficulty. *Journal of Learning Disabilities, 46*(5), 428–443. doi: 10.1177/0022219411436214

Mazzocco, M.M.M. (2007). Issues in defining mathematical learning disabilities and difficulties. In D. B. Berch & M.M.M. Mazzocco (Eds.), *Why is math so hard for some children: The nature and origins of mathematical learning difficulties and disabilities* (pp. 29–47). Baltimore, MD: Brookes.

Mazzocco, M.M.M., Devlin, K. T., & McKenney, S. L. (2008). Is it a fact? Timed arithmetic performance of children with mathematical learning disabilities (MLD) varies as a function of how MLD is defined. *Developmental Neuropsychology, 33*(3), 318–344. doi: 10.1080/87565640801982403

Mazzocco, M.M.M., Feigenson, L., & Halberda, J. (2011). Impaired acuity of the approximate number system underlies mathematical learning disability. *Child Development, 82*, 1224–1237. doi: 10.1111/j.1467-8624.2011.01608.x

Mazzocco, M.M.M., & Grimm, K. J. (2013). Growth in rapid automatized naming from grades K to 8 in children with math or reading disabilities. *Journal of Learning Disabilities, 46*(6), 517–533. doi: 10.1177/0022219413477475

Mazzocco, M.M.M., & Hanich, L. B. (2010). Math achievement, numerical processing, and executive functions in girls with Turner syndrome: Do girls with Turner syndrome have math learning disability? *Learning and Individual Differences, 20*(2), 70–81. doi: 10.1016/j.lindif.2009.10.011

Mazzocco, M.M.M., Murphy, M.M., Brown, E., Rinne, L., & Herold, K. H. (2013). Persistent consequences of atypical early number concepts. *Frontiers in Psychology, 4.* doi: 10.3389/fpsyg.2013.00486

Mazzocco, M.M.M., Myers, G. F., Lewis, K. E., Hanich, L. B., & Murphy, M. M. (2013). Limited knowledge of fraction representations differentiates middle school students with mathematics learning disability (dyscalculia) versus low mathematics achievement. *Journal of Experimental Child Psychology, 115*(2), 371–387. doi: 10.1016/j.jecp.2013.01.005

Mazzocco, M.M.M., Quintero, A., Murphy, M. M., & McCloskey, M. (2015). Genetic syndromes as model pathways to mathematical learning difficulties: Fragile X, Turner, and 22q deletion syndromes. In D. B. Berch, D. C. Geary, & K. Mann Koepke (Eds.), *Mathematical cognition and learning series: Neural substrates and genetic influences* (Volume 2, pp. 325–357). London, UK: Elsevier.

Mazzocco, M.M.M., & Thompson, R. E. (2005). Kindergarten predictors of math learning disability. *Learning Disabilities Research & Practice, 20*(3), 142–155. doi: 10.1111/j.1540-5826.2005.00129.

McCloskey, M. (2007). Quantitative literacy and developmental dyscalculias. In D. B. Berch & M.M.M. Mazzocco (Eds.), *Why is math so hard for some children: The nature and origins of mathematical learning difficulties and disabilities* (pp. 415–429). Baltimore, MD: Brookes.

Morgan, P. L., Farkas, G., & Wu, Q. (2009). Five-year growth trajectories of kindergarten children with learning difficulties in mathematics. *Journal of Learning Disabilities, 42*(4), 306–321. doi: 10.1177/0022219408331037

Murphy, M. M., & Mazzocco, M.M.M. (2008). Rote numeric skills may mask underlying mathematical disabilities in girls with Fragile X syndrome. *Developmental Neuropsychology, 33*(3), 345–364. doi: 10.1080/87565640801982429

Murphy, M. M., Mazzocco, M.M.M., Hanich, L. B., & Early, M. C. (2007). Cognitive characteristics of children with mathematics learning disability (MLD) vary as a function of the cutoff criterion used to define MLD. *Journal of Learning Disabilities, 40*(5), 458–478. doi: 10.1177/00222194070400050901

National Assessment of Educational Progress (NAEP). (2015). *The nation's report card.* Retrieved from http://nces.ed.gov/nationsreportcard/

National Mathematics Advisory Panel. (2008). *Foundations for success: The final report of the National Mathematics Advisory Panel.* US Department of Education. Retrieved from www.ed.gov/about/bdscomm/list/mathpanel/report/final-report.pdf

Nosworthy, N., Bugden, S., Archibald, L., Evans, B., & Ansari, D. (2013). A two-minute paper-and-pencil test of symbolic and nonsymbolic numerical magnitude processing explains variability in primary school children's arithmetic competence. *PLOS ONE, 8*(7). doi: 10.1371/journal.pone.0067918

Olsson, L., Östergren, R., & Träff, U. (2016). Developmental dyscalculia: A deficit in the approximate number system or an access deficit? *Cognitive Development, 39*, 154–167. doi: 10.1016/j.cogdev.2016.04.006

Park, J., & Brannon, E. M. (2013). Training the approximate number system improves math proficiency. *Psychological Science, 24*(10), 2013–2019. doi: 10.1177/0956797613482944

Petrill, S. A., & Kovas, Y. (2015). Individual differences in mathematics ability: A behavioral genetic approach. In D. B. Berch, D. C. Geary, & K. Mann Koepe (Eds.), *Development of mathematical cognition: Neural substrates and genetic influences* (pp. 299–323). London, UK: Elsevier.

Petrill, S., Logan, J., Hart, S., Vincent, P., Thompson, L., Kovas, Y., & Plomin, R. (2012). Math fluency is etiologically distinct from untimed math performance, decoding fluency, and untimed reading performance: Evidence from a twin study. *Journal of Learning Disabilities, 45*(4), 371–381. doi: 0022219411407926.

Piazza, M., Facoetti, A., Trussardi, A. N., Berteletti, I., Conte, S., Lucangeli, D., Dehaene, S., & Zorzi, M. (2010). Developmental trajectory of number acuity reveals a severe impairment in developmental dyscalculia. *Cognition, 116*, 33–41. doi: 10.1016/j.cognition.2010.03.012

Price, G. R., Mazzocco, M.M.M., & Ansari, D. (2013). Why mental arithmetic counts: Brain activation during single-digit arithmetic predicts high school math scores. *The Journal of Neuroscience, 33*(1), 156–163. doi: 10.1523/JNEUROSCI.2936-12.2013

Raghubar, K. P., Barnes, M. A., & Hecht, S. A. (2010). Working memory and mathematics: A review of developmental, individual difference, and cognitive approaches. *Learning and Individual Differences, 20*(2), 110–122. doi: 10.1016/j.lindif.2009.10.005

Reynvoet, B., Smets, K., & Sasanguie, D. (2016). "Number sense": What's in a name and why should we bother? In A. Henik (Ed.), *Continuous issues in numerical cognition: How many or how much* (pp. 195–214). Cambridge, MA: Academic Press.

Richardson, F. C., & Suinn, R. M. (1972). The mathematics anxiety rating scale: Psychometric data. *Journal of Counseling Psychology, 19*(6), 551–554. doi: 10.1037/h0033456

Rittle-Johnson, B., & Alibali, M. W. (1999). Conceptual and procedural knowledge of mathematics: Does one lead to the other? *Journal of Educational Psychology, 91*, 175–189. doi: 10.1037/0022-0663.91.1.175

Rubinsten, O., & Sury, D. (2011). Processing ordinality and quantity: The case of developmental dyscalculia. *PLOS ONE, 6*(9). doi: 10.1371/journal.pone.0024079

Sarnecka, B. W. (2015). How numbers are like the earth (and unlike faces, loitering or knitting) In D. Barner & A. Baron (Eds.), *Core knowledge and conceptual change* (pp. 151–170). New York, NY: Oxford University Press.

Sasanguie, D., Verschaffel, L., Reynvoet, B., & Luwel, K. (2016). The development of symbolic and non-symbolic number line estimations: Three developmental accounts contrasted within cross-sectional and longitudinal data. *Psychologica Belgica, 56*(4), 382–405.

Shalev, R. S. (2007). Prevalence of developmental dyscalculia. In M.M.M. Mazzocco & D. B. Berch (Eds.), *Why is math so hard for some children? The nature and origins of mathematical learning difficulties and disabilities* (pp. 49–60). Baltimore, MD: Brookes.

Siegel, L. S., & Ryan, E. B. (1989). The development of working memory in normally achieving and subtypes of learning disabled children. *Child Development, 60*(4), 973–980.

Siegler, R. S., & Opfer, J. E. (2003). The development of numerical estimation evidence for multiple representations of numerical quantity. *Psychological Science, 14*(3), 237–250. doi: 10.1111/1467-9280.02438

Siegler, R. S., & Robinson, M. (1982). The development of numerical understandings. *Advances in Child Development and Behavior*, 16, 241–312. doi: 10.1016/S0065-2407(08)60072-5

Stanovich, K. E., & Siegel, L. S. (1994). Phenotypic performance profile of children with reading disabilities: A regression-based test of the phonological-core variable-difference model. *Journal of Educational Psychology, 86*(1), 24–53. doi: 10.1037/0022-0663.86.1.24

Stock, P., Desoete, A., & Roeyers, H. (2010). Detecting children with arithmetic disabilities from kindergarten: Evidence from a 3-year longitudinal study on the role of preparatory arithmetic abilities. *Journal of Learning Disabilities, 43*(3), 250–268. doi: 10.1177/0022219409345011

Stuebing, K. K., Fletcher, J. M., Branum-Martin, L., & Francis, D. J. (2012). Simulated comparisons of three methods for identifying specific learning disabilities based on cognitive discrepancies. *School Psychology Review, 41*(1), 3–22.

Stuebing, K. K., Fletcher, J. M., LeDoux, J. M., Lyon, G. R., Shaywitz, S. E., & Shaywitz, B. A. (2002). Validity of IQ-discrepancy classifications of reading disabilities: A meta-analysis. *American Educational Research Journal, 39*(2), 469–518. doi: 10.3102/00028312039002469

Tosto, M. G., Asbury, K., Mazzocco, M.M.M., Petrill, S. A., & Kovas, Y. (2016). From classroom environment to mathematics achievement: The mediating role of self-perceived ability and subject interest, *Learning and Individual Differences, Aug.* (50), 260–269.

Tosto, M., Petrill, S., Halberda, J., Trzaskowski, M., Tikhomirova, T., Bogdanova, O., Ly, R., Wilmer, J., Naiman, D., Germine, L., Plomin, R., & Kovas, Y. (2014). Why do we differ in number sense? Evidence from a genetically sensitive investigation. *Intelligence, 43*(100), 35–46. doi: 10.1016/j.intell.2013.12.007

Vanbinst, K., Ansari, D., Ghesquière, P., & De Smedt, B. (2016). Symbolic numerical magnitude processing is as important to arithmetic as phonological awareness is to reading. *PLOS ONE, 11*(3). doi: 10.1371/journal.pone.0151045

Van Loosbroek, E., Dirkx, G. S., Hulstijn, W., & Janssen, F. (2009). When the mental number line involves a delay: The writing of numbers by children of different arithmetical abilities. *Journal of Experimental Child Psychology, 102*(1), 26–39. doi: 10.1016/j.jecp.2008.07.003

Vukovic, R. K. (2012). Mathematics difficulty with and without reading difficulty: Findings and implications from a four-year longitudinal study. *Exceptional Children, 78*(3), 280–300. doi: 10.1177/001440291207800302

Wang, Z., Lukowski, S. L., Hart, S. A., Lyons, I. M., Thompson, L. A., Kovas, Y., Mazzocco, M.M.M., Plomin, R., & Petrill, S. A. (2015). Is math anxiety always bad for math learning? The role of math motivation. *Psychological Science, 26*(12), 1863–1876. doi: 10.1177/0956797615602471

Willcutt, E. G., Petrill, S. A., Wu, S., Boada, R., DeFries, J. C., Olson, R. K., & Pennington, B. F. (2013). Comorbidity between reading disability and math disability concurrent psychopathology, functional impairment, and neuropsychological functioning. *Journal of Learning Disabilities, 46*(6), 500–516. doi: 10.1177/0022219413477476

Wilson, A. J., Revkin, S. K., Cohen, D., Cohen, L., & Dehaene, S. (2006). An open trial assessment of "The Number Race," an adaptive computer game for remediation of dyscalculia. *Behavioral and Brain Functions, 2*(1), 1. doi: 10.1186/1744-9081-2-20

Wu, Q., Morgan, P. L., & Farkas, G. (2014). Does minority status increase the effect of disability status on elementary school children's academic achievement? *Remedial and Special Education, 35*(6), 366–377. doi: 10.1177/0741932514547644

Wu, S. S., Willcutt, E. G., Escovar, E., & Menon, V. (2014). Mathematics achievement and anxiety and their relation to internalizing and externalizing behaviors. *Journal of Learning Disabilities, 47*(6), 503–514. doi: 10.1177/0022219412473154

Yerkes, R. M., & Dodson, J. D. (1908). The relation of strength of stimulus to rapidity of habit-formation. *Journal of Comparative Neurology and Psychology, 18*(5), 459–482.

Four

HOW SLD MANIFESTS IN WRITING

Nancy Mather
Barbara J. Wendling

DEFINITION, ETIOLOGY, AND INCIDENCE
OF WRITING DISABILITIES

Writing is an essential skill for education, communication, social interactions, and employment. In our contemporary society, e-mail and text messages have become the preferred means of communication replacing face-to-face encounters and even telephone conversations. This reliance on electronic communications has increased the need to have adequate writing skills. If individuals cannot communicate in writing they will struggle throughout their school years, and their employment opportunities may be limited. Learning to write can be particularly challenging to individuals with a specific learning disability (SLD) in written expression.

Similar to the writing process itself, writing disabilities are complex and multifaceted. Written expression requires fine-motor skill, knowledge of writing conventions, oral language, and reasoning. A writer must employ and integrate many diverse abilities to write legibly, spell, and translate thoughts into writing. Difficulty in any one aspect of writing can contribute to difficulty in another. For example, poor handwriting or poor spelling often affects the quality and quantity of written output. Thus, writing is a highly demanding task that has been described as "an immense juggling act" (Berninger & Richards, 2002, p. 173).

Essentials of Specific Learning Disability Identification, Second Edition.
Edited by Vincent C. Alfonso and Dawn P. Flanagan
© 2018 John Wiley & Sons, Inc. Published 2018 by John Wiley & Sons, Inc.

Definition

A disorder of written expression is coded in the *Diagnostic and Statistical Manual of Mental Disorders* (5th ed.) (*DSM-5;* American Psychiatric Association, 2013) as an SLD with impairment in written expression. The written expression disorder is a "specifier" under the general SLD heading. In the Individuals with Disabilities Education Improvement Act (IDEA 2004, P.L. 108-446), written expression is identified as one of the eight areas for eligibility under the category of SLD.

The *DSM-5* and IDEA 2004 requirements for a diagnosis of a specific learning disorder with impairment in written expression are similar but not identical. The *DSM-5* requires that the difficulty with written expression has been present for at least 6 months and that despite targeted interventions the individual is unable to perform academically at a level appropriate for his or her age. Furthermore, the disorder must significantly interfere with academic or occupational performance or activities of daily living as confirmed by individually administered standardized achievement measures and comprehensive clinical assessment.

Under IDEA 2004, identification of an SLD in writing requires documentation that the individual does not achieve adequately for his or her age or meet grade-level standards when provided with appropriate learning experiences and instruction. States must adopt criteria for determining the presence of an SLD. The criteria must not require the use of a severe discrepancy between intellectual ability and achievement, must permit the use of a process based on the individual's response to intervention, and may permit the use of alternative research-based methods (e.g., identifying a relevant pattern of strengths and weaknesses).

DSM-5 and IDEA 2004 require that exclusionary factors be considered before making a diagnosis of SLD with impairment in written expression. Other disorders (e.g., intellectual or sensory disabilities) or adverse conditions (e.g., lack of proficiency in the language of instruction or inadequate education or instruction) must be ruled out before a diagnosis of SLD can be confirmed. Additionally, under the guidelines of the *DSM-5* and IDEA, poor handwriting or poor spelling alone is insufficient for a diagnosis of an SLD with impairment in written expression. The writing difficulties must interfere with the ability to express oneself in writing.

Students with SLD often struggle with the development of both handwriting and spelling, the foundational skills of writing in the primary grades. These difficulties with spelling continue to persist at the secondary level (Williams, Walker, Vaughn, & Wanzek, 2017). Weaknesses in these lower-level skills are often then the reasons for their difficulty with written expression. Figure 4.1 illustrates how Maggie, a sixth-grade student, feels about her persistent difficulty with spelling as she writes: "I like writing, but I hate spelling."

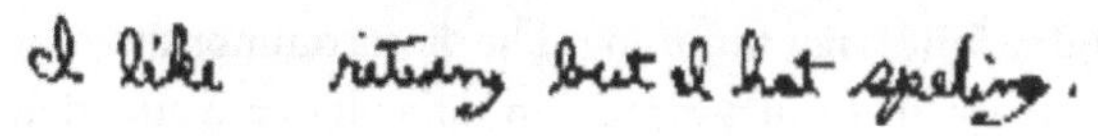

Figure 4.1. Maggie's Writing

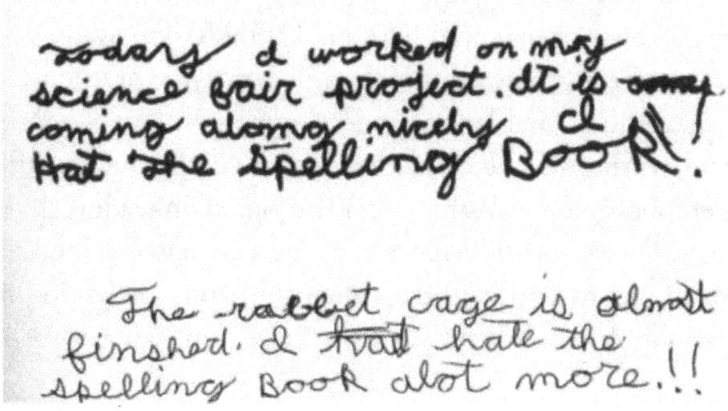

Figure 4.2. Kevin's Writing

In his journal, Kevin, a seventh-grade student, expresses similar sentiments about his spelling book (Figure 4.2).

Etiology

Individuals with writing disabilities are a heterogeneous group and many have other learning or behavior difficulties. An isolated disorder in written expression is considered rare (Bernstein, 2013). Due to comorbidity with other disorders as well as limited research in written language disorders, the causes are not well documented or understood. Evidence suggests that causes for poor writing stem from a variety of factors, including medical, neurobiological, neuropsychological, behavioral, and environmental. Medical conditions such as carbon monoxide poisoning or fetal alcohol syndrome have been linked to writing disorders (Bernstein, 2008) as has trauma to the parietal lobe of the brain (National Institute for Neurological Disorders and Stroke [NINDS], 2009). Adverse reactions to medications may also have an impact on written expression (Andrade, Bhakta, & Fernandes, 2010). Results from family and twin studies indicate that a genetic component is involved (e.g., Bernstein, 2008; Raskind, 2001). Individuals with specific language impairments and delays are certainly at risk for writing difficulties. Neuropsychological causes may include difficulties with fine-motor skills, language, visual-spatial abilities, attention, memory, or sequencing skills. Because writing tasks require planning, organizational skills, and sustained attention and effort, the relationship between certain behavior-related issues and writing is not surprising. The most common attention and behavior problems associated with written expression difficulties are attention-deficit hyperactivity disorder (ADHD) and oppositional defiant disorder.

The causes of writing problems will also vary based on the type of writing difficulty. For example, a problem with spelling may occur because of a limited ability to recall the orthography (written symbols) of a language or poor phonological awareness, whereas a problem in written expression is more likely to stem from inadequate oral language development.

In many cases, writing difficulties may not be noted until sometime after first grade, because more emphasis in the classroom may be placed on reading development. In fact, an individual's writing difficulties may not be observed until the student transitions from third to fourth grade, when the nature of writing requirements changes, the writing demands increase dramatically, and state testing often occurs.

Incidence

The prevalence of students with some type of SLD is typically estimated to be between 4% and 5% of the total US school-age population. Individuals with SLDs represent 36% of the total receiving special education services (National Center for Education Statistics [NCES], 2013, Table 204.30). Within the SLD category, the prevalence of written expression impairment appears similar to that of reading disability. Problems with written expression are estimated to occur in 2% to 8% of school-age children, with a higher prevalence of boys than girls (Katusic, Colligan, Weaver, & Barbaresi, 2009; Wiznitzer & Scheffel, 2009). The number of individuals with only a specific writing disability is difficult to pinpoint because individuals with writing disability often have comorbid conditions, such as disorders in reading, math, attention, or behavior. In a study addressing the incidence of written language disorders, Katusic et al. (2009) found that 75% of the sample of students with written language disorders ($N = 806$) in a large birth cohort were also experiencing problems in reading. Thus, only about one-fourth of the students with writing disabilities did not have a reading disability.

Teachers, however, have reported a much higher incidence of handwriting difficulties, estimating that nearly one-third of their male students and about 10% of their female students struggle with handwriting (Rosenblum, Weiss, & Parush, 2004). These findings suggest that writing disabilities have been underdiagnosed. This is partially due to comorbidity issues but also to the lack of emphasis on written language by researchers and educators alike. Evidence of the lack of instructional focus on writing in US schools can be found in reviewing the National Assessment of Educational Progress (NAEP) findings. According to the

Nation's Report Card: Writing 2007 (Salahu-Din, Persky, & Miller, 2008), less than one-third of fourth- and eighth-graders and less than one-fourth of 12th-graders were found to be proficient in writing. This information is based on the results from

DON'T FORGET

Writing disabilities tend to be underdiagnosed even though the prevalence rate is similar to that of reading disabilities.

the last paper-and-pencil version of the NAEP writing test. Beginning in 2011 a computer-based writing assessment was administered to eighth- and 12th-graders. The results, although not comparable to the 2007 results due to the change in format, were similar. Approximately one-fourth of eighth- and 12th-graders performed at the proficient level or higher (NCES, 2012).

SUBTYPES OF WRITING DISABILITY

Individuals who struggle with writing may have difficulty with one or more aspects of written language. Symptoms that may signal an impairment in written expression include difficulties with spelling, grammar and punctuation, and clarity and organization of written expression (*DSM-5*, 2013). Furthermore, problems such as low self-esteem and poor social skills should be considered because these symptoms are associated with learning disorders in general.

Berninger (1996) suggested that when assessing writing, an evaluator should consider the various "constraints" affecting writing. Understanding the multidimensional impact of constraints such as limited instruction, specific cognitive or linguistic weaknesses, limited cultural experiences, and poor motivation can help inform the type and extent of accommodations and instruction needed, because the various constraints affect different aspects of writing skill. In some cases, the problem is primarily with motor skills, which affects the development of handwriting. Other times, the problem is primarily code-based, affecting spelling; and in still others, it is primarily language-based, affecting expression. Frequently, the problems are combined, which complicates the diagnosis and treatment of the individual's writing difficulties.

Basically, three associated learning disabilities can affect writing acquisition and development: *dysgraphia, dyslexia,* and *oral language impairments* (Berninger & May, 2011). Many practitioners categorize individuals with an SLD affecting written language into two groups: those who experience

DON'T FORGET

Proficiency with basic writing skills underlies written expression. Problems with handwriting and spelling may contribute to written expression difficulties.

difficulty with basic writing skills and those who experience difficulty with written expression. Difficulties with the lower-level basic writing skills include the transcription skills of handwriting and spelling. Dysgraphia and dyslexia primarily affect these transcription skills. Difficulties with the higher-level written expression or text-generation skills primarily stem from oral language impairments or, in some cases, significant problems with executive functioning.

Dysgraphia

Dysgraphia has been described as a neurological disorder characterized by writing disabilities (NINDS, 2009), but definitions of dysgraphia vary. Some indicate that dysgraphia is essentially a type of motor disorder that manifests itself in poor-quality script (Deuel, 1994; Hamstra-Bletz & Blote, 1993). Other definitions associate dysgraphia with the inability to spell familiar and novel words (Miceli & Capasso, 2006). Still other definitions indicate that dysgraphia is not a unitary disorder and that an individual may demonstrate poor functioning in any or all of the different facets of writing performance (Wiznitzer & Scheffel, 2009).

For the purposes of this chapter, dysgraphia is viewed as a primary impairment in fine-motor skills and the production of written forms, which can then affect handwriting and spelling development. Individuals with dysgraphia struggle with the motoric aspects of writing, having weaknesses in motor control and the execution of specific motor movements. They often have difficulty with letter-writing skills, difficulty with legibility (how easily others can recognize their letters), delayed automaticity (how many letters they can write in 15 seconds), and speed (the amount of time required to complete a writing task) (Berninger & Wolf, 2009a, 2009b). These handwriting difficulties are often accompanied by problems with spelling (Berninger, 2004; Gregg, 2009). Individuals with dysgraphia may have any level of intellectual and oral language abilities. They may have no difficulty in reading or mathematics, with the exception of writing numbers.

Early identification of writing problems requires that attention be given to children who are struggling with the development of handwriting and spelling, because these are the foundational skills of writing in the primary grades. For children whose poor motor coordination causes poor handwriting, a diagnosis of developmental coordination disorder may be appropriate.

Figures 4.3 and 4.4 illustrate the writing of Dan, a student with above-average reading ability but severe problems with spelling and handwriting. The first sample is from fifth grade and the second is from seventh grade. As you can see, over the 2 years, neither his handwriting nor spelling shows much improvement.

Severe difficulties with handwriting can continue into adulthood. Figure 4.5 illustrates an excerpt from Toby's lecture notes, a 22-year-old college senior with

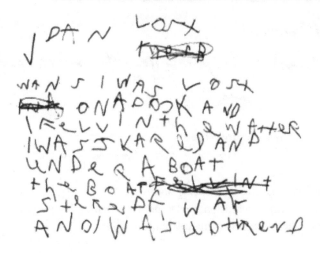

Figure 4.3. Dan's Fifth-Grade Writing Example

Translation. Lost
Once I was lost on a dock and I fell in the water. I was scared and under a boat. The boat steered away and I was up. The end.

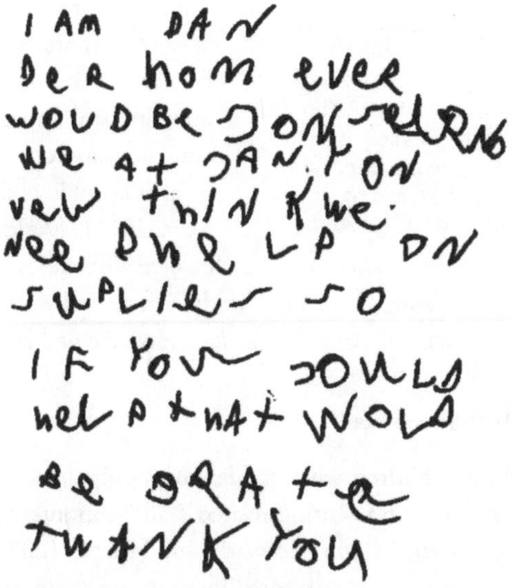

Figure 4.4. Dan's Seventh-Grade Writing Example

Partial translation: I am Dan. Dear whomever would be considerate . . . we at Canyon View think we need help on supplies so if you could help that would be great. Thank you.

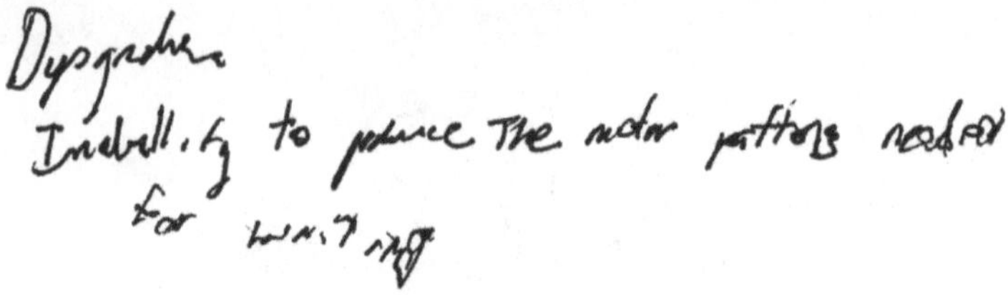

Figure 4.5. Toby's Lecture Notes

Translation: Dysgraphia, inability to produce the motor patterns needed for writing

dysgraphia who has average reading ability but nearly illegible handwriting. He was writing down a definition of dysgraphia. Clearly, Toby needs to write his papers and take his exams using a laptop or tablet.

Dyslexia

A number of individuals with writing disabilities may be diagnosed with dyslexia, a disorder that affects reading and spelling. In fact, poor spelling is often described as the hallmark of dyslexia (Gregg, 2009). Decoding (word reading) and encoding (word spelling) involve many of the same processes. These skills require mastery of the alphabetic principle or understanding how sounds and symbols correspond. For many individuals, problems in decoding and encoding stem from the same primary roots: poor phonological or orthographic abilities (Berninger & May, 2011). Dyslexia and dysgraphia involve difficulties with the symbolic aspects of language—reading or writing words. Often, individuals with dyslexia or dysgraphia have average intellectual abilities and adequate oral language skills.

> **CAUTION**
> ....
> Poor spelling with adequate ability to express ideas in writing is often typical of dyslexia or dysgraphia. Even though IDEA 2004 includes only the one broad category of written expression, poor spelling and handwriting are often symptomatic of a specific writing disability and should not be ignored.

Oral Language Impairments

As early as preschool, children with oral language impairments lag behind their typically developing peers on writing-related skills (Puranik & Lonigan, 2012). Among first-grade students, Costa, Edwards, and Hooper (2016) found that one-fourth of the students were at risk for difficulties in reading and writing. Oral language abilities were more impaired in elementary age students with reading and writing disabilities than in students with writing disabilities alone (Costa et al.,

≡ *Rapid Reference 4.1*

Definitions of Terms

Lexical knowledge. Vocabulary; knowledge of the meaning of words and the relationships among words

Morphology. The meaning units of language (e.g., prefixes, suffixes, and roots)

Orthography. The marks, including letters, numbers, and punctuation, that make up a written language

Syntactic knowledge. Knowledge of grammar and the rules governing word order and sentence structure

2016). In addition, students with dual impairments had more weaknesses in cognitive abilities and executive functioning.

As they progress in school, students with oral language impairments continue to exhibit difficulties with written expression because they lack the necessary lexical, morphological, orthographic, and syntactic knowledge to express their thoughts. (See Rapid Reference 4.1 for definitions of these terms.)

Students may also have difficulty with handwriting and spelling. When limited oral language is the primary problem, the individual will have difficulties in oral and written expression. When language is not the primary problem, the individual will be more capable in oral expression than in written expression, which is often true in students with dyslexia or dysgraphia. In all cases, it is important to explore the individual's performance in basic

DON'T FORGET

Individuals with dyslexia or dysgraphia are often far more capable with oral expression than with written expression (Kronenberger & Dunn, 2003).

writing skills as well as his or her abilities to employ the executive functions required to plan, organize, and revise writing. Poor basic writing skills or poor executive functions can be possible reasons or contributing factors for problems in written expression.

HOW WRITING DIFFICULTIES MANIFEST DEVELOPMENTALLY

Handwriting, spelling, and written expression all follow different developmental courses, although a problem in one area can influence development in another area. A student with poor handwriting has fewer opportunities to practice spelling; a student with poor spelling may limit word choices only to those he or she knows how to spell; and a student with problems in ideation or expression may write simple sentences and repetitive ideas, resulting in slow development of spelling and vocabulary. Often, students who have difficulties with writing seem to become stuck in a developmental phase until appropriate feedback and interventions are provided.

Handwriting

Warning signs of future writing difficulties are visible in children's earliest writing attempts. Awkward pencil grips, illegible writing, saying words aloud while writing, avoiding writing tasks, or fatiguing quickly can all signal potential writing problems. According to Levine (1987), handwriting proficiency typically develops in the following stages: (1) *imitation* (preschool to kindergarten), when children pretend to write by copying others; (2) *graphic presentation* (first and second grade), when children learn how to form letters and to write on a line with proper spacing; (3) *progressive incorporation* (late second to fourth grade), when letters are produced with less effort; and (4) *automatization* (fourth through seventh grade), when children write rapidly, easily, and efficiently. In the final stages, students develop personalized styles and increase their writing rates.

Students who struggle with handwriting often initially have difficulty learning to form letters and then have trouble writing with ease. In general, when compared to their classmates, students with SLD demonstrate slower rates of handwriting speed (Weintraub & Graham, 1998).

Spelling

For most children, knowledge of phoneme (sound) and grapheme (letter) correspondences develops naturally over the preschool and early elementary years, progressing from the skill of knowing letter names and sounds to being able to break apart (segment) the individual sounds within words. As general guidelines, the majority of first-grade students can segment words into syllables; by second grade, most children can segment words into individual phonemes, and orthography, morphology, and syntax begin to increase in importance (see Rapid Reference 4.1 for definitions). Once a writer is able to sequence sounds correctly, he or she must then pay attention to various letter patterns and spelling options. As students' knowledge of orthographic patterns develops, they recognize and use permissible letter sequences. They are able to sequence common letter strings in the correct order (e.g., *ight*). Although unexpected letters and irregular spelling patterns may be memorized, securing these images is more difficult than securing words that conform to common, regular spelling patterns (Ehri, 2000).

As spelling improves, the writer develops increasing awareness of the spelling of irregular words, affixes (prefixes and suffixes), as well as the spellings of words derived from Greek, Latin, and other languages. Several researchers have studied how spelling skill evolves and have proposed various models to explain the stages or phases of spelling development (e.g., Bear, Invernizzi, Templeton, & Johnston, 2016; Ehri, 2000; Gentry, 1982; Henderson, 1990). Rapid Reference 4.2 illustrates the phases of spelling development as proposed by Bear et al. (2016).

In addition, one must consider spelling development within the context of a specific language (e.g., Spanish has more regular phoneme-grapheme correspondence than

≡ Rapid Reference 4.2

An Overview of Phases of Spelling Development

Letter-Name Alphabetic Spelling: Ages 5 to 8

- Progresses from using scribbles to using the names of the letters as cues to represent the sound
- Learns to segment the sounds within words
- Comprises three periods: early (pre-phonemic to semi-phonemic), middle (phonetic), and late (transitional to correct)

Within Word Pattern Spelling: Ages 7 to 10

- Spells pre-consonantal nasals (e.g., the *m* in *jump*), consonant blends (e.g., *bl*- and -*st*), and consonant and vowel digraphs (e.g., *ph* or *oa*)
- Spells most consonant-vowel-consonant-silent *e* (CVCe) words correctly (e.g., *five*)
- Spells some vowel teams correctly (e.g., *ea, oa, ai*)
- Spells some homophones correctly (e.g., *bear* and *bare*)

Syllables and Affixes: Ages 9 to 14

- Spells words of more than one syllable
- Starts to consider syllables and affixes
- Makes errors at place where the syllables and affixes meet (e.g., *hopful* for *hopeful*)
- Makes errors on unaccented second syllables (e.g., *mountin* for *mountain*)

Derivational Relations Spelling: Age 10 to Adulthood

- Spells common word derivations (e.g., *big, bigger, biggest*)
- Spells words of Greek and Latin origin correctly (e.g., *psychology* or *aquatic*)
- Uses spelling rules correctly when adding suffixes (e.g., doubling the final consonant [*stop* → *stopped*] or dropping the final e [*like* → *liking*] when adding a suffix that begins with a vowel)

English). Thus, students learning more-consistent orthographies learn to spell more quickly than those who are learning to spell less-consistent orthographies. Phonological development may be universal to the development of all alphabetic languages, whereas the way sounds are mapped to letters is more language specific, making spelling in some languages easier than others (Goswami, 2006). In addition, the nature of the orthography of the native language will influence how children attempt to spell the English words that they are learning (Joshi, Hoien, Feng, Chengappa, & Boulware-Gooden, 2006).

> **DON'T FORGET**
>
> ....
>
> A child's primary language must be considered when analyzing his or her spelling development.

Written Expression

As noted, one area of written language can affect development and performance in another area. If a writer has to stop and think about how to spell a word, an already developed idea may be forgotten (Graham, Berninger, Abbott, Abbott, & Whitaker, 1997). For the development of written expression, beginning writers often progress from scribbles to strings of letters, to single words, to lists and unconnected complete sentences, and then to complete connected sentences that are integrated to produce stories, paragraphs, or essays. Sentence syntax increases in complexity, as does the use of a variety of sentence structures that include embedded clauses. Whereas a less-skilled writer may use just simple sentences or compound sentences, more advanced writers use different types of sentence structures to help maintain a reader's interest. As written language skills develop, students increase their knowledge of awareness of audience, organization, cohesion (unity of the ideas), and text structure.

> **DON'T FORGET**
>
> ....
>
> Ignoring problems in basic writing skills may delay the identification of a disability in written expression.

COGNITIVE CORRELATES AND DIAGNOSTIC MARKERS OF AN SLD IN WRITTEN EXPRESSION

Writing involves the integration of many different cognitive and linguistic factors at several levels: *subword* (e.g., phonology, orthography, and morphology); *word* (e.g., spelling and vocabulary); *sentence* (e.g., syntax); and *text* (e.g., cohesion and type of text structure) (Englert & Raphael, 1988; Gregg, 1995, 2009; Gregg &

Mather, 2002). These factors then influence the writer's ability to plan, draft, and edit (Englert, Raphael, Anderson, Anthony, & Stevens, 1991; MacArthur & Graham, 1993). Text generation and text revising, the most complex of the writing skills, involve numerous cognitive and linguistic capacities (e.g., idea generation, reasoning, oral language, and knowledge of syntax and vocabulary) (McCloskey, Perkins, & Van Divner, 2009). Careful analysis of the processing requirements of writing tasks can help determine which aspects of cognitive processing are involved; differential diagnosis requires careful examination of multiple subcomponent processes (Hale & Fiorello, 2004). The quality of written products can be increased or constrained by a multitude of factors (Hooper et al., 1994).

Since the early 1990s, Berninger (2009) and her colleagues have carefully examined the various predictors of handwriting, spelling, and composing. In a review of the findings from their years of research, the best predictors of hand-writing have been orthographic coding, the ability to form mental representations of written words, and graphomotor planning for sequential finger movements, which controls motor output. The best predictors of spelling have been measures of phonological and orthographic coding, as well as vocabulary knowledge in first through third grade. The best predictors of composition fluency—the number of words written within a time limit—and composition quality have been ortho-graphic coding, handwriting automaticity, and working memory. Spelling had a significant relationship to compositional fluency only in the primary grades, whereas handwriting automaticity had a significant relationship from first through sixth grade. In fact, automatic letter writing has been identified as the best predictor of composition length and quality for elementary and high school students (Connelly, Campbell, MacLean, & Barnes, 2006; Jones, 2004). Thus, competence in written language is based on the fluency and quality of the response (Hale & Fiorello, 2004).

Using contemporary Cattell-Horn-Carroll theory, the cognitive abilities related to written expression include the broad abilities of auditory processing (Ga), long-term retrieval (Glr), cognitive processing speed (Gs), crystallized intelligence (Gc), short-term working memory (Gwm), and fluid reasoning (Gf) (Flanagan, Ortiz, & Alfonso, 2013; Floyd, McGrew, & Evans, 2008). Auditory processing, in particular the narrow ability of phonetic coding, is important in segmenting sounds for spelling. Associative memory (a narrow Glr ability) and perceptual speed (a narrow Gs ability) are involved in mapping the sounds to their corresponding letters, another skill essential for spelling. Crystallized intelligence is a store of acquired knowledge and includes orthographic knowledge, knowledge of morphology, and lexical knowledge, all of which contribute to spelling and written expression. Short-term working memory is engaged during the writing process. For example, short-term working memory is involved in maintaining the idea to be communicated while transcribing the words. Fluid reasoning includes the ability to think logically and apply acquired knowledge to new situations, which are essential for written expression.

In addition, the process of expressing oneself in writing requires executive functions, such as attention, working memory, planning, and self-regulating behaviors. Ineffective or inconsistent use of executive function capacities can affect any aspect of the writing process and may be at the core of many written language problems (Dehn, 2008; Hale & Fiorello, 2004; McCloskey et al., 2009). These executive functions are also often impaired in individuals with attention-deficit disorders, which helps explain the high prevalence of writing disabilities in that population (Mayes & Calhoun, 2006, 2007).

COMPONENTS OF THE DIAGNOSTIC APPROACH TO IDENTIFYING AN SLD IN WRITTEN EXPRESSION

An assessment of written language disorders requires a multisource, multi-method diagnostic approach that includes standardized assessments as well as informal assessments, including curriculum-based measurements (CBMs) and classroom work samples. During the assessment process, writing samples should be obtained using different methods (e.g., copying, dictation, spontaneous writing) and under different conditions (e.g., timed, untimed). Results from a recent study demonstrated that numerous writing samples are needed to obtain a reliable estimate of young struggling students' writing capabilities (Graham, Hebert, Sandbank, & Harris, 2016). For example, 11 compositions were needed to obtain a reliable estimate of writing quality. Furthermore, how well students wrote in one genre only weakly predicted their writing skill in another genre.

> **C A U T I O N**
> ....
> Several writing samples are needed to obtain a reliable estimate of struggling writers' capabilities (Graham et al., 2016).

The evaluator should be clear about the reasons for testing, what writing skills are developmentally appropriate for the individual being assessed, as well as the types of questions being asked so that the assessment is designed to address all major domains of concern (Hooper et al., 1994). Because writing leaves a permanent record of performance, the individual's difficulties can be easily observed and analyzed. The purpose of a comprehensive evaluation is to identify the nature and severity of the impairment in handwriting, spelling, or written expression and then recommend the most appropriate interventions (Fletcher, Lyon, Fuchs, & Barnes, 2007). The evaluator's goal is to pinpoint the specific areas of writing difficulty and to identify the specific

DON'T FORGET

When students have reading and writing difficulties, a thorough language evaluation can be a critical element.

cognitive or linguistic correlates that are impeding the development of writing skills. When students have reading and writing difficulties, a thorough language evaluation can be a critical element for identifying their complex learning needs (Costa et al., 2016).

Prior to conducting a comprehensive evaluation, valuable information about the student's writing skills can be gathered through the use of formative assessments, such as CBMs. Specific procedures are incorporated into CBMs to assess and monitor a student's performance in spelling or written expression. Instructional decisions are made using the data collected from administered CBM probes with criteria for goals and progress rates determined by comparison to a normative group (Deno, Fuchs, Marston, & Shin, 2001). Progress monitoring is then paired with instructional modifications, and data-based decision rules are used for interpreting graphed CBM data to determine the effectiveness of the instructional interventions (Stecker, Fuchs, & Fuchs, 2005). This ongoing progress-monitoring data can help teachers make appropriate instructional decisions based on a student's responsiveness (Jung, McMaster, & delMas, 2017). If a Response to Intervention (RTI) model is in place, this type of information should be readily available. However, even without an RTI model in place, information from CBMs may be incorporated as part of pre-referral data or as a means to monitor progress after an evaluation has been conducted.

Handwriting

Three types of graphomotor disorders are prevalent in the adolescent and adult population with SLD and ADHD: *symbolic deficits, motor speed deficits,* and *dyspraxia* (Deuel, 1992; Gregg, 2009). Gregg explains these different disorders as follows. With symbolic deficits, the writer has specific phonemic, orthographic, and morphemic weaknesses that affect only writing, not drawing. These linguistic problems often co-occur in individuals with dyslexia. With motor speed deficits, the writer is capable of good handwriting, but letters and words are produced slowly. Individuals with ADHD often exhibit motor speed deficits (Deuel, 1992). With dyspraxia, the writer has limited ability to learn and perform voluntary motor activities, which affects writing and drawing.

In assessing handwriting, it is important to evaluate overall legibility, letter formation errors, and writing rate. The individual's posture, pencil grip, and paper position also should be considered. Legibility is often best determined by attempting to read a student's papers. Letter formation errors are identified by examining words and letters more closely. Writing speed is often measured by asking a student to copy a short passage for one minute or to write the letters of the alphabet as quickly as possible. In younger children, difficulties with handwriting usually result from a combination of fine-motor problems, limited ability to revisualize letters, and difficulty remembering the motor patterns for making the letter forms. With older children, problems often center on overall legibility and the fluency and automaticity of writing speed. A skill is automatic when it is mastered so well that minimal conscious attention and effort are required (Dehn, 2008). The speed and automaticity of graphomotor processing are the cornerstones for developing fluent text-generation skills, because the automatic motor routines free up cognitive resources needed for generating ideas into text (McCloskey et al., 2009).

> **DON'T FORGET**
> ....
> Fluent writing skills require automaticity and ease with graphomotor production.

Basic Writing Skills

Many standardized tests are available for assessing aspects of basic writing skills, such as the Woodcock-Johnson IV Tests of Achievement (Schrank, Mather, & McGrew, 2014a) or the Kaufman Test of Educational Achievement (3rd ed.) (Kaufman & Kaufman, 2014). In addition, analyses of classroom writing samples can help determine a student's knowledge of punctuation and capitalization rules as well as the types and frequency of spelling errors. If spelling difficulties are present, which is often the case in students with SLD in writing, it is important to consider the student's knowledge of phonology, orthography, and morphology.

Phonology

Phonological processes are critical for the development of spelling skills because spelling requires an awareness of the internal structure of words (Bailet, 1991; Blachman, 1994). Even spelling problems in high school students and young adults reflect specific deficits in the phonological aspects of language (Bruck, 1993;

Moats, 1995). The most-important phonological awareness ability for spelling is segmentation, the ability to break apart the speech sounds (Ehri, 2006; Smith, 1997). This abil-

> ## DON'T FORGET
> Segmentation skill is critical to spelling ability.

ity enables an individual to place the graphemes representing the phonemes in correct order. Segmentation can be tested using standardized tests or informal procedures. In addition, an individual's ability to spell nonsense words conforming to English spelling patterns can help reveal his or her knowledge of phoneme-grapheme correspondences and ability to sequence sounds. Students with weaknesses in phonological awareness often have trouble putting sounds in order and they confuse similar sounds, such as /p/ and /b/ and /t/ and /d/. For example, Kristen, a third-grade student, spelled the word *potato* as *btado*.

Orthography

Students with weaknesses in orthography have particular difficulties remembering letter sequences and spelling words that contain irregular spelling patterns (e.g., *once*) because they do not have mental images of words stored in memory or word-specific memory (Ehri, 2000). Results from one study suggested that high-functioning college students with dyslexia use phonological skills to spell familiar words, but they still have difficulty memorizing orthographic patterns and recalling spelling rules. This difficulty results in inconsistent spellings of irregular and less-familiar words (Kemp, Parrila, & Kirby, 2009). A student's understanding of orthographic conventions can be measured with a standardized test, such as the Test of Orthographic Competence (Mather, Roberts, Hammill, & Allen, 2008) or with informal procedures, such as having a student spell words that contain irregular elements, for example, *once, said,* and *again*. Students with weaknesses in orthography have difficulty recalling the images of words and when spelling will regularize the irregular element of the word, spelling *once* as *wuns* and *said* as *sed*.

Figure 4.6 shows the spellings of Matthew, a fifth-grade student. The evaluator first showed Matthew the correctly spelled word for 10 seconds and then covered it up and asked him to write the word from memory. As can be seen, Matthew spells words the way they sound, rather than how they look. Rapid Reference 4.3 describes the types of spelling errors that are more indicative of problems in phonology versus orthography.

they   thay

again   agn

could   cud

because   bcus

once   wuns

only   onle

night   nite

very   vere

Figure 4.6. Matthew's Spellings

⇒ *Rapid Reference 4.3*

Are Spelling Errors More Related to Phonological or Orthographic Awareness?

Phonology

The writer

- Does not put sounds in order
- Adds or omits sounds
- Represents phonemes with incorrect graphemes
- Confuses similar sounding speech sounds (e.g., /b/ and /p/-voiced and -unvoiced consonant pairs)
- Has trouble with vowel sounds

Orthography

The writer

- Presents all sounds in order but the graphemes are incorrect
- Reverses letters (e.g., b and d) transposes words (e.g., saw and was)
- Misspells common high-frequency words
- Regularizes the spelling of the irregular element in words (e.g., thay for they and sed for said)

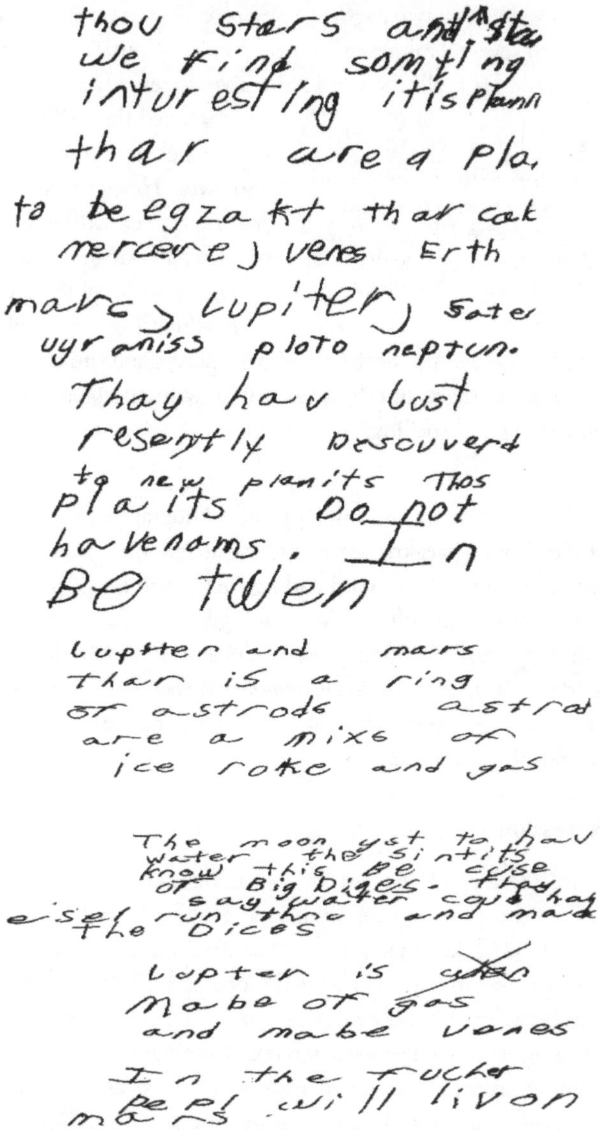

thou stars and stars
we find somting
inturesting it's plann
thar are a pla
to be egzakt thar cak
mercere, veres Erth
mars, Lupiter, Sater
uyraniss ploto neptun.
Thay hav bust
resently Discouverd
to new planits Thos
plaits Do not
havenoms. In
Be twen
Lupter and mars
thar is a ring
of astrods astrat
are a mixs of
ice roke and gas

The moon yst to hav
water the sintits
know this be cuse
of Big Diges. thay
say water coud hay
eisel run thro and mad
the Dices

Lupter is ~~water~~
mabe of gas
and mabe vanes

In the fucher
pepl will livon
mars

Figure 4.7. Steve's Report on Space

Translation: Through stars and stars we find something interesting. It is planets. There are 9 planets to be exact. They're called Mercury, Venus, Earth, Mars, Jupiter, Saturn, Uranus, Pluto, Neptune. They have just recently discovered two new planets. Those planets do not have names. In between Jupiter and Mars there is a ring of asteroids. Asteroids are a mix of ice, rock, and gas. The moon used to have water. The scientists know this because of the big ditches. They say water could have easily run through and made the ditches. Jupiter is made of gas and maybe Venus. In the future, people will live on Mars.

Figure 4.7 shows the first two pages of a report on planets by Steve, another fifth-grade student with severe weaknesses in orthography. Notice the types of spelling errors that he makes. He spells the word *exact* as *egzact,* exactly as it sounds. He has not mastered the spelling of common high-frequency words, such as *there* and *have.* He reverses the letter *J* in *Jupiter,* as well as the letter *d* in the word *made* (*mabe*). He lacks awareness of common English spelling rules, such as that English words rarely end with the letter *v* (e.g., *hav*). Also notice the erratic spacing and variation in letter size. Steve knows a lot about space, but the quality of his written expression is affected by his poor handwriting and spelling.

> **C A U T I O N**
>
> Spelling involves phonological and orthographic knowledge. Difficulty may be caused by weaknesses in one or both aspects of linguistic knowledge.

Morphology

Morphology also interacts with phonology and orthography to affect the spelling of words. Students with weaknesses in morphology—the meaning elements of words—often have trouble with word endings (e.g., verb tense, plurals) as well as the spelling of prefixes and suffixes. Morphology also influences how words are spelled, because the spelling often preserves meaning, rather than letter-sound connections (e.g., *music* and *musician, hymn* and *hymnal*). As a component of orthographic knowledge, an evaluator should explore the writer's knowledge and use of varied morphological patterns.

Written Expression

Knowledge and mastery of the writing process are considered to be essential components of written expression (Baker & Hubbard, 1995). Unfortunately, poor writers tend to lack knowledge of the entire writing process and are less likely than others to revise text to improve clarity (Hooper et al., 1994). Because reciprocal influences exist between oral and written language, oral language abilities will affect an individual's abilities to compose written text (Berninger & Wolf, 2009b). Thus, when evaluating a student's ability to express ideas, an assessment should also include measures of receptive and expressive oral language. In addition, an evaluator should explore how the student performs on tasks requiring working memory and executive functioning. Individuals with good memory abilities are able to write more complex sentences and juggle multiple writing tasks (Dehn, 2008; Swanson & Siegel, 2001). Even with well-developed basic writing skills, written expression places considerable demands on working memory because the act of constructing ideas can never become fully automatized (Dehn, 2015).

Furthermore, an evaluator should consider a writer's declarative knowledge (e.g., knowledge of topics), procedural knowledge (e.g., knowledge of strategies used to produce various text genres), and conditional knowledge (e.g., which strategies or text structures to employ for a particular audience) (Hooper et al., 1994).

Cognitive-Linguistic Abilities

A comprehensive evaluation of the individual's cognitive and linguistic abilities is an important component of the diagnostic approach. Determining which abilities are intact and which are impaired is necessary to understanding why the individual is struggling with writing and is helpful in planning the most effective instructional program. Tests such as the Woodcock-Johnson IV Tests of Cognitive Abilities (Schrank, McGrew, & Mather, 2014) and Woodcock-Johnson IV Tests of Oral Language (Schrank, Mather, & McGrew, 2014b) provide comprehensive assessment of the underlying abilities related to writing. For example, the

> **DON'T FORGET**
> ....
> Oral language is the cornerstone of written language.

evaluator can assess many of the cognitive correlates mentioned previously: working memory, processing speed, comprehension-knowledge, fluid reasoning, long-term retrieval, and auditory processing. In addition, executive functions, such as attention, are important to writing performance and should be explored.

EXAMPLES OF TREATMENT PROTOCOLS

Many students who have been diagnosed as having a specific learning disability in written expression are spending all of their day in general education classrooms. Similar to their peers, they are being asked to produce clear, coherent writing to a variety of topics and demands in a timely fashion. In contrast to oral language and reading disabilities, less is known about the treatment of writing disabilities (Fletcher et al., 2007; Graham & Harris, 2014; Graham & Perin, 2007). This may explain why many students who struggle with writing make little improvement in skill across grades. Poor writing cannot just be attributed to SLD; in fact, two out of three students in fourth grade do not write well enough to meet class expectations, and as many as 70% of students in Grades 4 through 12 are deficient in writing skills (Persky, Daane, & Jin, 2003). One problem is that some teachers devote limited time to writing instruction (Applebee & Langer, 2011). Another problem is that some teachers feel inadequately prepared to teach writing (Brindle, Graham, Harris, & Hebert, 2016). Thus, an effective writing curriculum requires that general and special education teachers are knowledgeable about writing instruction and work together to help students improve their writing skills. In addition, as a general principle, Berninger and May (2011) recommended that writing instruction should focus on all levels of language—subword, word, and text—for example, moving from subword letter writing to word spelling and then from word spelling to text composing. Procedural knowledge should be taught until it becomes automatic, such as ensuring mastery of phoneme-grapheme correspondences for spelling.

In selecting treatments for individuals with writing disabilities, an evaluator first has to consider (1) the area or areas of written language that are affected, (2) the severity of the writing difficulties, and (3) how and where services will be delivered. For example, a student with dysgraphia is likely to benefit from instruction to improve keyboarding skill or the use of voice-recognition software, whereas a student with weaknesses in written expression will need to learn strategies to help with ideation and organization.

The evaluator also needs to consider the types and extent of accommodations and adaptations that the student will require in the classroom and ensure that they will be implemented. A national survey of primary-grade teachers revealed that although general education teachers believed it is important to adjust their writing instruction for struggling writers, they viewed 20 adaptations for struggling writers as being slightly to moderately acceptable (Graham, Harris, Bartlett, Popadopoulou, & Santoro, 2016). Graham et al. (2016) found that the most common adaptations teachers provided were extra encouragement and extra time, whereas the least common and acceptable were instruction using technology and composing via dictation. In addition, more-experienced teachers tended to make more adaptations.

Rapid Reference 4.4 includes seven recommendations provided by Cutler and Graham (2008) to improve primary grade writing instruction, followed by recommendations by Graham and Perin (2007) for improving writing instruction in middle and high schools. A recent meta-analysis of interventions for teaching writing concluded that an effective writing curriculum should include goal setting, strategy instruction, text structure instruction, feedback, and peer interactions (Koster, Tribushinina, De Jong, & van den Bergh, 2015).

Several types of evidence-based programs have also been shown to result in beneficial outcomes for struggling writers. After an intervention or interventions have been selected, the duration and intensity of the services must be determined as well as the specific ways to monitor and document an individual's progress. Rapid Reference 4.5 provides a summary from a recent meta-analysis of writing interventions for elementary-level students (Graham, Kiuhara, McKeown, & Harris, 2012).

Handwriting

In some school districts, handwriting instruction begins with manuscript writing and progresses to cursive writing, at the end of the second or beginning of the third

≡ *Rapid Reference 4.4*

Recommendations for Improving Writing Instruction

Recommendations for Writing Instruction in the Elementary Grades

- Increase the amount of time students spend writing.
- Have students spend more time writing expository text.
- Teach skills and writing strategies (e.g., teaching text structures explicitly).
- Foster students' interest in and motivation for writing.
- Encourage connections for writing between home and school.
- Make computers a central part of the writing program.
- Provide professional development for teachers.

Source: Cutler and Graham (2008).

Recommendations for Writing Instruction Middle and High School

- Teach students strategies for planning, revising, and editing their compositions (e.g., self-regulated strategy development [SRSD] see Rapid Reference 4.10 further on in this chapter).
- Teach students how to summarize texts.
- Have adolescents work together to plan, draft, revise, and edit their compositions.
- Encourage students to set specific, reachable goals for the writing that they are to complete.
- Use computers and word processors as instructional supports for writing assignments.
- Use sentence-combining activities to help students construct more complex sentence structures.
- Engage students in prewriting to help them generate or organize their ideas.
- Engage students in analyzing concrete information and data to help them develop ideas and content for a particular writing task.
- Use a process writing approach that combines a number of writing instructional activities, which stress extended writing opportunities and writing for authentic audiences and provide individualized instruction.
- Provide students with models of good writing to read and analyze.
- Use writing as a tool for learning content material.

Source: Graham and Perin (2007).

grade. In other school districts, instruction in cursive writing has been abandoned. Opinions vary on whether this is a good or bad idea. A general consensus also does not exist regarding whether students with handwriting difficulties should be taught manuscript or cursive writing first; some students find printing to be easier, whereas others find cursive to be easier. Methods that teach manu-cursive, such as

≡ *Rapid Reference 4.5*

Explicit Teaching of Writing Processes, Skills, or Knowledge
- Strategy instruction
- Adding self-regulation to strategy instruction
- Text structure instruction
- Creative or imagery instruction
- Teaching transcription skills

Scaffolding or Supporting Students' Writing
- Prewriting activities
- Peer assistance when writing
- Product goals
- Assessing writing

Additional Interventions
- Word processing
- Extra writing
- Comprehensive writing programs

Source: Graham, Kiuhara, et al. (2012).

D'Nealian (Thurber, 1983), a continuous-stroke method that is a mixture of the two styles, are probably the most effective, because a student has to master only one writing style. Instructional programs for handwriting have several common elements, which are summarized in Rapid Reference 4.6.

≡ *Rapid Reference 4.6*

Common Elements for Handwriting Instructional Programs

- Opportunities to practice handwriting: With older students, teachers can provide functional opportunities for writing (e.g., filling out job applications, bank forms, etc.).
- Teachers can model correct letter formation with direct instruction of how to form the letters.
- Teachers can provide opportunities to practice letter formation by tracing over models (e.g., dotted letters), with gradual fading of the models.
- For younger students, teachers can provide primary paper with a middle line to foster the correct size of letters. As skill develops, provide students with standard paper.

The following four principles are effective for teaching students letter formation: (1) forming letters with verbal cues and tracing until the letters and the patterns become automatic; (2) copying letters and then practicing writing letters in isolation and then within words; (3) encouraging them to evaluate their own handwriting; and (4) helping them until they acquire a clear, legible writing style (Mather, Wendling, & Roberts, 2009). Berninger (2009) describes the results from a prior large-scale study where the most effective method for teaching letter formation was the use of number arrow cues combined with writing letters from memory.

Word processors can help students bypass handwriting difficulties, enabling them to produce neat, clean copies of their written work. Because of their severe difficulties with handwriting, some students should begin word processing instruction as early as second or third grade. To become efficient at word processing, students require instruction in keyboarding skills and how to operate the various functions of a word processing program.

Basic Writing Skills

Because of the pervasiveness of spelling problems among students with SLD, quality spelling instruction is essential. Traditional approaches to spelling, such as having students study for and take weekly spelling tests, or more holistic approaches, such as assuming children will learn to spell by writing, are ineffective for students who struggle. Students with SLD require explicit instruction that provides multiple opportunities for practice and immediate corrective feedback (Williams et al., 2017).

Although orthographic knowledge and knowledge of linguistic principles increase developmentally, many students with SLD develop more slowly in spelling skill than their peers. Thus, spelling is the major area of focus for instruction in basic writing skills. In addition, some students also require direct teaching of syntax and punctuation and capitalization rules. To determine appropriate spelling interventions, first it is necessary to assess and determine a student's level of underlying lexical or orthographic knowledge (Baumann & Kame'enui, 2004). Rapid Reference 4.7 describes the general research-based principles that will result in the most-effective spelling instruction.

Words with irregular elements are particularly difficult for students with dyslexia. Although practitioners often divide words into the categories of regular and irregular, this is an oversimplifi-cation of linguistic reality (Moats, 2010). Some words have only one irregular element such as the *ai* in the word *said*. Others seem truly

DON'T FORGET
....
An irregular word may just have one irregular element.

≡ Rapid Reference 4.7

Research-Based Principles for Effective Spelling Instruction

- Present spelling words in lists, rather than in sentences.
- Encourage students to pronounce the sounds in the words slowly as they attempt to spell the words.
- Provide students with frequent and systematic review of the words they are learning.
- Determine words that are appropriate for the students by analyzing their present level of skill development.
- Do not ask students to write words several times as a study technique. Instead, have them write a word from memory without looking at the word.
- Pay special attention to the teaching of irregular words, those that do not conform to English spelling patterns (e.g., *once*). Some students will benefit from tracing, saying the letter names, and then writing these types of words from memory.

unpredictable (e.g., *colonel).* Moats explained that the spellings of most English words can be explained on the basis of sound patterns, spelling conventions, word sense, and word history. So even a word such as *colonel* makes some sense when we learn that it comes from the Old Italian word *colonello,* which means "the commander of a column of troops."

Written Expression

Teaching writing as a process is an effective way to improve an individual's written expression (Graham, Kiuhara, et al., 2012). As part of the writing process, explicit strategies are taught that focus on planning, problem-solving, and self-monitoring, and these strategies help improve composition ability (Fletcher et al., 2007). It is difficult, however, for students to use strategies if they are not fluent in the lower-level skills of handwriting and spelling (Graham & Perin, 2007) or they do not understand when and how to use the strategy. Rapid Reference 4.8 lists the recommendations to improve written expression from the Institute for Education Sciences' practice guide *Teaching Elementary School Students to be Effective Writers* (Graham, Bollinger, et al., 2012).

Provide Daily Time to Write

The National Commission on Writing in America's Schools and Colleges (2003) found that providing students with adequate time to write was an essential

═ *Rapid Reference 4.8*

**Recommendations from Teaching Elementary
School Students to Be Effective Writers**

1. Provide daily time for students to write.
2. Teach students to use the writing process for a variety of purposes.
   a. Teach students the writing process.
   b. Teach students how to write for different purposes.
3. Teach students to become fluent with handwriting, spelling, sentence construction, and word processing.
4. Create an engaged community of writers.

component of an effective writing instruction program. However, surveys of elementary teachers indicate that little time is devoted to writing (Cutler & Graham, 2008). Dedicated instruction time is needed so students can learn the skills and strategies necessary to be effective writers and then time is needed so students can practice what they are learning. Graham, Kiuhara, et al. (2012) recommend 1 hour a day be devoted to writing beginning in first grade: 30 minutes of instruction followed by 30 minutes to practice writing. Integrating writing into content areas maximizes instructional time and provides additional practice time.

Teach Writing as a Process
Writing is a process used to communicate thoughts and ideas. It requires self-direction and the integration of cognitive and linguistic abilities to achieve the writer's purpose. The components of the writing process include planning, drafting, sharing, revising, editing, evaluating, and, in some cases, publishing. Rapid Reference 4.9 lists the components of the writing process and provides example strategies for each step. Students need to learn that writing is a flexible and recursive process that requires moving back and forth through the various components of the writing process. Using word processing technology can make the writing process easier for students.

One well-researched example of an approach to writing instruction is self-regulated strategy development (SRSD). This approach to teaching strategies has been tested in more than 40 instructional writing studies with elementary and secondary students (Graham & Harris, 2009; Graham, Harris, & McKeown, 2013; Graham, Kiuhara, et al., 2012; Koster et al., 2015). Numerous applications of SRSD have been created to help students enrich their writing vocabularies, improve their

≡ Rapid Reference 4.9

Components of the Writing Process and Example Strategies

Planning. Brainstorm ideas, outline and prioritize main points.
POW: Pick ideas, Organize notes, Write (Harris, Graham, Mason, & Friedlander, 2008)

Drafting. Imitate an author's writing (e.g., form).
Generate sentences orally or in writing.

Sharing. Peer sharing: Read to peer who provides feedback.
Author's chair: Read to class to see if questions arise.

Revising. Peer revising: Insert a question mark if something is not understood; insert a carat if more information would be helpful.

Editing. COPS: Capitalization, Overall appearance, Punctuation, Spelling (Schumaker et al., 1981)

Evaluating. Self-monitor: Ask a series of questions about the writing.

CAUTION

When students with SLD are taught strategies in general education settings, they may not receive explicit, intensive instruction that provides ample opportunities for practice and review (Schumaker & Deshler, 2009). They often do not receive individualized feedback on their practice attempts, and because mastery is not required, they do not acquire the writing strategies. Thus, specific instructional conditions must be in place if students with SLD are to improve their writing abilities.

abilities to produce narrative and expository written text, and enhance their understandings of the higher-level cognitive processes required for composition. Using SRSD, students are taught different strategies and techniques to guide them through the writing process and help them monitor their writing behavior. Rapid Reference 4.10 presents the stages of SRSD instruction as developed by these authors. An online module for learning and implementing SRSD is available from the Iris Center: SRSD: Using Learning Strategies to Enhance Student Learning (iris. peabody.vanderbilt.edu).

Teach Writing for Different Purposes

Learning to write well for different purposes is important for success in school, work, and life. Helping students learn to recognize and use common organizational patterns or genres can help them succeed when writing for a specific purpose such as writing to inform, narrate, persuade, or describe. Direct instruction in the

≡ *Rapid Reference 4.10*

Stages of SRSD Instruction

Stage 1: Develop and activate background knowledge. At this beginning stage, the teacher models and explains any pre-skills that the students need to learn to understand the strategy. Sample compositions are read and discussed.

Stage 2: Discuss it. Students and teachers discuss the goals and benefits of strategy use.

Stage 3: Model it. The teacher models how the strategy is used, sets goals for what he or she plans to achieve, and then assesses whether the goals were met.

Stage 4: Memorize it. Students engage in activities to help them memorize the strategy steps.

Stage 5: Support it. The teacher provides scaffolds, prompts, and guidance as students apply the strategies to their writings.

Stage 6: Independent performance. At this final stage, students are able to use the strategy correctly on their own.

different types of text structures—narrative (e.g., story grammar) and expository or informational (e.g., compare-contrast, cause-effect, or sequential paragraphs and essays)—helps students learn to plan and organize their writing. Through direct, explicit instruction, teachers model the different text structures and then provide guided practice so students learn how to use each text structure. Gradually, responsibility for writing shifts from the teacher to the student.

DON'T FORGET

Students with writing disabilities require instruction that is individualized, sequential, explicit, and systematic.

One example of a research-based approach for teaching text structure is cognitive strategy instruction in writing (CSIW) developed by Englert (2009). The CSIW curriculum incorporates think sheets and graphic organizers to help students understand and self-evaluate their compositions.

Teach Basic Writing Skills

In order to focus on the higher-level task of written expression, individuals must develop fluency with underlying basic skills. As lower-level transcription skills become more automatic, writers can allocate their attention to higher-level writing abilities (Jung et al., 2017). When an individual is fluent with handwriting or word processing, spelling, and sentence construction, he or she can devote cognitive resources to developing and communicating ideas. Instructional focus varies depending on the developmental level of the individual. For example, young writers need to learn how to hold a pencil correctly and practice accurate and fluent letter formation. During early elementary years, first- and second-grade students can begin learning word processing skills with a program such as Read, Write, and Type (www.talkingfingers.com). Students can master the spellings of commonly used words at each grade level and expand their understanding of orthography and morphology.

Create an Engaged Community of Writers

Not only is it necessary to teach the writing process and basic writing skills but also it is important to develop an environment that is supportive and motivating. One way to enhance a sense of community is through collaboration. Working together with teachers or peers engages the student in the writing process and provides a safe place to write. When participating in writing, teachers can model good writing and demonstrate the importance of writing. To further motivate writers, teachers should provide opportunities for students to choose their own topics. Students who are engaged and motivated tend to write more frequently.

CONCLUSION

Writing is one of the most complex human functions; it is a critical communication skill for academic and occupational success as well as social and behavioral well-being (Graham & Harris, 2014; Katusic et al., 2009). However, many developing writers do not develop proficiency with this essential skill. Less than one-third of fourth-graders and one-fourth of eighth- and 12th-graders were proficient on the most recent NAEP writing test. Writing, referred to as the "neglected R" (National Commission on Writing in America's Schools and Colleges, 2003), has not received the same level of attention as has reading from educators and researchers alike.

The causes of writing disabilities are not well-documented and clouded by high comorbidity with other learning or behavioral difficulties. Perhaps this helps explain why writing disabilities are underdiagnosed and, in many cases, addressed long after the onset of a student's difficulties. There is also a need for high-quality research on effective writing interventions (Graham & Harris, 2014). If the goal is to develop skilled writers, then effective teaching practices must be identified and employed. We hope future research will lead to a better understanding of writing disabilities, as well as increased understanding of the most effective instructional practices. Our students are thankful for the help and guidance they receive. As shown in Figure 4.8, Peter thanked his sixth-grade teacher: "Miss O. I am sorry I

Miss O I am
sara I cald you a
old gottoday You have
relly helpf me with my
writting this year.
Your frend
Peter

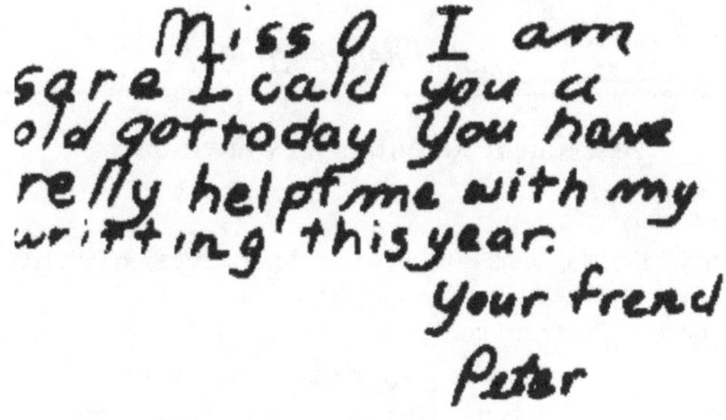

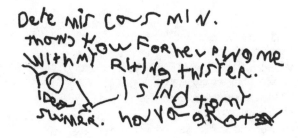

Figure 4.8. Peter's Note to His Teacher

Figure 4.9. Dan's Note to His Teacher

Translation: Dear Ms. Caseman, thank you for helping me with my writing this year. You listened to my ideas. Have a great summer. Dan

called you an old goat today. You have really helped me with my writing this year. Your friend, Peter."

Similar sentiments were expressed by Dan, the fifth-grade student we discussed, who has severe dysgraphia (see Figure 4.9).

RESOURCES

Practitioners need to be aware of the assessment tools as well as the instructional materials for written language. Rapid Reference 4.11 lists several assessment tools

≡ *Rapid Reference 4.11*

Assessment Resources for Practitioners

Motor and Handwriting

Beery-Buktenica Developmental Test of Visual-Motor Integration (6th ed.): www.pearsonclinical.com

Bruininks-Oseretsky Test of Motor Proficiency (2nd ed.): www.pearsonclinical.com

Peabody Developmental Motor Scales (2nd ed.): www.proedinc.com

Process Assessment of the Learner (2nd ed.) (PAL-II) Diagnostics for Reading and Writing: www.pearsonclinical.com

Informal checklists for observing and analyzing handwriting

Spelling

Subtests from Kaufman Test of Educational Achievement, (3rd ed.) (KTEA-3) and Wechsler Individual Achievement Test (3rd ed.) (WIAT-III): www.pearsonclinical.com

Tests from Woodcock-Johnson IV Tests of Achievement (WJ IV ACH): www.hmhco.com/hmh-assessments

Subtest from Wide Range Achievement Test (4th ed.) (WRAT-4): www.wpspublishing.com

Word Identification and Spelling Test (WIST): www.proedinc.com

Test of Written Spelling (5th ed.) (TWS-5): www.proedinc.com

Test of Orthographic Competence (TOC): www.proedinc.com

Informal spelling inventories

Curriculum-based measures

Composition

Oral and Written Language Scales, Second Edition (OWLS-II) Written Expression Scale: www.pearsonclinical.com

Test of Written Expression (TOWE): www.proedinc.com

Test of Written Language (4th ed.) (TOWL-4): www.proedinc.com

Writing Process Test (WPT): www.proedinc.com

Writing rubrics

Curriculum-based measures

Subtests from the Kaufman Test of Educational Achievement (3rd ed.) (KTEA-3)

Subtests from the Wechsler Individual Achievement Test (3rd ed.) (WIAT-III): www.pearsonclinical.com

Tests from the Woodcock-Johnson IV Tests of Achievement (WJ IV ACH): www.hmhco.com/hmh-assessments

Cognitive-Intellectual Abilities

Differential Ability Scales (2nd ed.) (DAS-II): www.pearsonclinical.com

Kaufman Assessment Battery for Children (2nd ed.) (KABC-II): www.pearsonclinical.com

Stanford Binet Intelligence Scales (5th ed.) (SB5): www.proedinc.com

Wechsler Intelligence Scale for Children (5th ed.) (WISC-V): www.pearsonclinical.com

Woodcock-Johnson IV Tests of Cognitive Abilities (WJ IV COG):
www.hmhco.com/hmh-assessments

for evaluating aspects of writing. Rapid Reference 4.12 lists examples of instructional materials for writing and is organized into handwriting, spelling, and composition categories followed by assistive technology and professional books. Rapid Reference 4.13 lists examples of useful writing apps (Cheesman, Winters, & McGuire, 2016).

≡ *Rapid Reference 4.12*

Instructional Resources for Practitioners

Handwriting or Keyboarding

Fonts4Teacher: www.fonts4teachers.com

Handwriting without Tears: www.hwtears.com

Read, Write, and Type: www.talkingfingers.com

Start Write: Handwriting Software: www.startwrite.com

The Handwriting Worksheet Wizard: www.startwrite.com

Writing aids (e.g., pencil grips, raised line paper): www.thepencilgrip.com or
www.therapro.com

Spelling

Franklin Spelling Tools: www.amazon.com

Patterns for Success in Reading and Spelling: www.proedinc.com

Phonics and Spelling Through Phoneme-Grapheme Mapping: www.voyagersopris.com

Scholastic Success With Spelling: www.scholastic.com

Sitton Spelling Sourcebook Series: www.sittonspelling.com

Spellography: www.voyagersopris.com

Word Journeys: Assessment-Guided Phonics, Spelling, and Vocabulary Instruction:
www.guilford.com

Words Their Way: Word Study for Phonics, Vocabulary, and Spelling Instruction
(6th ed.): www.pearsonhighered.com

Wordy Qwerty: www.talkingfingers.com

Composition
Draft Builder® www.donjohnston.com/draftbuilder
Excellence in Writing: www.writing-edu.com
Inspiration: www.inspiration.com/inspiration
Kidspiration: www.inspiration.com/kidspiration
Write: Outloud: www.donjohnston.com/writeoutloud

Assistive Technology
Co-Writer Solo: www.donjohnston.com/cowriter
Dragon Naturally Speaking: www.nuance.com/Dragon
Neo or Neo2 Portable Word Processors
WordQ and SpeakQ: www.goqsoftware.com

Examples of Recent Professional Books
Best Practices in Writing Instruction (2nd ed.) (Graham, MacArthur, & Fitzgerald, Eds., 2013)
Handbook of Writing Research (2nd ed.) (MacArthur, Graham, & Fitzgerald, Eds., 2015)
Helping Students with Dyslexia and Dysgraphia Make Connections: Differentiated Instruction Lesson Plans in Reading and Writing (Berninger & Wolf, 2009a).
Teaching Basic Writing Skills: Strategies for Effective Expository Writing Instruction (Hochman, 2009)
Teaching Elementary School Students to Be Effective Writers (Graham, Bollinger, et al., 2012)
Teaching Students with Dyslexia and Dysgraphia: Lessons from Teaching and Science (Berninger & Wolf, 2009b)
Writing Assessment and Instruction for Students with Learning Disabilities (Mather et al., 2009)
Writing Better: Effective Strategies for Teaching Students with Learning Difficulties (Graham & Harris, 2014)

≡ *Rapid Reference 4.13*

Examples of Useful Apps

Spelling and Grammar Correction Programs and Apps
- *Ginger Software.* This program-app corrects spelling and grammar. www.gingersoftware.com

- *Spell Check Plus.* This website corrects spelling and grammar while working on an Internet-connected computer. http://spellcheckplus.com
- *Franklin Spelling Correctors.* This collection of portable electronic spelling correctors corrects handwritten spelling. www.franklin.com

Examples of Speech-to-Text and Word Prediction Programs and Apps

- *Dragon Naturally Speaking.* This is a speech-to-text program-app. MacSpeech Scribe is the Apple version marketed by the same company. www.nuance.com/dragon
- *Co-Writer 7.* This is a word prediction program-app. www.donjohnston.com/cowrite
- *WordQ.* This is a word-prediction program-app. www.goqsoftware.com/product-details/wordq
- *Write: OutLoud.* This program-app gives auditory feedback while typing. www.donjohnston.com/writeoutloud

Examples of Graphic Organizer Programs and Apps

- *Inspiration* (Grade 6–adult) and *Kidspiration* (kindergarten–Grade 6) are graphic-organizer programs-apps. With a single click or tap, the diagram converts to an outline form. Levels within the outline or diagram can be repositioned using drag-and-drop. Once the outline is complete, the document can be exported to Microsoft Word, PowerPoint, or PDF versions. www.inspiration.com.
- *DraftBuilder 6.* This software-app breaks down the writing process into three manageable steps: (1) brainstorming, (2) note-taking, and (3) writing the first draft. This structure assists students to generate ideas and organize them to form a well-organized paper. www.donjohnston.com/draftbuilder
- *Cmap Tools.* This is a free graphic-organizer website, which also provides research and information on concept maps and graphic organizers. http://cmap.ihmc.us

Source: Cheesman et al. (2016).

🐿 TEST YOURSELF 🐿

1. **IDEA 2004 indicates that a student can be identified as having an SLD in either basic writing skills or written expression. True or false?**
2. **An individual with an SLD in written expression always has limited oral language. True or false?**
3. **Why is it important to consider the individual's handwriting skills?**
   (a) Handwriting is predictive of the quality of written expression.
   (b) Handwriting automaticity is an important predictor of composition fluency.
   (c) Poor handwriting can interfere with spelling and composition.
   (d) All of the above are true.
   (e) None of the above is true.

4. **The most important phonological skill for spelling is:**
   (a) Blending
   (b) Segmenting
   (c) Deleting
   (d) Substituting

5. **If a fifth-grade student spells the word *they* as *thay* it suggests a weakness in:**
   (a) Phonological awareness
   (b) Morphological awareness
   (c) Orthographic awareness
   (d) Semantic awareness

6. **Spelling is developmental in nature. True or false?**

7. **Writing disabilities have high comorbidity with other learning or behavioral difficulties. True or false?**

8. **Dysgraphia is a disorder that always affects just handwriting. True or false?**

9. **When evaluating an individual for a specific learning disability in written expression, consider:**
   (a) Performance on handwriting tasks
   (b) Performance on spelling tasks
   (c) Performance on oral language tasks
   (d) All of the above
   (e) B and c

10. **Effective instruction for written expression should teach:**
    (a) Writing as a process
    (b) Strategies
    (c) Text structures
    (d) All of the above

Answers: 1. False; 2. False; 3. d; 4. b; 5. c; 6. True; 7. True; 8. False; 9. d; 10. d.

REFERENCES

American Psychiatric Association. (2013). *Diagnostic and statistical manual of mental disorders* (5th ed.). Washington, DC: Author.

Andrade, C., Bhakta, S. G., & Fernandes, P. P. (2010). Familial vulnerability to an unusual cognitive adverse effect of topiramate: Discussion of mechanisms. *Indian Journal of Psychiatry, 52,* 260–263.

Applebee, A. N., & Langer, J. A. (2011). A snapshot of writing instruction in middle and high school. *English Journal, 100*(6), 14–27.

Bailet, L. L. (1991). Beginning spelling. In A. M. Bain, L. L. Bailet, & L. C. Moats (Eds.), *Written language disorders: Theory into practice* (pp. 1–21). Austin, TX: PRO-ED.

Baker, S., & Hubbard, D. (1995). Best practices in the assessment of written expression. In A. Thomas & J. Grimes (Eds.), *Best practices in school psychology* (3rd ed., pp. 717–730). Bethesda, MD: National Association of School Psychologists.

Baumann, J. F., & Kame'enui, E. J. (2004). *Vocabulary instruction: Research to practice*. New York, NY: Guilford.

Bear, D. R., Invernizzi, M., Templeton, S., & Johnston, F. (2016). *Words their way: Word study for phonics, vocabulary, and spelling instruction* (6th ed.). Upper Saddle River, NJ: Pearson.

Berninger, V. W. (1996). *Reading and writing acquisition: A developmental neuropsychological perspective*. Boulder, CO: Westview Press.

Berninger, V. W. (2004). Understanding the graphia in dysgraphia. In D. Dewey & D. Tupper (Eds.), *Developmental motor disorders: A neuropsychological perspective* (pp. 328–350). New York, NY: Guilford.

Berninger, V. W. (2009). Highlights of programmatic, interdisciplinary research on writing. *Learning Disabilities Research & Practice, 24*, 69–80.

Berninger, V. W., & May M. O. (2011). Evidence-based diagnosis and treatment for specific learning disabilities involving impairments in written and/or oral language. *Journal of Learning Disabilities, 44*, 167–183.

Berninger, V. W., & Richards, T. (2002). *Brain literacy for educators and psychologists*. San Diego, CA: Academic Press.

Berninger, V. W., & Wolf, B. J. (2009a). *Helping students with dyslexia and dysgraphia make connections: Differentiated instruction lesson plans in reading and writing*. Baltimore, MD: Brookes.

Berninger, V. W., & Wolf, B. J. (2009b). *Teaching students with dyslexia and dysgraphia: Lessons from teaching and science*. Baltimore, MD: Brookes.

Bernstein, B. E. (2008). *Learning disorder: Written expression*. Retrieved from http://emedicine.medscape.com/article/918389-overview

Bernstein, B. E. (2013). *Written expression learning disorder*. Retrieved from http://emedicine.medscape.com/article/1835883

Blachman, B. A. (1994). Early literacy acquisition: The role of phonological awareness. In G. P. Wallach & K. G. Butler (Eds.), *Language learning disabilities in school-age children and adolescents* (pp. 253–274). New York, NY: Merrill.

Brindle, M., Graham, S., Harris, K. R., & Hebert, M. (2016). Third and fourth grade teacher's practices in teaching writing: A national study. *Reading and Writing, 29*, 929–954.

Bruck, M. (1993). Component spelling skills of college students with childhood diagnoses of dyslexia. *Learning Disability Quarterly, 16*, 171–184.

Cheesman, E. A., Winters, D. C., & McGuire, P. M. (2016). In N. Mather & L. Jaffe (Eds.), *Woodcock-Johnson IV: Recommendations, reports, and strategies* (pp. 392–408). Hoboken, NJ: Wiley.

Connelly, V., Campbell, S., MacLean, M., & Barnes, J. (2006). Contribution of lower-order skills to the written composition of college students with and without dyslexia. *Developmental Neuropsychology, 29*, 175–196.

Costa, L. C., Edwards, C. N., & Hooper, S. R. (2016). Writing disabilities and reading disabilities in elementary school students: Rates of co-occurrence and cognitive burden. *Learning Disability Quarterly, 39*, 17–30.

Cutler, L., & Graham, S. (2008). Primary grade writing instruction: A national survey. *Journal of Educational Psychology, 100*, 907–919.

Dehn, M. J. (2008). *Working memory and academic learning: Assessment and intervention.* Hoboken, NJ: Wiley.

Dehn, M. J. (2015). *Essentials of working memory assessment and intervention.* Hoboken, NJ: Wiley.

Deno, S. L., Fuchs, L. S., Marston, D., & Shin, J. (2001). Using curriculum-based measurement to establish growth standards for students with learning disabilities. *School Psychology Review, 30*, 507–524.

Deuel, R. K. (1992). Motor skill disorder. In S. R. Hooper, G. W. Hynd, & R. E. Mattison (Eds.), *Developmental disorders: Diagnostic criteria and clinical assessment* (pp. 239–282). Hillsdale, NJ: Erlbaum.

Deuel, R. K. (1994). Developmental dysgraphia and motor skill disorders. *Journal of Child Neurology, 10*, 6–8.

Ehri, L. C. (2000). Learning to read and learning to spell: Two sides of a coin. *Topics in Language Disorders, 20*(3), 19–36.

Ehri, L. C. (2006). Alphabetics instruction helps students learn to read. In R. M. Joshi & P. G. Aaron (Eds.), *Handbook of orthography and literacy* (pp. 649–677). Mahwah, NJ: Erlbaum.

Englert, C. S. (2009). Connecting the dots in a research program to develop, implement, and evaluate strategic literacy interventions for struggling readers and writers. *Learning Disabilities Research & Practice, 24*, 104–120.

Englert, C. S., & Raphael, T. E. (1988). Constructing well-formed prose: Process, structure and metacognitive knowledge. *Exceptional Children, 54*, 18–25.

Englert, C. S., Raphael, T. E., Anderson, L., Anthony, H., & Stevens, D. (1991). Exposition: Reading, writing, and the metacognitive knowledge of learning disabled students. *Learning Disabilities Research, 5*, 5–24.

Flanagan, D., Ortiz, S., & Alfonso, V. (2013). *Essentials of Cross-Battery Assessment* (3rd ed.). Hoboken, NJ: Wiley.

Fletcher, J. M., Lyon, G. R., Fuchs, L. S., & Barnes, M. A. (2007). *Learning disabilities: From identification to intervention.* New York, NY: Guilford.

Floyd, R. G., McGrew, K. S., & Evans, J. J. (2008). The relative contribution of the Cattell-Horn-Carroll cognitive abilities in explaining writing achievement during childhood and adolescence. *Psychology in the Schools, 45*, 132–144.

Gentry, J. R. (1982). An analysis of developmental spelling in GYNS AT WRK. *Reading Teacher, 36*, 192–200.

Goswami, U. (2006). Orthography, phonology, and reading development: A cross-linguistic perspective. In R. M. Joshi & P. G. Aaron (Eds.), *Handbook of orthography and literacy* (pp. 463–480). Mahwah, NJ: Erlbaum.

Graham, S., Berninger, V. W., Abbott, R. D., Abbott, S. P., & Whitaker, D. (1997). Role of mechanics in composing of elementary school students: A new methodological approach. *Journal of Educational Psychology, 89*, 170–182.

Graham, S., Bollinger, A., Booth Olson, C., D'Aoust, C., MacArthur, C., McCutchen, D., & Olinghouse, N. (2012). *Teaching elementary school students to be effective writers: A practice guide* (NCEE 20124058). Washington, DC: National Center for Education Evaluation and Regional Assistance, Institute of Education Sciences, US Department of Education. Retrieved from http://ies.ed.gov/ncee/wwc/publications_reviews.aspx#pubsearch

Graham, S., & Harris, K. R. (2009). Almost 30 years of writing research: Making sense of it all with the *Wrath of Khan*. *Learning Disabilities Research & Practice, 24,* 58–68.

Graham, S., & Harris, K. R. (2014). *Writing better: Effective strategies for teaching students with learning difficulties.* Baltimore, MD: Brookes.

Graham, S., Harris, K. R., Bartlett, B. J., Popadopoulou, E., & Santoro, J. (2016). Acceptability of adaptations for struggling writers: A national survey with primary-grade teachers. *Learning Disability Quarterly, 39,* 5–16.

Graham, S., Harris, K. R., & McKeown, D. (2013). The writing of students with learning disabilities, meta-analysis of SRSD writing intervention studies, and future directions: Redux. In H. L. Swanson, K. R. Harris, & S. Graham (Eds.), *Handbook of learning disabilities* (2nd ed., pp. 405–438). New York, NY: Guilford.

Graham, S., Hebert, M., Sandbank, M. P., & Harris, K. R. (2016). Assessing the writing achievement of young struggling writers: Application of generalizability theory. *Learning Disability Quarterly, 39,* 72–82.

Graham, S., Kiuhara, S., McKeown, D., & Harris, K. R. (2012). A meta-analysis of writing instruction for students in the elementary grades. *Journal of Educational Psychology, 104,* 879–896.

Graham, S., MacArthur, C. A., & Fitzgerald, J. (Eds.). (2013). Best practices in writing instruction (2nd ed.). New York, NY: Guilford.

Graham, S., & Perin, D. (2007). *Writing next: Effective strategies to improve writing of adolescents in middle and high schools.* A report to the Carnegie Corporation of New York. Washington, DC: Alliance for Excellent Education.

Gregg, N. (1995). *Written expression disorders.* Dordrecht, The Netherlands: Kluwer.

Gregg, N. (2009). *Adolescents and adults with learning disabilities and ADHD: Assessment and accommodation.* New York, NY: Guilford.

Gregg, N., & Mather, N. (2002). School is fun at recess: Informal analyses of written language for students with learning disabilities. *Journal of Learning Disabilities, 35,* 7–22.

Hale, J. B., & Fiorello, C. A. (2004). *School neuropsychology: A practitioner's handbook.* New York, NY: Guilford.

Hamstra-Bletz, L., & Blote, A. W. (1993). A longitudinal study on dysgraphic handwriting in primary school. *Journal of Learning Disabilities, 26,* 689–699.

Harris, K. R., Graham, S., Mason, L.H., & Friedlander, B. (2008). *Powerful writing strategies for all students.* Baltimore, MD: Brookes.

Henderson, E. H. (1990). *Teaching spelling* (2nd ed.). Boston, MA: Houghton Mifflin.

Hochman, J. C. (2009). *Teaching basic writing skills: Strategies for effective expository writing instruction.* Longmont, CO: Sopris West.

Hooper, S. R., Montgomery, J., Swartz, C., Reed, M. S., Sandler, A. D., Levine, M. D., ... & Wasileski, T. (1994). Measurement of written language expression.

In G. R. Lyon (Ed.), *Frames of reference for the assessment of learning disabilities: New views on measurement issues* (pp. 375–417). Baltimore, MD: Brookes.

Jones, D. (2004, December). Automaticity of the transcription process in the production of written text (Doctorate thesis). Graduate School of Education, University of Queensland, Australia.

Joshi, R. M., Hoien, T., Feng, X., Chengappa, R., & Boulware-Gooden, R. (2006). Learning to spell by ear and by eye: A cross-linguistic comparison. In R. M. Joshi & P. G. Aaron (Eds.), *Handbook of orthography and literacy* (pp. 569–577). Mahwah, NJ: Erlbaum.

Jung, P., McMaster, K. L., & delMas, R. C. (2017). Effects of early writing intervention delivered within a data-based instruction framework. *Exceptional Children, 83*, 281–297.

Katusic, S. K., Colligan, R. C., Weaver, A. L., & Barbaresi, W. J. (2009). The forgotten learning disability: Epidemiology of written-language disorder in a population-based birth cohort (1976–1982), Rochester, MN. *Pediatrics, 123*, 1306–1313.

Kaufman, A. S., & Kaufman, N. L. (2014). *Kaufman Test of Educational Achievement* (3rd ed.). New York, NY: Pearson.

Kemp, N., Parrila, R. K., & Kirby, J. R. (2009). Phonological and orthographic spelling in high-functioning adult dyslexics. *Dyslexia: The Journal of the British Dyslexia Association, 15*, 105–128.

Koster, M. P., Tribushinina, E., De Jong, P., & van den Bergh, H. H. (2015). Teaching children to write: A meta-analysis of writing instruction research. *Journal of Writing Research, 7*, 299–324.

Kronenberger, W. G., & Dunn, D. W. (2003). Learning disorders. *Neurologic Clinics, 21*, 941–952.

Levine, M. (1987). *Developmental variations and learning disorders.* Cambridge, MA: Educators Publishing Service.

MacArthur, C., & Graham, S. (1993). Integrating strategy instruction and word processing into a process approach to writing instruction. *School Psychology Review, 22*, 671–682.

MacArthur, C., Graham, S., & Fitzgerald, J. (Eds.). (2015). *Handbook of writing research* (2nd ed.). New York, NY: Guilford.

Mather, N., Roberts, R., Hammill, D., & Allen, E. (2008). *Test of Orthographic Competence.* Austin, TX: PRO-ED.

Mather, N., Wendling, B. J., & Roberts, R. (2009). *Writing assessment and instruction for students with learning disabilities.* San Francisco, CA: Jossey-Bass.

Mayes, S. D., & Calhoun, S. L. (2006). WISC-IV and WISC-III profiles in children with ADHD. *Journal of Attention Disorders, 9*, 486–493.

Mayes, S. D., & Calhoun, S. L. (2007). Challenging the assumptions about the frequency and coexistence of learning disability types. *School Psychology International, 28*, 437–448.

McCloskey, G., Perkins, L. A., & Van Divner, B. (2009). *Assessment and intervention of executive function difficulties.* New York, NY: Routledge.

Miceli, G., & Capasso, R. (2006). Spelling and dysgraphia. *Cognitive Neuropsychology, 23*, 110–134.

Moats, L. C. (1995). *Spelling: Development, disability, and instruction.* Timonium, MD: York Press.

Moats, L. C. (2010). *Speech to print: Language essentials for teachers* (2nd ed.). Baltimore, MD: Brookes.

National Center for Education Statistics (NCES). (2012). *The nation's report card: Writing 2011* (NCES 2012-470). Washington, DC: Institute of Education Sciences, US Department of Education.

National Center for Education Statistics (NCES). (2013). *Digest of education statistics: 2013.* US Department of Education. Retrieved from http://nces.ed.gov/programs/digest

National Commission on Writing in America's Schools and Colleges. (2003). *Neglected R: The need for a writing revolution.* Princeton, NJ: College Entrance Examination Board.

National Institute for Neurological Disorders and Stroke (NINDS). (2009). Dysgraphia information page. Retrieved from www.ninds.nih.gov/disorders/dysgraphia/dysgraphia .htm

Persky, H. R., Daane, M. C., & Jin, Y. (2003). *The nation's report card: Writing 2002.* (NCES 2003-529). US Department of Education. Institute of Education Sciences. National Center for Education Statistics. Washington, DC: Government Printing Office.

Puranik, C. S., & Lonigan, C. J. (2012). Early writing deficits in preschoolers with oral language difficulties. *Journal of Learning Disabilities, 45,* 179–190.

Raskind, W. H. (2001). Current understanding of the genetic basis of reading and spelling disability. *Learning Disability Quarterly, 24,* 144–157.

Rosenblum, S., Weiss, P. L., & Parush, S. (2004). Handwriting evaluation for developmental dysgraphia: Process versus product. *Reading and Writing, 17,* 433–458.

Salahu-Din, D., Persky, H., & Miller, J. (2008). *The nation's report card: Writing 2007* (NCES 2008-468). National Center for Education Statistics, Institute of Education Sciences, US Department of Education. Retrieved from http://nces.ed.gov/nationsreportcard/pubs/ main2007/2008468.asp

Schrank, F. A., Mather, N., & McGrew, K. S. (2014a). *Woodcock-Johnson IV Tests of achievement.* Itasca, IL: Houghton Mifflin Harcourt.

Schrank, F. A., Mather, N., & McGrew, K. S. (2014b). *Woodcock-Johnson IV Tests of Oral Language.* Itasca, IL: Houghton Mifflin Harcourt.

Schrank, F. A., McGrew, K. S., & Mather, N. (2014). *Woodcock-Johnson IV Tests of Cognitive Abilities.* Itasca, IL: Houghton Mifflin Harcourt.

Schumaker, J. B., & Deshler, D. D. (2009). Adolescents with learning disabilities as writers: Are we selling them short? *Learning Disabilities Research & Practice, 24,* 81–92.

Schumaker, J. B., Deshler, D. D., Nolan, S., Clark, F. L., Alley, G. R., & Warner, M. M. (1981). *Error monitoring: A learning strategy for improving academic performance of LD adolescents* (Research Report No. 32). Lawrence, KS: University of Kansas Institute for Research in Learning Disabilities.

Smith, C. R. (1997, February). *A hierarchy for assessing and remediating phonemic segmentation difficulties.* Paper presented at the Learning Disabilities Association International Conference, Chicago, IL.

Stecker, P. M., Fuchs, L. S., & Fuchs, D. (2005). Using curriculum-based measurement to improve student achievement: Review of research. *Psychology in the Schools, 42,* 795–819.

Swanson, H. L., & Siegel, L. (2001). Learning disabilities as a working memory deficit. *Issues in Education: Contributions from Educational Psychology, 7,* 1–48.

Thurber, D. (1983). Write on! With continuous stroke point. *Academic Therapy, 18*, 389–395.

Weintraub, N., & Graham, S. (1998). Writing legibly and quickly: A study of children's ability to adjust their handwriting to meet common classroom demands. *Learning Disabilities Research & Practice, 13*, 146–152.

Williams, K. J., Walker, M. A., Vaughn, S., & Wanzek, J. (2017). A synthesis of reading and spelling interventions and their effects on spelling outcomes for students with learning disabilities. *Journal of Learning Disabilities, 50*, 286–297.

Wiznitzer, M., & Scheffel, D. L. (2009). Learning disabilities. In R. B. David, J. B. Bodensteiner, D. E. Mandelbaum, & B. Olson (Eds.), *Clinical pediatric neurology* (pp. 479–492). New York, NY: Demos Medical Publishing.

Five

HOW SLD MANIFESTS IN ORAL EXPRESSION AND LISTENING COMPREHENSION

Nickola Wolf Nelson
Elisabeth H. Wiig

INTRODUCTION

Students with specific learning disabilities (SLDs) may have problems with oral expression and listening comprehension as part of their learning disability profile whether or not such difficulties contributed originally to identifying them as having SLD. Relationships between oral and written language difficulties are complex and intertwined. They can occur in multiple patterns and emerge in different sequences and at different ages. Consider the following three situations.

In the first situation, students with oral language difficulties are identified in preschool or early elementary as having specific language impairment (SLI; Leonard, 1998; Rice & Wexler, 2001). These young children may produce language marked by fewer different words and shorter sentences than peers and with more grammatical errors involving pronouns, verb phrases, and complex sentence structures. Adults may conclude that such students' receptive language is better than their expressive language, and, in fact, many may respond appropriately to simple requests but have difficulty expressing their ideas when formulating original discourse. The problem is that such apparent advantages for listening comprehension over oral expression may mask problems of language comprehension (listening or reading comprehension) that may become apparent in later grades when academic language becomes longer and more complex. Problems

Essentials of Specific Learning Disability Identification, Second Edition.
Edited by Vincent C. Alfonso and Dawn P. Flanagan
© 2018 John Wiley & Sons, Inc. Published 2018 by John Wiley & Sons, Inc.

with vocabulary, sentence structure, and discourse organization tend not to be restricted to input or output modalities; rather, they affect all primary modalities—listening and reading comprehension and oral and written expression.

In early childhood, however, the problems with reading comprehension and written expression for such children are not yet apparent, whereas their oral language difficulties are. As preschoolers and in the early elementary grades, students with oral language difficulties may be found eligible for special education under the category of speech/language impaired in the Individuals with Disabilities Education Improvement Act (IDEA 2004). (Note that here, speech/language impaired is abbreviated as S/LI, not SLI; SLI stands for *specific language impaired*, which is not an eligibility category named in IDEA.) While proceeding through the early grades and receiving speech-language intervention, children with S/LI may begin to sound okay when they talk; at this point, their language problems may be more obvious in their struggles to learn to read and write than when listening and speaking. Although not all children with SLI show problems with early reading development, some evidence suggests that they are two times more likely to have phonological awareness and reading problems than their peers (see Catts, Adlof, Hogan, & Weismer, 2005; Ramus, Marshall, Rosen, & van der Lely, 2013). By second or third grade, many may be tested and identified as having SLD instead of or in addition to their identification as having S/LI.

Partial evidence that some children shift from the S/LI category to the SLD category in federal-count data was reported by Mashburn and Myers (2010). They conducted a secondary data analysis for one cohort followed longitudinally from kindergarten to Grade 5. Figure 5.1 shows the pattern that is revealed when the data for these two categories are extracted from the researchers' data table. Although it is not altogether clear that the same children are switching from S/LI to SLD categories, it is striking that, as the proportion of special education students with SLD rises, the proportion of students with S/LI falls. The categorical shift represented in scenario one is consistent with a classification profile described by Silliman and Berninger (2011; see also Berninger & Wolf, 2016) as "oral and written language learning disability" (OWL LD), which includes a "preschool history of oral language struggles or delays" as well as "persisting oral and written language problems in the school-age years" (Silliman & Berninger, 2011, p. 14).

In a second situation, some students proceed through the preschool years with no concerns about their language development, but they are identified as having problems when they struggle to learn reading decoding and spelling in early elementary school. Some of these students also may show weaknesses in spoken expression, listening comprehension, and vocabulary, but at a mild enough level that they are not identified early. Others have weaknesses almost exclusively in the

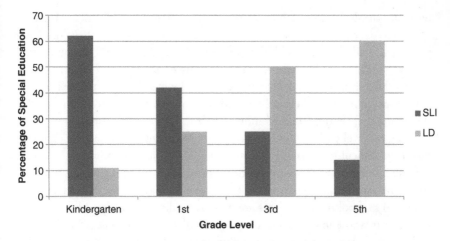

Figure 5.1. Proportions of Special Education Students Eligible Based on Having Speech/Language Impairment (S/LI) or Learning Disability (LD), Showing Decreases in S/LI Co-Occurring with Increases in LD

Note: This original figure was constructed using values from a table in Mashburn and Myers (2010) based on secondary analysis of a data set gathered by the US Department of Education (2000) for the Early Childhood Longitudinal Study—Kindergarten Cohort (ECLS–K).

© N. W. Nelson (2016). Shared with permission of the author.

areas of reading decoding, spelling, and reading fluency (perhaps in spite of having been served through a multitiered system of support) while demonstrating particularly strong abilities in spoken expression and listening comprehension. In fact, a diagnostic feature of this group may be a pattern with markedly higher listening comprehension than reading comprehension scores on standardized tests that are co-normed (e.g., Badian, 1999). This is because the students' reading decoding difficulties interfere with their reading comprehension but not their listening comprehension. This pattern of reading and spelling difficulties accompanied by generally intact language comprehension and expression is consistent with a diagnosis of *dyslexia* (Berninger & Wolf, 2016; Bishop & Snowling, 2004; Catts et al., 2005).

Students with dyslexia may demonstrate reading decoding and fluency problems long after their peers become fluent readers, consequently requiring extra time to understand higher level texts, although they may do so successfully with the extra time (Scarborough, 2005). They also tend to avoid writing tasks and may make excessive spelling and grammatical errors when they attempt to produce original texts. In such cases, it could be tempting to conclude that oral language is intact, whereas written language is impaired, but that explanation would fail to recognize the degree to which these students' oral language difficulties at the level of phonology and word structure knowledge contribute to their decoding problems, while leaving vocabulary learning and sentence- and discourse-level language skills (e.g., vocabulary, syntax, and discourse) basically intact.

In a third situation, students with SLD may be identified for the first time as having special needs in their early or middle elementary school years. Initially for this group, there may be no indication of disorder in the areas of oral expression or listening comprehension; however, later in development it may become clear that they have difficulties of language comprehension (whether reading or listening) that are interfering with their educational progress. Even though these students' comprehension difficulties may be marked, they may be overlooked in early elementary school if the students are good at reading decoding and fluency for simple texts whose linguistic challenges (vocabulary and sentence structure) tend to be tightly controlled. Corresponding language expression weaknesses also may be overlooked if students sound okay when they talk. What people may not notice is that the student produces mostly simple sentence constructions, some of which incorporate logical inconsistencies (e.g., "He fell off his bike because he hurt his leg.").

When these students' comprehension difficulties do become apparent in middle elementary or later grades, alternative hypotheses may be generated to explain the late-emerging difficulties. One hypothesis might be that the student is simply not trying or is generally a slow learner, but that may mask a language-learning disability. Another might be that the student is showing the effects of another primary deficit, such as an auditory processing disorder, inadequate short-term-memory capacity, or attention-deficit hyperactivity disorder (ADHD). Evidence of comorbidities of language and learning disabilities with such diagnoses abound (e.g., Leonard, 1998; Mueller & Tomblin, 2012; Tomblin & Mueller, 2012), and assessment in any of these areas could provide evidence supportive of that hypothesis. It would be critical, however, not to ignore evidence of language weaknesses.

Our concern would be that, without comprehensive language assessment, language weaknesses could be overlooked, which might be at the root of comprehension difficulties. For example, it is difficult, if not impossible, to separate auditory processing difficulties from language processing difficulties. Even though nonlinguistic auditory stimuli might be used in assessment protocols for diagnosing auditory processing disorder, there is no clear evidence that students' abilities to detect distinctions and sequencing of acoustic stimuli are not affected by the skills they have developed for processing phonological cues in language.

Similarly, when memory or attention problems are evident, it is important to ask, Memory for what? Attention for what? A student who is having difficulty understanding language and encoding it internally is less likely to pay attention to it or remember it. Attention and behavioral concerns may appear to co-occur with language impairments at particularly high rates, but there may be multiple reasons for that, including sampling bias (Tomblin & Mueller, 2012) and dependence between behavior rating scales, such as those for identifying attention deficits, and tests of language and communication, which measure the same things (Redmond, 2002). Within students, attention and memory may be fully adequate for activities that are not language based, such as playing a video game, creating a work of art, or assembling a model-building kit. Apparent problems of short-term memory could be thoroughly intertwined with difficulty encoding language syntactically and phonologically. Individual student profiles need to be considered, proceeding with caution in making assumptions about causality.

When students struggle to comprehend and formulate complex academic language, spoken or written, in spite of relatively intact sound-word structure knowledge and being able to read aloud with surprising accuracy, some researchers have suggested that this represents a "specific comprehension deficit" (Bishop & Snowling, 2004; Nation, Clarke, Marshall, & Durand, 2004; Ramus et al., 2013). Increasingly, it is understood that such sentence-discourse-level problems may be associated with weak formulation of expressive language as well as comprehension difficulties (Leonard, 2009). Consistent with this, Catts et al. (2005) argued that the term *specific language impairment alone* (or *SLI without dyslexia*) would better reflect this condition, showing the non-phonological language difficulties that cross receptive and expressive modalities, even though phonological language abilities, as well as reading decoding and word recognition abilities, could be basically intact.

> **DON'T FORGET**
>
> When a student has academic difficulties and avoids curricular activities, it may be tempting to assume that a student "could if he [or she] would [try]," but stronger relationships with students are built when the diagnostician or clinician can take the understanding position that a student "would if he [or she] could." This includes professionals communicating that they recognize that this work is difficult, but together they will figure out how to make things better and learning easier.

Longitudinal studies have pointed to the possibility that students whose primary difficulties are in the area of language comprehension could have had lexical and grammatical weaknesses in their younger years that were subclinical to measurement (Alonzo, Yeomans-Maldonado, Murphy, Bevens, & Language and

Reading Research Consortium (LARRC), 2016; Catts, Adlof, & Weismer, 2006; Scarborough, 2005). For some students, these problems become apparent in later grades when the demands of language complexity, including vocabulary and syntax in disciplinary literacy, such as in math or science, exceed the student's inadequate abilities (Fang, 2012; Shanahan & Shanahan, 2012). By looking for language roots for academic problems, teams of psychologists, special educators, and speech-language pathologists may have a meaningful and treatable place to start, rather than looking primarily at cognitive processing deficits that tend to co-occur.

These three situations are not exhaustive, and they should not be viewed as explaining invariable subtypes of SLD, but they do show how S/LI may morph into SLD over time, or how SLD may involve a language component that remains hidden. These three situations also support notions that language disorders *are* learning disabilities and that learning disabilities *are* language disorders (Sun & Wallach, 2014). In real life, patterns of oral and written language difficulties involve many variations and blurry boundaries, but theoretical accounts and empirical studies are accumulating evidence that problems such as dyslexia and specific language impairment can be differentiated. However, the distinctions are based on different patterns of strengths and weaknesses by language levels (*phonological,* also called *sound-word level,* versus *non-phonological,* also called *sentence-discourse level*). Despite tradition, they are not differentiated based on receptive-versus-expressive or even oral-versus-written modalities (Bishop & Snowling, 2004; Catts et al., 2005, 2006; Nelson, 2016; Ramus et al., 2013).

Additionally, the patterns reported here as situations point to the importance of thorough assessment of oral as well as written language when identifying SLD. In this way, they point to the importance of focusing on language comprehension and expression as complex, multifaceted processes, which should be attended to in intervention after being identified through assessment, as explained in later sections of this chapter.

DEFINITION, ETIOLOGY, AND INCIDENCE OF LANGUAGE DISABILITIES

Although language disorders characterized by difficulty with oral expression and listening comprehension are named in definitions of SLD, they are not always recognized as being part of the same category. Research on overlaps, distinctions, and genetic foundations of language and learning disabilities is ongoing and may contribute to deeper understandings. For now, however, it is helpful to consider current definitions and practices.

Definition

One of the challenges in understanding how SLD manifests in oral expression and listening comprehension is the lack of common terminology and definitions across disciplines and internationally for relating language disorders and learning difficulties (Bishop, 2014; Nelson, 2016). That language disorders are inherent in learning disabilities, however, should not be in question. Consider the emphasis on language in the original definition of SLD as encoded in the IDEA. This definition, which has been retained from the first iteration of the law to its most recent revisions in 2004, reads as follows:

> The term "specific learning disability" means a disorder in one or more of the basic psychological processes involved *in understanding or in using language, spoken or written* [emphasis added] that may manifest itself in the imperfect ability to listen, think, speak, read, spell, or do mathematical calculations. (IDEA 2004, §602.30, Definition)

According to this definition, reading and writing are not simply dependent on underlying language abilities; they are language abilities. Similarly, difficulties in using language when listening and speaking are not only language disorders; they are learning disabilities. We propose that by assessing similar language skills in different modalities diagnosticians can describe a student's pattern of language strengths and weaknesses, and then teams may use that information to provide a richer educational experience for students with SLD.

A second key resource to consider when defining language disorders and learning disabilities is the *Diagnostic and Statistical Manual of Mental Disorders* (5th ed.) (*DSM-5;* American Psychiatric Association, 2013). The definition of language disorders in this resource changed substantively from the fourth to the fifth edition. Two key differences were removal of the distinction between "Expressive" and "Mixed Receptive-Expressive" types, which were part of the definition in the *DSM-IV,* and removal of reference to discrepancies with nonverbal intellectual ability as a criterion for identification. Instead, *DSM-5* referenced discrepancies from expectations for students of the same chronological age (CA). The *DSM-5* codes are cross-listed with codes from the *International Statistical Classification of Diseases and Related Health Problems* (10th rev.) (*ICD-10*) (World Health Organization, 2005). These are reproduced in the following excerpts.

The diagnostic criteria for "Language Disorder" (code 315.39 in the *DSM-5*; code, F80.9 in the *ICD-10*) include the following:

A. Persistent difficulties in the acquisition and use of language across modalities (i.e., spoken, written, sign language, or other) due to deficits in comprehension or production that include the following: (1) Reduced vocabulary (word knowledge and use). (2) Limited sentence structure (ability to put words and word endings together to form sentences based on the rules of grammar and morphology). (3) Impairments in discourse (ability to use vocabulary and connect sentences to explain or describe a topic or series of events or have a conversation. (p. 42)

Beyond naming problems at the word, sentence, and discourse levels in Part A, Part B specifies that "Language abilities are substantially and quantitatively below those expected for age" (i.e., using CA referencing rather than cognitive referencing), and they should result in functional limitations affecting communication, social participation, academic achievement, or occupational performance. Part C indicates that the onset of symptoms must be in the early developmental period, and Part D excludes language difficulties that are attributable to hearing or other sensory impairment, motor dysfunction, another medical or neurological condition, intellectual disability, or global developmental delay. It is these exclusionary criteria that make the definition of language disorder in *DSM-5* consistent with the diagnosis of *specific language impairment (SLI)* or *primary language disorder,* which are other terms for the same condition. Additionally, the *DSM-5* allows that language disorder may be comorbid with other neurodevelopmental disorders, including "specific learning disorder (literacy and numeracy), attention deficit/hyperactivity disorder, autism spectrum disorder, and developmental coordination disorder" (p. 44).

The removal of the distinction between receptive and expressive language disorders in *DSM-5* has implications for understanding oral expression and listening comprehension related to students with SLD. It is not that expressive and receptive language processes are indistinguishable when they occur

> **DON'T FORGET**
> ....
> The term *specific language impairment (SLI)* is used in the research literature to label school-age children, adolescents, and young adults for whom language disabilities are of a primary nature and do not result from emotional disorders, cognitive delays, sensory impairments, or language differences (Leonard, 1998); however, it is not a term used in IDEA, which uses *speech/language impaired.*
>
> The terms *SLI + dyslexia* (Ramus et al., 2013), *language learning disability* (Sun & Wallach, 2014); *language literacy disorder* (Nelson, 2016); and *oral written language learning disability* (OWL LD; Berninger & Wolf, 2016) are synonyms for mixed disorders of oral and written language. The lack of consensus on terminology is a problem (Bishop, 2014; Nelson, 2016).

naturally, because they are, or that listening skills are identical to speaking skills or reading to writing, because they are not; rather, it is difficult, if not impossible, to design a formal test that can assess language input in isolation from language output. Beyond the constrictions of isolating these processes from the influence of sensori-motor input-output modalities, however, the underlying language constructs share more similarities than differences (see Figure 5.2 for a representation of the basic

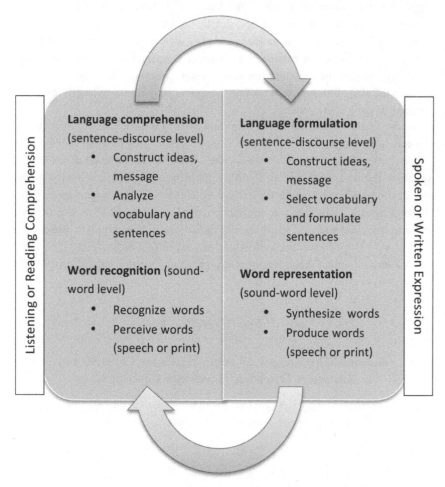

Figure 5.2. Graphic Representation of Similarities Across Modalities (Oral and Written, Receptive and Expressive) in the Language-Level Latent Constructs at the Sentence-Discourse Level and Sound-Word Level, Despite Sensori-motor Differences in Input-Output Channels

Source: © N. W. Nelson, 2016. Reproduced with permission.

constructs). Evidence for this comes from factor analysis of traditional formal test results that tends to show a single latent construct, or highly correlated vocabulary and syntax constructs, rather than expressive and receptive language as representing two separate factors that are distinguishable (Lonigan & Milburn, 2017; Tomblin & Zhang, 2006). This is in spite of the fact that many formal tests continue to allow the computation of composite scores for receptive and expressive language abilities that imply that they do represent separable, independent latent constructs. We note, however, that the receptive-expressive distinction reflects a long-standing tradition in standardized assessments, and clinicians and publishers may be reluctant to abandon it, even though factor analysis and other evidence suggests that "expressive language disorders" cannot be uniquely separated from "receptive language disorders" (Leonard, 2009). Other reasons separate categories have been challenged are summarized in Rapid Reference 5.1.

Interestingly, in contrast to the definition of SLD in IDEA, which emphasizes the role of language, the definition of "specific learning disorder" in *DSM-5* lists six categories that may represent "difficulties learning and using academic skills" (p. 66) without naming oral expression and listening comprehension among them, perhaps to avoid overlap with the definition in *DSM-5* of *language disorder*. The list of academic skills that may be identified as reflecting SLD in the *DSM-5* includes the following: (1) word reading difficulties; (2) reading comprehension difficulties; (3) spelling difficulties; (4) written expression difficulties; (5) difficulties mastering number sense, number facts, or calculation; and (6) difficulties with

---

≡ *Rapid Reference 5.1*

Reasons Why Receptive Versus Expressive Categories of Language Disorders Have Been Challenged

- Details of oral language that are important for identifying language disabilities, such as using morphology grammatically (e.g., verb tense, auxiliary *is*), are difficult to evaluate through comprehension.
- Many children classified by tests as having an expressive language disability may be reclassified as having a receptive-expressive disability a year later (Conti-Ramsden & Botting, 1999).
- Using factor analysis on standardized language test results, a single-dimension model (i.e., combined receptive and expressive) or one that separates problems on the basis of language level (i.e., vocabulary [word] and syntax [sentence]) best explains the nature of language disabilities (Lonigan & Milburn, 2017; Tomblin & Zhang, 2006).

mathematical reasoning. Problems with impairment of reading (accuracy, fluency, or comprehension) are coded as 315.00 (corresponding to the *ICD-10* code of F81.0). A note in this area indicates that "*Dyslexia* is an alternative term used to refer to a pattern of learning difficulties characterized by problems with accurate or fluent word recognition, poor decoding, and poor spelling abilities" (p. 67). We note, additionally, that all of these six types of academic skills involve language processing skills, even though they are not named as such.

Similarly, problems with impairment in written expression are coded as 315.2 (corresponding to the *ICD-10* code of F81.81). They involve spelling accuracy, grammar and punctuation accuracy, and clarity or organization of written expression. Again, these are all language abilities, with close connections to oral language abilities at the word, sentence, and discourse levels, although that is not explicit in the *DSM-5* definition of SLD.

Finally, problems with impairment in mathematics are coded as 315.1 (corresponding to the *ICD-10* code of F81.2). They involve number sense, memorization of arithmetic facts, accurate or fluent calculation, and accurate math reasoning. Although such skills may dissociate from oral language, a number of language abilities, including using language for metalinguistic and executive functions, may play a role in mathematical proficiency. These include the ability to understand and retain a series of verbal instructions for conducting mathematical procedures, using self-talk to guide computational accuracy, using vocabulary and syntax knowledge to make sense of math story problems and to perform mathematical reasoning operations, and using language skills to fact check one's mathematical calculations.

In clinical and educational practice, language disabilities are commonly identified by the language domains that are affected. In this taxonomy, language disabilities are classified as affecting primarily language content (meaning-semantics), language structure or form (phonology, morphology, and syntax), and language use (contextual use–pragmatics) or combinations of these three domains (see Rapid Reference 5.2 for definitions).

This categorization system results in identification of individual profiles of strengths and weaknesses across language domains. It is reflected in standardized language tests that provide composite scores or index scores for abilities related to language content versus language structure or form. Some standardized language tests also include behavioral rating scales to establish criterion-referenced measures for language use in context (pragmatics), and some use direct assessment tasks to assess social communication. A classification system based on language domains has the advantage of corresponding to grade-level curriculum standards for, among others, English and language arts.

⩵ *Rapid Reference 5.2*

Language Domain Definitions

- *Phonology* refers to speech sounds and how they are combined to make meaningful words.
- *Morphology* refers to the smallest units of meaning (morphemes) in language, with every word constituting at least one morpheme and additional grammatical morphemes added to indicate, among other functions, the third person (-s) and tense of verbs (-ed), auxiliary verb (is), and comparisons (-er and -est).
- *Syntax* refers to the rules used for combining words into simple sentences with one clause or for forming complex sentences with multiple clauses and embeddings.
- *Semantics* refers to the word content (vocabulary) and conventions for combining words to form meaningful units of expression.
- *Pragmatics* refers to social conventions for using words, sentences, and expressions in informal or formal social interactions and other forms of discourse. An example is asking for permission by saying, "May I . . ."

Difficulties that are focused in the domain of language use in context (pragmatics) are classified in the *DSM-5* as "social (pragmatic) communication disorder" (Code 315.39; *ICD-10* code F80.89). This condition is diagnosed when students have unusual difficulty with language use and nonliteral (figurative) language, but do not meet the criteria for diagnosis of autism spectrum disorder (ASD) or intellectual disability.

An emerging alternative to the domain-specific categorization system for identifying types of language disorders among school-age children and adolescents is one that is based on language levels rather than language domains. Assessment focused on language levels also relates to curricular standards, and it carries the added advantage of representing relationships between oral and written language. In much of the literature (e.g., Bishop & Snowling, 2004; Catts et al., 2005; Ramus et al., 2013), the two language levels of this system have been characterized as *phonological* and *non-phonological,* but they also may be characterized as *sound-word level knowledge* (phonological), which contributes to skills such as word pronunciation, reading decoding, spelling, contrasted with *sentence-discourse level knowledge,* which contributes to skills needed for language comprehension and formulation (Nelson, 2016).

The terminology of *phonological* and *non-phonological* was stimulated by support for a phonological hypothesis related to skills underlying the ability to read and write individual words in alphabetic languages. Scarborough (2005) noted that this was a "beautiful hypothesis," but she added that it was inconsistent with a number of "ugly facts." A key element of Scarborough's argument was that the phonological hypothesis, although a good explanation for reading problems in the primary grades, was not as good at explaining reading difficulties among children who were either younger or older than these early readers. Instead, Scarborough pointed to research that showed that non-phonological language elements (e.g., vocabulary, syntax, and discourse) could explain variance in reading abilities better in the preschool and later school-age years.

Consistent with the view that phonological and non-phonological language abilities play critical roles in reading and writing, as well as in specific language impairment, Bishop and Snowling (2004) proposed the two-dimensional quadrant model that is illustrated in Figure 5.3 (with circled constructs based on work by Ramus et al., 2013). This model provides a framework for explaining how typical development differs from dyslexia, SLI, mixed SLI + dyslexia, and related problems. When the two dimensions are plotted against each other, four major

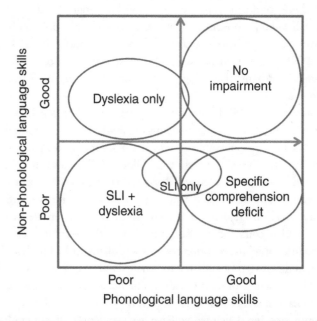

Figure 5.3. Two-Dimensional Quadrant Model Proposed by Bishop and Snowling (2004) to Reflect Relationships Between Dyslexia and Specific Language Impairment, Supported by Their Evidence and Evidence from Other Longitudinal Studies (Catts et al., 2005, 2006), with Evidence for Subtypes Added Based on Ramus et al. (2013).

Note: SLI = specific language impairment; SLI + dyslexia = oral written language learning disability (OWL LD; Berninger & Wolf, 2016; Silliman & Berninger, 2011).

patterns are explained. In the upper-right-hand quadrant, phonological and non-phonological language skills are average or above, representing typical development of oral and written language. In the upper-left-hand quadrant, poor phonological skills at the sound-word level co-occur with good listening comprehension and oral expression at the sentence-discourse level. This is the profile of classical dyslexia, in which problems of reading and writing co-occur with average or better oral language skills (except at the level of word structure knowledge). The lower-left-hand quadrant represents a profile in which phonological and non-phonological language skills both are low, representing mixed oral and written language difficulties. Bishop and Snowling (2004) characterized this pattern as *classical SLI,* but Ramus and colleagues called it *SLI + dyslexia,* differentiating it from *SLI-only.* Ramus and colleagues (2013) presented additional evidence that SLI-only could be distinguished from SLI + dyslexia by the absence of problems involving phonological skills and reading decoding in SLI-only. Similarly, Catts et al. (2005) argued that the label *SLI-only* (i.e., SLI without reading decoding problems) was preferable to *poor comprehender* for characterizing problems represented in the lower-right-hand quadrant. They noted that this would represent how students with the SLI-only profile can have difficulty with language expression as well as comprehension, as also suggested by Leonard (2009). When Catts et al. (2006) presented evidence for the profile in the lower-right quadrant, they adopted the more frequently used label of *specific comprehension deficit.*

Based on factor analysis, Ramus et al. (2013, p. 636) concluded that their results agreed with Bishop and Snowling's (2004) "that non-phonological and phonological language skills are the two main sources of variance in language abilities among SLI, dyslexia and control children." They also showed, however, that specific language impairment and dyslexia do not always co-occur and that the nature of any phonological factor may differ between the two groups. They identified a *phonological representation* factor underlying the problems for the SLI-only group, which could be assessed primarily with speech perception, speech production, and nonword repetition tasks. It was distinguished from a *phonological skills* factor underlying problems for the dyslexia-only or dyslexia + SLI group, which could be assessed primarily with phonemic awareness, rapid naming, and digit span tasks. Finally, Ramus et al. (2013) noted that a separate subgroup with specific comprehension deficit would have few problems with either phonological skills or phonological representation, consistent with the quadrant model.

As Catts et al. (2006) observed, the phonological and non-phonological dimensions of the quadrant model are consistent with the simple view of reading (SVR; Gough & Tunmer, 1986; Hoover & Gough, 1990; Tunmer & Chapman, 2007, 2012). According to the SVR, reading comprehension can be explained as the product of two dimensions—reading decoding (a sound-word level or phonological skill) and language comprehension (a sentence-discourse level or non-phonological skill). The SVR was expanded by Tunmer and Chapman (2012) to incorporate vocabulary knowledge, noting that vocabulary could explain additional variance in reading decoding and language comprehension. Tunmer and Chapman supported this addition with evidence, as did Catts et al. (2006) and Ramus et al. (2013). The SVR also could explain why reading comprehension might be lower than listening comprehension, which Badian (1999) observed to be a diagnostic feature of dyslexia. That is, even though language comprehension is generally intact in dyslexia, reading comprehension would be affected indirectly by the problems of reading decoding, at least in the early stages of learning to read. Later in development, by drawing on this strength, and perhaps supported by intervention, it would be possible for students with dyslexia to demonstrate relatively intact reading comprehension in spite of ongoing challenges with fluent and accurate reading decoding (Catts et al., 2005; Scarborough, 2005).

Etiology

Many factors are involved in the development of language, including genetic, intrinsic cognitive and linguistic factors, extrinsic familial and educational factors, and social-emotional and contextual factors. Thus, problems involving any of these contributing factors could explain why children and adolescents with SLD and SLI have difficulty learning language. Although SLDs are presumed to be related to neurodevelopmental factors, which could in turn be explained by genetic ones, few clues have been found to explain the exact nature of the causal chain. It is wise to keep in mind Fisher's (2006) cautionary note:

> Genes do not specify behaviours or cognitive processes; they make regulatory factors, signaling molecules, receptors, enzymes, and so on, that interact in highly complex networks, modulated by environmental influences, in order to build and maintain the brain. (p. 270).

Consistent with the view that SLI can be differentiated from dyslexia, separate genes have been implicated for each. For example, the FOX-P2 gene on chromosome 18 has been isolated in families with SLI and particular difficulty with past-tense verb learning (Finley, 2005). Evidence showed further that this gene is necessary for synaptogenesis in Brodman's area 41b (auditory association area). However, Finley (2005) cautioned that "the same ability requires virtually all the cortical areas, most of the genes, and highly elaborated language experience" (p. 212). In the area of reading, research has implicated the DCDC2 gene as affecting neuronal migration in people with reading disability. Meng et al. (2005) estimated that as high as 20% of cases with dyslexia could be traced to the DCDC2 gene. This team used a statistical approach to study and compare specific DNA markers in 153 families with dyslexia. They noted that brain circuits must communicate with each other, but, in dyslexia, circuits are disrupted and compensatory brain circuits are inefficient.

Contemporary theories of language acquisition may hold some clues as to how this might work by positing computational models for learning the statistical probabilities associated with linguistic regularities and establishing related neural networks. Supporting such theories, researchers have used evoked response potentials to explore why college-age students with dyslexia may have difficulty isolating speech perception data from perceptual noise (Jaffe-Dax, Raviv, Jacoby, Loewenstein, & Ahissar, 2015). The findings from this research suggest that a specific computational deficit, stemming from poor automatic integration of stimulus statistics, could account for some of the phonological symptoms of dyslexia.

Research on the neurological bases for language disabilities also points to variations in the development of critical neuroanatomical structures. For example, neurologists have developed an anatomical risk index that combines measures of brain volume, asymmetrical development, and other anatomical differences that are either specific or nonspecific for language disabilities, dyslexia, and schizophrenia (Leonard et al., 2002). Supporting this index, children with high negative risk index scores show inferior performance on listening comprehension, oral expression, and reading measures (Leonard, Eckert, Given, Virginia, & Eden, 2006). These findings link language disabilities and dyslexia through shared neurological risk factors, a link that is often seen in educational practice and that has been described previously in this chapter. Other studies have documented anomalies in the cerebellar-frontal circuit associated with problems of rapid automatic naming and reading but without primary spoken language impairment (Eckert et al., 2003).

Functional neuroimaging studies have pointed to possible causative factors, as well. Early work with positron emission tomography (PET) showed evidence that some areas of brain work in isolation of others in dyslexia (Paulesu et al., 1996). Other fMRI research has implicated the cerebellum, which is known for its role in coordinating motor activity. This research shows that the cerebellum plays a role in integrating perceptual and cognitive processes involved in reading (Fulbright et al., 1999). Additionally, fMRI research with poor readers has shown over-activation in the left anterior region (Broca's area) accompanied by under-activation in posterior regions (Wernicke's, angular gyrus, occipitotemporal lobe) (Shaywitz, Lyon, & Shaywitz, 2006). Taking this one step further, Shaywitz et al. (2004) demonstrated changes in activity in left occipitotemporal systems for skilled reading in children after a phonologically based intervention.

With advances in neuroimaging and the corresponding shift away from gross anatomical differences to cerebral functions, attention became focused on white-matter development (Fields, 2008). The brain's white matter contains millions of axons that are covered with myelin, a fatty substance that surrounds and insulates the axons of some nerve cells. The axons connect neurons in different regions of the brain, and neural impulses travel about 100 times faster along neurons when the axons are adequately covered with myelin. Knowledge of white-matter development and functions opens new avenues for explaining difficulty with the phonological loop (connections between auditory perception and speech production attributed to the arcuate fasciculus) and how executive functions that may be demonstrated by children with language disorders may become increasingly prominent during adolescence when myelination is incomplete.

Incidence

Reports of prevalence for language disabilities vary, depending on factors such as severity and type of disability, age of identification, and criteria for inclusion and definition. An epidemiological study of children in kindergarten reported an overall prevalence rate of 7.4% for SLI, with a higher rate among boys (8%) than girls (6%) (Tomblin, Mainela-Arnold, & Zhang, 2007). Other studies have indicated prevalence rates from 6% to 8% of school-age children (Gilger & Wise, 2004), and an estimated 50% of children with early language disabilities later experience reading difficulties (Catts et al., 2005). A study of 8-year-olds estimated the prevalence rate for language disabilities to be 6.3%, and the ratio of boys to girls to be nearly double (1.8 to 1) (Pinborough-Zimmerman et al., 2007). Reports of prevalence of dyslexia range more widely, depending on how dyslexia is defined and when students are assessed. Dyslexia prevalence was estimated at 5% to 17% by Shaywitz and Shaywitz (2001).

Prevalence of mixed disorders of SLI + SLD is not well documented because of the federal rules for unduplicated counts in school systems. That is, students are represented only in the count for S/LI, which includes speech disorders as well as language disorders, or in the count for SLD, but not both, depending on which is considered *primary*. The prevalence of co-occurring language and literacy disorders varies across grade level (Catts et al., 2005), but it could be estimated at 5% to 10% of the school-age population and much higher if subclinical weaknesses in one area or the other are considered (review Figure 5.1).

DEVELOPMENTAL MANIFESTATIONS

Becoming proficient with language requires the acquisition of words. Words, in turn, are constructed of phonemes and morphemes and may be represented by orthography. Words, which represent language content and grammatical functions, become components of sentences combined based on a grammar of implicit rules governing inflectional, syntactic, and discourse organization. By learning vocabulary, sentence structure, and discourse structure, speakers, who are also listeners, gain proficiency at formulating messages and understanding them. This process begins before birth with the formation of a neurodevelopmental system that is predisposed to establish social connections and to learn language.

Children can establish eye contact at birth, and they respond to phonological distinctions in infancy (Kuhl, 2004). Within the first year of life, most respond to familiar words and phrases. By 12 to 18 months, they produce their first words and attempt to imitate words produced by others, often in the context of joint action routines (Bruner, 1975). Sometime after age 2, vocabulary learning increases to such a degree that it may be called a *vocabulary explosion*. Also at about age 2, most children begin to combine single words into two-word utterances and to add inflectional endings, such as plurals or possessives. The handy rule of thumb is to expect two-word phrases by about age 2 years and three-word phrases by about age 3 years. After age 3, grammatical development for many toddlers advances quickly. By kindergarten, most children are capable of combining sentences, subordinating them, and embedding one within another, even though they may still be making developmental errors involving morphology and verb and pronoun inflection (e.g., "Him hitted me 'cause him mad").

CAUTION

It is often assumed that late-talking children will have significant language difficulties or develop a language disability. This assumption has not been supported by several studies (Rice, Taylor, & Zubrick, 2008; Weismer, 2007). For example, Weismer (2007) reported that only 8.8% of late talkers end up with impaired language at age 5 years. The same study indicated that a late-talking child's comprehension of language at 2½ years of age is the best predictor of language production at age 4½ years.

Toddlers also demonstrate discourse-level abilities and use them for varied social purposes and make use of verbal symbols and nonverbal facial expressions and gestures. Examples include commenting, telling and understanding stories, sharing feelings, arguing and protesting, as well as making requests. Although these early developmental milestones are relatively predictable across cultures and languages, they are not invariable. Being late to achieve these milestones is not a strong predictor of later difficulty, however. In fact, research has shown that many children who are clearly "late talkers" catch up with their peers by the preschool years.

The follow sections offer a brief primer on the acquisition of language in the areas of content, form, and use in the preschool years. These skills set the foundation for higher-level skills supporting listening comprehension and spoken expression over the school-age years.

Acquisition of Content

Language content (i.e., meaning) is represented in words but also in language units larger than words, such as different vocabulary referring to the same concepts across sentences; sentences that can be worded differently but mean the same thing; and discourse for conveying stories, information, or conversation. Meaning can be conveyed via nonliteral means as well as literally and with nonverbal means (i.e., through gesture and tone) as well as with words. Vocabulary plays a key and essential role in conveying the content of a message, but syntax can communicate relationships beyond the level of single word, and discourse can communicate more complex meanings beyond sentences.

During the preschool and school years, children develop large vocabularies, associated concepts, and combinatorial rules (i.e., semantics) that interface with syntactic structures to convey meaning. This aspect of a person's linguistic system develops and is modified throughout the individual's lifetime. One view is that semantic language systems are acquired through analogical comparisons that develop from an initial focus on concrete similarities to comparisons of abstract relational similarities in a process of progressive alignment (Gentner & Namy, 2006).

Only recently have scientists begun to understand how words are mapped in the brain (Huth, de Heer, Griffiths, Theunissen, & Gallant, 2016). By using fMRI technology and sophisticated analysis techniques while participants listened to hours of stories, Huth and colleagues (2016) were able to create a semantic atlas showing regions across the brain where particular words and sets of related words are organized into intricate patterns represented with a surprising degree of consistency across individuals. Using this technology, it is possible that future research may reveal why some types of conceptual vocabulary are particularly difficult for individuals with SLI and SLD. These include the understanding and use of prepositions, space and time references (e.g., using *forward* for space or time), antonyms (e.g., *inward* and *outward*), synonyms (e.g., *configuration* for *pattern*), abstract words (e.g., *ethics*), and figurative expressions (e.g., *bridging the generation gap*). Meanwhile, it is important for examiners to probe for information about a student's awareness of semantic relationships that extend beyond the picture pointing and naming tasks used in many formal vocabulary tests.

Acquisition of Structure

Knowledge of language structure is needed at all language levels—sounds, words, sentences, and discourse. At the level of sounds, the child must learn phonological rules for processing speech-sound sequences and combining speech sounds (phonemes) into words. Ramus et al. (2013) termed this *phonological representation*. To become literate, children also must become aware of the individual phonemes that make up words. Ramus et al. (2013) termed these *phonological skills*. The phonological system does not function in isolation but interfaces with the syntactic system (morphology and syntax). As noted previously, phonological skills support listening and speaking and the acquisition of literacy skills for reading and writing. In typically developing children, phonemic representation develops in infancy and interfaces with meaning so that by 18 months, most children understand about 150 words and use about 50 words for communicating. This learning process requires language-specific listening (i.e., categorical perception) and computational strategies for recognizing repeated speech-sound (phonemic) patterns and combinations of speech sounds into words (Kuhl, 2004).

The young child also must acquire linguistic rules for interpreting and expressing number, tense, comparison, and reference marked by pronouns (morphology) and verb structures. The morphological rule system is generally acquired during the preschool and early elementary school years and is usually well established by grades 3 through 4. However, learning words with Latin and Greek roots and with a variety of derivational morphemes may proceed into secondary school and throughout life.

The early syntactic rule system applies to forming simple sentences with two or three words, and the typical child acquires these rules during the preschool years concurrently with the acquisition of morphology. Coordinated clauses with the words *and, but, or,* and *so* develop during the late preschool years. Typical children at age 5 can produce and comprehend complex sentences with subordinated clauses. Clauses, which are underlined in these examples, may be adverbial (e.g., "She left before he did."), nominal (e.g., "She decided that he was her friend."), or relative (e.g., "She told the woman who was driving the bus."). Compound and complex sentence structures are later refined by increasing length, moving subordinate clauses to the beginning of sentences, and degree of abstraction (Fang, 2012; Nippold, Hesketh, Duthie, & Mansfield, 2005; Shanahan & Shanahan, 2012). An example of a nominalized sentence common in the language of science would be "That extinction is imminent for this species has to be considered." Such sentences are particularly difficult to process because they differ from the word order of simple sentences, requiring more reliance on working memory (Ehren, Murza, & Malani, 2012).

During the preschool and early grades, children with language disabilities exhibit difficulties in acquiring rules for using auxiliaries, such as *be* and *do*, third-person singular -*s*, regular past-tense endings (e.g., -*ed*), and irregular forms of nouns and verbs. They use word endings inconsistently compared to typically developing children, and the percentage of accurate identifications of children with and without language disabilities (predictive values), based on the use of morphology approximate or exceed 80% (Bedore & Leonard, 1998; Joanisse, 2004).

School-age children and adolescents with language disabilities show deficits in the use of complex syntax during conversational dialogue and in comprehending or producing narrative and expository discourse. They typically produce shorter and simpler sentences and use fewer subordinate clauses (Nippold, Mansfield, Billow, & Tomblin, 2008). Among 15-year-olds with a history of early language disabilities (from Grade 1), evidence shows ongoing differences in syntactic competence from their typically developing peers (Nippold, Mansfield, Billow, & Tomblin, 2009). Specifically, the language disabilities of these adolescents are reflected by lower density in number of clauses and less use of nominal clauses in discourse and by syntactic deficits on standardized language tests. Moreover, the discourse and syntax measures correlate significantly, indicating that errors in the spontaneous use of syntax for socialization also occur on formal tasks featured in standardized tests. This also is consistent with evidence of a separate factor at the sentence-discourse level, comprising both sentence- and discourse-level measures (Nelson, 2016).

Acquisition of Use

The conventions for social and academic communication in context (pragmatics) are driven by the human need for expressing intentions, controlling oneself and others, and adapting to cultural-linguistic expectations. Pragmatic skill involves much more than being polite or acting in a socially appropriate manner. It draws on understanding expectations for using different forms of discourse with different types of communication partners in different settings. Discourse-level skill develops over the school-age years along with syntax. Although preschool-age children and even toddlers can convey elements of personal narratives, the ability to organize complete narrative episodes grows over the school-age years. Skill with the macrostructure of expository texts increases as well, along with skill with other forms of academic and disciplinary specific discourse.

One of the important pragmatic functions in academic contexts is to elicit and share information through questioning. Children with language disabilities tend to have problems understanding and using higher-level *wh-* questions (e.g., "Why?" "How?"), even when asked in the context of illustrations (Deevy & Leonard, 2004). *Wh-* questions that require inferential thinking (i.e., going beyond the facts given in a simultaneously spoken and read text) also present significant difficulties (Wiig & Wilson, 1994). In addition, children and adolescents with language disabilities have difficulties interpreting intentions that are expressed indirectly and may appear to ignore indirect requests such as "Shouldn't you take your shoes off?" and "The books need straightening before recess." They also have difficulties engaging in interactions that require complex intentions such as apologizing, persuading, and negotiating terms. These difficulties can lead to assumptions of behavioral problems when it is actually language that is the problem.

COGNITIVE CORRELATES OF LANGUAGE DEVELOPMENT AND DISORDERS

Competent language users can create and comprehend an infinite variety of utterances by combining the units of language in an infinite variety of ways using predictable conventions (this property of language is called *combinatorial*). To do so in real time requires competence not only with language knowledge and skills but also with cognitive correlates that enable processing to occur rapidly and synchronously within functional neural networks. Attention, working memory, and executive functions are examples of general cognitive processes that must be recruited for this to occur. They enhance the ability to receive, process, interpret, retain, retrieve, and produce language at normal rates of speech and listening, often guided by metalinguistic awareness, self-organizational strategies, and purpose. In this section, we consider how cognitive correlates, such as attention and executive function, short-term memory, working memory, word retrieval, and processing speed, all can contribute to variation in listening comprehension and spoken expression and how they can affect measures of language performance.

Attention

Attention is needed for concentration, focusing, and consciousness. It is an aspect of human cognition that can be controlled in the presence of limited capacity or

≋ Rapid Reference 5.3

Types of Attention

Sustained attention maintains attention over time; it is controlled by the reticular formation, brain stem, and frontal regions of the brain.

Selective attention allows a person to focus on a single stimulus and block distracters; it is mediated by temporal, parietal, and striatal regions of the brain.

Inhibiting responses and dividing and shifting attention comprise the executive level of the attentional system; it is mediated by the frontal lobes.

resources (Anderson, Anderson, & Anderson, 2006). Attentional deficits vary in nature and degree across disorders and involve different brain structures (see Rapid Reference 5.3). Digit span forward is an example of an assessment task that requires focused attention. Story retelling also involves sustained and selective attention. These resources are more likely to be engaged if a person knows that retelling will be expected. Then executive controls, which are discussed in the next section, can be employed to facilitate their application.

Attentional capacities and executive functions increase throughout childhood, along with maturation of the central nervous system and frontal lobes in particular (Manly et al., 2001). Selective attention develops between ages 6 and 13 years. Stable sustained attention develops later, with growth in all aspects of attention between ages 8 and 10 years and a spurt in development occurring about age 11. Impaired attention, especially response inhibition, is prevalent in ADHD and is associated with frontal lobe dysfunction (Semrud-Clikeman et al., 2000). Children with ADHD perform poorly on measures of attention, indicating pervasive deficits in the integrity of the attentional system (Anderson et al., 2006).

High rates of comorbidity of language and literacy disorders and ADHD are reported, but the nature of the relationship is unclear, and readers should keep in mind that association does not imply causation (Tomblin & Mueller, 2012). One hypothesis is that processing speed deficits could be a common feature underlying both (Boada, Willcutt, & Pennington, 2012). Although exact mechanisms are unknown, it is important to consider the role of attention deficits during formal and informal assessment to provide appropriate support during language intervention and in the classroom. Because formal language testing is conducted in a one-to-one environment, it is not the best context for assessing attention issues that may arise in the classroom.

Thinking further about causality, some evidence suggests that deficits or inefficiencies in language ability may make a student more dependent on cognitive resources, such as sustained attention, as well as vice versa. Montgomery, Evans, and Gillam (2009) found associations between sustained attention and simple sentence comprehension for students with SLI but not for typically developing peers. They found that comprehension of simple sentences, as well as complex ones, by students with SLI required significant auditory vigilance, sustained attention, and resource capacity allocation. It is easy to see how tiring this extra effort could be, making it difficult for children with SLI to sustain the effort to listen attentively in the classroom.

Related to the question "Attention to what?" Berninger, Abbott, Cook, and Nagy (2016) found that measures of attention and executive function predicted more variance in composite scores for subword, word, and syntax-text levels of language when those measures involved language processing than when they were not specifically related to language. Berninger and colleagues (2016) also found that inhibition related to focused attention uniquely predicted outcomes for the oral language system.

Executive Functions

Attention is closely related to executive functions, which include selective attention, cognitive inhibition (i.e., interference control), control of working memory, and cognitive flexibility (i.e., ability to shift set). Cognitive flexibility is needed to attend to semantic cues from multiple angles, making it possible to understand figurative meanings, analogies, and words with multiple meanings. Executive functions are associated with a growing awareness that one can exert control over attention and ignore distractors. This involves learning to tune out auditory or cognitive noise while in the midst of a purposeful task. It also involves recruiting working memory to hold elements of a task in store while actively working on them (Diamond, 2013). Executive functions help individuals perform complex tasks that require coordination of multiple domains and levels of language skills, whether they involve listening, speaking, reading, or writing. Writing tasks, however, provide particularly rich opportunities to provide assessment and intervention for executive functions (Bashir & Singer, 2006; Harris, Graham, Mason, & Friedlander, 2008).

Short-Term Memory

Short-term (immediate) memory capacities are central in language acquisition and use. Auditory short-term memory is used to retain spoken language for a short

≡ Rapid Reference 5.4

Short-Term Memory

Short-term auditory memory capacity was defined classically by Miller (1956) as seven unrelated items, plus or minus two. Competent language users can re-auditorize and retain linguistic units in short-term memory using what Baddeley (1986, 1996) termed the *phonological loop*. The ability to re-auditorize may be less available to students with phonological deficits. Digit span tasks often are used to measure short-term auditory memory. Nonword repetition and sentence repetition tasks also measure memory for language at the sound-word level and sentence level. By taxing short-term memory, such tasks require application of phonological or syntactic skills to assist in retention and repetition.

Visual short-term memory, which is important for reading and other visual processing tasks, is limited to four unrelated units in adults (Awh, Barton, & Vogel, 2007). Learning strategies for chunking units and encoding relationships to make them meaningful can contribute to greater capacity in either auditory or visual modality.

time, lasting only a few seconds, to allow time for comprehension (see Rapid Reference 5.4). A child's or adult's short-term auditory memory is measured as the number of language units (i.e., sounds, syllables, or words) he or she can hear and produce in 2 seconds, and this relationship between production speed and time remains stable throughout life (Cowan, 1996). Short-term auditory memory deficits may interfere with processing and understanding lengthy or complex information such as sentences that incorporate multiple subordinated or embedded clauses (e.g., relative clauses). Children with language disabilities tend to have inadequate short-term auditory memory capacities for real-time processing and chunking and, therefore, interpreting what is heard. Procedural memory, which is involved in sequential learning, such as for acquiring syntax, is also inadequate in children with language disabilities, and the deficits affect learning beyond the linguistic domain (Tomblin et al., 2007; Ullman & Pierpoint, 2005).

Working Memory

Working memory makes it possible to hold information in mind, similar to a buffer store, while processing, interpreting, or responding to it (see Rapid Reference 5.5). Adequate working memory capacities are essential for interpreting spoken language as well as for integrating thought and language for complex oral

≡ Rapid Reference 5.5

Working Memory

Baddeley (1986, 1996) proposed a model for working memory with three distinct subsystems: (1) a phonological loop, activating verbal information in memory; (2) a visual-spatial sketch pad, activating visual information in memory; and (3) a modality-free central executive. Montgomery, Gillam, and Evans (2016) extended this research by comparing Baddeley's and other researchers' working memory explanations of listening comprehension deficits to syntax explanations. They concluded logical points in favor of WM explanations, but they also noted that more work needs to be done to develop an integrated theory of memory and language comprehension processes.

expression. Developmental relationships have been found between working memory and inhibitory control, which may serve as general-purpose functions to guide complex cognition and behavior (Roncadin, Pascual-Leone, Rich, & Dennis, 2007). However, over time, this may change. Dual-task efficiency for shifting between two tasks or dimensions correlates positively with working memory in children ages 6 through 11 years and with efficiency for inhibiting responses to nonessential stimuli in children ages 12 through 17 years. This indicates that with age and experience, strategic processes rather than general-purpose resources may determine performance on complex tasks with competing stimulus or response demands.

Research also supports a connection between language disabilities and inadequate working memory for spoken language (Adams & Gathercole, 2000; Weismer, Evans, & Hesketh, 1999; Weismer, Plante, Jones, & Tomblin, 2005). In children with language impairments, the maturation and integration of working memory and inhibitory cognitive control to form strategic processes appear delayed to a degree that negatively affects the acquisition and use of complex sentence structure and cognitive content.

When formulating messages for oral expression, working memory is used to store information temporarily about an intended utterance until the motor processes involved in speech production can be executed. Inadequate storage may account for some of the expressive language difficulties of students with SLI (Montgomery, 2003). Working memory constraints also may limit the capacity of children with SLI to fully extract and represent the meaning of the longer sentences that they are attempting to comprehend. Supporting this view, evidence suggests that complex and simple sentences place significant demands on working memory resources for children with SLI (Montgomery, 2003; Montgomery & Evans, 2009).

Montgomery (2003) has noted that understanding spoken language represents the smooth integration of language-specific knowledge, strategies for managing the processing of the language, and additional cognitive controls. It is reasonable, therefore, to see that the processing of semantics, lexical units, and syntax and morphology in sentence comprehension requires linguistic knowledge and the allocation of attention and memory resources. Children with specific language disabilities also will encounter difficulties in comprehension due to storage as well as speed of manipulating linguistic units (Leonard et al., 2007).

Processing Speed

Deficits in processing speed may be a contributing factor to language disabilities, dyslexia, and other reading disabilities in children, adolescents, and adults (Boada et al., 2012; Leonard et al., 2007; Wiig, Zureich, & Chan, 2000; Wolf, Bowers, & Biddle, 2000). Frontal and temporal-parietal brain regions and subcortical structures mediate processing speed, depending on whether the input is auditory or visual. Processing speed appears related to the extent of myelination, dendritic branching, and neurochemical or biophysical factors (Colombo, 2004). Higher levels of processing speed have been linked to greater working memory capacity and inductive reasoning abilities (Kail, 2007). Evidence also suggests that processing speed is not domain-specific but rather affects many domains and represents activation of integrative neuronal networks, as suggested by observed associations between general intelligence and processing speed (Ho, Baker, & Decker, 2005).

Processing and naming speed for familiar visual stimuli (e.g., colors and shapes) can differentiate children with language disabilities from those with typical development. Children and adolescents with and without language disabilities show similar, linear patterns of increase in visual processing speed and naming speed (i.e., decreased naming time) for single-dimension (colors or forms) and dual-dimension (color-form combinations) stimuli (Wiig et al., 2000) (see Rapid Reference 5.6). In typically developing children, processing speed and naming speed for color-form combinations stabilize between ages 13 and 15 years. By contrast, processing speed and naming speed, especially for dual-dimension stimuli (e.g., a red circle), remain significantly slower in children with language disabilities. Among children with significant processing speed and naming speed deficits for color-form combinations (i.e., with longer naming times), close to 50% exhibit severe language disabilities (i.e., total language standard scores at 70 or below) (Wiig et al., 2000).

≡ Rapid Reference 5.6

....

Speed of Processing

Single-dimension naming (e.g., colors or forms) measures reaction + retrieval + response time, or *perceptual speed.*

Dual-dimension naming (e.g., color-form combinations) measures perceptual speed + cognitive overhead that results from increased demands on attention, visual working memory, and set shifting, or *cognitive speed.*

Neuroimaging of regional cerebral blood flow (rCBF) during rapid naming of color-form combinations reveals that cortical blood flow increases significantly in the temporal-parietal regions bilaterally and decreases in frontal regions (Wiig, Nielsen, Minthon, & Warkentin, 2002).

Functional magnetic resonance imaging (fMRI) validates rCBF and shows concurrent activation of subcortical regions, including the hippocampus (Wiig, Nielsen, Londos, & Minthon, 2009).

The question that clinicians must ask is, "What are the most efficient ways to help children and adolescents to improve their success in classroom activities involving language?" Although processing speed may be a marker of language, literacy, and academic difficulty, trying to increase processing speed as a general ability may be less productive than working on the language skills that may be contributing to the deficits in speed in the first place.

Word Retrieval

Word-retrieval problems, also called *word-finding problems* or *dysnomia,* involve difficulties retrieving words stored in long-term memory. These difficulties tend to correlate with deficits in processing speed. They are observed in children with language disabilities during tasks that require controlled access to the stored lexicon, such as naming objects on confrontation, associative naming, verbal fluency, sentence completion, and thematic speaking and writing (German & Newman, 2004; McGregor, Newman, Reilly, & Capone, 2002). When typically developing students respond to associative naming tasks, such as naming animals, they demonstrate organized semantic grouping (e.g., naming a group of farm animals and then switching to a series of zoo or jungle animals). Such a strategy can facilitate retrieval, but it presumes the organization of semantic networks, which may be a problem for some students with language disorders.

Unsuccessful attempts at retrieving a particular word to fit a verbal context may result in circumlocution. This involves describing the entity to be named (e.g., ". . . the thing that . . .") in lieu of naming it. Other naming errors involve substituting highly associated words (e.g., *fork* for *knife*) or words with shared prefixes (e.g., *telephone* for *television*). Spontaneous speech is often interrupted by prolonged pauses and the use of placeholders (e.g., ". . . well, well, you see . . .") to maintain audience attention. Neuroimaging research indicates that naming the same animals or objects from visual or auditory stimulation activates the same left inferior-temporal region (Tranel, Grabowski, Lyon, & Damasio, 2005).

This suggests that the mediation between word forms and their conceptual representations is independent of input modality. These findings may explain the pervasive nature of word-retrieval deficits in children with language and reading disabilities and their relationship to semantic problems that contribute to poor language comprehensions demonstrated by students with SLI and SLD when reading or listening. Word-finding difficulties are greatest when there are few cues for retrieval or associative links are weak, which has implications for the need to build more elaborate semantic networks in the process of expanding vocabulary in order to build stronger associative links.

COMPONENTS OF A COMPREHENSIVE DIAGNOSTIC APPROACH

Assessment of oral expression and listening comprehension generally takes place in the context of comprehensive language assessment, which may include the administration of standardized, norm-referenced tests and informal, criterion-referenced, or dynamic measures. It also involves gathering input about the student's strengths and weaknesses from parents, teachers, and students. It is helpful to keep in mind that a student's performance in any given context is controlled by a combination of intrapersonal variables (i.e., what the student brings to the context) as well as interpersonal and contextual variables (i.e., demands of the context). Rapid Reference 5.7 provides examples of these.

Norm-referenced testing has come under increasing scrutiny in recent years, with some school systems turning to alternatives allowed under IDEA, such as measuring change in the context of Response to Intervention programing to identify learning disabilities. Although multiple methods may provide a more-complete picture, we contend that norm-referenced tests continue to provide critical, if not essential, information for identifying language and literacy disorders among school-age students. The danger of failing to assess comprehensive elements of oral and written language or failing to assess elements beyond narrowly defined skills is that other aspects of a student's immediate needs

≡ *Rapid Reference 5.7*

....

Intra- and Interpersonal Variables

Intrapersonal variables can be related to (1) linguistic knowledge (e.g., phonology, morphology, syntax, semantics, and pragmatics or sound-word and sentence-discourse knowledge); (2) cognitive factors (e.g., memory, executive functions, reasoning, and problem-solving); and (3) social-emotional variables (e.g., self-awareness, confidence, self-regulation, and social skills).

Interpersonal or contextual variables can be related to (1) the school setting (e.g., environment, interactions, and school culture); (2) the curriculum (e.g., grade level, curriculum objectives, and learning outcomes); (3) society in general (e.g., culture, religion, societal roles, functions, and settings); and (4) the linguistic and cognitive demands of the assessment task.

Standardized testing seeks to control the context so that it is ostensibly the same for every student of the same age taking the same test. This assumes participants have experienced similar expectations in their schools and homes; however, that is a reasonable assumption for most students but not students who enter the test-taking context with linguistic or cultural experiences that differ widely from expectations of the test. When standardized testing is problematic, flexible and informal assessment methods may provide more valid information. Standardized tests should never be modified or translated for an individual participant. Such modifications invalidate scoring and compromise the test's future use with that person. Dynamic, informal assessment is a better solution for cultural-linguistic mismatches.

may be overlooked. The broader danger is that the student's comprehensive individualized educational needs may not be met.

Goals of Assessment

Assessment of oral expression and listening comprehension can be conducted for various purposes. Common goals of norm-referenced assessment include (1) contribution to identification of disability for the purpose of establishing eligibility for special education, (2) profiling patterns of strengths and weaknesses for the purpose of differential diagnosis of subtypes and intervention planning, and (3) detecting whether scores are significantly different when a student has been tested at two points in time for the purpose of understanding the student's needs or measuring progress. Goals of curriculum-based language assessment include assessing performance in natural contexts to understand influences of contextual factors and probing change in the context of curricular performance and intervention. Curriculum-based language assessment may be preferable for students whose cultural-linguistic experiences do not match those of available formal tests.

Assessment for Identifying Disability

Norm-referenced assessments of oral expression and listening comprehension contribute key information for identifying language-literacy disorder in all combinations (e.g., *SLI, SLI + dyslexia*, or *dyslexia*), which may be characterized by multiple labels (e.g., *language disorder, learning disability, oral and written language learning disability*), including both labels recognized by schools in the United States (i.e., *speech/language impaired, specific learning disability*). Under the regulations of IDEA, an individualized education program (IEP) committee determines whether a student meets criteria for a recognized disability and needs special education. To inform decisions about language-literacy disorders, standardized norm-referenced testing may be completed by school psychologists, speech-language pathologists, and other literacy or special education professionals. IEP committees who convene for the purpose of identifying disability and establishing eligibility for special education include a student's parent or guardian and general education teacher as well as professionals who can interpret the results of standardized testing and an administrator who can make placement commitments on behalf of the school district.

The objective of an expert diagnostician of language-literacy disabilities is to obtain reliable and valid measures and observations that can describe a student's difficulties dynamically in relation to the contexts in which the student is expected to perform. Ideally such testing should assess a representative sample of relevant language content, structure, and use across all language levels (i.e., sound, word, sentence, discourse) and across relevant modalities, which, for most school-age students, are listening, speaking, reading, and writing.

A major contribution of norm-referenced testing (sign language for some) is to identify whether a student meets criteria as having a language disorder or has abilities that fall within the range of normal (i.e., not impaired). Norm-referenced tests traditionally have been used to compare a given child's performance to a representative normative sample of same-age peers. The normative sample may or may not include students with the disability in question, but research has shown that tests are more discriminative when the normative sample does *not* include students with the disorder being targeted (Peña, Spaulding, & Plante, 2006).

Some norm-referenced tests focus on specific aspects of language development, such as tests of phonological awareness (e.g., Wagner, Torgesen, Rashotte, & Pearson, 2013); receptive and expressive vocabulary (e.g., Brownell, 2010;

Dunn & Dunn, 2007); basic concepts (e.g., Bracken, 2006; Wiig, 2004); syntax (e.g., Rice & Wexler, 2001); narrative language (e.g., Gillam & Pearson, 2004); and metalinguistics (Wiig & Secord, 2014); among others. Some tests, which may be called *batteries*, are broader in scope, comprising multiple subtests and tasks. Some of these are aimed primarily at assessing varied components of oral language, such as the Comprehensive Assessment of Spoken Language (CASL; Carrow-Woolfolk, 1999) or Test of Language Development–Intermediate (4th ed.) (TOLD-I:4; Hammill & Newcomer, 2008). One widely used oral language test, the Clinical Evaluation of Language Fundamentals (5th ed.) (CELF-5; Wiig, Semel, & Secord, 2013), incorporates probes of reading comprehension and written expression as well. The Oral-Written Language Scales (OWLS; Carrow-Woolfolk, 2011) offer separate scales for assessing oral and written language. The Woodcock-Johnson (4th ed.) (WJ-IV; Schrank, Mather, & McGrew, 2014) comprises three batteries. They measure *cognition* (including phonemic awareness as a cognitive skill), *achievement* (including tests of reading and writing across sound-word and sentence-discourse levels), and *oral language,* which was added in the fourth edition.

One new assessment tool—the Test of Integrated Language and Literacy Skills (TILLS; Nelson, Plante, Helm-Estabrooks, & Holtz, 2016)—is designed to measure the components of the quadrant model. That is, the TILLS measures the two dimensions—sound-word and sentence-discourse abilities—across listening, speaking, reading, and writing modalities. Among its parallel subtests across modalities are three sound-word subtests that use pseudowords—nonword repetition, nonword spelling, and nonword reading; two sentence-discourse subtests that use short "stories" using complex syntactic structures of academic language—listening comprehension and reading comprehension; and two sentence-discourse subtests that measure aspects of narrative discourse—story retelling and written expression-discourse score. Because the subtests of the TILLS are co-normed, they can be represented as a profile of sound-word-level and sentence-discourse-level skills across oral and written modalities (illustrated in the section "Assessment for Profiling Strengths and Weaknesses").

Norm-referenced tests provide a variety of scores, some of which are more psychometrically sound than others (see Rapid Reference 5.8 for an explanation of problems with validity of age- and grade-level scores). In comprehensive language tests, subtest scores can be summed to form a total language score or a composite score. Examiners should consult technical manuals of specific tests to learn whether composite scores represent hypothetical constructs (e.g., receptive versus expressive language or oral versus written language), or whether they are supported by factor analysis, such as the sound-word and sentence-discourse composites on

≡ *Rapid Reference 5.8*

....

Scores on Norm-Referenced Tests

Raw scores represent the actual point scores earned on a test or subtest.

Standard scores are derived to be on a common scale so they can be compared. Total or composite scores on language tests are often scaled with a mean of 100 and standard deviation of 15. Subtest scores are often scaled with a mean of 10 and standard deviation of 3.

Age- and grade-equivalent scores represent raw scores at the average for a particular chronological age group or grade level, defining a child who does not exist. They are interpolated in a way that ignores the naturally occurring overlap in performance across adjacent age groups or grade levels. Thus, they tend to be misleading and unreliable, sometimes suggesting that children are behind when they are not.

Percentile-rank scores indicate the relative standing based on the percentage of scores that occur above and below the student's score. Two distinct types of percentile scores may be reported in test manuals:

a. Actual percentile ranks reflect the percentage of participants who scored above the score in question in the empirical data for the standardization sample

b. Normal curve equivalent (NCE) percentiles reflect the percentage of people in a hypothetical normal distribution who would score above the score in question if the distribution were exactly normal

   The problem is that responses to language measures at different ages generally are *not* distributed normally. That is because different skills are just emerging, actively developing, or nearing completion at different ages. This produces skewed normative samples. One way to identify that a test manual is reporting NCE percentile scores is that they are identical across tests, which is not the case for true percentile ranks. For example, a standard score of 100 always corresponds to a NCE percentile of 50 because 50% of a hypothetically normal bell curve falls above the mean, but an actual percentile rank is not as predictable.

Co-normed test scores are those that have been developed using a common standardization group. They enable profiling and comparison of subtest scores. Scores from tests with different standardization samples cannot be compared directly because differences may reflect differences in the samples rather than within students. Scores from co-normed tests can be compared.

Percentile-rank and standard scores can be compared across ages to indicate growth.

Composite scores may or may not be based on factor analysis or other evidence. Test manuals should provide information about whether *identification core* composite scores are based on evidence to maximize sensitivity, specificity, and predictive values for differentiating between children with and without language disabilities. As a general rule of thumb, sensitivity and specificity should exceed 80%.

the TILLS (Nelson et al., 2016). Single subtest scores should be used for decision making only if a test's manual shows that the test was standardized in a manner to avoid systematic order effects (e.g., by using random sequences of subtests in establishing subtest norms).

If a test is to be used for the purpose of identifying a disorder, the test's manual should provide evidence supporting the selection of subtests that make up one or more age-based "identification core" composite scores for the test. The set of subtests that makes up an identification core composite score is rarely the same across the full age range of the test. Therefore, this evidence should establish the particular set of subtests within critical age bands whose scores yield the optimal balance between sensitivity (i.e., accuracy in identifying a high percentage of children known to have disorders by other current standards) and specificity (i.e., accuracy in identifying a high percentage of children without disorders known not to have the disorder in question by other current standards). It is critical that examiners employ these evidence-based cut scores to make identification decisions supported by evidence for a particular norm-referenced test and not on policy dictates that are constant. In other words, it is problematic to use a specific cut-off score, such as −1.5 or −2.0 SD below the mean. The use of invariant cut scores for identifying disability violates the 2004 IDEA mandate that assessment procedures must be valid for the purpose for which they are used. A single standard cut-score criterion applied across tests can underestimate disability for some tests and overestimate it for others (Spaulding, Plante, & Farinella, 2006).

Assessment for Profiling Strengths and Weaknesses

Language comprehension and oral expression are highly dependent on sentence- and discourse-level knowledge, which, along with vocabulary, should be assessed and profiled as part of comprehension assessment. These should be assessed in such a way that they can be contrasted with sound-word-level skills. An assessment profile that exposes weaknesses at the sentence-discourse level and relates them to strengths or weaknesses at the sound-word level may help to explain problems in reading comprehension as well as listening comprehension. Strengths at the sentence-discourse level and a pattern in which listening comprehension exceeds reading comprehension could be indicative of a specific reading impairment (often called *dyslexia*). Weaknesses in sentence-discourse-level skills in the presence of strong sound-word-level abilities in the areas of reading, decoding, and spelling could suggest a pattern of SLI that may not have been identified previously, which may be called *specific comprehension deficit* (Alonzo et al., 2016; Bishop & Snowling, 2004; Catts et al., 2005; Catts, Bridges, Little, & Tomblin, 2008).

Profiles can be helpful for showing relationships of listening comprehension and oral expression to each other, to component skills that contribute to each, and to similar skills used in other modalities (e.g., for reading comprehension and written expression). Profiles should be constructed using tasks that are similar enough that comparisons are meaningful, and they should be co-normed using the same standardization sample so that comparisons are valid (see Rapid Reference 5.8). Profiles can be used to explore component skills individually (e.g., vocabulary, syntax, and different discourse genres) to the degree that is possible. Such skills also should be explored in complex curriculum-relevant tasks that require their integration as part of gathering more fine-grained information about the nature of a student's strengths and weaknesses.

As noted previously in this chapter, it is difficult if not impossible to assess comprehension and expression in isolation of one another. Examples of formal tasks for assessing integrated language comprehension and formulation include narrative retelling, summarizing expository texts or documentaries, giving directions for playing a game, following spoken directions on paper or via actions, generating a response to a simulated social scene, answering questions after hearing a passage read aloud, combining sentences or sentence components orally, recalling sentences, and telling how vocabulary words are related in specific ways. Students who have comprehension deficits do not necessarily demonstrate the same level of difficulty with different discourse genres. For example, students with OWL LD may find narrative discourse relatively easier than expository discourse, whereas students with ASD may find expository discourse relatively easier than narrative discourse, but individual students' patterns may differ unrelated to particular subtypes.

Figure 5.4 provides an example of two students' differing test profiles, using data from the TILLS (Nelson et al., 2016). Figure 5.4a shows a profile for student A, a 9-year-1-month-old third-grader, who earned a sound-word composite standard score of 65 and a sentence-discourse composite standard score of 79. This profile suggests a need to work on both sound-word structure knowledge and on semantic relationships and social discourse. Although this student shows strength on the phonemic awareness task, the student's nonword repetition score is borderline, and the nonword reading, nonword spelling, and written expression word scores all suggest that the student has not generalized this phonemic awareness capability to reading decoding and spelling. Another thing that is remarkable about this student's profile is the drop in scores from immediate story retelling (administered first) to delayed story retelling (requested retelling of the same story about 15 minutes later). This student forgot the story entirely and retold material from the listening comprehension subtest instead. In addition to

(a)

		Oral Language										Written Language						
		Sound/Word Level				Sentence/Discourse Level						Sound/Word Level				Sent/Disc Level		
		PA	NW Rep	DSF	DSB	VA	LC	FD	SR	DSR	SC	NW Read	RF	NW Spell	WE-Word	RC	WE-Disc	WE-Sent
Standard Score		9	7	6	4	3	7	4	7	0	3	6	4	4	1	2	13	6

(b)

		Oral Language										Written Language						
		Sound/Word Level				Sentence/Discourse Level						Sound/Word Level				Sent/Disc Level		
		PA	NW Rep	DSF	DSB	VA	LC	FD	SR	DSR	SC	NW Read	RF	NW Spell	WE-Word	RC	WE-Disc	WE-Sent
Standard Score		1	9	6	4	8	7	3	10	9	6	2	0	4	1	5	2	10

Figure 5.4. Profiles for Two Students Who Completed the Test of Integrated Language and Literacy Skills (TILLS; Nelson et al., 2016). Both Demonstrate Oral Written Language Learning Disability (OWL LD) but with Differing Profiles of Strengths and Weaknesses at Sound-Word and Sentence-Discourse Levels. (a) Student A, a 9-year-1-Month-Old Third-Grade Girl Has a Sound-Word Composite Standard Score of 65 and a Sentence-Discourse Composite Standard Score of 79. (b). Student B, a 9-year-4-Month-Old Third-Grade Boy Has a Sound-Word Composite Standard Score of 48 and a Sentence-Discourse Composite Standard Score of 73.

Note: Key: PA = Phonemic Awareness; NW Rep = Nonword Repetition; DSF = Digit Span Forward; DSB = Digit Span Backward; VA = Vocabulary Awareness; LC = Listening Comprehension; FD = Following Directions; SR = Story Retelling; DSR = Delayed Story Retelling; SC = Social Communication; NW Read = Nonword Reading; RF = Reading Fluency; NW Spell = Nonword Spelling; WE-Word = Written Expression–Word; RC = Reading Comprehension; WE-Disc = Written Expression–Discourse; WE-Sent = Written Expression–Sentence.

Source: From the Test of Integrated Language and Literacy Skills™ © 2016 Brookes Publishing Co.; used with permission of Brookes Publishing.

word study related to vocabulary and word structure, this student could benefit from learning strategies for remembering new material in the curriculum that might be understood but then forgotten. Memory deficits could also be a contributor to this student's low score on following directions, but memory alone cannot explain this student's difficulties at the sound-word and sentence-discourse levels.

Figure 5.4b shows a profile for student B, who earned a sound-word composite standard score of 48 and a sentence-discourse composite standard score of 73. This student has a similar profile to student A in some respects, but does not show the same strength in phonemic awareness as student A. However, this student demonstrates strong skills on vocabulary awareness, which student A did not. This demonstrates that student B was able to pick two out of three words (e.g., *kite–airplane–train*) that go together and tell why and then to switch cognitive set to pick out two other words from the same set of three and tell why they go together in a different way. Student B also could complete the story retelling task equally well on immediate retelling and delayed retelling, even though following directions was as problematic for him as it was for student A. On the companion Student Language Scale (SLS; Nelson, Howes, & Anderson, 2018), student B's general education teacher responded to the question about what one thing would help him do better at school by recommending "clearly establishing expectations in simple [underlining in original] non-complex steps."

As noted previously in this chapter and illustrated with these two examples, integrated language skills can reflect a combination of language knowledge and related cognitive abilities (attention, memory, executive function, etc.). Disentangling the effects of cognitive and linguistic factors may be difficult. To do so, examiners might consider whether a particular assessment task incorporates cognitive factors such as memory and attention deliberately as a controlled aspect of the measurement construct or whether the task reflects attempts to minimize the influence of memory (e.g., by providing the three words in print in the vocabulary awareness task previously described). An example of an assessment task

CAUTION

Many norm-referenced tests of intelligence, language, and learning provide composite or index scores. There can be a temptation to compare composite or index standard scores based on the examiner's perceived needs or to compare scores that come from different tests. This can lead to faulty interpretations of a student's strengths or weaknesses. The standard scores on two sets of composite or index scores should be compared only when there is no overlap in subtest content (i.e., when they are orthogonal) and when composite or subtest scores come from a test that was co-normed on the same standardization sample.

that intentionally incorporates memory demands into language assessment is a nonword repetition task, such as the one on the TILLS, or a sentence repetition task, such as recalling sentences on the CELF-5 (Wiig et al., 2013). Direction-following and story-retelling tasks also incorporate memory for different types of discourse as a purposeful measurement trait. Delayed story retelling (on the TILLS) taps into short-term memory, but of a different type.

Assessment for Documenting Change

Norm-referenced tests are not well suited for monitoring progress based on intervention or within a Response to Intervention framework (Fuchs, Mock, Morgan, & Young, 2003). This is because they sample broadly, often with the goal of minimizing the number of items assessed at any one level within a particular subtest. Although formal tests are not good for progress monitoring, they can be used to document change over more extended time periods (e.g., 6 months), that is, if they have been validated for that purpose.

The TILLS and the WJ-IV are examples of formal tests that report data regarding how much of a difference is required to document a "true difference" between scores earned by a particular student at two points in time. For the TILLS, "true change" scores are provided in 68% and 90% confidence intervals of a student's score, which reflect the standard error of the estimate (SEE) for each subtest. These values were calculated using test-retest reliability data (correlations) to account for the score variance that might be expected simply by testing students at two points in time. The "true change" values provide the number of standard points that would have to increase (or decrease) from the first to second testing session for the clinician to conclude that true change had occurred on that measure. Even so, change scores should be interpreted with caution. For example, a student could move to a higher age bracket for the second testing. That could require passing more items to reach the same standard score relative to the older age group, which could make it appear that the student has not progressed, even though the same score is mostly due to a psychometric artifact.

When the purpose of assessment is to monitor progress in response to intervention or to decide whether formal assessment and special services might be needed, a better approach is to use standardized probes that can be repeated at more frequent intervals, such as monthly or biweekly. These tap into an integrated version of the targeted skill to observe whether the student can generalize it to similar naturalistic tasks with new content. Probes should not simply repeat the intervention task, and care should be taken not to send unhelpful signals to students. For example, reading lists of words repeatedly until they can be read more fluently could create the impression that reading success is defined by the number of words that can be read correctly within a minute rather than understanding what one has read.

Probes may be designed to assess sentence-discourse abilities that are associated with listening comprehension or oral expression. For example, students could be asked to summarize excerpts from their actual grade-level textbooks read aloud. Their efforts then could be scored with rubrics or by quantifying the number of content units retained and the results could be graphed. Or students could be asked to list new vocabulary words from a particular lesson. Their knowledge of the new words could be probed immediately and repeatedly over additional days to assess retention and retrieval.

Dynamic assessment offers another framework for assessing change within a facilitative environment, such as within an intervention session. Dynamic assessment involves the three general phases: test-teach-retest. It can be particularly helpful in curriculum-based language assessment and intervention, as illustrated in the following section. It also can be particularly useful for assessing the learning potential of culturally linguistically diverse students for whom formal norm-referenced testing, particularly in their second language, is inappropriate.

Curriculum-Based Assessment and Intervention

Curriculum-based language assessment (CBLA) can be differentiated from other forms of curriculum-based measurement (CBM) by the primary question it is designed to answer (Nelson, 1989, 2010). CBM uses repeated probes to answer whether the student is learning a designated aspect of the curriculum, such as how to read single words fluently. CBLA uses actions guided by four questions to address the question of whether the student has the language skills to learn a designated aspect of the curriculum: (1) What does the context require? (This is followed by analysis of the cognitive-linguistic demands of the curricular task.) (2) What does the student currently do when attempting the task? (This is accompanied by ongoing analysis of strengths and weaknesses as the student attempts the task.) (3) What might the student learn to do differently? (This involves the use of dynamic assessment techniques to figure out what works best to help the student make new connections.) (4) How should the task be modified to help the student be more successful without making him or her dependent on the help? (This involves consideration of the need for accommodations or for new ways to present the information to the student.)

CBLA depends on information gathered during formal assessment and information gathered from those who know the student best (e.g., parent, teacher, and student) to identify and prioritize aspects of the curriculum that are particularly problematic for the student. This can be done with the assistance of behavioral observations that focus on language and communication (e.g., listening, speaking, reading, and writing) and by asking about the student's ability to respond to grade-level curriculum standards (Wiig & Secord, 2003). Prioritization of parts of the curriculum to target also can be facilitated by using rating scales with multiple informants (e.g., the Student Language Scale; Nelson et al., 2018).

Once an area of the curriculum has been selected, a text sample, math story problem, or other language sample is drawn from that part of the curriculum, so it can be used for dynamic assessment and intervention. For example, a teacher or clinician could read a passage to a student and request an independent retelling or summarization. This performance would be analyzed to identify aspects of the task that the student may have overlooked or has not yet mastered. Then, the information from this "test" step can be used to inform the "teach" step, in which the adult mediates the task by framing, focusing, and feeding back information the student might use to make sense of the task. Finally, the adult mediator moves to the second "test" phase by removing the instructional scaffolds and making sure that the student can now apply such skills and strategies more independently and with a novel set of curricular materials. Finally, the adult leads the IEP team in deciding whether the student needs accommodations or modification in how the task is presented within the curriculum.

CONCLUSION

Whether formal or informal, standardized or individualized assessment techniques are primary. The process of learning about a student's strengths and weaknesses in listening comprehension and oral expression plays a key role in knowing what to do next for students with SLD. Without this piece, it would be easy to overlook information that could provide the key to understanding students with SLD and how to help them.

🐾 TEST YOURSELF 🐾

1. **Which description best fits children with *specific language impairment*?**
    (a) They are unlikely to be identified until later in their school-age years because their oral language is better than their written language.

   (b) They are likely to produce shorter sentences with more grammatical errors and fewer different words than same-age peers.

   (c) They are likely to have problems with oral expression, but not with listening or reading comprehension.

2. **Which description best fits children with *dyslexia*?**

   (a) In later grades, they may take longer than peers to comprehend higher-level written texts because of reading decoding weaknesses, but, due to their relatively strong sentence-discourse-level language skills, they may comprehend grade-level texts successfully.

   (b) In early grades they often show oral language difficulties, but they are unlikely to show problems with phonological awareness, reading decoding, and spelling.

   (c) They are unlikely to be identified until later grades because their problems are primarily in the area of language comprehension.

3. **Which description best fits children with *specific comprehension deficit*?**

   (a) They may be difficult to identify early because their reading decoding skills are better than their language comprehension skills.

   (b) What is "specific" is that their language comprehension is better than their language expression.

   (c) Their oral comprehension is better than their reading comprehension because of their reading decoding problems.

4. **Which of the following best represents a primary message of this chapter?**

   (a) Oral and written language developments are separate developmental achievements.

   (b) Reading and writing are related to basic language abilities.

   (c) Reading and writing *are* language abilities.

5. **A key reason that the *DSM-5* definition of language disorder removed the subtype distinction between receptive and expressive subtypes is the lack of scientific evidence that language comprehension can be measured separately from language expression. True or false?**

6. **Which of the following is *not* generally listed as one of the five language domains?**

   (a) Phonology

   (b) Morphology

   (c) Syntax

   (d) Attention

   (e) Pragmatics

7. **Language skills can be distinguished based on whether they are "phonological" or "non-phonological." Which of the following skills would represent the non-phonological dimension?**

   (a) Reading nonsense words out loud

   (b) Spelling nonsense words

    (c) Repeating nonsense words out loud

    (d) Repeating a word, but without its initial sound

    (e) Retelling a story

8. **Current DNA testing enables diagnosticians to pinpoint the presence of genetic markers for specific language impairment. True or false?**

9. **Which of the following does *not* fit in the group of cognitive correlates of language development?**

    (a) Attention

    (b) Syntax

    (c) Working memory

    (d) Executive function

10. **Which of the following is an example of a contextual variable that should be considered during assessment of language?**

    (a) Social-emotional variables demonstrated by the child

    (b) Sentence-discourse-level knowledge in comprehension and formulation

    (c) The language demands of the curriculum

    (d) Cognitive correlates

Answers: 1. b; 2. a; 3. a; 4. c; 5. True; 6. d; 7. e; 8. False; 9. b; 10. c.

REFERENCES

Adams, A. M. & Gathercole, S. W. (2000). Limitations in working memory: Implications for language development. *International Journal of Language and Communication Disorders, 35,* 95–116.

Alonzo, C. N., Yeomans-Maldonado, G., Murphy, K. A., Bevens, B., & Language and Reading Research Consortium (LARRC).(2016). Predicting second grade listening comprehension using pre-kindergarten measures. *Topics in Language Disorders, 36,* 312–333.

American Psychiatric Association. (2013). *Diagnostic and statistical manual of mental disorders* (5th ed.). Washington, DC: Author.

Anderson, V., Anderson, D., & Anderson, P. (2006). Comparing attentional skills in children with acquired and developmental nervous system disorders. *Journal of the International Neuropsychological Society, 12,* 519–531.

Awh, E., Barton, B., & Vogel, E. K. (2007). Visual working memory represents a fixed number of items regardless of complexity. *Psychological Science, 18,* 622–628.

Baddeley, A. S. (1986). *Working memory.* Oxford, UK: Clarendon Press.

Baddeley, A. S. (1996). Working memory. *Science, 255,* 556–559.

Badian, N. A. (1999). Reading disability defined as a discrepancy between listening and reading comprehension: A longitudinal study of stability, gender differences, and prevalence. *Journal of Learning Disabilities, 32,* 138–148.

Bashir, A. S. & Singer, B. D. (2006). Assisting students in becoming self-regulated writers. In T. Ukrainetz (Ed.), *Contextualized language intervention: Scaffolding pre-K–12 literacy achievement* (pp. 565–598). Eau Claire, WI: Thinking Publications.

Bedore, L. & Leonard, L. (1998). Specific language impairment and grammatical morphology: A discriminant function analysis. *Journal of Speech, Language and Hearing Research, 41,* 1185–1192.

Berninger, V., Abbott, R., Cook, C. R., & Nagy, W. (2016). Relationships of attention and executive functions to oral language, reading, and writing skills and systems in middle childhood and early adolescence. *Journal of Learning Disabilities,* 1–16. doi: 10.1177/0022219415617167

Berninger, V. W. & Wolf, B. J. (2016). *Dyslexia, dysgraphia, OWL LD, and dyscalculia* (2nd ed.). Baltimore, MD: Brookes.

Bishop, D.V.M. (2014). Ten questions about terminology for children with unexplained language problems. *International Journal of Language and Communication Disorders, 49,* 389–415.

Bishop, D.V.M. & Snowling, M. J. (2004). Developmental dyslexia and specific language impairment: Same or different? *Psychological Bulletin, 130*(6), 858–886.

Boada, R., Willcutt, E. G., & Pennington, B. F. (2012). Understanding the comorbidity between dyslexia and attention-deficit/hyperactivity disorder. *Topics in Language Disorders, 32,* 264–284.

Bracken, B. (2006). *Bracken Basic Concept Scale.* San Antonio. TX: Pearson.

Brownell, R. (2010). *Receptive and Expressive One-Word Picture Vocabulary Tests* (4th ed.). San Antonio, TX: Pearson.

Bruner, J. (1975). The ontogenesis of speech acts. *Journal of Child Language, 2,* 1–19.

Carrow-Woolfolk, E. (1999). *Comprehensive Assessment of Spoken Language (CASL).* Bloomington, MN: Pearson Assessments.

Carrow-Woolfolk, E. (2011). *Oral and Written Language Scales (OWLS).* Torrance, CA: Western Psychological Services.

Catts, H. W., Adlof, S. M., Hogan, T. P., & Weismer, S. E. (2005). Are specific language impairment and dyslexia distinct disorders? *Journal of Speech, Language, and Hearing Research, 48*(6), 1378–1396.

Catts, H. W., Adlof, S. M., & Weismer, S. E. (2006). Language deficits in poor comprehenders: A case for the simple view of reading. *Journal of Speech, Language, and Hearing Research, 49,* 278–293.

Catts, H. W., Bridges, M. S., Little, T. D., & Tomblin, J. B. (2008). Reading achievement growth in children with language impairments. *Journal of Speech, Language, and Hearing Research, 51,* 1569–1579.

Colombo, J. (2004). Visual attention in infancy: Process and product in early cognitive development. In M. I. Posner (Ed.), *Cognitive neuroscience of attention* (pp. 329–341). New York, NY: Guilford.

Conti-Ramsden, G., & Botting, N. (1999). Classification of children with specific language impairment: Longitudinal considerations. *Journal of Speech, Language, and Hearing Research, 42,* 1195–1204.

Cowan, N. (1996). Short-term memory, working memory, and their importance in language processing. *Topics in Language Disorders, 17,* 1–18.

Deevy, P., & Leonard, L. (2004). The comprehension of wh- questions in children with specific language impairment. *Journal of Speech, Language, & Hearing Research, 47,* 802–815.

Diamond, A. (2013). Executive functions. *Annual Review of Psychology, 64,* 135–168.

Dunn, L. M., & Dunn, D. M. (2007). *Peabody Picture Vocabulary Test* (4th ed.). San Antonio, TX: Pearson.

Eckert, M. A., Leonard, C. M., Richards, T. L., Aylward, E. H., Thomson, J., & Berninger, V. W. (2003). Anatomical correlates of dyslexia: Frontal and cerebellar findings. *Brain, 126,* 482–494.

Ehren, B. J., Murza, K. A., & Malani, M. D. (2012). Disciplinary literacy from a speech-language pathologist's perspective. *Topics in Language Disorders, 32,* 85–98. doi: 10.1097/ TLD.0b013e318244e8d4

Fang, X. (2012). Language correlates of disciplinary literacy. *Topics in Language Disorders, 32,* 19–34.

Fields, R. D. (2008, March). *Scientific American,* pp. 54–61.

Finley, B. L. (2005). Rethinking developmental neurobiology. In M. Tomasello & D. I. Slobin (Eds.), *Beyond nature-nurture: Essays in honor of Elizabeth Bates* (pp. 195–218). Mahwah, NJ: Erlbaum.

Fisher, S. A. (2006). Tangled webs: Tracing the connections between genes and cognition. *Cognition, 101,* 270–297.

Fuchs, D., Mock, D., Morgan, P. L., & Young, C. L. (2003). Responsiveness-to-intervention: Definitions, evidence and implications for the learning disabilities construct. *Learning Disabilities Research and Practice, 18,* 157–171.

Fulbright, R. K., Jenner, A. R., Mencl, W. E., Pugh, K. R., Shaywitz, B. A., Shaywitz, S. E., . . . & Gore, J. C. (1999). The cerebellum's role in reading: A functional MR imaging study. *American Journal of Neuroradiology, 20,* 1925–1930.

Gentner, D., & Namy, L. L. (2006). Analogical processes in language learning. *Current Directions in Psychological Science, 15,* 297–301.

German, D. J., & Newman, R. S. (2004). The impact of lexical factors on children's word-finding errors. *Journal of Speech, Language, and Hearing Research, 47,* 624–636.

Gilger, J. W., & Wise, S. W. (2004). Genetic correlates of language and literacy impairments. In C. A. Stone, E. R. Silliman, B. J. Ehren, & K. Apel (Eds.), *Handbook of language and literacy disorders* (pp. 25–48). New York, NY: Guilford.

Gillam, R. B., & Pearson, N. A. (2004). *Test of Narrative Language (TNL).* Austin, TX: PRO-ED.

Gough, P. B., & Tunmer, W. E. (1986). Decoding and reading disability. *Remedial and Special Education, 7,* 6–10.

Hammill, D. D., & Newcomer, P. L. (2008). *Test of Language Development—Intermediate* (4th ed.). Austin, TX: PRO-ED.

Harris, K. R., Graham, S., Mason, L. H., & Friedlander, B. (2008). *Powerful writing strategies for all students.* Baltimore, MD: Brookes.

Ho, H-Z., Baker, L. A., & Decker, S. N. (2005). Covariation between intelligence and speed of cognitive processing: Genetic and environmental influences. *Behavior Genetics, 18,* 247–261.

Hoover, W. A., & Gough, P. B. (1990). The simple view of reading. *Reading and Writing, 2,* 127–160.

Huth, A. G., de Heer, W. A., Griffiths, T. L., Theunissen, F. E., & Gallant, J. L. (2016). Natural speech reveals the semantic maps that tile human cerebral cortex. *Nature, 532,* 453–472. doi: 10.1038/nature17637

Jaffe-Dax, S., Raviv, O., Jacoby, N., Loewenstein, Y., & Ahissar, M. (2015). A computational model of implicit memory captures dyslexics' perceptual deficits. *The Journal of Neuroscience, 35,* 12116–12126.

Joanisse, M. F. (2004). Specific language impairments in children phonology, semantics, and the English past tense. *Current Directions in Psychological Science, 13*(4), 156–160.

Kail, R. V. (2007). Longitudinal evidence that increases in processing speed and working memory enhance children's reasoning. *Psychological Science, 18,* 312–313.

Kuhl, P. K. (2004). Early language acquisition: Cracking the speech code. *Neuroscience, 5,* 831–843.

Leonard, C. M., Eckert, M. A., Given, B., Virginia, B., & Eden, G. (2006). Individual differences in anatomy predict reading and oral language impairments in children. *Brain, 129,* 3329–3342.

Leonard, C. M., Lombardino, L. J., Walsh, K., Eckert, M. A., Mockler, J. L., Rowe, L. A., . . . & DeBose, C. B. (2002). Anatomical risk factors that distinguish dyslexia from SLI predict reading skill in normal children. *Journal of Communication Disorders, 35*(6), 501–531.

Leonard, L. B. (1998). *Children with specific language impairment.* Cambridge, MA: MIT Press.

Leonard, L. B. (2009). Is expressive language disorder an accurate diagnostic category? *American Journal of Speech-Language Pathology, 18,* 115–123.

Leonard, L. B., Weismer, S. E., Miller, C. A., Francis, D. J., Tomblin, J. B., & Kail, R. V. (2007). Speed of processing, working memory, and language impairment in children. *Journal of Speech, Language, and Hearing Research, 50,* 408–428.

Lonigan, C., & Milburn, T. (2017). Identifying the dimensionality of oral language skills of children with typical development in preschool through fifth grade. *Journal of Speech, Language, and Hearing Research, 60,* 2185–2198.

Manly, T., Anderson, V., Nimmo-Smith, I., Turner, A., Watson, P., & Robertson, I. (2001). The differential assessment of children's attention: The Test of Everyday Attention for Children (TEA-Ch), normative sample and ADHD performance. *Journal of Child Psychology and Psychiatry, 42,* 1065–1081.

Mashburn, A. J., & Myers, S. S. (2010). Advancing research on children with speech-language impairment: An introduction to the early childhood longitudinal study—Kindergarten cohort. *Language, Speech, and Hearing Services in Schools, 41,* 61–69.

McGregor, K. K., Newman, R. M., Reilly, R., & Capone, N. C. (2002). Semantic representation and naming in children with specific language impairment. *Journal of Speech, Language, and Hearing Research, 45,* 998–1014.

Meng, H., Smith, S. D., Hager, K., Held, M., Liu, J., Olson, R. K., . . . & Somlo, S. (2005). DCDC2 is associated with reading disability and modulates neuronal development in the brain. *Proceedings of the National Academy of Sciences of the United States of America, 102*(47), 17053–17058.

Miller, G. (1956). The magical number seven plus or minus two: Some limits in our capacity for processing information. *Psychological Review, 63,* 81–97.

Montgomery, J. W. (2003). Working memory and comprehension in children with specific language impairment: What we know so far. *Journal of Communication Disorders, 36,* 221–231.

Montgomery, J. W., & Evans, J. L. (2009). Complex sentence processing and working memory in children with specific language impairment. *Journal of Speech, Language, and Hearing Research, 52,* 269–288.

Montgomery, J. W., Evans, J. L., & Gillam, R. (2009). Relationship of auditory attention on complex sentence comprehension in children with specific language impairment: A preliminary study. *Applied Psycholinguistics, 30,* 123–151.

Montgomery, J. W., Gillam, R. B., & Evans, J. L. (2016). Syntactic versus memory accounts of the sentence comprehension deficits of specific language impairment: Looking back, looking ahead. *Journal of Speech, Language, and Hearing Research, 59,* 1491–1504. doi: 10.1044/2016_JSLHR-L-15-0325

Mueller, K. L., & Tomblin, J. B. (2012). Examining the comorbidity of language impairment and attention-deficit/hyperactivity disorder. *Topics in Language Disorders, 32,* 228–246.

Nation, K., Clarke, P., Marshall, C. M., & Durand, M. (2004). Hidden language impairments in children: Parallels between poor reading comprehension and specific language impairment? *Journal of Speech, Language, and Hearing Research, 47*(1), 199–211.

Nelson, N. W. (1989). Curriculum-based language assessment and intervention. *Language, Speech, and Hearing Services in Schools, 20*(2), 170–184.

Nelson, N. W. (2010). *Language and literacy disorders: Infancy through adolescence.* Boston, MA: Allyn & Bacon.

Nelson, N. W. (2016). Language XX: What shall it be called and why does it matter? *International Journal of Speech-Language Pathology, 18,* 229–240. doi: 10.3109/17549507.2015.1126643

Nelson, N. W., Howes, B. M., & Anderson, M. A. (2018). *Student language scale and manual.* Baltimore, MD: Brookes.

Nelson, N. W., Plante, E., Helm-Estabrooks, N., & Hotz, G., (2016). *Test of Integrated Language and Literacy Skills (TILLS).* Baltimore, MD: Brookes.

Nippold, M. A., Hesketh, L. J., Duthie, J. K., & Mansfield, T. C. (2005). Conversational versus expository discourse: A study of syntactic development in children, adolescents, and adults. *Journal of Speech, Language, and Hearing Research, 40,* 1048–1064.

Nippold, M. A., Mansfield, R. C., Billow, J. L., & Tomblin, J. B. (2008). Expository discourse in adolescents with a history of language impairments: Examining syntactic development. *American Speech-Language Pathology, 17,* 256–266.

Nippold, M. A., Mansfield, R. C., Billow, J. L., & Tomblin, J. B. (2009). Syntactic development in adolescents with a history of language impairments: A follow-up investigation. *American Journal of Speech-Language Pathology, 18,* 241–251.

Paulesu, E., Frith, U., Snowling, M., Gallagher, A., Morton, J., Frackowiak, R.S.J., & Frith, C. D. (1996). Is developmental dyslexia a disconnection syndrome? Evidence from PET scanning. *Brain, 119,* 143–157.

Peña, E. D., Spaulding, T. J., & Plante, E. (2006). The composition of normative groups and diagnostic decision making: Shooting ourselves in the foot. *American Journal of Speech-Language Pathology, 15*, 247–254.

Pinborough-Zimmerman, J., Satterfield, R., Miller, J., Bilder, D., Hossain, S., & McMahon, W. (2007). Communication disorders and comorbid intellectual disability, autism, and emotional/behavioral disorders. *American Journal of Speech-Language Pathology, 16*, 359–367.

Ramus, F., Marshall, C. R., Rosen, S., & van der Lely, H.K.J. (2013). Phonological deficits in specific language impairment and developmental dyslexia: Towards a multidimensional model. *Brain, 136*, 630–645.

Redmond, S. M. (2002). The use of rating scales with children who have language impairments. *The American Journal of Speech-Language Pathology, 11*, 124–138.

Rice, M., Taylor, C., & Zubrick, S. (2008). Language outcomes of 7-year-old children with and without a history of late language emergence at 24 months. *Journal of Speech, Language, and Hearing Research, 51*, 394–407.

Rice, M. L., & Wexler, K. (2001). *Rice Wexler Test of Early Grammatical Impairment.* San Antonio, TX: The Psychological Corporation/Pearson.

Roncadin, C., Pascual-Leone, J., Rich, J. B., & Dennis, M. (2007). Developmental relations between working memory and inhibitory control. *Journal of the International Neuropsychological Society, 13*, 59–67.

Scarborough, H. S. (2005). Developmental relationships between language and reading: Reconciling a beautiful hypothesis with some ugly facts. In H. W. Catts & A. G. Kamhi (Eds.), *The connections between language and reading disabilities* (pp. 3–22). Mahwah, NJ: Erlbaum.

Schrank, F. A., Mather, N., & McGrew, K. S. (2014). *Woodcock-Johnson IV* [Tests of Cognitive Abilities, Tests of Achievement, Tests of Oral Language]. Rolling Meadows, IL: Riverside.

Semrud-Clikeman, M., Steingard, R., Filipek, P., Biederman, J., Bekken, K., & Renshaw, P. (2000). Using MRI to examine brain-behavior relationships in males with attention deficit disorder with hyperactivity. *Journal of the American Academy of Child and Adolescent Psychiatry, 39*, 477–484.

Shanahan, T., & Shanahan, C. (2012). What is disciplinary literacy and why does it matter? *Topics in Language Disorders, 32*, 7–18. doi: 10.1097/TLD.0b013e318244557a

Shaywitz, B. A., Lyon, G. R., & Shaywitz, S. E. (2006). The role of functional magnetic resonance imaging in understanding reading and dyslexia. *Developmental Neuropsychology, 30*(1), 613–632.

Shaywitz, B. A., Shaywitz, S. E., Blachman, B. A., Pugh, K. R. Fulbright, R. K., Skudlarski, P., . . . & Gore, J. C. (2004). Development of left occipitotemporal systems for skilled reading in children after a phonologically based intervention. *Biological Psychiatry, 55*, 926–933.

Shaywtiz, S. E., & Shaywitz, B. A. (2001). The neurobiology of reading and dyslexia. *Focus on Basics Connecting Research and Practice, 5* (A), 11–15.

Silliman, E. R., & Berninger, V. W. (2011). Cross-disciplinary dialogue about the nature of oral and written language problems in the context of developmental, academic, and phenotypic profiles. *Topics in Language Disorders, 31*, 6–23. doi: 10.1097/TLD.0b013e31820a0b5b

Spaulding, T. J., Plante, E., & Farinella, K. A. (2006). Eligibility criteria for language impairment: Is the low end of normal always appropriate? *Language, Speech, and Hearing Services in Schools, 37*, 61–72.

Sun, L., & Wallach, G. P. (2014). Language disorders are learning disabilities: Challenges on the divergent and diverse paths to language learning disability. *Topics in Language Disorders, 34*, 25–38.

Tomblin, J. B., Mainela-Arnold, E., & Zhang, X. (2007). Procedural learning in adolescents with and without specific language impairments. *Language Learning Development, 3*, 269–293.

Tomblin, J. B., & Mueller, K. L. (2012). How can comorbidity with attention-deficit/hyperactivity disorder aid understanding of language and speech disorders? *Topics in Language Disorders, 32*, 198–206.

Tomblin, J. B., & Zhang, X. (2006). The dimensionality of language ability in school-age children. *Journal of Speech, Language, and Hearing Research, 49*, 1193–1208.

Tranel, D., Grabowski, T. J., Lyon, J., & Damasio, H. (2005). Naming the same entities from visual or from auditory stimulation engages similar regions of the left inferotemporal cortices. *Journal of Cognitive Neuroscience, 17*, 1293–1305.

Tunmer, W. E., & Chapman, J. W. (2007). Language-related differences between discrepancy-defined and non-discrepancy-defined poor readers: A longitudinal study of dyslexia in New Zealand. *Dyslexia, 13*(1), 42–66.

Tunmer, W. E., & Chapman, J. W. (2012). The simple view of reading redux: Vocabulary knowledge and the independent components hypothesis. *Journal of Learning Disabilities, 45*, 453–466.

Ullman, M., & Pierpoint, E. (2005). Specific language impairment is not specific to language: The procedural deficit hypothesis. *Cortex, 41*, 399–433.

US Department of Education, National Center for Education Statistics.(2000). *ECLS-K base year restricted-use child file* [CD-ROM and user's manual] (NCES No. 2000-097). Washington, DC: Author.

Wagner, R. K., Torgesen, J. K., Rashotte, C. A., & Pearson, N. A. (2013). *Comprehensive Test of Phonological Processing* (2nd ed.). San Antonio, TX: PRO-ED.

Weismer, S. E. (2007). Typical talkers, late talkers, and children with specific language impairment: A language endowment spectrum? In R. Paul (Ed.), *Language disorders from a developmental perspective* (pp. 83–101). Mahwah, NJ: Erlbaum.

Weismer, S. E., Evans, J., & Hesketh, L. J. (1999). An examination of verbal working memory capacity in children with specific language impairment. *Journal of Speech, Language, and Hearing Research, 42*, 1249–1260.

Weismer, S. E., Plante, E., Jones, M., & Tomblin, J. B. (2005). A functional magnetic resonance imaging investigation of verbal working memory in adolescents with specific language impairment. *Journal of Speech, Language, and Hearing Research, 48*, 405–425.

Wiig, E. H. (2004). *Wiig Assessment of Basic Concepts*. Greenville, SC: Super Duper Publications.

Wiig, E. H., Nielsen, N. P., Londos, E., & Minthon, L. (2009). A quick test of cognitive speed as a measure of normal aging and aging with dementia. In Q. Gariepy & R. Menard (Eds.), *Handbook of cognitive aging: Causes, processes and effects* (pp. 151–179). New York, NY: Nova Science Publishers.

Wiig, E. H., Nielsen, N. P., Minthon, L., & Warkentin, S. (2002). *A quick test of cognitive speed (AQT)*. San Antonio, TX: Pearson/Psych Corp.

Wiig, E. H., & Secord, W. (2003). *Classroom Performance Assessment (CPA)*. Sedona, AZ, and Arlington, TX: Red Rock Publications & Schema Press.

Wiig, E. H., & Secord, W. A. (2014). *Clinical Evaluation of Language Fundamentals Metalinguistics* (5th ed.). San Antonio, TX: Pearson.

Wiig, E. H., Semel, E., & Secord, W. A. (2013). *Clinical Evaluation of Language Fundamentals* (5th ed.). San Antonio, TX: Pearson.

Wiig, E. H., & Wilson, C. C. (1994). Is a question a question? Differential patterns in question answering by students with LLD. *Language, Speech, and Hearing Services in Schools, 25*, 250–259.

Wiig, E. H., Zureich, P., & Chan, H. N. (2000). A clinical rationale for assessing rapid, automatic naming in children with language disorders. *Journal of Learning Disabilities, 33*, 369–374.

Wolf, M., Bowers, P. G., & Biddle, K. (2000). Naming-speed processes, timing, and reading: A conceptual review. *Journal of Learning Disability, 33*, 387–407.

World Health Organization. (2005). *International statistical classification of diseases and related health problems* (10th rev.). Geneva, Switzerland: Author.

Six

NONVERBAL LEARNING DISABILITIES

Margaret Semrud-Clikeman

The construct of nonverbal learning disabilities (NLDs) is a fairly new diagnosis and was first introduced by Myklebust and Johnson (Johnson, 1987; Myklebust, 1975). This constellation of areas of difficulty was further researched by Byron Rourke and colleagues in the 1980s and 1990s. The incidence of NLD has been estimated to be approximately 1% of the general population or 5% of the population of individuals with learning disabilities (Rourke, 1988). Cognitive and academic difficulties have been identified in the areas of visual-spatial processing, mathematics, handwriting, social cognition, and in some cases attention (Pennington, 2008; Rourke, Ahmad, Collins, Hayman-Abello, & Warriner, 2002). Cognitive and academic strengths include a well-developed vocabulary, reading recognition ability, and rote language skills (Rourke & Tsatsanis, 2000).

One of the difficulties with the construct of NLD is that the definition has continued to evolve and different clinical laboratories and practitioners use various methods for identifying

C A U T I O N
....
There is no universally agreed-on definition of an NLD.

individuals with NLD (Mammarella & Cornoldi, 2014; Ris & Nortz, 2008). In the original work with NLD, spatial and temporal perception, handwriting, and mathematics were identified as key components for the disorder as well as a

Essentials of Specific Learning Disability Identification, Second Edition.
Edited by Vincent C. Alfonso and Dawn P. Flanagan.
© 2018 John Wiley & Sons, Inc. Published 2018 by John Wiley & Sons, Inc.

significant discrepancy between verbal and performance IQ (typically expressed on a Wechsler battery) with verbal abilities being higher than performance.

Currently, NLD is characterized by deficits in three broad areas of dysfunction: motoric skills, visual-spatial organizational-memory skills, and social abilities (Mammarella & Cornoldi, 2014).

ROURKE'S PIONEERING WORK

After several decades of clinical research, Byron Rourke conceptualized NLD as a set of assets and deficits. The primary features are the key features that in turn cause difficulties with other areas of functioning that are not the main deficit (Rourke, 1989). Thus, Rourke has characterized children with NLD as having strong verbal skills and deficits in tactile-visual deficits that subsequently affect attention, memory, problem-solving, and social competence (Rourke, 1995). In this conceptualization, the social competence difficulties described originally by Myklebust are hypothesized to be a result of problems with visual-spatial processing.

> **DON'T FORGET**
> ....
> One of the first studies on NLD was conducted by Rourke in 1988 and published in *The Clinical Neuropsychologist, 4*, 293–330. He found that children with NLD showed more difficulty with mathematics compared to reading, visual-spatial deficits, and tactile-kinesthetic problems.

HYPOTHESIZED ETIOLOGY OF NLD

The early conceptualizations of NLD theorized that this disorder stemmed from a neurological dysfunction of white matter (Goldberg & Costa, 1981; Rourke, 1995). White matter is surrounded by the gray matter of the brain and is made up of myelinated fibers that transmit neural impulses across the brain from back to front and left to right. This hypothesis also allowed for the inclusion of children with some genetic and medical conditions. For this reason, in addition to children without apparent congenital or acquired neurological dysfunction, Rourke and associates began to incorporate the neurological disorders of fetal alcohol syndrome, velocardiofacial syndrome (VCFS), traumatic brain injury, Asperger's syndrome (AS), William's syndromes, and Turner syndromes (TS) as having some or all of the features of NLD (Rourke, Rourke, & van der Vlugt, 2002). The overlap of NLD with these diagnoses will be discussed in the next section.

One of the controversies in NLD is whether NLD and high-functioning autism (HFA; previously called AS) are variants of the same disorder or whether

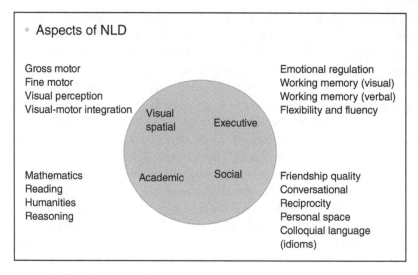

Figure 6.1 How Does NLD Present?

NLD is a separate disorder. Many children with HFA and NLD also have attentional difficulties as well as mood symptoms of anxiety and depression. Some individuals theorize that NLD is best used as a model for understanding AS (Schultz, Romanski, & Tsatsanis, 2000; Volkmar & Klin, 2000); others suggest that AS is a more-severe form of NLD (Brumback, Harper, & Weinberg, 1996) or that AS and NLD are separate disorders (Davis & Broitman, 2011). Three excellent reviews (Fine, Semrud-Clikeman, Bledsoe, & Musielak, 2011; Ris & Nortz, 2008; Spreen, 2011) provide somewhat different conclusions on whether NLD is a useful category. Fine et al. (2011) and Ris and Nortz (2008) conclude that the diagnosis is a useful way of conceptualizing the various areas of difficulty that these children have whereas Spreen (2011) does not find that it is useful in clinical practice. One of the areas that has been lacking in the past are demonstrations of differences in the brain structure of individuals with autism spectrum disorder (ASD) and NLD. Figure 6.1 provides information as to the common behaviors and symptoms seen in NLD.

NEUROIMAGING FINDINGS

Models for NLD and HFA suggest differences in the trajectory for the developing brain during gestation that affects how a child perceives social interactions. Findings from neuroimaging studies of individuals with ASD have found a larger white matter volume compared to individuals with typical neurodevelopment, which is particularly present at younger ages (Abell et al., 1999).

The amygdala is the area of the brain (see Rapid Reference 6.1) in the temporal lobe that is responsible for the processing of emotional information. This structure is identified as a key unit in the network that allows people to respond appropriately to facial expressions and is part of the neural networks important for social understanding (Schultz, Romanski, et al., 2000). Early experience in social interactions is also important for the development of empathy, theory of mind, and social reciprocity. Schultz, Gauthier, et al. (2000) concluded that "early emotional learning failures could cause a cascade of neurodevelopmental events, including the emergence of profoundly disturbed social relatedness" (p. 190). For children with NLD the disruption may not be as drastic as for children with HFA. Similarly, Rourke (1995) emphasized difficulties with connectivity between limbic structures and the frontal lobe rather than impairment of specific regions. Larger volumes of white matter have been found in the amygdalar regions in children with ASD (Groen, Teluj, Buitelaar, & Tendolkar, 2010; Nacewicz, Dalton, & Johnstone, 2006).

≡ Rapid Reference 6.1

Areas of the Brain

Frontal lobes. Important for the processing of others' emotions, changing behavior to fit the situation, cognitive flexibility, working memory, and insight into one's behavior

Parietal lobes. Important for the processing of visual-spatial skills as well as sensory-motor abilities and knowledge of where the body is in space

White matter. Long processes of nerves that are myelinated (have a white fatty sheath) and located inside the brain; myelination allows the neural impulses to move more quickly

Gray matter. The nuclei of nerves that lie on the outside of the brain

Corpus callosum. A large bundle of white matter fibers that connect the two hemispheres

Amygdala. Processes emotions; important for understanding empathy and the feelings of others

Hippocampus. Important for new learning and memory; provides the emotional tone for memories

Anterior cingulate gyrus. Important for self-monitoring; an area crucial for changing behaviors to fit the situation

The hippocampus has also been evaluated. The hippocampus is adjacent to the amygdala and is related to short-term memory as well as the processing of the emotional content of memories. It has been found that the hippocampal volume, particularly in the left hemisphere, is larger in children with ASD (Groen et al., 2010). It is hypothesized that these differences are adaptive for the developing brain and result when the brain is overwhelmed with processing emotional learning experiences. These areas then form more connections in an attempt to organize information streaming into the brain. The amygdala and hippocampus have also been implicated in the processing of emotions and emotional tone as well as selection of appropriate responses to stimuli (Gazzaniga, Ivry, & Mangun, 2013). There are also rich connections among the amygdala, hippocampus, and frontal lobe that make up what is known as the social processing circuit. Thus, the amygdalar-hippocampal-frontal circuit may be particularly important for mediating emotional perception and regulation and is compromised in children with social reciprocity difficulties (Amaral, 2002; Schultz, Gauthier, et al., 2000). In the only study located including an NLD sample, the NLD group did not show increased volume of the amygdala and hippocampal regions. By contrast, the ASD group had much larger amygdala-hippocampal regions compared to the control group and the NLD group (Semrud-Clikeman, Fine, Bledsoe, & Zhu, 2013a).

These findings have important implications for our understanding of NLD as well as of ASD and AS. These regions have many reciprocal connections, which, in turn, can lead to increased excitation in both structures, possibly involving the development of larger volume and increased connectivity in these structures (Abu-Akel, 2003). A previous finding supports the hypothesis that these regions interact strongly when the system is stressed (Hull, 2002) and when a child experiences high anxiety, often seen in children with ASD but not in those with NLD (Juranek et al., 2006).

An additional structure that has been studied in ASD, and to a lesser extent in NLD, is the anterior cingulate cortex (ACC; Abu-Akel, 2003). This structure plays a major role in attention and emotional processing (Posner & Raichle, 1994) as well as the attribution of mental states to the self and to others (Gusnard, Akbudak, Shulamn, & Raichle, 2001). It has also been suggested that the ACC is involved in basic social orienting in autism (Adolphs, 2001; Mundy, 2003). The ACC has been found to be smaller in children with ASD and NLD compared to controls (Semrud-Clikeman, Fine, Bledsoe, & Zhu, 2013b). A smaller volume of the ACC in children with AS or NLD may be related to difficulty in the evaluation and self-monitoring of behavior.

In a preliminary finding, differences in the splenium of the corpus callosum have been reported with the NLD group showing the smallest volume of the splenium (Fine, Musielak, Bledsoe, & Semrud-Clikeman, 2014). The splenium is the farthest area of the corpus callosum and connects the parietal lobes. As the reader may recall the parietal lobes are responsible for understanding visual-spatial tasks as well as integration of knowledge. Finding a smaller volume in this region indicates that there is less transmission across hemispheres in this area. It is likely that this is related to the difficulties that children with NLD have with visual-spatial and mathematics problems. It is important to note that this difference was not found in children with diagnoses of AS or typical neurodevelopment.

These neuroimaging findings suggest that there are similarities and differences between individuals with HFA and NLD. Each group shows differences in the ACC and experiences difficulty with directing behaviors, assessing their impact on others, and processing social stimuli—all tasks believed to reside in the ACC. Only the HFA group shows larger amygdala and hippocampal volumes. This suggests that the more extreme behaviors that are seen in this group are related to the social processing network of the amygdala-hippocampal-frontal connections. The NLD group shows smaller splenial measures, which have been related to problems with visual-spatial processing. Such differences in this region are found solely for the NLD group and not the HFA group. These findings begin to suggest that these may be related, but different, disorders. The following section discusses the neuropsychological findings in children with NLD and may serve to provide additional information as to how these children function.

NEUROPSYCHOLOGICAL FINDINGS

Children with NLD or HFA or AS have characteristic similarities and important differences. Similarities include social interaction difficulties and some motor skills. There are also differences between these groups in selected areas (Fine, Semrud-Clikeman, & Bledsoe, 2012). Children with NLD are consistently found to have difficulties with visual-spatial skills, mathematics, reading comprehension of abstract passages, fine-motor ability, a significant split between verbal and perceptual skills on an IQ measure, and visual-constructive skills with social skills being impaired, but not as substantially as for those with ASD (Fine & Semrud-Clikeman, 2011; Mammarella & Cornoldi, 2014). Children with ASD have been found to show more difficulties in theory of mind, stereotyped behaviors, and emphasis on routine. It is also striking that NLD, but not ASD, symptoms frequently occur in some genetic conditions, which will be discussed further on in this chapter. Children with NLD demonstrate strengths in rote language and sight word vocabulary. Weaknesses include mathematics calculation, reading comprehension (at older grades), visual-spatial skills, attention, and possibly in executive

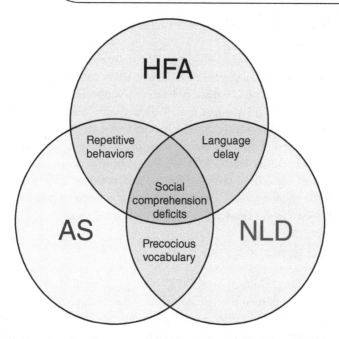

Figure 6.2 Overlapping Features of Children with NLD, AS, and HFA

functioning. Figure 6.2 provides a schematic of the general areas thought to be compromised in children with NLD. The following section discusses each of these areas in more detail.

Verbal-Performance Intelligence Quotient (IQ) Differences

In several cases seen in our clinic, children with significant differences between their verbal and perceptual ability on the Wechsler Intelligence Scale for Children (WISC) have been diagnosed with NLD. In the early literature, this was one of the main ways of identifying NLD. Unfortunately, this method identifies children as NLD who may have other difficulties. Approximately 20% to 25% of the population has a significant difference between verbal and performance abilities yet few of these children have NLD. Using the verbal-performance difference to diagnose NLD results in many false positive diagnoses.

Children with NLD are not the only group that evidences a significant difference between verbal and performance

CAUTION

The verbal-performance difference by itself is not diagnostic of NLD.

abilities. Children with AS also have been found to be more likely to demonstrate such a difference in skills with the NLD group showing a larger magnitude of difference (Semrud-Clikeman, Walkowiak, Wilkinson, & Christopher, 2010). Others have also found that there is a verbal-performance discrepancy in children with autism (Klin, Pauls, Schultz, & Volkmar, 2005) and children with autism with a discrepantly higher verbal or performance IQ showing more difficulty with social functioning (Black, Wallace, Sokoloff, & Kenworthy, 2009). One conclusion from this research is that the discrepancy between verbal and performance ability alone is not sufficient for a diagnosis of NLD (Ris & Nortz, 2008) but should be used as one piece of evidence. This conclusion was echoed earlier by Rourke and associates (Pelletier, Ahmad, & Rourke, 2001). Unfortunately, many clinicians continue to diagnose NLD based almost solely on this discrepancy.

Language

Generally speaking, children with NLD have good vocabularies. By contrast, difficulty is present in their ability to understand the meaning of what is being said (semantics) and the ability to use language appropriately in social situations (pragmatics); also termed *pragmatic language.* In this case a child with NLD experiences significant difficulties with understanding the nuances of language including idioms and humor (Semrud-Clikeman & Glass, 2010). Particular difficulty is found in the use of pragmatic language when social referencing is involved (Humphries, Cardy, Worling, & Peets, 2004; Worling, Humphries, & Tannock, 1999).

Achievement

Children with NLD have been found to demonstrate good single-word reading skills with later difficulties found in reading comprehension particularly with inferential reasoning (i.e., "Why do you think this character feels this way?") (Fine & Semrud-Clikeman, 2011). Solving mathematics problems has also been noted, particularly when children are required to line up numbers in math problems or need to comprehend the higher-level abstract concepts required in division, data presentation (charts, graphs), algebra, geometry, and trigonometry. When children with NLD were asked to solve more simplified types of mathematical word problems, they were as successful as other children (Forrest, 2004). These findings suggest it might not be mathematics, per se, that are problematic for the child but rather problems that require higher-order (more-abstract) thinking as well as working memory and planning and organization.

Visual-Spatial Skills

Studies have found difficulties with visual-spatial skills and visual-motor ability to be present in children with NLD (Mammarella & Cornoldi, 2014; Semrud-Clikeman, Walkowiak, Wilkinson, & Christopher, 2010). In addition, difficulties with visual-spatial tasks and with visual-motor ability have been found to correlate significantly with social skills (Semrud-Clikeman, Walkowiak, Wilkinson, & Christopher, 2010). Visual abstract reasoning has also been found deficient in children with NLD (Semrud-Clikeman, Walkowiak, Wilkinson, & Christopher, 2010). These findings support Rourke's contention that visual-spatial and perceptual difficulties may underlie the social difficulties frequently found in children with NLD.

Motor skills have also been evaluated in children with NLD. Several studies have found children with NLD to have difficulty placing pegs in a pegboard quickly (Harnadek & Rourke, 1994; Wilkinson-Smith & Semrud-Clikeman, 2014). In a study that compared children with two subtypes of attention-deficit hyperactivity disorder (ADHD), AS, and NLD, it was found that the NLD group performed poorly on this measure bilaterally and the AS group showed difficulty solely with the left hand (Semrud-Clikeman, Walkowiak, Wilkinson, & Christopher, 2010).

Handwriting is an area of particular challenge for children with NLD, including difficulties with letter formation, letter spacing, and word spacing, particularly in the early grades. Asking the child to print the alphabet as quickly as possible is an informal test for these skills. Children with NLD have difficulty forming the letters and may do this quickly or so painstakingly it takes an inordinate amount of time to write anything. As tasks become more abstract and complex, visual-spatial and visual-motor difficulties increase. Difficulties can be found in these areas in children with ADHD and ASD due to other reasons than visual-motor deficits, namely, impulsivity or anxiety.

Executive Functioning

Executive functions are just beginning to be evaluated in children with NLD. These are skills that are related to planning, organization, attention, and emotional regulation. These skills also include the ability to arrive at conclusions based on information presented, to manage novel experiences and information, and to plan and organize information and materials (Forrest, 2007; Rourke, 2000; Semrud-Clikeman, 2003). Novel tasks are particularly difficult for children with NLD. For example, the first time the Block Design subtest from the Wechsler scales is

DON'T FORGET

Executive functions, although not well-studied in children with NLD, may be the most problematic issue for these children. They may also interact with problems with visual-spatial analysis as well as social skills. Further study of executive function in children with NLD is needed.

administered, it is a relatively new task for the child. It has been found to be among the more challenging tasks for children with NLD (Pelletier et al., 2001). As tasks become increasingly more complex and require memory and reasoning, a child with NLD experiences more difficulty than a child with typical development (Ris et al., 2007; Strang & Rourke, 1985). Working memory, sequencing of information, and cognitive flexibility have also been found to be problematic for children with NLD (Semrud-Clikeman, Walkowiak, Wilkinson, & Butcher, 2010).

Attention is a related construct to executive functioning. Rourke (2000) believed that the attentional problems frequently seen in children with NLD are more related to visual-spatial deficits rather than to attention per se. This was an untested hypothesis. One study looked at this area directly and found that social perception measures were related strongly to executive functioning but not to attention or visual-spatial skills (Fine, Semrud-Clikeman, Butcher, & Walkowiak, 2008).

The implication of these findings suggests that visual-perception may not be as directly related to NLD as to complex cognitive functioning involved with executive functioning (Semrud-Clikeman, Walkowiak, Wilkinson, & Christopher, 2010; Semrud-Clikeman, Walkowiak, Wilkinson, & Minne, 2010). Difficulty with planning and organization seems to be the greatest contributor to difficulty with novel reasoning in children with NLD (see Rapid Reference 6.2).

≋ Rapid Reference 6.2

Title: The role of the right hemisphere for processing of social interactions in normal adults using functional magnetic resonance

Authors: Margaret Semrud-Clikeman, Jodene Fine, and David Zhu

Publication date: 2011

Findings: The right hemisphere is more active in understanding social interactions compared to the left hemisphere, particularly in the amygdala, frontal lobe, and the fusiform gyrus—the network important for social processing.

Journal: *Neuropsychobiology, 64,* 47–52

Social Perception and Psychopathology

In the past, some researchers have suggested that children with NLD show higher rates of depression and anxiety and possible suicidality (Pelletier et al., 2001), whereas others have not found this relationship, particularly in samples that are community based rather than in residential treatment or in psychiatric clinics (Antshel & Joseph, 2006; Bloom & Heath, 2010; Forrest, 2007; Yu, Buka, McCormick, Fitzmaurice, & Indurkhya, 2006). Mild symptoms of social withdrawal and sadness have been found particularly in adolescence when peer relationships become very important (Semrud-Clikeman et al., 2010). Sadness and problems with emotional modulation are likely related to the child's difficulty in recognizing nonverbal cues in social situations (Semrud-Clikeman et al., 2010). Thus, if a child who misidentifies nonverbal cues acts accordingly to the mistaken perception, then it is likely that the feedback from peers will not be positive and may result in the child withdrawing even further from social interactions.

Interpretation of ambiguous or vague social interaction is particularly difficult for children with NLD when verbal cues are not present (Semrud-Clikeman & Glass, 2008). The difficulty children with NLD have in interpreting humor (e.g., puns, jokes, cartoons, and non sequiturs) appears to be more related to higher-order reasoning required for understanding humor rather than visual-spatial deficits.

NEUROLOGICAL AND GENETIC DISORDERS WITH NLD SYMPTOMS

NLD may be present as a sole diagnosis. It has also been found to be associated with several genetic, metabolic, and neurodevelopmental disorders. A neurological examination of children with co-occurring neurological disorders may show problems with pencil control, drawing, and fine-motor movements and may demonstrate problems with staying focused on tasks. For these children, it is not common to detect problems on an MRI or on neurological examination.

DON'T FORGET

Selected genetic syndromes seem to share some symptoms with NLD. This finding can help us understand the neural underpinnings of NLD.

Turner Syndrome

The reader may recall that females have two X chromosomes. TS results when one X chromosome is either missing or incomplete. It occurs in approximately 1 in

2,500 girls and is associated with short stature, webbed neck, and a low hairline. Most girls with TS have, overall, average cognitive ability. Numerous studies have revealed neuropsychological deficits in girls with TS similar to those seen in children with NLD (Hong, Scarletta, Kent, & Kesler, 2009; Kesler, 2007). There is a marked difference between verbal and performance abilities with the performance skills much lower than the verbal skills. Language is generally good, but problems with pragmatic language are present. Frequently these girls have attention difficulties as well. Mathematics skills are often weaker compared to reading, and visual-spatial skills are the weakest area for these girls (Hong et al., 2009). These difficulties are seen from toddlerhood through adulthood with adults with TS showing even more deficits in visual-spatial ability that becomes more problematic over time (Green et al., 2014).

Consistent with the widening difficulty in visual-spatial skills, Green et al. (2014) showed a different trajectory in girls with TS compared with controls. When comparing the same brains at time one and time two (roughly ages 8 and 9 years), left parietal white matter volume and right parietal cortical thickness were smaller in girls with TS at time two. This finding is important because it suggests that the visual-spatial cortex of the brain (parietal lobe) develops differently in girls with TS and that there may be a critical period for effective intervention, likely between the ages of 8 and 9.

> **DON'T FORGET**
> ....
> The long arm on a chromosome is q and the short arm is p.

22q11 Deletion Syndrome

22q11 deletion syndrome (velocardiofacial syndrome, DiGeorge syndrome, Shprintzen syndrome) has an estimated prevalence of 1 in 2,000 (Shprintzen, 2008). As is in the title of the disorder, it is a deletion of the long arm (q) of chromosome 22. Children with this syndrome also frequently experience difficulties with heart disease; a lack of potassium, which causes trouble with bone formation, cleft palate, short stature, and facial features that are somewhat unusual; and a deficiency in fighting off diseases and illnesses (i.e., T-cell immunodeficiency) (Robin & Shprintzen, 2005). This syndrome has also been called *velocardiofacial syndrome* due to the cleft palate and nasal speech. These children often have an intellectual disability as well as ASD and ADHD. Several psychiatric symptoms may be present, including anxiety disorder, phobias, and bipolar disorder (Schoch et al., 2014). In addition, research has found a relative weakness in visual-spatial ability, executive functioning, mathematics, and attention in relation to a lower

IQ (Henry et al., 2002; Lepach & Petermann, 2011). This pattern is reminiscent of NLD although the IQ is lower than would be expected. Neuroimaging has found reduced gyri in the frontal and parietal lobes, which are associated with visual-spatial skill formation (Schaer et al., 2006).

Neurofibromatosis Type I

Neurofibromatosis type I (NF1) is the most common disorder relating to tumors inside or outside of the body. It is abnormality on the 17th chromosome in the long arm (also called *17q11.2*) and has an estimated incidence of 1 in 3,000. Many children with NF1 also have learning disabilities (30% to 40%), visual-perceptual difficulties (56%) (Eliason, 1986), as well as attentional deficits and lower than expected overall IQ (Cutting, Koth, & Denckla, 2000; Hofman, Harris, Bryan, & Denckla, 1994). Some researchers have found children with NF1 to have language difficulties, and most researchers have found more nonverbal deficits in these children. Thus, the most-prevalent type of cognitive deficit in NF1 is most consistent with a modified NLD phenotype (visual-spatial deficit, attention problems, academic deficits).

Nephropathic Cystinosis

Nephropathic cystinosis is a rare autosomal recessive disorder in which the amino acid cystine accumulates in lysosomes inside the cell nucleus because there is a deficiency in transporting the cysteine outside of the cell body. This deficiency is the result of difficulties on the short arm (*p*) of chromosome. The incidence of cystinosis is estimated at approximately 1 in 100,000 individuals worldwide, with a carrier rate estimated at 1 in 158. This information is important because carriers may be at increased risk for subtle cognitive differences similar to those found in individuals with cystinosis. The earliest and most common clinical feature of cystinosis is Fanconi syndrome (FS) involving the kidneys, which begins in the first year of life. FS is an inability of the kidneys to reabsorb glucose, amino acids, and other important nutrients. Children with FS often have symptoms consistent with NLD (Ballantyne, Spilkin, & Trauner, 2013; Trauner, Spilkin, Williams, & Babchuck, 2007). They have great difficulty with visual-motor coordination (Trauner et al., 2007). Arithmetic skills may also be deficient. Although overall social-emotional functioning is good, subtle social difficulties may be present (Delgado, Schatz, Nichols, & Trauner, 2005) as well as subtle challenges in executive functioning (Ballantyne et al., 2013). Thus, the cognitive and behavioral profile of children with FS meets the commonly accepted definition of NLD.

Neuroimaging studies of cognition in cystinosis have shown consistency with the neurocognitive profile. A study that evaluated the white matter tracts of the brain found reduced white matter in the parietal lobes, which correlated significantly with difficulties with visual-spatial skills (Bava et al., 2010). As a result of this study, it was concluded that the lowered amount of white matter tracts may have led to a difference in the development of the neural networks that are related to visual-spatial function—a key element of difficulty in NLD.

Summary of Neurocognitive Difficulties

As the reader can surmise, these genetic syndromes have neurocognitive difficulties consistent with those found in children with NLD without a known medical cause. Importantly, the brain structural abnormalities that have been found in these syndromes involve the parietal and parietal-frontal lobe connections, areas that are important for visual-spatial analysis. Further studies to identify specific genes or gene interactions may help to clarify the underlying neural mechanisms that underlie normal development of visual-spatial skills as well as how to better assist those individuals who are found to have NLD in the future. The following brief case study highlights several points made in this chapter.

CASE STUDY

Background information: Kate is a 10-year-old female who was referred to our clinic because she experienced difficulty with visual-spatial skills, making friends, and social understanding. Her teacher was concerned that Kate had Asperger's syndrome. Her Verbal Comprehension Index (VCI) was 119, Perceptual Reasoning Index (PRI) was 60; her Wechsler Individual Achievement Test (WIAT) Math standard score was 65 and Reading was 132. She was described as having few friends and had great difficulty reading facial and behavioral cues but had typical language development.

Her mother completed the Autism Diagnostic Interview–Revised (ADI-R). Kate was rated a 9 in social reciprocity (cut-off is 10), a 2 in communication (cutoff is 8), and had one restricted-repetitive behavior symptom (cutoff is 3).

She was administered the Rey Complex Figure (see Figure 6.3).

Instead, Kate's looked like Figure 6.4.

Kate evidenced good performance on a measure that required her to interpret emotional cues, but she performed poorly in her ability to process facial expressions and nonverbal cues. On executive functioning tests, she did well on tests of theory of mind as well as taking another's perspective (Sorting and

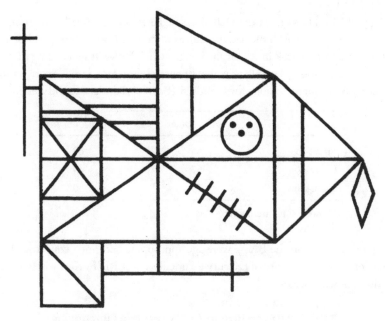

Figure 6.3 Rey Complex Figure

Figure 6.4 Kate's Rendition of the Rey Complex Figure

Theory of Mind tasks from the Delis-Kaplan Tests of Executive Functioning [D-KEFS]). On the D-KEFS she had difficulty on trails with sequencing numbers but not letters or on the task in which she had to switch between sequencing numbers and letters. She showed excellent verbal fluency ability. Standard T-score on some Behavior Assessment System for Children (BASC) scales are found here:

	BASC Parent	BASC Teacher
Attention	65	68
Depression	67	69
Social skills*	35	30

* Lower scores are poorer

All other scales on the BASC were age appropriate and not a concern. On the Behavior Rating Inventory of Executive Functioning (BRIEF) Kate was rated high on the following scales:

Behavior Rating Inventory of Executive Functioning

	Parent	Teacher
Working memory	70	72
Planning and organization	65	73

Interview with Kate and her mother: Kate has one or two friends but experiences difficulties making new friends. She indicated that she is frequently sad because she feels left out of social interactions. At times, she has been teased because she doesn't understand the meaning behind what is being said or she misinterprets the meaning of sarcasm and humor. She doesn't show sufficient symptoms for a diagnosis of depression. Kate has participated in social skills groups and seems to understand basic social skills but has difficulty applying them in the real world. Kate and her mother deny that she has any difficulty with stereotyped behaviors or intense interests outside of a usual 10-year-old girl. Language development was normal and she has always been interested in other children. Her ability to color and print was always difficult from preschool to present day. Mathematics continues to be a challenge for her. Reading recognition has always been good but now that she is in the fourth grade she is experiencing difficulties with reading comprehension, particularly when the passages require inferential thinking. Kate can be inattentive in a large-group setting but can attend when in a smaller group. In school Kate has no Section 504 Plan or individualized education program (IEP) and is currently failing mathematics and written language. Her teachers report that she has difficulty with math facts as well as being able to write a coherent passage. Handwriting is extremely poor. Basic reading and spelling skills are within grade expectations.

Based on the data provided, answer the following questions:

1. What diagnosis is most appropriate for Kate? And why?
2. What other tests might help to understand Kate better?
3. What other diagnoses should be considered?

Responses

1. NLD—difficulties with visual-spatial skills, social skills, math skills, verbal-performance difference. She does not meet the criteria for HFA—no stereotyped behaviors or intense interests.
2. Perhaps a continuous performance measure and a parent report scale or consideration should be given to a measure of adaptive functioning. Because working memory is a difficulty, it is possible the use of some measures that directly measure memory could be beneficial—for instance the California Verbal Learning Test–Child Revision or parts of the NEPSY.
3. The most common differential diagnosis is HFA, but ADHD might be considered as well as a mood disorder.

CONCLUSION

There are conflicting views of what NLD consists of and whether this diagnosis is useful. Research consistently shows that some children demonstrate significant difficulties with visual-spatial reasoning, mathematics, handwriting, and in some cases social cognition and attention. Strengths are commonly seen in reading recognition, spelling, vocabulary, and language. Although neuroimaging and neuropsychological studies have found similarities between NLD and HFA, these same studies have found differences. Similarities in neural development are present in the region of the brain that is involved with self-monitoring and changing of behavior (ACG). Differences are present in the connection between the parietal lobe solely in the NLD group, whereas the HFA group shows more difficulty in the amygdala-hippocampal-frontal lobe connections. These differences, although seemingly subtle, likely contribute to the emotional regulation challenges that are present in children with HFA as well as the stereotyped behaviors and the intense interests. None of these issues is as present in children with NLD. Neuro-psychologically, children with NLD also demonstrate more difficulty in visual-spatial processing compared to those with HFA. Although both groups do have difficulty understanding nonverbal cues, only the HFA group also has difficulty understanding emotional cues.

In addition, there is emerging evidence from findings in children with specific genetic syndromes that NLD symptoms are present and correlate well with neuroimaging findings. These findings suggest that these disorders, although related, are likely different in scope and in underlying neurological pathology. Further study is needed to determine whether NLD is on the same spectrum as ASD but is expressed as a less-severe disorder. A longitudinal study is needed to determine how NLD is expressed in adulthood and whether it differs from HFA at that point.

At this time, schools do not classify children with NLD as having a special education need unless there is significant difficulty in mathematics. Social difficulty has been suggested as a special education need, but it has never been categorized as a special education category in the schools. Generally, children with NLD, if not qualifying under mathematics learning disability, are served under a Section 504 particularly if they have ADHD or significant handwriting challenges. Although it is important to recognize that visual-spatial skills may be an important part of NLD, emerging research suggests that executive function deficits may contribute to NLD more than visual-spatial difficulties.

🐟 TEST YOURSELF 🐟

1. **Usually individuals with NLDs have deficits in:**
   (a) Attention
   (b) Executive functions
   (c) Visual-spatial skills
   (d) Mathematics
   (e) All of the above

2. **Children with NLD and those with HFA show more similarities than differences. True or false?**

3. **Neuroimaging has found the following structure to be most compromised in children with NLD:**
   (a) Frontal lobe
   (b) Parietal lobe

(c) Occipital lobe

(d) Temporal lobe

(e) A and b

(f) C and d

4. **Genetic syndromes have been found to show commonality with NLD. The most common genetic syndrome with these characteristics is:**

(a) Velocardiofacial syndrome

(b) Turner syndrome

(c) Neurofibromatosis type I

(d) Cystinosis

5. **Children with NLD are more likely to commit suicide. True or false?**

6. **The incidence of NLD is**

(a) 2% of the population

(b) 5% of the LD population

(c) 10% of the ASD population

(d) 2% of the ADHD population

Answers: 1.e; 2. False; 3. e; 4. c; 5. False; 6. b.

REFERENCES

Abell, F., Krams, M., Ashburner, J., Passingham, R., Friston, K., Frackowiak, R., . . . & Frith, U. (1999). The neuroanatomy of autism: A voxel-based whole brain analysis of structural scans. *Cognitive Neuroscience, 10*(8), 1647–1651.

Abu-Akel, A. (2003). A neurobiological mapping of theory of mind. *Brain Research Reviews, 43*, 29–40.

Adolphs, R. (2001). The neurobiology of social cognition. *Current Opinion in Neurobiology Cognitive Neuroscience, 11*(2), 231–239.

Amaral, D. G. (2002). The primate amygdala and the neurobiology of social behavior: Implications for understanding social anxiety. *Biological Psychiatry, 51*, 11–17.

Antshel, K., & Joseph, G.-R. (2006). Maternal stress in nonverbal learning disorder: A comparison with reading disorder. *Journal of Learning Disabilities, 39*, 194–205.

Ballantyne, A. O., Spilkin, A. M., & Trauner, D. A. (2013). Executive function in nephropathic cystinosis. *Cognitive and Behavioral Neurology*, (26), 14–22.

Bava, S., Theilmann, R. J., Sach, M., May, S. J., Frank, L., Hesselink, J. R., . . . & Trauner, D. A. (2010). Developmental changes in cerebral white matter microstructure in a disorder of lysosomal storage. *Cortex, 46*, 206–216.

Black, D. O., Wallace, G. L., Sokoloff, J. L., & Kenworthy, L. (2009). Brief report: IQ split predicts social symptoms and communication abilities in high-functioning children with autism spectrum disorders. *Journal of Autism and Developmental Disorders, 39*, 1613–1619.

Bloom, E., & Heath, N. (2010). Recognition, expression, and understanding facial expression of emotion in adolescents with nonverbal and general learning disabilities. *Journal of Learning Disabilities, 43,* 180–192.

Brumback, R. A., Harper, C. R., & Weinberg, W. A. (1996). Nonverbal learning disabilities, Asperger's syndrome, pervasive developmental disorder—should we care? *Journal of Child Neurology, 11,* 427–429.

Cutting, L. E., Koth, C. W., & Denckla, M. B. (2000). How children with neurofibromatosis type 1 differ from "typical" learning disabled clinic attenders: Nonverbal learning disabilities revisited. *Developmental Neuropsychology, 17,* 29–47.

Davis, J. M., & Broitman, J. (2011). *Nonverbal learning disabilities in children: Bridging the gap between science and practice.* Boston, MA: Springer.

Delgado, G., Schatz, A., Nichols, S., & Trauner, D. A. (2005). Behavioral profiles of children with infantile nephropathic cystinosis. *Developmental Medicine & Child Neurology, 47,* 403–407.

Eliason, M. J. (1986). Neurofibromatosis: Implications for learning and behavior. *Journal of Developmental and Behavioral Pediatrics, 7,* 175–179.

Fine, J. G., Musielak, K., Bledsoe, J., & Semrud-Clikeman, M. (2014). Corpus callosal findings in children with developmental disorders. *Child Neuropsychology, 20,* 641–661.

Fine, J. G., & Semrud-Clikeman, M. (2011). Nonverbal learning disabilities. In A. Davis (Ed.), *Handbook of pediatric neuropsychology* (pp. 721–734). New York, NY: Springer.

Fine, J. G., Semrud-Clikeman, M., & Bledsoe, J. (2012). Nonverbal learning disability. In A. Davis (Ed.), *Handbook of pediatric neuropsychology* (pp. 721–734). New York, NY: Springer.

Fine, J. G., Semrud-Clikeman, M., Bledsoe, J., & Musielak, K. (2011). A critical review of the NLD literature as a developmental disorder. *Child Neuropsychology, 17,* 418–443.

Fine, J. G., Semrud-Clikeman, M., Butcher, B., & Walkowiak, J. (2008). Brief report: Attention effect on a measure of social perception. *Journal of Autism and Developmental Disorders, 38,* 1797–1802.

Forrest, B. J. (2004). The utility of math difficulties, internalized psychopathology, and visual-spatial deficits to identify children with nonverbal learning disability syndrome: Evidence for a visual-spatial disability. *Child Neuropsychology, 10,* 129–146.

Forrest, B. J. (2007). Diagnosing and treating right hemisphere disorders. In S. J. Hunter & J. Donders (Eds.), *Pediatric neuropsychological intervention* (pp. 175–192). Cambridge, UK: Cambridge University Press.

Gazzaniga, M. S., Ivry, R. B., & Mangun, G. R. (2013). *Cognitive neuroscience: The biology of the mind* (4th ed.). New York, NY: W.W. Norton.

Goldberg, E., & Costa, L. D. (1981). Hemisphere differences in the acquisition and use of descriptive systems. *Brain and Language, 14,* 144–173.

Green, T., Chromik, L. C., Mazaika, P. K., Fierro, K., Raman, M. M., Lazzeroni, L. C., . . . Reiss, A. L., (2014). Aberrant parietal cortex developmental trajectories in girls with Turner syndrome and related visual-spatial cognitive development: A preliminary study. *American Journal of Medical Genetics B: Neuropsychiatric Genetics, 165B,* 531–540.

Groen, W., Teluj, M., Buitelaar, J., & Tendolkar, I. (2010). Amygdala and hippocampus enlargement during adolescence in autism. *Journal of the American Academy of Child & Adolescent Psychiatry, 49,* 552–560.

Gusnard, D. A., Akbudak, E., Shulamn, M. E., & Raichle, M. E. (2001). Medial prefrontal cortex and self-referential mental activity: Relation to a default mode of brain function. *Proceedings of the National Academy of Science of the United States of America, 98,* 4259–4264.

Harnadek, M.C.S., & Rourke, B. P. (1994). Principal identifying features of the syndrome of nonverbal learning disabilities in children. *Journal of Learning Disabilities, 27*(3), 144–154.

Henry, J. C., van Amelsvoort, T., Morris, R. G., Owen, J., Murphy, D.G.M., & Murphy, K. C. (2002). An investigation of the neuropsychological profile in adults with velo-cardio-facial syndrome (VCFS). *Neuropsychologia, 40,* 471–478.

Hofman, K. J., Harris, E. L., Bryan, R. N., & Denckla, M. B. (1994). Neurofibromatosis type 1: The cognitive phenotype. *Journal of Pediatrics, 124,* S1–S8.

Hong, D. S., Scarletta, K. J., Kent, J., & Kesler, S. R. (2009). Cognitive profile of Turner syndrome. *Developmental Disability Research Review, 15,* 270–278.

Hull, A. M. (2002). Neuroimaging findings in post-traumatic stress disorder—systematic review. *British Journal of Psychiatry, 131,* 102–110.

Humphries, T., Cardy, J. O., Worling, D. E., & Peets, K. (2004). Narrative comprehension and retelling abilities of children with nonverbal learning disabilities. *Brain and Cognition, 56,* 77–88.

Johnson, D. J. (1987). Nonverbal learning disabilities. *Pediatric Annals, 16*(2), 133–141.

Juranek, J., Filipek, P. A., Berenji, G. R., Modahl, C., Osann, K., Spence, A., & Berenji, G. R. (2006). Association between amygdala volume and anxiety level: Magnetic resonance imaging (MRI) study in autistic children. *Journal of Child Neurology, 21,* 1051–1058.

Kesler, S. R. (2007). Turner syndrome. *Child and Adolescent Psychiatric Clinics of North America, 16,* 709–722.

Klin, A., Pauls, D. L., Schultz, R. T., & Volkmar, F. R. (2005). Three diagnostic approaches to Asperger's syndrome: Implications for research. *Journal of Autism and Developmental Disorders, 35*(2), 221–234.

Lepach, A. C., & Petermann, F. (2011). Nonverbal and verbal learning: A comparative study of children and adolescents with 22q11 deletion syndrome, non-syndromal nonverbal learning disorder, and memory disorder. *Neurocase, 17,* 480–490.

Mammarella, I., & Cornoldi, C. (2014). An analysis of the criteria used to diagnose children with nonverbal learning disorder (NLD). *Child Neuropsychology, 20,* 255–280.

Mundy, P. (2003). Annotation: The neural basis of social impairments in autism; The role of the dorsal medial-frontal cortex and anterior cingulate system. *Journal of Child Psychology & Psychiatry & Allied Disciplines, 44,* 793–809.

Myklebust, H. R. (1975). *Progress in learning disabilities* (Vol. 3). New York, NY: Grune & Stratton.

Nacewicz, B. M., Dalton, K. M., & Johnstone, T. (2006). Amygdala volume and nonverbal social impairment in adolescent and adult males with autism. *Archives of General Psychiatry, 63,* 1417–1428.

Pelletier, P. M., Ahmad, S. A., & Rourke, B. P. (2001). Classification rules for basic phonological processing disabilities and nonverbal learning disabilities: Formulation and external validity. *Child Neuropsychology, 7*(2), 84–98.

Pennington, B. F. (2008). *Diagnosing learning disabilities.* New York, NY: Guilford.

Posner, M. I., & Raichle, M. E. (1994). *Images of mind.* New York, NY: Scientific American Library.

Ris, D. M., Ammerman, R. T., Waller, N., Walz, N. C., Oppenheimer, S., Brown, T. M., et al. (2007). Taxonicity of nonverbal learning disabilities. *Journal of the International Neuropsychological Society, 13,* 50–58.

Ris, D. M., & Nortz, M. J. (2008). Nonverbal learning disorder. In J. E. Morgan, & J. H. Ricker (Eds.), *Textbook of clinical neuropsychology: Studies on neuropsychology, neurology, and cognition* (pp. 346–359). New York, NY: Elsevier Psychology Press.

Robin, N. H., & Shprintzen, R. J. (2005). Defining the clinical spectrum of deletion 22q11.2. *The Journal of Pediatrics, 147,* 90–96.

Rourke, B. P. (1988). The syndrome of nonverbal learning disabilities: Developmental manifestations in neurological disease and dysfunction. *The Clinical Neuropsychologist, 4,* 293–330.

Rourke, B. P. (1989). *Nonverbal learning disabilities: The syndrome and the model.* New York, NY: Guilford.

Rourke, B. P. (1995). The NLD syndrome and the white matter model. In B. P. Rourke (Ed.), *Syndrome of nonverbal learning disabilities: Neurodevelopmental manifestations* (pp. 1–26). New York, NY: Guilford.

Rourke, B. P. (2000). Neuropsychological and psychosocial subtyping: A review of investigations within the University of Windsor laboratory. *Canadian Psychology, 41,* 34–51.

Rourke, B. P., Ahmad, S. A., Collins, D. W., Hayman-Abello, B. A., & Warriner, E. M. (2002). Child clinical/pediatric neuropsychology: Some recent advances. *Review of Psychology, 53,* 309–339.

Rourke, B. P., Rourke, S., & van der Vlugt, H. (2002). *Practice of child-clinical neuropsychology.* Lisse, The Netherlands: Swets & Zeitlinger.

Rourke, B. P., & Tsatsanis, K. D. (2000). Nonverbal learning disabilities. In A. Klin, F. R. Volkmar, & S. S. Sparrow (Eds.), *Asperger syndrome* (pp. 231–253). New York, NY: Guilford.

Schaer, M., Schmidt, J. L., Glaser, B., Lazeyras, F., Delavelle, J., & Eliez, J. (2006). Abnormal patterns of cortical gyrification in velo-cardio-facial syndrome (deletion 2211.2): An MRI study. *Psychiatry Research: Neuroimaging, 146,* 1–11.

Schoch, K., Harrell, W., Hooper, S. R., Ip, E. H., Saldana, S., Kwapil, T. R., & Shashi, V. (2014). Applicability of the nonverbal learning disability paradigm for children with 22q11.2 deletion syndrome. *Journal of Learning Disabilities, 47,* 153–166.

Schultz, R. T., Gauthier, I., Klin, A., Fulbright, R. K., Anderson, A. W., Volkmar, F. R., & Skudlarski, P. (2000). Abnormal ventral temporal cortical activity during face discrimination among individuals with autism and Asperger's syndrome. *Archives of General Psychiatry, (4),* 331–340.

Schultz, R. T., Romanski, L. M., & Tsatsanis, K. D. (2000). Neurofunctional models of autistic disorder and Asperger syndrome: Clues from neuroimaging. In A. Klin, F. R. Volkmar, & S. S. Sparrow (Eds.), *Asperger's syndrome* (pp. 172–209). New York, NY: Guilford.

Semrud-Clikeman, M. (2003). Executive functions and social communication disorders. *Perspectives, 29,* 20–22.

Semrud-Clikeman, M., Fine, J. G., Bledsoe, J., & Zhu, D. C. (2013a). Magnetic resonance imaging volumetric findings in children with Asperger's syndrome, nonverbal learning disability, or healthy controls. *Journal of Clinical and Experimental Neuropsychology, 35,* 540–550.

Semrud-Clikeman, M., Fine, J., Bledsoe, J., & Zhu, D. (2013b). Volumetric differences among children with Asperger's disorder, nonverbal learning disabilities, and controls on MRI. *Journal of Clinical and Experimental Neuropsychology, 5,* 540–550.

Semrud-Clikeman, M., & Glass, K. L. (2008). Comprehension of humor in children with nonverbal learning disabilities, verbal learning disabilities and without learning disabilities. *Annals of Dyslexia, 58,* 163–180.

Semrud-Clikeman, M., & Glass, K. (2010). The relation of humor and child development: Social, adaptive, and emotional aspects. *Journal of Child Neurology, 25,* 1248–1260.

Semrud-Clikeman, M., Walkowiak, J., Wilkinson, A., & Butcher, B. (2010). Differences on direct and indirect executive function measures among children with Asperger's syndrome, ADHD: Combined type, ADHD: Predominately inattentive type, and controls. *Journal of Autism and Developmental Disorders, 40,* 1017–1027.

Semrud-Clikeman, M., Walkowiak, J., Wilkinson, A., & Christopher, G. (2010). Neuro-psychological findings in nonverbal learning disabilities. *Developmental Neuropsychology, 35,* 582–600.

Semrud-Clikeman, M., Walkowiak, J., Wilkinson, A., & Minne, E. (2010). Behavior and social perception in children with Asperger's disorder, nonverbal learning disability, or ADHD. *Journal of Abnormal Child Psychology, 38,* 509–519.

Shprintzen, R. J. (2008). Velo-cardio-facial syndrome: 30 years of study. *Developmental Disabilities Research Reviews, 14,* 3–10.

Spreen, O. (2011). Nonverbal learning disabilities: A critical review. *Child Neuropsychology, 17,* 418–443.

Strang, J. D., & Rourke, B. P. (1985). Arithmetic disability subtypes: The neuropsychological significant of specific arithmetical impairment in childhood. In B.P. Rourke (Ed.), *Neuropsychology of learning disabilities: Essentials of subtype analysis* (pp. 167–186). New York, NY: Guilford.

Trauner, D. A., Spilkin, A. M., Williams, J., & Babchuck, L. (2007). Evidence for an early effect of the cystinosin gene on neural function: Specific cognitive deficits in young children with cystinosis. *Journal of Pediatrics, 151,* 192–196.

Volkmar, F. R., & Klin, A. (2000). Diagnostic issues in Asperger's syndrome. In A. Klin, F. R. Volkmar, & S. S. Sparrow (Eds.), *Asperger's syndrome* (pp. 172–209). New York, NY: Guilford.

Wilkinson-Smith, A., & Semrud-Clikeman, M. (2014). Are fine-motor impairments a defining feature of nonverbal learning disabilities in children? *Applied Neuropsychology: Child, 3,* 52–59.

Worling, D. E., Humphries, T., & Tannock, R. (1999). Spatial and emotional aspects of language inferencing in nonverbal learning disabilities. *Brain and Language, 70,* 220–239.

Yu, J., Buka, S., McCormick, M. C., Fitzmaurice, G. M., & Indurkhya, A. (2006). Behavioral problems and the effects of early intervention on eight-year-old children with learning disabilities. *Maternal and Child Health Journal, 10,* 329–338.

Part Two

METHODS AND MODELS OF SPECIFIC LEARNING DISABILITY IDENTIFICATION

Seven

A RESPONSE TO INTERVENTION (RTI) APPROACH TO SLD IDENTIFICATION

Jack M. Fletcher
Jeremy Miciak

Supported in part by grant P50 HD052117, "Texas Center for Learning Disabilities," from the Eunice Kennedy Shriver National Institute of Child Health and Human Development (NICHD). The content is solely the responsibility of the authors and does not necessarily represent the official views of the NICHD or the National Institutes of Health.

CLASSIFICATION AND IDENTIFICATION

From the beginning of the history of the concept of specific learning disabilities (SLDs), defining and identifying children and adults with SLD has been controversial (Doris, 1993). The fundamental issue, regardless of the descriptive label, is how to identify a subgroup of people from a larger population of people with learning, achievement, and (historically) behavioral difficulties that are representative of the concept of SLD (Fletcher, Lyon, Fuchs, & Barnes, 2007). In this chapter, we focus on approaches to identification of SLD that are implemented as part of a Response to Intervention (RTI) framework.

Fundamental to understanding any approach to identification of SLD is an understanding of classification, a process present in many scientific disciplines. Classifications permit the division of a larger set of observations into smaller subgroups based on a set of attributes that define how the observations are similar

Essentials of Specific Learning Disability Identification, Second Edition.
Edited by Vincent C. Alfonso and Dawn P. Flanagan
© 2018 John Wiley & Sons, Inc. Published 2018 by John Wiley & Sons, Inc.

and dissimilar. The assignment of the observations to the smaller subgroups is *identification* and represents an operationalization of the definitions that emerge from the classification. The relation of classification and identification is apparent in many scientific disciplines. For example, biologists have created complex criteria by which plants and animals are identified as different species. The *Diagnostic and Statistical Manual of Mental Disorders* (5th ed.) *(DSM-5)*, produced by the American Psychiatric Association (2013), is an example of a hypothetical classification of mental and behavioral disorders that, as in other areas of medicine, is largely categorical and uses signs and symptoms for identification (also called *diagnosis*). For SLD, classifications operate when the child's difficulties in school are identified as SLD and not as an intellectual disability or oral language problem. The various identification frameworks outlined in this book differ in how criteria for identification of SLD are operationalized, but they do not differ in the critical aspect of SLD that differentiates it from other academic problems: *unexpected underachievement.* The differences among these identification models emerge in how the classification is operationalized as a set of criteria for identification of children into subgroups.

Thus, any approach to identification derives from a classification that provides a characterization of the attributes specific to the subgroups to be identified. These attributes may be used to differentiate specific subgroups from the many different subgroups of the larger population of people who experience learning, achievement, and behavioral difficulties (Morris & Fletcher, 1988). At the heart of the classification are hypothesized constructs that represent the nature of the different subgroups, such as SLD, intellectual disability, attention-deficit hyperactivity disorder (ADHD), and other subgroups that may experience learning, achievement, and behavioral difficulties (e.g., children with depression or motivational difficulties). The result is a classification of different disorders that, in turn, lead to identification (or diagnostic) criteria that are then operationalized into a measurement system (definition) that permits determination of subgroup membership. The classification, and the resultant operational definitions and criteria, are also hypotheses that require continual evaluation. The measurement model is observable and operationalizes subgroups that are inherently unobservable. Thus, SLD is not directly observable but is operationalized by articulating the classification and the measurement model used to operationalize it. See Rapid Reference 7.1 for definitions of important terms used in this chapter.

Classifications tend to describe subgroups and, sometimes, individuals that represent ideal types, or prototypes. They are usually hierarchical and arranged in terms of larger to smaller classes that all share at least one common attribute but differ on other attributes. However, especially for subgroups such as SLD, in

≡ *Rapid Reference 7.1*

··

Classification Terminology

Taxonomy. The science of classification

Classification. An organization of entities into classes, usually hierarchical, and proceeding from larger to smaller subgroups based on shared and non-shared attributes; the classes may not be observable, representing hypothetical prototypes of each class

Identification (or diagnosis). The assignment of entities to a classification

Definition. A method for operationalizing identification into a classification

which the primary attributes are dimensional—that is, exist on a continuum with no natural demarcations (see Fletcher et al., 2007)—deciding about subgroup membership involves the placement of individuals along a set of multiple, correlated dimensions. Because there are no natural demarcations, the decisions that stem from the measurement model are inherently arbitrary and significantly influenced by the measurement error inherent in the procedures used to operationalize the classification. Measurement error is an especially significant problem if rigid cut points are applied and no considerations are made for the correlations among dimensions (Francis et al., 2005).

DON'T FORGET

··

SLD is fundamentally a dimensional classification in which the attributes exist on a continuum and for which there are no natural demarcations of specific categories. Other dimensional disorders include ADHD and, in medicine, obesity and hypertension. In any dimensional disorder, categories and thresholds are arbitrary and there is measurement error that leads to potential unreliability of individuals relative to thresholds.

Good classifications are reliable and not dependent on the specific measurement model so that they can be replicated despite variations in the measurement model. They also identify most of the people of interest (i.e., have adequate coverage). Most important, good classifications are valid not simply because subgroups can be identified but because the subgroups making up a valid classification can be differentiated on variables not used to establish the subgroups (Skinner, 1981). For example, if SLD is identified as a discrepancy between IQ and achievement, there should be systematic differences between low achievers who meet IQ-discrepancy criteria and low achievers who do not demonstrate an IQ discrepancy on cognitive, behavioral, and other variables not used to define the subgroups

≡ Rapid Reference 7.2

Characteristics of Good Classifications

- **Reliable.** Replicates across different approaches to operationalizations (internal validity)
- **Valid.** Differentiates classes on variables not used to define them (external validity)
- **Coverage.** Identifies the majority of the entities of interest
- **Effective.** Facilitates communication and prediction

(e.g., intervention response). Good classifications that meet these criteria facilitate communication, prediction, and other activities (see Rapid Reference 7.2).

In this chapter, the identification of SLD in the context of an RTI service-delivery framework is presented with these ideas about classifications, measurement models, and their reliability and validity as guiding principles. First, the concept of SLD is discussed as a classification hypothesis. Second, identification is discussed in terms of different methods. We present an approach to identification that aligns with the 2004 Individuals with Disabilities Education Improvement Act (IDEA 2004), not because it is a gold standard but because the concepts in IDEA 2004 are aligned with a classification that includes the essential components of the SLD concept (Fletcher et al., 2007). We then review some of the available reliability and validity evidence involving identification of SLD in an RTI framework.

WHAT IS SLD?

Historically, the SLD construct has been invoked in reference to the idea of "unexpected underachievement." Although early efforts to implement a classification of SLD based on this construct were too broad and included children with primary behavior problems (Doris, 1993), the construct has always attempted to represent people who struggle to master reading, writing, and mathematics, despite the absence of conditions known to interfere with mastery of academic skills, such as a sensory disorder, intellectual disability, emotional and behavioral

DON'T FORGET

Exclusionary criteria represent attributes that, by definition, preclude membership in a class (e.g., intellectual disability precludes SLD). Inclusionary criteria are attributes that indicate membership in a class, but are usually necessary and not sufficient (e.g., low achievement is necessary but not sufficient for identification of SLD).

difficulties that interfere with motivation or effort, and factors such as economic disadvantage, minority language status, and poor instruction. In the next few sections we discuss the evolution of the concept of SLD based on diagnosis by exclusion toward identification criteria that are more inclusionary.

Exclusionary Definitions

Early attempts to identify SLD focused on excluding "known" causes of low achievement. The exclusionary clauses in the federal statutory definition of SLD, which involved absence of sensory or motor disorders, intellectual disability, and behavioral disorders of presumed environmental origin (US Office of Education, 1968), have their roots in the earliest attempts to identify behavior disorders in children that were due to brain disorders (Still, 1902). Similarly, early descriptions of dyslexia as "word blindness" in a seemingly bright child attending a good school also used evidence of adequate intellectual functioning and educational opportunities to exclude certain forms of reading disabilities (Morgan, 1896). The first formal definitions of *minimal brain dysfunction* (Clements, 1966) included the exclusionary criteria present in the US federal statutory definition of SLD: "The term does not include children who have learning disabilities, which are primarily the result of visual, hearing, or motor handicaps, or mental retardation, or emotional disturbance, or of environmental, cultural, or economic disadvantage" (US Office of Education, 1968, p. 34).

The notion inherent in these early attempts to define and operationalize SLD is that "unexpected underachievement" can be identified simply by specifying conditions in which underachievement is due to presumably known causes that are excluded as factors in SLD. The classification underlying this approach to identification distinguishes SLD from sensory disorders, intellectual disabilities, behavioral problems, and environmental factors related to low achievement. However, the provisions about environmental factors related to low achievement (e.g., environmental disadvantage) were originally in place in the federal definition of SLD to prevent pooling of funds provided under special education and civil rights legislation (i.e., Title I; Doris, 1993). Not surprisingly, this approach to operationalizing a classification of SLD was not successful because the resulting subgroup was heterogeneous (Rutter, 1978), and assumptions about environmental factors, such as "cultural disadvantage," were difficult to operationalize (Kavale & Forness, 1985). As Ross (1976) stated,

Stripped of clauses which specify what a learning disability is not, this definition is circular, for it states, that a learning disability is an inability to

≋ Rapid Reference 7.3

Methods for SLD Identification

Aptitude-achievement discrepancy. SLD is identified in the presence of a "significant" discrepancy between aptitude (different IQ scales, listening comprehension) and achievement, usually with exclusionary criteria and often with no criterion for absolute low achievement.

Low achievement. SLD is indicated by the presence of absolute low achievement relative to chronological age expectations, usually with exclusionary criteria.

Cognitive discrepancy. SLD is indicated by a pattern of intraindividual strengths and weaknesses on measures of cognitive processes, usually with some linkage to expected relations of achievement and cognitive function (weakness) and evidence of strengths in other cognitive processes.

Hybrid model. SLD is indicated by two inclusionary criteria, inadequate instructional response, and absolute low achievement, with exclusionary criteria representing other disorders.

learn. It is a reflection of the rudimentary state of knowledge, in this field, that every definition in current use has its focus on what the condition is not, leaving what it is unspecified and thus ambiguous. (p. 11)

Examples of common methods for SLD identification are provided in Rapid Reference 7.3.

Moving Toward Inclusionary Definitions

The changes since early efforts to define SLD on the basis of exclusionary criteria can be understood as an effort to identify inclusion criteria that specify which people meet criteria for SLD. What is important is that the underlying notion of SLD as "unexpected underachievement" and the classification framework that distinguishes SLD from intellectual disabilities and behavior disorders is unchanged. The challenge is determining *inclusionary* criteria that reliably and validly identify people with SLD, as opposed to another form of achievement problem.

DON'T FORGET

Moving from exclusionary to inclusionary definitions of SLD does not change the underlying notion of SLD as "unexpected underachievement" or the classification framework that distinguishes SLD from other disorders.

Aptitude-Achievement Discrepancy Methods

Early efforts to use a discrepancy of higher aptitude and lower achievement have long been proposed. Although the most well-known method uses IQ scores to operationalize aptitude, variations in which IQ composite is used (e.g., verbal IQ, nonverbal or performance IQ, composite or Full Scale IQ), even in listening comprehension, have been proposed and evaluated (Fletcher et al., 2007). The use of an aptitude-achievement discrepancy as an inclusionary criterion has failed in part because this approach to measurement does not yield a subgroup of children who are poor achievers and can be validly differentiated from other low achievers on the basis of attributes not used to define the subgroups. In a meta-analysis of 46 studies, Stuebing et al. (2002) reported negligible aggregated effect size differences on behavioral (−0.05) and achievement variables (−0.12). There was a small effect size difference on cognitive variables (0.30) not used to define the subgroups, but negligible differences on measures of phonological awareness, rapid naming, verbal memory, and vocabulary. They also reported that the heterogeneity in estimates of effect sizes could be explained by variations in how IQ discrepancy and low achievement were defined.

In other domains, the long-term prognosis of reading disabilities does not vary with IQ discrepancy (Francis, Shaywitz, Stuebing, Shaywitz, & Fletcher, 1996). In the area of intervention response, Fuchs and Young (2006) concluded from a review of 13 studies that IQ was a good predictor of intervention response. However, an empirical meta-analysis of these 13 articles, along with nine additional studies, found that IQ accounts for only small amounts (< 1%) of the unique variance in response to reading intervention (Stuebing, Barth, Molfese, Weiss, & Fletcher, 2009). More recent neuroimaging studies have not found differences in brain activation for IQ-discrepant and non-discrepant poor readers (Simos, Rezaie, Fletcher, & Papanicolaou, 2013; Tanaka et al., 2011). Thus, there is little evidence that supports classifications of SLD based on IQ-achievement discrepancy criteria.

> **DON'T FORGET**
> ....
> IQ-achievement discrepant and low-achieving poor readers do not show robust differences in external validity studies, including behavior, achievement, cognitive processes, prognosis, intervention response, and brain activation. Aptitude-achievement methods have been studied in relation to a variety of indices of aptitude, including listening comprehension, and in relation to math and other domains, and in speech and language disorders, with little evidence of validity (Fletcher et al., 2007).

Low-Achievement Methods

Given the concerns about the validity of classifications based on IQ-achievement discrepancy, some have proposed that SLD be identified on the basis of absolute low achievement, so that anyone scoring below the 25th percentile may belong to the SLD subgroup (Siegel, 1992). Grouping students according to achievement strengths and weaknesses (e.g., reading versus math disabilities) does lead to subgroups that can be reliably and validly differentiated (Willcutt et al., 2013). Indeed, the strongest evidence for the validity of the SLD construct comes from research studies on cognition, genetics, and brain function that demonstrate differentiation of children with reading and math difficulties from children with intellectual disabilities, ADHD and no achievement problems, and typically developing children (Fletcher et al., 2007). As such, *low achievement is a necessary but not sufficient condition for identification of SLD,* and it represents a clear inclusionary criterion.

> **CAUTION**
> ....
> The mere presence of low achievement does not necessarily indicate SLD.

If the SLD classification is multidimensional, then multiple measurements are needed to identify SLD. In this context, low achievement is stipulated as the inclusionary criterion, and exclusionary criteria are added to rule out the presence of other disabilities and the environmental factors associated with low achievement, resulting in a subgroup that has different kinds of SLD (e.g., basic reading, reading fluency, reading comprehension, mathematics computations and problem-solving, and written language). Thus, the task is to rule out other disabilities and environmental factors as "causes" of underachievement and specify the domain(s) in which underachievement may occur. In fact, a review of the literature on the classification of SLD using the criteria for reliable and valid classifications provided previously suggests that this approach to SLD identification has the strongest evidence of any measurement model (Fletcher et al., 2007).

The weakness of the low-achievement method for SLD identification is its inability to sort people according to putative causes of low achievement. For example, it is difficult to demonstrate major differences in the cognitive and neural correlates of low achievement between economically advantaged and disadvantaged children. In addition, it does not seem reasonable to stipulate that children for whom environmental

> **DON'T FORGET**
> ....
> Low achievement is a necessary, but not sufficient, condition for SLD identification and should be considered an inclusionary criterion.

factors seem to operate cannot also possess the attributes of SLD. The issue is still whether there are additional inclusionary criteria that would help identify people as SLD and also have a relation with intervention planning and response (Kavale & Forness, 1985).

C A U T I O N

Children from environmentally disadvantaged backgrounds may possess the attributes of SLD; therefore, the extent to which such disadvantage may be a contributing or primary cause of learning difficulties should be evaluated carefully.

Cognitive Discrepancy Methods

Recently, there have been increasing calls to move toward SLD-identification models that assess cognitive processing patterns of strengths and weaknesses (PSW models; Hale et al., 2010). These methods require a cognitive strength and a cognitive weakness that is related to achievement. The validity evidence typically cited is that cognitive measures are correlated with achievement (Johnson, 2014; Kudo, Lussier, & Swanson, 2015). In addition, the fact that application of these methods produces different cognitive profiles and psychosocial profiles of SLD is also cited (Backenson et al., 2015; Fenwick et al., 2015), along with case studies. This evidence base is not compelling. Showing that cognitive measures and achievement are correlated does not establish that such measures are related to intervention outcomes, much less provide value-added information to identification. Any statistical method will generate profiles, but the mere generation of profiles does not establish reliability and validity, especially if the validity studies are largely post hoc (Morris & Fletcher, 1988). From a classification perspective, the reliability and validity of PSW methods cannot be established via case studies, especially for a high-prevalence problem such as SLD.

The reliability and validity of these methods should be established by comparing low-achieving students who meet criteria for SLD based on PSW criteria with low-achieving students who do not meet these criteria. However, these PSW models have not been investigated extensively from a classification perspective. Indeed, few large-scale studies have investigated PSW models, and claims about validity are therefore limited.

Recent studies using these methods have raised questions about whether intraindividual cognitive discrepancies, as operationalized by PSW frameworks, represent a reliable and valid classification; further evidence is necessary if these models are to be recommended for adoption. In contrast to the aptitude-achievement and low-achievement literature previously discussed, there is not a significant body of empirical classification research making comparisons across LD and low-achieving groups using PSW methods or comparisons of identification rates across methods. In one recent study, Miciak et al. (2016) used a large intervention database with extensive assessments of cognitive functions to determine if status as SLD under common operationalizations of PSW methods predicted differential treatment response, which would be expected if PSW status has relevance for planning interventions. There was little evidence of value-added increments relative to baseline assessments of reading skills. Indeed, individual cognitive assessments in the absence of the application of PSW methods did not contribute significantly to the prediction of treatment outcomes. This paralleled a recent meta-analysis by Stuebing et al. (2014), which found that different cognitive measures explained extremely small amounts of growth in response to intervention when initial status in reading skills was taken into account. In another recent meta-analysis, Burns et al. (2016) examined the role of cognitive and neuropsychological tests in relation to different aspects of intervention. (i.e., screening, planning, intervention design, and outcomes). The authors reported a small effect of cognitive tests across these dimensions (Hedges' $g = .17$), which was much smaller than the effect of reading fluency ($g = .43$) and phonological awareness ($g = .48$). They recommended a focus on direct assessments of academic achievement and not on the correlates.

Such findings highlight the central controversy regarding the necessity of an assessment of cognitive processes as part of the SLD identification process: the value that such assessments *add* to intervention planning and outcomes. One significant reason that an assessment of cognitive processes may be unnecessary is that cognitive processes are correlated with achievement. Thus, what value is added by measuring correlates (psychological processes) when the "manifestations" (achievement) are part of the measurement model? It is difficult for a correlate to contribute independently of the manifestations. Additionally, contrary to proponents' assertions (Hale et al., 2010; Reynolds & Shaywitz, 2009), there is not a strong evidence base suggesting that classifications based on cognitive strengths and weaknesses yield unique subgroups of students or that such assessments can be used to tailor interventions to students' unique cognitive profile(s). Indeed, three recent comprehensive literature reviews on different approaches to matching individual characteristics to intervention, including learning styles, aptitude-by-treatment interactions, neuropsychological profiles, and personality-by-treatment interactions, have found a fragmented evidence base that largely did not find the interactions of person-level attributes and differential RTI that these

C A U T I O N

The evidence base supporting cognitive discrepancies as a valid tool for identifying SLD subgroups that respond differentially to interventions is weak.

hypotheses would predict (Burns et al., 2016; Kearns & Fuchs, 2013; Pashler, McDaniel, Rohrer, & Bjork, 2008).

The strongest evidence for the aptitude-by-treatment interactions posited by advocates of a cognitive discrepancy model actually comes from studies that operationalize strengths and weaknesses in the achievement domain. For example, Connor, Morrison, Fishman, Schatschneider, and Underwood (2007) showed that when teachers geared reading interventions based on strengths and weaknesses in decoding and comprehension, differential outcomes were apparent. More generally, the fact that children with SLD in reading show improved reading performance when provided reading but not math instruction (Morris et al., 2012) may seem trivial, but in fact it supports the idea of aptitude-by-treatment interactions—strong support for the concept of the specificity of SLD. Whether such findings extend to cognitive discrepancies has not been established. These are hypotheses that warrant continued investigation, especially in the context of a measurement framework that involves multiple attributes (i.e., baseline academic performance in addition to cognitive performance).

> **DON'T FORGET**
> ....
> Planning interventions based on strengths and weaknesses in the achievement domain has a strong evidence base.

Provision of Adequate Instruction

In addition to low achievement, the other potential attribute of an approach to the classification of SLD is the evaluation of instructional response. Most definitions of SLD indicate that inadequate instruction is one of the environmental factors that should be treated as an exclusionary factor (Fletcher et al., 2007). For example, IDEA 2004 states that children may not be identified as SLD if there is no evidence of adequate instruction in reading or math. Concerns about the adequacy of instruction component has taken on a new emphasis since the early 2000s because of consensus reports indicating that many children are identified as SLD and placed in special education despite inadequate core instructional programs (Donovan & Cross, 2002). Perhaps the most significant change in IDEA 2004 is the provision that indicates that, regardless of the identification model,

> to ensure that underachievement in a child suspected of having a specific learning disability is not due to lack of appropriate instruction in reading or math, the group must consider, as part of the evaluation . . . (1) Data that demonstrate that prior to, or as a part of, the referral process, the child was provided appropriate instruction in regular education settings, delivered by qualified personnel; and (2) Data-based documentation of repeated

assessments of achievement at reasonable intervals, reflecting formal assessment of student progress during instruction, which was provided to the child's parents. (Individuals with Disabilities Education Improvement Act of 2004, 2006)

DON'T FORGET

....

Inadequate instructional response is an inclusionary characteristic of SLD in models derived from RTI service-delivery frameworks.

Under this language, instructional response is not just exclusionary. Because data must be collected that measure student progress and the quality of instruction, instructional response is an inclusionary criterion, with inadequate instructional response representing evidence of "unexpected underachievement."

A Hybrid Method: The Importance of Instructional Response

This discussion of history, classification, and the development of multi-criteria identification models is prefatory to any discussion of an identification model for SLD. Fletcher et al. (2007) argued that the evidence supports a hybrid model of classification consistent with a consensus group of researchers convened by the US Department of Education Office of Special Education Programs (Bradley, Danielson, & Hallahan, 2002). This group suggested three primary criteria, the first two of which are clearly inclusionary (Bradley et al., 2002, p. 798):

1. Student demonstrates low achievement.
2. There is insufficient response to effective research-based interventions. A systematic plan for assessing change in performance must be established prior to intervention.
3. Exclusion factors such as mental retardation, sensory deficits, serious emotional disturbance, language minority children (where lack of proficiency in English accounts for measured achievement deficits), and lack of opportunity to learn should be considered.

Rapid Reference 7.4 lists criteria for SLD identification that are consistent with those outlined by Bradley et al. (2002).

Identifying people with SLD, whether as part of the process stipulated in IDEA 2004, in a clinic outside of school, and through research, requires multiple criteria. Researchers and practitioners may argue about how these attributes are operationalized and whether other attributes are needed, but these three sets of criteria seem to align with the notion of unexpected underachievement. The difference in this hybrid model relative to cognitive discrepancy and other low-achievement

⟻ Rapid Reference 7.4

....

Criteria for Identification of SLD in a Hybrid Model That Integrates Low Achievement and Components of RTI

- Insufficient response to effective research-based interventions based on assessments of progress and the quality and fidelity of instruction
- Demonstration of absolute low achievement in word reading, reading fluency, reading comprehension, mathematics computation, mathematics problem-solving, and written expression
- Exclusionary factors such as intellectual disability, sensory deficits, serious emotional disturbance, language minority status, and lack of opportunity to learn do not explain inadequate instructional response

models is that the primary criterion for "unexpected" is based on instructional response. *What better evidence for unexpected underachievement is there than evidence that the person has not responded to quality instruction?*

In this hybrid model and in methods that emerge in the context of RTI implementations, intractability to quality instruction is a marker for unexpected underachievement and a necessary component for SLD iden-

C A U T I O N
....
No matter which model is used for identification, a single criterion is never adequate to indicate SLD.

DON'T FORGET
....
No child should be identified as SLD without evidence of intractability in response to adequate instruction.

tification, as in all the classification models reviewed in this chapter. As such, intractability constitutes an *inclusionary* attribute. Moreover, this component is essential whether the identification model stems from an RTI process or a process that includes some form of cognitive discrepancy. Only if an achievement deficit is present and the child demonstrates intractability in response to adequate instruction is there evidence that the low achievement is unexpected.

RTI AND SLD IDENTIFICATION

The advantage of an SLD identification process that emerges from an RTI service-delivery system is that the instructional response components are embedded in the identification process, streamlining eligibility decisions and directly linking special education services with those provided in general education. RTI service-delivery frameworks also permit a more flexible approach to assessment in which tools are selected according to hypotheses about the basis for inadequate instructional response. Individual educational plans stem directly from the comprehensive evaluation. Consistent with IDEA 2004, identification incorporates multiple sources of data.

What Is an RTI Framework?

Purpose and Structure

The most important consideration in understanding RTI models is that they are not implemented for the primary purpose of SLD identification (see Rapid Reference 7.5). Rather, the primary goal is the prevention and remediation of academic and behavioral difficulties through effective classroom and supplemental instruction, including those provided by all entitlement programs. As such, RTI is a framework for effectively delivering and coordinating services in schools. Thus, RTI frameworks permit the generation of data that are relevant to identification of SLD and that lead to different approaches to referral and placement decisions related to SLD (Fletcher & Vaughn, 2009a).

> **C A U T I O N**
> ....
> RTI is a framework for service delivery. Identification is a secondary objective, which derives from screening and progress monitoring, but also requires additional criteria.

In an RTI framework, universal screening of students for achievement and behavioral difficulties occurs two to three times yearly. Children who are at risk have access to tiered, or layered, interventions that begin in the general education classroom and increase in

≡ *Rapid Reference 7.5*
....

What Is RTI?

The primary goal of RTI is to improve academic and behavioral outcomes for all students by eliminating discrepancies between actual and expected performance. RTI also does the following:

- Offers a set of processes for coordinating high-quality service delivery in schools
- Takes a multitiered, layered instructional approach that prevents problems first and then brings increasingly intense interventions to students who don't respond
- Facilitates making instructional decisions based on data
- Integrates entitlement programs with general education

≡ Rapid Reference 7.6

Characteristics of Most RTI Frameworks

- Universal, population-based screening and progress monitoring; decision making based on data to modify instruction
- Implementation of evidence-based interventions in the general education classroom with supplemental and intensive intervention
- A coordinated, seamless system of service delivery, connecting prevention and remediation
- Data that provide information relevant to eligibility for special education
- Parent involvement and team-based decision making

intensity depending on the students' instructional response. Intensity is increased by providing more time, teaching in smaller groups, and varying curricula and interventions to meet the needs of the individual student. Rapid Reference 7.6 includes common characteristics of most RTI frameworks.

The need for more-intense interventions is measured by brief assessments of progress, often based on a curriculum-based measurement (CBM) framework (Fuchs & Fuchs, 1998; Kovaleski, VanDerHeyden, & Shapiro, 2013). If a child progresses through multiple layers of intervention and does not show adequate instructional response relative to some benchmark established by the school, district, or state, the child may be considered for special education because of the evidence that instruction within the general education curriculum has not been adequate to meet the student's instructional needs. At this point, a comprehensive evaluation would occur. Controversy attends the issue of appropriate benchmarks. However, the interpretation of these benchmarks is facilitated by links with some sort of national reference, as well as state requirements for annual yearly progress, which is clearly possible from a

DON'T FORGET

The primary goal of an RTI framework is the prevention and remediation of academic and behavioral difficulties through effective classroom and supplemental instruction, including those provided by all entitlement programs.

DON'T FORGET

Benchmarks are most interpretable when linked to a national reference as well as state requirements for annual yearly progress.

CBM framework (Fuchs & Fuchs, 2004). For instructional decision making, tying measures to the curriculum where progress is indexed to local benchmarks is reasonable. Nevertheless, care should be taken in using local standards for a legal eligibility requirement, unless there is a clear link with national standards and evidence of reliability and validity.

One myth about RTI models is that they require a child to complete multiple levels of intervention before special education is considered. In fact, a child can be referred for special education evaluation at any point in the RTI process (Kovaleski et al., 2013). Referral, however, begs the question of what special education can provide. In some instances, the child may need the civil rights protections afforded by IDEA 2004 or may have problems that are not addressed by the RTI framework (e.g., a speech and language disorder or concerns about a pervasive developmental disorder). Similar to identification approaches to SLD implemented before IDEA 2004, the evaluation process must consider what services and protections the referred child may require. The difference is that in RTI the primary goal is to identify treatment needs; eligibility determination is not isolated from efforts at intervention.

DON'T FORGET

A child may be referred for special education at any point in the RTI process.

Implementation Frameworks

There are many approaches to the implementation of RTI frameworks, which are best considered not as a single model but as a set of processes with variation in how the processes are implemented (Fletcher & Vaughn, 2009a). These approaches have at least two historical origins representing efforts to implement prevention programs in schools. The first origin represents efforts to prevent behavior problems using a school-wide prevention approach (Donovan & Cross, 2002; Walker, Stiller, Serverson, Feil, & Golly, 1998). These models often use a *problem-solving* process, whereby a team identifies a behavioral or academic problem, chooses an intervention to address the problem, evaluates the outcome of the intervention, and then proposes new interventions if the problem has not been resolved (Reschly & Tilly, 1999).

The second origin derives from research on preventing reading difficulties in children. These approaches use *standardized protocols* to deliver interventions that increase in intensity and differentiation depending on the child's instructional response. An example of such an approach is the three-tier model of instructional delivery in reading that begins in general education (Tier 1),

≡ Rapid Reference 7.7

Overarching Approaches to RTI Implementation

- **Problem-solving model.** A shared decision-making team is organized at a school, composed of administrators, teachers, and itinerant professionals. Based on screening and progress-monitoring data, the team identifies a behavioral or academic problem and an intervention to address the problem, evaluates the outcome of the intervention, and then proposes new interventions if the problem has not been resolved. This model has its origins in RTI implementations involving behavioral difficulties, but it is also used for academic problems.
- **Standard protocol.** Based on universal screening and progress-monitoring data, children are identified as at risk. Interventions are usually standardized at each tier and increase in intensity and differentiation depending on the child's instructional response. These models originated in efforts to enhance reading instruction outcomes.

adds supplemental instruction in the form of additional small-group instruction for 20 to 40 minutes per day for about 20% of students who do not respond to enhanced general education instruction (Tier 2), and provides more intensive instruction for longer periods of time, usually in smaller groups, for about 5% of students who do not respond to general education and supplemental intervention (Tier 3). The problem-solving and standardized treatment protocol models reflect the impact of public health models of health care delivery that distinguish primary, secondary, and tertiary levels of intervention and increase intensity and differentiation (and cost) depending on the individual's response to treatment (Vaughn et al., 2009, 2010). Rapid Reference 7.7 summarizes approaches to RTI implementation, and Rapid Reference 7.8 identifies specific issues that schools should consider when implementing RTI.

What constitutes the comprehensive evaluation? These models share common features, including (1) universal screening, to identify students at risk for academic and behavioral difficulties; (2) progress monitoring, to evaluate response to interventions; and (3) increasingly intensive interventions that begin with high-quality, differentiated general education instruction and subsequent supplemental programs, which increase time in, and differentiation of, instruction (Jimerson, Burns, & VanDerHeyden, 2016). These three components provide data that may lead to referral for a *comprehensive evaluation* to determine eligibility for special education under SLD or another disability category or eligibility for other entitlement programs. The objectives of RTI service-delivery frameworks

≡ *Rapid Reference 7.8*

Sampling of Issues School Districts Should Consider When Implementing RTI Frameworks

- Leadership, from superintendent to teacher and community, must be on board
- Role of parents
- How to screen and monitor progress
- Criteria for inadequate response
- Number of tiers
- Organization of curriculum and relation to tiers
- How to target professional development
- Standard protocol versus problem-solving model
- Role of special education and assessment professionals

focus on the provision of quality, evidence-based instruction, a necessary component for any SLD-identification model.

RTI frameworks do not exist for SLD identification; these frameworks have been adopted by school districts for many reasons, most of which are focused on improved outcomes for all students (Spectrum K12, 2008). When districts adopt high-quality RTI frameworks that follow research recommendations, there is considerable evidence of improved achievement and behavioral outcomes as well as a reduction in special education referrals (Jimerson et al., 2016). However, these improvements in student achievement are not guaranteed, as a recent report commissioned by the National Center for Educational Evaluation and Regional Assistance demonstrated (Balu et al., 2015). In this report, student performance at 146 impact schools with self-reported implementation of RTI frameworks was evaluated. The study design compared performance of students who scored just below the cut point for intervention to students who scored just above. Surprisingly, the students assigned to intensive interventions as part of the RTI framework did not perform better than the comparison students, and students in first grade performed even worse. Clearly, just implementing RTI was not sufficient; the details matter. In this study, the research team had very little control over the implementation at schools. There was considerable variability in the cut points to assign students to intervention, the duration and intensity of those interventions, the quality and content of instruction, as well as the use of progress monitoring to make instructional decisions.

These results suggest that schools and districts may need external support in order to implement RTI frameworks successfully. The results also suggest that schools and districts should pay careful attention to practice recommendations for RTI, including (1) universal screening; (2) differentiated instruction for all

> **C A U T I O N**
>
> Implementation of RTI frameworks may require considerable discussion and negotiation at a district level and may take several years to scale effectively. The administrative hierarchy, from the superintendent to the teacher, must be on board.

students; (3) intensive, systematic interventions for those who score below benchmarks; (4) ongoing progress monitoring; and (5) increasingly intensive interventions for students who do not demonstrate adequate progress to Tier 2 instruction (Gersten et al., 2008). Small-scale, empirical studies that implement this framework in carefully controlled settings demonstrate positive effects (VanDerHeyden, Witt, & Gilbertson, 2007; Vaughn et al., 2012).

Applications to Identification of SLD

The difference in the referral and eligibility process in an RTI framework versus a traditional approach is demonstrated in Figure 7.1 (Fletcher et al., 2007). The first difference is the importance placed on universal screening and continuous progress monitoring. On the left side, the traditional approach does not involve universal screening or progress monitoring, both of which are apparent in the model on the right side of the figure based on RTI. The second difference involves how students are referred for special education. An educator or parent initiates the referral in a traditional model, an approach known to relate to gender and minority disproportionality (Donovan & Cross, 2002). In an RTI framework, referral emerges because of inadequate instructional response, and progress monitoring continues whether the student is identified with SLD or not. The third difference is the idea of multiple treatments and modification of instruction based on progress. Multiple treatments and modifying instruction based on progress are implicit in the traditional model but explicit in the RTI framework. The fourth difference relates to special education. The traditional model sets aside special education as a separate service; the RTI service-delivery framework links general and special education and continues progress monitoring.

> **DON'T FORGET**
>
> Any model for SLD identification requires a comprehensive evaluation, including those provided in the context of RTI, as well as evidence of inadequate instructional response.

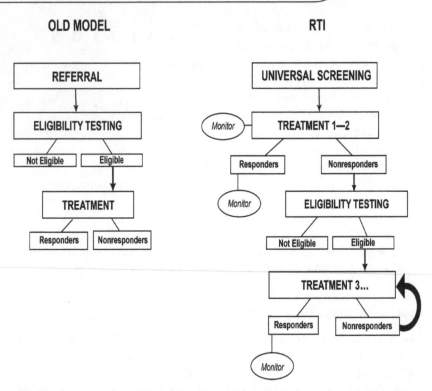

Figure 7.1. Comparison of a Traditional Model of Identification for SLD with a Model Based on RTI. From Fletcher et al. (2007). Copyright 2007 by Guilford Press. Reprinted with permission.

Other differences occur in the comprehensive evaluation. In a model based on RTI, much is already known about the student because of screening, progress monitoring, and the nature of interventions that have not been effective. As such, the student comes to the eligibility process with data and specific questions that represent hypotheses about the basis for effective instructional response, which form the basis for the comprehensive evaluation. Assessments are tailored to specific questions about the instructional needs of the child and the basis for inadequate response. As part of the evaluation, the child can be given IQ tests, assessments of cognitive processes, behavioral assessments, or any procedure deemed necessary to understand inadequate instructional response and to determine whether special education services are appropriate interventions (Fletcher et al., 2007). There is no requirement or expectation that the same evaluation be done with each and every child or that the assessment process assess cognitive processes (Zirkel, 2013).

The Comprehensive Evaluation

The flexibility concerning assessment, which IDEA 2004 defines as a "comprehensive data-gathering process," should occur regardless of the identification framework but leads to the concern that identification is based solely on the data used to screen students and monitor progress (Dixon, Eusebio, Turton, Wright, & Hale, 2010; Reynolds & Shaywitz, 2009). Not only is this illegal in terms of the provisions of IDEA 2004 but also it is inconsistent with the classification of SLD and the fact that multiple criteria are needed. However, in some instances, the only formal data may be that based on instructional response data and the adequacy of instruction (Kovaleski et al., 2013). There is no requirement in IDEA 2004 that all the components of identification be formally assessed (vision, hearing, limited English proficiency, intellectual disability, behavioral problem, etc.), but the evaluation still should consider these components and make eligibility decisions based on multiple sources of information. *When appropriate,* these domains may be assessed through further psycho-educational assessment.

Eligibility decisions could be made when the only formal data are based on instructional response and the adequacy of instruction, but it is recommended that additional formal assessment be included for evaluations of SLD (Kovaleski et al., 2013). The comprehensive evaluation should formally address the two attributes that are necessary for identification of SLD—low achievement and instructional response. In addition, the comprehensive evaluation needs to address the possible presence of other disabilities and contextual factors that may influence achievement. For these reasons, it is recommended that a comprehensive evaluation for SLD include a brief evaluation using norm-referenced achievement tests; data on instructional response; data on the adequacy of instruction; and, at a minimum, assessments of developmental and medical history and teacher-parent rating scales to screen for behavioral factors that may contribute to low achievement.

> **C A U T I O N**
> ....
> Data on inadequate instructional response are rarely sufficient to satisfy requirements of IDEA 2004, much less identify SLD. However, this does not mean that every possible attribute or concern must be formally evaluated.

Establish Low Achievement

Low achievement is one of two inclusionary criteria in the hybrid model of SLD identification presented in this chapter. Thus, firmly establishing low achievement should be a part of most comprehensive evaluations for SLD. As outlined in Fletcher et al. (2007, Chapter 4), norm-referenced assessments of achievement can be used that are brief and based on hypotheses about the nature and scope of academic impairment for the specific child. In this context, norm-referenced achievement tests nicely complement data on instructional response and provide additional information supporting the identification of a child as SLD. Progress-monitoring tools for assessing instructional response may not be as reliable and sensitive to change for all eight academic domains in IDEA 2004 (e.g., reading comprehension). Additionally, the use of instructional response, as measured by CBMs, as the sole criterion for the identification of inadequate responders, demonstrates low reliability for identification decisions, and different measures and criteria will result in different identification decisions for individual children (Barth et al., 2008; Brown-Waesche, Schatschneider, Maner, Ahmed, & Wagner, 2011). Finally, to minimize testing time, use of norm-referenced assessments of academic achievement in the hybrid model should be brief and based on hypotheses about the specific nature and scope of academic impairment (Fletcher et al., 2007). There is no need to assess all eight domains of IDEA 2004 if the nature of the achievement problem is easily established. Why complete extensive assessments of reading comprehension and written expression for children who have problems with word recognition and spelling?

One other advantage to the inclusion of norm-referenced assessments of achievement is that the resultant patterns of difficulty can be tied to the research base on different types of SLD (Fletcher et al., 2007). There is a great deal known about the cognitive and neural correlates of reading, math, and written expression difficulties. Additionally, by identifying the achievement domains in which the student has weaknesses, decisions about instruction can be aligned with a robust evidence base of effective academic interventions for students with SLD (e.g., Gersten

> **DON'T FORGET**
>
> There is an extensive body of research on SLD and different academic skills, spanning the range from cognitive processes to neural correlates and genetics, as well as emotional and behavioral correlates and environmental factors. This research has fueled investigation on intervention (Fletcher et al., 2007).

et al., 2008; Swanson, 1999). For some students, the area of academic impairment may be limited (e.g., word reading) and the resultant intervention plan will be limited. However, for some students with problems in multiple domains a more comprehensive intervention plan may be needed.

≋ Rapid Reference 7.9

Methods for Assessing Instructional Response

- **Final status.** Compares norm-referenced and criterion-referenced post-intervention achievement scores to a benchmark
- **Slope-discrepancy.** Compares rates of growth to the average rate for a reference group, usually with a progress-monitoring assessment
- **Dual-discrepancy.** Compares rates of growth and level of performance on a progress-monitoring assessment to identify inadequate response

Source: Fuchs and Deshler (2007).

Assess Intervention Response

Fuchs and Deshler (2007) identified three major approaches to identifying students as meeting one criterion for SLD based on instructional response, including (1) final status, (2) slope-discrepancy, and (3) dual-discrepancy (see Rapid References 7.9 and 7.10). *Final status* methods compare norm-referenced and criterion-referenced post-intervention achievement scores to a benchmark based on local or national norms. *Slope-discrepancy* methods compare rates of growth to the average rate for a reference group, and *dual-discrepancy* methods use rates of growth and level of performance on a progress-monitoring assessment to identify inadequate response. All three approaches are examples of discrepancy models, but the last two incorporate assessments of change (Fuchs & Fuchs, 1998)

≋ Rapid Reference 7.10

Characteristics Differentiating Adequate and Inadequate Responders to Reading Instruction

- Inadequate responders tend to be older, more economically disadvantaged, more likely male, and more likely to have repeated grades.
- Behavioral difficulties are more common in inadequate responders, especially inattention.
- Assessments of phonological awareness, rapid naming, and different oral language skills may more reliably differentiate adequate and inadequate responders.
- IQ scores are weaker discriminators of responder status relative to more-specific assessments of cognitive processes.

and use progress-monitoring assessments. (For more information on these approaches, see Jimerson et al., 2016.)

As with any cut point–based criterion used to identify a component of SLD, the cut points associated with these methods are arbitrary. Much of the controversy involves whether benchmarks can be local or based on some type of national standardization. The use of intervention response data to monitor progress and adjust instruction, for which local benchmarks are at the discretion of the district, is very reasonable and strongly supported by research (Stecker, Fuchs, & Fuchs, 2007). For identification purposes, intervention response criteria should have some form of national standardization whenever possible. In general, for identification purposes, there is little evidence that assessments of slope provide value-added information to assessments of growth (Fletcher et al., 2014). However, growth is critical for providing information on student progress, achievement of goals, and the need to modify instruction, with a strong evidence base supporting the utility of progress monitoring for these purposes as an essential part of instruction (Kovaleski et al., 2013; Stecker et al., 2007).

Assess Contextual Factors

If the concerns that led to referral involve other disabilities, the assessment may need to be more comprehensive and address the presence of other disabilities and the exclusionary criteria, which are better considered as contextual factors affecting treatment planning. A more-comprehensive evaluation should address specific hypotheses about the child and could include many components, including (1) assessments of IQ and adaptive behavior to identify intellectual disabilities, (2) assessments and procedures to identify pervasive developmental disorders, (3) an evaluation of English proficiency for students in the process of learning English, and (4) assessments of speech and language. Behavior rating scales from parents and teachers should be routinely completed as screening measures for comorbid disorders (e.g., ADHD) and other contextual factors that may explain low achievement; these contextual factors must be considered in formulating a treatment plan. However, not every child needs to be assessed for every potential problem; the comprehensive assessment should be based on specific hypotheses that emerge from progress-monitoring data and the student's response to targeted, preventive interventions.

More generally, disability determination is two-pronged. If the student is evaluated outside of an RTI framework, additional consideration of evidence that an identified disorder (first prong) leads to adaptive impairment (i.e., an educational need; second prong) must also be considered, because disability determination always has these two prongs. In an RTI framework, adaptive impairment is determined first (i.e., evidence that the child does not achieve at grade level despite quality instruction), and the establishment of eligibility involves determining the basis for this intractability. In other identification models, the assessment of adaptive impairment may be subjective and partly responsible for the confusion that emerges when an interdisciplinary team denies eligibility despite a diagnosed disorder that sometimes, but not always, interferes with school performance. Just having a disorder is not sufficient to identify the disorder as a disability.

> **DON'T FORGET**
>
> Disability determination has two components. There must be evidence of a problem and evidence that the problem has consequences for adaptation or an educational need. In an RTI framework, the adaptive consequences are identified first and then the problem is specified.

Reliability Issues Are Universal for All Methods

The reliability of classifications based on an RTI approach is difficult to address because there is no gold standard for determining inadequate response (or more broadly which child "truly" demonstrates an SLD). In the absence of a gold standard, the identification decisions emerging from RTI service-delivery frameworks can be compared across different operationalizations or compared to alternative models for SLD identification. Decisions about setting benchmarks and acceptable levels of error (i.e., false positives and false negatives) can be made based on considerations of student need, the validity of emergent groups, and resource availability and allocation. There are inherent trade-offs involved, because efforts to minimize false negatives (missing an inadequate responder) will result in a larger number of false positives (identifying an adequate responder as inadequate). In general, we recommend that schools and districts emphasize minimizing false negatives because academic interventions are generally low cost, low risk, and more effective when administered early.

> **CAUTION**
>
> Because SLDs are dimensional, there is no gold standard or true positive for any classification model. Identification is always relative to the criteria used to operationalize the classification.

Regardless of whether identification is based on the assessment of instructional response, low achievement, or some type of cognitive discrepancy, any psychometric approach based on cut points is inherently unreliable; different students will be identified by different measures, different criteria, or different cut points

(Francis et al., 2005). Students near the cut point are very similar and will change group membership (i.e., adequate versus inadequate responders). This is certainly true for the assessment of intervention response (Barth et al., 2008; Brown-Waesche et al., 2011). The problem can be easily understood by considering a study by Fletcher et al. (2014). In this study, comparisons were made of different methods for assessing instructional response in reading. Identification of inadequate responders based on assessments of final status at the end of an intervention or on indices incorporating growth (slope) showed low agreement concerning which students were inadequate responders. Subsequent data simulations demonstrated that even slight reductions in the reliability of the measures resulted in large reductions in agreement between identification decisions of adequate and inadequate responders. When the simulation simultaneously accounted for the imperfect correlation between reading measures, the imperfect reliability of the measures, and the different norming populations on which scores would be based, agreement dropped dramatically. These reductions in agreement on response status are due to measurement issues that are not specific to the measures or the procedures used; they reflect reliability issues inherent to any psychometric approach to group identification based on cut points. Altogether, these inherent limitations suggest that multiple criteria and measures should be used, which is why the use of norm-referenced assessments of achievement in a hybrid model is encouraged.

The same problems with the reliability of individual decisions and lack of overlap across methods have been demonstrated for low-achievement and IQ-discrepancy methods (Francis et al., 2005; Macmann, Barnett, Lombard, Belton-Kocher, & Sharpe, 1989). In a series of studies of PSW methods, Miciak and colleagues demonstrated that different PSW methods showed poor overlap (Miciak, Fletcher, et al., 2014; Miciak et al., 2016) and that just manipulating highly correlated achievement tests while holding the cognitive correlate constant led to low reliability in individual decisions (Miciak, Taylor, Denton, & Fletcher, 2015). In a simulation of PSW methods, Stuebing, Fletcher, Branum-Martin, and Francis (2012) found that these methods identified low numbers of children as SLD, that the decisions were highly accurate for "not-SLD" decisions, but that "yes-SLD" decisions had a high false-positive rate. This study was replicated by Kranzler, Floyd, Benson, Zaboski, and Thibodaux (2016), who used the normative data from the Woodcock-Johnson III Psychoeducational Test Battery (Woodcock, McGrew, &

C A U T I O N
....
Many studies find poor overlap across methods used to identify inadequate responders, suggesting a need for multiple criteria.

Mather, 2001) to create classification decisions based on a PSW approach. Similar to Stuebing et al. (2012), they found a low number of people were identified with SLD. Accuracy was very high for "not-LD" decisions but not for "yes-LD" decisions because of a high false-positive rate.

Validity Issues

Hypothetical classifications are also evaluated by comparing the emergent subgroups on variables not used to identify the members. Thus, identification from an RTI framework should yield subgroups that are different on external dimensions, such as academic level, cognitive, characteristics, behavior, intervention response, and brain-activation patterns. If the subgroups resulting from an RTI framework differ on these external dimensions, the classification (inadequate versus adequate responder) accrues validity. In contrast with other proposed models for LD identification (e.g., aptitude-achievement discrepancy, cognitive-discrepancy frameworks), there is a robust and growing evidence base for responder status as a valid and educationally meaningful classification. Two literature reviews summarizing early research on RTI frameworks found consistent, moderate-to-large differences between adequate and inadequate responders on a number of dimensions, including academic level, cognitive characteristics, and behavior (Al Otaiba & Fuchs, 2002; Nelson, Benner, & Gonzalez, 2003).

These findings have been replicated in subsequent years across diverse samples. For example, Fletcher et al. (2011) compared performance in typically achieving, adequately responding, and inadequately responding first-graders on assessments of phonological awareness, rapid naming, expressive and receptive language, working memory, vocabulary-verbal knowledge, and nonverbal problem-solving. Multivariate statistical tests demonstrated that inadequate responders—across the different measures used to define them—differed from the responder group and the typical group.

Similarly, Miciak, Stuebing, et al. (2014) investigated the cognitive attributes of adequate and inadequate responders in a sample of adolescents identified by final status indicators in decoding, fluency, and comprehension. The groups were compared on cognitive measures, including phonological awareness, rapid naming, verbal knowledge, and nonverbal reasoning. Results indicated that the adequate responder group scored highest on academic and cognitive variables. The groups with reading deficits in only fluency or in fluency, comprehension, and decoding (global impairment) scored lowest on both cognitive and academic measures, with the differences reflecting the greater severity of the globally impaired group. The

DON'T FORGET

Validity studies show consistent differences between adequate and inadequate responders in cognitive and demographic characteristics.

C A U T I O N

Cognitive differences between adequate and inadequate responders may represent a continuum of severity as opposed to qualitatively different subgroups.

pattern was different for the poor comprehenders, reflecting greater difficulties with vocabulary and listening comprehension. However, these differences simply reflect differences in the correlations of different reading domains and cognition. Taken together, these studies provide validity for identifying inadequate responders in the context of a RTI model by providing evidence for the effective isolation of inadequate responders as a subgroup unique to other students who struggle with academic skills.

OTHER ISSUES WITH THE HYBRID METHOD

Other concerns about identification of students as SLD in an RTI framework have been identified (Fuchs & Deshler, 2007; Hale et al., 2010; Reynolds & Shaywitz, 2009) and addressed elsewhere (e.g., Consortium for Evidence-Based Early Intervention Practices, 2010; Fletcher & Vaughn, 2009b; Gresham, 2009). Some argue that an assessment of cognitive processes is required because the statutory definition of SLD in federal regulations identifies SLD as "a disorder of psychological processes". In addition to the discussion in the preceding section on cognitive discrepancy models of identification, it is important to recognize that word reading, math computations, and so on are *cognitive processes* that have been specifically studied from cognitive, neuroimaging, and genetic frameworks. Identification in an RTI framework does not routinely include assessments of IQ or cognitive processes when the concern is SLD because of the weak evidence that such assessments contribute to intervention planning. Nor are such assessments required by law (Zirkel, 2013).

Concerns that identification in an RTI framework will not identify "gifted" children with SLD (Reynolds & Shaywitz, 2009) hinges on whether the construct of "giftedness" can be reliably measured and whether the idea that a person can be gifted and have characteristics of SLD is valid. The specific concern is whether children identified in any model must demonstrate characteristics of absolute low achievement. The question only emerges if the identification model posits the existence of some general attribute that represents aptitude for learning and predicts treatment response, which is not supported by evidence (Fletcher et al., 2007; Fletcher & Vaughn, 2009a, 2009b; Stuebing et al., 2009). As Fletcher and Vaughn

(2009b) discussed, if some type of composite IQ score is the measure of aptitude, a regression-corrected discrepancy *may be* meaningful for students in the upper ranges of IQ. However, discrepancies involving very high IQ and lower achievement that is not demonstrative of absolute low achievement (e.g., less the 25th percentile) is often a regression artifact (Reynolds, 1984). Assuming a population correlation of .60 for IQ and achievement, a 1.5 standard error discrepancy would require achievement scores 32 points lower at IQ levels of 130 (Fletcher et al., 1994). As opposed to relying on IQ-achievement discrepancies, it may be more reasonable to ensure that achievement domains are broadly measured using norm-referenced assessments. In particular, many students may have problems with automaticity that can be identified with fluency assessments. In sum, the identification of students as gifted tends to be driven by a reliance on IQ and a failure to correct for correlations of IQ and achievement and to broadly assess achievement domains as recommended in the hybrid model. It may well be that "gifted" students with SLD exist. But IQ-discrepancy by itself does not indicate SLD (Kavale & Flanagan, 2007), just as poor instructional response by itself is not adequate to identify SLD.

Similarly derived concerns exist about whether children with IQ scores in the borderline low-average range (70 to 80) (so-called slow learners) are misplaced. As summarized previously, IQ is not strongly associated with treatment response, prognosis, or other attributes that would make it an important attribute requiring routine measurement. The best way to assess aptitude for learning is to put a person in an intervention and measure his or her growth. Slow learners learn more slowly.

> ## C A U T I O N
> Although children considered "gifted" and SLD may exist, research has not found effective approaches to identifying these students. Many students identified because of high IQ and relative achievement discrepancies reflect a failure to account for regression to the mean.

> ## C A U T I O N
> The idea that slow learners can be identified on the basis of IQ scores in the 70 to 80 range does not have much research support.

CONCLUSION

This chapter reviewed a hybrid approach to SLD identification that emerges from an RTI service-delivery framework. This hybrid approach directly addresses the three identification criteria required by IDEA 2004 (and which are required regardless of the model for SLD identification used): (1) low achievement, (2) inadequate response to intervention, and (3) a consideration of contextual and exclusionary factors. As with all approaches to SLD identification that rely on forming groups based on cut points applied to continuous and imperfect psychometric data, the individual identification decisions emerging from this hybrid model will differ across operationalizations and testing occasions. This is true of all identification models. However, when comparing identification models stemming from RTI frameworks with other identification methods based on low achievement or some form of IQ or cognitive discrepancy, it is important to recognize that the differences are at the measurement level, not the underlying conceptualization of the SLD construct.

More generally, identification of SLD within RTI service-delivery frameworks is not a panacea for the issues with measurement and determination of discrepancies that have long plagued psychometric models of identification. Approaches that incorporate assessments of instructional response are based on discrepancies with age and treatment response but are simpler because they do not require the use of difference scores between two or more psychometric tests. These methods are also no better than the quality of the instructional services provided, but this is also true for any model of SLD identification. Regardless of the identification model, the SLD construct requires multiple criteria for identification. These criteria must include instructional response as an inclusionary criterion, and the use of rigid cut points that attempt to treat SLD as a categorical distinction will perpetuate the identification issues of great concern to educational practitioners, policy makers, and parents. At the very least, confidence intervals should be used to account for the measurement error of the tests. It is disheartening to see many states adopt criteria purporting to derive from RTI models that specify a rigid cut point, which likely will have the effect of perpetuating adversarial relations of schools and parents concerning the issue of who is eligible as opposed to what services are being provided and how much growth the student is showing. SLD is a supportable and defensible construct that can be reliably and validly identified, but there is a need to anchor research on identification in a classification framework and constantly evaluate the reliability and validity of the classification.

🐟 TEST YOURSELF 🐟

1. In SLD, classification occurs when an individual is diagnosed with LD. True or false?

2. Which of the following statements are true for aptitude-achievement discrepancy?

   (a) Differences in cognitive functions between IQ-discrepant and non-discrepant poor readers are small for cognitive variables not used to define the groups.

(b) Children with an IQ-achievement discrepancy have a better response to intervention.

(c) The long-term development of reading is better in IQ-discrepant than in non-discrepant poor readers.

(d) A variety of measures has been used to operationalize aptitude in aptitude-achievement discrepancy models.

3. **Which statements are true for low-achievement models of identification?**

(a) Low achievement per se is a reliable indicator of SLD.

(b) Low achievement is necessary but not sufficient for identification of SLD.

(c) There is a strong evidence base supporting the validity of classifications of SLD based on low-achievement models.

(d) Absolute low achievement is a requirement for any model of SLD identification.

4. **The primary goal of RTI models is the identification of the right child as SLD. True or false?**

5. **Which statements best characterize referral for special education in an RTI model?**

(a) Children are never referred; they are screened and identified at the end of the RTI process.

(b) Referral is made in the context of universal screening, progress monitoring, and intervention response, with special education as part of the continuum of service delivery.

(c) Referral is not needed because RTI models do not require a comprehensive evaluation.

(d) RTI models are often recommended for districts that have gender and minority disproportionality in special education.

6. **Comprehensive assessments in an RTI model and a traditional model may not differ for some children. True or false?**

7. **Identification in an RTI model is more straightforward than a traditional model because no discrepancy scores are involved. True or false?**

8. **Which of the following components is *not* included in most RTI models?**

(a) Universal screening

(b) Progress monitoring

(c) Increasingly intense interventions

(d) Assessment of cognitive strengths and weaknesses

9. **There is a strong evidence base supporting classifications of SLD based on cognitive strengths and weaknesses. True or false?**

10. **Issues with RTI models for identification include which of the following?**

(a) Weak overlap of different methods for identifying inadequate responders

(b) Insufficient development of evidence-based interventions in some academic domains

252 ESSENTIALS OF SPECIFIC LEARNING DISABILITY IDENTIFICATION

(c) That scaling an RTI model is an intensive process requiring close collaborations among administrators, teachers, school professionals, and parents

(d) Absence of reliable screening tools and measures for progress monitoring

Answers: 1. False; 2. a, d; 3. b, c; 4. False; 5. b, d; 6. True; 7. False; 8. d; 9. False; 10. a, b, c.

REFERENCES

Al Otaiba, S., & Fuchs, D. (2002). Characteristics of children who are unresponsive to early literacy intervention: A review of the literature. *Remedial and Special Education, 23*(5), 300–316.

American Psychiatric Association. (2013). *Diagnostic and statistical manual of mental disorders* (5th ed.). Washington, DC: Author.

Backenson, E. M., Holland, S. C., Kubas, H. A., Fitzer, K. R., Wilcox, G., Carmichael, J. A., . . . & Hale, J. B. (2015). Psychosocial and adaptive deficits associated with learning disability subtypes. *Journal of Learning Disabilities, 48*(5), 511–522.

Balu, R., Zhu, P., Doolittle, F., Schiller, E., Jenkins, J., & Gersten, R. (2015). *Evaluation of response to intervention practices for elementary school reading* (NCEE 2016–4000). Washington, DC: National Center for Education Evaluation and Regional Assistance, Institute of Education Sciences, US Department of Education.

Barth, A. E., Stuebing, K. K., Anthony, J. L., Denton, C. A., Mathes, P. G., Fletcher, J. M., & Francis, D. J. (2008). Agreement among response to intervention criteria for identifying responder status. *Learning and Individual Differences, 18*(3), 296–307.

Bradley, R., Danielson, L., & Hallahan, D. P. (Eds.). (2002). *Identification of learning disabilities: Research to practice*. London, UK: Routledge.

Brown-Waesche, J. S., Schatschneider, C., Maner, J., Ahmed, Y., & Wagner, R. (2011). Examining agreement and longitudinal stability among traditional and RTI-based definitions of reading disability using the affected-status agreement statistic. *Journal of learning Disabilities, 44*(3), 296–307. doi: 0022219410392048

Burns, M. K., Petersen-Brown, S., Haegele, K., Rodriguez, M., Schmitt, B., Cooper, M., . . . & VanDerHeyden, A. M. (2016). Meta-analysis of academic interventions derived from neuropsychological data. *School Psychology Quarterly, 31*(1), 28–42.

Clements, S. D. (1966). Task force one: Minimal brain dysfunction in children. *National Institute of Neurological Diseases and Blindness, Monograph, 3.*

Connor, C. M., Morrison, F. J., Fishman, B. J., Schatschneider, C., & Underwood, P. (2007). Algorithm-guided individualized reading instruction. *Science—New York Then Washington, 315*(5811), 464.

Consortium for Evidence-Based Early Intervention Practices. (2010). *A response to the Learning Disabilities Association of America (LDA) white paper on specific learning disabilities (SLD) identification*. Illinois State Board of Education. Retrieved from www.isbe.net/Documents/LDA_SLD_white_paper_response.pdf

Dixon, S. G., Eusebio, E. C., Turton, W. J., Wright, P. W., & Hale, J. B. (2010). *Forest Grove School District v. T. A.* Supreme Court case: Implications for school psychology practice. *Journal of Psychoeducational Assessment, 29*(2), 103–113. doi: 0734282910388598

Donovan, M. S., & Cross, C. T. (2002). *Minority students in special and gifted education, committee on minority representation in special education.* Washington, DC: National Academy of Education.

Doris, J. L. (1993). Defining learning disabilities: A history of the search for consensus. In G. R. Lyon, D. B. Gray, J. F. Kavanagh, & N. A. Krasnegor (Eds.), *Better understanding learning disabilities: New views for research and their implications for education and public policies* (pp. 97–116). Baltimore, MD: Brookes.

Fenwick, M. E., Kubas, H. A., Witzke, J. W., Fitzer, K. R., Miller, D. C., Maricle, D. E., . . . & Hale, J. B. (2015). Neuropsychological profiles of written expression learning disabilities determined by concordance-discordance model criteria. *Applied Neuropsychology: Child, 5*(2), 1–14. doi: 10.1080/21622965.2014.993396

Fletcher, J. M., Lyon, G. R., Fuchs, L. S., & Barnes, M. A. (2007). *Learning disabilities: From identification to intervention.* New York, NY: Guilford.

Fletcher, J. M., Shaywitz, S. E., Shankweiler, D. P., Katz, L., Liberman, I. Y., Stuebing, K. K., . . . & Shaywitz, B. A. (1994). Cognitive profiles of reading disability: Comparisons of discrepancy and low achievement definitions. *Journal of Educational Psychology, 86*(1), 6.

Fletcher, J. M., Stuebing, K. K., Barth, A. E., Denton, C. A., Cirino, P. T., Francis, D. J., & Vaughn, S. (2011). Cognitive correlates of inadequate response to reading intervention. *School Psychology Review, 40*(1), 3.

Fletcher, J. M., Stuebing, K. K., Barth, A. E., Miciak, J., Francis, D. J., & Denton, C. A. (2014). Agreement and coverage of indicators of response to intervention: A multi-method comparison and simulation. *Topics in Language Disorders, 34*(1), 74.

Fletcher, J. M., & Vaughn, S. (2009a). Response to intervention: Preventing and remediating academic difficulties. *Child Development Perspectives, 3*(1), 30–37.

Fletcher, J. M., & Vaughn, S. (2009b). Response to intervention models as alternatives to traditional views of learning disabilities: Response to commentaries. *Child Development Perspectives, 3*(1), 48–50.

Francis, D. J., Fletcher, J. M., Stuebing, K. K., Lyon, G. R., Shaywitz, B. A., & Shaywitz, S. E. (2005). Psychometric approaches to the identification of LD: IQ and achievement scores are not sufficient. *Journal of Learning Disabilities, 38*(2), 98–108.

Francis, D. J., Shaywitz, S. E., Stuebing, K. K., Shaywitz, B. A., & Fletcher, J. M. (1996). Developmental lag versus deficit models of reading disability: A longitudinal, individual growth curves analysis. *Journal of Educational Psychology, 88*(1), 3.

Fuchs, D., & Deshler, D. D. (2007). What we need to know about responsiveness to intervention (and shouldn't be afraid to ask). *Learning Disabilities Research & Practice, 22*(2), 129–136.

Fuchs, D., & Young, C. L. (2006). On the irrelevance of intelligence in predicting responsiveness to reading instruction. *Exceptional Children, 73*(1), 8–30.

Fuchs, L. S., & Fuchs, D. (1998). Treatment validity: A unifying concept for reconceptualizing the identification of learning disabilities. *Learning Disabilities Research & Practice, 25*(1), 33–45.

Fuchs, L. S., & Fuchs, D. (2004). Determining adequate yearly progress from kindergarten through grade 6 with curriculum-based measurement. *Assessment for Effective Intervention, 29*(4), 25–37.

Gersten, R., Compton, D., Connor, C. M., Dimino, J., Santoro, L., Linan-Thompson, S., & Tilly, W. D. (2008). *Assisting students struggling with reading: Response to intervention and multi-tier intervention for reading in the primary grades: A practice guide* (NCEE 2009–4045). Washington, DC: National Center for Education Evaluation and Regional Assistance, Institute of Education Sciences, US Department of Education. Retrieved from http://ies.ed.gov/ncee/wwc/publications/practiceguides

Gresham, F. M. (2009). Evolution of the treatment integrity concept: Current status and future directions. *School Psychology Review, 38*(4), 533–541.

Hale, J., Alfonso, V., Berninger, V., Bracken, B., Christo, C., Clark, E., . . . & Dumont, R. (2010). Critical issues in response-to-intervention, comprehensive evaluation, and specific learning disabilities identification and intervention: An expert white paper consensus. *Learning Disability Quarterly, 33*(3), 223–236.

Individuals with Disabilities Education Improvement Act of 2004, 34 C.F.R. §300-301 (2006).

Jimerson S. R., Burns M. K., & VanDerHeyden, A. M. (2016). *Handbook of response to intervention: The science and practice of assessment and intervention.* Springfield, IL: Charles E. Springer.

Johnson, E. S. (2014). Understanding why a child is struggling to learn: The role of cognitive processing evaluation in LD identification. *Topics in Language Disorders, 34*(1), 59–73. Retrieved from http://dx.doi.org/10.1080/21622965.2014.993396

Kavale, K. A., & Flanagan, D. P. (2007). Ability-achievement discrepancy, response to intervention, and assessment of cognitive abilities/processes in specific learning disability identification: Toward a contemporary operational definition. In A. A. Editor (Ed.), *Handbook of response to intervention* (pp. 130–147). New York, NY: Springer.

Kavale, K. A., & Forness, S. R. (1985). Learning disability and the history of science: Paradigm or paradox? *Remedial and Special Education, 6*(4), 12–24.

Kearns, D. M., & Fuchs, D. (2013). Does cognitively focused instruction improve the academic performance of low-achieving students? *Exceptional Children, 79*(3), 263.

Kovaleski, J. F., VanDerHeyden, A. M., & Shapiro, E. S. (2013). *The RTI approach to evaluating specific learning disabilities.* New York, NY: Guilford.

Kranzler, J. H., Floyd, R. G., Benson, N., Zaboski, B., & Thibodaux, L. (2016). Classification agreement analysis of Cross-Battery Assessment in the identification of specific learning disorders in children and youth. *International Journal of School and Educational Psychology, 4*(3), 124–136.

Kudo, M. F., Lussier, C. M., & Swanson, H. L. (2015). Reading disabilities in children: A selective meta-analysis of the cognitive literature. *Research in Developmental Disabilities, 40*, 51–62.

Macmann, G. M., Barnett, D. W., Lombard, T. J., Belton-Kocher, E., & Sharpe, M. N. (1989). On the actuarial classification of children: Fundamental studies of classification agreement. *The Journal of Special Education, 23*(2) 127–149.

Miciak, J., Fletcher, J. M., Stuebing, K. K., Vaughn, S., & Tolar, T. D. (2014). Patterns of cognitive strengths and weaknesses: Identification rates, agreement, and validity for learning disabilities identification. *School Psychology Quarterly, 29*(1), 21.

Miciak, J., Stuebing, K. K., Vaughn, S., Roberts, G., Barth, A. E., & Fletcher, J. M. (2014). Cognitive attributes of adequate and inadequate responders to reading intervention in middle school. *School Psychology Review, 43*(4), 407–427.

Miciak, J., Taylor, W. P., Denton, C. A., & Fletcher, J. M. (2015). The effect of achievement test selection on identification of learning disabilities within patterns of strengths and weaknesses framework. *School Psychology Quarterly, 30,* 321–334.

Miciak, J., Williams, J. L., Taylor, W. P., Cirino, P. T., Fletcher, J. M., & Vaughn, S. (2016). Do processing patterns of strengths and weaknesses predict differential treatment response? *Journal of Educational Psychology, 108*(6), 898–909.

Morgan, W. P. (1896). A case of congenital word blindness. *British Medical Journal, 2*(1871), 1378.

Morris, R., & Fletcher, J.M. (1988). Classification in neuropsychology: A theoretical framework and research paradigm. *Journal of Clinical and Experimental Neuropsychology, 10,* 640–658.

Morris, R., Lovett, M. W., Wolf, M., Sevcik, R., Steinbach, K., Frijters, J., & Shapiro, M. (2012). Multiple-component remediation for developmental reading disabilities: IQ, socioeconomic status, and race as factors in remedial outcome. *Journal of Learning Disabilities, 45*(2), 99–127.

Nelson, J. R., Benner, G. J., & Gonzalez, J. (2003). Learner characteristics that influence the treatment effectiveness of early literacy interventions: A meta-analytic review. *Learning Disabilities Research & Practice, 18*(4), 255–267.

Pashler, H., McDaniel, M., Rohrer, D., & Bjork, R. (2008). Learning styles concepts and evidence. *Psychological Science in the Public Interest, 9*(3), 105–119.

Reschly, D., & Tilly, W. D., III (1999). Reform trends and system design alternatives. In D. Reschly, W. D. Tilly III & J. Grimes (Eds.), *Special education in transition: Functional assessment and noncategorical programming* (pp. 19–48). Longmont, CO: Sopris West.

Reynolds, C. R. (1984). Critical measurement issues in learning disabilities. *The Journal of Special Education, 18,* 451–476.

Reynolds, C. R., & Shaywitz, S. E. (2009). Response to intervention: Ready or not? Or, from wait-to-fail to watch-them-fail. *School Psychology Quarterly, 24*(2), 130.

Ross, A. D. (1976). *Psychological aspects of learning disabilities and reading disorders.* New York, NY: McGraw-Hill.

Rutter, M. (1978). Prevalence and types of dyslexia. *Dyslexia: An Appraisal of Current Knowledge, 1,* 3–28.

Siegel, L. S. (1992). An evaluation of the discrepancy definition of dyslexia. *Journal of Learning Disabilities, 25*(10), 618–629.

Simos, P. G., Rezaie, R., Fletcher, J. M., & Papanicolaou, A. C. (2013). Time-constrained functional connectivity analysis of cortical networks underlying phonological decoding in typically developing school-aged children: A magnetoencephalography study. *Brain and Language, 125*(2), 156–164.

Skinner, H. A. (1981). Toward the integration of classification theory and methods. *Journal of Abnormal Psychology, 90*(1), 68.

Spectrum K12 Solutions/The Council of Administrators of Special Education. (2008). *Response to intervention (RTI) adoption survey.* Washington, DC: The Council of Administrators of Special Education.

Stecker, P. M., Fuchs, L. S., & Fuchs, D. (2007). Using curriculum-based measurement to improve student achievement: Review of research. *Psychology in the Schools, 42*(8), 795–819.

Still, G. F. (1902). The Goulstonian lectures on some abnormal psychical conditions in children. *The Lancet, 4103,* 1008–1012.

Stuebing, K. K., Barth, A. E., Molfese, P. J., Weiss, B., & Fletcher, J. M. (2009). IQ is not strongly related to response to reading instruction: A meta-analytic interpretation. *Exceptional Children, 76*(1), 31–51.

Stuebing, K. K., Barth, A. E., Trahan, L. H., Reddy, R. R., Miciak, J., & Fletcher, J. M. (2014). Are children cognitive characteristics strong predictors of responses to intervention? A meta-analysis. *Review of Educational Research, 85*(3), 395–429.

Stuebing, K. K., Fletcher, J. M., Branum-Martin, L., & Francis, D. J. (2012). Simulated comparisons of three methods for identifying specific learning disabilities based on cognitive discrepancies. *School Psychology Review, 41*(1) 3–22.

Stuebing, K. K., Fletcher, J. M., LeDoux, J. M., Lyon, G. R., Shaywitz, S. E., & Shaywitz, B. A. (2002). Validity of IQ-discrepancy classifications of reading disabilities: A meta-analysis. *American Educational Research Journal, 39*(2), 469–518.

Swanson, H. L. (1999). Reading research for students with LD: A meta-analysis of intervention outcomes. *Journal of Learning Disabilities, 32*, 504–522. doi: 10.1177/002221949903200605

Tanaka, H., Black, J., Hulme, C., Leanne, S., Kesler, S., Whitfield, G., . . . & Hoeft, F. (2011). The brain basis of the phonological deficit in dyslexia is independent of IQ. *Psychological Science, 22*, 1442–1451.

US Office of Education. (1968). *First annual report of the National Advisory Committee on Handicapped Children*. Washington, DC: US Department of Health, Education and Welfare.

VanDerHeyden, A. M., Witt, J. C., & Gilbertson, D. (2007). A multi-year evaluation of the effects of a response to intervention (RTI) model on identification of children for special education. *Journal of School Psychology, 45*, 225–256.

Vaughn, S., Cirino, P. T., Wanzek, J., Wexler, J., Fletcher, J. M., Denton, C. D., . . . & Francis, D. J. (2010). Response to intervention for middle school students with reading difficulties: Effects of a primary and secondary intervention. *School Psychology Review, 39*(1), 3.

Vaughn, S., Wanzek, J., Murray, C. S., Scammacca, N., Linan-Thompson, S., & Woodruff, A. L. (2009). Response to early reading intervention examining higher and lower responders. *Exceptional Children, 75*(2), 165–183.

Vaughn, S., Wexler, J., Leroux, A., Roberts, G., Denton, C., Barth, A., & Fletcher, J. (2012). Effects of intensive reading intervention for eighth-grade students with persistently inadequate response to intervention. *Journal of Learning Disabilities, 45*(6), 515–525.

Walker, H., Stiller, B., Severson, H. H., Feil, E. G., & Golly, A. (1998). First step to success: Intervening at the point of school entry to prevent antisocial behavior patterns. *Psychology in the Schools, 35*, 259–269.

Willcutt, E. G., Petrill, S. A., Wu, S., Boada, R., DeFries, J. C., Olson, R. K., & Pennington, B. F. (2013). Comorbidity between reading disability and math disability: Concurrent psychopathology, functional impairment, and neuropsychological functioning. *Journal of Learning Disabilities, 46*(6), 500–516.

Woodcock, R. W., McGrew, K. S., & Mather, N. (2001). *Woodcock-Johnson III Tests of Cognitive Abilities* (pp. 371–401). Rolling Meadows, IL: Riverside Publishing.

Zirkel, P. A. (2013). A comprehensive evaluation of the Supreme Court's *Forest Grove* decision? *Journal of Psychoeducational Assessment, 31*(3), 313–317. doi: 0734282912468576

Eight

USING STUDENT RESPONSE TO INTERVENTION TO IDENTIFY SLD

Requirements, Recommendations, and Future Research

Matthew K. Burns
Kathrin E. Maki
Kristy Warmbold-Brann
June L. Preast

H ow to best identify students with a specific learning disability (SLD) is one of the most frequently and passionately debated issues in the history of education or psychology. The notable shortcomings of the discrepancy model left the field without a widely accepted method to identify students with SLD, when in 2004 the federal special education law changed. The 2004 amendments to the Individuals with Disabilities Education Act (IDEA) responded to long-standing criticisms of the ability-achievement discrepancy model for SLD identification by stating that local educational agencies (LEAs)

. . . shall not be required to take into consideration whether a child has a severe discrepancy between achievement and intellectual ability in oral expression, listening comprehension, written expression, basic reading skill, reading comprehension, mathematical calculation, or mathematical reasoning. (P.L. 108-446 §614 [b][6][A])

Essentials of Specific Learning Disability Identification, Second Edition.
Edited by Vincent C. Alfonso and Dawn P. Flanagan
© 2018 John Wiley & Sons, Inc. Published 2018 by John Wiley & Sons, Inc.

The federal law was also revised to state that an LEA "may use a process that determines if the child responds to scientific, research-based intervention as a part of the evaluation procedures" (P.L. 108-446 §614 [b][6][A]; §614 [b][2 & 3]). The latter provision gave birth to what is now called Response to Intervention (RTI), which has become a commonly used method of identifying SLD. In this chapter, we provide an overview of RTI and its legal basis, discuss frequently implemented components of RTI frameworks and the research base for them, provide an overview of assessments used within them, and discuss strengths, limitations, areas for future research, and resources.

WHAT IS RTI?

There are multiple ways to define RTI, but we describe it as the use of assessment data to allocate resources most efficiently in order to enhance learning for all students (Burns & VanDerHeyden, 2006; VanDerHeyden & Burns, 2010). Therefore, the RTI decision-making framework applies to instructional and intervention decisions beyond SLD identification and generally involves providing effective instruction for students within general education, conducting universal screening in which the reading or mathematics skills of every student is quickly assessed, providing increasingly intensive services based on student needs, closely monitoring student progress, and identifying those students who do not respond adequately to the most-intensive general education interventions as having an SLD (see Rapid Reference 8.1).

RTI is essentially a series of problem analyses. A strong RTI model answers three analyses questions: (1) Is there a class-wide need? (2) What is the category of the problem? and (3) What is the causal variable? We discuss these three questions

≋ *Rapid Reference 8.1*

What RTI Involves

- Providing effective instruction for students within general education
- Conducting universal screening in which the reading or mathematics skills of every student is quickly assessed
- Providing increasingly intense services based on student needs
- Closely monitoring student progress
- Identifying those students who do not respond adequately to the most-intensive general education interventions as learning disabled

≡ Rapid Reference 8.2

···

An Effective RTI Model Should Answer These Questions

- Is there a class-wide need?
- What is the category of the problem?
- What is the causal variable?

in the following as the basis for RTI practice and also summarize assessment tools and decision rules used for each (see Rapid Reference 8.2).

Class-Wide Need

There is an alarming number of students in K–12 schools who cannot read proficiently (34% in fourth grade and 35% in eighth grade; National Center for Educational Statistics, 2013), and 83% of African American fourth-graders in this country could not read at grade level (Children's Defense Fund, 2014). Therefore, it is not unusual to implement an RTI framework in a school in which more than 50% of the students would be identified as needing additional support from universal screenings. In fact, we have all worked in classrooms of 20 to 25 or even 30 students in which every single student was reading below benchmark standards. Imagine attempting to conduct small-group reading interventions with every student in a third-grade classroom with 25 students. It is just not possible.

Effective RTI implementation is dependent on two major assumptions. The first assumption is that a quality core instructional program is in place and implemented with fidelity, and the second is that no more than approximately 25% of the students require intervention. Of course, the two assumptions are closely intertwined because quality core instruction leads to fewer students requiring intervention, and both enhance the likelihood that more-targeted intervention efforts will be successful.

The importance of reducing the number of students who need intervention as the first step in an RTI model allows for success of subsequent intervention activities. Picture a K–8 building with 650 students in which only 40% are proficient (60% need intervention) and at which a well-meaning problem-solving team meets to develop individualized plans for each student who is struggling. If 60% of the 650 students need intervention, then 390 students need intervention.

> ## C A U T I O N
> ....
> Most schools have too many students who need interventions to have a successful problem-solving team.

If the problem-solving team meets each week for 38 weeks, then they have to discuss and develop plans for more than 10 students each meeting! There is not a problem-solving team in the country that can do quality problem analysis for 10 students each, and there would not be enough resources to implement the individualized interventions for that many students. The solution is to first provide quality core instruction and to implement class-wide interventions (Tier 1) so the number of students needing supplemental intervention decreases to 20% or 130 students.

Screening Tools

We see the scenario just described all of the time, and we can ensure that it is a model that is doomed to failure unless schools address Tier 1 first. Therefore, the first problem-analysis question has to address class-wide needs and is answered with universal screening data. The National Center on Response to Intervention reviewed several screening tools and described them at www.rti4success.org/resources/tools-charts/screening-tools-chart. Following we discuss two commonly used approaches to screening.

Curriculum-based measurements (CBMs) are brief assessments that are often used for universal screening. There are proprietary CBMs for early literacy, reading, mathematics, and writing that are available for free or for minimal costs from one of several different CBM platforms (Aimsweb, https://aimsweb.pearson.com/, Dynamic Indicators of Basic Early Literacy Skills, https://dibels.uoregon.edu/, Formative Assessment System for Teachers, www.fastbridge.org/, System to Enhance Educational Performance, www.isteep.com/login.aspx, and easyCBM, https://dibels.uoregon.edu/assessment/reading/). There is considerable research regarding the psychometric properties of CBM for screening decisions from which the data appear sufficiently reliable for initial screening decisions (Kilgus, Methe, Maggin, & Tomasula, 2014; Lembke, Carlisle, & Poch, 2016).

Many school districts use commercially prepared measures of reading and mathematics to conduct universal screening in reading, math, and writing. The Texas Primary Reading Inventory: Screening (TPRI) measures reading development for kindergarten through Grade 3 via an individually administered assessment (Texas Education Agency, 2010), Star Reading and Star Math (Renaissance Learning, 2003, 2011) for students in Grades 2 through 12 with individually administered 10-minute sessions on a computer, and the Measures of Academic Progress (MAP; Northwest Evaluation Association, 2012) for students in Grades 2 through 10 with individually administered assessment sessions on a computer. The three assessments mentioned here were rated well by the National Response to Intervention Center (see www.rti4success.org/resources/tools-charts/screening -tools-chart) and are commonly used, but they cost between $9 and $13.50 per student for the computer-based assessments. The TPRI is less costly (approximately $190 per kit plus approximately $1 per student booklet), but it is administered one-on-one.

There are few advantages of the commercially available reading and math tests over CBM as screeners, especially with younger students. CBM does not capture more-advanced reading and math skills (e.g., comprehension and problem-solving) as well as the more-fluency-based skills (e.g., oral reading fluency, letter identification, math fact fluency, and computation). Thus, the group-administered measures may be better screeners with students at fifth grade and above, but they cost considerably more to use.

Decision Rule

Decisions from CBMs or group-administered reading and math measures can be made comparing the data to national or local norms (as available). Screening decisions usually rely on the 25th or 40th percentiles, with students scoring below the criterion being identified as needing additional support (Tier 2). We recommend using the more liberal criterion of the 40th percentile because schools would rather overidentify than miss students who need support, but those are decisions that need to be made by local school personnel.

Decision rules for identifying class-wide needs are not well established. The screening data are organized according to classrooms. It makes intuitive sense to identify any classroom with more than 20% of the students scoring below the benchmark criterion (e.g., 40th percentile) as exhibiting a class-wide need. However, research regarding class-wide interventions (see following section) was all conducted using the class median as the criterion to identify a class-wide need. In other words, the median score was computed for the screening measure used in each classroom, and those medians that fell below the benchmark criterion (e.g., 40th percentile) suggested a class-wide need.

Intervention

Whenever a large number of students score below the national benchmark criterion, then a class-wide intervention should be implemented. Research has consistently demonstrated that effective class-wide interventions can increase proficiency of the students while substantially reducing the number of students who need additional support (Burns et al., 2015; Burns, Pulles, Helman, & McComas, 2016; VanDerHeyden, McLaughlin, Algina, & Snyder, 2012;

VanDerHeyden, Witt, & Gilbertson, 2007). Peer-assisted learning strategies (PALS; Mathes, Howard, Allen, & Fuchs, 1998) was one of the first interventions to address class-wide need by partnering students into heterogeneous dyads and completing a 26-week curriculum that involves practicing letter sounds, segmenting and blending words, reading sight words, and reading a brief story that has key words that the student practiced reading in the previous section.

PALS has consistently been shown to increase the reading skills of first-grade students who are at risk for reading failure (Mathes et al., 1998). Burns et al. (2015) found that implementing a class-wide intervention that focused on partner reading and paragraph shrinking with second- and third-graders increased their reading skills and reduced the percentage of students who needed supplemental support (Tier 2) down to 20%. Similar results were found for students for reading (Burns, Pulles, et al., 2016) and mathematics (VanDerHeyden et al., 2012; VanDerHeyden & Codding, 2015).

> **DON'T FORGET**
> ....
> Implementing a class-wide intervention that focused on partner reading and paragraph shrinking with second- and third-graders increased their reading skills and reduced the percentage of students who needed supplemental support (Tier 2) down to 20%.

Category of the Deficit

The fictitious K–8 school previously mentioned with 650 students, 60% of whom need additional support, would benefit from class-wide interventions. However, successful class-wide methods may reduce the number of students who need support to 20%, but that is still 130 students and still too many for in-depth problem analysis and individualized interventions. Therefore, a strong Tier 2 intervention is needed in which students are grouped based on similar need and receive interventions matched to those needs.

A previous synthesis of research concluded that interventions were more effective if they targeted student need. For example, if a student struggled with reading comprehension and demonstrated adequate reading fluency, then the intervention should focus on reading comprehension; however, a student who struggled with reading comprehension, fluency, and decoding would benefit most from a decoding intervention. A meta-analysis of 26 small-group reading-intervention studies found moderate effects when the intervention targeted a specific skill ($g = 0.65$) but only small to moderate effects ($g = 0.35$) for comprehensive interventions that were composed of multiple components (e.g., phonics, fluency, and comprehension in one intervention; Hall & Burns, in press).

Given that interventions are more effective if they target a specific skill,

> **DON'T FORGET**
> ....
> Interventions are more effective if they target what the student actually needs.

the second problem analysis question in an RTI framework is to identify which general skill the intervention should target, and this can happen only after a class-wide intervention has reduced the number of students who need support. Once that number decreases to approximately 20% (e.g., 5 out of 25 students), then school teams can examine universal screening data to determine what broad category of the problem should be addressed for students receiving Tier 2 interventions.

Diagnostic Assessments

Once a student is identified as needing intervention, then additional data are collected to determine what skills each student needs. The decision at this point must still be a simplified (i.e., categorical) problem analysis. For reading, skills can be targeted using the areas of reading identified by the National Reading Panel (National Reading Panel [US], National Institute of Child Health, & Human Development [US], 2000): phonemic awareness, phonics, fluency, and vocabulary and comprehension. Mathematics skills are usually isolated by assessing the skills represented within the scope and sequence of a given curriculum.

The goal of diagnostic assessment is to determine what intervention is most appropriate, and it is usually done by identifying the most fundamental skill in which a student struggles. For instance, if a student struggles with reading comprehension but had adequate reading fluency, then the intervention should focus on comprehension. However, if a student struggled with comprehension, fluency, and decoding, then the intervention would target decoding. Most reading tests used for screening focus on comprehension (e.g., Star Reading and MAP) and serve as indicators of how well a student understands what he or she reads. Fluency can be assessed with grade-level oral reading fluency CBM probes. Decoding can be assessed with measures of word attack, pseudoword reading, or nonsense word reading. However, percentage of words read correctly can also be used as a proxy for decoding. Percentage of words read correctly has strong instructional utility that is consistently supported in the literature (Burns, 2007; Hosp & Ardoin, 2008; Treptow, Burns, & McComas, 2007).

Interventionists can simply divide the number of words read correctly in 1 minute by the total number of words read (words correct plus errors) and multiply by 100%. The research-based criterion of 93% or higher is used to determine the level of accuracy with which a student reads (Gickling & Armstrong, 1978; Treptow et al., 2007). Students reading less than 93% of the words correctly are likely struggling to decode the text (Burns, Haegele, & Peterson-Brown, 2014). Finally, there are several measures of phonemic awareness such as initial sound fluency, phoneme segmentation fluency, or any standardized measure, such as those available within the Comprehensive Test of Phonological Processing (Wagner, Torgesen, & Rashotte, 1999).

Math data usually consist of a series of single-skill (e.g., single-digit multiplication, double-digit subtraction with regrouping), CBM-like probes. Interventionists take the sequence of skills outlined in a curriculum and develop a single-skill probe for each. The assessments are then given to determine the most foundational skill at which the student demonstrates an instructional level.

Data for diagnostic decisions are usually interpreted with instructional-level criteria. As stated, students who read less than 93% of the words correctly while reading contextualized text are demonstrating difficulty reading the text with sufficient accuracy. Other measures, such as decoding and phonemic awareness, can be interpreted with a criterion of 90% (Burns, 2004). However, math data are interpreted somewhat differently. Burns, VanDerHeyden, and Jiban (2006) empirically derived math criteria to which data can be compared and found that 14 to 31 digits correct per minute for second- and third-graders and 24 to 49 digits correct per minute for fourth- and fifth-grade students represented an instructional level. Thus, interventionists should administer single-skill probes until a student scores within the instructional level range, which would represent the skill that should be targeted for Tier 2 intervention.

Monitoring Student Progress
Although there is some debate about how to screen student skills best, there is some agreement that CBM is ideally suited to monitor student progress. The National Center on Intensive Intervention rates several tools to monitor student progress, and almost all of the positively reviewed tools are some form of CBM (see www .intensiveintervention.org/chart/progress-monitoring). Student progress should be monitored approximately once per week for students receiving a Tier 2 intervention.

Decision Rules
Once data are collected with weekly progress-monitoring assessments, they are best interpreted through a dual discrepancy in which student level and rate of growth are interpreted (Fuchs, 2003). Students who score below the seasonal benchmark criterion are considered to be discrepant from level expectations. Rate of growth is more difficult to interpret, and to explain fully would exceed the scope

of this chapter. Simply stated, growth is often computed as an increase in unit per week, which is then compared to normative or individual expectations. For example, reading benchmark scores might be 22 words read correctly (WRC) per minute in the fall, 38 WRC in the winter, and 54 WRC in the spring, which would equal an average increase of 1.00 WRC increase per minute per week for the norm group. Student rates of growth that were less than 1.00 would suggest a discrepancy in expectation for growth. Speece and Case (2001) compared the dual-discrepancy model to ability-achievement discrepancy model and low-reading achievement, with validity methods supporting the dual discrepancy for identifying students with reading-learning disabilities. Burns and Senesac (2005) found that students who were dually discrepant after intervention scored significantly lower on a reading measure than did their peers who were also at risk but who demonstrated adequate growth during the intervention.

Intervention

Once the intervention target is broadly identified (i.e., category of the problem), then students can be grouped based on the screening and diagnostic data to receive an intervention (Tier 2). For example, all of the fourth-grade students who needed decoding could be grouped into groups of about five and receive a decoding intervention (e.g., REWARDS; Archer, Gleason, & Vachon, 2006), but those who need reading fluency could be grouped and receive an intervention that addresses that component skill (e.g., Six-Minute Solution; Adams & Brown, 2007).

If done well, Tier 2 interventions can be quite effective. In our K–8 school with 650 students, a strong class-wide intervention can first reduce the number of students who need support from 390 to 130, and then a strong Tier 2 intervention that targets student needs can reduce the number of students down even further to perhaps 30 to 60 students.

Causal Variable

There will always be students with intense needs. A school may implement a strong core instructional program (Tier 1) and a highly effective small-group intervention program that is well matched to student need (Tier 2), but there will still remain 5% to 10% of the students who need even further additional support. It is this small group of students who need in-depth problem analysis and individualized interventions usually developed with the support of a problem-solving team (Tier 3). If the number of students who need support is decreased from 390 to 130, and again from 130 to 60, then the problem-solving team could analyze student data for one or two students each week and develop effective individualized intervention plans. However, many problem-solving teams do not have a framework to examine student data at this level.

Problem analysis within Tier 3 should focus on identifying the causal variable or the environmental variable or condition that is within the control of school personnel and is most closely related to the problem. Daly, Witt, Martens, and Dool (1997) provided a framework for analyzing student data based on their review of the research literature. They proposed that student failure could be explained by five hypotheses that could be used to guide interventions. The first hypothesis was that the student did not want to do the activity, which suggested the need to add incentives for performance. Second, the student failed because of a lack of practice, which required providing additional repetition. Third, the student needed more help with the task, which was addressed with explicit instruction and interventions that involve high modeling. Fourth, the student had never been asked to perform the task in a manner that was consistent with the requirement, which was remediated by using conditions that matched required performance to how the student learned to complete the task. Finally, the task was too hard, which was addressed by using material that represented an instructional level.

Monitoring Student Progress

As is the case for Tier 2 interventions, the progress of students receiving a Tier 3 intervention should be closely monitored with CBM. Students receiving a Tier 3 intervention should be assessed at least once each week and perhaps twice weekly with the same measures used for a Tier 2 intervention. Student progress is also monitored with the dual-discrepancy approach previously described.

Intervention

There is considerable research supporting the five hypotheses outlined by Daly et al. (1997) that are usually tested with brief experimental analyses (BEAs), which involves delivering multiple interventions over a brief period of time and assessing their effectiveness with brief measures (Jones & Wickstrom, 2002). For example Andersen, Daly, and Young (2013) compared reading fluency with six students after three conditions: (1) providing a reward for reading more fluently, (2) implementing an intervention with multiple instructional components, and (3) a control condition. The results indicated that the multicomponent intervention led to the highest reading fluency for three of the students, and the reward-only condition led to highest fluency for three other students. Thus, three students likely had a reading deficit (needed more help) and three were demonstrating a motivational issue (did not want to do it). The data from the BEA indicated the type of intervention that should be used for each student to ensure the highest likelihood of success.

The Daly et al. (1997) framework testing through BEAs has consistently been used to identify interventions with positive effects for reading fluency (Burns &

Wagner, 2008; Daly, Martens, Hamler, Dool, & Eckert, 1999), early literacy (Petursdottir et al., 2009), mathematics (Carson & Eckert, 2003), and writing (Burns, Ganuza, & London, 2009). A meta-analysis of relevant research found large effects from 13 studies that examined reading fluency (Burns & Wagner, 2008).

To describe adequately the problem-analysis process within Tier 3 would go beyond the scope of this chapter. Readers are referred to Daly et al. (1997) for a description of a particularly useful framework to guide data-analysis when identifying a causal variable within Tier 3. However, we again caution that without an effective Tier 1 and Tier 2, school personnel have little hope for an effective Tier 3.

WHAT IS THE LEGAL BASIS FOR RTI?

The reauthorization of IDEA in 2004 resulted in considerable changes in the identification of SLD. Whereas prior to 2004 states exclusively used ability-achievement discrepancy to identify SLD (Reschly & Hosp, 2004), the IDEA reauthorization allowed for the use of an RTI process for SLD identification. IDEA consequently required states to allow SLD to be identified using RTI and outlawed states from requiring use of ability-achievement discrepancy in SLD identification.

Although the reauthorization of IDEA in 2004 outlines the requirement that states allow for use of RTI in SLD identification, federal law does not describe how RTI should be implemented or used in SLD identification (Maki, Floyd, & Roberson, 2015). Thus, identification of SLD through RTI is determined by individual states resulting in considerable variability in the operationalization of SLD identification under RTI (Hauerwas, Brown, & Scott, 2013; Zirkel & Thomas, 2010). Additionally, because all states must allow for use of RTI in SLD identification but are not required to use RTI, there is also variability in SLD-identification practices across states (Maki et al., 2015) and within them (Hoover, Baca, Wexler-Love, & Saenz, 2008). A recent review of SLD identification practices in the United States found that approximately 20% of all states currently require sole use of RTI in SLD identification (Maki et al., 2015).

> **DON'T FORGET**
> ....
> Approximately 20% of all states currently require sole use of RTI in SLD identification.

Although all states must allow for its use, there is also great variability in how RTI frameworks are implemented for SLD identification within state regulations.

Some states incorporate only the federal language regarding use of "a process that determines if the child responds to scientific, research-based intervention as a part of the evaluation procedures" (P.L. 108-446 §300.307[a][2]), but other states outline additional criteria that must be included within an RTI framework for SLD identification. For instance, some states require a minimum number of progress-monitoring data points, a minimum number interventions implemented, student achievement below a given percentile rank (e.g., below the 5th percentile), and data regarding intervention implementation fidelity (Maki et al., 2015). Such differences in state regulations regarding SLD identification under RTI can result in variability in the prevalence rate of SLD as well as the students being identified with SLD. Variability in state SLD RTI regulations and consequently student identification decisions are problematic given the high-stakes nature of special education identification decisions (Salvia, Ysseldyke, & Bolt, 2012).

IS RTI RESEARCH BASED?

There are multiple descriptions of RTI models in their entirety that provide data to support their effectiveness (e.g., Marston, Lau, Muyskens, & Wilson, 2016; McNamara & Hollinger, 2003; Shapiro, 2016). Meta-analytic research with 21 studies found large effects for systemic (e.g., reductions in special education referrals, $d = 1.28$) and student outcomes (e.g., increased reading scores, $d = 0.72$) (Burns, Appleton, & Stehouwer, 2005). Although Burns et al. (2005) found large effects, the studies rarely used an experimental design. VanDerHeyden et al. (2007) used a multiple-baseline design to examine outcome with schools that staggered RTI implementation start dates. There was an experimentally supported link between RTI implementation and reductions in the number of students evaluated for special education services and an elimination of the disproportional rate at which ethnic minority and male students were referred for special education evaluations.

A recent federally funded study with 146 schools across 13 states found disappointing results for RTI implementation, but the study did not actually examine the effects of RTI. The report by Balu et al. (2015) found that RTI implementation had no effect for second- and third-graders and potentially negative effects for students in first grade. The study used a regression-discontinuity design, which meant that students just below the cut point were compared to those just above it. Shinn and Brown (2016) questioned if that was the correct sample to study because RTI efforts were initially designed to help students well below proficiency standards. Moreover, Shinn and Brown (2016) pointed out that schools used very different approaches to identify students in need of intervention and assessed RTI implementation through self-report surveys of teachers who may or may not have been knowledgeable about the RTI implementation or about RTI in general, and many of the students in the control group also received the intervention. Thus, the data provided by Balu et al. (2015) cannot be used to evaluate the effectiveness of RTI.

The more important finding by Balu et al. (2015) was that there were a wide number of RTI practices, some of which were linked to better student outcomes. The authors noted on page 100 of the report that "across the impact sample schools, there is significant variation in the estimated impacts of reading interventions on reading outcomes" and "certain RtI practices and student body characteristics are associated with the varying magnitude of the estimated impacts across schools." Gersten et al.'s (2008) review of the literature found strong evidence for providing systematic Tier 2 interventions that focused on three or fewer foundational skills and were delivered in small groups of students for 20 to 40 minutes three to five times each week. There was moderate evidence for universal screening and low evidence for other aspects. For mathematics, Gersten et al. (2009) found strong evidence for explicit and systematic Tier 2 interventions that included activities such as modeling problem-solving, verbalizing thought processes, guided practice, corrective feedback, and frequent review, and instruction that taught solving word problems focusing on common underlying structures. There was moderate evidence for universal screening, using visual representations, and building basic fact fluency. The authors found low evidence for monitoring progress, including motivational strategies in interventions and in-depth treatment of whole numbers.

Deciding if something is evidenced-based or not is not a yes or no answer; similar to validity, research is not dichotomous (i.e., valid or not valid). There are considerable data suggesting positive effects on student learning, but the practices in which schools engage vary substantially and some practices are more effective than others. Thus, if schools select and implement the practices associated with strong effects, then they can be confident that they are implementing an evidence-based practice. Additional research is needed to understand better the effects of RTI on student learning.

DOES RTI IDENTIFY SLD?

It is difficult to evaluate how well an SLD identification model actually identifies SLD because there is no gold standard as to how to define SLD operationally. In other words, we are validating a test based on how well it aligns with something that we are not sure how to measure. There have been several attempts to validate the RTI process by examining the reading and cognitive correlates of non-responders, which we describe in the following paragraphs.

A study with 151 elementary-aged students who were all at risk for reading difficulties found that students who demonstrated adequate response to intervention scored significantly better ($d = 0.64$ to 0.87) on reading measures that were external to the RTI process than did students who did not demonstrate an adequate response (Burns & Senesac, 2005). The study might have been the first one to find a difference among students identified as SLD and those at risk and not identified as SLD. Almost 20 years of research about the IQ-achievement discrepancy model found that students identified as SLD had similar reading skills as those not identified as discrepant (Algozzine & Ysseldyke, 1982, 1983; Stuebing et al., 2002). The lower reading skills among students who would be identified as SLD with an RTI model compared to those who were at risk, but not SLD has been replicated at least once ($d = 0.77$ to 1.12; Burns, Silberglitt, Christ, Gibbons, & Coolong-Chaffin, 2016).

Further research examined different academic and cognitive skills between students for whom a reading intervention was not successful and those who did demonstrate adequate response. Nonresponders consistently scored lower on measures of word identification, word attack, sight-word efficiency, and phonemic decoding (Johnson & Swanson, 2011; Miciak, Stuebing, et al., 2014; Toste et al., 2014). Most measures of cognitive correlates were not significantly different between responders and non-responders, with the exception of rapid naming (Johnson & Swanson, 2011; Miciak, Stuebing, et al., 2014; Nelson, Benner & Gonzalez, 2003), but even rapid naming resulted in a small increment in variance explained beyond reading skills and only for rapid-naming measures that involved letters (Fletcher et al., 2011).

It is unclear if RTI truly identifies SLD, but no SLD identification model has been adequately validated to identify SLD. Over time, SLD has become synonymous with the concept of unexpected underachievement (Fletcher, 2012). Historically, unexpected underachievement has been viewed as achievement that is significantly below student cognitive ability (Fletcher, 2009) and is caused by psychological processing deficits (Mastropieri & Scruggs, 2005). Unexpected underachievement has been described as a critical marker of SLD with low achievement alone an insufficient indicator of SLD (Kavale & Forness, 2000). Rather, significant discrepancy between expected (i.e., based on cognitive ability) and actual achievement historically has been viewed as necessary to define unexpected underachievement and, therefore, to identify SLD.

> **C A U T I O N**
> ....
> It is unclear if RTI actually identifies SLD, but no SLD diagnostic model has been adequately validated to identify SLD.

Using RTI for SLD identification may inherently change conceptual understanding of the construct (Kavale & Spaulding, 2008; Scruggs & Mastropieri, 2002). Lack of response to evidence-based instruction and intervention is not necessarily indicative of the historical markers defining SLD (i.e., unexpected underachievement caused by psychological processing deficits; Batsche, Kavale, & Kovaleski, 2006). It is clear that RTI identifies underachievers through below-expected achievement and growth. However, it is less clear if RTI differentiates between expected and unexpected underachievement because it does not assess individual student cognitive abilities (Kavale & Spaulding, 2008). Instead RTI reconceptualizes unexpected underachievement to be based on comparisons of growth to a norm group while participating in research-based interventions rather than with single indicators such as IQ or a measure of cognitive processing. It is unclear if this approach to determining unexpected underachievement is superior to others, but as previously described, research has provided evidence for differentiated reading skills between responders and nonresponders, which is certainly a step in the right direction.

STRENGTHS OF AN RTI APPROACH TO IDENTIFYING SLD

Although there are legitimate criticisms of RTI and much research to be done, there are several strengths that are unique to this particular SLD identification model, which we discuss here. The ability-achievement discrepancy method has frequently been termed a "wait-to-fail" approach to LD identification because a student must exhibit a "severe"-enough discrepancy between ability and achievement before he or she can be identified, which typically is not evident until later elementary years (Compton et al., 2012). By contrast, proponents of RTI models for SLD identification assert that this approach allows for effective and early identification because it uses a systematic method to ensure that students receive timely and effective support as soon as student difficulties are evident (Kavale, Kauffman, Bachmeier, & LeFever, 2008). Consequently, when schools implement RTI frameworks, students participate in interventions as part of the evaluation process as opposed to other SLD identification methods (e.g., ability-achievement discrepancy and pattern of strengths and weaknesses; PSW), which make SLD identification decisions in isolation from intervention implementation.

A second strength for RTI is that assessment data are gathered for the purpose of information instruction and intervention (Salvia et al., 2012). Ability-achievement discrepancy and PSW SLD identification methods have been criticized for lacking treatment validity (Miciak, Fletcher, Stuebing, Vaughn, & Tolar, 2014; Vaughn & Fuchs, 2006) because ability-achievement discrepancy and PSW do not directly link assessment data to intervention. Although there is some research suggesting that cognitive processes can be trained (Melby-Lervag & Hulme, 2013), such cognitive processes training effects do not translate into improved student achievement (Burns, Petersen-Brown, et al., 2016; Kearns & Fuchs, 2013; Melby-Lervag & Hulme, 2013). Conversely, RTI assessments rely on student achievement data, which monitor student progress on specific skills over a period of time (Fletcher, Lyon, Fuchs, & Barnes, 2007). Moreover, RTI models link assessment to treatment, an integral component of any valid classification decision-making system (Cromwell, Blashfield, & Strauss, 1975; Fletcher et al., 2007). Therefore, RTI assessment data can be directly used for intervention planning based on student skill needs.

Third, RTI does not need to make high-inference decisions when identifying SLD. When analyzing student needs in schools, it is important to gather assessment data so that low-inference decisions can be made in order to ensure consistent identification decision making (Christ & Arañas, 2015). Ability-achievement discrepancy and PSW SLD identification methods result in high-inference decisions because they do not directly and repeatedly measure student skill needs (Miciak, Fletcher, et al., 2014). Conversely, assessment data gathered within RTI frameworks directly measure student skills and needs resulting in low-inference decisions (Kovaleski, VanDerHeyden, & Shapiro, 2013). These assessment data, therefore, can be directly used for intervention planning aligned with student skill needs.

Fourth, RTI decisions are made with multiple pieces of data, which could result in improved psychometrics over other approaches to SLD identification. Special education identification decisions are arguably one of the most high-stakes decisions that occur in schools. Reliability of data used for high-stakes decisions should exceed .90 for any one subgroup (Salvia et al., 2012). However, difference scores calculated within ability-achievement discrepancy and PSW identification

≡ Rapid Reference 8.3

Strengths of an RTI Approach to Identifying SLD

- RTI allows for effective and early identification because it systematically ensures that students receive timely and effective support as soon as student difficulties are evident.
- Assessment data are gathered for instruction and intervention.
- RTI does not need to make high-inference decisions when diagnosing SLD.
- RTI decisions are made with multiple pieces of data across time.

methods have been shown to be unreliable (Francis et al., 2005; Stuebing, Fletcher, Branum-Martin, & Francis, 2012). Conversely, RTI relies on multiple assessment points over a period of time rather than assessment data collected at one time point such as ability-achievement discrepancy and PSW. The collection of assessment data over time and use of multiple data points in decision making has been shown to result in more reliable decisions than single-time-point assessment data (Burns, Scholin, Kosciolek, & Livingston, 2010; Fletcher, 2012; Fletcher, Denton, & Francis, 2005). Thus, to ensure consistent SLD identification decisions, it is imperative that the assessment data being used in such decisions result in reliable decisions.

LIMITATIONS OF AN RTI APPROACH TO IDENTIFYING SLD, AND FUTURE RESEARCH

RTI is being implemented with high frequency in K–12 schools, but there are areas of concern and additional research that is needed. We describe some of these concerns here.

Identifying SLD with RTI requires use of repeated assessments over a period of time in order to show that a student does not respond to intervention. CBMs are used to monitor student progress within RTI, which were developed in the 1980s as a means to monitor student progress in alignment with specific curriculum, particularly for students receiving special education services (Christ, Zopluoglu, Monaghen, & Van Norman, 2013). In subsequent years, CBM has been developed to provide information on student progress within broad skills (e.g., reading, math, and writing) independent of specific curricula. During the early development of CBM materials in the 1980s and in subsequent years, most of the research on CBM focused on reading (Wayman, Wallace, Wiley, Ticha, & Espin, 2007). Moreover, CBM reading (CBM-R) materials are implemented at greater frequency than other CBM subject areas in schools (Christ et al., 2013), which is likely a reflection of the research focus on CBM-R.

There is considerable research regarding the use of CBM-R, particularly in reading fluency, to screen student reading skills as well as to monitor student progress in reading. Moreover, schools have many options when looking for CBM-R materials to monitor student progress. However, the research regarding CBM in other subject areas, such as math and writing, is limited compared to research regarding CBM-R (Wayman et al., 2007). Although there are math computation and writing CBM, such materials are used less frequently than CBM-R in schools. Moreover, approximately 50% of students identified with SLD are identified with an SLD in reading, but there are eight areas of SLD in which students can receive special education services (P.L. 108-446 §300.309). Despite the fact that there are eight areas of SLD under IDEA, materials for monitoring student progress in other areas (e.g., reading comprehension, oral language, listening comprehension) are lacking (Kavale et al., 2008; McMaster, Parker, & Jung, 2012). However, this limitation regarding lack of adequate assessments for these SLD achievement areas is not specific to RTI but an overarching limitation regarding SLD identification in general. In addition, students can be identified with SLD in high schools, but RTI models are less clearly defined at the secondary level and much less frequently implemented than in elementary school (Spectrum-K12, 2010).

Although early intervention and identification has been viewed as a benefit of RTI over ability-achievement discrepancy, research regarding the reliability of decisions made with CBM show that student progress must be monitored for a considerable length of time in order to make reliable decisions. Although the reliability of decisions increases with repeated assessment, data obtained from CBM assessments have still been shown to result in unreliable decisions. Christ and colleagues (i.e., Christ, Zopluoglu, Long, & Monaghen, 2012; Christ et al., 2013) have shown that less than 14 weeks of data are likely to result in decisions based on measurement error, consequently resulting in unreliable decisions regarding student progress. Moreover, reliability of decisions varies across the number of probes used (Christ et al., 2013) and model used to interpret the data (Burns et al., 2010). Therefore, schools must ensure that they collect adequate CBM assessment data over an adequate period of time in order to make reliable SLD identification decisions within RTI frameworks and that they are using a validated model to interpret the data.

Another concern is how difficult it is to implement RTI. Some have suggested that the reason the ability-achievement discrepancy model failed was because it was not correctly implemented (Scruggs & Mastropieri, 2002), which is especially concerning given the substantial relative ease of implementing an IQ and achievement test in comparison to school-wide prevention and reform that is RTI. Thus, many have identified implementation integrity as a potential fatal flaw in the RTI approach (Noell & Gansle, 2016; Ysseldyke, 2005).

Perhaps the most alarming concern about RTI implementation is the lack of consensus on how to identify nonresponse. There have been multiple studies that have compared different approaches to nonresponse, including comparison of data to an aim line and dual discrepancy (Burns et al., 2010) and comparing different dual-discrepancy criteria (Burns & Senesac, 2005; Burns, Silberglitt, et al., 2016; Toste et al., 2014). Although research has consistently identified

≡ Rapid Reference 8.4

···

Limitations of an RTI Approach to Identifying SLD

- There is considerable research regarding the use of CBM for reading, but research regarding CBM in other subject areas such as math and writing is limited.
- Approximately 50% of students identified with SLD are identified with an SLD in reading, but RTI procedures in the other areas of SLD are not as clear as for reading.
- Decisions made with progress-monitoring data must be taken over a considerable length of time so that 12 to 14 data points can be collected.
- It is difficult to effectively implement RTI.
- There is a lack of consensus on how to identify student nonresponse.

the superiority of dual discrepancy over other approaches (Burns & Senesac, 2005; Speece & Case, 2001), which approach is best to define a dual discrepancy is not known.

CONCLUSION

RTI is being commonly implemented in K–12 schools, and 20% of states require RTI to identify SLD. RTI is essentially a problem analysis framework in which school personnel identify class-wide needs, categorical problems, and causal variables through intensive problem analysis. Moreover, RTI relies on quality core instruction, intensive interventions, and closely monitoring student progress with reliable sources of data.

Although there are concerns about RTI, such as a lack of consensus about how to identify nonresponse, we conclude by paraphrasing a famous quote by Winston Churchill. In our opinion, RTI is the worst way to identify a child with SLD except every other way. It is unclear if RTI actually identifies SLD, but it is unclear if any model actually identifies SLD, and RTI at least focuses on improving student learning in the process. RTI remains a practice with considerable potential. We have yet to realize the full potential of the model 12 years after it was included in federal law, mostly because of concerns listed in this chapter. The field may never agree on how to best identify SLD or even how to best achieve RTI's considerable promise, but perhaps the RTI framework could change the focus of the debate from how to most accurately identify SLD to how to most effectively help students learn. Given the number of students who struggle with reading and math in schools, and the poor outcomes of students identified with SLD, that would be a move that we would welcome.

RESOURCES

National Center for Intensive Intervention. Supports data-based individuation for Tier 3 students with severe academic and behavior needs. The site also provides tool charts for academic and behavior progress monitoring and interventions. www.intensiveintervention.org/

National Center on RTI. Offers essential components of RTI, webinars, modules, and tools charts for screening, progress monitoring, and academic interventions. www.rti4success.org/

RTI Action Network Access. An SLD-identification toolkit. Also includes instructional videos for implementing RTI. www.rtinetwork.org/

RTI applications, Volume 1: Academic and behavioral interventions (Burns, Riley-Tillman, & VanDerHeyden, 2012): Guides readers in selecting interventions in a RTI framework.

RTI applications, Volume 2: Assessment, analysis, and decision making (Riley-Tillman, Burns, & Gibbons, 2013): Offers decision-making recommendations for assessment in an RTI framework to determine if the student is responding to the intervention.

The RTI approach to evaluating learning disabilities (Kovaleski et al., 2013): Details procedures for using RTI to evaluate eligibility for learning disabilities.

🐾 TEST YOURSELF 🐾

1. **Which of these components is *not* part of a typical RTI model?**
   (a) Universal screening
   (b) Tiered interventions
   (c) Closely monitoring student progress
   (d) Quality core instruction
   (e) All of the above are parts of a typical RTI model.

2. **How has most research identified a class-wide need?**
   (a) Percentage of students below benchmark criterion is equal to or more than 50%.
   (b) Median score for the class is below the benchmark criterion.

    (c) Percentage of students below criterion is equal to or more than 20%.

    (d) Class average is below the benchmark criterion.

    (e) All of the above are true.

3. **A student who struggles with comprehension, fluency, and decoding would likely respond best to what type of reading intervention?**

    (a) Phonemic awareness

    (b) Oral language

    (c) Fluency

    (d) Decoding

    (e) Leveled text

4. **Which of the following is the definition of a causal variable?**

    (a) The environmental variable that is within control of school personnel that is most closely related to the problem

    (b) The underlying cognitive process in which the student is deficient and that is causing the academic problem

    (c) The variable within the student's developmental history that is causing the problem

    (d) The dependent variable in a functional analysis of academic skill

    (e) None of the above

5. **All states must allow for use of RTI in SLD identification. True or false?**

6. **On which of the following measures do nonresponders consistently score lower than students who respond adequately to intervention?**

    (a) Word identification

    (b) Sight-word efficiency

    (c) Phonemic decoding

    (d) Oral language

    (e) None of the above

7. **Decisions using progress-monitoring data that are made with less than 12 to 14 data points could be based on what?**

    (a) Measurement error

    (b) Reliable data

    (c) Valid measures

    (d) Student self-report

    (e) Parental judgment

8. **There is no consensus about how to best operationalize student response and nonresponse. True or false?**

Answers: 1. e; 2. b; 3. c; 4. a; 5. True; 6. d; 7. a; 8. True.

REFERENCES

Adams, G., & Brown, S. (2007). *The six-minute solution: A reading fluency program.* Longmont, CO: Sopris West.

Algozzine, B., & Ysseldyke, J. (1982). Classification decisions in learning disabilities. *Educational and Psychological Research, 2,* 117–129.

Algozzine, B., & Ysseldyke, J. (1983). Learning disabilities as a subset of school failure: The over-sophistication of a concept. *Exceptional Children, 50,* 242–246.

Andersen, M. N., Daly, E. J., & Young, N. D. (2013). Examination of a one-trial brief experimental analysis to identify reading fluency interventions. *Psychology in the Schools, 50,* 403–414.

Archer, A. L., Gleason, M., & Vachon, V. (2006). *Rewards: Multisyllabic word reading strategies: Teacher's guide.* Longmont, CO: Sopris West.

Balu, R., Zhu, P., Doolittle, F., Schiller, E., Jenkins, J., & Gersten, R. (2015). *Evaluation of response to intervention practices for elementary school reading.* NCEE 2016–4000. Washington, DC: National Center for Education Evaluation and Regional Assistance.

Batsche, G. M., Kavale, K. A., & Kovaleski, J. F. (2006). Competing views: A dialogue on response to intervention. *Assessment for Effective Intervention, 32,* 6–19.

Burns, M. K. (2004). Empirical analysis of drill ratio research: Refining the instructional level for drill tasks. *Remedial and Special Education, 25,* 167–175.

Burns, M. K. (2007). Reading at the instructional level with children identified as learning disabled: Potential implications for response-to-intervention. *School Psychology Quarterly, 22,* 297.

Burns, M. K., Appleton, J. J., & Stehouwer, J. D. (2005). Meta-analytic review of responsiveness-to-intervention research: Examining field-based and research-implemented models. *Journal of Psychoeducational Assessment, 23,* 381–394.

Burns, M. K., Ganuza, Z. M., & London, R. M. (2009). Brief experimental analysis of written letter formation: Single-case demonstration. *Journal of Behavioral Education, 18,* 20–34.

Burns, M. K., Haegele, K., & Peterson-Brown, S. (2014). Screening for early reading skills: Using data to guide resources and instruction. In R. J. Kettler, T. A. Glover, C. A. Albers, & K. A. Feeney-Kettler (Eds.), *Universal screening in educational settings: Identification, implementation, and interpretation* (pp. 171–198). Washington, DC: American Psychological Association.

Burns, M. K., Karich, A. C., Maki, K. E., Anderson, A., Pulles, S. M., Ittner, A., . . . & Helman, L. (2015). Identifying classwide problems in reading with screening data. *Journal of Evidence-Based Practices for Schools, 14,* 186–204.

Burns, M. K., Petersen-Brown, S., Haegele, K., Rodriguez, M., Schmitt, B., Braum, M., . . . & VanDerHeyden, A. M. (2016). Meta-analysis of academic interventions derived from neuropsychological data. *School Psychology Quarterly, 31,* 28–42.

Burns, M. K., Pulles, S. M., Helman, L., & McComas, J. J. (2016). Intervention-based assessment frameworks: An example of a tier 1 reading intervention in an urban school. In S. L. Graves & J. Blake (Eds.), *Psychoeducational assessment and intervention for ethnic minority children: Evidence-based approaches* (pp. 165–182). Washington, DC: American Psychological Association.

Burns, M. K., Riley-Tillman, T. C., & VanDerHeyden, A. M. (2012). *RTI applications: Academic and behavioral interventions* (Vol. 1). New York, NY: Guilford.

Burns, M. K., Scholin, S. E., Kosciolek, S., & Livingston, J. (2010). Reliability of decision-making frameworks for response to intervention for reading. *Journal of Psychoeducational Assessment, 28*(2), 102–114.

Burns, M. K., & Senesac, B. K. (2005). Comparison of dual discrepancy criteria for diagnosis of unresponsiveness to intervention. *Journal of School Psychology, 43*, 393–406.

Burns, M. K., Silberglitt, B., Christ, T. J., Gibbons, K. A., & Coolong-Chaffin, M. (2016). Using oral reading fluency to evaluate response to intervention and to identify students not making sufficient progress. In K. D. Cummings & Y. Petscher (Eds.), *The fluency construct* (pp. 123–140). New York, NY: Springer.

Burns, M. K., & VanDerHeyden, A. M. (2006). Using response to intervention to assess learning disabilities: Introduction to the special series. *Assessment for Effective Intervention, 32*, 3–5.

Burns, M. K., VanDerHeyden, A. M., & Jiban, C. (2006). Assessing the instructional level for mathematics: A comparison of methods. *School Psychology Review, 35*, 401–418.

Burns, M. K., & Wagner, D. (2008). Determining an effective intervention within a brief experimental analysis for reading: A meta-analytic review. *School Psychology Review, 37*, 126–136.

Carson, P. M., & Eckert, T. L. (2003). An experimental analysis mathematics instructional components: Examining the effects of student-selected versus empirically selected interventions. *Journal of Behavioral Education, 12*, 35–54.

Children's Defense Fund. (2014). *The state of America's children.* Retrieved from www.childrensdefense.org/library/state-of-americas-children/

Christ, T. J., & Arañas, Y. A. (2015). Best practices in problem analysis. In P. Harrison & A. Thomas (Eds.), *Best practices in school psychology* (Vol. VI, pp. 87–98). Bethesda, MD: National Association of School Psychologists.

Christ, T. J., Zopluoglu, C., Long, J., & Monaghen, B. (2012). Curriculum-based measurement of oral reading: Quality of progress monitoring outcomes. *Exceptional Children, 78*, 356–373.

Christ, T. J., Zopluoglu, C., Monaghen, B., & Van Norman, E. R. (2013). Curriculum-based measurement of oral reading: Multi-study evaluation of schedule, duration, and dataset quality on progress monitoring outcomes. *Journal of School Psychology, 51*, 19–57. doi: http://dx.doi.org/10.1016/j.jsp.2012.11.001

Compton, D. L., Gilbert, J. K., Jenkins, J. R., Fuchs, D., Fuchs, L. S., Cho, E., . . . & Bouton, B. (2012). Accelerating chronically unresponsive children to tier 3 instruction: What level of data is necessary to ensure selection accuracy? *Journal of Learning Disabilities, 45*(3), 204–216.

Cromwell, R. L., Blashfield, R. K., & Strauss, J. S. (1975). Criteria for classification systems. In N. Hobbs (Ed.), *Issues in the classification of children* (pp. 4–25). San Francisco, CA: Jossey-Bass.

Daly, E. J., III, Martens, B. K., Hamler, K. R., Dool, E. J., & Eckert, T. L. (1999). A brief experimental analysis for identifying instructional components needed to improve oral reading fluency. *Journal of Applied Behavior Analysis, 32*, 83–94.

Daly, E. J., III, Witt, J. C., Martens, B. K., & Dool, E. J. (1997). A model for conducting a functional analysis of academic performance problems. *School Psychology Review, 26*, 554–574.

Fletcher, J. M. (2009). Dyslexia: The evolution of a scientific concept. *Journal of the International Neuropsychological Society, 15*, 501–508.

Fletcher, J. M. (2012). Classification and identification of learning disabilities. In B. Wong & D. L. Butler (Eds.), *Learning about learning disabilities* (4th ed., pp. 1–25). Waltham, MA: Academic Press.

Fletcher, J. M., Denton, C., & Francis, D. J. (2005). Validity of alternative approaches for the identification of learning disabilities operationalizing unexpected underachievement. *Journal of Learning Disabilities, 38*(6), 545–552.

Fletcher, J. M., Lyon, G. R., Fuchs, L. S., & Barnes, M. A. (2007). *Learning disabilities: From identification to intervention*. New York, NY: Guilford.

Fletcher, J. M., Stuebing, K. K., Barth, A. E., Denton, C. A., Cirino, P. T., Francis, D. J., & Vaughn, S. (2011). Cognitive correlates of inadequate response to intervention. *School Psychology Review, 40*, 2–22.

Francis, D. J., Fletcher, J. M., Stuebing, K. K., Lyon, G. R., Shaywitz, B. A., & Shaywitz, S. E. (2005). Psychometric approaches to the identification of LD: IQ and achievement scores are not sufficient. *Journal of Learning Disabilities, 38*, 98–108.

Fuchs, L. S. (2003). Assessing intervention responsiveness: Conceptual and technical issues. *Learning Disabilities Research & Practice, 18*, 172–186.

Gersten, R., Beckman, S., Clarke, B., Foegen, A., Marsh, L., Star, J., & Witzel, B. (2009). *Assisting students struggling with mathematics: Response to intervention for elementary and middle schools*. Institute of Educational Sciences, National Center for Education Evaluation and Regional Assistance. Washington, DC: US Department of Education.

Gersten, R., Compton, D., Connor, C. M., Dimino, J., Santoro, L., Linan-Thompson, S., & Tilly, W. D. (2008). *Assisting students struggling with reading: Response to intervention and multi-tier intervention in the primary grades*. Institute of Educational Sciences, National Center for Education Evaluation and Regional Assistance. Washington, DC: US Department of Education.

Gickling, E. E., & Armstrong, D. L. (1978). Levels of instructional difficulty as related to on-task behavior, task completion, and comprehension. *Journal of Learning Disabilities, 11*, 559–566.

Hauerwas, L. B., Brown, R., & Scott, A. N. (2013). Specific learning disability and response to intervention: State-level guidance. *Exceptional Children, 80*, 101–120.

Hoover, J. J., Baca, L., Wexler-Love, E., & Saenz, L. (2008). *National implementation of response to intervention (RTI)*. Retrieved from www.nasdse.org/Portals/O/ NationalImplementationofRTl-ResearchSummary.pdf

Hosp, J. L., & Ardoin, S. P. (2008). Assessment for instructional planning. *Assessment for Effective Intervention, 33*, 69–77.

Johnson, D.E.D., & Swanson, H. L. (2011). Cognitive characteristics of treatment-resistant children with reading disabilities: A retrospective study. *Journal of Psychoeducational Assessment, 29*, 137–149.

Jones, K. M., & Wickstrom K. F. (2002). Done in sixty seconds: Further analysis of the assessment model for academic problems. *School Psychology Review, 31*, 554–568.

Kavale, K. A., & Forness, S. R. (2000). What definitions of learning disability say and don't say: A critical analysis. *Journal of Learning Disabilities, 33*, 239–256. doi: http://dx.doi.org/ 10.1177/002221940003300303

Kavale, K. A., Kauffman, J. M., Bachmeier, R. J., & LeFever, G. B. (2008). Response-to-intervention: Separating the rhetoric of self-congratulation from the reality of specific learning disability identification. *Learning Disability Quarterly, 31*, 135–150.

Kavale, K. A., & Spaulding, L. S. (2008). Is response to intervention good policy for specific learning disability? *Learning Disabilities Research & Practice, 23*(4), 169–179. doi: 10.1111/j.1540-5826.2008.00274.x

Kearns, D. M., & Fuchs, D. (2013). Does cognitively focused instruction improve the academic performance of low-achieving students? *Exceptional Children, 79*, 263–290.

Kilgus, S. P., Methe, S. A., Maggin, D. M., & Tomasula, J. L. (2014). Curriculum-based measurement of oral reading (R-CBM): A diagnostic test accuracy meta-analysis of evidence supporting use in universal screening. *Journal of School Psychology, 52*, 377–405.

Kovaleski, J., VanDerHeyden, A. M., & Shapiro, E. S. (2013). *The RTI approach to evaluating learning disabilities.* New York, NY: Guilford.

Lembke, E. S., Carlisle, A., & Poch, A. (2016). Using curriculum-based measurement fluency data for initial screening decisions. In K. D. Cummings & Y. Petscher (Eds.), *The fluency construct* (pp. 91–122). New York, NY: Springer.

Maki, K. E., Floyd, R. G., & Roberson, T. (2015). State learning disability eligibility criteria: A comprehensive review. *School Psychology Quarterly, 30*, 457–469.

Marston, D., Lau, M., Muyskens, P., & Wilson, J. (2016). Data-based decision-making, the problem-solving model, and response to intervention in the Minneapolis Public Schools. In S. Jimerson, M. K. Burns, & A. M. VanDerHeyden (Eds.), *Handbook of response to intervention* (pp. 677–692). New York, NY: Springer.

Mastropieri, M. A., & Scruggs, T. E. (2005). Feasibility and consequences of response to intervention: Examination of the issues and scientific evidence as a model for the identification of individuals with learning disabilities. *Journal of Learning Disabilities, 38*, 525–531.

Mathes, P. G., Howard, J. K., Allen, S. H., & Fuchs, D. (1998). Peer-assisted learning strategies for first-grade readers: Responding to the needs of diverse learners. *Reading Research Quarterly, 33*, 62–94.

McMaster, K. L., Parker, D., & Jung, P. G. (2012). Using curriculum-based measurement for beginning writers within a response to intervention framework. *Reading Psychology, 33* (1–2), 190–216. doi: 10.1080/02702711.2012.631867

McNamara, K., & Hollinger, C. (2003). Intervention-based assessment: Evaluation rates and eligibility findings. *Exceptional Children, 69*, 181–193.

Melby-Lervag, M., & Hulme, C. (2013). Is working memory training effective? A meta-analytic review. *Developmental Psychology, 49*, 1–22.

Miciak, J., Fletcher, J. M., Stuebing, K. K., Vaughn, S., & Tolar, T. D. (2014). Patterns of cognitive strengths and weaknesses: Identification rates, agreement, and validity for learning disabilities identification. *School Psychology Quarterly, 29*, 21–37.

Miciak, J., Stuebing, K. K., Vaughn, S., Roberts, G., Barth, A. E., & Fletcher, J. M. (2014). Cognitive attributes of adequate and inadequate responders to reading intervention in middle school. *School Psychology Review, 43*, 407–427.

National Center for Educational Statistics. (2013). *The nation's report card: A first look: 2013 mathematics and reading* (NCES 2014-451). Washington, DC: Institute of Education Sciences, US Department of Education.

National Reading Panel (US), National Institute of Child Health, & Human Development (US). (2000). *Report of the national reading panel: Teaching children to read; An evidence-based assessment of the scientific research literature on reading and its implications for reading instruction: Reports of the subgroups.* Washington, DC: National Institute of Child Health and Human Development, National Institutes of Health.

Nelson, J. R., Benner, G. J., & Gonzalez, J. (2003). Learner characteristics that influence the treatment effectiveness of early literacy interventions: A meta-analytic review. *Learning Disabilities Research and Practice, 18*(4), 255–267.

Noell, G. H., & Gansle, K. A. (2016). Assuring the response to intervention process has substance: Assessing and supporting intervention implementation. In S. Jimerson, M. K. Burns, & A. M. VanDerHeyden (Eds.), *Handbook of response to intervention: The science and practice of multitiered systems of support* (2nd ed., pp. 407–420). New York, NY: Springer.

Northwest Evaluation Association. (2012). *Measures of academic progress for math.* Portland, OR: Author.

Petursdottir, A. L., McMaster, K., McComas, J. J., Bradfield, T., Braganza, V., Koch-McDonald, J., . . . & Scharf, H. (2009). Brief experimental analysis of early reading interventions. *Journal of School Psychology, 47*, 215–243.

Renaissance Learning. (2011). *Star math.* Wisconsin Rapids, WI: Author.

Renaissance Learning. (2003). *Star reading.* Wisconsin Rapids, WI: Author.

Reschly, D. J., & Hosp, J. L. (2004). State SLD identification policies and practices. *Learning Disability Quarterly, 27*, 197–213. doi: http://dx.doi.org/10.2307/1593673

Riley-Tillman, T. C., Burns, M. K., & Gibbons, K. (2013). *RTI applications: Assessment, analysis, and decision making* (Vol 2). New York, NY: Gilford.

Salvia, J., Ysseldyke, J., & Bolt, S. (2012). *Assessment in special and inclusive education.* Belmont, CA: Wadsworth.

Scruggs, T. A., & Mastropieri, M. A. (2002). On babies and bathwater: Addressing the problems of identification of learning disabilities. *Learning Disability Quarterly, 25*, 155–168.

Shapiro, E. S. (2016). Evaluating the impact of response to intervention in reading at the elementary level across the state of Pennsylvania. In S. Jimerson, M. K. Burns, & A. M. VanDerHeyden (Eds.), *Handbook of response to intervention: The science and practice of multitiered systems of support* (2nd ed., pp. 661–676). New York, NY: Springer.

Shinn, M. R., & Brown, R. (2016). *Much ado about little: The dangers of disseminating the RTI outcome study without careful analysis.* Retrieved from www.rtinetwork.org/images/content/blog/rtiblog/shinn%20brown%20ies%20report%20review.pdf

Spectrum-K12. (2010). Response to intervention adoption survey. Retrieved from http://rti.pearsoned.com/docs/RTIsite/2010RTIAdoptionSurveyReport.pdf

Speece, D. L., & Case, L. P. (2001). Classification in context: An alternative approach to identifying early reading disability. *Journal of Educational Psychology, 93*, 735–749.

Stuebing, K. K., Fletcher, J. M., Branum-Martin, L., & Francis, D. J., (2012). Evaluation of the technical adequacy of three methods for identifying specific learning disabilities based on cognitive discrepancies. *School Psychology Review, 41*, 3–22.

Stuebing, K. K., Fletcher, J. M., LeDoux, J. M., Lyon, G. R., Shaywitz, S. E., & Shaywitz, B. A. (2002). Validity of IQ-discrepancy classifications of reading disabilities: A meta-analysis. *American Educational Research Journal, 39*, 469–518.

Texas Education Agency. (2010). *The Texas primary reading inventory: Screening*. Austin, TX: Author.

Toste, J. R., Compton, D. L., Fuchs, D., Fuchs, L. S., Gilbert, J. K., Cho, E., . . . & Bouton, B. D. (2014). Understanding unresponsiveness to tier 2 reading intervention: Exploring the classification and profiles of adequate and inadequate responders in first grade. *Learning Disability Quarterly, 37*, 192–203.

Treptow, M. A., Burns, M. K., & McComas, J. J. (2007). Reading at the frustration, instructional, and independent levels: The effects on students' reading comprehension and time on task. *School Psychology Review, 36*, 159–166.

VanDerHeyden, A. M., & Burns, M. K. (2010). *Essentials of response to intervention*. New York, NY: Wiley.

VanDerHeyden, A. M., & Codding, R. S. (2015). Practical effects of classwide mathematics intervention. *School Psychology Review, 44*, 169–190.

VanDerHeyden, A., McLaughlin, T., Algina, J., & Snyder, P. (2012). Randomized evaluation of a supplemental grade-wide mathematics intervention. *American Educational Research Journal, 49*, 1251–1284.

VanDerHeyden, A. M., Witt, J. C., & Gilbertson, D. (2007). A multi-year evaluation of the effects of a response to intervention (RTI) model on identification of children for special education. *Journal of School Psychology, 45*, 225–256.

Vaughn, S., & Fuchs, L. S. (2006). A response to "Competing views: A dialogue on response to intervention": Why response to intervention is necessary but not sufficient for identifying students with learning disabilities. *Assessment for Effective Intervention, 32*, 58–61.

Wagner, R. K., Torgesen, J. K., & Rashotte, C. A. (1999). *Comprehensive test of phonological processing*. Austin, TX: PRO-ED.

Wayman, M. M., Wallace, T., Wiley, H. I., Ticha, R., & Espin, C. A. (2007). Literature synthesis on curriculum-based measurement in reading. *The Journal of Special Education, 41*, 85–120.

Ysseldyke, J. (2005). Assessment and decision making for students with learning disabilities: What if this is as good as it gets? *Learning Disability Quarterly, 28*, 125–128.

Zirkel, P. A., & Thomas, L. B. (2010). State laws and guidelines for implementing RTI. *Teaching Exceptional Children, 43*(1), 60–73.

Nine

COGNITIVE NEUROSCIENTIFIC CONTRIBUTIONS TO THEORETICAL UNDERSTANDING OF SLD

Scott L. Decker
Rachel M. Bridges
Tayllor Vetter

C ontemporary understanding of specific learning disabilities (SLDs) is characterized more by disagreement than agreement, with differences of opinion ranging from theoretical and conceptual to practical and applied. However, aside from general consensus that SLD is characterized by unexpected low achievement, the recognition that underlying causes of learning disabilities are "neurological," or brain-based in origin, is widely recognized by most major organizations. For example, the Learning Disabilities Association of America states, "Specific Learning Disabilities is a chronic condition of presumed *neurological* origin . . ." (Association for Children with Learning Disabilities, 1986, p. 15). Similarly, the National Joint Committee on Learning Disabilities (NJCLD) defines learning disabilities as ". . . a general term that refers to a heterogeneous group of disorders manifested by significant difficulties in the acquisition and use of listening, speaking, reading, writing, reasoning, or mathematical abilities. These disorders are intrinsic to the individual, presumed to be due to *central nervous system* dysfunction . . ." (1989, p. 1, emphasis added), which was identified by Hammill (1990) as the strongest of all definitions. This neurological basis also holds true for defining specific types of learning disabilities.

Essentials of Specific Learning Disability Identification, Second Edition.
Edited by Vincent C. Alfonso and Dawn P. Flanagan
© 2018 John Wiley & Sons, Inc. Published 2018 by John Wiley & Sons, Inc.

For example, the International Dyslexia Association (IDA, 2002, emphasis added) defined dyslexia as ". . . a specific learning disability that is *neurological* in origin" (para 1).

Together, these excerpts illustrate the acknowledgment of SLD occurring within the nervous system, and specifically the brain, as pervasive and well established. However, despite the unanimity in recognition of learning disabilities as a "neurological" condition, only quite recently have psychologists begun to integrate neuropsychological approaches into school-based practice effectively. This chapter aims to provide evidence for the utility of neuropsychology in the identification and conceptualization of learning disabilities by discussing (1) the history of learning disabilities, (2) contemporary issues in learning disability identification, (3) the value of neuropsychological evaluations, and (4) future directions for application of the neuropsychological approach to learning disabilities.

HISTORY OF SLD

The recognition and comprehension of learning disabilities originated with European neurologists who studied brain-injured adults. Researchers such as Franz Joseph Gall and John Baptiste Bouillaud linked specific areas of brain injury to cognitive impairments (Catani, 2005; Hallahan & Mercer, 2001). A heightened understanding of the relationship between localization and functioning was established in the 1860s and 1870s through the work of Paul Broca and Carl Wernicke, who linked specific areas of the temporal lobe to language processing. Such foundational research on impairments from brain injuries influenced early investigations of reading disabilities. In the 1870s, Sir William Broadbent and Adolph Kussmaul reported separate cases of adults, who were otherwise intelligent, as unable to read due to brain injury—a deficit coined as *word blindness* by Kussmaul. Later, Scottish ophthalmologist John Hinshelwood determined injury to the left angular gyrus as related to this deficit (Hallahan & Mercer, 2001; Pickle, 1998; Shaywitz, 2003).

The preceding findings prompted W. Pringle Morgan to examine a 14-year-old boy with *congenital* word blindness, who displayed symptoms similar to those in the adult cases with deficits by injury (Hallahan & Mercer, 2001; Morgan, 1896). The similarities across acquired and congenital word blindness prompted Hinshelwood to publish on the topic, and he noted the possible heritability of the disability, reporting on six cases within the same family, and also postulated on a disproportionate number of males as displaying its symptoms. Moreover, Hinshelwood encouraged the use of specialized instruction for children with the deficit (Hallahan & Mercer, 2001; Hinshelwood, 1917).

Through sparked interest from such European research, academics and clinicians in the United States began studying the brain-behavior relationship in learning disabilities, with Samuel Orton, Grace Fernald, Marion Monroe, and Samuel Kirk as foundational contributors (Hallahan & Mercer, 2001). Although Fernald, Marion, and Kirk supported the development of interventions for children with learning disabilities, Orton's research evolved into the contemporary objection of the intelligent quotient as representative of cognitive ability. Additionally, Orton extended Hinshelwood's theory involving the angular gyrus, arguing that reading involves not only this structure but also several additional neurological areas due to the complexity of the task. Finally, Orton was one of the first to integrate multisensory training into reading instruction for children with learning disabilities, further demonstrating the complex involvement of the brain in reading (Hallahan & Mercer, 2001; Hulme, 2014; Orton, 1937).

Between 1960 and 1975, the term *learning disability* was defined as its own category and became recognized by federal law (Hallahan & Mercer, 2001). Samuel Kirk is often cited as the creator of this term in his first edition of *Educating Exceptional Children*. In his work, Kirk defined learning disability as "a retardation, disorder, or delayed development in one or more of the processes of speech, language, reading, writing, arithmetic, or other school subject resulting from a psychological handicap . . ." (Kirk & Bateman, 1962, p. 73). Kirk further noted that learning disabilities are not caused by "cerebral dysfunction and/or emotional or behavioral disturbances" and are not a result of other factors.

This period also marked disagreement on the importance of including underlying neurological causes in the definition of learning disabilities. Although medical professionals preferred to define minimal brain damage instead of learning disabilities, emphasizing the role of brain dysfunction, educators favored a definition that focused on the discrepancy between intelligence and achievement (Hallahan & Mercer, 2001; Kavale & Forness, 1995). The National Advisory Committee on Handicapped Children (NACHC) integrated these definitions in the late 1960s, providing a description that could be used as a basis for funding programs. This definition also qualified learning disabilities as *specific learning disabilities,* indicating that specific areas of cognitive processing weaknesses manifest in academic performance in reading, math, spelling, and so on. The Children with Specific Learning Disabilities Act of 1969 was then passed, which used the NACHC definition to provide services for children with learning disabilities (Hallahan & Mercer, 2001).

In 1975, Congress passed Public Law (P.L.) 94-142, in which learning disabilities were given an official category and children within this classification became eligible for funding of services. In order to implement P.L. 94-142, the US

DON'T FORGET

....

In 1975, Congress passed Public Law (P.L.) 94-142, in which learning disabilities were given an official category and children within this classification became eligible for funding of services.

Department of Education (USDOE) defined SLD similarly to NACHC's definition, including vocabulary that is indicative of the neurological origins of learning disabilities. In 1981, the NJCLD expanded on the neurological underpinnings by noting, "These disorders are intrinsic to the individual and are presumed to be due to central nervous system dysfunction" (Hammill, Leigh, McNutt, & Larsen, 1981, p. 336). Despite these references to neurological influences on learning disabilities, the USDOE determined that evidence of an ability-achievement discrepancy would determine whether a child identifies as having a learning disability under P.L. 94-142.

P.L. 94-142 has undergone the following revisions since its origination in 1975: (1) the Individuals with Disabilities Education Act (IDEA) in 1997 and (2) the Individuals with Disabilities Education Improvement Act (IDEIA) in 2004. However, the federal definition of SLD has remained virtually unchanged. Additionally, in more recent years, criticism of the traditional discrepancy model of identification has arisen. Although other methods of learning disability identification continue to emerge (i.e., Response to Intervention, pattern of strengths and weaknesses), it is arguable that concerns regarding efficacy are influencing researchers to return to the roots of SLD: the neuropsychological basis.

In the 1980s and 1990s, researchers began evidencing the biological basis of learning disabilities through postmortem studies, neuroimaging studies, and hereditary factor studies (Hallahan & Mercer, 2001). In sum, without the introductory work of European researchers, ongoing research of modern neuropsychologists, and successive brain-behavior link that has been recognized, the current stance of providing adequate educational opportunities for children with learning disabilities would not hold. Moreover, the current framework in which SLDs are construed unfortunately would remain unchanged.

PRELIMINARY APPLICATIONS OF NEUROPSYCHOLOGICAL THEORY: SIGNIFICANT BUT FLAWED

Although initial investigations supported the neurological basis of SLD, inaccurate neuropsychological theories yielded limited applications and thus seemingly have been fleeting. Such imprecision can be traced back to the 1800s with German physician Franz Joseph Gall's erroneous theory of phrenology—a pseudoscience of the localization of intellectual qualities based on skull measurements (Hallahan & Mercer,

2001; Head, 1926; Wiederholt, 1974).
Unfortunately, this domain of thought
outweighed many of his constructive
findings, leaving him generally viewed
as a charlatan. Succeeding foundational
research has also been criticized, exem-
plified by Hinshelwood's findings that

C A U T I O N

Although early research did support a
neurological basis of SLD, initial
attempts to generalize imprecise
theories to behavioral interventions
yielded inefficacy.

linked noninjured children to adults with brain lesions have been argued to exclude
environmental and contextual factors (Coles, 1987). Moreover, ignoring such
variables limited the empirical value of these conclusions.

Orton's view of SLD was also influenced by faulty models of neurological
functioning. Based on the notion that children with SLD have reverse cerebral
dominance (switch of language dominance from left to right hemisphere), Orton
emphasized the importance of investigating differences in hemispheric functioning (Hallahan & Mercer, 2001). The term *strephosymbolia* was conceived to
differentiate the disorder he was observing from one that is visual in nature, as
word-blindness implies (Orton, 1928). Even so, this observation contributed to a
multisensory treatment approach, emphasizing phonology, which has been
maintained until the current time.

Yet, even more recent cases display fault, with the work of Doman (1974) and
Delacato (1959) demonstrating particular salience. These authors developed the
program of "Neurological Organization" for children with language and visual-
perceptual processing disabilities, under the following postulations: The growth of
the individual recapitulates that of the species, individuals with brain damage need
be instructed in hemispheric dominance, and educational methods must alter the
brain itself, not simply symptoms (Delacato, 1959, 1963, 1966; Hallahan &
Mercer, 2001); such assumptions were far ahead of their time (Hallahan & Mercer,
2001). Nonetheless, this method showed transient recognition, because it was
criticized for its demanding training requirements and questionable theoretical
foundation (Hallahan & Mercer, 2001; Robbins & Glass, 1969).

The aforementioned inaccuracies, among others, may prompt modern professionals to be hesitant in accepting a neurological framework. As illustrated historically,
it is clear that a neurological conceptualization is quite pertinent for understanding the
underlying causal factors of SLD. However, the issue at hand is not that such
approaches were brain-based but rather that they were built on speculative theory.
Without a substantive framework, these propositions are negligible and potentially
wasteful of resources on ineffective practice. Thus, moving forward, instead of
abandoning the neurological lens due to historical error, it is imperative to use
contemporary empirical techniques in order to solidify understanding of SLD.

NEUROCOGNITIVE CONNECTIVITY FRAMEWORK: AN INTEGRATIVE MODEL OF CONTEMPORARY NEUROSCIENCE FOR UNDERSTANDING SLD

Despite an extensive history of acknowledging the manifestation of SLD in the brain, understanding of the neurological basis of these disabilities remained vague; little could be said other than that SLD began "in the brain." In part, the limited awareness stemmed from technological restrictions in brain imaging. However, starting in the 1970s, rapid developments in brain-imaging technology have provided tremendous opportunity to expose and refine the neurological correlates of SLD.

> **DON'T FORGET**
> ··
> Recent developments in brain-imaging technology have provided tremendous opportunity to expose and refine the neurological correlates of SLD.

The prevailing obstacle is not that more research on the brain is needed but rather a succinct integration is necessary. Additionally, detailed anatomical analysis and activation maps using complex and sophisticated brain-imaging machinery do not provide intuition that can be readily interpreted by individuals who lack extensive training in neuroscience disciplines. In lieu of detailed examination of neuroscientific findings from specific studies, a more-general integrative framework is necessary to reflect on how brain-imaging studies have contributed to the field of learning disabilities.

At large, contemporary brain research has advanced the understanding of SLD in a variety of ways. In general, modern brain-imaging studies have verified the historically consensual observation that children with SLD have unique neurological differences in brain functioning as compared to neurotypical children. However, there are many competing perspectives of SLD with substantial contradictions. For example, the "social construction" view of SLD typically proposes there is no inherent difference between children with and without SLD, and the SLD category is a mechanism of racial privilege (Dudley-Marling, 2004; Sleeter, 1986). Similarly, "behavioral" perspectives do not differentiate SLD from general learning problems and often view academic failure as a contextual problem frequently attributed to instructional practice (Reschly, Cooling-Chaffin, Christenson, & Gutkin, 2007). Although social and contextual effects certainly influence learning, contemporary neuroscientific research demonstrating neurological differences in children with SLD compared to children without SLD (Decker, Hale, & Flanagan, 2013; Miller & Defina, 2009) help narrow and focus theoretical perspectives of SLD. Specifically, neurological findings support the involvement of a pattern of strengths and weaknesses in cognitive processes that create significant difficult learning in a standard educational environment. Indeed, the mainstream resistance to cognitive and neuropsychological assessment in school psychology is highly influenced by the lack of training many school psychologists have about the brain (Decker, 2008).

C A U T I O N

The mainstream resistance to cognitive and neuropsychological assessment in school psychology is highly influenced by the lack of training many school psychologists have about the brain.

In addition to supporting the importance of unique cognitive attributes in SLD, contemporary research has provided a more-precise understanding of the neurological origins of SLD—one that goes beyond describing the condition as "neurological." Specifically, functional neuroimaging data have linked cognitive deficits in children with SLD to specific brain functioning. For example, it has been found that individuals with mathematics learning disabilities (MLDs) exhibit disturbances in the left parietal and prefrontal brain areas, which have been linked to problems in math (Geary, 2013). Beyond MLD, functional neuroimaging has validated children with dyslexia reveal decreased activation in the left occipitotemporal cortex as well as deficiencies in the motor and attentional systems related to reading (Paulesu, Danelli, & Berlingeri, 2014).

Unfortunately, neuroscientific investigations of SLD, despite providing major breakthroughs in understanding learning and attention problems, have made little impact on diagnostic assessment practices in clinical and school practice. In part, the problem is less to do with the need for more research but with the difficulty in synthesizing the major assumptions and findings across the large number of studies that have already been completed. However, there are broad assumptions concerning the nature of the brain that are supported by contemporary neuroscientific research that have relevance for understanding SLD. Although limited, Rapid Reference 9.1 provides four empirically tested assumptions derived from cognitive neuroscience.

≡ Rapid Reference 9.1

Assumptions of Contemporary Neuropsychological Theory

- The brain consists of multiple functional networks.
- Different networks are used for different cognitive demands.
- Different types of academic learning (reading, math, writing, etc.) have different cognitive demands and, thus, use different brain networks.
- Brain networks involved in different cognitive demands must be functionally connected (share information) for efficient learning to occur.

Understanding functions of the brain in terms of networks rather than specific anatomical locations has been a considerable development in modern neuroscience (Bullmore & Sporns, 2009). There are numerous networks in the brain, without clear differentiation; however, the various networks are characterized by specific patterns of connectivity (Sporns, 2011; van den Heuvel & Sporns, 2013). Similar to how different cities are connected by a network of airports, brain networks have hubs or central nodes with high connectivity and other regions with low connectivity. The specific model of network connectivity in the brain has been described as a "small-world" network (Bassett & Bullmore, 2006).

Particular brain regions engage various networks that are involved in distinct cognitive tasks. The most-prominent networks that have direct functional links to cognition involve perceptual regions, such as the occipital lobe's involvement in visual processing and temporal region's involvement in auditory processing. The term *functional connectivity* is used to describe the correlated neuronal activity of these various regions (Bowyer, 2016). However, this term is not only conceptual but also refers to the measurement basis of brain connectivity using fMRI and EEG methodologies. Functional connectivity refers to the cross-temporal correlation of measured brain activity in different regions of the brain (Bowyer, 2016; Honey et al., 2009).

An emerging view in contemporary neuroscience is that SLD is caused by problems in brain connectivity within specific brain networks that are important for academic learning (Paulesu et al., 1996; Rippon, Brock, Brown, & Boucher, 2007). The term *neurocognitive connectivity (NCC)* framework will be used in this chapter to explain the unique pattern of cognitive strengths and weaknesses in children with SLD. Additionally the NCC framework provides integration across empirical findings that extend beyond neuroscience and include development, cognition, genetics, and behavior.

As a simplification to demonstrate the basic assumptions of an NCC framework for understanding SLD, consider the cognitive demands of learning to read in early grades; the early stages of reading involve "word decoding." Decoding involves, first, a *visual analysis* of letters and *visual recognition* of letter patterns or groups of letters. Next, letter groups must be associated with language sounds (*phonology*). To read a word, the letter sounds of different letters in the word must be blended. Finally, the blended letter sounds must be recognized as a word that is already stored in the child's vocabulary (*semantics*).

Specific cognitive processes involved in word decoding are linked to specific brain networks in different areas of the brain. First, the *visual analysis* of letters primarily involves brain networks in the occipital lobe in the most posterior region of the brain. By contrast, the second step of *phonology* involves auditory sound representations

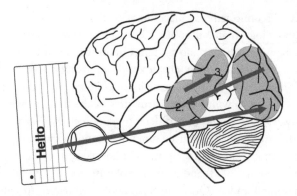

Figure 9.1. NCC Framework of Word Recognition: Corresponding Cognitive and Neurological Processes

1. **Decode.** Visual analysis of letters and visual recognition of letter patterns occurs in the occipital lobe after the individual has viewed the word.
2. **Phonology.** Visual letter groups are associated with the language sounds and sound blending occurs in the superior temporal lobe.
3. **Semantics.** Blended sounds are recognized as words in stored vocabulary in neurological areas in close proximity to where phonological processing occurred.

that are localized to the temporal regions of the brain, more specifically, in the superior temporal region. Third, closely associated with auditory sound representations are the receptive languages areas, which involve networks in close proximity to auditory sound representations region, because language is learned through sound. See Figure 9.1 for a visual representation of these steps. However, "language" goes beyond sound to involve semantic representation or word meanings, which involves more distributed brain networks in the brain. Given that word decoding involves cognitive processes in two different regions of the brain, academic learning of word decoding requires networks from these two different areas of the brain to be connected. Reduced connectivity between brain networks involved in specific learning tasks reduces learning efficiency. Reduced learning efficiency of academic tasks due to individual differences in atypical brain connectivity is the underlying cause of SLD.

DON'T FORGET

Reduced learning efficiency of academic tasks due to individual differences in atypical brain connectivity is the underlying cause of SLD.

Numerous studies involving brain imaging support the NCC framework for SLD. One of the first studies investigating brain connectivity differences between children with dyslexia and typically developing children found that children with dyslexia had "disconnected" language areas of the brain that corresponded to deficits in phonology (Paulesu et al., 1996). Here, it was proposed that weak connectivity between anterior and posterior brain regions in the left hemisphere resulted in phonological deficits characteristic of many children with reading problems. Differences in brain connectivity in children with learning disabilities has also been linked to white matter structures of the brain, which serve as the major "highways" for connecting different brain regions (Silani et al., 2005; Temple, 2002). Additionally, reduced functional connectivity has been associated with deficits in integrating orthography and phonology in children with dyslexia (Cao, Bitan, & Booth, 2008) and predictive of differences between children with dyslexia and normal readers (Quaglino et al., 2008). Moreover, specific patterns of brain connectivity are linked to specific types of learning problems (Fields, 2008; Pugh et al., 2000).

Meta-analytic research has supported clear changes in brain activity as a result of reading interventions. Specifically, researchers found that children with reading difficulties exhibited different amounts of functional connectivity in the frontal lobe compared to children without reading difficulties. However, after participating in different reading interventions, a difference in frontal connectivity no longer existed (Barquero, Davis, & Cutting, 2014). Furthermore, recent literature suggests children with double deficits (phonological and rapid-naming deficits) have more atypical brain connectivity than children with only a single deficit (Norton et al., 2014), which demonstrates a linear relationship between atypical connectivity and learning problems. These findings indicate treatment outcomes of children with dyslexia, in comparison to a control group, are dependent on the normalization of brain connectivity in specific regions of the brain (Richards & Berninger, 2008)—a concept that has major implications for directing future neurological interventions.

Children with reading disabilities are not alone in evidence of atypical brain connectivity. Children with different types, as well as subtypes, of SLD have different patterns of atypical brain connectivity. For example, recent research has demonstrated differentiated functional connectivity in brain regions involved in word processing among fMRI data for children with dysgraphia, dyslexia, and oral and written language learning disabilities (Berninger, Richards, & Abbott, 2015). Specifically, brain areas to which these regions are connected, as well as the total number of functional connections, varied across diagnosis.

Disruptions in brain connectivity extend beyond dyslexia; data suggest such patterns have also been found in children with developmental dyscalculia (Rosenberg-Lee et al., 2015). Interestingly, brain areas implicated in dyscalculia are different than dyslexia due to the different neurocognitive demands inherent in learning math (Ashkenazi, Black, Abrams, Hoeft, & Menon, 2013; Butterworth, Varma, & Laurillard 2011; Kucian & von Aster, 2015). Similar to dyslexia, dyscalculia is being viewed as a "disconnection syndrome" in specific brain regions involved in math calculations (Kucian et al., 2014). For instance, children with dyscalculia display decreased fractional anisotropy in the superior longitudinal fasciculus as well as significant insufficiencies in fibers of the superior longitudinal fasciculus—an area theorized to be essential in numerical processing (Kucian, Plangger, O'Gorman, & von Aster, 2013). In other words, different types of SLD (dyslexia, dyscalculia, dysgraphia, etc.) are associated with different patterns of atypical connectivity in different regions of the brain.

The NCC perspective (of viewing SLD in terms of connectivity) provides a fresh perspective not only for understanding SLD but also for grasping neurological disorders at large (Stam, 2014). Abnormal patterns of brain connectivity have been linked to numerous developmental and psychiatric conditions, and reduced symptomatology in these conditions is dependent on the normalization in brain network connectivity (Voytek & Knight, 2015). For example, atypical patterns of connectivity have been found in individuals with schizophrenia (Su, Hsu, Lin, & Lin, 2015), epilepsy (Widjaja et al., 2015), substance abuse, and Alzheimer's disease (Qin et al., 2015), to name a few.

IMPLICATIONS FOR THE ASSESSMENT AND TREATMENT OF SLD

Evidence for the neurological basis of SLD yield several suggestions for improved identification and intervention procedures. A discussion of theoretical and applied implications follows.

Theoretical

As previously mentioned, SLD research is characterized more by incongruity than consensus. Additionally, caution should be taken when attempting to generalize neuropsychological theories to applied practice, given historic inaccuracies. However, the modern convergence that focuses on brain connectivity as important for understanding SLD may have important implications for the assessment and treatment of children with SLD.

C A U T I O N

SLD research is characterized more by incongruity than consensus.

For example, validation of definitional terms used to define SLD has been a long-standing issue of contention. Specifically, the term *psychological processes*, used in reference to the cognitive deficits characteristic of SLD, implies the problem as psychological (or inside the person's head). However, the vagueness in using this definitional term has fueled political debates among differing perspectives on understanding SLD. Similarly, attributing SLD to "the brain" lacks theoretical clarity. Although contemporary neuroscience substantiates the neurological origins of SLD, the NCC framework provides greater specificity to the underlying causes of SLD. Although the definitions of SLD need not use the complexity of neuro-psychological jargon (i.e., left parietal-temporal connectivity), NCC provides a theoretical framework to investigate the "cognitive constructs" for defining SLD.

Complex cognitive activity emerges from neuronal activity as part of an integrated network structure to exchange information throughout the brain (van den Heuvel & Sporns, 2013). Although the degree to which disconnected brain networks manifests as discrepancies between different type of behavioral measures is not precisely known, reasonable inferences can be made based on the theory. For example, Cattell-Horn-Carroll (CHC) theory is a hierarchical model of the structure of cognitive abilities (Carroll, 1993). Of the many broad abilities, some are characterized by perceptual components of cognitive tasks such as auditory and visual tasks (Ga and Gv, respectively). Consequently, such tasks likely involve brain networks associated with these perceptual modalities. Other broad abilities such as short-term memory (Gsm) and memory retrieval (Glr) involve brain networks associated with the retrieval and maintenance of memory representations, which are known to be supported by multiple distributed net-works in the brain. Although the point here is not to provide a definitive map of brain networks involved in CHC abilities, the correspondence between brain networks and cognitive tasks may help provide a model of understanding patterns of behavioral performance on cognitive measures. For example, a child's deficits in Ga tasks likely correspond to specific network hubs in specific regions of the brain (superior temporal region). Knowing a child has specific deficits in auditory perception as evidenced by behavioral performance across Ga measures provides insight into interpreting other cognitive measures. For example, many Gsm tests involve auditory input. A pattern of deficits on Gsm tests involving low performance on tasks with auditory stimuli helps provide a more-specific description of the cognitive problem that cannot be captured by broad composite scores on Ga and Gsm tests alone.

Assessment and Identification

Neuropsychological approaches to assessment of children with SLD has grown in interest, especially among school psychologists (Decker, 2008). A long-standing debate concerning SLD has been the ideal mode of identification. For instance, the use of cognitive tests has a record of contention within the field. Historically, measures of cognition were required by US federal guidelines for SLD identification. However, IQ scores were the basis of using such cognitive measures. Consistent with a contemporary neuropsychological view, SLD is defined by *specific* cognitive deficits that arise from connectivity problems in particular regions of the brain. The use of IQ scores, which is an amalgam of different cognitive tests compiled into a single score, lacks the specificity and sensitivity for capturing the exact cognitive deficits associated with SLD (Decker et al., 2013).

Supporting an NCC framework, causal links have been made between changes in brain networks and reading interventions (Shaywitz & Shaywitz, 2008). Consistent with a cognitive strengths and weaknesses approach, reduced connectivity in specific brain networks will cause impaired performance on specific cognitive and academic tests. The consistency and inconsistency in cognitive and academic performance supports an assessment model in which meaningful differences across and between cognitive and academic measures help pinpoint underlying learning problems. For example, children with dyslexia often have deficits in phonological awareness. However, SLD, in general, can be caused by other types of cognitive deficits including working memory, language, or attention. Although the profile of cognitive strengths and weaknesses is well known, the underlying theoretical cause of the uneven profile of cognitive abilities in children with SLD has remained a mystery. Within the NCC framework, an uneven profile of cognitive skills may correspond to network hub functionality in the brain. Some preliminary research may already suggest this is likely the case (Adelstein et al., 2011; Bassett et al., 2009; Cole, Yarkoni, Repovš, Anticevic, & Braver, 2012; Li et al., 2009; Shimono, Mano, & Niki, 2012; van den Heuvel, Stam, Kahn, & Pol, 2009; Zalesky & Fornito, 2009).

> **DON'T FORGET**
> ....
> Although the profile of cognitive strengths and weaknesses is well known, the underlying theoretical cause of the uneven profile of cognitive abilities in children with SLD has remained a mystery.

Just as brain networks provide a common denominator for cognitive and academic weaknesses in phonology that changes with intervention (Shaywitz & Shaywitz, 2008), there is promise that other interventions involving different brain networks will be similarly effective. Although it is unfeasible to do brain imaging of children in school for diagnostic purposes, a comprehensive battery of tests involving different brain networks that overlap with academic cognition is essential. Within the NCC framework of this chapter, the value of cognitive tests can be clarified. First, and historically noted, cognitive test performance provides a "gauge" to differentiate typical from atypical cognitive development. Second, such tests provide an indication of cognitive functioning that is less dependent on instructional learning experiences. For example, rapid object-naming measures provide a degree of prompt lexical access, which is known to be involved in some types of SLD. Similarly, phonological awareness provides an indicator of abilities to represent and manipulate speech-language sounds—a skill also linked to some types of SLD. Weaknesses on these particular cognitive measures provide valuable information on the underlying deficit that is causing the learning problem. Ultimately all cognition is dependent on brain connectivity, and cognitive measures provide a more-specific guide of brain hub disconnectivity than academic measures alone. Moreover, in aiding to specify the underlying cognitive deficit, these measures provide information to guide and select more-targeted intervention. Evaluating the correspondence between cognitive test performance and brain hub involvement will likely be a future direction of neurocognitive research.

Intervention and Treatment

Most academic learning tasks, even at the earliest developmental stages, involve numerous subcomponent skills, which in turn involve different cognitive components. Cognitive assessment provides an evaluation of core component skills involved in academic learning. In contrast to instructional approaches, which are primarily based on behavioral learning theorists, there is not an inherent basis for identifying and describing cognitive subcomponents of academic tasks, which excludes it from being the focus of intervention.

However, such attitudes lack specification of discrete subskills and cognitive processes inherent in educational learning. As previously reviewed, normalization of brain connectivity corresponds to improved learning. Similarly, intervention approaches that target the underlying problem improve academic skills. For example, intervening with phonology improves reading for children with dyslexia, whereas intervening with magnitude estimation helps children with dyscalculia.

In emphasizing the role of brain connectivity, the NCC perspective may provide an important theoretical foundation for guiding interventions. Essentially, children with SLD have weak connections in particular areas of the brain that reduce integration of associative learning that is involved in specific academic tasks. Interventions that facilitate connectivity of these brain regions should result in improved performance or create the conditions for improving the efficiency of learning.

An important role emerging from NCC involves a revised understanding of attention, which has historically been difficult to define. Attention has been classically defined as a description of information held in awareness at a particular moment in time; it can become more or less focused and can shift; it involves exogenous (environmental) influences as well as endogenous (within the person) influences. More contemporary research has found links between attention and brain connectivity. Specifically, attention is a cognitive mechanism that facilitates the binding or connectivity of different brain networks. Attention is important because it is influenced by task demands and volitional control; thus, it is amenable through interventions.

Last, the NCC framework may provide a conceptual framework for explaining novel therapies that have been used in SLD. Neurofeedback (NF) has been one method used to directly change brain connectivity. This treatment involves a brain-computer interface for operant conditioning of brain activity, in which patients are trained to direct their own EEG activity. Positive outcomes have been reported for various disabilities, including SLD. For instance, case and experimental studies have demonstrated changes in brain connectivity from NF in children with dyslexia that resulted in improved spelling (Breteler, Arns, Peters, Giepmans, & Verhoeven, 2010); improved reading (from 1.2 grade levels to upwards of 2 grade levels; Coben, Wright, Decker, & Morgan, 2015; Walker & Norman, 2006); and improved phonological skills (Nazari, Mosanezhad, Hashemi, & Jahan, 2012).

CONCLUSION

This chapter reviews the history of SLD, with particular focus on the importance of brain-based models of learning to explain behavioral symptoms of SLD. Although a neurological basis of SLD has been long suspected, the cognitive-neuropsychological basis of SLD remained a mystery. Contemporary neuroscientific studies, benefitting from advances in brain-imaging technology, have provided greater specification in distinct brain regions found to be diverging between children with SLD and children developing neurotypically. Similarly, greater clarity of the cognitive demands in academic learning has provided more detailed models of cognitive processes in education.

The integration of cognitive and neuroscience investigations of SLD is converging to suggest specific brain regions, or networks, are explicitly engaged during academic learning. Additionally, education requires integrated, or connected, brain networks dedicated to the differential processing demands in learning. The NCC framework is offered to synthesize the emerging theme of neuroscientific investigations, suggesting SLD is caused by reduced connectivity in brain networks involved in academic learning. Patterns of connectivity correspond to different displays of learning disabilities. Implications of viewing SLD as a brain network connectivity problem are discussed with relevance to theory, assessment, and intervention. Although research supporting a disconnectivity model of SLD has been reinforced by neuroscientific investigations, additional research in the applied and practical applications of the model is necessary.

🐾 TEST YOURSELF 🐾

1. Contemporary understanding of SLD is characterized more by disagreement than agreement, with differences of opinion ranging from theoretical and conceptual to practical and applied. True or false?

2. Learning disabilities were given an official category and children within this classification became eligible for funding of services under which Public Law?
   (a) 105-17
   (b) 94-142
   (c) 108-446
   (d) 99-457

3. Assumptions of contemporary neuropsychological theory include the following except:
   (a) Different networks are used for different cognitive demands.
   (b) Different types of academic learning (reading, math, writing, etc.) have different cognitive demands and, thus, use different brain networks.
   (c) There is no connection between the brain and SLD.
   (d) Brain networks involved in different cognitive demands must be functionally connected (share information) for efficient learning to occur.

4. Although the profile of cognitive strengths and weaknesses is well known, the underlying theoretical cause of the uneven profile of cognitive abilities in children with SLD has remained a mystery. True or false?

5. SLD, in general, can be caused by other types of cognitive deficits, including:
   (a) Working memory
   (b) Language
   (c) Attention
   (d) All of the above

Answers: 1. True; 2. b; 3. c; 4. True; 5. d.

REFERENCES

Adelstein, J. S., Shehzad, Z., Mennes, M., DeYoung, C. G., Zuo, X. N., Kelly, C., . . . & Milham, M. P. (2011). Personality is reflected in the brain's intrinsic functional architecture. *PLOS ONE, 6*(11), e27633.

Ashkenazi, S., Black, J. M., Abrams, D. A., Hoeft, F., & Menon, V. (2013). Neurobiological underpinnings of math and reading learning disabilities. *Journal of Learning Disabilities, 46*(6), 549–569.

Association for Children with Learning Disabilities. (1986). ACLD description: Specific learning disabilities. *ACLD Newsbriefs,* pp. 15–16.

Barquero, L. A., Davis, N., & Cutting, L. E. (2014). *Neuroimaging of reading intervention: A systematic review and activation likelihood estimate meta-analysis. PLOS ONE, 9*(1), e83668.

Bassett, D. S., & Bullmore, E. D. (2006). Small-world brain networks. *The Neuroscientist, 12*(6), 512–523.

Bassett, D. S., Bullmore, E. T., Meyer-Lindenberg, A., Apud, J. A., Weinberger, D. R., & Coppola, R. (2009). Cognitive fitness of cost-efficient brain functional networks. *Proceedings of the National Academy of Sciences, 106*(28), 11747–11752.

Berninger, V. W., Richards, T. L., & Abbott, R. D. (2015). Differential diagnosis of dysgraphia, dyslexia, and OWL LD: Behavioral and neuroimaging evidence. *Reading and Writing, 28*(8), 1119–1153.

Bowyer, S. M. (2016). Coherence a measure of the brain networks: Past and present. *Neuropsychiatric Electrophysiology, 2*(1), 1.

Breteler, M. H., Arns, M., Peters, S., Giepmans, I., & Verhoeven, L. (2010). Improvements in spelling after QEEG-based neurofeedback in dyslexia: A randomized controlled treatment study. *Applied Psychophysiology and Biofeedback, 35*(1), 5–11.

Bullmore, E., & Sporns, O. (2009). Complex brain networks: Graph theoretical analysis of structural and functional systems. *Nature Reviews Neuroscience, 10*(3), 186–198.

Butterworth, B., Varma, S., & Laurillard, D. (2011). Dyscalculia: From brain to education. *Science, 332*(6033), 1049–1053.

Cao, F., Bitan, T., & Booth, J. R. (2008). Effective brain connectivity in children with reading difficulties during phonological processing. *Brain and Language, 107*(2), 91–101.

Carroll, J. B. (1993). *Human cognitive abilities: A survey of factor analytic studies.* Cambridge, UK: Cambridge University Press.

Catani, M. (2005). The rises and falls of disconnection syndromes. *Brain, 128*(10), 2224–2239.

Coben, R., Wright, E. K., Decker, S. L., & Morgan, T. (2015). The impact of coherence neurofeedback on reading delays in learning disabled children: A randomized controlled study. *NeuroRegulation, 2*(4), 168.

Cole, M. W., Yarkoni, T., Repovš, G., Anticevic, A., & Braver, T. S. (2012). Global connectivity of prefrontal cortex predicts cognitive control and intelligence. *Journal of Neuroscience, 32*(26), 8988–8999.

Coles, G. (1987). *The learning mystique: A critical look at "learning disabilities."* New York, NY: Pantheon Books.

Decker, S. L. (2008). School neuropsychology consultation in neurodevelopmental disorders. *Psychology in the Schools, 45*(9), 799–811.

Decker, S. L., Hale, J. B., & Flanagan, D. P. (2013). Professional practice issues in the assessment of cognitive functioning for educational applications. *Psychology in the Schools*, *50*(3), 300–313.

Delacato, C. (1959). *The treatment and prevention of reading problems*. Springfield, IL: Thomas.

Delacato, C. (1963). *The diagnosis and treatment of speech and reading problems*. Springfield, IL: Thomas.

Delacato, C. (1966). *Neurological organization and reading*. Springfield, IL: Thomas.

Doman, G. (1974). *What to do about your brain-injured child or your brain-damaged, mentally retarded, mentally deficient, cerebral-palsied, spastic, flaccid, rigid, epileptic, autistic, athetoid, hyperactive child*. Garden City Park, NY: Avery.

Dudley-Marling, C. (2004). The social construction of learning disabilities. *Journal of Learning Disabilities*, *37*(6), 482–489.

Fields, R. D. (2008). White matter in learning, cognition and psychiatric disorders. *Trends in Neurosciences*, *31*(7), 361–370.

Geary, D. C. (2013). Early foundations for mathematics learning and their relations to learning disabilities. *Current Directions in Psychological Science*, *22*(1), 23–27.

Hallahan, D. P., & Mercer, C. D. (2001). *Learning disabilities: Historical perspectives*. Paper written for the Office of Special Education Programs, US Department of Education, and presented at the OSEP's LD Summit conference, August 27–28, Washington, DC.

Hammill, D. D. (1990). On defining learning disabilities: An emerging consensus. *Journal of Learning Disabilities*, *23*(2), 74–84.

Hammill, D. D., Leigh, J. E., McNutt, G., & Larsen, S. C. (1981). A new definition of learning disabilities. *Learning Disability Quarterly*, *4*(4), 336–342.

Head, H. (1926). *Aphasia*. Cambridge, UK: Cambridge University Press.

Hinshelwood, J. (1917). Congenital word-blindness. *The Lancet*, *190*(4922), 980.

Honey, C. J., Sporns, O., Cammoun, L., Gigandet, X., Thiran, J. P., Meuli, R., & Hagmann, P. (2009). Predicting human resting-state functional connectivity from structural connectivity. *Proceedings of the National Academy of Sciences*, *106*(6), 2035–2040.

Hulme, C. (2014). *Reading retardation and multi-sensory teaching*. New York, NY: Routledge.

International Dyslexia Association (IDA). (2002). Definition of dyslexia. Retrieved from https://dyslexiaida.org.

Kavale, K. A., & Forness, S. R. (1995). *The nature of learning disabilities: Critical elements of diagnosis and classification*. New York, NY: Routledge.

Kirk, S. A., & Bateman, B. (1962). Diagnosis and remediation of learning disabilities. *Exceptional Children*, *29*(2), 73–78.

Kucian, K., Ashkenazi, S. S., Hänggi, J., Rotzer, S., Jäncke, L., Martin, E., & von Aster, M. (2014). Developmental dyscalculia: A dysconnection syndrome? *Brain Structure and Function*, *219*(5), 1721–1733.

Kucian, K., Plangger, F., O'Gorman, R., & von Aster, M. (2013). Operational momentum effect in children with and without developmental dyscalculia. *Frontiers in Psychology*, *4*.

Kucian, K., & von Aster, M. (2015). Developmental dyscalculia. *European Journal of Pediatrics*, *174*(1), 1–13.

Li, Y., Liu, Y., Li, J., Qin, W., Li, K., Yu, C., & Jiang, T. (2009). Brain anatomical network and intelligence. *PLOS Computational Biology, 5*(5), e1000395.

Miller, D. C., & Defina, P. A. (2009). The application of neuroscience to the practice of school neuropsychology. In D. C. Miller (Ed.), *Best practices in school neuropsychology: Guidelines for effective practice, assessment, and evidence-based intervention* (p. 141). Hoboken, NJ: Wiley.

Morgan, W. P. (1896). A case of congenital word blindness. *British Medical Journal, 2*(1871), 1378.

National Joint Committee on Learning Disabilities. (1989, September 18). Letter from NJCLD to member organizations. Topic: Modifications to the NJCLD definition of learning disabilities. Washington, DC: Author.

Nazari, M. A., Mosanezhad, E., Hashemi, T., & Jahan, A. (2012). The effectiveness of neurofeedback training on EEG coherence and neuropsychological functions in children with reading disability. *Clinical EEG and Neuroscience, 43*(4), 315–322.

Norton, E. S., Black, J. M., Stanley, L. M., Tanaka, H., Gabrieli, J. D., Sawyer, C., & Hoeft, F. (2014). Functional neuroanatomical evidence for the double-deficit hypothesis of developmental dyslexia. *Neuropsychologia, 61*, 235–246.

Orton, S. T. (1928). Specific reading disability—strephosymbolia. *Journal of the American Medical Association, 90*(14), 1095–1099.

Orton, S. T. (1937). *Reading, writing and speech problems in children.* New York, NY: W. W. Norton & Co.

Paulesu, E., Danelli, L., & Berlingeri, M. (2014). Reading the dyslexic brain: Multiple dysfunctional routes revealed by a new meta-analysis of PET and fMRI activation studies. *Frontiers in Human Neuroscience, 8*, 830.

Paulesu, E., Frith, U., Snowling, M., Gallagher, A., Morton, J., Frackowiak, R. S., & Frith, C. D. (1996). Is developmental dyslexia a disconnection syndrome? *Brain, 119*(1), 143–157.

Pickle, J. M. (1998). Historical trends in biological and medical investigations of reading disabilities: 1850–1915. *Journal of Learning Disabilities, 31*(6), 625–635.

Pugh, K. R., Mencl, W. E., Shaywitz, B. A., Shaywitz, S. E., Fulbright, R. K., Constable, R. T., . . . & Liberman, A. M. (2000). The angular gyrus in developmental dyslexia: Task-specific differences in functional connectivity within posterior cortex. *Psychological Science, 11*(1), 51–56.

Qin, Y. Y., Li, Y. P., Zhang, S., Xiong, Y., Guo, L. Y., Yang, S. Q., . . . & Zhu, W. Z. (2015). Frequency-specific alterations of large-scale functional brain networks in patients with Alzheimer's disease. *Chinese Medical Journal, 128*(5), 602.

Quaglino, V., Bourdin, B., Czternasty, G., Vrignaud, P., Fall, S., Meyer, M. E., . . . & de Marco, G. (2008). Differences in effective connectivity between dyslexic children and normal readers during a pseudoword reading task: An fMRI study. *Neurophysiologie Clinique/Clinical Neurophysiology, 38*(2), 73–82.

Reschly, A. L., Coolong-Chaffin, M., Christenson, S. L., & Gutkin, T. (2007). Contextual influences and response to intervention: Critical issues and strategies. In S. R. Jimerson, M. K. Burns, & A. M. VanDerHeyden (Eds.), *Handbook of response to intervention* (pp. 148–160). Minneapolis, MN: Springer.

Richards, T. L., & Berninger, V. W. (2008). Abnormal fMRI connectivity in children with dyslexia during a phoneme task: Before but not after treatment. *Journal of Neurolinguistics*, *21*(4), 294–304.

Rippon, G., Brock, J., Brown, C., & Boucher, J. (2007). Disordered connectivity in the autistic brain: Challenges for the "new psychophysiology." *International Journal of Psychophysiology*, *63*(2), 164–172.

Robbins, M. P., & Glass, G. V. (1969). The Doman-Delacato rationale: A critical analysis. In J. Hellmuth (Ed.), *Educational therapy* (Vol. 2, pp. 321–377). Seattle, WA: Special Child.

Rosenberg-Lee, M., Ashkenazi, S., Chen, T., Young, C. B., Geary, D. C., & Menon, V. (2015). Brain hyper-connectivity and operation-specific deficits during arithmetic problem solving in children with developmental dyscalculia. *Developmental Science*, *18*(3), 351–372.

Shaywitz, S. E. (2003). *Overcoming dyslexia: A new and complete science-based program for reading problems at any level.* New York, NY: Knopf.

Shaywitz, S. E., & Shaywitz, B. A. (2008). Paying attention to reading: The neurobiology of reading and dyslexia. *Development and Psychopathology*, *20*(04), 1329–1349.

Shimono, M., Mano, H., & Niki, K. (2012). The brain structural hub of interhemispheric information integration for visual motion perception. *Cerebral Cortex*, *22*(2), 337–344.

Silani, G., Frith, U., Demonet, J. F., Fazio, F., Perani, D., Price, C., . . . & Paulesu, E. (2005). Brain abnormalities underlying altered activation in dyslexia: A voxel-based morphometry study. *Brain*, *128*(10), 2453–2461.

Sleeter, C. E. (1986). Learning disabilities: The social construction of a special education category. *Exceptional Children*, *53*(1), 46–54.

Sporns, O. (2011). The human connectome: A complex network. *Annals of the New York Academy of Sciences*, *1224*(1), 109–125.

Stam, C. J. (2014). Modern network science of neurological disorders. *Nature Reviews Neuroscience*, *15*(10), 683–695.

Su, T. W., Hsu, T. W., Lin, Y. C., & Lin, C. P. (2015). Schizophrenia symptoms and brain network efficiency: A resting-state fMRI study. *Psychiatry Research: Neuroimaging*, *234*(2), 208–218.

Temple, E. (2002). Brain mechanisms in normal and dyslexic readers. *Current Opinion in Neurobiology*, *12*(2), 178–183.

van den Heuvel, M. P., & Sporns, O. (2013). Network hubs in the human brain. *Trends in Cognitive Sciences*, *17*(12), 683–696.

van den Heuvel, M. P., Stam, C. J., Kahn, R. S., & Pol, H.E.H. (2009). Efficiency of functional brain networks and intellectual performance. *Journal of Neuroscience*, *29*(23), 7619–7624.

Voytek, B., & Knight, R. T. (2015). Dynamic network communication as a unifying neural basis for cognition, development, aging, and disease. *Biological Psychiatry*, *77*(12), 1089–1097.

Walker, J. E., & Norman, C. A. (2006). The neurophysiology of dyslexia: A selective review with implications for neurofeedback remediation and results of treatment in twelve consecutive patients. *Journal of Neurotherapy*, *10*(1), 45–55. doi 10.1300/J184v10n01_04

Widjaja, E., Zamyadi, M., Raybaud, C., Snead, O. C., Doesburg, S. M., & Smith, M. L. (2015). Disrupted global and regional structural networks and subnetworks in children with localization-related epilepsy. *American Journal of Neuroradiology, 36*(7), 1362–1368.

Wiederholt, J. L. (1974). Historical perspectives on the education of the learning disabled. In L. Mann & D. Sabatino (Eds.), *The second review of special education* (pp. 103–152). Philadelphia: JSE Press.

Zalesky, A., & Fornito, A. (2009). A DTI-derived measure of cortico-cortical connectivity. *IEEE Transactions on Medical Imaging, 28*(7), 1023–1036.

Ten

INTEGRATING INSTRUCTIONALLY RELEVANT SLD DIAGNOSES, PATTERNS OF STRENGTHS AND WEAKNESSES, AND POSITIVE HOME-SCHOOL PARTNERSHIPS

Free and Appropriate Public Education for *All*

Nicole Lynn Alston-Abel
Virginia Berninger

This chapter is based in part on research on defining and treating specific learning disabilities, which was supported by HD P50HD071764 from the Eunice Kennedy Shriver National Institute of Child Health and Human Development (NICHD) at the National Institutes of Health (NIH).

OVERVIEW

In this chapter we position legal and professional issues in identifying and teaching students with specific learning disabilities (SLDs) in the United States within their historic context in education, the Every Student Succeeds Act (ESSA) enacted in 2015 at the federal level and still being implemented in states, and the relevance of the voices of school practitioners and researchers. We make a case for flexible approaches to linking assessment to instruction for meeting the needs of students who struggle in learning to read, write, listen, speak, and do math because they have SLDs, live in poverty, or are members of other cultural and language groups historically associated

Essentials of Specific Learning Disability Identification, Second Edition.
Edited by Vincent C. Alfonso and Dawn P. Flanagan.
© 2018 John Wiley & Sons, Inc. Published 2018 by John Wiley & Sons, Inc.

with underachievement. On the one hand, it was a mistake to use culture, language, or low socioeconomic status (SES) as an exclusionary criterion for pull-out specialized instruction. On the other hand, there is urgency to reverse the overrepresentation of minority students in special education and meet the educational needs of diverse students and those living in poverty. Thus, best professional practices are (1) evidence-based (e.g., using developmental profiles, learning profiles, and pheno-type profiles for identifying patterns of strengths and weaknesses [PSWs]); (2) culturally, linguistically, and socioeconomically sensitive; and (3) aim to provide free and appropriate public education (FAPE) for *all* (see Blankstein & Noguera, 2015; Organisation for Economic Co-operation and Development, 2014).

HISTORIC CONTEXT

The first national law in 1975 granting students with educationally handicapping conditions the right to FAPE was the result of collaborations among parents of students with SLDs or with developmental disabilities (DDs) including what is now called *intellectual disability*. The widespread use of discrepancy definitions (between full or total scale scores on intelligence tests and scores on achievement tests) used to qualify students for special education services and individualized educational programs (IEPs) resulted in large part from the need to differentiate those with and without intellectual disabilities; but this approach has not been shown in research to be valid for identifying SLDs (e.g., Stuebing, Fletcher, Marin, & Francis, 2012). Even when the Verbal Comprehension Index of the Wechsler scales is used rather than a Full Scale score to predict expected reading and writing achievement, weighted working memory components for supporting language learning contribute uniquely and substantially to the prediction (e.g., Niedo, Abbott, & Berninger, 2014; Sanders, Berninger, & Abbott, 2017). Nor has the use of Response to Intervention (RTI) in the early grades to avoid "wait to fail" and to prevent SLDs been shown to be valid for identifying SLDs (e.g., Fletcher, Barth, & Stuebing, 2009; Fletcher et al., 2011; Waesche, Schatschneider, Maner, Ahmed, & Wagner, 2011), which may persist despite early intervention (Sanders et al., 2017).

Although the 1989 Interagency Report to Congress authorized more federal funding for research by the National Institutes of Health (NIH) and the United States Department of Education (now the Institute of Educational Sciences [IES]) on identifying SLDs and teaching students with SLDs, since then neither researchers nor state policies have reached a consensus on how to define SLDs for purposes of instructionally relevant differential diagnosis. See Berninger (2015), Berninger and Niedo (2014), and Berninger and Wolf (2016) for an overview of these and other past and current historical issues in the field of SLDs.

Thus, one goal of this chapter is to share findings from one programmatic line of research, which was federally funded by the National Institute of Child Health and Human Development (NICHD) (1989–2008 and 2011–2016) as a consequence of the interagency report.

CURRENT ISSUES IN RESEARCH AND TRANSLATION SCIENCE OF RESEARCH INTO PRACTICE

Two sets of recent findings in this programmatic research are featured for students with a single SLD or co-occurring SLDs, which epidemiological studies at the Mayo Clinic show affect one in five school-age children and youths (for an overview, see Colligan & Katusic, 2015). The first set of findings (summarized in Wolf & Berninger, 2015) shows that SLDs are definable using developmental profiles, learning profiles, and phenotype profiles (Berninger, 2015; Silliman & Berninger, 2011). These profiles are based on PSWs using a new measurement approach that combines categorical classification and variables along continuous distributions (Widiger & Trull, 2007). The second set of findings (summarized in Berninger & Richards, 2015) verifies that there is indeed more than one kind of SLD and the plural suffix in specific learning disabili*ties* is evidence-based at the behavioral and brain levels of analyses (Berninger, Richards, & Abbott, 2015).

Details of these recent findings are explained in the "Research Lessons" section, which provides updates since Berninger (2011) that are relevant for educational practitioners in translating research on SLDs into educational practice. However, this chapter also calls attention to the relevance of PSWs for educating the one in four students living in poverty (for review of the evidence, see Berliner, 2012, 2103; Berninger & Morphy, 2016; Duncan & Murnane, 2011; Luby et al., 2013) and those who are involuntary immigrants in the United States (i.e., Native Americans and African Americans) (Ladson-Billings, 2006).

Three themes underlie application of PSWs to these three target student populations, who are not always mutually exclusive. First, the focus is on best professional practices rather than government regulations. Second, those government regulations are generally designed for defining eligibility for special services rather than day-to-day best professional practices in schools for assessment-instruction links for *proactively* helping students who struggle with reading, writing, oral language, and math become successful learners. Third, the focus is not on eligibility criteria for special education services alone but rather on using developmental profiles, learning profiles, and phenotype profiles to identify all of those who need modifications in their general educational programs (inclusive settings) to become successful learners. The hope is that educational practitioners on interdisciplinary teams can apply this approach grounded in PSWs proactively and flexibly to help all students become successful learners throughout the school day and make progress from the beginning to the end of the school year.

Thus, we make a case that to meet the goal of ESSA for success of all students, educational professionals in schools need to provide FAPE for students with SLDs, students living in poverty, *and* students who are racial, cultural, and linguistic minorities (Berninger, McHale-Small, Dunn, & Alston-Abel, 2016). To do so, we draw on the voice of an educational practitioner who encounters and manages these issues on a daily basis in schools and add this real-world experience to the lessons from research.

VOICE OF EDUCATOR: EXPERIENCE USING PSWs

In this section the first author, an educational practitioner who is a former teacher now a school psychologist, and whose daily professional work involves all three groups discussed in this chapter for helping all students succeed (FAPE for all), shares from her experience in translating research knowledge into practice in real-world school settings, During her doctoral program she participated in the grant-supported programmatic research featured in this chapter. Now she works in a school serving diverse students: 75% qualify for free and reduced lunch; they live in families of African American (18%), European American (1 %), Hispanic (42%), Native American (0.7%), and Pacific Islander (11%) and other heritages including mixed. Innovative practices initiated by the administration at this school include (1) providing extended learning opportunities after school that include snacks to meet the educational and nutritional needs of students in low-income families and (2) developing more flexible discipline practices that focus on positive behavior support and intervention and restorative justice as an alternative to suspending students and putting them at risk for getting into trouble on the streets.

IDENTIFYING STUDENTS FOR SPECIALIZED INSTRUCTION

Examples from the first author's school practice illustrate application of PSWs to (1) identify who needs specialized instruction—in general education and special education—and (2) translate research evidence and her clinical and teaching experience into practice in a culturally sensitive way (e.g., Banks & Banks, 2011; Jones, 2009; McCardle & Berninger, 2015; Washington & Thomas-Tate, 2009; Worrell, 2005) tailored to individual students. Her work is not done when she completes her assessment and writes an assessment report. Rather, she works with teachers and parents to translate the assessment results, interpreted in reference to a PSW, into a plan for individually tailored instructional intervention, and she gathers evidence regarding whether that works for the individual student (White, 2009). If the student is not responding, she reaches out to the special education or general education teacher to modify the instructional approach until the student does respond successfully.

On a daily basis, educational professionals are faced with making myriad decisions surrounding how to serve every student in the best ways possible. Unlike private schools, charter schools, or university research settings, public schools are required to serve all who enter, without regard to family background, socio-economic status, or behavioral challenges. Child Find laws also require that students with disabilities be identified and provided with appropriate services. Students with visible physical or severe and profound disabilities are most often identified by physicians, and they are provided services without much controversy. However, students with invisible disabilities inside the brain or mind, such as SLDs, are not as easily identified and are subject to much greater regulatory control by the government as to who should be served.

The experience of effective educators and research findings have demonstrated that the educational needs of students are often more complex than allowed for under the eligibility criteria specified in government regulations. Yet, these educational needs can be identified through assessment targeted to the difficulties an individual student faces and examination of profile of strengths and weaknesses in the assessment results. For example, students from low-income families and minority groups including immigrant families frequently enter kindergarten with deficits in vocabulary knowledge and limited exposure to foundational academic skills. Such is the case even for immigrants from areas such as the US territories in the Marshall Islands and other Pacific Islands, which maintain Native languages and English in their educational systems. Members of an interdisciplinary team in a school setting may encounter these students first during an intervention meeting with teachers who are concerned about the students' knowledge deficits or slow academic progress and request either guidance on targeted interventions or assessment to determine if the students have a disability. It is during these meetings when conflict often first becomes apparent between best professional practices learned in training programs and state implementation of special education laws.

Consider the case of a student with limited vocabulary. Is it because the student is learning English as a second language and is an English language learner (ELL)? Or does the student have an undiagnosed communication disorder? Or does the student come from a home environment with limited English language exposure or home literacy activities? Or did the student not participate in a preschool program that fosters emerging literacy? The school psychology practitioner has to determine whether or not to conduct an evaluation and if so what the nature of that evaluation should be. If an evaluation is initiated, the practitioner may be pressured to follow state procedures for qualifying a student for special education services, even if the student's developmental, medical, family history, and current issues in the classroom do not fit textbook legal cases; best professional practices would be to engage first in problem-solving consultation of the interdisciplinary team with the classroom teacher to try out some modified approaches to the classroom instructional program.

Moreover, traditionally, state regulations have specified a standard assessment battery, as if a one-size-fits-all approach to evaluating students works. This standard battery approach is not justified when serving diverse populations. For example, in the case of *Larry P. v. Riles* (Wade, 1980), the court found that if African American students were assessed using standard cognitive assessments, they were more likely to be found to have an intellectual disability than if other more-appropriate approaches that take into account linguistic and cultural differences were used. At issue is the reality of bias in standard assessment batteries that are not sensitive to cultural and linguistic diversity. The normative sample for measures in those batteries may or may not reflect a student's ethnic or socioeconomic background and may unintentionally inaccurately measure the individual's cognitive aptitude or oral language and related reading and writing skills.

What the PSW approach provides is an alternative to the overly formulaic approach to assessment, namely, flexibility to look at multiple aspects of cognition, language, and other processes that subtests assess, rather than just at a full-scale or total-test score, and consider how a student's cultural and language background may influence his or her vocabulary and other language skills on formal testing. For example, a student who was a second language learner but also had a severe communication disorder scored in the average range (SS = 90) using the Mental Processing Index of the Kaufman Assessment Battery for Children, Second Edition, but close to the intellectually delayed range (General Intellectual Ability [GIA] = 71) on the overall score on the Woodcock-Johnson IV Tests of Cognitive Abilities.

Professional judgment, based on observation of response to specific items and examination of the profile of strengths and weaknesses across measures on different batteries, led to the conclusion that the difference between the two overall scores reflected the student's cultural and language background that influenced understanding directions (receptive language) and oral responses (expressive language) during formal testing. If a discrepancy criterion was required based on one test, this student would not qualify for receiving specialized instruction in reading, written language, or math. However, because the school district allowed professional judgment based on examining PSWs within the cognitive domain, the first author was able to make a case that the student qualified for specialized instruction due to severe deficits in long-term memory and retrieval fluency, which significantly affected ability to encode new information in working memory and automatically recall previously learned information from long-term memory. Such difficulties are hallmark characteristics of SLDs (for review of evidence, see Berninger & Swanson, 2013). If practitioners are limited in which assessments they are permitted to give or are rigid in what assessments they choose to give and how they interpret those assessments, they are likely to misdiagnose students as "slow learners" or "low achieving" or attribute their learning deficits only to their ELL status. Instead, some students may indeed have an SLD and require specialized instruction to become successful learners.

Another example of how students can be affected by tests that rely heavily on the crystalized knowledge (learned factual declarative knowledge) as a component in a full-scale cognitive index is a student with limited or differing vocabulary. For example, the first author asked one student, "Where would you find a jury?" The student response was "in a jury box." When queried by the examiner, the student response was "on a dresser" to the question, "Where is the jury box?" Was the student wrong? Technically, according to standardized procedures used in norming, yes. However, this minority student had no experience with courts, and came from a part of the country where *jewelry* was pronounced *jury*. Although most of this students' subtest scores were in the average range—at or above the population mean, performance on three subtests, which are each heavily reliant on prior knowledge or experience, lowered her WJ4 General Intellectual Ability (GIA) to a standard score of 82. Does this score truly reflect all of the student's cognitive abilities? Or is it a limited snapshot? Or is it instructionally relevant for helping her achieve optimal academic success for her profile of strengths and weaknesses?

Thus, the voice of experience has yielded this evidence-based lesson for real-world school settings: When working with diverse populations, it is important to use a flexible approach from initial test(s) selection to confirming findings with other assessments tools to analyzing whether and how cultural and linguistic diversity may contribute to some of the assessment findings. Rapid Reference 10.1 provides some assessment questions to consider.

DON'T FORGET

When working with diverse populations, it is important to use a flexible approach from initial test(s) selection to confirming findings with other assessments tools to analyzing whether and how cultural and linguistic diversity may contribute to some of the assessment findings.

≡ Rapid Reference 10.1

Assessment Questions to Consider

Factor	Possible Considerations
Is the student an English language learner or is a language other than English spoken in the home?	*Assessment for language dominance (which language is used most often and with whom) may be warranted. *Parent Interview questions could include the following: • Is this child's development in his or her native language similar to or different from siblings? • Has the student attended school where another language is used for instruction? • What language does the child usually speak at home?
Does the student show signs of a communication disorder? *This is especially important for test selection. Assessment tools vary in terms of the language required to understand and follow oral directions, to provide verbal responses, and to use verbal mediation to complete tasks.*	*Receptive language • Is the student able to follow multiple-step directions? • Does the student retain information? *Expressive language • Does the student express his or her ideas clearly? • Is the student's written language clear and understandable? • Does the student speak as much as same-aged peers? *Are there signs of mixed receptive and expressive language difficulties?
Has the student been exposed to literacy?	*What were the child's early learning experiences? • Did the child attend preschool or day care before starting kindergarten? • Does the parent read with the child at home?
Are there executive functioning concerns?	*Does the student struggle with organization? • Does the student attend to the details in assignments?

	• Is the student able to perform multistep problem-solving?
	• Can the student keep track of assignments and materials?
	• Can the student remember what he or she is supposed to do from one moment to the next?
	• Does the student show evidence of planning (first, next, then, last)?
Could any of these challenges affect student performance on specific tasks?	*Does the subtest allow for demonstration or reteaching to ensure that the student understands the task?
	• Does the task rely on prior knowledge for successful completion?
	• Does student performance vary significantly depending on the amount of verbal output required?
	• Is the student able to sustain attention long enough to complete the task successfully?
Has performance on a single or a few subtests significantly skewed overall results?	*In looking at the cognitive profile in its entirety, does the composite reflect performance on the majority of the measures administered?
What are the task demands on subtests when performance was low?	*Are there similarities in task demands that students do especially poorly on (i.e., accessing prior knowledge, verbal output, executive functions)?
	• If yes, could domains or abilities measured by those subtests be reassessed in a different format?

DESIGNING, IMPLEMENTING, AND EVALUATING RESPONSE TO SPECIALIZED INSTRUCTION

The issue is not simply the validity of using specific assessment tools but one of how multiple tools are used for looking at an individual student holistically: incorporating developmental, educational, medical, and family history; using referral questions to choose relevant assessments; and linking assessment results to individually tailored instruction. Task demands of individual subtests should be taken into account when interpreting performance to identify deficit skills that the student has to overcome. Cognition is a complex process involving multiple mental activities operating individually and in conjunction with one another. A weakness in any one or combination of these mental activities can result in learning difficulties for a student. Using the lens of a PSW rather than global scores more accurately identifies the nature of those learning difficulties and helps professionals plan specially designed instructional activities for individual students. For SLDs, there is no simple, one-size-fits-all way to design such instruction. State and local regulations regarding the identification of SLDs often create constraints that leave out students who are truly in need of specially designed instruction whether in the general education or special education classroom.

RESEARCH LESSONS: EVIDENCE-BASED PROFILES FOR DIAGNOSING AND TREATING SLDs

One line of research illustrates the normal variation among all learners leading to learning differences versus the biologically based (genetic and brain) variations underlying SLDs involving language learning. Another line of research validates another three-tier model than the one that has been widely implemented in schools. Yet another line of research supports multicultural diversity. See each of the headings that follow.

Normal Variation Versus Biologically Based SLDs

Seven kinds of funded research projects contributed to a model specifying which PSW to assess for purposes of assessment and instruction: cross-sectional assessment studies of typically developing students, longitudinal overlapping cohort assessment studies of typically developing students, randomized controlled instructional studies of at-risk readers and writers in school settings, design experiments at the university for improving reading and writing achievement of students with diagnosed SLDs, a multigenerational family genetics study of dyslexia (and co-occurring dysgraphia in some individuals), brain imaging studies of different kinds of SLDs before and after specialized instruction, and behavioral and biological studies on defining and treating persisting SLDs during middle childhood and early adolescence. See Berninger and Richards (2010) for an overview of this programmatic research. Collectively these and other studies funded by a Javitz grant from the US Department of Education on math supported the following approaches to identifying SLDs in reading, writing, oral language, and math (see Berninger, 2007a, 2007b, 2011, 2015, Chapters 7, 8, 9, 10, 11; Sanders et al., 2017).

First, rule out developmental disabilities and other neurogenetic or medical conditions that are associated with reading, writing, oral language, or math learning difficulties but for other reasons than SLDs (see Batshaw, Pellegrino, Roizen, 2007;

Berninger, 2007a, 2007b, 2015, Chapters 7, 8, 10, 11; Berninger, Swanson, & Griffin, 2014). To do so, collect data on developmental, medical, and educational history through questionnaires and interviews, observe during instruction in the classroom, interview teachers, and assess the five domains of development: cognitive, language, sensorimotor, social-emotional, and attention executive functions.

Second, for those students who appear to be otherwise typically developing without developmental disabilities or medical conditions, but are struggling in specific academic skills, assess *learning profiles* (achievement in key reading, writing, oral language, and math skills). Also assess *phenotype profiles*—the working memory components that support learning oral and written language and math and are behavioral markers of underlying genetic bases. For specific guidelines on what to include in the assessments and related differential diagnosis that follows, see Berninger (2015, Chapter 9), Berninger and Richards (2010), Sanders et al. (2017), and Silliman and Berninger (2011). In general, normed measures of supervisory attention (focus, switch, sustain, self-monitor) that involve tasks requiring *paying attention to language* (coordinating the two developmental domains of attention/executive functions and of language) have been found to be the relevant phenotypes for diagnosing SLDs rather than attention-deficit hyperactivity disorder diagnosis based on symptom ratings (Berninger, Abbott, Cook, & Nagy, 2016). Also note that a cross-battery approach can be used now that many of the widely used tests in schools have subtests that assess the research-validated skills in learning profiles and phenotype profiles. Best professional practices are to assess the validated constructs and are not tied to a single test for doing so. See Rapid Reference 10.2 for phenotype profile measures.

Third, based on the PSWs in the learning profiles for multileveled language by ear, mouth, eye, and hand and multicomponent working memory phenotypes supporting language and math learning (Berninger & Richards, 2010, Figure 1; Berninger & Swanson, 2013), the following conditions can be diagnosed:

- *Dysgraphia* (impaired sub-word letter writing in the learning profile and weaknesses in orthographic coding or finger sequencing or both in the phenotype profile)
- *Dyslexia* (impaired oral word reading [real words and pseudowords] and written spelling [real words and pseudowords] in the learning profile and weaknesses in one or more of the following—phonological coding, orthographic coding, phonological loop, or orthographic loop—in the phenotype profile)
- *Oral and written language learning disability (OWL LD)* (impaired syntax in listening comprehension, reading comprehension, oral expression, and written expression or a subset of these language skills in the learning

≡ Rapid Reference 10.2

Phenotype Profile for Language Learning Mechanism

- Three word forms for storage and processing
  - Orthographic
  - Phonological
  - Morphological
- Syntax buffer for storage of multiple words
- Two loops for integrating internal codes and output systems
  - Phonological loop
  - Orthographic loop
- Panel of executive functions for regulating language learning
  - Focused/selective attention
  - Switching attention
  - Sustaining attention
  - Self-monitoring

Sources: Berninger (2007b); Berninger et al. (2010), Berninger & Richards (2010).

profile and weaknesses in aural, oral, reading, or written syntax or morphology or a subset of these skills in the phenotype profile)
- Likewise, *dyscalculia* can be diagnosed on the basis of impaired numeral writing, math-fact retrieval, and calculation in the learning profile and one or more weaknesses in counting along the mental number line, place value, and part-whole relationships in the phenotype profile.

Research has supported this model of instructionally relevant differential diagnosis of SLDs, based on converging evidence from (1) comprehensive assessment at Tier 3 for those who struggle beyond the primary grades and in spite of early intervention (Berninger et al., 2015; Lyman, Sanders, Abbott, & Berninger, 2017; Sanders et al., 2017), (2) response to early Tier 1 intervention in the schools (Berninger, 2008), and (3) response to instruction including components specific to SLD diagnosis (Berninger & Dunn, 2012; Berninger, Nagy, Tanimoto, Thompson, & Abbott, 2014; Berninger & O'Malley May, 2011; Tanimoto, Thompson, Berninger, Nagy, & Abbott, 2015). However, note that some students will meet criteria for more than one SLD in cascading fashion across adjacent levels of language to the left of the level that shows the hallmark impairment (*sub-word* letter writing only, *word* reading and spelling with or without letter writing difficulty, or *syntax* with or without letter writing or word reading or spelling difficulties (Berninger et al., 2015).

Thus, in designing individually tailored instruction it is important to (1) teach to all levels of language close in time, (2) implement instruction in small groups that allow for social interaction among learners and with teachers, (3) weave in learning activities that are intellectually engaging and capitalize on individual students' strengths (for example, in hands-on problem-solving activities) and interests, and (4) give students hope they can overcome their struggles (Berninger, 2015, Chapters 4, 5, 6; Berninger & Wolf, 2016; Thompson et al., 2017). Overall, this interdisciplinary research has also supported the "other three-tier model," which is described next.

> **C A U T I O N**
> ....
> When designing individually tailored instruction it is important to (1) teach to all levels of language close in time, (2) implement instruction in small groups that allow for social interaction among learners and with teachers, (3) weave in learning activities that are intellectually engaging and capitalize on individual students' strengths (for example, in hands-on problem-solving activities) and interests, and (4) give students hope they can overcome their struggles.

The Other Three-Tier Model

Tier 1 is a grade-appropriate screen intervene model for prevention tailored to individuals in K to 6. Screening measures validated in the cross-sectional studies at each grade level K to 6 (Berninger, 2007a, 2007b) can be used to identify target skills for providing evidence-based, assessment-linked supplementary instruction (e.g., lessons in Berninger & Abbott, 2003). Response to instruction can then be monitored to evaluate whether individual students are responding to instruction as indicated by improved scores in their initial weaknesses prior to intervention in that they improve on those skills and they reach levels of peers the same age. For evidence regarding implementation of this approach in early-grade classrooms with low-income, diverse students, see Berninger, Dunn, Lin, and Shimada (2004). Tier 2 is problem-solving consultation based on branching diagnosis. See Berninger (2015) and associated websites and User Guides in Berninger 2007a and 2007b with Tier 2 guidelines for consulting with classroom teachers and the rest of the interdisciplinary team in problem-solving issues that may arise with any student at any time in his or her schooling.

Tier 3 is differential diagnosis and treatment planning for SLDs based on developmental profiles, learning profiles, and phenotype profiles. After assessment, results are used to diagnose an SLD and should inform design of individually tailored specialized instruction and consulting with parents and teachers. One contribution of a PSW approach is the flexibility it offers for Tier 3 identification of students who have SLDs, but differ in cognitive abilities. For example, those students with SLDs whose cognitive abilities fall in the superior or very superior range may score at or near the population mean in their learning profiles and significantly higher than peers with average cognitive abilities and SLDs; yet those with superior or better versus average cognitive abilities may not differ in the hallmark phenotypes associated with dyslexia, which mark the genetic bases for this SLD (Berninger & Abbott, 2013; Lyman et al., 2017).

Although skills in writing, reading, and oral language achievement and phenotypes associated with carefully defined SLDs have a genetic basis (Abbott, Raskind, Matsushita, Richards, Price, & Berninger, 2017; Raskind, Peters, Richards, Eckert, & Berninger, 2012), cutting-edge epigenetics research (e.g., Cassiday, 2009; Riddihough & Zahn, 2010) is showing that behavioral markers of underlying genetic vulnerability can change in response to environmental influences. Thus, progress monitoring throughout the secondary and postsecondary grades is warranted in individuals with personal and family history of SLDs or who fail to respond to early intervention because genetic vulnerability may remain even when behavioral improvement is observed in response to instruction at one time point in development (see Samuelsson et al., 2008). Not only accommodations but also instructional interventions may be needed at the secondary and postsecondary levels to assist some individuals (Nielsen et al., 2016).

There is also a brain basis for SLDs. Research has identified not only specific locations in the brain and specific neural networks where students with and without SLDs differ but also the nature of differences in the structural and functional connectivity for reading and writing tasks and the number of connections involved (Berninger et al., 2015; Richards et al., 2015; Richards, Nagy, Abbott, & Berninger, 2016). Thus, an SLD may be an invisible disability that makes it more difficult to learn oral language, written language, and/or math skills because of inefficiencies in how the multiple brain regions involved in the complex reading, writing, oral language, and math systems are interconnected. Recent research has also shown that instruction aimed across levels of language close in time and multiple language systems (by ear, eye, hand, and mouth) changes brain connectivity on multiple language tasks in the reading brain (submitted), multiple cognitive and language tasks in writing (Richards, Berninger, Yagel, Abbott, & Peterson, 2017), and the brain's mental self-government for managing language learning in the complex human connectome (Berninger, Richards, & Abbott, 2017; Richards, Abbott, Yagle, Peterson, Raskind, & Berninger, 2017). Without identification and appropriate treatment, significant social emotional problems (especially internalizing disorders) may occur in individuals with SLDs, which are invisible disorders but nevertheless real (Nielsen et al., 2017).

Research Evidence for Multicultural Sensitivity

Research has also shown the importance of taking into account whether dialect speakers of Black English are or are not code-switchers between the English spoken at home and at school (Washington & Thomas-Tate, 2009). Likewise, effective instruction for Native Americans involves integration of literacy instruction with the oral tradition and building effective community-school relationships (McCardle & Berninger, 2015).

CONCLUSION

In this section we emphasize three take-home messages that provide cautions for practitioners.

Caution 1: Creating Positive Rather Than Adversarial School-Home Relationships

A questionnaire completed by parents annually for 5 years (first through fifth grade or third through seventh grade) showed that not only instructional activities at school but also home literacy activities contributed significantly to their child's reading achievement and writing achievement (Alston-Abel & Berninger, 2017). Reaching out to parents in proactive ways can build positive relationships between home and school for nurturing students' learning.

Rather than waiting for parents to seek legal intervention, which may result in costly lawsuits, an alternative, effective approach is to reach out proactively to parents to create positive collaborations with them regarding their child's education.

Caution 2: Best Professional Practices Guide Day-to-Day Educational Practices in Assessment and Instruction *and* Federal Laws Protect Civil Rights

Professionals on interdisciplinary teams should draw on the best professional practices of their respective disciplines for their professional work in assessment and instruction in schools. The federal laws for students with educational handicapping conditions are designed to guarantee their civil rights but not to substitute for best professional practices of the educational professionals in educating the students with educational handicapping to learn and achieve at appropriate levels for grade or their developmental or learning profiles.

Caution 3: Combining Evidence-Based and Culturally Sensitive Practices for FAPE for *All*

Combining the voice of educational professionals with research evidence has illustrated how the PSW model can be applied to the evidence-based, other three-tier model for those who have SLDs, live in poverty, or are members of diverse minority groups. Educational practitioners should proactively strive to achieve FAPE for *all*, which is the spirit of the law underlying the Individuals with Disabilities Education Improvement Act for special education and ESSA for general education. FAPE for all can be achieved in inclusionary settings for all but those with severe developmental disabilities and does not require costly pull out for most students.

> **DON'T FORGET**
>
> PSW is an effective approach for identifying instructional needs and planning instruction that can be used in a variety of ways shown to work in educational practice and research. It is not tied to a single conceptual model or test battery. Neither educational practice nor research has shown there is a one-size-fits-all approach that works for all students. A more-appropriate individually tailored question is, "What works for whom for what and where in the curriculum?" See Berninger and Dunn (2012).

TEST YOURSELF

1. **The best practices role of the school psychologist is:**
   (a) Assessing students to determine if they qualify for special education services according to the criteria of the state and the local school(s) where they work.
   (b) Assessing schoolwide Response to Intervention for curriculum in place in a local school.
   (c) Protecting the school district from law suits by parents.
   (d) Working with general education and special education teachers and other members of the interdisciplinary team in a school to optimize the achievement of all students through evidence-based assessment and intervention informed by the voice of practitioner experience.

2. **What is the "other three-tier model"?**
   (a) Proactively prevent learning problems in all students through screening and intervention.

   (b) Provide problem-solving consultation for teachers and parents for any student who struggles.

   (c) Assess strengths and weaknesses of individual students to identify current instructional needs and plan, implement, and evaluate instruction and other interventions to meet those individual needs.

   (d) All of the above.

3. **The purpose of psychoeducational assessment in schools is solely to determine eligibility for special education services. True or false?**

4. **When considering assessment for an English language learner, which of the following should occur?**

   (a) The student should not be assessed because they don't speak English.

   (b) Find out what languages other than English are spoken in the home, which one(s) the student uses most often and with whom (i.e., language dominance), and what the student's level of proficiency with English is to determine if assessment in English could be considered valid.

   (c) Evaluators should automatically choose nonverbal assessments.

   (d) The evaluator should use his or her standard battery of assessments to evaluate.

5. **In what ways can language influence performance on cognitive assessments?**

   (a) Regional pronunciation of words can influence the way students interpret and respond to questions.

   (b) Performance can reflect a student's prior knowledge and literacy exposure or lack thereof.

   (c) The use of verbal mediation can influence a student's performance on nonverbal tasks.

   (d) All of the above are true.

6. **Task analysis is an important step in understanding a student's performance on an assessment. True or false?**

7. **A phenotype of dyslexia is:**

   (a) Letters turned backwards.

   (b) Impaired word decoding in reading.

   (c) Below-average intelligence.

   (d) Expressive language deficits.

8. **The component deficits of dyscalculia are:**

   (a) Impaired math-fact retrieval.

   (b) Lack of understanding of place value.

   (c) Weakness in counting along a mental number line.

   (d) All of the above.

9. **The primary consideration when conducting assessments is compliance with state and local regulations. True or false?**

10. Rigid adherence to a particular assessment methodology or battery provides equitable treatment to all students. True or false?

Answers: 1. d; 2. d; 3. False; 4. b; 5. d; 6. True; 7. b; 8. d; 9. False; 10. False.

REFERENCES

Abbott, R., Raskind, W., Matsushita, M., Richards, T., Price, N., & Berninger, V. (2017). Dysgraphia, dyslexia, and OWL LD during middle childhood and early adolescence: Evidence for genetic effects on hallmark phenotypes. *Biomarkers and Genes, 1*(1), 1–10. doi: 10.15761/BG.1000103

Alston-Abel, N., & Berninger, V. (2017). Relationships between home literacy practices and school achievement: Implications for school-home collaboration and consultation practices. *Journal of Educational and Psychological Consultation.* Retrieved from www.tandfonline .com/1oi/hepc20

Banks, J., & Banks, C. (Eds.). (2011). *Handbook of research on multicultural education.* Flagstaff, AZ: Northern Arizona University.

Batshaw, M., Pellegrino, L., & Roizen, N. (2007). *Children with disabilities* (6th ed.). Baltimore, MD: Brookes.

Berliner, D. C. (2012). Effects of inequality and poverty vs. teachers and schooling on America's youth. *Teachers College Record, 116*(1), Retrieved March 1, 2013, from www .tcrecord.org/content.asp?contentid=16889

Berliner, D. C. (2013). Inequality, poverty and the socialization of America's youth for the responsibilities of citizenship. *Theory into Practice, 52*(3), 203–209. doi: 10.1080/00405841.2013.804314

Berninger, V. (2007a). *Process assessment of the learner* (2nd ed.). San Antonio, TX: Pearson. [Diagnostic for Math (PAL-II M) and user guide on CD with guidelines for Tiers 1, 2, and 3 assessment-intervention]

Berninger, V. (2007b). *Process assessment of the learner* (2nd ed.). San Antonio, TX: Pearson. [Diagnostic for Reading and Writing (PAL-II RW) and user guide on CD with guidelines and resources for Tiers 1, 2, and 3 assessment-intervention]

Berninger, V. (2008). Defining and differentiating dyslexia, dysgraphia, and language learning disability within a working memory model. In E. Silliman& M. Mody (Eds.), *Language impairment and reading disability-interactions among brain, behavior, and experience* (pp. 103–134). New York, NY: Guilford.

Berninger, V. (2011) Evidence-based differential diagnosis and treatment of reading disabilities with and without comorbidities in oral language, writing, and math for prevention, problem-solving consultation, and specialized instruction. In D. Flanagan & V. Alfonso (Eds.), *Essentials in specific learning disability identification* (pp. 203–232). New York, NY: Wiley.

Berninger, V. W. (2015). *Interdisciplinary frameworks for schools: Best professional practices for serving the needs of all students.* Washington, DC: American Psychological Association. [Advisory board and companion websites with readings and resources]

Berninger, V., & Abbott, S. (2003). *PAL research-supported reading and writing lessons: Instructional manual and reproducibles.* San Antonio, TX: Harcourt/PsyCorp.

Berninger, V., & Abbott, R. (2013). Children with dyslexia who are and are not gifted in verbal reasoning. *Gifted Child Quarterly, 57*, 223–233. doi 10.1177/0016986213500342

Berninger, V., Abbott, R., Cook, C., & Nagy, W. (2016). Relationships of attention and executive functions to oral language, reading, and writing skills and systems in middle childhood and early adolescence. *Journal of Learning Disabilities,* pp. 1–16. doi: 10.1177/0022219415617167

Berninger, V., Abbott, R., Swanson, H. L., Lovitt, D., Trivedi, P., Lin, S., Gould, L., Youngstrom, M., Shimada, S., & Amtmann, D. (2010). Relationship of word- and sentence-level working memory to reading and writing in second, fourth, and sixth grade. *Language, Speech, and Hearing Services in Schools, 41*, 179–193.

Berninger, V., Dunn, A., Lin, S., & Shimada, S. (2004). School evolution: Scientist-practitioner educators creating optimal learning environments for ALL students. *Journal of Learning Disabilities, 37*, 500–508.

Berninger, V., & Dunn, M. (2012). Brain and behavioral response to intervention for specific reading, writing, and math disabilities: What works for whom? In B. Wong & D. Butler (Eds.), *Learning about LD* (4th ed., pp. 59–89). London, UK: Elsevier/Academic Press.

Berninger, V., McHale-Small, M., Dunn, A., & Alston-Abel, N. (2016). Best professional practices in school psychology for helping all students succeed. Translating Every Child Succeeds Act (ESSA) into interdisciplinary teamwork. *The School Psychologist, 70*(1), 7–15. Published online by Division 16 of the American Psychological Association at http://apadivision16.org/the-school-psychologist-tsp/

Berninger, V., & Morphy, P. (2016, February). Strategies for underperforming schools: Research shows one of the leading causes of low school achievement in the United States is poverty. Posted article on *The SES Indicator*. American Psychological Association. Retrieved from www.apa.org/pi/ses/resources/indicator/

Berninger, V., Nagy, W., Tanimoto, S., Thompson, R., & Abbott, R. (2014, October 30). Computer instruction in handwriting, spelling, and composing for students with specific learning disabilities in grades 4 to 9. *Computers and Education, 81*, 154–168. Retrieved from www.ncbi.nlm.nih.gov/pmc/articles/PMC4217090

Berninger, V., & Niedo, J. (2014). Individualizing instruction for students with oral and written language difficulties. In J. Mascolo, D. Flanagan, & V. Alfonso (Eds.), *Essentials of planning, selecting and tailoring intervention: Addressing the needs of unique learners* (pp. 231–264). New York, NY: Wiley.

Berninger, V., & O'Malley May, M. (2011). Evidence-based diagnosis and treatment for specific learning disabilities involving impairments in written and/or oral language. *Journal of Learning Disabilities, 44*, 167–183.

Berninger, V., & Richards, T. (2010). Inter-relationships among behavioral markers, genes, brain, and treatment in dyslexia and dysgraphia. *Future Neurology,* 5, 597–617. doi: 10.2217/fnl.10.22

Berninger, V., & Richards, T. (2015, October). Research confirms what many teachers know: Learning disabilities are plural. *Examiner.* Posted on website of the International Dyslexia Association.

Berninger, V., Richards, T., & Abbott, R. (2015). Differential diagnosis of dysgraphia, dyslexia, and OWL LD: Behavioral and neuroimaging evidence. *Reading and Writing. An Interdisciplinary Journal, 28*, 1119–1153. doi: 10.1007/s11145-015-9565-0 A2

Berninger, V., Richards, T., & Abbott, R. (2017). Brain and behavioral assessment of executive functions for self-regulation of levels of language in reading brain. *Journal of Nature and Science*, *3*(11), e464. Retrieved from www.jnsci.org/content/464

Berninger, V., & Swanson, H. L. (2013). Diagnosing and treating specific learning disabilities in reference to the brain's working memory system. In H. L. Swanson, K. Harris, & S. Graham (Eds.), *Handbook of learning disabilities* (2nd ed., pp. 307–325). New York, NY: Guilford.

Berninger, V., Swanson, H. L., & Griffin, W. (2014). Understanding developmental and learning disabilities within functional-systems frameworks: Building on the contributions of J. P. Das. In T. Papadopoulos, R. Parrilla, & J. Kirby (Eds.), *Cognition, intelligence, and achievement* (pp. 397–418). Chennai, India: Elsevier.

Berninger, V., & Wolf, B. (2016). *Teaching students with dyslexia, dysgraphia, OWL LD, and dyscalculia: Lessons from teaching and science* (2nd ed.). Baltimore, MD: Brookes.

Blankstein, A., & Noguera, P. (Eds.). (2015). *Excellence through equity: Five principles of courageous leadership to guide achievement for every student.* Thousand Oaks, CA: Corwin.

Cassiday, L. (2009). *Mapping the epigenome: New tools chart chemical modifications of DNA and its packaging proteins* (pp. 11–16). Retrieved September 14, 2009, from www.gen.on-line.org

Colligan, R., & Katusic, S. (2015). Overview of epidemiological studies of incidence of learning disabilities with annotated research references from the Mayo Clinic, Rochester, MN. In V. W. Berninger, *Interdisciplinary frameworks for schools: Best professional practices for serving the needs of all students.* Washington, DC: American Psychological Association.

Duncan, G., & Murnane, R. (Eds.). (2011). *Whither opportunity? Rising inequality, schools, and children's life chances.* New York, NY: Russell Sage Foundation.

Fletcher, J., Barth, A., & Stuebing, K. (2009). A response to intervention (RTI) approach. In D. Flanagan & V. Alfonso (Eds.), *Essentials in specific learning disability identification* (pp. 115–144). New York, NY: Wiley.

Fletcher, J., Stuebing, K., Barth, A., Denton, C., Cirino, P., Francis, D., & Vaughn, S. (2011). Cognitive correlates of inadequate response to reading intervention. *School Psychology Review, 40,* 3–22.

Jones, L. (2009). (Ed.). *The psychology of multiculturalism in schools: A primer for practice, training and research.* Bethesda, MD: National Association of School Psychologists Press.

Ladson-Billings, G. (2006). 2006 presidential address. From the achievement gap to the education debt: Understanding achievement in US schools. *Educational Researcher, 35,* 3–12.

Luby, J., Belden, A., Botterton, K., Marrus, N., Harms, M., Babb, C., Barch, D., et al. (2013). The effects of poverty on childhood brain development. The mediating effect of caregiving and stressful life events. *Journal of the American Medical Association Pediatrics, 167,* 1135–1142. doi: 10.1001/jamapediatrics.2013.3139

Lyman, R., Sanders, E., Abbott, R., & Berninger, V. (2017). Translating interdisciplinary research on language learning into identifying specific learning disabilities in verbally gifted and average children and youth. *Journal of Behavioral and Brain Research, 7*(6). doi: 10.4236/jbbs.2017.76017

McCardle, P., & Berninger, V. (Eds.). (2015). *Narrowing the achievement gap for Native American students: Paying the educational debt.* New York, NY: Routledge.

Niedo, J., Abbott, R., & Berninger, V. (2014). Predicting levels of reading and writing achievement in typically developing, English-speaking 2nd and 5th graders. *Learning and*

Individual Differences, *32C*, 54–68. Retrieved from www.ncbi.nlm.nih.gov/pmc/articles/PMC4058427

Nielsen, K., Abbott, R., Griffin, W., Lott, J., Raskind, W., & Berninger, V. (2016). Evidence-based reading and writing assessment for dyslexia in adolescents and young adults. *Learning Disabilities. A Multidisciplinary Journal*, *21*, 38–56. doi: 10.18666/LDMJ-2016-V21-I1-6971

Nielsen, K., Haberman, K., Todd, R., Abbott, R., Mickail, T., & Berninger, V. (2017). Emotional and behavioral correlates of persisting specific learning disabilities in written language (SLDs-WL) during middle childhood and early adolescence. *Journal of Psycho-educational Assessment.* doi: 10.1177/0734282917698056

Organisation for Economic Co-operation and Development. (2014, June). *United States: Tackling high inequalities: Creating opportunities for all.* Retrieved from www.oecd.org/social/Tackling-high-inequalities.pdf

Raskind, W., Peters, B., Richards, T., Eckert, M., & Berninger, V. (2012). The genetics of reading disabilities: From phenotype to candidate genes. *Frontiers in Psychology*, *3*, 601. doi: 10.3389/fpsyg.2012.00601

Richards, T. L., Abbott, R. D., Yagle, K., Peterson, D., Raskind, W., & Berninger, V. (2017). Self-government of brain's response to instruction informed by cingulo-opercular network for adaptive control and working memory components for language learning. *Journal of Systems and Integrative Neuroscience*, *3(4)*, 1–12. doi: 10.15761/JSIN.1000173

Richards, T., Berninger, V., Yagel, K., Abbott, R., & Peterson, D. (2017). Changes in DTI diffusivity and fMRI connectivity cluster coefficients for students with and without specific learning disabilities in written language: Brain's response to writing instruction. *Journal of Nature and Science*, *3(4)*, e350, 1–11. Retrieved from www.jnsci.org/content/350

Richards, T. L., Grabowksi, T., Askren, K., Boord, P., Yagle, K., Mestre, Z., . . . Berninger, V. (2015). Contrasting brain patterns of writing-related DTI parameters, fMRI connectivity, and DTI-fMRI connectivity correlations in children with and without dysgraphia or dyslexia. *Neuroimage Clinical*, *8*, 408–421. Retrieved from www.ncbi.nlm.nih.gov/pmc/articles/PMC4473717

Richards, T., Nagy, W., Abbott, R., & Berninger, V. (2016). Brain connectivity associated with cascading levels of language. *Journal of Systems and Integrative Neuroscience*, *2*, 219–229. doi: 10. 15761/JSIN. 1000139

Riddihough, G., & Zahn, L. (2010). What is epigenetics? Introduction to special issue on epigenetics. *Science*, *330*, 611.

Samuelsson, S., Byrne, B., Olson, R., Hulslander, J., Wadsworth, S., Corley, R., . . . DeFres, J. C. (2008). Response to early literacy instruction in the United States, Australia, and Scandinavia: A behavioural-genetic analysis. *Learning and Individual Differences*, *18*, 289–295.

Sanders, E., Berninger, V., & Abbott, R. (2017). Sequential prediction of literacy achievement for specific learning disabilities contrasting in impaired levels of language in grades 4 to 9. *Journal of Learning Disabilities.* doi: https://doi.org/10.1177/0022219417691048

Silliman, E. R., & Berninger, V. W. (2011). Cross-disciplinary dialogue about the nature of oral and written language problems in the context of developmental, academic, and phenotypic profiles. *Topics in Language Disorders*, *31*, 6–23. Retrieved from http://journals.lww.com/topicsinlanguagedisorders/Fulltext/2011/01000/Cross_Disciplinary_Dialogue_about_the_Nature_of.3.aspx

Stuebing, K., Fletcher, J., Marin, L., & Francis, D. (2012). Evaluation of the technical adequacy of three methods for identifying specific learning disabilities based on cognitive discrepancies. *School Psychology Review, 41*, 3–22.

Tanimoto, S., Thompson, R., Berninger, V., Nagy W., & Abbott, R. (2015, April 26). Computerized writing and reading instruction for students in grades 4 to 9 with specific learning disabilities affecting written language. *Journal of Computer Assisted Learning, 1*(81), 154–168.

Thompson, R., Tanimoto, S., Lyman, R., Geselowitz, K., Begay, K., Nielsen, K., . . . Berninger, V. (2017). Effective instruction for persisting dyslexia in upper grades: Adding hope stories and computer coding to explicit literacy instruction. *Education and Information Technology.* doi 10.1007/s10639-017-9647-5.

Waesche, J. B., Schatschneider, C., Maner, J. K., Ahmed, Y., & Wagner, R. K., (2011). Examining agreement and longitudinal stability among traditional and RTI-based definitions of reading disability using the affected-status agreement statistic. *Journal of Learning Disabilities, 44*, 296–307.

Wade, D. (1980, Summer). Racial discrimination in IQ testing—*Larry P. v. Riles. DePaul Law Review, 29*, Article 12.

Washington, J., & Thomas-Tate, S. (2009). How research informs cultural-linguistic differences in the classroom: The bi-dialectical African American child. In S. Rosenfield & V. Berninger (Eds.), *Implementing evidence-based academic interventions in school settings* (pp. 147–163). New York, NY: Oxford University Press.

White, O. (2009). A focus on the individual: Single-subject evaluations of response to intervention. In S. Rosenfield & V. Berninger (Eds.), *Implementing evidence-based academic interventions in school settings* (pp. 531–558). New York, NY: Oxford University Press.

Widiger, T., & Trull, T. (2007). Plate tectonics in the classification of personality disorder: Shifting to a dimensional model. *American Psychologist, 62*, 71–83.

Wolf, B., & Berninger, V. (2015, March 20). Specific learning disabilities: Plural, definable, diagnosable, and treatable. *Dyslexia Connections.* International Dyslexia Association (IDA) Newsletter for Parents.

Worrell, F. C. (2005). Cultural variation within American families of African descent. In C. Frisby & C. Reynolds (Eds.), *The comprehensive handbook of multicultural school psychology* (pp. 137–172). Hoboken, NJ: Wiley.

Eleven

DUAL DISCREPANCY/CONSISTENCY OPERATIONAL DEFINITION OF SLD

Integrating Multiple Data Sources and Multiple Data-Gathering Methods

Dawn P. Flanagan
Vincent C. Alfonso
Megan C. Sy
Jennifer T. Mascolo
Erin M. McDonough
Samuel O. Ortiz

Portions of this chapter are from Flanagan and Alfonso (2017). Text reproduced and adapted with permission.

D espite several decades of inquiry into the nature of specific learning disability (SLD), the federal definition of SLD (34 CFR Part 300.8(c) 10; see the first "Don't Forget") has remained the same for 30 years. As such, the federal definition of SLD does not reflect the best thinking about the SLD construct (Kavale, Spaulding, & Beam, 2009). With no change in the federal definition of SLD, attention was placed on articulating ways to operationalize it with the intent of improving the practice of SLD identification (Flanagan, Ortiz, Alfonso, & Mascolo, 2002, 2006; Kavale & Flanagan, 2007; Kavale & Forness,

Essentials of Specific Learning Disability Identification, Second Edition.
Edited by Vincent C. Alfonso and Dawn P. Flanagan
© 2018 John Wiley & Sons, Inc. Published 2018 by John Wiley & Sons, Inc.

2000; Kavale et al., 2009). For more than three decades, the main operational definition of SLD has been the "discrepancy criterion." Discrepancy was first introduced in Bateman's (1965) definition of LD and was later formalized in the federal regulations as follows:

(1) The child does not achieve commensurate with his or her age and ability when provided with appropriate educational experiences, and (2) the child has a *severe discrepancy between achievement and intellectual ability* in one or more areas relating to communication skills and mathematics abilities. (US Office of Education [USOE], 1977, p. 65083; emphasis added)

Several problems with the traditional ability-achievement discrepancy approach to SLD identification have been discussed extensively in the literature (see Hale, Wycoff, & Fiorello, 2011, for a review) and, therefore, will not be repeated here. With the reauthorization of IDEA in 2004, and the corresponding de-emphasis on the traditional ability-achievement discrepancy criterion for SLD identification, there have been a number of attempts to operationalize the federal definition, many of which are presented in this book (see Rapid Reference 11.1 for examples).

DON'T FORGET

....

2004 IDEIA Definition of SLD

A disorder in one or more of the basic psychological processes involved in understanding or using language, spoken or written, which manifests itself in the imperfect ability to listen, think, speak, read, write, spell, or do mathematical calculations. This includes conditions such as perceptual disabilities, brain injury, minimal brain dysfunction, dyslexia, and developmental aphasia.

The purpose of this chapter is to provide a research-based operational definition of SLD that is consistent with the federal definition of SLD and the third option specified in the procedures for identifying SLD (34 CFR Part 300.309; see next "Don't Forget") included in the 2006 regulations that accompany the Individuals with Disabilities Education Improvement Act of 2004 (IDEIA). This third option involves the evaluation of a pattern of strengths and weaknesses (PSW) that is consistent with the SLD construct via a combination of tests of cognitive and academic abilities and neuropsychological processes (see Fiorello, Flanagan, & Hale, 2014). Flanagan and colleagues' dual discrepancy/ consistency (DD/C) operational definition of SLD is used as the basic conceptual structure for the independent evaluation of SLD (i.e., Flanagan, Ortiz, & Alfonso, 2013; Flanagan et al., 2002; McDonough & Flanagan, 2016).

After describing the DD/C operational definition of SLD (referred to as *DD/C model* for short), this chapter demonstrates how to link assessment findings to

≡ Rapid Reference 11.1

Examples of How the 2004 Federal Definition of SLD Has Been Operationally Defined

- Absolute low achievement (see Lichtenstein & Klotz, 2007, for a discussion)
- Ability-achievement discrepancy (see Zirkel & Thomas, 2010, for a discussion)
- Dual discrepancy, including a discrepancy in rate of learning and a discrepancy in level of learning relative to typically achieving peers (e.g., Fuchs & Fuchs, 1998)
- Failure to respond to scientifically based intervention (e.g., Fletcher, Lyon, Fuchs, & Barnes, 2007; Chapters 7 and 8, this book)
- Pattern of academic and cognitive strengths and weaknesses (also called *alternative research-based* approaches or *third-method* approaches; e.g., Hale et al., 2011; Hale, Flanagan, & Naglieri, 2008; Chapter 12, this book)

Note: All examples include a consideration of exclusionary factors as specified in the federal definition of SLD.

---

educational strategies and recommendations. Finally, this chapter provides a step-by-step approach to conducting a PSW analysis following the DD/C model using the Cross-Battery Assessment Software System (X-BASS v2.0; Flanagan, Ortiz, & Alfonso, 2017). Case studies that follow the DD/C model are presented in Chapter 13.

THE DUAL DISCREPANCY/ CONSISTENCY OPERATIONAL DEFINITION OF SLD

Flanagan and colleagues first proposed their operational definition of SLD in the early 2000s (Flanagan et al., 2002). Since that time they have modified and refined their operational definition periodically to ensure that it reflects the most-current theory, research,

DON'T FORGET

Federal Regulations Permit the Use of a PSW Model for SLD Identification

Evaluation documentation must consider whether the student exhibits a PSW

- In performance, achievement, or both
- Relative to age, state-approved grade-level standards, or intellectual development
- That is determined by the group to be relevant to the identification of SLD using appropriate instruments

Source: (34 CFR 300.311(a)(5)), (34 CFR 300.309(a)(2)(ii))

and thinking with regard to (1) the nature of SLD, (2) the methods of evaluating various elements and concepts inherent in SLD definitions, and (3) criteria for establishing SLD as a discrete condition separate from undifferentiated low achievement and overall below-average ability to think and reason, particularly for the purpose of acquiring, developing, and applying academic skills (e.g., Flanagan & Alfonso, 2017; Flanagan, Alfonso, & Mascolo, 2011; Flanagan, Alfonso, & Ortiz, 2012; Flanagan, Ortiz, Alfonso, & Mascolo, 2006). The most recent iteration of Flanagan and colleagues' operational definition of SLD (i.e., the DD/C model) is presented in Rapid Reference 11.2.

This definition encourages a continuum of data-gathering methods, beginning with curriculum-based measures (CBMs) and progress monitoring and culminating in norm-referenced tests of cognitive and academic abilities and neuropsychological processes for students who demonstrate an inadequate response to high-quality instruction and intervention—a process long advocated (e.g., Reynolds & Shaywitz, 2009a). This type of systematic approach to understanding learning difficulties can emanate from any well-researched theory (see Flanagan & Alfonso, 2017; Flanagan, Ortiz, et al., 2006; Flanagan et al., 2002, 2013; Hale et al., 2011; McCloskey, Whitaker, Murphy, & Rogers, 2012; McDonough & Flanagan, 2016). The DD/C definition is grounded primarily in CHC theory, but it has been extended to include important neuropsychological functions that are not explicit in CHC theory (e.g., executive functions and orthographic processing).

The DD/C model provides a framework for organizing assessment data to evaluate whether an individual's PSW is consistent with the SLD construct. The essential elements in evaluation of SLD in the DD/C definition, as illustrated in Rapid Reference 11.2, include (1) academic ability analysis, (2) evaluation of mitigating and exclusionary factors, (3) cognitive ability and processing analysis, (4) PSW analysis, and (5) evaluation of interference with learning for purposes of special education eligibility. These elements are depicted as distinct levels in Rapid Reference 11.2 and together form the DD/C operational definition of SLD.

As may be seen in Rapid Reference 11.2, the "Nature of SLD" column includes a description of what SLD is and what it is not. Overall, the levels represent an adaptation and extension of the recommendations offered by Kavale and colleagues (e.g., Kavale & Forness, 2000, Kavale et al., 2009), but they also include concepts from a variety of other researchers (e.g., Fletcher-Janzen & Reynolds, 2008; Geary, Hoard, & Bailey, 2011; Hale et al., 2016; Hale & Fiorello, 2004; Reynolds & Shaywitz, 2009a, 2009b; Siegel, 1999; Stanovich, 1999; Vellutino, Scanlon, & Lyon, 2000; Chapter 10, this book).

It is assumed that the levels of evaluation depicted in Rapid Reference 11.2 are undertaken after pre-referral assessment activities have been conducted and when

═ Rapid Reference 11.2

The Dual Discrepancy/Consistency (DD/C) Operational Definition of SLD

Level	Nature of SLD[1]	Focus of Evaluation	Examples of Evaluation Methods and Data Sources	Criteria for SLD	SLD Classification and Eligibility
1	Difficulties in one or more areas of academic achievement, including (but not limited to)[2] Basic Reading Skill, Reading Comprehension, Reading Fluency, Oral Expression, Listening Comprehension, Written Expression, Math Calculation, and Math Problem Solving	**Academic Achievement:** Performance in specific academic skills [e.g., Grw (Reading Decoding, Reading Fluency, Reading Comprehension, Spelling, Written Expression), Gq (Math Calculation, Math Problem Solving), and Gc (Communication Ability, Listening Ability)]	Response to quality instruction and intervention via progress monitoring; performance on norm-referenced, standardized achievement tests; evaluation of work samples; observations of academic performance; teacher-parent-student interview; history of academic performance; and data from other members of the multidisciplinary team (MDT) (e.g., speech-language pathologist, interventionist, reading specialist)	Performance in one or more academic areas is weak or *deficient*[3] (despite attempts at delivering quality instruction) as evidenced by converging data sources. Note that low scores are not sufficient to meet this condition. These scores must also represent *unexpected underachievement* (as defined in Rapid Reference 11.14)	Necessary
2	SLD does not include a learning problem that is the result of visual, hearing, or	**Exclusionary Factors:** Identification of potential primary causes of academic	Data from the methods and sources listed at Levels 1 and 3; behavior rating scales; medical	Performance is not *primarily* attributed to these exclusionary factors, although	

(continued)

Level	Nature of SLD[1]	Focus of Evaluation	Examples of Evaluation Methods and Data Sources	Criteria for SLD	SLD Classification and Eligibility
	motor disabilities; of intellectual disability; of social or emotional difficulty or disorder; or of environmental, educational, cultural, or economic disadvantage.	skill weaknesses or deficits, including intellectual disability, cultural or linguistic difference, sensory impairment, insufficient instruction or opportunity to learn, organic or physical health factors, social-emotional or psychological difficulty or disorder	records; prior evaluations; interviews with current or past professionals such as counselors, psychiatrists, etc.	one or more of them may contribute to learning difficulties. (Consider using the Exclusionary Factors Form, which is included in Rapid Reference 11.6.)	
3	A disorder in one or more of the basic psychological or neuro-psychological processes involved in understanding or in using language, spoken or written; such disorders are presumed to originate from central nervous system dysfunction.	**Cognitive Abilities and Processes:** Performance in cognitive abilities and processes (e.g. Gv, Ga, Glr, Gsm, Gs); specific neuropsychological processes (e.g. attention, executive functioning, orthographic processing; rapid automatic naming); and learning efficiency (e.g. associative memory; free recall memory; meaningful memory)	Performance on norm-referenced tests, evaluation of work samples, observations of cognitive performance, task analysis, testing limits, teacher-parent-student interview, history of academic performance, and records review	Performance in one or more cognitive abilities or neuropsychological processes (related to academic skill deficiency) is weak or deficient[3] as evidenced by converging data sources. Note that low scores are not sufficient to meet this condition. The cognitive ability or process in question must also be domain-specific (as defined in Rapid Reference 11.13)	

4

The SLD is a discrete condition differentiated from generalized learning deficiency by generally average or better ability to think and reason and a learning skill profile exhibiting significant variability, indicating a pattern of cognitive and academic strengths and weaknesses.

Pattern of Strengths and Weaknesses Marked by a Dual-Discrepancy/ Consistency (DD/C):

Determination of whether academic skill weaknesses or deficits are *unexpected and related to domain-specific* cognitive weaknesses or deficits; pattern of data reflects a below-average aptitude-achievement consistency with at least *average ability* to think and reason

Data gathered at all previous levels as well as any additional data following a review of initial evaluation results (e.g., data gathered for hypothesis testing; data gathered via demand analysis and limits testing)

Circumscribed below-average aptitude-achievement consistency; circumscribed ability-achievement and ability-cognitive aptitude *discrepancies,* with at least average ability to think and reason; clinical judgment supports the impression that the student's overall ability to think and reason will enable him or her to benefit from tailored or specialized instruction or intervention, compensatory strategies, and accommodations, such that his or her performance rate and level will likely approximate more typically achieving, nondisabled peers

Use the Cross-Battery Assessment Software System (X-BASS v2.0; Ortiz et al., 2017) to conduct the PSW analysis.

Sufficient for SLD identification

(*continued*)

Level	Nature of SLD[1]	Focus of Evaluation	Examples of Evaluation Methods and Data Sources	Criteria for SLD	SLD Classification and Eligibility
5	SLD has an adverse impact on educational performance.	**Special Education Eligibility:**[4] Determination of least restrictive environment (LRE) for delivery of instruction and educational resources	Data from all previous levels and MDT meetings	Student demonstrates significant difficulties in daily academic activities that cannot be remediated, accommodated, or otherwise compensated for *without the assistance of individualized special education services.*	Necessary for special education eligibility

[1] This column includes concepts inherent in the federal definition IDEIA (2004), Kavale et al.'s (2009) definition, Hamison and Holmes's (2012) consensus definition, and other prominent definitions of SLD (see Chapter 1). Thus, the most-salient prominent SLD markers are included in this column.

[2] Poor spelling with adequate ability to express ideas in writing is often typical of dyslexia and dysgraphia. Even though IDEIA 2004 includes only the broad category of written expression, poor spelling and handwriting are often symptomatic of a specific writing disability and should not be ignored (Wendling & Mather, 2009).

[3] Weak performance is typically associated with standard scores in the 85–89 range, whereas deficient performance is often associated with standard scores that are greater than one standard deviation (SD) below the mean. Interpretations of weak or deficient performance based on standard scores that fall in the weak and deficient ranges are bolstered when they have ecological validity (e.g., when there is evidence that the abilities or processes identified as weak or deficient manifest in everyday classroom activities that require these abilities and processes).

[4] The major SLD may be accompanied by secondary learning difficulties that should be considered when planning the more-intensive, individualized special education instruction directed at the primary problem. For information on linking assessment data to intervention, see Mascolo, Alfonso, and Flanagan (2014).

Source: Adapted from Flanagan and Alfonso (2017) and Flanagan et al. (2013).

a focused evaluation of specific abilities and processes through standardized testing is deemed necessary. Evaluation of the presence of a learning disability assumes that an individual has been referred for testing specifically because of observed learning difficulties. However, prior to formal testing, it is expected that remediation of academic skill weaknesses via a Response to Invention (RTI) service delivery model or a multitiered system of support (MTSS) was attempted with little success. Moreover, prior to beginning SLD assessment, other significant data sources should have already been gathered and considered within the context of the intervention activities. These data may include results from informal testing, direct observation of behaviors, work samples, reports from people familiar with the individual's difficulties (e.g., teachers, parents), and information provided by the individual him- or herself. Each level of the DD/C model is summarized next.

DON'T FORGET

The operational definition of SLD presented in Rapid Reference 11.2 is based primarily on CHC theory, but it encourages a continuum of data-gathering methods, beginning with curriculum-based measures (CBMs) and progress monitoring and culminating in norm-referenced tests of cognitive abilities and neuropsychological processes for students who demonstrate an inadequate response to intervention.

CAUTION

Most individuals have statistically significant strengths and weaknesses in their cognitive ability and processing profiles. Intraindividual differences in cognitive abilities and processes are commonplace in the general population (McGrew & Knopik, 1996; Oakley, 2006). Therefore, statistically significant variation in cognitive and neuropsychological functioning in and of itself must not be used as de facto evidence of SLD. Instead, the pattern must reflect what is known about the nature of SLD (see Rapid Reference 11.2).

Level 1: Analysis of Specific Academic Skills

Level 1 focuses on the basic concept of SLD: that underlying ability and processing deficits affected skill development adversely, which contributed to underachievement. In other words, intrinsic cognitive weaknesses or deficits often manifest in observable phenomena, particularly academic achievement. Thus, the first component of the DD/C operational definition of SLD involves documenting that some type of *learning* dysfunction exists. In the DD/C definition, the presence of a *weakness* or *normative weakness or deficit* (see Rapid Reference 11.3) established through standardized testing, and supported through other means, such as clinical

≡ Rapid Reference 11.3

Definition of Weakness and Normative Weakness or Deficit

Term or Concept	Meaning Within the Context of DD/C	Comments
Weakness	Performance on standardized, norm-referenced tests that falls *below average* (when average is defined as standard scores between 90 and 110 [inclusive], based on a scale having a mean of 100 and an SD of 15). Thus, a weakness is associated with standard scores of 85 to 89 (inclusive).	Interpreting scores in the very narrow range of 85–89 requires clinical judgment, because abilities associated with these scores may or may not pose significant difficulties for the individual. Interpretation of any cognitive construct as a weakness for the individual should include ecological validity (i.e., evidence of how the weakness manifests in real-world performances, such as classroom activities).
Normative Weakness or Deficit	Performance on standardized, norm-referenced tests that falls greater than one SD below the mean (i.e., standard scores < 85). This type of weakness is often referred to as "population relative" or "inter-individual." The terms *normative weakness* and *deficit* are used interchangeably.	The range of 85–115, inclusive, is often referred to as the range of *normal limits* because it is the range in which nearly 70% of the population falls on standardized, norm-referenced tests. Therefore, scores within this range are sometimes classified as *within normal limits*. As such, any score that falls outside and below this range is a normative weakness *as compared to most people*. Notwithstanding, the meaning of any cognitive construct that emerges as a normative weakness is enhanced by ecological validity.

Source: Flanagan and Alfonso (2017).

observations of academic performance, work samples, and parent and teacher reports, is a necessary but insufficient condition for SLD determination. Level 1 includes the first criterion that is considered necessary for determining the presence of SLD.

Accordingly, the process at Level 1 involves comprehensive measurement of the major areas of academic achievement (e.g., reading, writing, math, and oral language) or any subset of these areas that is the focus and purpose of the evaluation. The academic areas that are generally assessed at this level in the operational definition include the eight areas of achievement specified in the federal definition of SLD (IDEIA, 2004). These eight areas are basic reading skill, reading fluency, reading comprehension, math calculation, math problem-solving, written expression, oral expression, and listening comprehension. Typically, the eight areas of academic achievement are measured using standardized, norm-referenced tests. The Wechsler Individual Achievement Test, Third Edition (WIAT-III; Wechsler, 2009), Kaufman Test of Educational Achievement, Third Edition (KTEA-3; Kaufman & Kaufman, 2014), and Clinical Evaluation of Language Fundamentals, Fifth Edition (CELF-5; Wiig, Semel, & Secord, 2013) batteries combined provide for measurement of all eight areas (see Rapid Reference 11.4). Nevertheless, it is important to realize that data on academic performance should come from multiple sources (see Rapid Reference 11.2, Level 1, column 4). Note that it is not necessary to assess all eight areas of academic achievement for all students who are referred for suspected SLD, unless required by district guidelines, for example. Instead, practitioners should focus their evaluation on the specific referral concerns and ensure that assessment is comprehensive in those areas.

Following the collection of data on academic performance, it is necessary to determine whether the student has a weakness or normative weakness or deficit in one or more specific academic skills.

Determining whether a student

> **C A U T I O N**
> ....
> The finding of low academic achievement is not sufficient for SLD identification because this condition alone may be present for a variety of reasons, only one of which is SLD.

has a weakness or normative weakness or deficit usually involves making normative-based comparisons of the student's performance against a representative sample of same-age or -grade peers from the general population. If weaknesses in the student's academic performance are not found (i.e., all scores suggest generally average or better performance relative to most people), then the issue of SLD may be moot because such weaknesses are a necessary component for SLD identification and diagnosis.

≡ *Rapid Reference 11.4*

Correspondence Among Subtests from the WIAT-III, KTEA-3, and CELF-5 and the Eight Areas of SLD Listed in the Federal Definition

SLD Area	WIAT-III	KTEA-3	CELF-5
Basic Reading Skills	Early Reading Skills Pseudoword Decoding Word Reading	Letter and Word Recognition Nonsense Word Decoding Phonological Processing Decoding Fluency	
Reading Fluency	Oral Reading Fluency	Silent Reading Fluency Word Recognition Fluency	
Reading Comprehension	Reading Comprehension	Reading Comprehension Reading Vocabulary	Reading Comprehension
Mathematics Calculation	Math Fluency—Addition Math Fluency—Subtraction Math Fluency—Multiplication Numerical Operations	Math Computation Math Fluency	
Mathematics Problem-Solving	Math Problem-Solving	Math Concepts and Applications	
Written Expression	Alphabet Writing Fluency Essay Completion Sentence Composition Spelling	Spelling Written Expression Writing Fluency	Structured Writing
Oral Expression	Oral Expression	Associational Fluency Object Naming Facility Oral Expression	Formulated Sentences
Listening Comprehension	Listening Comprehension	Listening Comprehension	Following Directions Linguistic Concepts Semantic Relationships Sentence Comprehension Understanding Spoken Paragraphs Word Structure

Source: Flanagan and Alfonso (2017).

Nevertheless, some students who struggle academically may not demonstrate academic weaknesses or deficits on standardized, norm-referenced tests of achievement, particularly very bright students, for a variety of reasons. For example, some students may have figured out how to compensate for

> ## DON'T FORGET
> ....
> **Weakness:** Standard scores between 85 and 89, inclusive
>
> **Normative Weakness or Deficit:** Standard scores < 85

their processing deficit(s). Therefore, it is important not to assume that a student with a standard score in the in the upper 80s or low 90s, for example, on a "broad reading" composite is "okay," particularly when a parent, teacher, or the student him- or herself expresses concern. Under these circumstances, a more-focused assessment of the CHC abilities and neuropsychological processes related to reading should be conducted. Conversely, the finding of low scores on norm-referenced achievement tests does not guarantee that there will be corresponding low scores on norm-referenced cognitive tests in areas that are related to the achievement area—*an important fact that was ignored in a recent investigation of the DD/C method* (i.e., Kranzler, Floyd, Benson, Zaboski, & Thibodaux, 2016). Below-average achievement may be the result of a host of factors, only one of which is weaknesses or deficits in related cognitive processes and abilities. Most practitioners know this to be true. See Flanagan and Schneider (2016) for a discussion.

As Rapid Reference 11.5 demonstrates, the presence of an academic weakness or normative weakness or deficit established through standardized testing, for example, and corroborated by other data sources, such as CBM, clinical observations of academic performance, work samples, and so forth, is a necessary (but insufficient) condition for SLD determination (Level 1 in Rapid Reference 11.2). At this initial level then, a student's academic performance is compared to that of same-age peers in the general population using norm-referenced tests, such as the WIAT-III and KTEA-3. When weaknesses or normative weaknesses or deficits in academic performance are found, and are corroborated by other data sources, the process advances to Level 2.

Level 2: Evaluation of Exclusionary Factors as Potential Primary and Contributory Reasons for Academic Skill Weaknesses or Deficits

Level 2 involves evaluating whether any documented weaknesses or deficits found through Level 1 evaluation are or are not *primarily* the result of factors that may be, for example, largely external to the child, or noncognitive in nature. Because there can be many reasons for weak or deficient academic performance, causal links to SLD should not be ascribed prematurely. Instead, reasonable hypotheses related to

≋ Rapid Reference 11.5

Factors That Inhibit and Facilitate Academic Performance

Academic Performance or Norm-Referenced Tests	Data-Gathering Methods	Examples of Factors That Inhibit Academic Performance	Examples of Factors That Facilitate Academic Performance
Weakness: SS = 85–89	Standardized tests (individual and group)	Exclusionary factors that are contributory, such as social-emotional and psychological disorders and culture and language difference	Familial support; good teacher-student relationship; others who believe in student's capabilities
Deficit: SS ≤ 85	Progress monitoring data; CBM data	Lack of sufficient resources	Self-determination, effort, perseverance
	Work samples, classroom observations	Poor communication between home and school	Adequate resources at the individual and classroom level
	Parent, teacher, and student interviews	Instruction not matched to student's instructional level	Good home-school collaboration and partnership
	Criterion referenced: benchmark assessment		Instruction matched to student's instructional level

Source: Flanagan and Alfonso (2017).

other potential causes should be developed. For example, cultural and linguistic differences are two common factors that can affect test performance and academic skill acquisition adversely and result in achievement data that appear to suggest SLD (see Chapter 14, this book). In addition, lack of motivation and effort, social-emotional disturbance, performance anxiety, psychiatric disorders, sensory impairments, intellectual disability, and medical conditions (e.g., hearing or vision problems) also need to be ruled out as potential explanatory correlates to any weaknesses or deficits identified at Level 1. Rapid Reference 11.6 provides

≡ Rapid Reference 11.6

Evaluation and Consideration of Exclusionary Factors for SLD Identification

An evaluation of specific learning disability (SLD) requires consideration of factors other than a disorder in one or more basic psychological processes that may be the primary cause of a student's academic skill weaknesses and learning difficulties. These factors include (but are not limited to) vision or hearing,[1] motor disabilities, intellectual disability (ID), social or emotional or psychological disturbance, environmental or economic disadvantage, cultural and linguistic factors (e.g., limited English proficiency), insufficient instruction or opportunity to learn and physical and health factors. These factors may be evaluated via behavior rating scales, parent and teacher interviews, classroom observations, attendance records, social and developmental history, family history, vision and hearing exams,[1] medical records, prior evaluations, and interviews with current or past counselors, psychiatrists, and paraprofessionals who have worked with the student. Noteworthy is the fact that students with (and without) SLD often have one or more factors (listed in the following) that **contribute** to academic and learning difficulties. However, the practitioner must rule out any of these factors as being the **primary** reason for a student's academic and learning difficulties to maintain SLD as a viable classification or diagnosis.

Vision (Check All That Apply):

☐ Vision test recent (within 1 year)

☐ Vision test outdated (> 1 year)

☐ Passed

☐ Failed

☐ Wears glasses

☐ History of visual disorder or disturbance

☐ Diagnosed visual disorder or disturbance

Name of disorder: _____

☐ Vision difficulties suspected or observed

(e.g., difficulty with far- or near-point copying, misaligned numbers in written math work, squinting or rubbing eyes during visual tasks such as reading, working on computers)

NOTES:_____

_____

_____

Hearing (Check All That Apply)[2]:

☐ Hearing test recent (within 1 year)

☐ Hearing test outdated (> 1 year)

☐ Passed

☐ Failed

☐ Uses hearing aids

☐ History of auditory disorder or disturbance

☐ Diagnosed auditory disorder or disturbance

☐ Name of disorder:_____

☐ Hearing difficulties suggested in the referral

(e.g., frequent requests for repetition of auditory information, misarticulated words, attempts to self-accommodate by moving closer to sound source, obvious attempts to speech read)

NOTES: _____

_____

_____

Motor Functioning (Check All That Apply):

☐ Fine-motor delay or difficulty

☐ Gross-motor delay or difficulty

☐ Improper pencil grip (specify type: _____)

☐ Assistive devices or aids used

(e.g., weighted pens, pencil grip, slant board)

☐ History of motor disorder

☐ Diagnosed motor disorder

Name of disorder: _____

☐ Motor difficulties suggested in the referral

(e.g., illegible writing; issues with letter or number formation, size, spacing; difficulty with fine-motor tasks such as using scissors, folding paper)

NOTES: _____

_____

_____

Cognitive and Adaptive Functioning (Check All That Apply):

☐ Significantly "subaverage intellectual functioning" (e.g., IQ score of 75 or below)
☐ Pervasive cognitive deficits (e.g., weaknesses or deficits in many cognitive areas, including *Gf* and *Gc*)
☐ Deficits in adaptive functioning (e.g., social, communication, self-care)

Areas of significant adaptive skill weaknesses (check all that apply):

☐ Motor skill   ☐ Communication   ☐ Socialization

☐ Daily living skills   ☐ Behavior or emotional skills ☐ Other

NOTES: _____

_____

_____

Social-Emotional and Psychological Factors (Check All That Apply):

☐ Diagnosed psychological disorder (Specify: _____)
☐ Date of diagnosis
☐ Family history significant for psychological difficulties
☐ Disorder presently treated—specify treatment modality (e.g., counseling, medication): _____
☐ Reported difficulties with social or emotional functioning (e.g., social phobia, anxiety, depression)
☐ Social-emotional or psychological issues suspected or suggested by referral
☐ Home-school adjustment difficulties
☐ Lack of motivation or effort
☐ Emotional stress
☐ Autism
☐ Present medications (type, dosage, frequency, duration) _____
☐ Prior medication use (type, dosage, frequency, duration) _____
☐ Hospitalization for psychological difficulties (date(s): _____)
☐ Deficits in social, emotional, or behavioral [SEB] functioning (e.g., as assessed by standardized rating scales)
Significant scores from SEB measures: _____

NOTES: _____

_____

_____

Environmental and Economic Factors (Check All That Apply):

☐ Limited access to educational materials in the home

☐ Caregivers unable to provide instructional support

☐ Economic considerations precluded treatment of identified issues (e.g., filling a prescription, replacing broken glasses, tutoring)

☐ Temporary crisis situation

☐ History of educational neglect

☐ Frequent transitions (e.g., shared custody)

☐ Environmental space issues (e.g., no space for studying, sleep disruptions due to shared sleeping space)

NOTES: _____

_____

_____

Cultural or Linguistic Factors (Check All That Apply)[3]:

☐ Limited number of years in United States (_____)

☐ No history of early or developmental problems in primary language

☐ Current primary language proficiency:

(Dates: _____ Scores: _____)

☐ Acculturative knowledge development

(Circle one: high   moderate   low)

☐ Language(s) other than English spoken in home

☐ Lack of or limited instruction in primary language (no. of years _____)

☐ Current English language proficiency:

(Date: _____ Scores: _____)

☐ Parental educational and socioeconomic level

(Circle one: high   moderate   low)

NOTES: _____

_____

_____

Physical and Health Factors (Check All That Apply):

☐ Limited access to health care

☐ Chronic health condition (specify: _____)

☐ Temporary health condition (date/ duration: _____)

☐ History of medical condition (date diagnosed _____)

☐ Medical treatments (specify: _____)

☐ Repeated visits to the school nurse

☐ Medication (type, dosage, frequency, duration: _____)

☐ Minimal documentation of health history or status

☐ Migraines

☐ Hospitalization (dates: _____)

☐ Repeated visits to doctor

NOTES: _____

_____

_____

Instructional Factors (Check All That Apply):

☐ Interrupted schooling (e.g., mid-year school move) Specify why: _____

☐ New teacher (past 6 months)

☐ Nontraditional curriculum (e.g., homeschooled)

☐ Days absent _____

☐ Retained or advanced a grade(s)

☐ Accelerated curriculum (e.g., AP classes)

NOTES: _____

_____

_____

Determination of Primary and Contributory Causes of Academic Weaknesses and Learning Difficulties (Check One):

☐ Based on the available data, it is reasonable to conclude that one or more factors is *primarily* responsible for the student's observed learning difficulties. Specify: _____

☐ Based on the available data, it is reasonable to conclude that one or more factors *contributes* to the student's observed learning difficulties. Specify:

_____

☐ *No* factors listed here appear to be the primary cause of the student's academic weaknesses and learning difficulties.

[1]For vision and hearing disorders, it is important to understand the nature of the disorder, its expected impact on achievement, and the time of diagnosis. It is also important to understand what was happening instructionally at the time the disorder was suspected and diagnosed.

With regard to hearing, even mild loss can affect initial receptive and expressive skills as well as academic skill acquisition. When loss is suspected, the practitioner should consult professional literature to further understand the potential impact of a documented hearing issue (see American Speech-Language-Hearing Association guidelines www.asha.org).

With regard to vision, refractive error (i.e., hyperopia and anisometropia), accommodative and vergence dysfunctions, and eye movement disorders are associated with learning difficulties whereas others vision problems are not (e.g., constant strabismus and amblyopia). As such, when a vision disorder is documented or suspected, the practitioner should consult professional literature to further understand the impact of the visual disorder (e.g., see American Optometric Association www.aoa.org).

[2]When there is a history of hearing difficulties and a learning disability diagnosis is being considered, hearing testing should be recent (i.e., conducted within the past 6 months).

[3]When evaluating the impact of language and cultural factors on a student's functioning, the practitioner should consider whether and to what extent other individuals with similar linguistic and cultural backgrounds as the referred student are progressing and responding to instruction in the present curriculum (e.g., if an LEP student is not demonstrating academic progress or is not performing as expected on a class- or district-wide assessment when compared to his or her peers who possess a similar level of English proficiency and acculturative knowledge, it is unlikely that cultural and linguistic differences are the sole or primary factors for the referred student's low performance). In addition, it is important to note that as the number of cultural and linguistic differences in a student's background increase, the greater the likelihood that poor academic performance is attributable primarily to such differences rather than a disability.

Note: All 50 US states specify eight exclusionary criteria. Namely, learning difficulties cannot be primarily attributed to (1) visual impairment, (2) hearing impairment, (3) motor impairment, (4) intellectual disability, (5) emotional disturbance, (6) environmental disadvantage, (7) economic disadvantage, and (8) cultural difference. Noteworthy is the fact that certain states have adopted additional exclusionary criteria including *autism* (CA, MI, VT, and WI), *emotional stress* (LA and VT), *home or school adjustment difficulties* (LA and VT), *lack of motivation* (LA and TN), and *temporary crisis situation* (LA, TN, and VT). Mascolo and Flanagan have integrated these additional criteria under "social-emotional and psychological factors" and "environmental and economic factors" and have added two additional categories, namely, "instructional factors" and "physical and health factors" to this form.

Source: Developed by Jennifer T. Mascolo and Dawn P. Flanagan. This form may be copied and disseminated.

an exclusionary factors form that can be used to systematically and thoroughly document that the exclusionary factors listed in the federal definition of SLD (as well as other factors) are evaluated. This form may also be found at www.crossbattery.com under "Resources." At Level 2, the practitioners must judge the extent to which any factors other than a cognitive weakness or weaknesses can be considered the *primary* reason for the academic performance difficulties.

Note that because the process of SLD determination does not necessarily occur in a strict linear fashion, evaluations at Levels 1 and 2 often take place concurrently, because data from Level 2 are often necessary to understand performance at Level 1. The circular arrows between Levels 1 and 2 in Rapid Reference 11.2 are meant to illustrate the fact that interpretations and decisions that are based on data gathered at Level 1 may need to be informed by data gathered at Level 2. Ultimately, at Level 2, the practitioner must judge the extent to which any factors other than a cognitive weakness or weaknesses can be considered the primary reason for academic performance difficulties. If performance cannot be attributed primarily to other factors, then the second criterion necessary for establishing SLD according to the operational definition is met and assessment may continue to the next level.

It is important to recognize that although factors such as having English as a second language may be present and may affect performance adversely, SLD may also be present. Certainly, children who may have vision problems, chronic illnesses, limited English proficiency, and so forth may also have SLD. Therefore, when these or other factors at Level 2 are present, or even when they are determined to be *contributing* to poor performance, SLD should not be ruled out. Rather, only when such factors are determined to be *primarily* responsible for weaknesses in learning and academic performance, not merely contributing to them, should SLD, as an explanation for dysfunction in performance, be discounted. Examination of exclusionary factors is necessary to ensure a fair and equitable interpretation of the data collected for SLD determination and, as such, is not intended to *rule in* SLD. Rather, careful examination of exclusionary factors is intended to rule out other possible explanations for deficient academic performance.

One of the major reasons for placing the evaluation of exclusionary factors at this (early) point in the SLD assessment process is to provide a mechanism that is efficient in time and effort and that may prevent the unnecessary administration of additional tests. However, it is noteworthy that it may not be possible to completely and convincingly rule out all the numerous potential exclusionary factors at this stage in the assessment process. For example, the data gathered at Levels 1 and 2 may be insufficient to draw conclusions about such conditions as developmental disabilities and intellectual disability, which often require more thorough and direct assessment (e.g., administration of an intelligence test and adaptive behavior scale). When exclusionary factors have been evaluated carefully and eliminated as possible *primary* explanations for poor academic performance— at least those that can be evaluated at this level—the process may advance to the next level.

Level 3: Performance in Cognitive Abilities and Neuropsychological Processes

The criterion at this level is like the one specified in Level 1 except that it is evaluated with data from an assessment of cognitive abilities, neuro-psychological processes, and learning efficiency. Analysis of data generated from the administration of standardized tests represents the most common method available by which cognitive and neuropsychological functioning in children is evaluated. However, other types of information and data are relevant to cognitive performance (see Rapid Reference 11.2, Level 3, column 4). Practitioners should seek out and gather data from other sources as a means of providing corroborating evidence for standardized test findings. For example, when test findings are found to be consistent with a student's performance in the classroom, a greater degree of confidence may be placed on test performance because interpretations of cognitive deficiency have ecological validity—an important condition for any diagnostic process (Flanagan & Alfonso, 2017; Flanagan et al., 2012; Hale & Fiorello, 2004; Mascolo et al., 2014).

A particularly salient aspect of the CHC-based operational definition of SLD is the concept that a weakness or deficit in a cognitive ability or process underlies difficulties in academic performance or skill development. Because research demonstrates that the relationship between the cognitive dysfunction and the manifest learning problems are causal in nature (e.g., Fletcher, Taylor, Levin, & Satz, 1995; Hale & Fiorello, 2004), in a probabilistic sense (Flanagan & Schneider, 2016), data analysis at this level should seek to ensure that identified weaknesses or deficits on cognitive tests bear an empirical relationship to those weaknesses or deficits in academic skills identified previously. It is this very notion that makes it necessary to draw on cognitive and neuropsychological theory and research to inform opera-tional definitions of SLD and increase the reliability and validity of the SLD identification process. Theory and its related research base not only specify the relevant constructs that ought to be measured at Levels 1 and 3 but also predict the way they are related. Furthermore, application of current theory and research provides a substantive empirical foundation from which interpretations and conclusions may be drawn. Rapid References 11.7, 11.8, and 11.9 provide a summary of the relations between CHC cognitive abilities and processes and reading, math, and writing achievement. These tables also provide a summary of the literature on the etiology of academic difficulties (see McDonough, Flanagan, Sy, & Alfonso, 2017, for a discussion).

The information contained in Rapid References 11.7 to 11.9 may be used to guide how practitioners organize their assessments at this level. That is, prior to selecting cognitive and neuropsychological tests, the practitioner should have knowledge of those cognitive abilities and processes that are most important for understanding academic performance in the area(s) in question (i.e., the area[s] identified as weak or deficient at Level 1). Evaluation of cognitive performance should be comprehensive, especially in the areas of suspected dysfunction. Evidence

DON'T FORGET
....

If no weaknesses or deficits in cognitive abilities or processes are found, then an essential criterion for SLD determination is not met.

DON'T FORGET
....

Because new data are gathered at Level 3, reevaluation or further consideration of exclusionary factors should be undertaken. The circular arrows between Levels 2 and 3 in Rapid Reference 11.2 are meant to illustrate the fact that interpretations and decisions that are based on data gathered at Level 3 may need to be informed by data gathered at Level 2. Likewise, data gathered at Level 3 are often necessary to rule out (or in) one or more exclusionary factors at Level 2. Reliable and valid identification of SLD depends in part on being able to understand academic performance (Level 1), cognitive performance (Level 3), and the relationship between them, as well as the many factors that may facilitate or inhibit such performances (Level 2).

of a cognitive weakness or deficit is a necessary condition for SLD determination.

Level 4: The Dual Discrepancy/Consistency Pattern of Strengths and Weaknesses

This level of evaluation is based on a theory- and research-guided examination of performance across academic skills, cognitive abilities, and neuropsychological processes to determine whether the student's PSW is consistent with the SLD construct. When the process of SLD identification has reached this level, three necessary criteria for SLD identification have already been met: (1) one or more weaknesses or deficits in academic performance, (2) one or more weaknesses or deficits in cognitive performance, and (3) exclusionary factors determined not to be the primary cause of the

≡ Rapid Reference 11.7

Summary of Relations Between CHC Domains and Reading Achievement and the Etiology of Reading Functions

CHC Broad Ability	Reading Achievement	Etiology of Reading Functions
Gf	**Inductive (I)** and **general sequential reasoning (RG)** abilities play a moderate role in *reading comprehension.* Executive functions such as planning, organization, and self-monitoring are also important.	Several cortical and subcortical structures are frequently implicated in *basic reading skills and word reading accuracy.* Recent work appears to identify dysfunction in a left hemispheric network that includes the occipitotemporal region, inferior frontal gyrus, and inferior parietal region of the brain (Fletcher, Simos, Papanicolaou, & Denton, 2004; Richlan, 2012; Richlan, Kronbichler, & Wimmer, 2009; Shaywitz et al., 2000; Silani et al., 2005). Numerous imaging studies have also found that dysfunctional responses in the left inferior frontal and temporoparietal cortices play a significant role with regard to phonological deficits (Skeide et al., 2015). Similar brain regions are activated on tasks involving *reading fluency,* but additional activation is observed in areas involved in eye movement and attention (Jones, Ashby, & Branigan, 2013). Further, there is also evidence for increased activation in the left occipitotemporal region, in particular the occipitotemporal sulcus, which is important for rapid processing of letter patterns (Dehaene & Cohen, 2011; Shaywitz et al., 2004).
Gc	**Language development (LD), lexical knowledge (VL),** and **listening ability (LS)** are important at all ages for *reading acquisition and development.* These abilities become increasingly important with age. Oral language, listening comprehension, and EF (planning, organization, self-monitoring) also important for *reading comprehension.*	
Gwm	**Memory span (MS)** and **working memory capacity (WM)** or attentional control are important for *overall reading* success. Phonological memory or WM for verbal and sound-based information may also be important.	
Gv	Orthographic processing (often measured by tests of perceptual speed that use orthographic units as stimuli) is related to *reading rate and fluency.*	

Ga	**Phonetic coding (PC)** or phonological awareness-processing is very important during the elementary school years for the development of *basic reading skills*. Phonological memory or WM for verbal and sound-based information may also be important.	Brain regions often associated with *reading comprehension* include the anterior temporal lobe, inferior temporal gyrus, inferior frontal gyrus, inferior frontal sulcus, and middle and superior frontal and temporal regions (Ferstl et al., 2008; Gernsbacher & Kaschak, 2003). More recent research has revealed a relationship between listening and reading comprehension and activation along the left superior temporal sulcus, which has been referred to by some as the *comprehension cortex* (Berl et al., 2010). However, broader pathways are also activated in reading comprehension, reflecting increased cognitive demand compared to listening.
Glr	**Naming facility (NA)** or **rapid automatic naming** (RAN; also called *speed of lexical access*) is very important during the elementary school years for *reading rate and fluency*. **Associative memory (MA)** is also important.	
Gs	**Perceptual speed (P)** abilities are important throughout school but particularly during the elementary school years.	Family and genetic factors have long been identified as crucial in reading achievement, with some researchers suggesting that a child with a parent with a reading disability is eight times more likely to be dyslexic compared to the general population (Pennington & Olson, 2005).
		Shared environmental factors include language and literacy environment during childhood (Wadsworth, Olson, Pennington, & DeFries, 2000) and quality of reading instruction.

Source: Flanagan, Ortiz, et al., 2006; Flanagan et al., 2013; McDonough et al., 2017; McGrew & Wendling, 2010; McGrew, LaForte, & Schrank, 2014).

academic and cognitive weaknesses or deficits. What has yet to be determined is whether the pattern of results is marked by an empirical or ecologically valid relationship between the identified cognitive and academic weaknesses, whether the individual's cognitive weakness or deficit is domain-specific, whether the

≡ Rapid Reference 11.8

Summary of Relations Between CHC Domains and Mathematics Achievement and the Etiology of Math Functions

CHC Broad Ability	Math Achievement	Etiology of Math Functions
Gf	**Reasoning inductively (I)** and **deductively with numbers (RQ)** is very important for *math problem-solving*. Executive functions such as set shifting and cognitive inhibition are also important.	The intraparietal sulcus in both hemispheres is widely viewed as crucial in processing and representing numerical quantity (*number sense*), although there may be differences in activation as a function of age (Ansari & Dhital, 2006; Ansari, Garcia, Lucas, Hamon, & Dhital, 2005; Dehaene, Molko, Cohen, & Wilson, 2004; Kaufmann et al., 2006; Kucian, von Aster, Loenneker, Dietrich, & Martin, 2008; Mussolin et al., 2010; Price & Ansari, 2013).
Gc	**Language development (LD), lexical knowledge (VL),** and **listening ability (LS)** are important at all ages for *math problem-solving*. These abilities become increasingly important with age. Number representation (e.g., quantifying sets without counting, estimating relative magnitude of sets) and number comparisons are related to overall *number sense*.	Regions of the left fronto-parietal cortex, including the intraparietal sulcus, angular gyrus, and supramarginal gyrus, have been consistently associated with *math calculation* (Ansari, 2008; Dehaene et al., 2004; De Smedt, Holloway, & Ansari, 2011). The dorsolateral prefrontal cortex has also been found to show increased activation during calculation, implying that executive functioning and working memory may be playing a role in the process (Davis et al., 2009).
Gwm	**Memory span (MS)** and **working memory capacity (WM)** or attentional control are important for *math problem-solving* and overall success in math.	
Gv	**Visualization (VZ),** including mental rotation, is important primarily for higher-level math (e.g., geometry, calculus) and *math problem-solving*.	

Ga		
Glr	**Naming facility (NA;** also called *speed of lexical access*) and **associative memory (MA)** are important for memorization and rapid retrieval of *basic math facts* and for accurate and fluent *calculation.*	A left hemisphere network that includes the precentral gyrus, inferior parietal cortex, and intraparietal sulcus, is often implicated in *math fact retrieval* (Dehaene & Cohen, 1995, 1997; Dehaene, Spelke, Pinel, Stanescu, & Tsivkin, 1999). Further, some researchers believe that rote math facts are retrieved from verbal memory, thereby requiring activation of the angular gyrus and other regions associated with linguistic processes (Dehaene & Cohen, 1995; Dehaene et al., 1999).
Gs	**Perceptual speed (P)** is important during all years, especially the elementary school years for *math calculation fluency.*	Prevalence of math disabilities is about 10 times higher in those with family members who had math disabilities (Shalev et al., 2001). Environmental factors, including motivation, emotional functioning (e.g., math anxiety), and suboptimal or inadequate teaching may also contribute to math difficulties (Szűcs & Goswami, 2013; Vukovic, Kieffer, Bailey, & Harari, 2013). Further, math achievement in particular may be associated with cultural or gender-based attitudes that may be transmitted in the family environment (e.g., Chiu & Klassen, 2010; Gunderson, Ramirez, Levine, & Beilock, 2011).

Source: Flanagan, Ortiz, et al., 2006; Flanagan et al., 2013; McDonough et al., 2017; McGrew & Wendling, 2010; McGrew et al., 2014).

≡ Rapid Reference 11.9

Summary of the Literature on Relations Between CHC Domains and Writing Achievement and the Etiology of Writing Functions

CHC Broad Ability	Writing Achievement	Etiology of Writing Functions
Gf	**Inductive (I)** and **general sequential reasoning (RG)** are consistently related to *written expression* at all ages. Executive functions such as attention, planning, and self-monitoring are also important.	Neural correlates of writing are less understood, but some studies have suggested that the cerebellum and parietal cortex, particularly the left superior parietal lobe, may be involved (Katanoda, Yoshikawa, & Sugishita, 2001; Magrassi et al., 2010). In addition, the frontal lobes have also been implicated and are considered crucial in planning, brainstorming, organizing, and goal setting, which are important for *written expression* (Shah et al., 2013).
Gc	**Language development (LD), lexical knowledge (VL),** and **general information (K0)** are important primarily after second grade and become increasingly important with age. Level of knowledge of syntax, morphology, semantics, and VL has a significant impact on clarity of *written expression* and text generation ability.	Functional neuroimaging studies have provided substantial evidence for the role of the ventral-temporal inferior frontal gyrus and the posterior inferior frontal gyrus in *spelling* (Rapp, Purcell, Hillis, Capasso, & Miceli, 2015; van Hoorn, Maathuis, & Hadders-Algra, 2013). Other areas that have been identified include the left ventral cortex, bilateral lingual gyrus, bilateral fusiform gyrus (Planton, Jucla, Roux, & Démonet, 2013; Purcell, Shea, & Rapp, 2014; Richards et al., 2005, 2006). However, many of these regions have also been associated with reading and are not distinct to spelling or writing disorders.
Gwm	**Memory span (MS)** is important to writing, especially *spelling* skills, whereas **working memory (WM)** has shown relations with *advanced writing skills* (e.g., written expression, synthesizing multiple ideas, ongoing self-monitoring).	
Gv	Orthographic processing (often measured by tests of perceptual speed that use orthographic units as stimuli) is particularly important for *spelling*.	
Ga	**Phonetic coding (PC)** or phonological awareness-processing is very important during the elementary school years (primarily before fifth grade) for *basic writing skills* and *written expression*.	Although there is a significant genetic component involved in the development of writing skills, this etiology is often shared with a broad variety of reading and language skills (Olson et al., 2013).

Glr	**Naming facility (NA;** also called *speed of lexical access*) has demonstrated relations with *writing fluency.* Storing and retrieving commonly occurring letter patterns in visual and motor memory are needed for *spelling.*
Gs	**Perceptual speed (P)** is important during all school years for *basic writing skills* and is related to *written expression* at all ages.

Source: Flanagan, Ortiz, et al., 2006; Flanagan et al., 2013; McDonough et al., 2017; McGrew & Wendling, 2010; McGrew et al., 2014).

individual's academic weakness or deficit (underachievement) is unexpected, and whether the individual displays at least average ability to think and reason. These four conditions form a specific PSW that is marked by two discrepancies and a consistency (DD/C). X-BASS is needed to determine whether the data demonstrate the DD/C pattern, because specific formulae and regression equations are necessary to make the determination. Each of these four conditions is described next and the "Don't Forget" summarizes the simple steps necessary to conduct a PSW analysis using X-BASS.

Relationship Between Cognitive and Academic Weaknesses

A student with an SLD has specific cognitive and academic weaknesses or deficits. When these weaknesses are related empirically or when there is

DON'T FORGET
....

The DD/C PSW analysis in X-BASS is simple to conduct and requires the following: (1) entering data that represent seven areas of cognitive ability or processing (i.e., Gf, Gc, Glr, Gsm, Gv, Ga, Gs) and one or more areas of academic achievement and transferring estimates of those cognitive and academic areas to a Data Organizer tab by clicking a button next to each estimate; (2) selecting estimates from the Data Organizer tab for inclusion in the PSW analysis by checking a box next to the estimate (or by clicking on the "select all" button), which automatically transfers estimates to a Strengths and Weaknesses tab; and (3) designating each of the cognitive and academic estimates as either a strength or a weakness. On completion of these simple steps, the DD/C PSW analysis is automatically calculated *and interpreted.* These steps are demonstrated in the last section of this chapter using scores from an evaluation conducted by one of the authors of this chapter (McDonough, 2017).

C A U T I O N

The term *causal* as used within the context of the DD/C model has been misconstrued to mean *deterministic*. That is, if we know the causal inputs, we can predict the outcome perfectly (Kranzler et al., 2016). However, just because the causal inputs may be known, the outcomes clearly and obviously cannot be predicted perfectly. Cognitive abilities are indeed causally related to academic abilities, but the relationship is *probabilistic*, not deterministic, and is of moderate size (Flanagan & Schneider, 2016). The finding of cognitive weaknesses raises the risk of academic weaknesses, it does not guarantee academic weaknesses (Flanagan & Schneider, 2016), as assumed by Kranzler et al. (2016). Likewise, it should not be assumed that the finding of academic weaknesses means that there are related cognitive weaknesses (again, as assumed by Kranzler et al., 2016). As most practitioners know, in many cases of academic weakness, there are no cognitive correlates. This is because academic weaknesses may be related to numerous factors, only one of which is a cognitive weakness.

an ecologically valid relationship between them, the relationship is referred to as a *below-average cognitive aptitude-achievement consistency* in the DD/C model. This consistency is a necessary marker for SLD because SLD is caused by cognitive processing weaknesses or deficits (e.g., Fletcher, 2008; Hale et al., 2010). Thus, there is a need to understand and identify the underlying cognitive ability or processing problems that contribute significantly to the individual's academic difficulties.

The term *cognitive aptitude* within the context of the DD/C definition represents the specific cognitive ability or neuropsychological processing weaknesses or deficits that are empirically related to the academic skill weaknesses or deficits. For example, if a student's basic reading skill deficit is related to cognitive deficits in phonological processing (a narrow Ga ability) and rapid automatic naming (a narrow Gr ability), then the combination of below-average narrow Ga and Gr performances represents his or her below-average cognitive aptitude for basic reading, meaning that these below-average cognitive performances are likely contributing to or causing difficulties acquiring basic reading skills. Moreover, the finding of below-average performance on measures of phonological processing, rapid automatic naming, and basic reading skills together represents a below-average cognitive aptitude-achievement consistency.

The concept of a below-average cognitive aptitude-achievement consistency reflects the notion that there are documented relationships between specific cognitive abilities and processes and specific academic skills. Empirically supported cognitive-achievement relationships were summarized in Rapid References 11.7 through 11.9. The finding of below-average performance in related cognitive and academic areas is an important marker for SLD in the DD/C model and in other alternative research-based approaches (e.g., Hale et al., 2011; McCloskey et al., 2012).

In the DD/C model, the criteria for establishing a below-average cognitive aptitude-achievement consistency are as follows:

- "Below-average" performance (i.e., less than 90, and more typically at least one SD or more below the mean) in the specific cognitive and academic areas that are considered weaknesses or deficits
- Evidence of an empirical relationship between the specific cognitive and academic areas of weakness and an ecologically valid relationship between these areas (see Rapid Reference 11.10 for details regarding how X-BASS determines consistency); to validate the relationship between the cognitive and academic areas of weakness, practitioners can document the way the cognitive weakness or deficit manifests in real-world performances (see Rapid Reference 11.11 for guidance)

Discovery of consistencies among cognitive abilities and processes and academic skills in the below-average (or lower) range could result from intellectual disability, pervasive developmental disorders, or generally below-average cognitive ability, which would negate two important markers of SLD—that cognitive weaknesses are domain-specific and that underachievement is unexpected. Therefore, identification of SLD should not rest on below-average cognitive aptitude-achievement consistency alone. A student with SLD typically has many cognitive capabilities. Therefore, in the DD/C model, the student must demonstrate a pattern of strengths or overall intellectual ability that is at least average.

At Least Average Ability to Think and Reason (g)

A specific learning disability is just that—specific. It is not general. As such, the below-average cognitive aptitude-achievement consistency ought to be circumscribed and represent a significantly different level of functioning as compared to the student's cognitive capabilities or strengths in other areas. Indeed, the notion that students with SLD are of generally average or better overall cognitive ability is well known and has been written about for decades (e.g., Hinshelwood, 1902; Orton, 1937). In fact, the earliest recorded definitions of learning disability were developed by clinicians based on their observations of individuals who experienced considerable difficulties with the acquisition of basic academic skills, despite their average or above-average general intelligence. According to Monroe (1932), "The children of superior mental capacity who fail to learn to read are, of course, spectacular examples of specific reading difficulty since they have such obvious abilities in other fields" (p. 23; see Mather, 2011). Indeed, "all historical approaches to SLD emphasize the *spared or intact abilities* that stand in stark contrast to the deficient abilities" (Kaufman, 2008, pp. 7–8, emphasis added).

Description of the Consistency Component of the DD/C Model and How It Is Determined Using X-BASS

Term or Concept	DD/C	X-BASS	Comments
Below-Average Aptitude-Achievement Consistency	Areas of cognitive and academic weakness are below average and there is an empirical or ecologically valid relationship between them.	For this component of the PSW analysis, X-BASS answers two specific questions and, based on the answers to those questions, provides a statement about the presence of Below-Average Aptitude-Achievement Consistency. The first question is, "Are the scores that represent the cognitive and academic areas of weakness actually weaknesses as compared to most people (i.e., below-average or lower compared to same-age peers from the general population)?" The program parses the cognitive and academic weakness scores into three levels—<85, 85–89 inclusive, and ≥ 90. Scores that are less than 85 are considered *normative* weaknesses; scores that are between 85 and 89 (inclusive) are considered weaknesses because they are below average; and scores of 90 or higher are not considered to be weaknesses. Next, the two scores (academic and cognitive) are examined relative to each other. When both scores are less than 85, the program will report a "Yes," meaning that both scores are normative weaknesses. If one score is less than 85 and the other is between 85 and 89, the program will report "Likely." If both	In some cases, the question of whether or not an individual's pattern of strengths and weaknesses is marked by a below-average aptitude-achievement consistency may not be clear based on the quantitative data alone. As such, it is always important to interpret an individual's pattern of strengths and weaknesses within the context of all available data sources (e.g., including exclusionary factors, behavioral observations, and work samples) and render a judgment about SLD based on the totality of the data.

scores are between 85 and 89 (inclusive), the program reports "Possibly" (because the scores are within normal limits, despite being classified as below average). The program will also report "Possibly" when one score is less than 85 and one is 90 or higher. If one score is between 85 and 89 (inclusive) and the other is 90 or higher, the program reports "Unlikely." and when both scores are 90 or higher, the program reports "No," indicating that the scores cannot be considered weaknesses as compared to most people.

The second question is, "Are the areas of cognitive and academic weakness related empirically?" The strength of the relationship between the cognitive and academic areas of weakness is reported automatically by X-BASS as either LOW (median intercorrelation < .3), Moderate (i.e., MOD) (median intercorrelation between .3 and .5), or HIGH (median intercorrelation > .5), based on a review of the literature (see Flanagan et al., 2013; McGrew & Wendling, 2010) and the technical manuals of cognitive and intelligence batteries (e.g., WJ IV, WISC-V).

Information regarding where the cognitive and academic weakness scores fall as compared to most people and the strength of the relationship between the two areas is used to answer the question, "Is there a below-average aptitude-achievement consistency?" The answer automatically generated by X-BASS will be either "Yes, Consistent," "No, Not Consistent," or "Possibly, Use Clinical Judgment." For example, if the cognitive and academic areas selected by the evaluator as weaknesses are associated with scores that fall below 85 and if the strength of the relationship between the areas of cognitive and academic weakness is moderate or high, then the program will report "Yes, Consistent."

General and Specific Manifestations of Weaknesses or Deficits in Cognitive Abilities and Processes

General and Specific Manifestations of a Fluid Reasoning (Gf) Weakness

CHC Broad Cognitive Abilities–Neuropsychological Functions	Brief Definition	General Manifestations of the Cognitive-Neuropsychological Weakness	Specific Manifestations of the Cognitive-Neuropsychological Weakness
Fluid Reasoning (Gf)	• Novel reasoning and problem-solving; ability to solve problems that are unfamiliar • Processes minimally dependent on prior learning • Involves manipulating rules, abstracting, generalizing, and identifying logical relationships • Fluid reasoning evident in inferential reasoning, concept formation, classification of unfamiliar stimuli, categorization, and extrapolation of reasonable estimates in ambiguous situations (Schneider & McGrew, 2012) • Narrow Gf abilities include Induction, General Sequential Reasoning (Deduction), and Quantitative Reasoning.	Difficulties with: • Higher-level thinking and reasoning • Transferring or generalizing learning • Deriving solutions for novel problems • Extending knowledge through critical thinking • Perceiving and applying underlying rules or process(es) to solve problems	Reading difficulties: • Drawing inferences from text • Abstracting main idea(s) Math difficulties: • Reasoning with quantitative information (word problems) • Internalizing procedures and processes used to solve problems • Apprehending relationships between numbers Writing difficulties: • Essay writing and generalizing concepts • Developing a theme • Comparing and contrasting ideas

General and Specific Manifestations of a Crystallized Intelligence (Gc) Weakness

CHC Broad Cognitive Abilities– Neuropsychological Functions	Brief Definition	General Manifestations of Cognitive- Neuropsychological Weakness	Specific Manifestations of the Cognitive-Neuropsychological Weakness
Crystallized Intelligence (Gc)	• Breadth and depth of knowledge and skills that are valued by one's culture • Developed through formal education as well as general learning experiences • Stores of information and declarative and procedural knowledge • Reflects the degree to which a person has learned practically useful knowledge and mastered valued skills (Schnieder & McGrew, 2012) • Narrow Gc abilities include General Verbal Information, Language Development, Lexical Knowledge, Listening Ability, Information About Culture, Communication Ability, and Grammatical Sensitivity.	Difficulties with: • Vocabulary acquisition • Knowledge acquisition • Comprehending language or understanding what others are saying • Fact-based and informational questions • Using prior knowledge to support learning • Finding the right words to use or say	Reading difficulties: • Decoding (e.g., word student is attempting to decode is not in his or her vocabulary) • Comprehending (e.g., poor background knowledge about information contained in text) Math difficulties: • Understanding math concepts and the vocabulary of math Writing difficulties: • Grammar (syntax) • Bland writing with limited descriptors • Verbose writing with limited descriptors • Inappropriate word use Language difficulties: • Understanding class lessons • Expressive language—"poverty of thought"

General and Specific Manifestations of an Auditory Processing (Ga) Weakness

CHC Broad Cognitive Abilities–Neuropsychological Functions	Brief Definition	General Manifestations of Cognitive-Neuropsychological Weakness	Specific Manifestations of the Cognitive-Neuropsychological Weakness
Auditory Processing (Ga)	• Ability to analyze and synthesize auditory information • One narrow aspect of Ga is a precursor to oral language comprehension (i.e, parsing speech sounds or Phonetic Coding). • In addition to Phonetic Coding, other narrow Ga abilities include Speech Sound Discrimination, Resistance to Auditory Stimulus Distortion, Memory for Sound Patterns (and others related to music).	Difficulties with: • Hearing information presented orally • Initially processing oral Information • Paying attention, especially in the presence of background noise • Discerning the direction from which auditory information is coming • Discriminating between simple sounds • Foreign language acquisition	Reading difficulties: • Acquiring phonics skills • Sounding out words • Using phonetic strategies Math difficulties: • Reading word problems Writing difficulties: • Spelling • Note-taking • Poor quality of writing

General and Specific Manifestations of a Long-Term Storage and Retrieval (Glr) Weakness

CHC Broad Cognitive Abilities—Neuropsychological Functions	Brief Definition	General Manifestations of Cognitive-Neuropsychological Weakness	Specific Manifestations of the Cognitive-Neuropsychological Weakness
Long-Term Retrieval (Glr)	• Ability to store information (e.g., concepts, words, facts), consolidate it, and fluently retrieve it at a later time (e.g., minutes, hours, days, and years) through association • In Glr tasks, information leaves immediate awareness long enough for the contents of primary memory to be displaced completely. In other words, Glr tasks (unlike Gsm tasks) do not allow for information to be maintained continuously in primary memory (Schneider & McGrew, 2012). • Glr abilities may be categorized as either learning efficiency or fluency. Learning efficiency narrow abilities include Associative Memory, Meaningful Memory, and Free Recall Memory; fluency narrow abilities involve either the production of ideas (e.g., Ideational Fluency, Associational Fluency), the recall of words (e.g., Naming Facility, Word Fluency), or the generation of figures (e.g., Figural Fluency, Figural Flexibility) (Schneider & McGrew, 2012).	Difficulties with: • Learning new concepts • Retrieving or recalling information by using association • Performing consistently across different task formats (e.g., recognition versus recall formats) • Rapid retrieval of information • Learning information quickly • Paired learning (visual-auditory) • Recalling specific information (words, facts) • Generating ideas rapidly	Reading difficulties: • Accessing background knowledge to support new learning while reading • Slow to access phonological representations during decoding • Retelling or paraphrasing what one has read Math difficulties: • Memorizing math facts • Recalling math facts and procedures Writing difficulties: • Accessing words to use during essay writing • Specific writing tasks (compare and contrast; persuasive writing) • Note-taking • Idea generation and production Language difficulties: • Expressive—circumlocutions, speech fillers, "interrupted" thought, pauses • Receptive—making connections throughout oral presentations (e.g., class lecture)

General and Specific Manifestations of a Processing Speed (Gs) Weakness

CHC Broad Cognitive Abilities—Neuropsychological Functions	Brief Definition	General Manifestations of Cognitive-Neuropsychological Weakness	Specific Manifestations of the Cognitive-Neuropsychological Weakness
Processing Speed (Gs)	• Speed of processing, particularly when required to focus attention for 1–3 minutes • Usually measured by tasks that require the ability to perform simple repetitive cognitive tasks quickly and accurately • Narrow Gs abilities include Perceptual Speed, Rate-of-Test-Taking, Number Facility, Reading Speed, and Writing Speed (note that the last two abilities are also listed under other broad CHC domains, including Grw).	Difficulties with: • Efficient processing of information • Quickly perceiving relationships (similarities and differences between stimuli or information) • Working within time parameters • Completing simple, rote tasks quickly	Reading difficulties: • Slow reading speed, which interferes with comprehension • Need to reread for understanding Math difficulties: • Automatic computations • Computational speed slow despite accuracy • Slow speed can result in reduced accuracy due to memory decay. Writing difficulties: • Limited output due to time factors • Labored process results in reduced motivation to produce Language difficulties: • Cannot retrieve information quickly—slow, disrupted speech; cannot get out thoughts quickly enough • Is slow to process incoming information, puts demands on memory store, which can result in information overload and loss of meaning

General and Specific Manifestations of a Visual Processing (Gv) Weakness

CHC Broad Cognitive Abilities–Neuropsychological Functions	Brief Definition	General Manifestations of Cognitive-Neuropsychological Weakness	Specific Manifestations of the Cognitive-Neuropsychological Weakness
Visual Processing (Gv)	• Ability to analyze and synthesize visual information • Ability to make use of simulated mental imagery (often in conjunction with currently perceived images) to solve problems (Schneider & McGrew, 2012) • There are many narrow Gv abilities, some of which include Visualization, Speeded Rotation, Closure Speed, Flexibility of Closure, Visual Memory and Spatial Scanning.	Difficulties with: • Recognizing patterns • Reading maps, graphs, and charts • Attending to fine visual detail • Recalling visual information • Appreciation of spatial characteristics of objects (e.g., size, length) • Recognition of spatial orientation of objects	Reading difficulties: • Orthographic coding (using visual features of letters to decode) • Sight-word acquisition • Using charts and graphs within a text in conjunction with reading • Comprehension of text involving spatial concepts (e.g., social studies text describing physical boundaries, movement of troops along a specified route) Math difficulties: • Number alignment during computations • Reading and interpreting graphs, tables, and charts Writing difficulties: • Spelling sight words • Spatial planning during writing tasks (e.g., no attention to margins, words that overhang a line) • Inconsistent size, spacing, position, and slant of letters

General and Specific Manifestations of a Short-Term (Working) Memory (Gsm) Weakness

CHC Broad Cognitive Abilities–Neuropsychological Functions	Brief Definition	General Manifestations of Cognitive-Neuropsychological Weakness	Specific Manifestations of the Cognitive-Neuropsychological Weakness
Short-Term (Working) Memory (Gsm)	• Ability to hold information in immediate awareness and use or transform it within a few seconds	Difficulties with: • Following multistep oral and written instructions • Remembering information long enough to apply it • Remembering the sequence of information • Rote memorization • Maintaining one's place in a math problem or train of thought while writing	Reading difficulties: • Reading comprehension (i.e., understanding what is read) • Decoding multisyllabic words • Orally retelling or paraphrasing what one has read Math difficulties: • Rote memorization of facts • Remembering mathematical procedures • Multistep problems and regrouping • Extracting information to be used in word problems Writing difficulties: • Spelling multisyllabic words • Redundancy in writing (word and conceptual levels) • Identifying main idea of a story • Note-taking

General and Specific Manifestations of an Attention Weakness

CHC Broad Cognitive Abilities–Neuropsychological Functions	Brief Definition	General Manifestations of Cognitive-Neuropsychological Weakness	Specific Manifestations of the Cognitive-Neuropsychological Weakness
Attention	• Attention is a complex and multifaceted construct used when an individual must focus on certain stimuli for information processing. In order to regulate thinking and to complete tasks of daily living such as schoolwork, it is necessary to be able to attend to auditory and visual stimuli in the environment. Attention can be viewed as the foundation of all other higher-order processing. Attention can be divided into five subareas: selective-focused attention, shifting attention, divided attention, sustained attention, and attentional capacity. • It is important to identify the exact nature of the attentional problem(s) prior to selecting an intervention, teaching strategies, modifying the curriculum, or making accommodations.	Difficulty with: • Being easily distracted • Attention to detail; making careless mistakes • Discerning demands of a task (e.g., where to begin or how to get started) • Being able to attend to tasks except for in short intervals • Changing activities • Applying a different strategy when task demands change • Attending to more than one thing or task at a time • Performing well when faced with multiple stimuli or an abundance of detail	Reading difficulties: • Loses one's place easily • Easily distracted while reading • Does not pick up important details in text Math difficulties: • Does not consistently attend to math signs • Frequent mistakes on word problems Writing difficulties: • Completing long assignments; following time lines

General and Specific Manifestations of Weaknesses in Executive Functions

CHC Broad Cognitive Abilities—Neuropsychological Functions	Brief Definition	General Manifestations of Cognitive-Neuropsychological Weakness	Specific Manifestations of the Cognitive-Neuropsychological Weakness
Executive Functioning	• Executive functioning is often understood as two broadly conceptualized areas that are related to the brain's frontal lobes: cognitive control and behavioral-emotional control. The **cognitive** aspects of executive functioning include concept generation (Gc/Glr), problem-solving (Gf), attentional shifting (attention; Gs), planning, organizing, working memory (Gsm), and retrieval fluency (Glr). The **behavioral/emotional** aspects of executive functioning relate to the inhibitory controls of behavior (e.g., impulsivity, regulation of emotional tone, etc.) (see Miller, 2010).	Difficulty with: • Learning new activities, generating concepts, and solving problems • Identifying goals and setting goals • Planning (e.g., begins project without necessary materials; does not allocate sufficient time to complete task) • Sequencing (e.g., may skip steps in multistep problems) • Prioritizing (e.g., not sure what's important when taking notes) • Organization (e.g., loses important papers; fails to turn in completed work; creates unrealistic schedule) • Initiation (e.g., has difficulty getting started on tasks, assignments, etc.) • Pace (e.g., often runs out of time on seatwork and exams; has difficulty completing homework due to unrealistic time line) • Shifting between activities flexibly; coping with unforeseen events • Self-monitoring (e.g., doesn't check to ensure that each step was completed; doesn't check work before submitting it) • Emotional control (e.g., may exhibit inappropriate or overreactive response to situations)	Reading difficulties: • Sequencing; telling a story chronologically • Prioritizing; extracting main idea and other important information • Problem-solving; drawing inferences from text Math difficulties: • Sequencing; remembering order of operations • Prioritizing; figuring out what is important when solving word problems • Shifting; attending to math signs on a page Writing difficulties: • Generating ideas to write about • Sequencing a story • Prioritizing main events in a story

Source: Examples were adapted from Packer & Pruitt, 2010.

Current definitions of SLD also recognize the importance of generally average or better overall ability as a characteristic of individuals with SLD. For example, the official definition of *learning disability* of the Learning Disabilities Association of Canada (LDAC) states, in part,

> Learning Disabilities refer to a number of disorders which may affect the acquisition, organization, retention, understanding or use of verbal or nonverbal information. These disorders affect learning in individuals who otherwise demonstrate *at least average abilities essential for thinking and/or reasoning.* (www.ldac-acta.ca/learn-more/ld-defined, emphasis added; see also Harrison & Holmes, 2012)

Unlike some definitions of SLD, such as Canada's (Harrison & Holmes, 2012), the 2004 IDEA definition does not refer to overall ability level. However, the 2006 federal regulations contain the following phrasing:

> (ii) The child exhibits a pattern of strengths and weaknesses in performance, achievement, or both, relative to age, State-approved grade-level standards, or intellectual development, that is determined by the group to be relevant to the identification of a specific learning disability . . .

Given the vagueness of the wording in the federal regulations, one could certainly infer that this phrase means that the cognitive and academic areas of concern are significantly lower than what is expected relative to same-age peers or relative to otherwise average intellectual development. Indeed, there continues to be considerable agreement that a student who meets criteria for SLD has some cognitive capabilities that are at least average relative to most people (e.g., Berninger, 2011; Feifer, 2012; Fiorello et al., 2014; Flanagan, Ortiz, & Alfonso, 2011; Geary et al., 2011; Hale & Fiorello, 2004; Hale et al., 2011; Harrison & Holmes, 2012; Kaufman, 2008; Kavale & Flanagan, 2007; Kavale & Forness, 2000; Kavale et al., 2009; Mather, 2011; McCloskey et al., 2012; Naglieri, 2011; Chapters 10 and 12, this book). Moreover, the criterion of overall average or better ability in cognitive domains is necessary for differential diagnosis (see Chapter 15, this book).

By failing to differentially diagnose SLD from other conditions that impede learning, such as intellectual disability, pervasive developmental disorders, and overall below-average ability to learn and achieve (formerly referred to as "slow learner"), the SLD construct loses its meaning and there is a tendency (albeit well-intentioned) to accept anyone under the SLD category who has learning difficulties for reasons other than specific cognitive dysfunction (e.g., Kavale & Flanagan, 2007; Kavale, Kauffman, Bachmeier, & LeFever, 2008; Mather & Kaufman, 2006; Reynolds & Shaywitz, 2009b; Chapter 15, this book). Although the underlying and varied causes of the learning difficulties of all students who struggle academically should be investigated and addressed, an accurate SLD diagnosis is necessary because it informs instruction (e.g., Hale et al., 2010). When practitioners adhere closely to the DD/C model, SLD can be differentiated from other disorders that also manifest as academic difficulty (e.g., Berninger, 2011; Della Toffalo, 2010; Flanagan et al., 2013).

Although it may be some time before consensus is reached on what constitutes "average or better ability" for the purpose of SLD identification, a student with SLD, generally speaking, ought to be able to perform academically at a level that approximates that of his or her more typically achieving peers when provided with individualized instruction as well as appropriate accommodations, curricular modifications, and the like. In addition, in order for a student with SLD to reach performances (in terms of rate of learning and level of achievement) that approximate his or her nondisabled peers, he or she must possess the ability to learn compensatory strategies and apply them independently, which often requires higher-level thinking and reasoning, including intact executive processes (e.g., Maricle & Avirett, 2012; McCloskey, Perkins, & Van Divner, 2009).

Determining otherwise average or better ability to think and reason (or average or better g) for a student who has a below-average cognitive aptitude-achievement consistency is not a straightforward task, however, and there is no agreed-on method for doing so. The main difficulty in determining whether an individual with specific cognitive weaknesses has otherwise average overall ability or g is that the global ability scores that are available on cognitive or intelligence batteries may be attenuated by the cognitive processing weakness(es). Most batteries have a total test score that is an aggregate of all (or nearly all) abilities and processes measured by the instrument. As such, in many instances, the individual's specific cognitive weaknesses or deficits attenuate the total test score on these instruments, which often masks overall cognitive ability or intellectual capacity. This problem with ability tests was noted as far back as the 1920s when Orton stated, "it seems probably that psychometric tests as ordinarily employed give an entirely erroneous and unfair estimate of the intellectual capacity of these [learning disabled] children" (1925, p. 582; see Mather, 2011). Perhaps for this reason intelligence and cognitive ability batteries have become more differentiated, offering a variety of specific cognitive ability composites and options for global ability composites.

The criterion of at least average ability to think and reason as described in the DD/C model is determined by X-BASS. To understand how X-BASS makes the determination of at least average overall ability, it is necessary to understand three terms as they are

DON'T FORGET

Many scholars use the term *overall cognitive ability* or *intellectual ability* interchangeably with the first factor that emerges in a factor analysis of cognitive tests—that is, Spearman's *g*. The estimates of overall intellectual ability referred to in this chapter are consistent with this conceptualization.

used in the DD/C model and in X-BASS: *strength*, g-*value*, and *Facilitating Cognitive Composite (FCC)*. These terms are defined in Rapid Reference 11.12 and elaborated on in "Using X-BASS for SLD Identification: Three Steps to Output." Essentially, X-BASS will calculate a proxy for *g* (i.e., the FCC) based on the cognitive areas that the user indicates are strengths for the individual. This estimate is based on a consideration of how many cognitive areas are designated as strengths, which ones were designated as strengths, and where the scores representing these cognitive areas fall relative to most people.

Even when it is determined that a student has overall average ability to think and reason along with a below-average cognitive aptitude-achievement consistency, these findings alone do not satisfy the criteria for a PSW consistent with the SLD construct in the DD/C model. This is because it is not yet clear whether the differences between the score representing overall ability (e.g., FCC) and those representing specific cognitive and academic weaknesses or deficits are statistically significant, meaning that such differences are reliable differences (i.e., not due to chance). Moreover, it is not yet clear whether the cognitive area(s) of weakness is *domain-specific* and whether the academic area(s) of weakness (or underachievement) is *unexpected.*

Domain-Specific Cognitive Weaknesses or Deficits: The First Discrepancy in the DD/C Definition of SLD

SLD has been described as a condition that is domain-specific. In other words, areas of cognitive weakness or deficit are circumscribed, meaning that although they interfere with learning and achievement, they are not pervasive and do not affect all or nearly all areas of cognition. According to Stanovich (1993), "The key deficit must be a vertical faculty rather than a horizontal faculty—a domain-specific process rather than a process that operates across a variety of domains" (p. 279). It is rare to find an operational definition that specifies a criterion for determining that the condition is "domain-specific." Some suggest that this condition is supported by a statistically significant difference between a student's overall cognitive ability and a score representing the individual's cognitive area of weakness (e.g., Naglieri, 2011).

However, a statistically significant difference between two scores means only that the difference is not due to chance; it does not provide information about the rarity or infrequency of the difference in the general population. Some statistically significant differences are common in the general population; others are not. Therefore, to determine if the cognitive area that was identified as a weakness by the evaluator is domain-specific, the difference between the individual's actual and expected performance in this area should be evaluated for statistical rarity. Rapid Reference 11.13 summarizes the specific criteria used in X-BASS to determine whether a cognitive area designated as a weakness is also domain-specific. This

Rapid Reference 11.12

Terms Used in the DD/C Model and in X-BASS Necessary to Understand How "At Least Average Overall Ability" Is Conceptualized and Calculated

Term or Concept	DD/C	X-BASS	Comments
Strength	Performance on standardized, norm-referenced tests that falls in the average range (standard scores between 90 and 110 [inclusive], based on a scale having a mean of 100 and an SD of 15) or higher; thus, a strength is associated with standard scores of 90 or higher	On the Strengths and Weaknesses Indicator tab, users must classify scores as either a strength or a weakness. The general guideline for a strength is that the farther a score falls above 90, the greater the probability that the construct it represents (e.g., short-term memory) facilitates performance in some way. **Caution:** The user may classify any score as a strength on the Strengths and Weaknesses Indicator tab, including scores that fall below average or lower. Selecting a score as a strength, regardless of where it falls relative to most people, does not guarantee that it will meet criteria for PSW.	Note that the term *strength* is typically assigned only to scores that are average (eg, a standard score of 90 or 95 or 100) for conducting a PSW analysis within the context of the DD/C operational definition. Ordinarily, average scores are just that—average—reflecting adequately developed skills or abilities. They are not strengths in the normative sense, although they may be strengths in the relative sense (both of which are described in the following). When the term *strength* is used to describe average performance in a PSW analysis it simply means that the ability area associated with the average score does not appear to interfere with or adversely affect the individual's learning. No other meaning should be ascribed to the word *strength* in the PSW analysis, as operationalized by DD/C.
g-Value	Not discussed in the DD/C definition but	The g-value is calculated automatically by X-BASS and assists in answering the question,	A low g-value (e.g., not enough areas designated as strengths) suggests that overall intellectual

is used to determine whether an estimate of overall intellectual ability is calculated	"How likely is it that the individual's pattern of cognitive strengths represents at least average overall ability?" The higher the g-value, the greater the likelihood that the individual's overall intellectual ability (i.e., estimate of g) is at least average, despite one or more specific cognitive weaknesses. (see X-BASS v2.0 for more details; Flanagan et al., 2017).	ability is below average or lower. In other words, a low g-value suggests that in all likelihood the individual's cognitive weaknesses are more pervasive or global rather than specific. In this case, an estimate of overall intellectual ability (i.e., FCC) is not calculated and the PSW analysis is not conducted. **Don't Forget:** Individuals with low overall intellectual ability and achievement are in need of services, but they do not meet the SLD criteria set forth in the DD/C definition. These individuals are perhaps best served at Tiers 2 and 3 of an RTI model.
Cognitive strengths that constitute at least average overall ability to think and reason—the Facilitating Cognitive Composite (FCC)	The DD/C definition requires that the examiner assess a minimum of seven CHC areas: Gf, Gc, Gsm, Glr, Gv, Ga, and Gs. Based on the CHC areas that were designated as strengths, a g-value is calculated. If the g-value is of sufficient magnitude, a composite is	When the g-value is of sufficient magnitude, a standard formula is used in X-BASS to calculate a composite based on all CHC scores that were designated as strengths by the user. The composite is called the Facilitating Cognitive Composite (FCC). Steps and formulae used in X-BASS to calculate a composite are summarized in X-BASS v2.0 (e.g., see the PSW-A Notes tab; Flanagan, Ortiz, & Alfonso, 2017).	If too few CHC scores were designated as strengths, then X-BASS will not calculate an FCC. A sufficient breadth of cognitive abilities must be designated as strengths for the FCC to be calculated because the FCC is expected to be an estimate of g or general intelligence without the attenuating effects of specific cognitive weaknesses. For example, if an individual had relative weaknesses in working memory and processing speed, the FCC would be akin to using the WISC-V General Ability Index (GAI) as an estimate of general intelligence rather than the FSIQ, because the GAI does not include explicit measures of working memory or processing speed.

(continued)

Term or Concept	DD/C	X-BASS	Comments
	calculated and is considered a proxy for g or overall cognitive ability. **Don't Forget:** In addition to the seven CHC areas, common neuropsychological domains that are often assessed in cases of suspected SLD include orthographic processing (OP), speed of lexical access (LA), cognitive efficiency (C and E). If any of these neuropsychological domains is evaluated, it may also be included in the PSW analysis.		Also, if the areas that are designated as strengths by the user are sufficient in number, yielding a g-value that suggests at least average overall ability, but the scores representing those areas are in the mid- to upper 80s, for example, the FCC may fall below 85. In earlier versions of X-BASS (e.g., v1.0), when an FCC fell below 85, the program did not report it and the PSW analysis was not conducted. The assumption here was that the individual's weaknesses were more pervasive and global rather than specific. Below-average cognitive and academic ability in and of itself is not consistent with the SLD construct. However, because clinical judgment may suggest that multiple data sources support SLD, despite a below-average FCC, current versions of X-BASS (v1.3 to 2.1) allow the user to continue with the PSW analysis by overriding the "at least average overall ability" criterion. However, in these instances, X-BASS reports that the pattern (if identified) is not consistent with the DD/C model. **Don't Forget:** Although neuropsychological domains (e.g., CE, LA) may be included in the PSW analysis, they are not included in the calculation of the FCC.

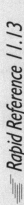

Rapid Reference 11.13

Terms Used in the DD/C Model and in X-BASS Necessary to Understand How a "Domain-Specific Weakness" Is Conceptualized and Calculated

Term or Concept	DD/C	X-BASS	Comments
Discrepancy 1: Cognitive weaknesses that are domain-specific and the ICC	The concept of at least average overall ability implies that any cognitive weaknesses that are observed are "circumscribed" or domain-specific, not pervasive.	In the PSW analysis conducted automatically in X-BASS, any cognitive scores that were designated as a weakness, regardless of magnitude, are labeled *Actual*. The FCC is used in a regression equation to calculate a "Predicted" score for the weak cognitive domain. For a cognitive weakness to be considered domain-specific, two conditions must be met: (1) the difference between the FCC and Actual (weakness) score must be statistically significant ($p < .05$) and (2) the difference between the Actual and Predicted scores must be considered unusual or rare in the general population. *Note that X-BASS corrects for false negatives.* When more than one cognitive weakness (among the seven CHC areas) is identified, then an ICC is automatically calculated. The purpose of the ICC is simply to provide a summary of the individual's cognitive weaknesses. For the PSW analysis, the user may select either the ICC or an individual cognitive ability or processing composite to represent a "cognitive weakness." More than one cognitive weakness may be examined for any individual.	Even if a weakness is considered domain-specific, the actual score may not be below average. The actual score must be below average to meet the criteria for "consistency" in the DD/C definition.

Rapid Reference introduces a new term that is used in X-BASS—the *Inhibiting Cognitive Composite* or *ICC*. The ICC is an aggregate of the estimates of cognitive abilities and processes that the evaluator designated as weaknesses.

Unexpected Underachievement: The Second Discrepancy in the DD/C Definition of SLD

The traditional ability-achievement discrepancy analysis was used to determine if an individual's underachievement (e.g., reading difficulty) was unexpected (i.e., the individual's achievement was not at a level that was commensurate with his or her overall cognitive ability). A particularly salient problem with the ability-achievement discrepancy approach was that a total test score from an intelligence test (e.g., FSIQ) was used as the estimate of overall ability. However, for individuals with SLD, the total test score was often attenuated by one or more specific cognitive weaknesses or deficits and therefore may have provided an unfair or biased estimate of the individual's actual overall intellectual capacity. Furthermore, when the total test score was attenuated by specific cognitive weaknesses or deficits, the ability-achievement discrepancy was often not statistically significant, which resulted in denying the student much-needed academic interventions and special education services (e.g., Aaron, 1995; Hale et al., 2011). For this reason, current intelligence tests and cognitive ability batteries offer alternatives to a total test score. For example, the WISC-V includes the GAI as an alternative to the FSIQ for use in comparison (discrepancy) procedures. Likewise, the WJ IV includes the Fluid-Crystallized (Gf-Gc) composite an alternative to the General Intellectual Ability (GIA) score. Flanagan and her colleagues have advocated for these types of alternatives for many years (e.g., see Appendix H in Flanagan, McGrew, & Ortiz, 2000; Appendix H in Flanagan et al., 2013). Rapid Reference 11.14 summarizes the specific criteria used in X-BASS to determine whether an academic area designated as a weakness represents unexpected underachievement.

In sum, an individual's scores from a comprehensive evaluation are evaluated at this level of the DD/C model (Level 4) to determine if they represent a PSW that is consistent with SLD. The pattern that suggests SLD is characterized by two discrepancies—one that defines SLD as a domain-specific condition and one that further defines SLD as unexpected underachievement—that is concomitant with a below-average cognitive aptitude-achievement consistency. Thus, a DD/C PSW includes the most salient diagnostic markers of SLD.

Level 5: Evaluation of Interference with Learning

When the SLD determination process reaches this point, presumably the criteria at each of the previous levels were met. In addition to the PSW requirement for

Terms Used in the DD/C Model and in X-BASS Necessary to Understand How "Unexpected Underachievement" Is Conceptualized and Calculated

Term or Concept	DD/C	X-BASS	Comments
Discrepancy 2: Academic weaknesses that represent unexpected underachievement	Individuals with at least average overall intellectual ability are expected to perform at about an average level academically, particularly when no other obvious factors are inhibiting academic performance. When a statistically significant pattern of general ability > academic achievement pattern is observed in the absence of any factors that may provide an explanation for the pattern, it is typically termed *unexpected underachievement*—the most salient diagnostic feature of SLD.	In the PSW analysis, an academic weakness represents unexpected underachievement when two conditions are met: (1) the difference between the FCC and Actual (weakness) score is statistically significant ($p < .05$) and (2) the difference between the Actual and Predicted scores is unusual or rare in the general population. *Note that X-BASS corrects for false negatives.*	Even if a weakness represents unexpected underachievement, the actual score may not be below average. The actual score must be below average to meet part of the criteria for "consistency" in the DD/C definition. **Don't Forget:** Because individuals benefit from explicit instruction, evidence-based interventions, strategy instruction, and the like, those individuals who have received such instruction and services may very well perform in the average range academically, which should not automatically rule out SLD, particularly when all other criteria are met. Results of a PSW analysis must always be considered within the context of the entire case history and current level and type of services provided to the individual.

SLD identification, a basic eligibility requirement contained in the legal and clinical prescriptions for diagnosing SLD refers to whether the suspected learning problem(s) result(s) in significant or substantial academic failure or other restrictions or limitations in daily life functioning.

The legal and diagnostic specifications of SLD necessitate that practitioners review the whole of the collected data and make a professional judgment about the extent of the adverse impact that any measured deficit has on an individual's performance in one or more areas of learning or academic achievement. Essentially, Level 5 analysis serves as a kind of quality control test designed to prevent the application of an SLD diagnosis in cases in which "real-world" functioning is not in fact impaired or substantially limited as compared to same-age peers in the general population, regardless of the patterns seen in the data.

This final criterion requires practitioners to take a very broad survey not only of the entire array of data collected during the assessment but also of the real-world manifestations and practical implications of any presumed disability. In general, if the criteria at Levels 1 through 4 were met, it is likely that, in the vast majority of cases, Level 5 analysis serves only to support conclusions that already have been drawn. However, in cases in which data may be equivocal or when procedures or criteria other than those specified in the DD/C model have been used, Level 5 analysis becomes an important safety valve, ensuring that any representations of SLD suggested by the data are indeed manifest in observable impairments in one or more areas of functioning in real-life settings.

The final section of this chapter walks the reader through three simple steps that ensure that the data necessary for conducting a PSW analysis following the DD/C model have been entered into X-BASS appropriately. Following these three steps, guidance on how to view and understand program output is provided.

USING X-BASS FOR SLD IDENTIFICATION: THREE STEPS TO PSW OUTPUT

While reading the information in this section, having the X-BASS program open will be helpful. The data that are used here are those from the case of Amanda (McDonough, 2017). Note that this case as originally presented by McDonough was modified here to demonstrate different features of X-BASS. As part of Amanda's evaluation for suspected SLD she was administered the WISC-V, WIAT-III, and selected tests from the CTOPP-2 (see Rapid Reference 11.15).

☰ Rapid Reference 11.15

WISC-V, WIAT-III, and CTOPP-2 Data from the Case of Amanda

Composites	Scores	Percentile Rank	Classification
Full Scale IQ Score	91	27	Average
Verbal Comprehension Index (VCI or Gc)	100	50	Average
Similarities	10		Average
Vocabulary	10		Average
Fluid Reasoning Index (FRI or Gf)	97	42	Average
Matrix Reasoning	9		Average
Figure Weights	10		Average
Visual Spatial Index (VSI or Gv)	81	16	Low average
Block Design	6		Below average
Visual Puzzles	7		Low average
Working Memory Index (WMI or Gsm)	85	16	Low average
Digit Span	8		Average
Picture Span	7		Low average
Processing Speed Index (PSI or Gs)	92	30	Average
Coding	8		Average
Symbol Search	9		Average
Naming Speed Index	99	47	Average
Naming Speed Literacy	98		Average
Naming Speed Quantity	102		Average
Symbol Translation Index	102	55	Average
Immediate Symbol Translation	102		Average
Delayed Symbol Translation	102		Average
Recognition Symbol Translation	104		Average
Storage and Retrieval Index	100	50	Average
Oral Language	96	53	Average
Listening Comprehension	96	39	Average
Oral Expression	98	45	Average

(*continued*)

Composites	Scores	Percentile Rank	Classification
Total Reading	76	5	Well below average
Basic Reading	81	10	Below average
Word Reading	77	6	Well below average
Pseudoword Decoding	85	16	Low average
Reading Comprehension and Fluency	73	4	Below average
Reading Comprehension	79	8	Well below average
Oral Reading Fluency	74	4	Well below average
Mathematics	90	25	Average
Math Problem-Solving	83	13	Below average
Numerical Operations	99	47	Average
Math Fluency	89	23	Average
Math Fluency–Addition	89	23	Average
Math Fluency–Subtraction	91	27	Average
Written Expression	82	12	Below average
Spelling	74	4	Well below average
Sentence Composition	94	34	Average
Phonetic Coding: Analysis	85	16	Low average
Phoneme Isolation	7	16	Low average
Segmenting Nonwords	8	25	Average
Phonetic Coding: Synthesis	49	0.1	Extremely below average
Blending Words	2	0.1	Extremely below average
Blending Nonwords	1	0.1	Extremely below average

Source: McDonough (2017).

Getting Started

X-BASS opens to a Welcome screen (see Figure 11.1). From this screen, click on the User Guide button for general operating instructions (see Figure 11.2). This tab provides just about all the information you will need to get started and contains many frequently asked questions about X-BASS. The User Guide may be printed for easy reference.

Cross-Battery Assessment Software System (X-BASS® v2.1)

Conceptualization by D.P. Flanagan, S.O. Ortiz, V.C. Alfonso; Programming by S.O. Ortiz and A.M. Dynda
Copyright © 2017 Samuel O. Ortiz, Dawn P. Flanagan & Vincent C. Alfonso. All Rights Reserved

Release: 2.1

Beginner Mode:

If you are new to XBA or X-BASS, click the "Beginner Mode" button for step by step guidance and assistance in using X-BASS. This option is strongly recommended for first time users of X-BASS.

Beginner Mode

Essentials of Cross-Battery Assessment, 3rd Edition remains the reference document necessary for understanding Cross-Battery Assessment (XBA) and the principles upon which the X-BASS is based.

X-BASS is an automated Cross-Battery data management system with integrated, single-entry data management across all programs (XBA Analyzer, PSW Analyzer, and C-LIM Analyzer) that facilitates data analysis and enhances interpretation. In addition, X-BASS includes enhanced features for data entry and organization, program navigation, composite and subtest selection, and automatic and selective graphing of scores. Special provisions for determination of specific learning disability via interactive PSW analyses and assistance with understanding test score validity for English language learners are also included.

Quick Start:

New users should read the User Guide. Advanced users can set the User Mode and go directly to the Start or Index tab.

Guide **Start** **Index**

What's New?

Click here to find out more about the new features and changes to the current version of X-BASS.

What's New

User Mode
○ Beginner
○ Intermediate
● Advanced

X-BASS ™

Cross-Battery Assessment
Software System 2.0

ACCESS CODE

Samuel O. Ortiz
Dawn P. Flanagan
Vincent C. Alfonso

WILEY

Cross-Battery **XBA**
Assessment

Figure 11.1 X-BASS Welcome Screen

Cross-Battery Assessment Software System (X-BASS® v2.1)

User Guide

Conceptualization by D.P. Flanagan, S.O. Ortiz, V.C. Alfonso; Programming by S.O. Ortiz and A.M. Dynda
Copyright © 2017 Samuel O. Ortiz, Dawn P. Flanagan & Vincent C. Alfonso. All Rights Reserved

Index   Tab Help   Start   Next Step

Data Organizer   S&W Indicator   PSW-A Data Summary

WISC-V WAIS-IV WPPSI-IV WIAT-III WJ IV COG WJ IV OL WJ IV ACH KABC-II KTEA-3 CAS2 DAS-II SB5

XBA Analyzer PSW Analyzer C-LIM Analyzer

NOTE: X-BASS does NOT use or calculate subtest raw scores and is NOT a test scoring program. Users of this software are responsible for following all test publishers' administration and scoring guidelines. All scores entered into X-BASS must be derived from use of each test's respective norms and via the specific procedures provided by the respective test publishers. All instructions regarding operation of X-BASS must be reviewed carefully prior to use.

FOR BEST VIEWING, SET YOUR WINDOW TO CORRESPOND TO THE WIDTH OF THIS LINE

User Guide and General Operating Instructions

New users should begin by scrolling down to read all the instructions and specific tab notes and click 'Beginner Mode' before proceeding. Users may click on the button below to the right to print the User Guide and General Operating Instructions for reference. Experienced users may set the desired mode manually and then click the Start button to go to the main tab and begin program operation.

Beginner Mode

X-BASS may now be run in three user modes. The default setting is the "Beginner Mode" which will display step by step guidance in using the program and applying XBA rules, in addition to the typical error, confirmation, results, and warning messages. This setting is recommended for first time users or users who are not yet very familiar with X-BASS operations and XBA procedures. "Intermediate Mode" displays only typical messages without much guidance. "Advanced Mode" suppresses all messages except results and critical ones or those that require user input. This mode is recommended only for experienced users of X-BASS; however, the mode can be changed at any time during program operation.

User Mode
○ Beginner - show all messages
○ Intermediate - show most messages
◉ Advanced - hide most messages

Troubleshooting   **Print User Guide**

Quick Start Instructions and Notes:

• Each time the program is opened, if an internet connection is available, it will automatically check for an updated version. If one is found, a pop up message will occur recommending download and installation of the update. Any pop up "Security Warning: Data connections disabled" messages can be dismissed or enabled. In addition, a black button at the bottom right of the Start tab allows for manually checking to see if an update to X-BASS is available.

• Clicking the Start button takes you to the "Start and Data Record Management" tab. There you can either enter new demographic information and create a new record or open a saved data record.

• Creating a new record takes you to the "Test Index and Main Navigation" tab; opening a saved record populates all data from that record and prompts you to click on the Index tab or stay on the Start tab.

• Select the core battery used in your assessment (or for ELLs, the C-LIM Index) and click on its button it to go to the tab for that battery.

• If entering data for a new record, enter the examinee's obtained composite and subtest scores on all appropriate tabs.

• X-BASS automatically evaluates or analyzes most composites for cohesion and provides a statement regarding whether the composite is cohesive. A recommendation for follow up is also provided.

• X-BASS provides percentile ranks for all composites and subtest scores and graphs all scores based on a 68% confidence interval (CI), unless the optional 90%CI or 95%CI is selected. Selection buttons for the CI are at the bottom of each tab.

Figure 11.2 User Guide Tab in X-BASS (Top Portion of Tab)

On the User Guide tab, click the round Start button in the upper-right corner, which takes you to the Start and Data Record Management tab (see Figure 11.3). Identifying information is entered on this tab. Figure 11.3 shows the identifying information that was entered for Amanda. Once this information is entered, click on the Create New Record button, which is the top button in the far-right column. The program will take a few seconds to create the new record and then automatically advance to the Test Index and Main Navigation tab (or Index tab for short; see Figure 11.4). As may been seen by the number of buttons on this tab, X-BASS has many functions and all of them can be accessed by clicking the appropriate button. Although this chapter only focuses on the DD/C PSW component of X-BASS, individual video tutorials are available at www .crossbattery.com that demonstrate additional functions of the software.

Step 1. Enter Individual Test Data and Cross-Battery Data into X-BASS and Transfer the Best Estimates of Cognitive and Academic Performance to the Data Organizer Tab

1.1 WISC-V Data. Click on the WISC-V button on the Index tab, which will automatically advance to the WISC-V Data Analysis tab (see Figure 11.5). All WISC-V data may be entered on this tab. Once data are entered, the program provides information regarding whether the indexes and global ability scores are cohesive and whether follow up assessment is considered necessary. The meaning of cohesion and follow-up are explained in the following "Don't Forget." Note that Figure 11.5 shows only the top of the WISC-V Data Analysis tab. Scrolling down this tab will reveal all the WISC-V indexes, global scores, and new clinical composites (see Flanagan & Alfonso, 2017, for details).

DON'T FORGET

Cohesion: A composite is considered cohesive when the variation in the scores that comprise it is not unusual in the general population. Common variation in scores comprising a composite suggests that the composite provides a good summary of the theoretically related abilities it was intended to represent.

Cohesion Analysis for WISC-V Index Scales

Finding	Interpretation
The difference between scaled scores is not significant or rare.	The difference between the scaled scores that comprise the index is not significant and a difference of this size occurs in more than 10% of the general population, which makes it relatively common. The composite is, therefore, cohesive and considered to be a good summary of the theoretically related abilities it was intended to represent.

(continued)

Finding	Interpretation
The difference between scaled scores is significant but not rare.	Although the difference between the scaled scores that comprise the index is significant, a difference of this size occurs in at least 10% of the general population, which makes it relatively common. Therefore, clinical judgment is needed to determine whether the composite is cohesive and likely to provide an adequate summary of the theoretically related abilities it was intended to represent.
The difference between scores is significant and rare.	The difference between the scaled scores that comprise the index is significant and considered rare, occurring in about 10% (or less) of the general population. Therefore, the index is not cohesive, meaning that it most likely is not a good summary of the theoretically related abilities it was intended to represent. Interestingly, even when a composite obscures important information about an individual's strengths and weaknesses due to unusual variation in the scores that comprise it, the composite is considered the best estimate of the latent construct it is intended to represent (see Schneider & Roman, 2018). Notwithstanding, further investigation of unusual variation is often warranted from a clinical standpoint (see Flanagan & Alfonso, 2017, for a discussion).

Follow-up: Regardless of index cohesion, it is important to consider whether follow-up assessment is necessary based on an analysis of where scaled scores within an index scale fall relative to each other and relative to most people. X-BASS analyzes each of these factors and then provides guidance regarding Primary Index Scale interpretation.

Examples of Follow-up Assessment

Additional Data Collection	Review of Existing Data
Investigation of narrow ability performance via administration of standardized, norm-referenced tests	Evaluation of existing data is given to determine if it corroborates current test performance (e.g., classroom work samples reveal manifestations of current cognitive ability weakness or deficit).
Informal assessment of the manifestations of an ability weakness or deficit (e.g., curriculum-based measures, state or local exams)	Outside evaluation corroborates current findings.
Formal and informal testing of hypotheses regarding variation in task characteristics and task demands	Professional, teacher, parent, or student report corroborates current findings.
Outside evaluation of disorder or condition that may adversely affect test performance (e.g., neuropsychological evaluation of attention-deficit hyperactivity disorder, psychological evaluation of emotional or personality functioning, functional behavioral assessment)	Error analysis explains inconsistencies in current data or reasons for weak or deficient performance.
Consultation with parents, teachers, or other professionals	Demand analysis explains inconsistencies in current data or reasons for weak or deficient performance.
Classroom observations in areas of concerns	Review attempted interventions.

Cross-Battery Assessment Software System (X-BASS® v2.1)

Start and Data Record Management

Conceptualization by D.P. Flanagan, S.O. Ortiz, V.C. Alfonso; Programming by S.O. Ortiz and A.M. Dynda
Copyright © 2017 Samuel O. Ortiz, Dawn P. Flanagan & Vincent C. Alfonso. All Rights Reserved

Tab Help | Next Step | Index

WISC-V | WAIS-IV | WPPSI-IV | WIAT-III | WJ IV COG | WJ IV ACH | WJ IV OL | KABC-II | KTEA-3 | CAS2 | DAS-II | SB5

To SET or change user mode for X-BASS, use the buttons to the right. Beginner Mode displays additional guidance and assistance in using the program. Intermediate mode displays typical informational and confirmational messages. Advanced mode suppresses all except critical messages.

User Mode: ○ Beginner ○ Intermediate ● Advanced

1. ENTER NAME [if new case]

*Name of Examinee:	Amanda Farris
Name of Evaluator:	Dr. Erin McDonough
Examinee's Age:	8 years 3 month(s)

2. ENTER DATES/GRADE

*Date of Evaluation:	1/4/2016	Use mm/dd/yyyy
*Date of Birth:	10/1/2007	If an error occurs, try yyyy/mm/dd.
*Examinee's Grade:	2	PK,K,1-12,12+

3. CREATE NEW DATA RECORD

Create New Record

Check box if examinee is current of former ELL ☐

DATA RECORD IS ACTIVE

OPEN SAVED DATA RECORD

Amanda Farris ▶

Save Current Record

Export Current Database

Import Saved Database

Clear Data/Reset Program

Delete Record

Check for Updates

To OPEN and activate a saved record from the database, select it from the dropdown menu on the right. Data records are listed in alphabetical order by first name. Once selected, all data associated with the record will be populated in the appropriate locations. Click the Index button at the upper right corner of this tab to begin reviewing and updating the saved data. The program can store and retrieve data for up to 500 cases.

To SAVE or update the current data record, click the blue "Save Current Record" button and continue working. Frequent saves are recommended.

To EXPORT and save the current database (for importation to a newer version of X-BASS), click the "Export Current Database" button. This action creates a file that can be used by updated versions of X-BASS to automatically transfer and merge the current database for use with the new version.

To IMPORT a saved database (for use in a newer version of X-BASS), click the "Import Saved Database" button. Note that you must have already exported the previous database using the older version of X-BASS. Once the older database has been properly saved, use this button to import it.

To CLEAR all scores, selections, and tab data in current use from the program, click the "Clear Data/Reset Program" button. CAUTION: This action is not reversible, removes data in current use, and resets the program to default values. Unsaved data and information will be permanently erased.

To DELETE a saved data record, select the record from the dropdown menu and click the "Delete Record" button. CAUTION: Make sure this is what you want to do because this action is not reversible.

To CHECK for updates to X-BASS, click the "Check for Updates" button. Note: an internet connection is required to determine if an update is available.

Figure 11.3 Start and Data Record Management Tab in X-BASS

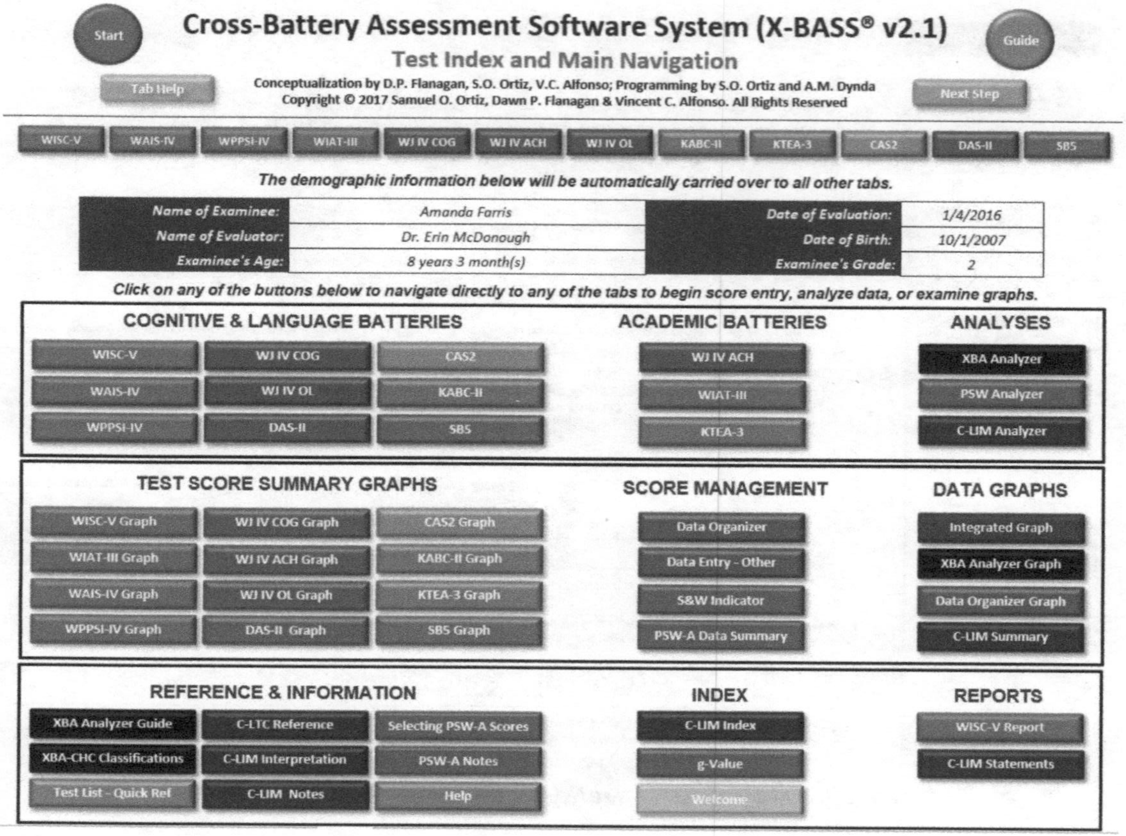

Figure 11.4 Test Index and Main Navigation Tab in X-BASS

Cross-Battery Assessment Software System (X-BASS® v2.1)

WISC-V® Data Analysis

XBA Analyzer
Data Organizer
C-LIM Summary

Start
Tab Help
Next Step
Index

WISC-V Graph
Integrated Graph
C-LIM Analyzer

Name: *Amanda Farris*

Grade: 2

Age: *8 years 3 month(s)*

Date: *1/4/2016*

(age range = 6.0 - 16:11)

WISC-V | WAIS-IV | WPPSI-IV | WIAT-III | WJ IV COG | WJ IV ACH | WJ IV OL | KABC-II | KTEA-3 | CAS2 | DAS-II | SB5

Index Name (check box for integrated graph)	Enter scores	PR	Transfer scores	Criteria for Cohesion: Is variability...		Follow up Recommendations
				significant or substantial?	Infrequent or uncommon?	Do the results suggest a need for follow up?
Subtest Name						
Verbal Comprehension Index (VCI/Gc)	100	50	☐	No	No	No, not considered necessary
				COHESIVE		**Gc:VL = 100** Transfer to Data Organizer
Similarities (Gc:VL,GfI)	10	50	☐			
Vocabulary (VL)	10	50	☐			
Information (K0)			☐			
Comprehension (K0)			☐			

The VCI provides an estimate of Crystallized Intelligence (Gc). Gc refers to an individual's knowledge base (or general fund of information) that develops as a result of exposure to language, culture, general life experiences, and formal schooling. Word knowledge as measured by the Vocabulary subtest was Average, and the ability to reason with words as measured by the Similarities subtest was Average relative to same age peers. The difference between the scores that comprise the VCI is not significant and a difference of this size is considered common in the general population. This means that the VCI is a good summary of Crystallized Intelligence. The individual's VCI of 100 (86-104) is classified as Average and is ranked at the 50th percentile, indicating performance as good as or better than 50% of same age peers from the general population.

Because the difference between the scores that comprise the VCI is not substantial (less than ½ SD) and both scores are at least average, follow up is not considered necessary.

Fluid Reasoning Index (FRI/Gf)	97	42	☐	No	No	No, not considered necessary
				COHESIVE		**Gf = 97** Transfer to Data Organizer
Matrix Reasoning (I)	9	37	☐			
Figure Weights (RG,RQ)	10	50	☐			
Picture Concepts (I)			☐			
Arithmetic (Gsm:MW,Gq:A3)			☐			

The FRI provides an estimate of Fluid Reasoning (Gf). Gf refers to a type of thinking that an individual may use when faced with a relatively new or novel task that cannot be performed automatically. Inductive reasoning as measured by the Matrix Reasoning subtest was Average and general sequential (deductive) reasoning and quantitative reasoning as measured by the Figure Weights subtest was Average relative to same age peers. The difference between the scores that comprise the FRI is not significant and a difference of this size is considered common in the general population. This means that the FRI is a good summary of Fluid Reasoning. The FRI of 97 (93-101) is classified as Average and is ranked at the 42nd percentile, indicating performance as good as or better than 42% of same age peers from the general population.

Because the difference between the scores that comprise the FRI is not substantial (less than ½ SD) and both scores are at least average, follow up is not considered necessary.

Figure 11.5 WISC-V Data Analysis Tab in X-BASS (Top Portion of Tab)

After entering all WISC-V data, evaluate the results of the cohesion and follow-up analyses. If indexes are cohesive and follow-up is not considered necessary, then click on the Transfer to Data Organizer button corresponding to each index. This button is in the far-right column of the WISC-V Data Analysis tab. For example, Figure 11.5 shows that the WISC-V VCI and FRI are cohesive, meaning that they each provide a good summary of the theoretically related abilities they were intended to represent. In addition, follow-up was not considered necessary for either of these Index scales. If the evaluator is confident that these indexes adequately represent the individual's performance in these cognitive domains (i.e., Gc:VL [Lexical Knowledge] for VCI, Gf [Fluid Reasoning] for FRI), then she or he may transfer the estimates of these abilities to the Data Organizer tab. In the case of Amanda, all her Index scales were cohesive and did not require follow-up. Therefore, in addition to VCI and FRI, the VSI (Gv:Vz [Visualization]), WMI (Gsm), PSI (Gs), and SRI (Glr) were transferred to the Data Organizer tab.

Note that the Data Organizer tab "holds" all the best estimates of the cognitive, academic, and neuropsychological constructs that were evaluated and transferred there until the user is ready to move forward with analysis of the data (see Step 2). When follow-up is considered necessary in any given domain, more than one estimate of performance in that domain may be transferred to the Data Organizer tab. For example, in the area of Glr, the individual may have performed in the average range on tests of Associative Memory (MA; Symbol Translation Index [STI]) and in the Well Below Average range on tests of Naming Facility (NA; Naming Speed Index [NSI]) and the difference between the STI and NSI may be statistically significant and unusual. In this case, two estimates of Glr (STI and NSI) may be transferred to the Data Organizer tab, in lieu of the SRI, to best represent the individual's range of performance (or strengths and weaknesses) in Glr. However, it is important to note that even when a composite is not cohesive (in this case, the SRI), it remains the best estimate of the latent construct (i.e., Glr; see Schneider & Roman, 2017). Notwithstanding, from a clinical standpoint, composites that are not cohesive often obscure important information about an individual's strengths and weaknesses within a cognitive domain. To best understand functioning in a broad cognitive ability domain when the broad ability composite is not cohesive, report and interpret the overall composite as the best estimate of the broad ability along with separate composites within the broad ability domain to assist in understanding strengths and weaknesses that are obscured by the broad ability composite. When separate composites are calculated in X-BASS, they should be used in PSW analysis because they are better representations of the individual's strengths and weaknesses within a broad ability domain, especially when they have ecological validity. The following "Don't Forget" provides a flowchart that illustrates best practices in reporting composites and determining which ones are most important for PSW analysis.

DON'T FORGET

Best Practices in Reporting and Interpreting Two-Subtest Composites with Emphasis on Cohesion and Follow up Assessment

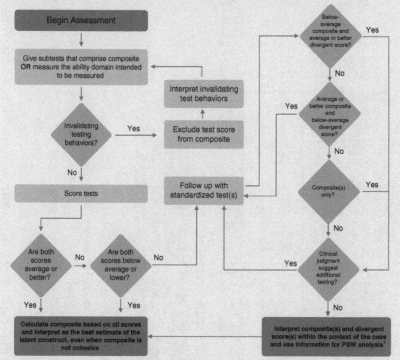

[1] For the purpose of PSW analysis, when composites are not cohesive and alternative composites are derived after follow-up assessment, they should be used in PSW analysis in lieu of a composite based on all scores because they better represent the individual's unique strengths and weaknesses, particularly when they have ecological validity.

Source: This flowchart was adapted from Schneider and Roman (2017).

1.2 CTOPP-2 Data. Because the WISC-V measures six of the required seven areas necessary to conduct a PSW analysis following the DD/C model, selected subtests of the CTOPP-2 were administered to measure the seventh area (i.e., Ga). Specifically, the evaluator administered the Blending Nonwords and Phoneme Isolation subtests. Amanda's performance on these subtests is shown in Figure 11.6. Whether you follow the flowchart in the previous "Don't Forget"

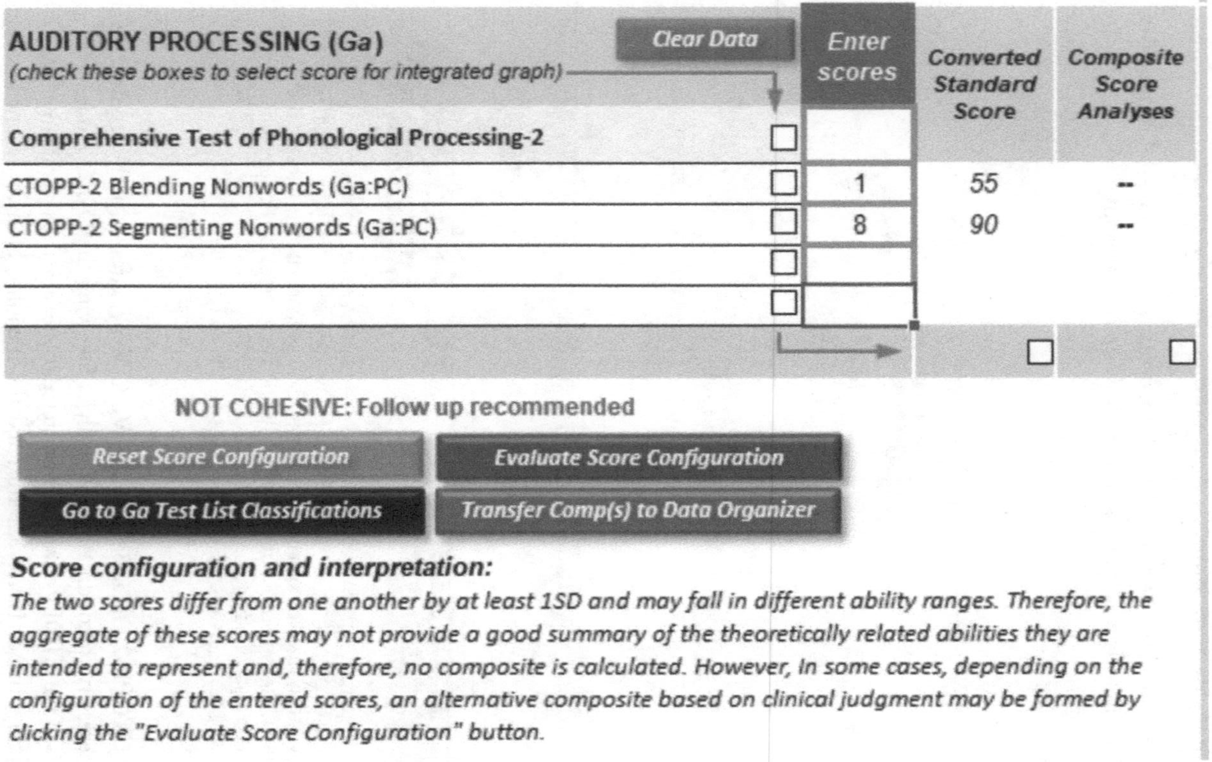

AUDITORY PROCESSING (Ga)
(check these boxes to select score for integrated graph)

	Enter scores	Converted Standard Score	Composite Score Analyses
Comprehensive Test of Phonological Processing-2			
CTOPP-2 Blending Nonwords (Ga:PC)	1	55	--
CTOPP-2 Segmenting Nonwords (Ga:PC)	8	90	--

NOT COHESIVE: Follow up recommended

[Clear Data]

[Reset Score Configuration]   [Evaluate Score Configuration]

[Go to Ga Test List Classifications]   [Transfer Comp[s] to Data Organizer]

Score configuration and interpretation:

The two scores differ from one another by at least 1SD and may fall in different ability ranges. Therefore, the aggregate of these scores may not provide a good summary of the theoretically related abilities they are intended to represent and, therefore, no composite is calculated. However, in some cases, depending on the configuration of the entered scores, an alternative composite based on clinical judgment may be formed by clicking the "Evaluate Score Configuration" button.

Figure 11.6 Analysis of Selected Subtests from the CTOPP-2 on the XBA Analyzer Tab of X-BASS: Follow-up Assessment on Lower Score Recommended

or the recommendations in X-BASS, the recommendation is to follow up on the lower score performance. The evaluator chose to follow up with two additional tests from the CTOPP-2 (i.e., Blending Words and Segmenting Nonwords). Amanda's performance on these additional subtests is shown in Figure 11.7. Given the substantial variation in Amanda's performance on the CTOPP-2 (i.e., $2\frac{2}{3}$ SD difference between her highest and lowest scores), the XBA Analyzer tab provided two separate estimates of Ga (also shown in Figure 11.7)—one that represents Phonetic Coding: Analysis (SS = 86) and one that represents Phonetic Coding: Synthesis (SS = 52). Following the guidance in the flowchart and in X-BASS, these composites best represent Amanda's strengths and weaknesses within the Ga domain and, therefore, should be transferred to the Data Organizer tab for inclusion in PSW analysis. The arrow in Figure 11.7 points to the button that transfers these composites to the Data Organizer tab.

However, note that the flowchart also indicates that even if a composite is not cohesive, it remains the best estimate of the measured construct. Therefore, the XBA Analyzer tab also includes an "Evaluate Score Configuration" button (which is directly above the button that the arrow is pointing to in Figure 11.7). When that button is clicked, an option will appear that allows a composite to be calculated based on all scores (see Figure 11.8). Once that option is selected, X-BASS reports a composite based on all scores (see Figure 11.9).

1.3. WIAT-III Data. Click on the WIAT-III button located at the top of any of the tabs already mentioned. All WIAT-III data may be entered on the WIAT-III Data Analysis tab. Once data are entered, the program provides information regarding whether the composites are cohesive and whether follow-up assessment is considered necessary. Figure 11.10 shows the WIAT-III Data Analysis tab with Amanda's data. Of note, there are composites on all achievement batteries that summarize different aspects of a broad domain, such as reading. For example, as may be seen in Figure 11.10, the WIAT-III Total Reading composite includes tests of basic reading skills (BRS), reading comprehension (RDC), and reading fluency (RDF). Although summary scores are useful in some instances and are often reported in psychoeducational evaluations, in X-BASS all achievement tests are classified according to the eight IDEA-specific areas of SLD. Therefore, achievement scores can be transferred to the Data Organizer tab only if they align with one of the eight areas. This is why there is no button in the far-right column of Figure 11.10 for the Total Reading score on the WIAT-III that would allow it to be transferred to the Data Organizer tab. However, because the WIAT-III Basic Reading Composite is composed of two subtests that were classified as BRS, the program allows the composite to be transferred to the Data Organizer tab (via the button in the far-right column next to "BRS = 81" in Figure 11.10).

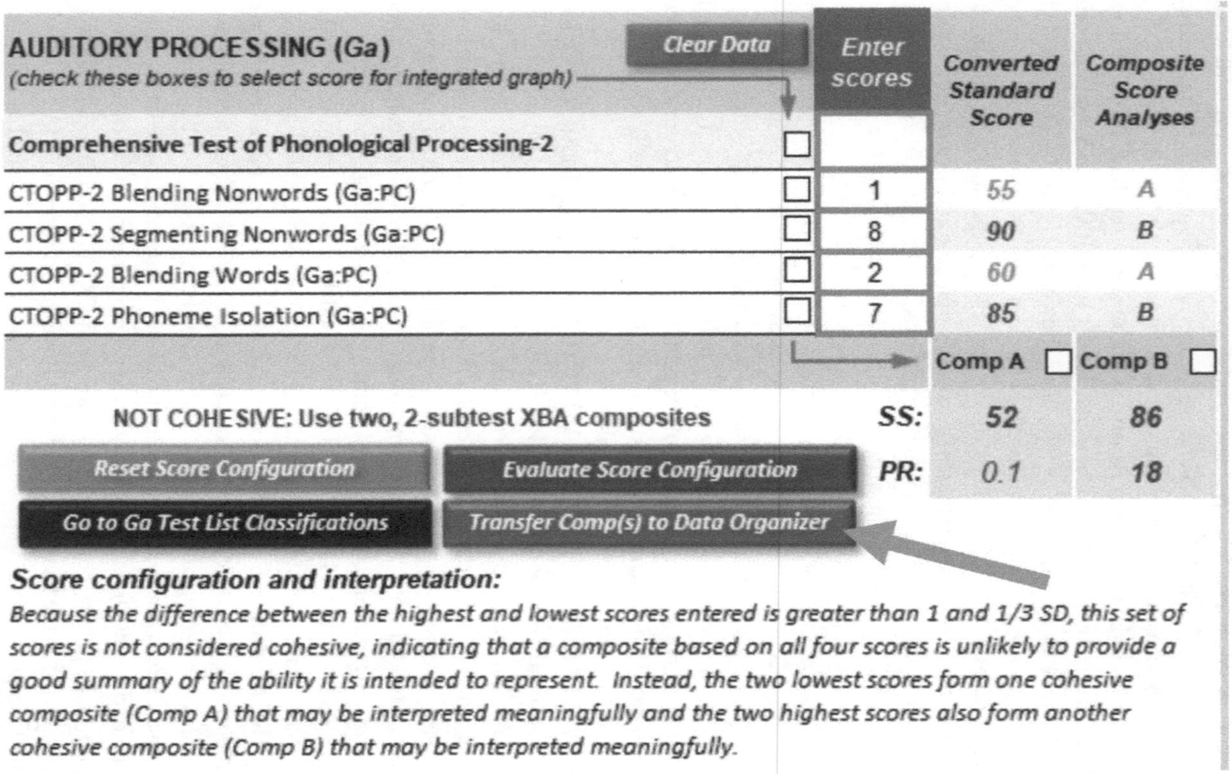

AUDITORY PROCESSING (Ga)
(check these boxes to select score for integrated graph)

Comprehensive Test of Phonological Processing-2	Enter scores	Converted Standard Score	Composite Score Analyses
CTOPP-2 Blending Nonwords (Ga:PC)	1	55	A
CTOPP-2 Segmenting Nonwords (Ga:PC)	8	90	B
CTOPP-2 Blending Words (Ga:PC)	2	60	A
CTOPP-2 Phoneme Isolation (Ga:PC)	7	85	B

Clear Data

	Comp A ☐	Comp B ☐
SS:	52	86
PR:	0.1	18

NOT COHESIVE: Use two, 2-subtest XBA composites

Reset Score Configuration	Evaluate Score Configuration
Go to Ga Test List Classifications	Transfer Comp(s) to Data Organizer

Score configuration and interpretation:

Because the difference between the highest and lowest scores entered is greater than 1 and 1/3 SD, this set of scores is not considered cohesive, indicating that a composite based on all four scores is unlikely to provide a good summary of the ability it is intended to represent. Instead, the two lowest scores form one cohesive composite (Comp A) that may be interpreted meaningfully and the two highest scores also form another cohesive composite (Comp B) that may be interpreted meaningfully.

Figure 11.7 Analysis of Follow-up Assessment Using Additional Tests from the CTOPP-2 on the XBA Analyzer Tab of X-BASS

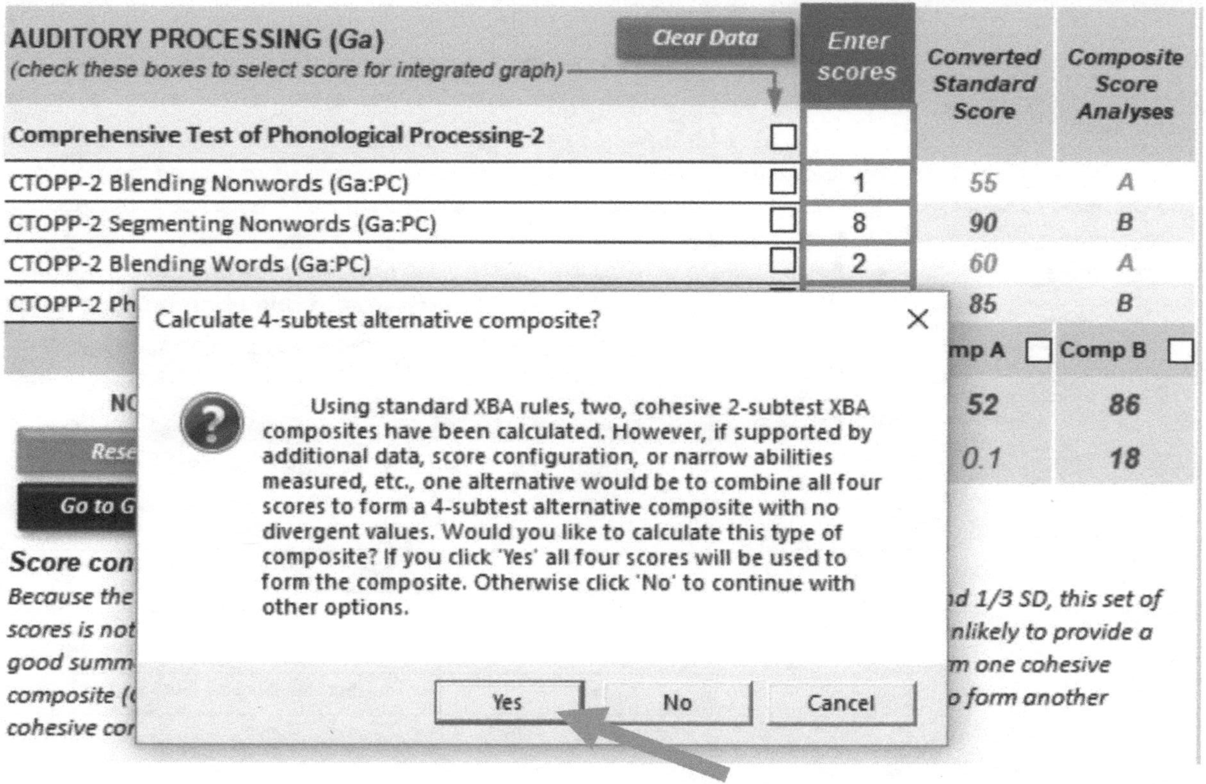

AUDITORY PROCESSING (Ga)
(check these boxes to select score for integrated graph)

Comprehensive Test of Phonological Processing-2	Clear Data	Enter scores	Converted Standard Score	Composite Score Analyses
	☐			
CTOPP-2 Blending Nonwords (Ga:PC)	☐	1	55	A
CTOPP-2 Segmenting Nonwords (Ga:PC)	☐	8	90	B
CTOPP-2 Blending Words (Ga:PC)	☐	2	60	A
CTOPP-2 Ph	☐		85	B
		Comp A ☐	Comp B ☐	
		52	86	
		0.1	18	

Calculate 4-subtest alternative composite?   ✕

❓ Using standard XBA rules, two, cohesive 2-subtest XBA composites have been calculated. However, if supported by additional data, score configuration, or narrow abilities measured, etc, one alternative would be to combine all four scores to form a 4-subtest alternative composite with no divergent values. Would you like to calculate this type of composite? If you click 'Yes' all four scores will be used to form the composite. Otherwise click 'No' to continue with other options.

[Yes]   [No]   [Cancel]

NO...
Rese...
Go to G...

Score con...
Because the
scores is not
good summ...
composite (...
cohesive co...

...d 1/3 SD, this set of
...nlikely to provide a
...m one cohesive
...o form another

Figure 11.8 Example of Option Provided by X-BASS to Allow Calculation of a Composite Based on All Tests That Were Administered, Regardless of Cohesion

Note: This feature of X-BASS was added based on the research conducted by Schneider and Roman (2017).

AUDITORY PROCESSING (Ga)
(check these boxes to select score for integrated graph)

Clear Data

Comprehensive Test of Phonological Processing-2	Enter scores	Converted Standard Score	Composite Score Analyses
CTOPP-2 Blending Nonwords (Ga:PC)	1	55	A
CTOPP-2 Segmenting Nonwords (Ga:PC)	8	90	A
CTOPP-2 Blending Words (Ga:PC)	2	60	A
CTOPP-2 Phoneme Isolation (Ga:PC)	7	85	A

Alt. Comp.

SS: **66**

PR: 1

Use the 4-subtest alternative composite

Reset Score Configuration

Evaluate Score Configuration

Go to Ga Test List Classifications

Transfer Comp(s) to Data Organizer

Score configuration and interpretation:
Although the four scores entered into this domain were either in different classification ranges or at least 1SD apart from each other, or both, an alternative composite has been formed using all four scores. Although this composite may be necessary for the purposes of SLD identification, particularly within a PSW framework, it may be clinically important to investigate the difference in performance relative to the narrow abilities being measured, particularly for any score that is about 1SD below the mean or lower.

Figure 11.9 Example Showing a Composite Based on All Scores

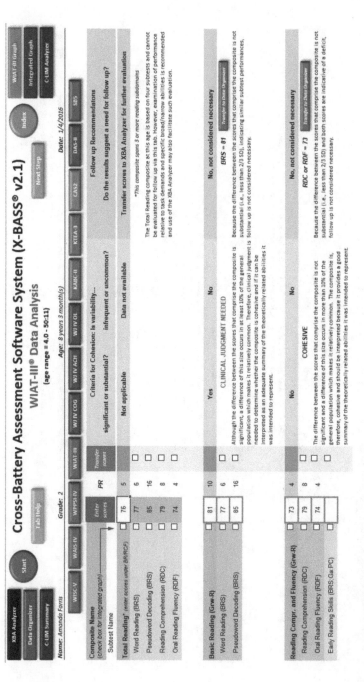

Figure 11.10 WIAT-III Data Analysis Tab in X-BASS

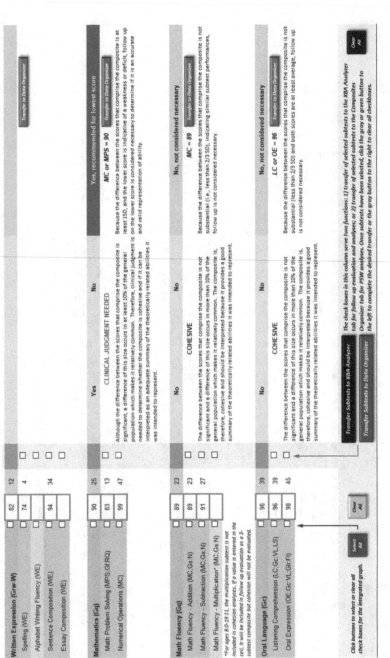

Figure 11.10 (Continued)

Note that the WIAT-III Reading Comprehension and Fluency composite is composed of a test of RDC and a test of RDF. Although this composite may be transferred to the Data Organizer tab, when the Transfer to Data Organizer button is pressed, a pop-up message will appear asking the evaluator whether she or he wants to transfer the composite to the RDC or RDF section of the Data Organizer tab. If the evaluator would prefer to transfer each subtest separately, then she or he should click on the box in the Transfer scores column to the right of the subtest scores and then scroll to the bottom of the tab and click on the Transfer Subtests to Data Organizer button (seen at the bottom of Figure 11.10). By clicking on this button, the Reading Comprehension subtest score will appear in the RDC section of the Data Organizer tab and the Oral Reading Fluency subtest score will appear in the RDF section of this tab. Figure 11.10 also shows that the subtests that comprise the Mathematics and Oral Language composites were selected for transfer to the Data Organizer tab, rather than the composites themselves, for the same reason—that is, these composites are each composed of subtests that measure two different IDEA-specific SLD areas.

Notice that the Written Expression composite in Figure 11.10 consists of subtests that have all been classified as the IDEA-specific SLD area of written expression (WE). As such, a cohesive WE composite may be transferred to the Data Organizer tab. In the case of Amanda, however, only two subtests were administered in the area of WE. Because these scores differ by over one SD, the boxes next to the subtest scores were selected for independent transfer to the Data Organizer tab. Overall, transferring achievement test scores separately (rather than the composites to which they contribute) allows estimates of specific skills to be evaluated independently in PSW analysis.

DON'T FORGET

Prior to transferring individual subtest scores to the Data Organizer tab, it is assumed that these scores are good representations of the individual's skill or ability in the areas represented by the scores. In other words, other data sources should be available that corroborate these score performances. If other data are not available, follow-up assessment may be warranted to investigate further score performances that suggest a weakness or deficit for the individual.

1.4. Cross-Battery (XBA) Data. Amanda's evaluator administered a test from the WJ IV and an additional test from the CTOPP-2 to follow up on her hypothesis that Amanda's reading difficulties may be related in part to an orthographic processing weakness or deficit. These data were entered into the Orthographic Processing (OP) section of the XBA Analyzer tab (see Figure 11.11). The OP XBA composite of 78 was transferred to the Data Organizer tab by clicking on the Transfer XBA Comp(s) to Data Organizer button.

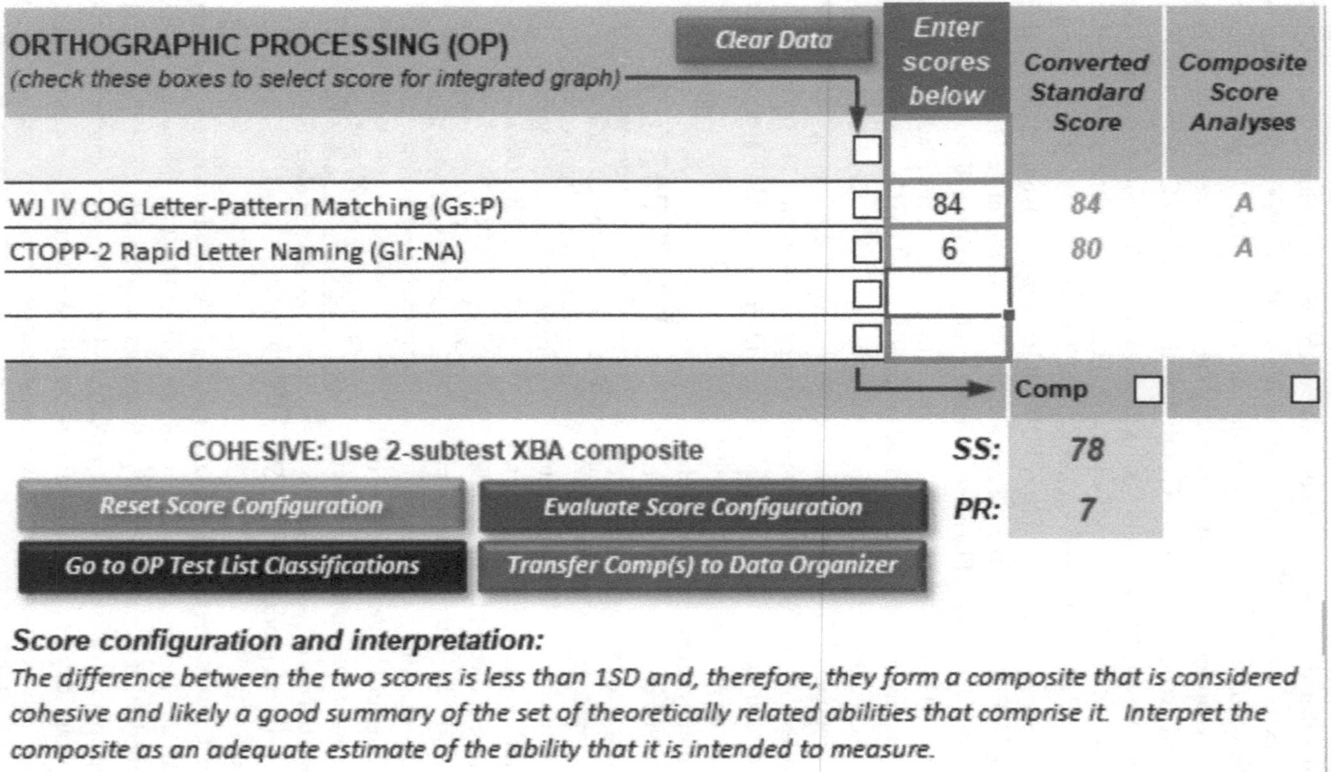

ORTHOGRAPHIC PROCESSING (OP)
(check these boxes to select score for integrated graph)

	Enter scores below	Converted Standard Score	Composite Score Analyses
☐			
WJ IV COG Letter-Pattern Matching (Gs:P)	84	84	A
CTOPP-2 Rapid Letter Naming (Glr:NA)	6	80	A
		Comp ☐	☐

COHESIVE: Use 2-subtest XBA composite

SS: 78   **PR:** 7

Reset Score Configuration	Evaluate Score Configuration
Go to OP Test List Classifications	Transfer Comp(s) to Data Organizer

Score configuration and interpretation:

The difference between the two scores is less than 1SD and, therefore, they form a composite that is considered cohesive and likely a good summary of the set of theoretically related abilities that comprise it. Interpret the composite as an adequate estimate of the ability that it is intended to measure.

Figure 11.11 Analysis of Selected Subtests on the XBA Analyzer Tab of X-BASS

Step 2. Select Scores from the Data Organizer Tab for Inclusion in the PSW Analysis

In Step 1, the best estimates of cognitive abilities and processes, academic achievement, and neuropsychological processes were transferred to the Data Organizer Tab. Figure 11.12 shows the Data Organizer tab with all of Amanda's data that were transferred from the WISC-V, WIAT-III, and XBA Analyzer tabs.

Step 2 requires that the evaluator select the scores from the Data Organizer tab that will be included in the PSW analysis by clicking the small box to the right of each score. Once selected, a check mark appears in the small box and the score itself is highlighted (see Figure 11.13). In most cases, all scores that were transferred to the Data Organizer tab are selected for inclusion in the PSW analysis. There may be times, however, when three scores are transferred to one or more of the CHC cognitive domains. Only two scores per CHC cognitive domain may be selected for inclusion in the PSW analysis. Up to three scores may be transferred to any of the IDEA-specific SLD areas, and up to three scores in each area may be selected for inclusion in the PSW analysis. Figure 11.13 shows some of the cognitive scores that were transferred from the WISC-V tab to the Data Organizer tab for inclusion in the PSW analysis. Note that the Data Organizer tab includes a button that is labeled "select ALL checkboxes" rather than selecting scores *individually* for inclusion in the PSW analysis; simply click this button and all scores on this tab will be selected automatically. If after all scores are selected and you wish to eliminate a score for some reason, then simply deselect it.

When a score is selected on the Data Organizer tab, it is automatically transferred to the Strengths and Weaknesses Indicator tab. After selecting all scores for inclusion in the PSW analysis, click on the top button in the far-right corner of the Data Organizer tab labeled S&W Indicator.

Step 3. Indicate Whether the Scores on the Strengths and Weaknesses Indicator Tab Represent a Strength or Weakness for the Individual

An individual's PSW ought to encompass the totality of the data gathered to the extent possible. The DD/C model encourages this perspective. Therefore, rather than simply selecting a single "strength" and a single "weakness" among many scores (as some PSW models require) the DD/C model requires that all scores representing cognitive, academic, and neuropsychological constructs be categorized by the evaluator as one or the other (as previously discussed in this chapter).

Cross-Battery Assessment Software System (X-BASS® v2.1)
Data Organizer and Score Summary

Conceptualization by D.P. Flanagan, S.O. Ortiz, V.C. Alfonso; Programming by S.O. Ortiz and A.M. Dynda
Copyright © 2017 Samuel O. Ortiz, Dawn P. Flanagan & Vincent C. Alfonso. All Rights Reserved

Start | Tab Help

XBA Analyzer | Data Entry - Other | C-LIM Summary

S&W Indicator | Data Organizer Graph | C-LIM Analyzer

Index | Next Step

WISC-V | WAIS-IV | WPPSI-IV | WIAT-III | WJ IV COG | WJ IV ACH | WJ IV OL | KABC-II | KTEA-3 | CAS2 | DAS-II | SB5

Selecting Scores for PSW Analyzer
Select All Checkboxes
Clear ALL Checkboxes

Name: Amanda Farris   **Age:** 8 years 3 month(s)   **Grade:** 2   **Date:** 1/4/2016

Guidelines for Selecting Best Composite Scores for SLD Evaluation

The purpose of this tab is to organize composites and subtests to assist in the selection of those to be used for evaluation of the pattern of strengths and weaknesses in the PSW Analyzer. Test names and scores can not be entered into this tab directly. Rather, this tab provides a summary of test battery and XBA composites that were transferred from other tabs because they were considered the best estimates of CHC abilities, academic areas, and selected neuropsychological domains. Use this tab to select the composites and subtest scores you would like to use in PSW analyses by clicking on the check box to the right of each one in any domain for which there are data. You may select up to two composites for each of the CHC broad ability (e.g., Gc, Gf, Gsm) and neuropsychological (e.g., Executive Functions, Orthographic Processing) domains and up to three scores for each of the academic areas. Note that you may also click on the "Data Organizer Graph" to view or print the information on this tab. For more information on how to select the best scores for use in PSW analyses, click the button to the right.

After you have made your selections, click the "S&W Indicator" button to continue with additional steps for conducting PSW analyses.

CRYSTALLIZED INTELLIGENCE (Gc)
Indicate which composite(s) you wish to use for PSW analyses. No more than two scores can be selected for this domain.

WISC-V Verbal Comprehension Index (Gc-VL)	100	☐ Test Comp Clear Score 1
		☐ Clear Score 2
		☐ Clear Score 3

FLUID REASONING (Gf)
Indicate which composite(s) you wish to use for PSW analyses. No more than two scores can be selected for this domain.

WISC-V Fluid Reasoning Index (Gf)	97	☐ Test Comp Clear Score 1
		☐ Clear Score 2
		☐ Clear Score 3

LONG-TERM STORAGE AND RETRIEVAL (Glr)
Indicate which composite(s) you wish to use for PSW analyses. No more than two scores can be selected for this domain.

WISC-V Storage and Retrieval Index (Glr)	100	☐ Test Comp Clear Score 1
		☐ Clear Score 2
		☐ Clear Score 3

SHORT-TERM MEMORY (Gsm)
Indicate which composite(s) you wish to use for PSW analyses. No more than two scores can be selected for this domain.

WISC-V Working Memory Index (Gsm)	85	☐ Test Comp Clear Score 1
		☐ Clear Score 2
		☐ Clear Score 3

VISUAL PROCESSING (Gv)
Indicate which composite(s) you wish to use for PSW analyses. No more than two scores can be selected for this domain.

WISC-V Visual Spatial Index (Gv/Vz)	81	☐ Test Comp Clear Score 1
		☐ Clear Score 2
		☐ Clear Score 3

AUDITORY PROCESSING (Ga)
Indicate which composite(s) you wish to use for PSW analyses. No more than two scores can be selected for this domain.

Auditory Processing (Ga)	49	☐ Comp A Clear Score 1
Auditory Processing (Ga)	85	☐ Comp B Clear Score 2
		☐ Clear Score 3

Figure 11.12 Data Organizer Tab in X-BASS

PROCESSING SPEED (Gs)

Indicate which composite(s) you wish to use for PSW analyses. No more than two scores can be selected for this domain.

WISC-V Processing Speed Index (Gs)	92	☐ Test Comp	Clear Score 1
		☐	Clear Score 2
		☐	Clear Score 3

DOMAIN SPECIFIC KNOWLEDGE (Gkn)

Indicate which composite(s) you wish to use for PSW analyses. No more than two scores can be selected for this domain.

☐		Clear Score 1
☐		Clear Score 2
☐		Clear Score 3

BASIC READING SKILLS (BRS)

Indicate which composite or subtests you wish to use for PSW analyses. All three scores may be selected for this domain.

WIAT-III Basic Reading Skills (BRS)	81	☐ Test Comp	Clear Score 1
WIAT-III Word Reading (BRS;Grw-R:RD)	77	☐ Subtest	Clear Score 2
WIAT-III Pseudoword Decoding (BRS;Grw-R:RD)	85	☐ Subtest	Clear Score 3

READING COMPREHENSION (RDC)

Indicate which composite or subtests you wish to use for PSW analyses. All three scores may be selected for this domain.

WIAT-III Reading Comprehension (RDC;Grw-R:RC)	79	☐ Subtest	Clear Score 1
		☐ Subtest	Clear Score 2
		☐ Subtest	Clear Score 3

READING FLUENCY (RDF)

Indicate which composite or subtests you wish to use for PSW analyses. All three scores may be selected for this domain.

WIAT-III Oral Reading Fluency (RDF;Grw-R:RS)	74	☐ Subtest	Clear Score 1
		☐	Clear Score 2
		☐	Clear Score 3

WRITTEN EXPRESSION (WE)

Indicate which composite or subtests you wish to use for PSW analyses. All three scores may be selected for this domain.

WIAT-III Written Expression (WE)	82	☐ Test Comp	Clear Score 1
WIAT-III Spelling (WE;Grw-W:SG)	74	☐ Subtest	Clear Score 2
WIAT-III Sentence Composition (WE;Grw-W:EU,WA)	94	☐ Subtest	Clear Score 3

MATH CALCULATION (MC)

Indicate which composite or subtests you wish to use for PSW analyses. All three scores may be selected for this domain.

WIAT-III Math Fluency (MC)	89	☐ Test Comp	Clear Score 1
WIAT-III Numerical Operations (MC;Gq:A3)	99	☐ Subtest	Clear Score 2
		☐	Clear Score 3

MATH PROBLEM SOLVING (MPS)

Indicate which composite or subtests you wish to use for PSW analyses. All three scores may be selected for this domain.

WIAT-III Math Problem Solving (MPS;Gq:A3;GfRQ)	83	☐ Subtest	Clear Score 1
		☐ Subtest	Clear Score 2
		☐ Subtest	Clear Score 3

ORAL EXPRESSION (OE)

Indicate which composite or subtests you wish to use for PSW analyses. All three scores may be selected for this domain.

WIAT-III Oral Expression (Gc:VL,Glr:Fl;OE)	98	☐ Subtest	Clear Score 1
		☐	Clear Score 2
		☐	Clear Score 3

LISTENING COMPREHENSION (LC)

Indicate which composite or subtests you wish to use for PSW analyses. All three scores may be selected for this domain.

WIAT-III Listening Comprehension (Gc:VL,LS;LC)	96	☐ Subtest	Clear Score 1
		☐	Clear Score 2
		☐	Clear Score 3

Figure 11.12 (Continued)

ORAL EXPRESSION (OE)

Indicate which composite or subtests you wish to use for PSW analyses. All three scores may be selected for this domain.

WIAT-III Oral Expression (Gc·VL,Glr:FI:OE) | 98 | ☐ Subtest | Clear Score 1
| | ☐ | Clear Score 2
| | ☐ | Clear Score 3

LISTENING COMPREHENSION (LC)

Indicate which composite or subtests you wish to use for PSW analyses. All three scores may be selected for this domain.

WIAT-III Listening Comprehension (Gc·VL,LS:LC) | 96 | ☐ Subtest | Clear Score 1
| | ☐ | Clear Score 2
| | ☐ | Clear Score 3

LEARNING EFFICIENCY (LE)

Indicate which composite(s) you wish to use for PSW analyses. No more than two scores can be selected for this domain.

☐ Clear Score 1
☐ Clear Score 2
☐ Clear Score 3

ORTHOGRAPHIC PROCESSING (OP)

Indicate which composite(s) you wish to use for PSW analyses. No more than two scores can be selected for this domain.

Orthographic Processing (OP) | 78 | ☐ Comp | Clear Score 1
| | ☐ | Clear Score 2
| | ☐ | Clear Score 3

Figure 11.12 (Continued)

Cross-Battery Assessment Software System (X-BASS® v2.1)

Data Organizer and Score Summary

Conceptualization by D.P. Flanagan, S.O. Ortiz, V.C. Alfonso; Programming by S.O. Ortiz and A.M. Dynda
Copyright © 2017 Samuel O. Ortiz, Dawn P. Flanagan & Vincent C. Alfonso. All Rights Reserved

XBA Analyzer	Start
Data Entry - Other	Tab Help
C-LIM Summary	

	S&W Indicator
Index	Data Organizer Graph
	C-LIM Analyzer

| Next Step |
| Selecting Scores for PSW Analyzer |
| Select ALL Checkboxes |
| Clear ALL Checkboxes |

Name: *Amanda Farris*   **Age:** *8 years 3 month(s)*   **Grade:** *2*   **Date:** *1/4/2016*

| WISC-V | WAIS-IV | WPPSI-IV | WIAT-III | WJ IV COG | WJ IV OL | WJ IV ACH | KABC-II | KTEA-3 | CAS2 | DAS-II | SB5 |

Guidelines for Selecting Best Composite Scores for SLD Evaluation

The purpose of this tab is to organize composites and subtests to assist in the selection of those to be used for evaluation of the pattern of strengths and weaknesses in the PSW Analyzer. Test names and scores can not be entered into this tab directly. Rather, this tab provides a summary of test battery and XBA composites that were transferred from other tabs because they were considered the best estimates of CHC abilities, academic areas, and selected neuropsychological domains. Use this tab to select the composites and subtest scores you would like to use in PSW analyses by clicking on the check box to the right of each one in any domain for which there are data. You may select up to two composites for each of the CHC broad ability (e.g., Gc, Gf, Gsm) and neuropsychological (e.g., Executive Functions, Orthographic Processing) domains and up to three scores for each of the academic areas. Note that you may also click on the "Data Organizer Graph" to view or print the information on this tab. For more information on how to select the best scores for use in PSW analyses, click the button to the right.

After you have made your selections, click the "S&W Indicator" button to continue with additional steps for conducting PSW analyses.

CRYSTALLIZED INTELLIGENCE (Gc)

Indicate which composite(s) you wish to use for PSW analyses. No more than two scores can be selected for this domain.

WISC-V Verbal Comprehension Index (Gc/VL)	100	☑ Test Comp	Clear Score 1
		☐	Clear Score 2
		☐	Clear Score 3

FLUID REASONING (Gf)

Indicate which composite(s) you wish to use for PSW analyses. No more than two scores can be selected for this domain.

WISC-V Fluid Reasoning Index (Gf)	97	☑ Test Comp	Clear Score 1
		☐	Clear Score 2
		☐	Clear Score 3

LONG-TERM STORAGE AND RETRIEVAL (Glr)

Indicate which composite(s) you wish to use for PSW analyses. No more than two scores can be selected for this domain.

WISC-V Storage and Retrieval Index (Glr)	100	☑ Test Comp	Clear Score 1
		☐	Clear Score 2
		☐	Clear Score 3

SHORT-TERM MEMORY (Gsm)

Indicate which composite(s) you wish to use for PSW analyses. No more than two scores can be selected for this domain.

WISC-V Working Memory Index (Gsm)	85	☑ Test Comp	Clear Score 1
		☐	Clear Score 2
		☐	Clear Score 3

VISUAL PROCESSING (Gv)

Indicate which composite(s) you wish to use for PSW analyses. No more than two scores can be selected for this domain.

WISC-V Visual Spatial Index (Gv/Vz)	81	☑ Test Comp	Clear Score 1
		☐	Clear Score 2
		☐	Clear Score 3

AUDITORY PROCESSING (Ga)

Indicate which composite(s) you wish to use for PSW analyses. No more than two scores can be selected for this domain.

Auditory Processing (Ga)	49	☑ Comp A	Clear Score 1
Auditory Processing (Ga)	85	☑ Comp B	Clear Score 2
		☐	Clear Score 3

Figure 11.13 Top Portion of Data Organizer Tab in X-BASS Showing That Scores Have Been Selected for Inclusion in PSW Analysis

The general guidelines for categorizing a cognitive score as either a strength or a weakness are as follows.

1. If the standard score representing a cognitive domain is about 90 or higher, and in the evaluator's clinical judgment the individual's cognitive performance in this domain does not appear to affect learning or academic achievement adversely, then the score may be categorized as a strength (for the PSW analysis). In cases in which the standard score is greater than 90, and perhaps much higher than 90, it is exceedingly likely that the cognitive domain represented by this score facilitates learning and academic performance and, therefore, should be categorized as a strength.

2. If the standard score representing a cognitive domain is less than 90, and in the evaluator's clinical judgment the individual's cognitive performance in this domain appears to affect learning or academic achievement adversely, then the score may be categorized as a weakness. In cases where the standard score is less than 85, it is exceedingly likely that the cognitive domain represented by this score inhibits learning and academic performance and, therefore, should be categorized as a weakness.

3. Because some cognitive domains with corresponding scores in the upper 80s and low 90s may be among the individual's highest scores, then even scores in the upper 80s may be judged by the evaluator to be strengths for the individual. Likewise, because some cognitive domains with corresponding scores in the upper 90s and lower 100s may be among the individual's lowest scores, then even scores in these ranges may be judged by the evaluator to be weaknesses for the individual. There is no cut point in X-BASS on this tab that designates a score as a strength or weakness. Due to a multiplicity of factors that affect an individual's score performances, clinical judgment it not only encouraged when making determinations about strengths and weaknesses but also necessary.

Categorizing all score performances as either strengths or weaknesses, taking into consideration where the scores fall relative to most people and where the scores fall relative to the individual's own capabilities, is important in understanding whether the individual meets criteria for SLD. Nevertheless, categorizing an individual's scores as either strengths or weaknesses is only one of many important considerations that assist in making an SLD determination.

Figure 11.14 shows Amanda's strengths and weaknesses in cognitive, achievement, and neuropsychological processing domains as indicated by her evaluator.

As shown in Figure 11.14, Amanda's strengths and weaknesses appear to follow the about 90 criterion closely, because most scores were at least a few points above

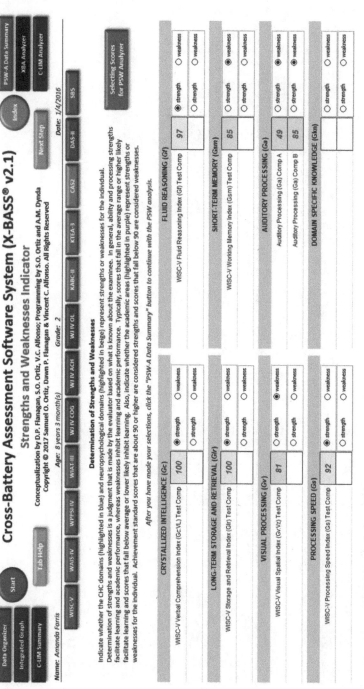

Figure 11.14 Strengths and Weaknesses Indicator Tab of X-BASS

BASIC READING SKILLS (BRS)

Test	Score	Strength	Weakness
WIAT-III Basic Reading Skills (BRS) Test Comp	81	O strength	● weakness
WIAT-III Word Reading (BRS;Grw-R:RD) Subtest	77	O strength	● weakness
WIAT-III Pseudoword Decoding (BRS;Grw-R:RD) Subtest	85	O strength	● weakness

READING FLUENCY (RDF)

Test	Score	Strength	Weakness
WIAT-III Oral Reading Fluency (RDF;Grw-R:RS) Subtest	74	O strength	● weakness
		O strength	O weakness
		O strength	O weakness

MATH CALCULATION (MC)

Test	Score	Strength	Weakness
WIAT-III Math Fluency (MC) Test Comp	89	● strength	O weakness
WIAT-III Numerical Operations (MC;Gq:A3) Subtest	99	● strength	O weakness
		O strength	O weakness

ORAL EXPRESSION (OE)

Test	Score	Strength	Weakness
WIAT-III Oral Expression (Gc:VL,Glr-Fl;OE) Subtest	98	● strength	O weakness
		O strength	O weakness
		O strength	O weakness

LEARNING EFFICIENCY (LE)

Test	Score	Strength	Weakness
		O strength	O weakness
		O strength	O weakness

READING COMPREHENSION (RDC)

Test	Score	Strength	Weakness
WIAT-III Reading Comprehension (RDC;Grw-R:RC) Subtest	79	O strength	● weakness

WRITTEN EXPRESSION (WE)

Test	Score	Strength	Weakness
WIAT-III Written Expression (WE) Test Comp	82	O strength	● weakness
WIAT-III Spelling (WE;Grw-W:SG) Subtest	74	O strength	● weakness
WIAT-III Sentence Composition (WE;Grw-W:EU,WA) Subtest	94	● strength	O weakness

MATH PROBLEM SOLVING (MPS)

Test	Score	Strength	Weakness
WIAT-III Math Problem Solving (MPS;Gq:A3;GRQ) Subtest	83	O strength	O weakness
		O strength	O weakness
		O strength	O weakness

LISTENING COMPREHENSION (LC)

Test	Score	Strength	Weakness
WIAT-III Listening Comprehension (Gc:VL,LS;LC) Subtest	96	● strength	O weakness
		O strength	O weakness
		O strength	O weakness

ORTHOGRAPHIC PROCESSING (OP)

Test	Score	Strength	Weakness
Orthographic Processing (OP) Comp	78	O strength	● weakness
		O strength	O weakness

Figure 11.14 (*Continued*)

or below 90 and corroborating data sources were available to support the evaluator's designations. One exception was Amanda's WIAT-III Math Fluency score of 89. If X-BASS was programmed to designate every score below 90 as a weakness, then this score would have showed up in Figure 11.14 as a weakness. Because X-BASS was designed deliberately to allow for clinical judgment, Amanda's Math Fluency score of 89 was considered a strength. The evaluator categorized Math Fluency as a strength because math is a personal strength for Amanda, the teacher reported math to be a relative strength for Amanda and indicated that she was performing as well as most students in the class in mathematics, and Amanda reported that she likes math and is confident in her math skills. Considering this information coupled with her other solid average math performances and her average processing speed, Amanda's evaluator judged Math Fluency to be a strength, indicating that her ability in this area is not likely to interfere with the continued development of her math skills.

After designating all scores as either strengths or weaknesses, X-BASS conducts a PSW analysis via an operationalization of the criteria set forth in the DD/C definition of SLD. The PSW output generated by X-BASS and guidance on how the user can select cognitive and academic areas of strength and weaknesses in lieu of the default output for the PSW analysis are presented next. To review a summary of the data that provide the input for the PSW analysis, click on the PSW-A Data Summary button at the top right of the Strengths and Weaknesses Indicator tab.

PSW-A Data Summary

The PSW-A Data Summary tab displays a few important terms, which were defined in Rapid References 11.12 through 11.14. In most cases, no additional information needs to be added to this tab, and no data need to be changed on this tab. The top portion of this tab (shown in Figure 11.15) summarized the CHC ability domains that were identified by the evaluator as strengths and weaknesses. In X-BASS, areas of strength are printed and highlighted in green and areas of weakness are printed and highlighted in red. Also, shown at the top of this tab are three estimates: (1) the g-value, (2) the FCC, and (3) the ICC.

Figure 11.15 shows that Amanda's g-value is .72, which is high. A high g-value (i.e., > .60) indicates that despite Amanda's cognitive areas of weaknesses (i.e., those printed in red and labeled with a W on this tab), it is very likely that her overall cognitive ability is at least average. When the g-value is high, X-BASS automatically calculates an FCC. Amanda's FCC is 96, indicating that, without the attenuating effects of her cognitive weaknesses, her overall intellectual capacity

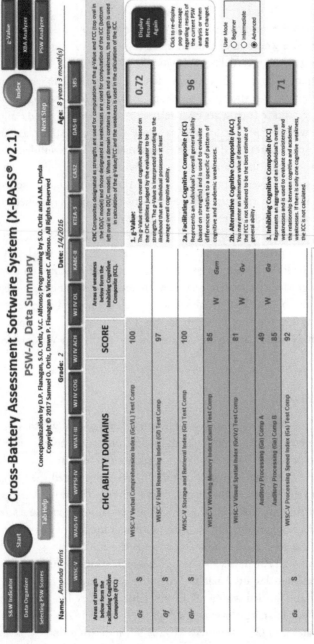

Figure 11.15 The PSW-A Data Summary Tab of X-BASS

	ACHIEVEMENT/SLD DOMAINS	SCORE	Areas of weakness below may be used as academic deficits in the DD/C model.		Composites or subtest scores designated as weaknesses may be used to represent academic deficits in PSW-A analyses (bottom right oval in the DD/C model). Only one academic weakness at a time is evaluated relative to a cognitive weakness and general ability, but any area may be selected in turn to examine other patterns of strengths and weaknesses on the PSW Analyzer tab.
	WIAT-III Basic Reading Skills (BRS) Test Comp	81			
	WIAT-III Word Reading (BRS;Grw-RRD) Subtest	77	W	BRS	
	WIAT-III Pseudoword Decoding (BRS;Grw-RRD) Subtest	85			
	WIAT-III Reading Comprehension (RDC;Grw-RRC) Subtest	79	W	RDC	
	WIAT-III Oral Reading Fluency (RDF;Grw-RRS) Subtest	74	W	RDF	
WE	WIAT-III Written Expression (WE) Test Comp	82			
S	WIAT-III Spelling (WE;Grw-W-SG) Subtest	74	W	WE	
	WIAT-III Sentence Composition (WE;Grw-WEEU;WA) Subtest	94			
MC	WIAT-III Math Fluency (MC) Test Comp	89			
S	WIAT-III Numerical Operations (MC;Gq-A3) Subtest	99			
MPS	WIAT-III Math Problem Solving (MPS;Gq-A3;Gf-RQ) Subtest	83			
OE S	WIAT-III Oral Expression (Gc-VL;Gr-F;OE) Subtest	98			
LC S	WIAT-III Listening Comprehension (Gc-VL;L-S;LC) Subtest	96			

Areas of strength below are likely consistent with the individual's overall general ability.

○ Score difference will be considered rare/infrequent when it occurs 5% of the time (very strict value, best for multiple comparisons or tests with low reliability)

● Score difference will be considered rare/infrequent when it occurs 10% of the time (default value, best for standard analyzes with composites and reliable tests)

○ Score difference will be considered rare/infrequent when it occurs 15% of the time (very liberal value, increases false positive rate–not recommended)

5. Rarity/Frequency of Difference – FCC/ACC to Academic Weakness
Select base rate level for determining whether the size of a difference occurs rarely or infrequently. The default value is 10%. A more conservative or liberal value may be appropriate. If multiple comparisons are made, a stricter value may be appropriate.

Figure 11.15 (Continued)

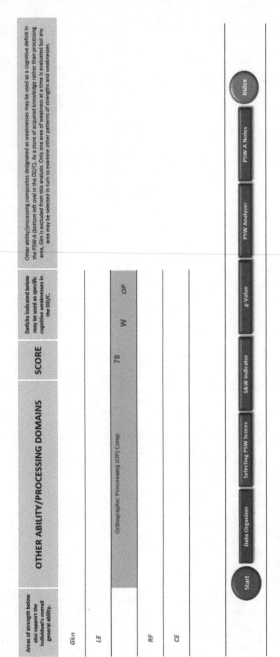

Figure 11.15 *(Continued)*

OTHER ABILITY/PROCESSING DOMAINS

Areas of strength below also support the individual's overall general ability.	SCORE	Deficits indicated below may be used as specific cognitive weaknesses in the DD/C.	Other ability/processing composites designated as weaknesses may be used as a cognitive deficit in the PSW-A (bottom left oval in the DD/C). As a store of acquired knowledge rather than processing area, Gc is excluded from this analysis. Only one area of weakness at a time is evaluated but any area may be selected in turn to examine other patterns of strengths and weaknesses.

Gkn

LE
Orthographic Processing (OP) Comp   78   W   OP

RF

CE

Start → Data Organizer → Selecting PSW Scores → S&W Indicator → ε Value → PSW Analyzer → PSW-A Notes → Index

is in the average range. Another way of conceptualizing the FCC is that it provides an indication that Amanda has at least average ability to think and reason—a defining characteristic of the PSW component in the DD/C model. Amanda's FCC suggests that she has many cognitive abilities and processes that ought to facilitate learning and academic performance. (For information on how the FCC was calculated, go to the Index tab on X-BASS, and click on PSW-A Notes in the References and Information section.)

> # DON'T FORGET
> ....
> The FCC is a proxy for psychometric g. It is an aggregate of a sufficient breadth of cognitive abilities that are typically part of global ability composites or alternative estimates of global ability on cognitive and intelligence tests, such as the GAI on the WISC-V and the Gf-Gc composite on the WJ IV. However, it differs from alternative estimates of global ability on current batteries because it always consists of only the individual's cognitive strengths and it will only be calculated when the individual has a sufficient breadth of cognitive strengths in the "right" areas (see the PSW-A Notes tab in X-BASS for more information).

Also listed in the top portion of the PSW-A Data Summary tab in Figure 11.15 is Amanda's ICC of 71, which is well below average. The ICC is an aggregate of Amanda's cognitive ability and processing weaknesses and suggests that such weaknesses will likely inhibit learning and academic achievement unless they are accommodated or compensated for in some way.

Notice that Figure 11.15 shows that the PSW-A Data Summary tab includes a space next to the Alternative Cognitive Composite or ACC. In some instances, the user may override the FCC with another composite. The ACC refers to any cognitive composite derived from an intelligence or cognitive ability battery that is a good estimate of overall cognitive ability and, in the evaluator's judgment, is a better estimate than the FCC. Typically, if either the *g*-value or FCC is reported in yellow there exists a question regarding whether the individual is of at least average cognitive ability. In this situation, clinical judgment is necessary to make that determination. If an alternative composite is considered a better estimate of overall ability as compared to the FCC, then it may be entered on this tab in the space provided.

The PSW analysis calculates the difference between Amanda's ICC, or any one of the scores that comprise it, and a score that was predicted by the FCC using a regression equation (as will be described next). The difference is considered rare if it occurs in about 10% of the population or less, which is the default value set in X-BASS. The evaluator may change the default value a priori (i.e., prior to advancing to the results of the PSW analysis) under certain circumstances. However, this value is the preferred value for examining score differences for SLD identification (e.g., Evans, 1990; Reynolds, 1985; Wright, 2002).

The next section of the PSW-A Data Summary tab in Figure 11.15 shows the Achievement or IDEA-specific SLD areas that were categorized by the evaluator as strengths and weaknesses for Amanda. Note that the PSW analysis calculates the difference between Amanda's academic weaknesses and a score that was pre-

C A U T I O N

Without a compelling reason to change the Frequency of the Difference for the actual and predicted cognitive comparison or the actual and predicted achievement comparison, the default difference should remain at 10%—the recommended default value.

dicted by the FCC using a regression equation (as will be described next). In this comparison, as in the actual and predicted score comparison for a cognitive area of weakness, the difference is considered rare if it occurs in about 10% of the population or less. Figure 11.15 shows that the default value was changed from 10% to 15% for this comparison. The evaluator changed the default value a priori (i.e., prior to conducting the PSW analysis) for the following reasons. First, Amanda has undergone at least 2 years of intervention services for reading difficulties and has reportedly made progress. Second, when Amanda began taking medication for ADHD her basic reading skills reportedly improved. Given these two factors, the evaluator suspected that her reading performance may be somewhat higher than it would have been without the added benefit of 2 years of intervention and medication. Therefore, a more liberal value was selected to ensure that any improvements she may have made in reading would not lead to a false negative (not identifying SLD in error), because Amanda is still below expectation despite intervention and other data sources suggest that she may have a learning disability.

The last section of the PSW-A Data Summary tab in Figure 11.15 shows other ability and processing domains that were not included in the previous sections. As may be seen in this Figure, Amanda's OP score of 78 was reported as a weakness. Note that these five additional areas may be included in the PSW analysis but do not contribute to the FCC if they are identified as strengths or to the ICC if they are identified as weaknesses. Once the information on the PSW-A Data Summary tab has been reviewed, the user may click on the top right button on this tab titled g-*Value*.

PSW-A g-Value Data Summary

The PSW-A *g*-Value Data Summary tab is shown in Figure 11.16. This tab is informational only. It provides an interpretation of the *g*-value (e.g., "*g*-Value = .72, Average overall ability is very likely"), the scale used to determine the likelihood that the *g*-value represents at least average overall ability (e.g., > .60 = average overall

Analysis and Interpretation of *g*-Value

Based on data entered in prior tabs, a *g*-Value is computed and displayed here. Users are advised to refer to the PSW-A Notes tab in X-BASS and to the relevant text in *Essentials of Cross-Battery Assessment, Third Edition* for a detailed discussion regarding the full meaning and proper use and interpretation of the *g*-Value.

The *g*-Value reflects overall cognitive ability based on the broad CHC abilities judged by the evaluator to be strengths for the individual using the following scale:

≤.50 = average overall ability is unlikely; .51 - .59 = more information needed; ≥.60 = average overall ability is very likely

| *g*-Value = | 0.72 | Average overall ability is very likely |

How likely is it that the individual's pattern of strengths indicates at least average overall cognitive ability?

LIKELY. Despite the presence of weaknesses in one or more cognitive domains, the evaluator indicated that the individual possesses average or better functioning in cognitive domains considered important for acquiring the academic skills typical for this grade level. In this case, the individual's overall ability ought to enable learning and achievement, particularly if the FCC/ACC is greater than or equal to 90 and when specific cognitive weaknesses are minimized through compensatory efforts, accommodations, and the like. If the FCC/ACC is between 85 and 89 inclusive, the criterion for at least average overall ability within the DD/C model should be supported by additional data and information.

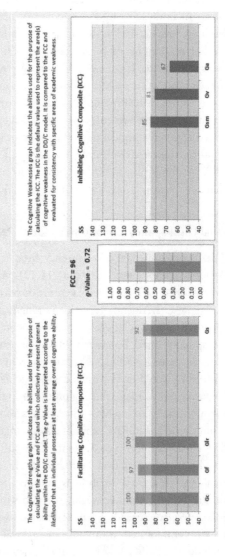

Figure 11.16 The *g*-Value Tab of X-BASS

ability is very likely), and the specific cognitive abilities and processes used to calculate the *g*-value, FCC, and ICC. The bottom of this tab answers the following question that is specific to the *g*-value: "How likely is it that the individual's pattern of strengths indicates at least average overall ability?" The answer to this question assists in understanding the importance of at least average overall ability in the learning process and is based on Amanda's *g*-value: Despite the presence of weaknesses in one or more cognitive ability domains, this individual displays average or better functioning in cognitive ability domains considered important for acquiring the academic skills typical for this grade level. The individual's overall cognitive ability is very likely to be average or better and, therefore, ought to enable learning and achievement, especially when specific cognitive weaknesses are minimized through compensatory efforts, accommodations, and the like.

Once the *g*-value information has been reviewed, the user may click on the PSW Analyzer button, located at the top right of the PSW-A *g*-Value tab. Note that this button is not visible in Figure 11.16.

Dual Discrepancy/Consistency Model: PSW Analyses for SLD

The Dual Discrepancy/Consistency Model: PSW Analysis for SLD tab (or PSW Analyzer tab for short; see Figure 11.17) provides the results of the PSW analysis following the DD/C model. There are three ovals on the PSW Analyzer tab. The top oval represents Amanda's cognitive strengths and includes the FCC of 96. Note that the top oval also includes a drop-down menu where Amanda's supporting academic strengths are listed. Because the FCC represents Amanda's cognitive capabilities that are anticipated to facilitate learning and achievement, it is expected that individuals with SLD would demonstrate areas of achievement that are consistent with their cognitive capabilities. Clicking on the drop-down menu in the top oval reveals the following areas of strength for Amanda that are consistent with her FCC: Oral Expression, Listening Comprehension, Math Calculation, and a specific area of Written Expression (i.e., Sentence Composition).

The bottom left oval in Figure 11.17 represents the individual's cognitive weakness. The PSW analysis is automatically conducted using the ICC as the default area of cognitive weakness (as shown in Figure 11.17). However, the user may select any area that was designated as a cognitive weakness from the drop-down menu located in the bottom left oval. For Amanda, this drop-down menu includes the WISC-V WMI and VSI, two auditory processing composites, and an orthographic processing composite.

The bottom right oval in Figure 11.17 represents the individual's academic weakness. The PSW analysis is automatically conducted using the first area that

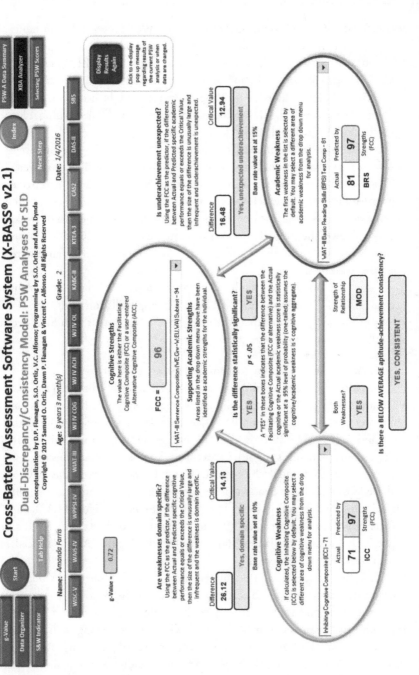

Figure 11.17 The PSW Analyzer Tab in X-BASS with ICC as the Default Cognitive Weakness

was marked as a weakness on the Strengths and Weaknesses Indicator tab in the order in which the IDEA-specific SLD areas are listed (i.e., BRS, RDC, RDF, WE, MC, MPS, OE, and LC). Because Amanda had a weakness in BRS, her WIAT-III Basic Reading Skills composite appears in the bottom right oval. The other areas of academic weakness included in the drop-down menu of the bottom-right oval for Amanda include WIAT-III Reading Comprehension, Oral Reading Fluency, Spelling, and Math Problem-Solving.

Because X-BASS automatically conducts a PSW analysis, it is important to decide a priori what areas of cognitive strength and weakness will be analyzed. The ICC is a good choice for the area of cognitive weakness because it provides an aggregate of all weaknesses. However, the ICC may contain estimates of cognitive abilities or processes that are not closely related to the academic area of weakness, which will lower the strength of the relationship between the ICC and the area of academic weakness. In that situation, it is important to select an alternative cognitive weakness.

Figure 11.17 shows the default values for the initial PSW analysis for Amanda (i.e., an ICC of 71 and the WIAT-III Basic Reading Skills composite of 81). The results of this analysis show that Amanda's PSW in consistent with SLD because the following conditions were met:

1. At least average ability to think and reason: FCC of 96
2. Domain-specific cognitive weakness: The difference between the FCC of 96 and the ICC of 71 is statistically significant (as indicated by the "yes" in the left center of the ovals in Figure 11.17), and the difference between the predicted (97) and actual (71) ICC is rare in the general population (about 10%), indicating that Amanda's cognitive areas of weakness are domain-specific.
3. Unexpected underachievement: The difference between the FCC of 96 and the WIAT-III Basic Reading Skills composite of 81 is statistically significant (as indicated by the "yes" in the right center of the ovals in Figure 11.17), and the difference between the predicted (97) and actual (81) Basic Reading Skills scores is rare in the general population (about 15%), indicating that Amanda's academic area of weakness is unexpected.
4. Below-average aptitude-achievement consistency: The scores that represent the areas of cognitive and academic weakness are below average as compared to most people, and there is an empirically established relationship between at least some of the areas that make up the ICC and basic reading skills. Amanda's ICC is made up of estimates of working memory, visual processing, and auditory processing. Although working memory and auditory processing (mainly phonological processing) are related to basic reading skills, visual processing (as

measured by the WISC-V VSI) is not. Therefore, it is likely that the strength of the relationship between the ICC and basic reading skills was tempered by the inclusion of visual processing in the ICC. Nevertheless, the data are sufficient to support a consistency between Amanda's areas of cognitive and academic weakness.

Amanda's evaluator decided a priori to run two analyses on the PSW Analyzer tab, one with phonological processing and basic reading skills as the areas of cognitive and academic weakness and the other with orthographic processing and oral reading fluency as the areas of cognitive and academic weakness, respectively. Figure 11.18 shows the results of this latter comparison. Note that whereas the strength of the relationship between the ICC and basic reading skills was moderate (see Figure 11.17), the strength of the relationship between phonological processing and basic reading skills is high (as reported in Chapter 8), and the strength of the relationship between orthographic processing and oral reading fluency is high (as may be seen in Figure 11.18). The results of the PSW analyses conducted with Amanda's data provided support for an SLD classification in the areas of basic reading skills and reading fluency.

The results of the PSW analysis are provided in written form as answers to four specific questions:

1. Did the individual's observed cognitive and academic performance meet criteria within the DD/C model consistent with PSW-based SLD identification?
2. Is there evidence of domain-specific weaknesses in cognitive functioning?
3. Is there evidence of unexpected underachievement?
4. Is there evidence of below-average aptitude-achievement consistency?

The answers to these four questions for Amanda, when orthographic processing and basic reading skills were selected as the areas of cognitive and academic weakness, respectively, are provided in Figure 11.19. Noteworthy is the fact that if the answer to the first question (i.e., "Did the individual's observed cognitive and academic performance meet criteria within the DD/C model consistent with PSW-based SLD identification?") is "yes," the output clearly states "this pattern of results does not automatically confirm the presence of SLD . . ." and if the answer is "no," the output clearly states "this pattern of results does not automatically rule out the presence of SLD . . ." The reason for these clarifications is that a classification or diagnosis of SLD should not rest on quantitative data alone or

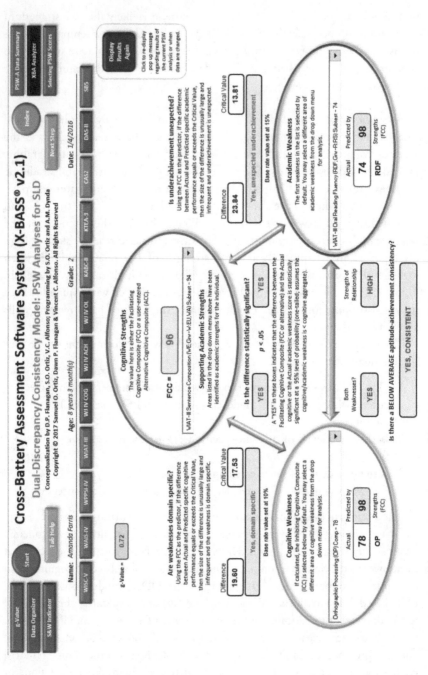

Figure 11.18 PSW Analyzer Tab of X-BASS with Orthographic Processing Selected as the Area of Cognitive Weakness

Dual-Discrepancy/Consistency Model: Summary of PSW Analyses for SLD

Name: *Amanda Farris* **Age:** *8 years 3 month(s)* **Grade:** *2* **Date:** *1/4/2016*

Did the individual's observed cognitive and academic performances meet criteria within the DD/C model consistent with PSW-based SLD identification?

YES. Based on the data selected for use in the PSW Analyzer, specific criteria for establishing a PSW consistent with SLD have been met. However, this pattern of results does not automatically confirm the presence of SLD. This pattern must be considered within the context of the entire case history of the individual. In addition, other data gathered through multiple methods need to be considered (e.g., information regarding exclusionary factors) when identifying or diagnosing SLD (see chapter 4 in Essentials of Cross-Battery Assessment, 3rd Ed.).

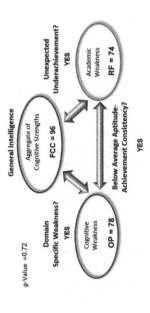

g-Value =0.72

General Intelligence

Aggregate of Cognitive Strengths — **FCC = 96**

Domain Specific Weakness? **YES** — Cognitive Weakness **OP = 78**

Unexpected Underachievement? **YES** — Academic Weakness **RF = 74**

Below Average Aptitude-Achievement Consistency? **YES**

1. Is there evidence of domain specific weaknesses in cognitive functioning?

YES. The difference between the individual's estimate of intact cognitive abilities (FCC=96) and the score representing the area of specific cognitive weakness (OP=78) is statistically significant. This finding means that there is likely a true or real difference between the estimate of overall cognitive strengths and the identified area of specific cognitive weakness for the individual. In addition, there is an unusually large difference between actual performance in the specific cognitive area (SS=78) and expected performance (SS=98) as predicted by overall cognitive strengths. That is, based on the individual's estimate of cognitive strengths, it was predicted that the individual would perform much better in the specific cognitive area. In fact, the size of the difference between the individual's actual and predicted performance in the specific cognitive area occurs very infrequently. The results of these analyses suggest that the individual's PSW consists of a domain-specific cognitive weakness (particularly when the actual SS<90), an inclusionary criterion for SLD.

2. Is there evidence of unexpected underachievement?

YES. The difference between the individual's estimate of intact cognitive abilities (FCC=96) and the score representing the area of specific academic weakness (RF=74) is statistically significant. This finding means that there is likely a true or real difference between the estimate of overall cognitive strengths and the identified area of specific academic weakness for the individual. In addition, there is an unusually large difference between actual performance in the specific academic area (SS=74) and expected performance (SS=98) as predicted by overall cognitive strengths. That is, based on the individual's estimate of cognitive strengths, it was predicted that the individual would perform much better in the specific academic area. In fact, the size of the difference between the individual's actual and predicted performance in the specific academic area occurs very infrequently. The results of these analyses suggest that the individual's PSW is marked by unexpected underachievement (particularly when the actual SS < 90), an inclusionary criterion for SLD.

3. Is there evidence of a below-average aptitude-achievement consistency?

YES. The specific cognitive (SS=78 for OP) and academic (SS=74 for RF) scores are indicative of normative weaknesses or deficits compared to same age peers (SS=85). There is research that supports a high relationship between OP (Orthographic Processing) and Reading Fluency which indicates that they are related. This combination of scores provides evidence that assists in explaining the nature of the individual's observed learning difficulties. Based on all of these considerations, these findings appear below average and appear to indicate overall support for the criterion regarding below average aptitude-achievement consistency.

Figure 11.19 Specific Questions About PSW Results Answered in X-BASS

discrepancy/consistency analyses alone. Other data gathered through multiple methods need to be considered and must corroborate any conclusions that are drawn from the PSW analysis.

CONCLUSION

This chapter provided a summary of the major components of the DD/C operational definition of SLD. This definition provides a common foundation for the practice of SLD identification and will likely be most effective when it is informed by cognitive and neuropsychological theory and research that supports (1) the identification and measurement of constructs associated with SLD, (2) the relationship between academic skills and cognitive abilities and processes, and (3) a defensible method of interpreting results. Of the many important components of the definition, the central focus was on specification of criteria at the various levels of evaluation that should be met to establish the presence of SLD. These criteria included identification of empirically related academic and cognitive abilities and processes in the below-average range, as compared to same-age peers from the general population; determination that exclusionary factors are not the primary cause of the identified academic and cognitive deficits; and identification of a pattern of performance that is marked by domain-specific cognitive weakness(es) and unexpected underachievement, with otherwise average ability to think and reason. When the criteria specified at each level of the operational definition are met, it may be concluded that the data gathered are sufficient to support a diagnosis of SLD in a manner consistent with IDEIA (2004) and its attendant regulations.

🪶 TEST YOURSELF 🪶

1. **An operational definition provides a process for the identification and classification of concepts that have been defined formally. True or false?**

2. **The CHC-based operational definition of SLD is arranged according to levels. At each level, the definition includes:**
   (a) Defining characteristics regarding the nature of SLD
   (b) The focus of evaluation for each characteristic
   (c) Examples of evaluation methods and relevant data sources
   (d) The criteria that need to be met to establish that an individual possesses a particular characteristic of SLD
   (e) All of the above

3. **Low academic achievement and a consideration of exclusionary factors are all that are necessary for a diagnosis of SLD. True or false?**

4. **According to IDEIA (2004) a student may have an SLD in all of the following academic areas except:**
   (a) Math calculation
   (b) Basic reading skill
   (c) Spelling
   (d) Listening comprehension

5. **Potential explanatory reasons for academic underachievement include:**
   (a) Lack of motivation
   (b) Social-emotional disturbance
   (c) Performance anxiety
   (d) Psychiatric disorders
   (e) All of the above

6. **A below-average aptitude-achievement consistency is a criterion for SLD identification in the CHC-based operational definition of SLD. True or false?**

7. **Children with SLD may require one or more of the following *except*:**
   (a) Individualized instruction
   (b) Grade retention
   (c) Accommodations
   (d) Curricular modifications

8. **The term *aptitude* within the context of the CHC-based operational definition of SLD represents the specific cognitive ability or neuropsychological processing deficits that are empirically related to the academic skill deficiency. True or false?**

9. **Basic psychological processes include all of the following *except*:**
   (a) Auditory working memory
   (b) Processing speed
   (c) Perseverance
   (d) Visual discrimination

10. **Flanagan and colleagues developed the PSW component of X-BASS for SLD identification to replace clinical judgment. True or false?**

Answers: 1. True; 2. e; 3. False; 4. c; 5. e; 6. True; 7. b; 8. True; 9. c; 10. False.

REFERENCES

Aaron, P. G. (1995). Differential diagnosis of reading disabilities. *School Psychology Review, 24,* 345–360.

Ansari, D. (2008). Effects of development and enculturation on number representation in the brain. *Nature Reviews: Neuroscience, 9*, 278–291.

Ansari, D., & Dhital, B. (2006). Age-related changes in the activation of the intraparietal sulcus during nonsymbolic magnitude processing: An event-related functional magnetic resonance imaging study. *Journal of Cognitive Neuroscience, 18*, 1820–1828.

Ansari, D., Garcia, N., Lucas, E., Hamon, K., & Dhital, B. (2005). Neural correlates of symbolic number processing in children and adults. *NeuroReport, 16*, 1769–1773.

Bateman, B. (1965). An educational view of a diagnostic approach to learning disorders. In J. Hellmuth (Ed.), *Learning disorders* (Vol. 1, pp. 219–239). Seattle, WA: Special Child Publications.

Berl, M. M., Duke, E. S., Mayo, J., Rosenberger, L. R., Moore, E. N., VanMeter, J., . . . & Gaillard, W. D. (2010). *Brain and Language, 114*, 115–125.

Berninger, V. W. (2011). Evidence-based differential diagnosis and treatment of reading disabilities with and without comorbidities in oral language, writing, and math: Prevention, problem-solving consultation, and specialized instruction. In D. P. Flanagan & V. C. Alfonso (Eds.), *Essentials of specific learning disability identification* (pp. 203–232). Hoboken, NJ: Wiley.

Chiu, M. M., & Klassen, R. M. (2010). Relations of mathematics self-concept and its calibration with mathematics achievement: Cultural differences among fifteen-year-olds in 34 countries. *Learning and Instruction, 20*, 2–17.

Davis, N., Cannistraci, C. J., Rogers, B. P., Catenby, J. C., Fuchs, L. S., Anderson, A. W., & Gore, J. C. (2009). The neural correlates of calculation ability in children: An fMRI study. *Magnetic Resonance Imaging, 27*, 1187–1197.

Dehaene, S., & Cohen, L. (1995). Towards an anatomical and functional model of number processing. *Mathematical Cognition, 1*, 83–120.

Dehaene, S., & Cohen, L. (1997). Cerebral pathways for calculation: Double disassociation between rote verbal and quantitative knowledge of arithmetic. *Cortex, 33*, 219–250.

Dehaene, S., & Cohen, L. (2011). The unique role of the visual word form area in reading. *Trends in Cognitive Science, 15*, 254–262.

Dehaene, S., Molko, N., Cohen, L., & Wilson, A. J. (2004). Arithmetic and the brain. *Current Opinion in Neurobiology, 14*, 218–224.

Dehaene, S., Spelke, E., Pinel, P., Stanescu, R., & Tsivkin, S. (1999). Sources of mathematical thinking: Behavioral and brain-imaging evidence. *Science, 284*, 970–974.

Della Toffalo, D. (2010). Linking school neuropsychology with response-to-intervention models. In D. C. Miller (Ed.), *Best practices in school neuropsychology: Guidelines for effective practice, assessment, and evidence-based interventions* (pp. 159–184). New York, NY: Guilford.

De Smedt, B., Holloway, I., & Ansari, D. (2011). Effects of problem size and arithmetic operation on brain activation during calculation in children with varying levels of arithmetical fluency. *NeuroImage, 57*, 771–781.

Evans, L. D. (1990). A conceptual overview of the regression discrepancy model for evaluating severe discrepancy between IQ and achievement scores. *Journal of Learning Disabilities, 23*(7), 406–412.

Feifer, S. G. (2012). Integrating RTI with cognitive neuropsychology: A scientific approach to reading. *Presentation given at the Fordham University 4th Annual Assessment Conference*, May 11. New York, NY.

Ferstl, E. C., Neumann, J., Bogler, C., & von Cramon, D. Y. (2008). The extended language network: A meta-analysis of neuroimaging studies on text comprehension. *Human Brain Mapping, 29*, 581–593.

Fiorello, C. A., Flanagan, D. P., & Hale, J. B. (2014). Response to the special issue: The utility of the pattern of strengths and weaknesses approach. *Learning Disabilities: A Multidisciplinary Journal, 20*(1), 55–59.

Flanagan, D. P., & Alfonso, V. C. (2017). *Essentials of WISC-V assessment.* Hoboken, NJ: Wiley.

Flanagan, D. P., Alfonso, V. C., & Mascolo, J. T. (2011). A CHC-based operational definition of SLD: Integrating multiple data sources and multiple data-gathering methods. In D. P. Flanagan & V. C. Alfonso (Eds.), *Essentials of specific learning disability identification* (pp. 233–298). Hoboken, NJ: Wiley.

Flanagan, D. P., Alfonso, V. C., & Ortiz, S. O. (2012). The Cross-Battery Assessment approach: An overview, historical perspective, and current directions. In D. P. Flanagan & P. L. Harrison (Eds.), *Contemporary intellectual assessment: Theories, tests and issues* (3rd ed., pp. 459–483). New York, NY: Guilford.

Flanagan, D. P., McGrew, K. S., & Ortiz, S. O. (2000). *The Wechsler Intelligence Scales and Gf-Gc theory: A contemporary approach to interpretation.* Needham Heights, MA: Allyn & Bacon.

Flanagan, D. P., Ortiz, S. O., & Alfonso, V. C. (2011). *Essentials of Cross-Battery Assessment with C/D ROM* (3rd ed.). Hoboken, NJ: Wiley.

Flanagan, D. P., Ortiz, S. O., & Alfonso, V. C. (2013). *Essentials of Cross-Battery Assessment* (3rd ed.). New York, NY: Wiley.

Flanagan, D. P., Ortiz, S. O., & Alfonso, V. C. (2017). *Cross-Battery Assessment software system, v2.0* (X-BASS). Hoboken, NJ: Wiley.

Flanagan, D. P., Ortiz, S. O., Alfonso, V. C., & Mascolo, J. (2002). *The achievement test desk reference (ATDR): Comprehensive assessment and learning disabilities.* Boston, MA: Allyn & Bacon.

Flanagan, D. P., Ortiz, S. O., Alfonso, V. C., & Mascolo, J. (2006). *The achievement test desk reference (ATDR): A guide to learning disability identification* (2nd ed.). Hoboken, NJ: Wiley.

Flanagan, D. P., & Schneider, W. J. (2016). Cross-Battery Assessment? XBA PSW? A case of mistaken identity: A commentary on Kranzler and colleagues' "Classification agreement analysis of Cross-Battery Assessment in the identification of specific learning disorders in children and youth." *International Journal of School & Educational Psychology, 4*(3), 137–145.

Fletcher, J. M. (Interviewee). (2008). Agora: The marketplace of ideas. Best Practices: Applying response to intervention (RTI) and comprehensive assessment for the identification of specific learning disabilities. [6-hour training program/DVD]. Bloomington, MN: Pearson.

Fletcher, J. M., Lyon, G. R., Fuchs, L. S., & Barnes, M. A. (2007). *Learning disabilities: From identification to intervention.* New York, NY: Guilford.

Fletcher, J. M., Simos, P. G., Papanicolaou, A. C., & Denton, C. (2004). Neuroimaging in reading research. In N. Duke & M. Mallette (Eds.), *Literacy research methods* (pp. 252–286). New York, NY: Guilford.

Fletcher, J. M., Taylor, H. G., Levin, H. S., & Satz, P. (1995). Neuropsychological and intellectual assessment of children. In H. Kaplan & B. Sadock (Eds.), *Comprehensive textbook of psychiatry* (6th ed., pp. 581–601). Baltimore, MD: Williams & Wilkens.

Fletcher-Janzen, E., & Reynolds, C. R. (Eds.). (2008). *Neuropsychological perspectives on learning disabilities in the era of RTI: Recommendations for diagnosis and intervention.* Hoboken, NJ: Wiley.

Fuchs, L. S., & Fuchs, D. (1998). Treatment validity: A unifying concept for reconceptualizing the identification of learning disabilities. *Learning Disabilities Research and Practice, 13,* 204–219.

Geary, D. C., Hoard, M. K., & Bailey, D. H. (2011). How SLD manifests in mathematics. In D. P. Flanagan & V. C. Alfonso (Eds.), *Essentials of specific learning disability identification* (pp. 43–64). Hoboken, NJ: Wiley.

Gernsbacher, M. A., & Kaschak, M. P. (2003). Neuroimaging studies of language production and comprehension. *Annual Reviews of Psychology, 54,* 91–114.

Gunderson, E. A., Ramirez, G., Levine, S. C., & Beilock, S. L. (2011). The role of parents and teachers in the development of gender-related math attitudes. *Sex Roles, 66,* 153–166.

Hale, J., Alfonso, V., Berninger, V., Bracken, B., Christo, C., Clark, E., . . . Dumont, R. (2010). Critical issues in response-to-intervention, comprehensive evaluation, and specific learning disabilities identification and intervention: An expert white paper consensus. *Learning Disability Quarterly, 33,* 1–14.

Hale, J. B., Chen, S. A., Tan, S. C., Poon, K., Fitzer, K. R., & Boyd, L. A. (2016). Reconciling individual differences with collective needs: The juxtaposition of sociopolitical and neuroscience perspectives on remediation and compensation of student skill deficits. *Trends in Neuroscience and Education, 5*(2), 41–51.

Hale, J. B., & Fiorello, C. A. (2004). *School neuropsychology: A practitioner's handbook.* New York, NY: Guilford.

Hale, J. B., Flanagan, D. P., & Naglieri, J. A. (2008). Alternative research-based methods for IDEA (2004): Identification of children with specific learning disabilities. *Communiqué, 36*(8), *1,* 14–15.

Hale, J. B., Wycoff, K. L., & Fiorello, C. A. (2011). RTI and cognitive hypothesis testing for identification and intervention of specific learning disabilities: The best of both worlds. In D. P. Flanagan & V. C. Alfonso (Eds.), *Essentials of specific learning disability identification* (pp. 173–201). Hoboken, NJ: Wiley.

Harrison, A. G., & Holmes, A. (2012). Easier said than done: Operationalizing the diagnosis of learning disability for use at the postsecondary level in Canada. *Canadian Journal of School Psychology, 27,* 12–34.

Hinshelwood, J. (1902). *Congenital word-blindness with reports of two cases.* London: John Bale, Sons & Danielsson.

Jones, M. W., Ashby, J., & Branigan, H. P. (2013). Dyslexia and fluency: Parafoveal and foveal influences on rapid automatized naming. *Journal of Experimental Psychology: Human Perception and Performance, 39,* 554–567.

Katanoda, K., Yoshikawa, K., & Sugishita, M. (2001). A functional MRI study on the neural substrates for writing. *Human Brain Mapping, 13,* 34–42.

Kaufman, A. S. (2008). Neuropsychology and specific learning disabilities: Lessons from the past as a guide to present controversies and future clinical practice. In E. Fletcher-Janzen & C. Reynolds (Eds.), *Neuropsychological perspectives on learning disabilities in an era of RTI: Recommendations for diagnosis and intervention* (pp. 1–13). Hoboken, NJ: Wiley.

Kaufman, A., & Kaufman, N. (2014). *Kaufman Test of Educational Achievement* (3rd ed.). Bloomington, MN: NCS Pearson.

Kaufmann, L., Koppelstaetter, F., Siedentopf, C., Haala, I., Haberlandt, E., Zimmerhackl, L. B., & Ischebeck, A. (2006). Neural correlates of the number-size interference task in children. *NeuroReport, 17,* 587–591.

Kavale, K. A., & Flanagan, D. P. (2007). Utility of RTI and assessment of cognitive abilities/ processes in evaluation of specific learning disabilities. In S. Jimerson, M. Berns, & A. VanDerHeyden (Eds.), *Handbook of response to intervention: The science and practice of assessment and intervention.* New York, NY: Springer Science.

Kavale, K. A., & Forness, S. R. (2000). What definitions of learning disability say and don't say: A critical analysis. *Journal of Learning Disabilities, 33,* 239–256.

Kavale, K. A., Kauffman, J. M., Bachmeier, R. J., & LeFever, G. B. (2008). Response-to-intervention: Separating the rhetoric of self-congratulation from the reality of specific learning disability identification. *Learning Disability Quarterly, 31,* 135–150.

Kavale, K. A., Spaulding, L. S., & Beam, A. P. (2009). A time to define: Making the specific learning disability definition prescribe specific learning disability. *Learning Disability Quarterly, 32,* 39–48.

Kranzler, J. H., Floyd, R. G., Benson, N., Zaboski, B., & Thibodaux, L. (2016). Classification agreement analysis of Cross-Battery Assessment in the identification of specific learning disorders in children and youth. *International Journal of School and Educational Psychology, 4*(3), 124–136.

Kucian, K., von Aster, M., Loenneker, T., Dietrich, T., & Martin, E. (2008). Development of neural networks for exact and approximate calculation: An FMRI study. *Developmental Neuropsychology, 33,* 447–473.

Lichtenstein, R., & Klotz, M. B. (2007). Deciphering the federal regulations on identifying children with specific learning disabilities. *Communiqué, 36*(3), *1,* 13–16.

Magrassi, L., Bongetta, D., Bianchini, S., Berardesca, M., & Arienta, C. (2010). Central and peripheral components of writing critically depend on a defined area of the dominant superior parietal gyrus. *Brain Research, 1346,* 145–154.

Maricle, D. E., & Avirett, E. (2012). The role of cognitive and intelligence tests in the assessment of executive functions. In *Contemporary intellectual assessment: Theories, tests, and issues* (3rd ed., pp. 820–828). New York: NY: Guilford.

Mascolo, J. T., Alfonso, V. C., & Flanagan, D. P. (Eds.). (2014). *Essentials of planning, selecting, and tailoring interventions for unique learners.* Hoboken, NJ: Wiley.

Mather, N. (2011). *Let's stop monkeying around: What we know about reading disabilities.* Verona, NY: New York Association of School Psychologists.

Mather, N., & Kaufman, N. (2006). Introduction to the special issue, part one: It's about the what, the how well, and the why. *Psychology in the Schools, 43,* 747–752.

McCloskey, G., Perkins, L. A., & Van Divner, B. (2009). *Assessment and intervention for executive function difficulties.* New York, NY: Routledge.

McCloskey, G., Whitaker, J., Murphy, R., & Rogers, J. (2012). Intellectual, cognitive, and neuropsychological assessment in three-tier service delivery systems in schools. In D. P. Flanagan and P. L. Harrison (Eds.), *Contemporary intellectual assessment: Theories, tests and issues* (3rd ed., pp. 852–881). New York, NY: Guilford.

McDonough, E. M. (2017). Illustrative case report. In D. P. Flanagan & V. C. Alfonso, *Essentials of WISC-V assessment*. Hoboken, NJ: Wiley.

McDonough, E., & Flanagan, D. P. (2016). Use of the Woodcock-Johnson IV in the diagnosis of specific learning disabilities in school-age children. In D. P. Flanagan & V. C. Alfonso (Eds.), *WJ IV clinical use and interpretation*. San Diego, CA: Academic Press.

McDonough, E. M., Flanagan, D. P., Sy, M., & Alfonso, V. C. (2017). Specific learning disorder. In S. Goldstein & M. DeVries (Eds.), *Handbook of DSM-5 disorders in children*. New York, NY: Springer.

McGrew, K. S., & Knopik, S. N. (1996). The relationship between intra-cognitive scatter on the Woodcock-Johnson Psycho-Educational Battery–Revised and school achievement. *Journal of School Psychology, 34*, 351–364.

McGrew, K. S., LaForte, E. M., & Schrank, F. A. (2014). *Technical manual: Woodcock-Johnson IV*. Rolling Meadows, IL: Riverside.

McGrew, K., & Wendling, B. (2010). Cattell-Horn-Carroll cognitive-achievement relations: What we have learned from the past 20 years of research. *Psychology in the School, 47*, 651–675.

Miller, D. C. (Ed.). (2010). *Best practices in school neuropsychology: Guidelines for effective practice, assessment, and evidence-based intervention*. Hoboken, NJ: Wiley.

Monroe, M. (1932). *Children who cannot read: The analysis of reading disabilities and the use of diagnostic tests in the instruction of retarded readers*. Oxford, England: University of Chicago Press.

Mussolin, C., De Volder, A., Grandin, A., Schlogel, X., Nassogne, M. C., & Noel, M. P. (2010). Neural correlates of symbolic number comparison in developmental dyscalculia. *Journal of Cognitive Neuroscience, 22*, 860–874.

Naglieri, J. A. (2011). The discrepancy/consistency approach to SLD identification using the PASS theory. In D. P. Flanagan & V. C. Alfonso (Eds.), *Essentials of specific learning disability identification* (pp. 145–172). Hoboken, NJ: Wiley.

Oakley, D. (2006). Intra-cognitive scatter on the Woodcock-Johnson Tests of Cognitive Abilities–Third Edition and its relation to academic achievement. *Dissertation Abstracts International: Section B: The Sciences and Engineering, 67*, 1199.

Olson, R. K., Hulslander, J., Christopher, M., Keenan, J. M., Wadsworth, S.J., Willcutt, E. G., . . . DeFries, J. C. (2013). Genetic and environmental influences on writing and their relations to language and reading. *Annals of Dyslexia, 63*, 25–43.

Orton, S. T. (1937). *Reading, writing, and speech problems in children*. New York, NY: W. W. Norton.

Packer, L. E., & Pruitt, S. E. (2010). *Challenging kids, challenged teachers*. Bethesda, MD: Woodbine Press.

Pennington, B. F., & Olson, R. K. (2005). *Genetics of dyslexia. The science of reading: A handbook*. Oxford, UK: Blackwell.

Planton, S., Jucla, M., Roux, F-E., & Démonet, J-F. (2013). The "handwriting brain": a meta-analysis of neuroimaging studies of motor versus orthographic processes. *Cortex, 49*, 2772–2787.

Price, G. R., & Ansari, D. (2013). Dyscalculia: Characteristics, causes, and treatments. *Numeracy, 6*, Article 2.

Purcell, J., Shea, J., & Rapp, B. (2014). Beyond the visual word form area: The orthography–semantics interface in spelling and reading. *Cognitive Neuropsychology, 31,* 482–510.

Rapp, B., Purcell, J., Hillis, A. E., Capasso, R., & Miceli, G. (2015). Neural bases of orthographic long-term memory and working memory in dysgraphia. *Brain, 138,* 1–17.

Reynolds, C. R. (1985). Critical measurement issues in learning disabilities. *Journal of Special Education, 18,* 451–476.

Reynolds, C. R., & Shaywitz, S. A. (2009a). Response to intervention: Prevention and remediation, perhaps, diagnosis, no. *Child Development Perspectives, 3,* 44–47.

Reynolds, C. R., & Shaywitz, S. A. (2009b). Response to intervention: Ready or not? Or, from wait-to-fail to watch-them-fail. *School Psychology Quarterly, 24,* 130–145.

Richards, T. L., Berninger, V. W., Nagy, W., Parsons, A., Field. K., & Richards, A. L. (2005). Brain activation during language task contrasts in children with and without dyslexia: Inferring mapping processes and assessing response to spelling instruction. *Educational and Child Psychology, 22,* 62–80.

Richards, T. L., Aylward, E. H., Berninger, V. W., Field, K. M., Grimme, A. C., Richards, A. L., . . . Nagy, W. (2006). Individual fMRI activation in orthographic mapping and morpheme mapping after orthographic or morphological spelling treatment in child dyslexics. *Journal of Neurolinguistics, 19,* 56–86.

Richlan, F. (2012). Developmental dyslexia: Dysfunction of a left hemisphere reading network. *Frontiers in Human Neuroscience, 6,* 120.

Richlan, F., Kronbichler, M., & Wimmer, H. (2009). Functional abnormalities in the dyslexic brain: A quantitative meta-analysis of neuroimaging studies. *Human Brain Mapping, 30,* 3299–3308.

Schneider, W. J., & McGrew, K. S. (2012). The Catell-Horn-Carroll model of intelligence. In D. P. Flanagan & P. L. Harrison (Eds.), *Contemporary intellectual assessment: Theories, tests, and issues* (3rd ed.) (pp. 99–144). New York, NY: Guilford.

Schneider, W. J., & Roman, Z. (2018). Fine-tuning Cross-Battery Assessment procedures: After follow-up testing, use all valid scores, cohesive or not. *Journal of the Psychoeducational Assessment, 36*(1), 34–54. doi: 10.1177/0734282917722861

Shah, C., Erhard, K., Ortheil, H. J., Kaza, E., Kessler, C., & Lotze, M. (2013). Neural correlates of creative writing: An fMRI study. *Human Brain Mapping, 34,* 1088–1101.

Shalev, R. S., Manor, O., Kerem, B., Ayali, M., Badichi, N., Friedlander, Y., & Gross-Tsur, V. (2001). Developmental dyscalculia is familial learning disability. *Journal of Learning Disabilities, 34,* 59–65.

Shaywitz, S. E., Pugh, K. R., Jenner, A. R., Fulbright, R. K., Fletcher, J. M., & Gore, J. C. (2000). The neurobiology of reading and reading disability (dyslexia). In M. L. Kamil, P. B. Mosenthal, P. D. Pearson, & R. Barr (Eds.), *Handbook of reading research* (Vol. 3, pp. 229–249). Mahwah, NJ: Erlbaum.

Shaywitz, B. A., Shaywitz, S. E., Blachman, B., Pugh, K. R., Fulbright, R. K., Skudlarski, P., . . . & Gore, J. C. (2004). Development of left occipitotemporal systems for skills reading in children after a phonologically based intervention. *Biological Psychiatry, 55,* 926–933.

Siegel, L. S. (1999). Issues in the definition and diagnosis of learning disabilities: A perspective on *Guckenberger v. Boston University. Journal of Learning Disabilities, 32,* 304–320.

Silani, L. S., Frith, U., Demonet, J. R., Fazio, F., Perani, D., Price, C., . . . & Paulesu, E. (2005). Brain abnormalities underlying altered activation in dyslexia: A voxel-based morphometry study. *Brain, 128,* 2453–2461.

Skeide, M. A., Kirsten, H., Kraft, I., Schaadt, G., Muller, B., Neef, N., . . . & Friederici, A. D. (2015). Genetic dyslexia risk variant is related to neural connectivity patterns underlying phonological awareness in children. *NeuroImage, 118,* 414–421.

Stanovich, K. E. (1993). The construct validity of discrepancy definitions of reading disability. In G. R. Lyon, D. B. Gray, J. F. Kavanagh, & N. A. Hrasnegor (Eds.), *Better understanding learning disabilities: New views from research and their implications for education and public policy* (pp. 273–307). Baltimore, MD: Brookes.

Stanovich, K. E. (1999). The sociopsychometrics of learning disabilities. *Journal of Learning Disabilities, 32,* 350–361.

Szűcs, D., & Goswami, U. (2013). Developmental dyscalculia: Fresh perspectives. *Trends in Neuroscience and Education, 2,* 33–37.

US Office of Education (USOE). (1977). Assistance to states for education of handicapped children: Procedures for evaluating specific learning disabilities. *Federal Register, 42*(250), 65082–65085.

van Hoorn, J. F., Maathuis, C. G., & Hadders-Algra, M. (2013). Neural correlates of paediatric dysgraphia. *Developmental Medicine and Child Neurology, 55,* 65–68.

Vellutino, F. R., Scanlon, D. M., & Lyon, G. R. (2000). Differentiating between difficult-to-remediate and readily remediated poor readers: More evidence against the IQ-achievement discrepancy definition of reading disability. *Journal of Learning Disabilities, 33,* 223–238.

Vukovic, R. K., Kieffer, M. J., Bailey, S. P., & Harari, R. R. (2013). Mathematics anxiety in young children: Concurrent and longitudinal associations with mathematical performance. *Contemporary Educational Psychology, 38,* 1–10.

Wadsworth, S. J., Olson, R. K., Pennington, B. F., & DeFries, J. C. (2000). Differential genetic etiology of reading disability as a function of IQ. *Journal of Learning Disabilities, 33,* 192–199.

Wechsler, D. (2009). *Wechsler Individual Achievement Test–Third Edition (WIAT-III).* San Antonio, TX: Pearson.

Wendling, B. J., & Mather, N. (2009). *Essentials of evidence-based academic interventions* (Vol. 57). Hoboken, NJ: Wiley.

Wiig, E. H., Semel, E., & Secord, W. A. (2013). *Clinical Evaluation of Language Fundamentals–Fifth Edition (CELF-5).* Bloomington, MN: NCS Pearson.

Wright, J. (2002). Best practices in calculating severed discrepancies between expected and actual academic achievement scores: A step-by-step tutorial. Retrieved June 1, 2010, from www.kasp.org/Documents/discrepancies.pdf.

Zirkel, P. A., & Thomas, L. B. (2010). State laws for RTI: An updated snapshot. *Teaching Exceptional Children, 42*(3), 56–63.

Twelve

PATTERN OF STRENGTHS AND WEAKNESSES MADE EASY

The Discrepancy/Consistency Method

Jack A. Naglieri
Steven G. Feifer

INTRODUCTION

There are many reasons why students experience academic failure (e.g., poor instruction, lack of motivation, visual problems, lack of exposure to books and reading, teaching methods that are not best for a student's particular style of learning, overall limited intellectual ability, a specific intellectual ability deficit, etc.). In this chapter, we focus on those students who have a disorder in one or more of the basic psychological processes that underlie academic success and failure, that is, a student with scores from a reliable and well-validated multi-dimensional test of basic psychological processes that shows strengths and weaknesses. This pattern of strengths and weaknesses (PSW) provides evidence of a disorder in basic psychological processes and supports eligibility for special education when the specific weakness in basic psychological process corresponds to a specific weakness in achievement test scores. These students can be identified only via a comprehensive assessment that uncovers the processing deficit(s) and associated academic failure, despite adequate instruction and a consideration of other exclusionary factors. This type of student would meet the criteria for a specific learning disability (SLD) as defined by the 2004 reauthorization of the

Essentials of Specific Learning Disability Identification, Second Edition.
Edited by Vincent C. Alfonso and Dawn P. Flanagan
© 2018 John Wiley & Sons, Inc. Published 2018 by John Wiley & Sons, Inc.

Individuals with Disabilities Education Improvement Act (2004; referred to as IDEA 2004; see Hale, Naglieri, Kaufman, & Kavale, 2004).

This chapter is about students who have a PSW in one or more of the basic psychological processes and academic weakness(s) that are associated with that processing failure. The academic difficulties these students struggle with may have been exacerbated by poor instruction, but inadequate teaching did not cause the difficulties. These students would likely benefit from frequent progress monitoring, but ongoing progress monitoring is not enough to ensure academic success. In order to understand the reasons for academic failure, these students need to be evaluated carefully by a qualified school psychologist or other assessment expert who can identify an SLD on the basis of a disorder in one or more of the basic psychological processes and corresponding academic failure.

Students with cognitive and academic processing deficits require instruction that is tailored to their unique learning needs. In order to identify and teach these students properly, an evaluation of basic psychological processes and their relationship to academic failure must be conducted. This procedure requires that reliable, valid, and theoretically sound measures of basic psychological processes are used and that the scores, compared to measures of academic skills, are aligned with the conceptualization of processing. This method is based on finding discrepancies between good and poor measures of basic psychological processes, discrepancies between good and poor academic achievement scores, and consistency between poor processing and poor academic achievement test scores. We present a straightforward method to conduct such an evaluation, which was originally described by Naglieri (1999), and is called the discrepancy/consistency method (DCM).

In this chapter, we present the DCM to relate information about a student's basic psychological processes with academic achievement for the purpose of SLD eligibility determination. The goal is to clarify exactly how identification of students with an SLD can be accomplished with recognition of the requirements stipulated by IDEA 2004 and federal regulations (for more information see Hale, Kaufman, Naglieri, & Kavale, 2006; Kavale, Kaufman, Naglieri, & Hale, 2005). In the remainder of this chapter, we address the question of how to measure basic psychological processes and how measuring them meets federal law. We use the DCM (presented with a case study) to show clearly how the basic measurement of psychological processing and achievement test scores can be analyzed. This analysis is followed by a discussion of the extent to which the approach we recommend is consistent with validity and fairness requirements presented in IDEA 2004. See Rapid Reference 12.1.

≡ *Rapid Reference 12.1*

A SLD is suggested when there is a (1) discrepancy among processing scores, (2) discrepancy among achievement scores, or (3) consistency between low processing and low achievement scores (assuming that the low scores are substantially below average).

PROCESSING AND SLD DETERMINATION

IDEA (2004) describes several important components of a comprehensive evaluation that that have relevance for SLD eligibility determination. First, a variety of assessment tools and strategies must be used to gather relevant information about the student. Second, the use of any single measure or assessment as the sole criterion for determining whether a student has a SLD is not permitted. Third, practitioners must use technically sound instruments to assess the relative contribution of cognitive and behavioral factors. Fourth, assessments must be selected and administered in a way that does not discriminate on the basis of race or culture, and these tests are administered in a form most likely to yield accurate information. Fifth, the measures used are reliable and valid for the purposes for which they were intended.

The federal regulations (*Federal Register, 2016*) clarified that states are not allowed to prohibit the use of a severe discrepancy between ability and achievement for SLD determination, and use of the traditional ability-achievement discrepancy was only discouraged. The following two points were also clarified: Screening to determine appropriate instructional strategies for curriculum implementation shall not be considered an evaluation for special education eligibility. RTI may be used as a part of the SLD eligibility process, but "determining why a child has not responded to research-based interventions requires a comprehensive evaluation" (p. 46647) and "RTI does not replace the need for a comprehensive evaluation" (p. 46648). What RTI does provide is greater assurance that (1) adequate learning experiences have been provided before initiating a comprehensive evaluation and (2) the child's failure to respond is not the result of inadequate instruction. These regulations also further clarify that the assessments used in the comprehensive evaluation "include those tailored to assess specific areas of educational need and not merely those that are designed to provide a single general intelligence quotient" (p. 43785). Despite these changes in the methodology for identifying SLD, the definition of this disorder was not changed. Section 602 of IDEA 2004 defines an SLD as shown in Rapid Reference 12.2.

≡ *Rapid Reference 12.2*

A. In general—The term *specific learning disability* refers to a disorder in one or more of the basic psychological processes involved in understanding or in using spoken or written language. The disorder may manifest itself in the imperfect ability to listen, think, speak, read, write, spell, or perform mathematical calculations.

B. Disorders included—Perceptual disabilities, brain injury, minimal brain dysfunction, dyslexia, and developmental aphasia.

C. Disorders not included—A learning problem that is primarily the result of visual, hearing, or motor disabilities, of mental retardation, of emotional disturbance, or of environmental, cultural, or economic disadvantage.

The definition of SLD and the method used to identify students with this disorder should be consistent (Hale et al., 2004, 2006; Kavale et al., 2005). Because IDEA (2004) clearly specifies that students must have a disorder in one or more of the basic psychological processes,

DON'T FORGET

A "disorder in one or more of the basic psychological processes" should meet two criteria: (1) the processing score is relatively lower than the student's average and (2) the processing score is low in relation to the national norm.

which is the underlying cause of an SLD, cognitive processes must be measured. A comprehensive evaluation of the basic psychological processes unites the statutory and regulatory components of IDEA 2004 and ensures that the methods used for identification more closely reflect the definition. Any defensible eligibility system would demand continuity between the statutory and regulatory definitions, and for this reason alone SLD determination requires the documentation of a basic psychological processing disorder. Moreover, the tools used for this assessment must meet the technical criteria included in IDEA 2004.

Given all these guidelines, it is reasonable to ask, "Exactly how can we conduct an evaluation of a student suspected of having an SLD?" The DCM was designed to answer this question. This is a conceptual approach that could be operationalized with any well-developed measures of basic psychological processes and academic achievement. The critical element of this approach is a reliable and valid measure of basic psychological processes. Practitioners should choose wisely when selecting published tests to use for this purpose (this chapter includes a summary of research on the critical issues to guide that decision). Keep in mind that the tools we select have a profound impact on what we learn about a student, how much we can assist, and how well our decisions can withstand scrutiny in a due process hearing. We now provide a more detailed description of the DCM with examples of how it works.

DCM

Naglieri (1999) first described the DCM for the identification of SLD. The method is based on a systematic examination of cognitive and academic achievement test scores. Determining if the processing scores show a PSW is accomplished by using a modified version of the method originally proposed by Davis (1959), popularized by Kaufman (1979), and Silverstein (1993). This so-called ipsative method determines when the student's scores are reliably different from the average score.

It is important to note that the ipsative approach, which is used in the DCM, is based on an analysis of theoretically defined measures of basic psychological processes that correspond to brain function (see Naglieri & Otero, 2011, 2017). We also recommend that analysis of differences among basic psychological processing scores be based on (1) a theoretically derived test of neurocognitive processing; (2) scales that represent the theory, not subtest scores; and (3) assessment of the academic skills that correspond to the measure of neurocognitive processes. Stated more exactly, we strongly recommend using scores from scales that reflect a specific neurocognitive theory for determining if there is a disorder in one or more of the basic psychological processes and scores that measure specific aspects of academic performance. We also advocate a two-dimensional analysis of processing scores: low scores in relation to the student's average processing score and low scores in relation to the national average.

> **DON'T FORGET**
> ....
> SLD is defined by IDEA (2004) as a "disorder in one or more of the basic psychological processes," so these must be measured for a diagnosis to be rendered.

Naglieri (1999) first suggested that a low score in basic psychological processes could provide evidence of a specific disorder in processing only if the score is also below the average range relative to students of the same age. Additionally, the student must have deficient academic performance. The student with a weakness in basic psychological processing is very likely to have significantly lower achievement scores and may be identified as exceptional (Naglieri, 2000). This approach is illustrated in Figure 12.1, which shows that SLD can be detected when there is a significant discrepancy between the student's high cognitive processing

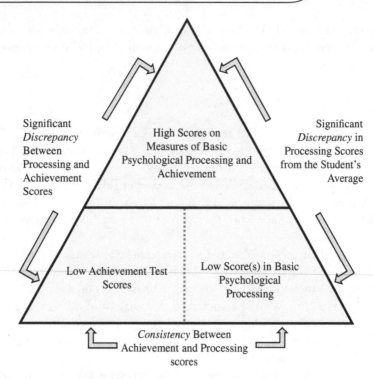

Figure 12.1. Discrepancy/Consistency Method for SLD Diagnosis

scores and some specific academic achievement, a significant discrepancy between the student's high and low cognitive processing scores (using the ipsative approach), and a consistency between the student's low processing and low achievement scores. This is a method to operationalize the PSW approach, which is discussed more fully elsewhere in Naglieri and Otero (2017).

Naglieri (1999) and Flanagan and Kaufman (2004) cautioned that, because the absolute value of a relative weakness could still be within the average range, a weakness that is low relative to the student's average and below the average category should be used to ensure that a student has "a disorder in the basic psychological processes" necessary for SLD identification (IDEA 2004, p. 11). To restate, the PSW should include significant variability in the cognitive processing scores and the lowest processing score is far enough below normal to be reasonably considered as a disorder (Naglieri, 1999). When there is a similar PSW in academic scores, a diagnosis of a SLD is supported, assuming that all exclusionary conditions are also met. All this is based on ensuring that the measures of basic psychological processes meet the technical requirements included in IDEA, that is, valid, reliable, nondiscriminatory, and more than general ability. The two important issues are (1) exactly how the DCM would work and (2) whether or not the tests recommended are sufficiently reliable and valid.

Using the DCM

In this chapter, we illustrate the use of the DCM with three instruments. First, the Cognitive Assessment System, Second Edition (CAS-2; Naglieri, Das, & Goldstein, 2014a) is used to measure basic psychological processes as defined by the planning attention simultaneous successive (PASS) theory. Second we use the Feifer Assessment of Reading (FAR; Feifer, 2015) and third the Feifer Assessment of Math (FAM; Feifer, 2016) as measures of academic performance that also involves PASS processes. Our goal is to show how SLD can be operationalized and such information used for diagnostic and instructional decision making. We are not suggesting that these are the only ways to use the DCM, but we do show that this approach has several advantages. First, it is parsimonious; there are four basic psychological processes to consider. Second, the integration of CAS-2 with FAR and FAM is theoretically sound and an elegant neurocognitive solution to the alignment of a disorder in basic psychological processes with academic difficulty. Third, this solution is consistent with requirements in IDEA 2004.

Specifics of the DCM

Using the DCM to determine if one or more of the four PASS scores could reflect a PSW is accomplished by comparing the difference between any individual PASS scale score with the average of the student's four PASS scores and the low score is below average. This method has been used often in intelligence testing (see Kaufman, 1994; Naglieri, 1999, 2011) because it has the advantage of providing statistical guidelines for examining individual profiles relative to the student's level of functioning. Once strengths and weaknesses in

> **DON'T FORGET**
> ....
> According to IDEA 2004, measurement of the basic psychological processes must be made using tests that are reliable and validated for that specific use.

PASS are detected, the scores from the CAS-2 can be compared to academic achievement scores on the FAR or FAM using values for significance found in Naglieri and Otero (2017). The steps for analyzing the CAS-2 are fully described by Naglieri and Otero (2017) and summarized here.

Assume that we have the following PASS scores for the CAS-2 12-subtest Extended Battery: Planning = 84, Simultaneous = 111, Attention = 96, and

Table 12.1 Differences Between PASS Standard Scores and the Student's Average PASS Score Required for Significance for the CAS-2 Extended and Core Batteries.

	Age	p	CAS-2 PASS Scales			
			Planning	Simultaneous	Attention	Successive
CAS-2 Extended	5–7	.05	9.5	9.3	8	9.4
		.10	8.5	8.3	7.2	8.4
	8–18	.05	9.3	8.3	9.5	9.1
		.10	8.4	7.4	8.6	8.2
CAS-2 Core	5–7	.05	11.2	10.1	9	10.7
		.10	10.1	9	8.1	9.6
	8–18	.05	10.2	9.1	10.9	10.4
		.10	9.2	8.1	9.8	9.3

Note: CAS-2 Extended has 12 subtests; CAS-2 Core has 8.

Successive = 93 for a student 8 years of age. The differences between each PASS score and the average are obtained by subtracting the mean score (96.0) from each PASS score. Negative values mean the score is below the average and positive scores indicate the value is above the average. Compare those difference scores to the values in Table 12.1. Differences between the individual score and average PASS score that are equal to or greater than the value in the table are significant. In this illustration, the Planning score of 84 is 12 points below the students' PASS average (a value of 8.4 is needed at $p = .10$) and well below average. This indicates that the Planning is significantly different from the average PASS score and the score is below the average range (90–109) and therefore designated as a weakness. By contrast, the Simultaneous score of 111 is above the student's average PASS score by 15 points (a value of 7.4 is needed) and is statistically significant. Because this score is in the above average range (110–119) it is designated as a strength. The Attention score of 96 is very similar to the student's average as is the Successive scale score of 93.

Once it has been established that there is a weakness (i.e., disorder) in one or more of the basic psychological processes (i.e., the weakness in PASS) then the PASS scores can be compared to achievement test scores. Any achievement test can be used; however, the use of an achievement measure that is aligned with PASS makes the connection between processing and academic failure more explicit.

Practitioners should look for discrepancies (significant differences) between high PASS scores and low scores on the FAR and FAM as well as consistencies (no significant differences) between low achievement and low PASS scores. The consistency between PASS and achievement scores indicates that the two measures are highly related; that is, they require the same kind of cognitive process despite a difference in test content.

What Is a Basic Psychological Process?

We use the terms *basic psychological process* and *cognitive process* to refer to a foundational neurocognitive ability that provides the means by which an individual functions in all settings and where each specific cognitive process provides a unique ability to perform. Our focus is on the PASS theory as described by Naglieri and Otero (2011, 2017) and as measured by the CAS-2. From this theory, successive processing is used to work with information that is arranged in a specific sequence and simultaneous processing is vital to seeing relationships among ideas. Attention is vital for focus of cognitive activity as well as resistance to distraction, and planning is the key to effective use of these processes and the entire base of knowledge and skills. Having several neurocognitive processing abilities affords us with the capability of completing the same task using different types or various combinations of processes. For example, a student may struggle to remember the sequence of letters needed to spell a long name (low in successive processing) but by organizing the string of letters into groups (using planning and simultaneous processes) the task can be achieved. Thus, changing the PASS processes a student uses can be an effective approach to intervention. See Rapid Reference 12.3.

PASS processes underlie all mental and physical activity. Through the application of these processes humans acquire all types of knowledge and skills to achieve fluency. However, it is very important to recognize that skills, such as reading decoding or math facts, also involve cognitive processes to varying degrees depending on the developmental level of the learner and the PASS

≋ Rapid Reference 12.3

Planning. Thinking about how you do what you decide to do

Attention. Being alert and resisting distractions

Simultaneous. Understanding how things go together to form a whole

Successive. Understanding how things go together in a specific order

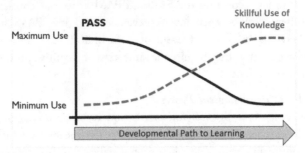

PASS + Knowledge = Skills

Figure 12.2. The Role of PASS on the Development Path to Learning

demands of the task. Naglieri and Otero (2007) describe this developmental learning process within the context of PASS as shown in Figure 12.2. The figure illustrates the role of PASS processing during learning. Initially, when there is little knowledge the learner has to rely on the ability to think (i.e., PASS). As knowledge is acquired, the role of PASS goes down and skillful or fluent application of knowledge results. For example, when a student sees and hears the word *book* for the first time there is an initial accumulation of knowledge. The student may look at the word and notice it starts with a *b*, then two letter *o*s, and ends with a letter *k*. Noticing these separate letters demands *attention,* the serial relationship of the letters involves *successive,* seeing the two *o*s as a group is *simultaneous,* and any analysis of how to manage the learning is *planning.* With good instruction and repetition, the word will be learned and the student will be able to read the word *book* fluently and with very little effort. At that point, the knowledge, which initially relied on PASS (and instruction, motivation, etc.), will become a skill and the word will be read fluently.

Assessment of basic psychological processes must be conducted using tests that are relatively free of academic content. Having measures of cognitive processes and achievement that do not have the same content maximizes the extent to which the two measures provide information that reflects the processing or academic construct efficiently rather than the combination of processing and academic skill. It is also critical to recognize that although achievement domains can be defined effectively by the content of the questions, processing tests are defined by the neurocognitive processing demands of the test questions and not by the content or modality. For example, the CAS-2 Successive processing scale is composed of three subtests that look very different. In one subtest (Word Series) high-imagery single-syllable words must be repeated in order as stated by the examiner; a second

(Visual Digit Span) requires that numbers, which were viewed, are recalled in order; and a third requires comprehension of the syntax of complex sentences. Despite the differences in these tasks, they all demand appreciation of the sequencing of the information—successive processing. The variety in modality and content strengthens the interpretation of the Successive scale on the CAS-2 because alternative interpretations are less plausible. For example, the description of word series as an auditory sequencing test is not supported because the visual sequencing test is included in the Successive processing scale. This is important because it helps understand how a student with poor successive processing can have an SLD in reading decoding and also have problems in math.

DON'T FORGET

Always ask the question, "What empirical evidence is there that supports a particular approach to measuring basic psychological processes?"

PASS Theory and Measurement

A. R. Luria's theoretical description of how the human brain functions is considered one of the most complete (Lewandowski & Scott, 2008). In his seminal works—*Human Brain and Psychological Processes* (1966), *Higher Cortical Functions in Man* (1980), and *The Working Brain* (1973)—Luria described the brain as a functional mosaic with parts that make specific contributions to a larger interacting network (Luria, 1973). That is, Luria stressed that no area of the brain functions without input from other areas so that cognition and behavior result from an interaction of complex brain activity across various areas. Luria's (1966, 1973, 1980) research on the functional aspects of the brain provided the basis for the PASS neurocognitive approach as an alternative to traditional notions of intelligence, which were initially described by Das, Naglieri, and Kirby (1994), operationalized by the CAS (Naglieri & Das, 1997), and more recently updated by Naglieri and Otero (2007) and Naglieri and Otero (2017). The four PASS processes represent a fusion of cognitive and neuropsychological constructs such as executive functioning (planning and attention); selective, sustain and shifting, attention (attention); visual-spatial processing of information into a coherent whole (simultaneous); and serial processing of information (successive; Naglieri & Das, 2005). The four PASS neurocognitive processes can be measured by the CAS-2, the CAS-2: Brief, and the CAS-2: Rating scale (Naglieri, Das, & Goldstein, 2014a, 2014b, 2014c). These individually administered measures are fully described in their respective test manuals and in the *Essentials of CAS-2 Assessment* (Naglieri & Otero, 2017). These four PASS neurocognitive processes are more fully described in the sections that follow.

Planning

Planning is a neurocognitive ability used to determine, select, and use strategies to solve problems when self-monitoring and self-correction are especially important (Naglieri & Otero, 2017). Planning is essential to all activities when there is the need for problem-solving. This includes an awareness of the need for a solution, monitoring how well things are going, consideration of alternative solutions that might be appropriate, and consideration of the relative value between continuing with a behavior or changing to a different one (Shadmehr, Smith, & Krakauer, 2010). Planning processing is also important when we reflect on the results of a completed task, recognizing what worked and what did not work, and considering other possible solutions in the future. These uniquely human activities are the responsibility of the frontal lobes of the brain (Goldberg, 2009).

To measure planning a test must allow a student to solve a novel problem for which there is no previously acquired strategy and minimal constraints should be placed on the way the student chooses to complete the task. For example, all of the Planning subtests on the CAS-2 and CAS-2: Brief (Naglieri et al., 2014a, 2014b) are best solved using strategies that the examinee decides to use after giving instructions that inform the student to complete the task using whatever method seems best. For this reason, the test scores reflect efficiency, measured by how long it takes to complete the task with the most correct responses.

Performance on academic tasks can also provide insights into a student's use of planning as well as the other PASS neurocognitive processes. Most any task can involve planning if the student has to make decisions about how to complete the task. For example, math computation demands evaluation of the task, consideration of the possible solutions, selection and use of the solution, checking to ensure that the solution was effective, and recognizing when the task is completed successfully. The same is true for writing, reading comprehension, evaluation of social situations, time management, and many other tasks that are best completed using a strategic (planning processing) approach. All PASS processes are involved in academic tasks (Naglieri & Rojahn, 2004) and these processes contribute to success on all reading and mathematics tests. The FAR (Feifer, 2015) and FAM (Feifer, 2016) tests offer a way to see how a student completes the task, for example, when a student spontaneously organizes verbal information that has to be recalled in a logical manner (planning) on the Word Recall subtest of the FAR. Similarly, a student may use a strategy (planning) to examine possible answers carefully (attention). This strategy can then be used to select an equation that best represents a mathematical word problem on the FAM.

We suggest that the CAS-2 and FAR and FAM together within a PSW model and DCM can provide an efficient and accurate assessment of SLDs in students.

This approach not only highlights cognitive and academic strengths and weaknesses but also provides a reliable and valid approach for SLD identification consistent with federal regulations. It also serves as a powerful framework to better inform intervention decision making. We begin our discussion with how planning and attention are expressed in mathematics.

The term *developmental dyscalculia* (*DD*) describes students with specific math-related deficits, including difficulty learning and retrieving mathematical facts, difficulty executing math calculation procedures when engaged in problem-solving, or lack of basic number sense and concept development skills to use a particular strategy when problem-solving (Rosselli, Matute, Pinto, & Ardila, 2006). Therefore, dyscalculia entails numerous cognitive and quantitative processes that underscore the development of mathematical achievement. One way to connect scores on a measure of cognitive processes with those obtained from an examination of academic knowledge is to use the FAM with the CAS-2. The FAM is specifically designed to examine the underlying neurodevelopmental processes that support the acquisition of proficient math skills. The test is composed of 19 individual subtests measuring various aspects of math fact retrieval, numeric and spatial memory, perceptual estimation skills, linguistic math concepts, and core number sense development. The FAM yields scores that reflect how a student solved the academic skills problems, which is consistent with the PASS theory as operationalized by the CAS-2 (see Rapid Reference 12.4). We demonstrate how this could work with a case example.

Case Study of William

William is a fourth-grade student whose rambunctious and playful personality has often led to academic and behavioral pitfalls in class. Though quite popular with peers, he tends to have a rather impulsive response style when problem-solving and often dives into an assignment with no particular strategy or plan. Unfortunately, poor planning is not a very prudent strategy when engaged in more complex mental operations such as solving mathematical word problems. For example, take a math word problem involving rate, time, and distance, when there is often too much information embedded within the problem. William often chooses the first numeral or data point presented in a hurried fashion and usually selects the wrong algorithm (strategy) to solve the problem. Planning, which is the essence of good executive functioning, is a necessary prerequisite for deciding "what to do when" and is very important when solving mathematical problems. Results of the CAS-2 provide important insight into William's ability to learn.

William's CAS-2 Full Scale score was in the below-average range and in the 19th percentile. Because this score reflects a combination of PASS processing

≡ Rapid Reference 12.4

•••

Math Subtypes as Measured by the FAM and PASS Processes

Math Subtype	Description	PASS Process
Procedural	A deficit in the ability to count, order, or sequence numbers, as well as difficulty remembering the sequence of mathematical procedures (e.g., algorithm) when problem-solving; consequently, when there is a breakdown in the procedural error system, the syntactical arrangement and execution of arithmetical procedures becomes compromised	Successive and Attention
Verbal	Difficulties encoding and retrieving overlearned math facts such as single-digit addition, single-digit subtraction, single-digit multiplication, and single-digit division; an inability to automatically retrieve stored math facts	Attention, Simultaneous, and Planning
Semantic	Consists of visual-spatial deficits hindering a variety of mathematically related skills including estimation skills, aligning numbers in columns when problem-solving, magnitude representations, and pattern recognition skills among objects; math difficulties stem from an inability to develop core number sense and magnitude representation	Simultaneous and Planning

strengths and weaknesses, emphasis should be placed on the separate PASS scores, which vary considerably. For instance, his simultaneous and successive processing scores were in the average range; however, William has cognitive weaknesses on the Planning and the Attention scales, which lead to poor control of thinking and acting and little use of strategies to focus attention and resist distractions. In fact, lower scores in Planning and Attention are typical for students with attention-deficit hyperactivity disorder (ADHD; Naglieri & Otero, 2011) and can be described as a problem with executive functioning (Naglieri et al., 2014c). Importantly, academic scores on the FAM mirror cognitive limitations on the

Table 12.2 William's PASS and Full Scale Scores from the CAS-2

PASS Scales	CAS-2 Standard Score	Percentile Rank	Difference from PASS Mean 91.2	Significantly Different (.05) from PASS Mean?	Strength (S) or Weakness (W)
Planning	77	6	−14.2	yes	W
Attention	82	12	−9.2	yes	W
Simultaneous	105	63	13.8	yes	
Successive	100	50	8.8	no	
CAS-2 Full Scale	92	30			

CAS-2, as shown in Table 12.2. The FAM yields three composite scales described in Rapid Reference 12.5.

The results of the FAM revealed significant deficits with the Semantic Index and, in particular, the Equation Building subtest due to poor planning and a tendency to select the first equation that best represented the word problem rather than a careful consideration of all choices. The Equation Building subtest requires students to select, though not solve, the proper equation that best represents a mathematical word problem and is part of the Semantic Index. William also performed very inconstantly on the Spatial Memory subtest, due primarily to his

≡ *Rapid Reference 12.5*

Scales on the FAM

Procedural Index. Measures the ability to count, order, and sequence numbers, as well as the ability to follow an algorithm or set of procedures used in calculating equations

Verbal Index. Measures the ability to automatically identify numbers, recall stored mathematical facts, and understand basic math terminology

Semantic Index. Measures the ability to determine magnitude representation, estimation skills, pattern-recognition skills, and quantitative reasoning when applying mathematical skills to solve real-world problems

Table 12.3 FAM Results for William

FAM Index	Standard Score (95% CI)	Percentile Rank	Qualitative Descriptor
Procedural Index	96 (+/−8)	39	Average
Verbal Index	101 (+/−8)	53	Average
Semantic Index	79 (+/−5)	8	Moderately below average
FAM Total Index	92 (+/−8)	30	Average

inconsistent attention span. He also became distracted by answer options that were similar to but not the correct answer. Table 12.3 depicts William's FAM profile of scores.

William's case illustrates how overall scores can be misleading because his overall FAM index score was consistent with his CAS-2 Full Scale score even though he clearly has specific weaknesses in the basic psychological processes of planning and attention with deficits in academic achievement. William makes careless mistakes due to impulsive problem-solving, which is most likely reflective of ADHD and is related to poor planning and attention. The DCM provides educators a way to conceptualize the relationships between the specific PASS processing and academic strengths to arrive at an accurate diagnosis. Clearly, William would meet IDEA 2004 criteria as a student with an SLD using the DCM and a PSW model. Once the disorder in basic psychological processing is established, then specific interventions can be considered (Naglieri & Feifer, 2017). For example, instructional modification may include color-coding math operational signs as well as color-coding important vocabulary terms embedded within word problems in order to trigger more consistent decision making. Cognitive interventions could include methods described by Naglieri and Pickering (2010), such as the handouts labeled Planning Facilitation and Overcoming Problems with Inattention. Additionally, specific strategies to stop, think, and create and plan when working, as well as targeted self-monitoring strategies to double-check work, would be beneficial as well. See Naglieri and Feifer (2017) for more information about interventions. Figure 12.3 illustrates William's profile of CAS-2 and FAM scores using the DCM approach.

Attention
The case of William also illustrates the role of attention in academic tasks. We use the term *attention* to designate a neurocognitive ability used to focus on a particular stimulus and inhibit responses. An optimal level of arousal is needed

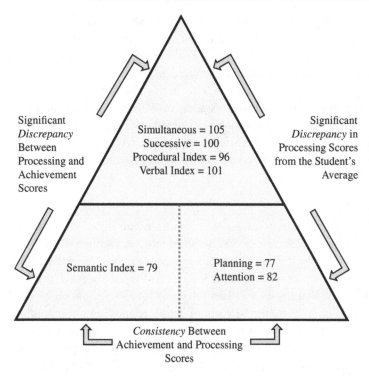

Figure 12.3. CAS-2 and FAM Results for Discrepancy/Consistency Method for the Case of William

for the more complex forms of attention that involve "selective recognition of a particular stimulus and inhibition of responses to irrelevant stimuli" (Luria, 1973, p. 271). Higher forms of attention are shown when a student demonstrates focused, selective, sustained, and effortful activity. The longer attention is needed for it, the more the activity requires vigilance. Brain structures such as the reticular formation enable an individual to focus selective attention toward a stimulus over a period of time without the loss of attention to other competing stimuli. Attentional processing assessed using CAS-2 subtests demand focused, selective, sustained, and effortful activity. Focused attention involves directed concentration toward a particular activity, selective attention provides the inhibition of responses to distracting stimuli, and sustained attention refers to the variation of performance over time, which can be influenced by the different amount of effort required to solve the test.

There are many academic tasks that are particularly dependent on attention. Clearly, everything a person does in and outside of school requires attention and resistance to distractions in the environment as well as distracting thoughts. Some tasks require more attention than others, particularly when the complexity of a task increases and a student has to select an answer from several options that look similar, as illustrated in the case of William. The key to detecting the role of attention in any specific activity is to notice the complexity of the stimuli. Whenever there are many things a student could attend to and what he or she has to focus on is less salient, attention will be required. Listening to the teacher when a fellow student is talking and being distracted by a text message or a sound outside of the room all illustrate what we measure on the Attention scale of the CAS-2 and the CAS-2 Rating scale.

Simultaneous

Simultaneous processing is used to integrate separate stimuli into a single whole where separate elements must be combined into a conceptual whole (Naglieri & Otero, 2017). The spatial aspect of simultaneous ability involves the perception of stimuli as a group or whole and the formation of visual images. The grammatical dimension of simultaneous processing allows for the integration of words into ideas through the comprehension of word relationships, prepositions, and inflections, so the person can obtain meaning. Thus, simultaneous processes involve nonverbal-spatial as well as verbal content. This ability is associated with the parietal-occipital-temporal brain regions. The distinguishing characteristic of CAS-2 subtests designed to measure simultaneous processing is the requirement that information must be organized into a coherent whole.

There are many academic tasks that are particularly dependent on simultaneous processing. These include, for example, recognizing sight words, whole-language instruction, comprehension of the meaning of a statement, paragraph or story, math word problems, and more advanced content such as geometry, chemistry, and so on. In this section, we examine how simultaneous processing can disrupt multiple aspects of the reading process as well as a how simultaneous processing can affect the ability to visualize mathematics. This can include poor reading comprehension because the student cannot see how to combine all the information into a cohesive whole or poor reading fluency due to an inability to take in the entire visual-spatial word form, thereby leading students to read at a slow pace and focusing on each sound of a word rather than the word as a whole. This tends to be a primary issue in surface dyslexia, which refers to poor reading fluency due to limitations with visual perceptual and orthographic processing (Feifer, 2015).

The FAR uses 15 individual subtests to measure various aspects of reading, including phonological development, orthographical processing, decoding skills, morphological awareness, reading fluency, and comprehension skills. The

≡ Rapid Reference 12.6

Reading Subtypes as Measured by the FAR and PASS Processes

Reading Subtype	Description	PASS Process
Dysphonetic	A deficit in the ability to use a phonological route to bridge letters and sounds; specific measures of phonemic awareness, decoding words and nonwords as well as decoding words in context comprise this domain	Successive, Attention
Surface	A deficit in the ability to automatically recognize words by taking in the visual perceptual and orthographic properties of the visual word form; specific measures of text perception, rapid naming, orthographic processing, and reading phonologically irregular words comprise this domain	Simultaneous, Attention
Mixed	The most severe type of reading disorder because these students lack the phonological processing skills to accurately identify words as well as the orthographic processing skills to automatically recognize the printed word form	Successive, Simultaneous, and Attention
Reading comprehension	A deficit in the ability to successfully derive meaning from print, despite adequate reading mechanics; specific measures of language development, working memory, executive functioning, and morphological processing comprise this domain	Planning, Attention

instrument measures four specific subtypes of reading disorders, all of which are derived from deficits in one or more PASS attributes (see Rapid Reference 12.6).

Case of Nick

Nick has been attending Bailey Elementary School since kindergarten and began receiving targeted academic interventions in first grade. According to school reports, Nick had difficulty acquiring basic sound-symbol associations, and his reading fluency was measured at just 27 words per minute correct on the

Table 12.4 Nick's PASS and Full Scale Scores from the CAS-2

PASS Scales	CAS-2		Difference from PASS Mean 92.0	Significantly Different (.05) from PASS Mean?	Strength (S) or Weakness (W)
	Standard Score	Percentile Rank			
Planning	100	50	8.0	no	
Attention	104	61	12.0	yes	
Simultaneous	74	4	−18.0	yes	W
Successive	90	25	−2.0	no	
CAS-2 Full Scale	92	30			

completion of first grade. Nick began receiving Tier 2 reading support services in second grade and worked with the school's reading specialist for approximately 30 minutes each day. He responded well to his reading intervention services and completed second grade reading approximately 57 words per minute accurately. Nevertheless, there were additional academic concerns on entering third grade. For instance, Nick was described as having difficulty with spelling and written language skills and was inconsistent with reading comprehension skills. He struggled to keep pace with his peers and often failed to complete his work in a timely manner. Table 12.4 depicts Nick's CAS-2 profile of scores.

Nick's overall CAS-2 Full Scale score was in the average range and at the 30th percentile compared to peers, but this score does not fully explain his PASS neurocognitive abilities. There were specific strengths noted in his Planning (100) and Attention (104) scales. He used a very efficient strategy when problem-solving and had little difficulty changing his plan based on the cognitive demands of the task. Furthermore, Nick worked very diligently and conscientiously throughout the test, refrained from making careless miscues, and focused his attention to the task at hand. However, there was a cognitive weakness noted on the Simultaneous processing scale (74), which can directly hinder a variety of academic skills such as spelling (difficulty conjuring up a visual spatial image of the printed word form), reading fluency, speed (difficulty automatically recognizing words as a conceptual whole), and mathematics (seeing patterns in numbers). Rapid Reference 12.7 describes each of the reading indices on the FAR.

≡ Rapid Reference 12.7

FAR Scales

Phonological Index. Measures the ability to use phonemic awareness and decoding skills to recognize words, nonwords, and words embedded within context

Fluency Index. Measures the ability to use visual perceptual and orthographical skills to rapidly retrieve and recognize words

Mixed Index. A combined measure of decoding skills and orthographic skills to accurately and automatically identify words in print

Comprehension Index. Measures the ability to derive meaning from print as well as underlying language skills, morphological processing skills, and executive functioning skills

Nick's achievement test scores correspond to the cognitive processing scales as shown by his pattern of scores on the FAR. He obtained a FAR total index score of 84, which, similar to the CAS-2 Full Scale score, was in the below-average range and at the 14th percentile compared to peers, but does not uniformly represent all of the scores the test yields. He performed adequately when decoding words in isolation as well as using decoding skills to accurately identify words embedded within the context of a story (successive processing). A relative strength was noted in his ability to answer targeted questions from story passages, because Nick had little difficulty deriving meaning from print.

A significant weakness was observed in the Fluency Index, which was in the moderately below-average range and at the 3rd percentile compared to peers. He worked slowly when rapidly identifying objects and letters, demonstrated poor text orthography skills, and had difficultly reading an isolated list of phonologically irregular words (i.e., *yacht, onion, debt,* etc.). Lower scores on rapid naming and text orthography tasks often stem from poor simultaneous processing and an inability to visualize the entire printed word form as a unique whole. This can lead to inconsistent spelling as well as slower print identification skills when reading. Nick would benefit from a targeted reading fluency intervention in order to increase text automatic recognition and fluency (i.e., Read Naturally, Great Leaps, RAVE-O, etc.). See Naglieri and Pickering (2010) and Naglieri and Feifer (2017) for more intervention options. Figure 12.4 illustrates Nick's profile of CAS-2 and FAR scores using the DCM method.

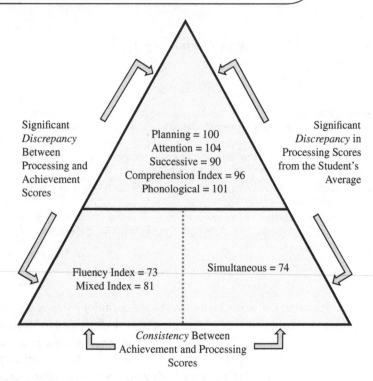

Significant *Discrepancy* Between Processing and Achievement Scores

Planning = 100
Attention = 104
Successive = 90
Comprehension Index = 96
Phonological = 101

Significant *Discrepancy* in Processing Scores from the Student's Average

Fluency Index = 73
Mixed Index = 81

Simultaneous = 74

Consistency Between Achievement and Processing Scores

Figure 12.4. CAS-2 and FAR Results for Discrepancy/Consistency Method for the Case of Nick

Simultaneous and Math

Case of Cheryl

Cheryl is an eighth-grade student who has consistently earned straight As throughout her educational career and has been a model student in class. She is a conscientious and attentive student and takes pride in her academic efforts. Cheryl has outstanding language development skills and is quite verbose and articulate in her manner. She has no history of math-related difficulties and has easily memorized most math facts. However, her advanced language and memory skills appear to be no match for the spatial types of skills needed to pass her geometry class, and this marked the first time in her academic career that Cheryl was failing a course. She especially struggled on problems involving spatial relationships and estimation skills, because Cheryl appeared out of her element when thinking in pictures and not in words. A review of her CAS-2 PASS scores provided an explanation for her learning difficulty, as seen in Table 12.5.

Table 12.5 Cheryl's PASS and Full Scale Scores from the CAS-2

PASS Scales	CAS-2 Standard Score	Percentile Rank	Difference from PASS Mean 102.6	Significantly Different (.05) from PASS Mean?	Strengths (S) or Weaknesses?
Planning	107	68	4.4	no	
Attention	124	95	21.4	yes	S
Simultaneous	82	12	−20.6	yes	W
Successive	108	70	5.4	no	
CAS-2 Full Scale	92	30			

Cheryl has a strength in the Attention scale (124) and a cognitive weakness on the Simultaneous scale (82) with average scores on Planning (107) and Successive processing (108). It is likely that she has compensated for simultaneous weakness by developing and using strategies (planning), having excellent ability to focus and resist distractions (attention), and good ability to work with and remember information in sequence (successive processing). However, geometry relies primarily on simultaneous processing to draw on a visual-spatial image, or gestalt, when dealing with questions of shape, size, relative position of figures, and the properties of space. Cheryl's cognitive weakness in simultaneous processing is hindering the acquisition of specific kinds of math skills.

Further testing with the FAM noted significant deficits with her semantic index, which involves a collection of subtests measuring skills such as spatial memory, perceptual estimation, and magnitude representation. In other words, the FAM provides evidence of how a particular cognitive processing deficit, as measured and defined by the CAS-2, specifically hinders mathematics. Her overall FAM index scores are shown in Table 12.6.

Cheryl's overall FAM Semantic Index score was in the below-average range and at the 12th percentile compared to peers. This represented an absolute weakness with mathematical skills. Nevertheless, Cheryl still had a strength in the verbal domain of math, because she was very quick to memorize single-digit addition, subtraction, multiplication, and division facts (this is dependent on using good strategies [planning] and remembering sequences of information [successive processing]). However, she had a poor understanding of the conceptual

Table 12.6 FAM Scores for Cheryl

FAM Index	Standard Score (95% CI)	Percentile Rank	Qualitative Descriptor
Procedural Index	84 (+/−8)	14	Moderately below average
Verbal Index	94 (+/−8)	34	Average
Semantic Index	70 (+/−5)	14	Moderately below average
FAM Total Index	82 (+/−8)	12	Below average

underpinnings of mathematics and struggled with an array of skills in the Semantic Index including poor estimation skills, poor magnitude representational skills, and limitations with spatial memory (simultaneous processing). In fact, Cheryl has the profile of a student with a cognitive weakness (simultaneous processing) and a mathematical weakness (Semantic Index), which was consistent with semantic dyscalculia.

It is important to note that Cheryl also has cognitive and academic strengths, which have been revealed using the DCM. This method shows the presence of a discrepancy within her PASS cognitive profile of strong cognitive processing and weak simultaneous processing. In addition, there is a consistency between her simultaneous score and her academic processing skills as represented by the Semantic Index score on the FAM. Targeted interventions should include teaching methods that allow Cheryl to touch, see, and feel spatial properties due to an inability to visualize them when problem-solving. This may include working with dice, dominoes, unifix cubes, vertical number lines, puzzles, tangible shapes, and more experiential learning to facilitate her spatial awareness skills. For more on intervention see Naglieri and Pickering (2010) and Naglieri and Feifer (2017). Figure 12.5 illustrates Cheryl's profile of CAS-2 and FAR scores using the DCM approach.

Successive

Successive processing is a neurocognitive ability that is used to work with information that is arranged in a specific serial order (Naglieri et al., 2014a). Successive processing is required to recognize, recall, and reason when success on any task demands the perception of stimuli in sequence, for example, the formation of sounds, letters, words. and movements into a specific order. This ability is necessary for the recall of information in order as well as phonological analysis and the syntax of language (Das et al., 1994). Deficits with successive processing are also associated with early reading problems in young students,

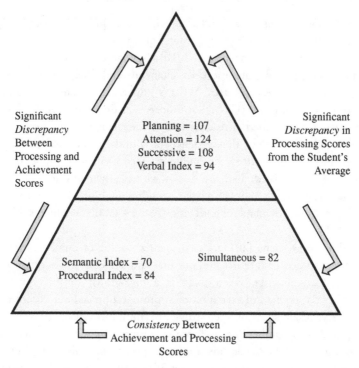

Figure 12.5. CAS-2 and FAR Results for Discrepancy/Consistency Method for the Case of Cheryl

because suck skill requires a student to learn sounds in a sequential order. This ability is associated with the temporal brain regions.

Many academic tasks demand successive processing, for example, counting, memorizing math facts, initial reading decoding of unfamiliar words, spelling, and sequencing of words to make a sentence. It is important to note that the overall meaning of a sentence demands simultaneous processing, but the ordering of the words to reflect the meaning requires successive processing. Successive processing is critical when a student is presented with very confusable words and must focus carefully on the pronunciation of sounds in order. Tests of phonological skills, reading decoding, and spelling all demand considerable successive processing. When serial information is grouped into a pattern (such as the number 55,366 organized into 55–3–66), then planning (i.e., using the strategy of chunking; see Naglieri & Pickering, 2010) and simultaneous processing (organizing the numbers into related groups) are also involved.

Math is a highly complex skill and often requires an underlying appreciation of ordering numbers, comprehending numeric quantities, and manipulating symbols in a sequential fashion (Feifer, 2016). Similar to reading and all other academic areas, planning, attention, simultaneous and successive processes are involved in various aspects of math. What is important to note is that although successive processing is a psychological process that underlies specific aspects of mathematics, it also underlies reading and written language skills as well. For instance, stitching together the sequence of sounds needed to spell requires successive processing, as does the ability to blend targeted phonemes when actively decoding a word. Perhaps this is why nearly two-thirds of children with a math learning disability also have a reading disability due, in part, to the successive processing demands of both tasks (Ashkenazi, Black, Abrams, Hoeft, & Menon, 2013).

According to Dehaene (2011), the sequential coding of numbers formulates the basis of the brain's internal number line and therefore relies on successive processing. Consequently, when there is a breakdown in this system, the syntactical arrangement and execution of arithmetical procedures becomes compromised. As a result, students often struggle to count forward and backward from various points on a number line, and routinely must "begin at 1" when counting or risk losing their place. In addition, successive processing deficits may impair the all-important algorithm or the internal set of procedures involved in calculating equations not committed to rote memory. This can involve recalling the sequences of steps necessary to perform multiple-step tasks such as long division, multiplying or dividing multiple-digit numbers, reducing fractions, and working with decimals. Last, there is often a breakdown in remembering the sequence of steps necessary to execute procedural operations due in part to limitations with successive processing (Feifer, 2016). Using the CAS-2 and FAR and FAM provides clinicians with a framework for a targeted, brain-based assessment of specific processing strengths and weaknesses that subserve reading and math skills as shown in the next case study.

Case of Peter

Peter struggled to remember the sequence of steps when doing math equations, basic math facts, and long passages when reading, when decoding words, and spelling hard words. What remained puzzling is that Peter had an outstanding memory for details and excelled when remembering specific aspects of a field trip or any type of experiential learning experience. Peter was initially referred for a school psychological evaluation while in third grade. The test results indicated no significant discrepancy between his ability and his achievement, both of which

Table 12.7 Peter's PASS and Full Scale Scores from the CAS-2

PASS Scales	CAS-2 Standard Score	CAS-2 Percentile Rank	Difference from PASS Mean 92.2	Significantly Different (.05) from PASS Mean?	Strength (S) or Weakness (W)
Planning	94	34	1.8	no	
Attention	94	34	1.8	no	
Simultaneous	102	55	9.8	yes	
Successive	79	8	−13.2	yes	W
CAS-2 Full Scale	92	30			

were in the average range. Furthermore, there were no attention or behavioral concerns reported as well. In fact, Peter was described as very polite and respectful in manner and put forth an excellent effort in school. He did not qualify for special education services, and the evaluation offered little with respect to targeted interventions or classroom accommodations to assist with learning.

Peter is currently in fifth grade and remains below grade level in reading and mathematics. He was referred for an updated assessment using a processing strengths and weaknesses approach to determine how Peter learns in order to identify more-specific and effective intervention strategies. Table 12.7 depicts Peter's CAS-2 profile of scores.

Consistent with previous intelligence testing, Peter's overall CAS-2 Full Scale score of 92 was in the average range and at the 27th percentile (see Table 12.8).

Table 12.8 Peter's Scores on the FAM

FAM Index	Standard Score (95% CI)	Percentile Rank	Qualitative Descriptor
Procedural Index	76 (+/−8)	5	Moderately below average
Verbal Index	81 (+/−8)	10	Below average
Semantic Index	98 (+/−5)	45	Average
FAM Total Index	86 (+/−8)	18	Below average

Most of his PASS scores are in the average range, with the exception of his successive (79) processing, which was a weakness. Lower scores on this scale reflect his difficulty working with information in a sequential order. It is important to note that difficulties with successive processing can hinder verbal information (i.e., remembering multiple-step directions) or nonverbal information (i.e., remembering longer algorithms or steps when engaged in more complex mathematics). Therefore, the next question that arises is how does poor successive processing directly affect Peter's reading and mathematical skills?

Further testing with the FAM noted significant deficits with Peter's Procedural Index, which involves a collection of sequence-based skills such as skip counting forward and backward from various points on a number line as well as recognizing patterns and sequences among number relationships. His overall FAM Total Index score was 86, which was in the below-average range and in the 18th percentile. Peter's core deficit with successive processing influences mathematics in a symbolic fashion (i.e., difficulty identifying number patterns) as well as a conceptual fashion (i.e., difficulty remembering the sequences of steps needed to solve more complex equations). In addition, Peter also struggled on the Verbal Index, which is a measure of automatic or reflexive problem-solving of single-digit math facts. He had difficulty retrieving basic math facts when timed, though his conceptual understanding of mathematics was sound (Semantic Index). Peter was also administered the FAR to determine the impact of his low successive processing with reading skills (see Table 12.9).

Table 12.9 Peter's Scores on the FAR

FAR Index	Standard Score (95% CI)	Percentile Rank	Qualitative Descriptor
Phonological Index	79 (+/−3)	8	Moderately below average
Fluency Index	92 (+/−8)	30	Average
Mixed Index	85 (+/−4)	16	Below average
Comprehension Index	90 (+/−10)	25	Average
FAR Total Index	84 (+/−4)	14	Below average

Peter obtained a FAR total index score of 84 +/−4, which is in the below-average range of functioning and in the 14th percentile (see Table 12.9). He especially had difficulty within the Phonological Index, which required Peter to use successive processing to chunk together individual sounds or phonemes in order to identify words. Instead, he tended to overly rely on his stronger simultaneous processing, as evidence by his good performance on the Fluency Index. For instance, Peter performed well on a task that required him to identify phonologically irregular words (i.e., *yacht, debt, onion,* etc.), though he had considerably more difficulty identifying words that were more readily decodable. In essence, Peter struggled on more decodable words because of his weakness in successive processing and resulting difficulty combining sounds in a sequential manner to identify targeted words. Instead, he was simply memorizing his way through books by using his strong simultaneous processing to take in the entire printed word form, a strategy much better suited for phonologically irregular words that cannot readily be decoded. Peter would benefit from an explicit phonological approach to reading (i.e., Fundations, Wilson, Orton-Gillingham, etc.) that allowed him to develop more automaticity with respect to blending sounds to recognize words.

Once again, the DCM provides a way to examine the specific processing strengths and weaknesses within Peter's neurocognitive abilities, as well as his academic skills, for eligibility determination and to develop targeted interventions. As can be seen from Figure 12.6, there was a significant discrepancy between Peter's successive processing and the rest of his psychological processing scores as measured by the CAS-2. In addition, the FAM indicated that his Procedural Index was a relative weakness, and FAR indicated that his Phonological Index was a weakness. Finally, there was a consistency between Peter's difficulties in the sequential aspect of mathematics (Procedural Index) and sequential aspects of reading (Phonological Index) and lower successive processing scores. Therefore, it is important to note that PASS basic psychological processes as measured by the CAS-2 help us understand variation in the development of numerous skills. Specific strategies to assist Peter in math may include learning how to chunk information, using mnemonic strategies to remember longer mathematical algorithms, practice number line fluency skills, and playing math games to develop greater procedural knowledge when problem-solving. See Naglieri and Pickering (2010) and Naglieri and Feifer (2017) for more information about interventions. Figure 12.6 illustrates Peter's profile of CAS-2 and FAR-FAM scores using the DCM approach.

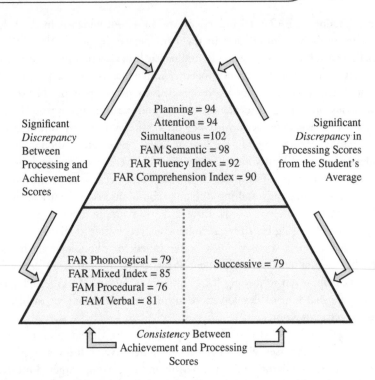

Figure 12.6 content:

Significant *Discrepancy* Between Processing and Achievement Scores

Planning = 94
Attention = 94
Simultaneous =102
FAM Semantic = 98
FAR Fluency Index = 92
FAR Comprehension Index = 90

Significant *Discrepancy* in Processing Scores from the Student's Average

FAR Phonological = 79
FAR Mixed Index = 85
FAM Procedural = 76
FAM Verbal = 81

Successive = 79

Consistency Between Achievement and Processing Scores

Figure 12.6. CAS-2, FAR, and FAM Results for Discrepancy/Consistency Method for the Case of Peter

VALIDITY OF THE PASS THEORY

IDEA 2004 and the DCM

The long-standing approach of using an ability-achievement discrepancy to determine if a child has an SLD is no longer required but is not disallowed in IDEA 2004, which also states that "the local educational agency may use a process that determines if the child responds to scientific, research-based intervention as a part of the evaluation procedures." Importantly, the Response to Intervention (RTI) method is allowed but not mandated (see §614(b) 6B of IDEA 2004). Instead of an ability achievement discrepancy or RTI, the analysis of the PSW in basic psychological processes (and achievement) originally proposed by Naglieri (1999) and suggested by others (Flanagan, Alfonso & Mascolo, 2011; Hale & Fiorello, 2004) has emerged as a viable method of SLD eligibility determination. The DCM described in the chapter provides a specific procedure for identifying SLD that is based on a PSW in basic psychological processes (PASS) and academic skills. Perhaps most important, using this method unifies the definition of SLD and the method used to identify children as suggested by Kavale et al. (2005) and Hale et al. (2004, 2006). These authors argued that because IDEA 2004 clearly states that children must have a disorder in "one or more of the basic psychological processes," a comprehensive evaluation of the basic psychological processes unites the statutory and regulatory components of the law (p. 11).

DOES THE DCM MEET IDEA 2004 REQUIREMENTS?

There had been an increasing emphasis on empirically supported methods of SLD eligibility determination in IDEA 2004. In order to demonstrate the science behind the DCM we are presenting, several of those requirements are discussed. Interested readers could read more on the validity of the PASS theory for SLD diagnosis and intervention in several other sources (Naglieri, 1999, 2005, 2008; Naglieri & Conway, 2009; Naglieri & Das, 1997, 2005; Naglieri & Otero, 2011, 2017) and, therefore, only a few points relevant to the DCM is summarized here.

> **DON'T FORGET**
> ....
> Always ask the question, "What empirical evidence is there that supports a particular approach to measuring basic psychological processes?"

IS COGNITIVE PROCESSING ASSESSMENT NONDISCRIMINATORY?

The need for fair assessment of diverse populations of students has become progressively more important as the US population continues to become more diverse. Recognizing this change, IDEA (2004) stresses that assessments must not discriminate on the basis of race, culture, or language background. Appropriate assessment of students who may have SLD from all race and ethnic groups must be accomplished using tools that are nondiscriminatory. At the heart of this issue is selection of the tools that can be most effectively used within a diverse context. Fagan (2000), Naglieri (2015), and Suzuki and Valencia (1997) argued that because processing tests do not rely on questions with language and quantitative content, they are more appropriate for assessment of culturally and linguistically diverse populations. Ceci (2000) suggested that a processing approach could (1) allow for early detection of disabilities before academic failure is experienced, (2) have better diagnostic utility, and (3) provide a way to better understand students' disabilities.

There is evidence that PASS cognitive processing scores differ minimally between race and ethnic groups and when the test is given in different languages.

DON'T FORGET
....

There is considerable evidence that the PASS theory as measured by the CAS can be appropriately used for culturally and linguistically diverse populations.

For example, PASS cognitive processing scores of 298 African American children and 1,691 Caucasian children were compared (Naglieri, Rojahn, Matto & Aquilino, 2005). Controlling for key demographic variables, regression analyses showed a CAS Full Scale mean standard score difference of 4.8 points in favor of Caucasian children. Similarly, Naglieri, Rojahn, and Matto (2007) examined the utility of the PASS theory with Hispanic children by comparing performance on the CAS of Hispanic and Caucasian children from the standardization sample ($N = 2,200$). The study showed that the two groups differed by 4.8 standard score points when demographics differences were statistically controlled. They also found that the correlations between achievement and the CAS scores did not differ significantly for the Hispanic and Caucasian samples (Naglieri, Rojahn, & Matto, 2007). These initial findings suggested that measuring neurocognitive abilities rather than traditional intelligence quotients (IQs) resulted in smaller differences between Hispanic and Caucasian groups. The next study of Hispanics provided additional insights into the value of PASS theory as measured by the CAS.

Comparisons of PASS scores obtained for the English and Spanish versions of the CAS have been conducted. Naglieri, Otero, DeLauder, and Matto (2007) compared PASS standard obtained on the CAS when administered in English and Spanish to bilingual children referred for reading problems. The children earned similar Full Scale scores on the English and Spanish versions of the CAS, using the regular norms conversion tables, which were highly correlated ($r = .96$). Deficits in successive processing were found on both versions of the test (consistent with the view that children with reading disabilities are poor in this process), and 90% of children who had a cognitive weakness on the English version of the CAS also had the same cognitive weakness on the Spanish version of the CAS. Otero, Gonzalez, and Naglieri (2012) replicated that study with another group of students referred for reading problems and found CAS Full Scale scores that differed by less than one point and a high correlation between the scores (.94). Similar results were reported for the CAS-2 Full Scale scores in the test manual (Naglieri et al., 2014a). Without controlling for demographic differences, Hispanics and non-Hispanics differed on the CAS-2 Full Scale scores by 4.5 points, and with controls for demographic characteristics, the difference was 1.8. Very similar results are reported in the CAS-2: Brief manual.

Natur (2009) compared Arabic-speaking Palestinian students using the Arabic version of the CAS to a matched sample of children from the United States. He found a very small difference between the Arab (Full Scale standard score mean of 101.0) and US (Full Scale standard score mean of 102.7) scores using the US norms. Naglieri, Taddei, and Williams (2013) found that Italian children's ($N = 809$) Full Scale standard score of 100.9 on the Italian version of the CAS (Naglieri & Das, 2006) was very similar to the Full Scale of 100.5 for a matched sample of US children ($N = 1,174$) from the original standardization sample. The samples' CAS standard scores were based on the US norms. Importantly, multigroup confirmatory factor analysis results supported the configural invariance of the CAS factor structure between Italians and Americans for the 5- to 7-year-old and 8- to 18-year-old age groups.

Race differences in PASS scores have also been studied. The CAS scores of 298 African American and 1,691 Caucasian children were compared by Naglieri et al., (2005). Controlling for key demographic variables, regression analyses showed a CAS Full Scale mean score difference of 4.8. They also found that correlations between the CAS scores and Woodcock-Johnson–Revised Tests of Achievement (WJ-R ACH; Woodcock, McGrew, & Mather, 2001) were very similar for African Americans (.70) and Caucasians (.64), illustrating the lack of predictive bias in the scores. This research was replicated by results for the CAS-2 and the CAS-2: Brief. The approach used to compare race groups was the same method described by Naglieri et al. (2005). After the effects of gender, region, parental education, and educational setting were statistically controlled a CAS-2 Full Scale standard difference of 4.5 score points was found. Similar findings are reported in that manual for the CAS-2: Brief.

The small differences by race and ethnicity, as well as the similarity in scores across different versions of the CAS (English versus Spanish, US versus Arabic, and US versus Italian samples), as well as the factorial similarity for the Italian and US samples strongly suggest that the neuropsychologically based PASS theory as measured by the CAS appears to be robust across cultures and language. These findings are best understood within the context of differences found on other ability tests, which is summarized next.

Table 12.10 provides a summary of standard score differences by race for the CAS (Naglieri & Das, 1997) and CAS-2 (Naglieri et al., 2014a), K-ABC and KABC-II (Kaufman & Kaufman, 1983, 2004), the Stanford-Binet-IV (SB-IV; Roid, 2003), the WISC-IV (Wechsler, 2003), and the Woodcock-Johnson Tests of Cognitive Abilities, Third Edition (WJ-III; Woodcock et al., 2001). The results for the WISC-IV are reported by O'Donnell (2009), the SB-IV by Wasserman and Becker (2000), and the WJ-III results are from Edwards and Oakland (2006). The race differences for the K-ABC normative sample were reported in that test's manual (Kaufman & Kaufman, 1983) and the findings for the KABC-II were

Table 12.10 Mean Standard Score Differences by Race on Several Ability Tests

Ability Test	Standard Score Difference	
Traditional IQ Tests		
	SB-IV**	12.6
	WISC-IV*	11.5
	WJ-III*	10.9
	WISC-IV**	10.0
Nontraditional Tests		
	K-ABC**	7.0
	K-ABC**	6.1
	KABC-II**	5.0
	CAS-2*	6.3
	CAS***	4.8
	CAS-2***	4.3

Note: Comparisons made using unmatched samples from the standardization samples are designated with*; samples matched on demographic characteristics are designated with **, and sample differences controlled using regression procedures are designated with ***.

summarized by Lichtenberger, Sotelo-Dynega, and Kaufman (2009). Differences for the CAS were reported by Naglieri et al. (2005) and in the test manual for the CAS-2 by Naglieri et al. (2014a). The results clearly show that measuring ability as a cognitive process as operationalized by the CAS, CAS-2, KABC, and KABC-II is associated with smaller race differences (see Naglieri & Otero, 2017, for more details).

There is an important difference between traditional IQ tests and those tests that take a cognitive processing approach to conceptualizing ability. That is, the content of the subtests is less academically laden, especially the CAS and CAS-2. We suggest that the exclusion of tests that demand knowledge of words (e.g., vocabulary, similarities) and math (e.g., arithmetic) and the inclusion of tests that represent a theoretical conceptualization of basic psychological processes play a critical role in reducing the differences between groups. It is important, however, to ask the question, "Does elimination of academic content reduce the validity of the processing test?" This question is perhaps most clearly addressed by studying the correlation between the scores from a test of processing with a test of achievement.

PASS Relationship to Achievement

Understanding the relationship between a test of ability or basic psychological processes with a test of achievement is complicated by the fact that IQ test questions measure very similar content to achievement tests (e.g., vocabulary, arithmetic word problems, phonological skills, etc.). For this reason, traditional IQ tests have an advantage over those measures that do not include verbal and quantitative test items (Naglieri & Bornstein, 2003). Despite that advantage, Naglieri (1999) initially reported that the correlations between achievement test scores with the CAS and K-ABC were as high as or higher than those found for the WISC-III and WJ-R. More recently, Naglieri (2015, 2016) examined the strength of the correlation between the WISC-V and WIAT-III using data from the test's manual (Table 5.12; Wechsler, 2014). In order to look at the relationship with and without the influence of those portions of the WISC-V, we require verbal knowledge used in the two procedures. First, the average correlation among all five WISC-V scales with the WIAT-III total was computed. Second, the average of the WISC-V scales when the Verbal Comprehension Index was excluded was obtained. This allows for a way to understand how correlated the Wechsler is when the most achievement-like scale (Verbal Comprehension, which includes questions that require knowledge, similarities, and vocabulary) is excluded. When combined with other test data, this method proves very revealing. The same approach was taken with data from the Woodcock-Johnson IV Test of Cognitive Abilities and Achievement (Schrank, McGrew, & Mather, 2014, Table 5.6) and the K-ABC-II (Kaufman & Kaufman, 2004). The findings are provided in Table 12.11.

What is most revealing about these results is the clear pattern across the WISC-V, WJ-III, and the KABC-II. The correlations between each of these tests and achievement was higher when the scales that demand verbal knowledge were included. The Verbal Comprehension scale and the WIAT-III give the best explanation why. The results were so highly correlated because of the similarity in content across the two tests. Some researchers (e.g., Lohman & Hagan, 2001) argue that this is evidence of validity; we suggest that correlations between achievement test scores and ability tests are artificially inflated because of the shared content. The correlations between the scales that do not require knowledge

Table 12.11 Average Correlations Between Ability and Achievement Including and Excluding the Most Academically Laden Scales on the Tests of Ability

Average Ability and Achievement Correlations			All Scales	Selected Scale Correlations
WISC-V	Verbal Comprehension	.74	.53	
WIAT-III	Visual Spatial	.46		.47
N = 201	Fluid Reasoning	.40		
	Working Memory	.63		
	Processing Speed	.34		
WJ-IV COG	Comprehension Knowledge	.50	.54	
WJ-IV ACH	Fluid Reasoning	.71		
N = 825	Auditory Processing	.52		
	Short-Term Working Memory	.55		.50
	Cognitive Processing Speed	.55		
	Long-Term Retrieval	.43		
	Visual Processing	.45		
KABC-II	Knowledge/GC	.70	.53	
WJ-III ACH	Sequential/Gsm	.43		.48
N = 167	Simultaneous/Gv	.41		
	Learning/Glr	.50		
	Planning/Gf	.59		
CAS	Planning	.57	.59	
WJ-III ACH	Simultaneous	.67		
N = 1,600	Attention	.50		
	Successive	.60		

are a more accurate estimate of the relationship between ability as measured by a specific test and achievement. In this summary, what is found is that the correlation for the CAS, which does not include these achievement-laden subtests, was .59, higher than all the others.

Do Exceptional Children Have Specific PASS Profiles?

Recently, Naglieri (2015) summarized reports found in the Wechsler Intelligence Scale for Children, Fourth Edition (WISC-IV; Wechsler, 2003) technical manual, the Woodcock-Johnson III Tests of Cognitive Abilities (WJ-III; Woodcock et al., 2001) from Wendling, Mather, and Schrank (2009), and CAS data from the technical manual and Naglieri et al. (2007). We have added the WISC-V (Wechsler, 2014) data from that test's manual to this comparison as shown in Figure 12.7. The findings must be considered with recognition that the samples were not matched on demographic variables across the various studies, the

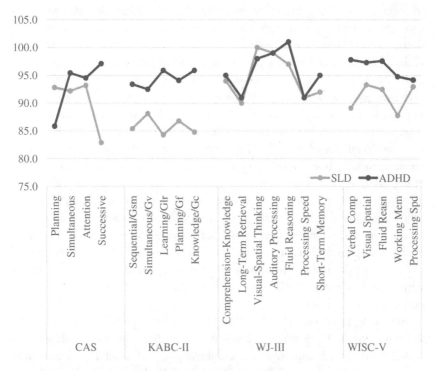

Figure 12.7. Ability Test Profiles for Students with Specific Learning Disabilities and Attention-Deficit Hyperactivity Disorder

accuracy of the diagnosis may not have been verified, and some of the sample sizes were small. Notwithstanding these limitations, the findings provide important insights into the extent to which these various tests are likely to yield scale-level profiles that are distinctive, thereby providing validity evidence for application of the DCM for SLD diagnosis. As is apparent from these data, the students with a specific reading decoding disability showed a specific PASS cognitive weakness that is different from those with ADHD. These findings provide support for use of the PASS theory and the DCM.

The profiles of the PASS processing standard scores obtained from children with reading decoding disability and ADHD are consistent with theoretical expectations and previous research (see Figure 12.7). For example, reading decoding is a common problem for many children that has been related to a cognitive weakness in successive processing. Das, Naglieri, and Kirby (1994) suggested that a successive processing deficit underlies a phonological skills deficit and is an associated reading decoding failure. Successive processing's involvement increases if the word is not easily recognized, and this process is even more important if the words are to be read aloud because articulation also requires a considerable amount of successive processing. For this reason, a test of phonemic skills, such as phonemic separation, is sensitive to reading failure (Das, Mishra, & Kirby, 1994). Several studies on the relationship between PASS and reading disability have shown that successive processing is an important ability that underlies phonological skills (Das, Parrila, & Papadopoulos, 2000). Finally, Huang, Bardos, and D'Amato (2010) studied PASS profiles on the CAS for large samples of students in regular education ($N = 1,692$) and students with learning disabilities ($N = 367$). They found 10 core PASS profiles for those in regular educational and eight unique profiles from students with SLD. Haung et al. (2010) concluded that "a student with a true LD has a relatively high chance of being accurately identified when using profiles analysis on [PASS] scores" (p. 28). They added that their "analysis has provided evidence for the use of the PASS theory and that it appears that it has sufficient applications for diagnosis for students suspected of having a LD" (p. 28). Individuals with ADHD have a different disorder in basic psychological processing. Is there a theoretical reason why individuals with ADHD have a weakness in planning? Yes, and the theory is borne out by the research.

According to Barkley (1997) "ADHD represents a profound disturbance in self-regulation and organization behavior across time" (p. vii). Children with ADHD (combined and hyperactive-impulsive types) exhibit problems with inhibition, poor planning, reduced self-monitoring, poor organization, impaired problem-solving, poor self-regulation, and problems developing, using, and monitoring strategies (Barkley, 2003; Hale, Fiorello, & Brown, 2005). These children are described as having difficulty with the basic psychological process of planning (Naglieri & Otero, 2011) and executive function, which are associated with the prefrontal lobes (Goldberg, 2009). Associating these symptoms to the frontal lobes as suggested by Goldberg provides a clear connection between the disorder and the PASS neurocognitive theory we have presented in this chapter and as described by Naglieri and Otero (2011, 2017). The data presented in this chapter for individuals with ADHD are also consistent with cross-cultural studies and findings by Van Luit, Kroesbergen, and Naglieri (2005) and Taddei and Venditti (2010), who found that Dutch and Italian children with ADHD, respectively, also earned their lowest score on the Planning scale of the CAS. Finally, Canivez and Gaboury (2010) also found support for the diagnostic utility of the PASS theory for those with ADHD.

CONCLUSION

The purpose of this chapter was to describe a procedure that can be used to identify children with SLD using the PSW model and the DCM. Our approach to defining and measuring basic psychological processes that form the foundation of the PSW is based on the PASS neurocognitive theory that has been extensively studied. We have shown how the DCM can be used within the PASS theory, which unites a test of basic psychological processes (CAS-2) with tests of reading (FAR) and math (FAM). We have also presented case studies and research evidence that illustrate the extent to which our approach meets requirements of IDEA 2004, that the assessment of SLDs is not discriminatory, and that the tools used are valid for this purpose. Our goal is to use new approaches to measuring cognition and achievement that, as the evidence presented in this chapter and elsewhere, are theoretically sound, empirically supported, and straightforward to use. Our hope is that we can help practitioners more accurately identify and instruct students with SLDs.

🐟 TEST YOURSELF 🐟

1. **The definition of an SLD used in IDEA 2004:**
    (a) Requires an ability achievement discrepancy
    (b) Is based on a disorder in one or more of the basic psychological processes
    (c) Requires having deficits in more than one academic area
    (d) Requires measuring words per minute

2. **The DCM requires that a "disorder" in basic psychological processing be:**
   (a) Low relative the norm
   (b) Low relative to the student's average
   (c) Neither a nor b
   (d) Both a and b

3. **IDEA 2004 requires that assessment of SLDs be determined using:**
   (a) A comprehensive evaluation
   (b) RTI only
   (c) Measures that are valid for the purposes for which they were intended
   (d) A and c only

4. **When using a PSW approach there should be:**
   (a) A "disorder" in basic psychological processes
   (b) Achievement test scores that align with the variation of processing scores
   (c) Both a and b

5. **According to IDEA 2004 an appropriate test of basic psychological processes should be:**
   (a) Nondiscriminatory
   (b) Reliable
   (c) Valid for the purpose for which it is used
   (d) All of the above

Answers: 1. b; 2. d; 3. d; 4. c; 5. d.

REFERENCES

Ashkenazi, S., Black, J. M., Abrams, D. A., Hoeft, F., & Menon, V. (2013). Neurobiological underpinnings of math and reading learning disabilities. *Journal of Learning Disabilities, 46,* 549–569.

Barkley, R. A. (1997). Behavioral inhibition, sustained attention, and executive functions: Constructing a unifying theory of ADHD. *Psychological Bulletin, 121*(1), 65–94. Retrieved from http://dx.doi.org/10.1037/0033-2909.121.1.65

Barkley, R. A. (2003). Attention-deficit/hyperactivity disorder. In E. J. Mash & R. A. Barkley (Eds.), *Child psychopathology* (2nd ed., pp. 75–143). New York, NY: Guilford.

Canivez, G. L., & Gaboury, A. R. (2010, August). *Cognitive Assessment System construct and diagnostic utility in assessing ADHD.* Paper presented at the 2010 Annual APA Convention, San Diego, CA.

Ceci, S. J. (2000). So near and yet so far: Lingering questions about the use of measures of general intelligence for college admission and employment screening. *Psychology, Public Policy, and Law, 6,* 233–252.

Das, J. P., Mishra, R. K., & Kirby, J. R. (1994). Cognitive patterns of dyslexics: Comparison between groups with high and average nonverbal intelligence. *Journal of Learning Disabilities, 27*, 235–242.

Das, J. P., Naglieri, J. A., & Kirby, J. R. (1994). *Assessment of cognitive processes.* Boston, MA: Allyn & Bacon.

Das, J. P., Parrila, R. K., & Papadopoulos, T. C. (2000). Cognitive education and reading disability. In A. Kozulin & Y. Rand (Eds.), *Experience of mediated learning* (pp. 276–291). New York, NY: Pergamon Press.

Davis, F. B. (1959). Interpretation of differences among averages and individual test scores. *Journal of Educational Psychology, 50*, 162–170.

Dehaene, S. (2011). *The number sense: How the mind creates mathematics.* Oxford, UK: Oxford University Press.

Edwards, O. W., & Oakland, T. D. (2006). Factorial invariance of Woodcock-Johnson III scores for African Americans and Caucasian Americans. *Journal of Psychoeducational Assessment, 24*(4), 358–366.

Fagan, J. R. (2000). A theory of intelligence as processing: Implications for society. *Psychology, Public Policy, and Law, 6*, 168–179.

Federal Register. (2016). Assistance to States for the Education of Children with Disabilities and Preschool Grants for Children with Disabilities Final Rule, *34*, 300–301.

Feifer, S. G. (2015). *Feifer Assessment of Reading (FAR).* Lutz, FL: PAR.

Feifer, S. G. (2016). *Feifer Assessment of Math (FAM).* Lutz, FL: PAR.

Flanagan, D. P., Alfonso, V. C., & Mascolo, J. T. (2011). A CHC-based operational definition of SLD: Integrating multiple data sources and multiple data-gathering methods. In D. P. Flanagan & V. C. Alfonso (Eds.), *Essentials of specific learning disability identification* (pp. 233–298). Hoboken, NJ: Wiley.

Flanagan, D. P., & Kaufman, A. S. (2004). *Essentials of WISC-IV assessment.* Hoboken, NJ: Wiley.

Goldberg, E. (2009). *The new executive brain: Frontal lobes in a complex world.* New York, NY: Oxford University Press.

Hale, J. B., & Fiorello, C. A. (2004). *School neuropsychology: A practitioner's handbook.* New York, NY: Guilford.

Hale, J. B., Fiorello, C. A., & Brown, L. (2005). Determining medication treatment effects using teacher ratings and classroom observations of children with ADHD: Does neuropsychological impairment matter? *Educational and Child Psychology, 22*, 39–61.

Hale, J. B., Kaufman, A. S., Naglieri, J. A., & Kavale, K. A. (2006). Implementation of IDEA: Using RTI and cognitive assessment methods. *Psychology in the Schools*, pp. 753–770.

Hale, J. B., Naglieri, J. A., Kaufman, A. S., & Kavale, K. A. (2004). Specific learning disability classification in the new Individuals with Disabilities Education Act: The danger of good ideas. *The School Psychologist, 58*(1), 6–13.

Huang, L. V., Bardos, A. N., & D'Amato, R. C. (2010). Identifying students with learning disabilities: Composite profile analysis using the Cognitive Assessment System. *Journal of Psychoeducational Assessment, 28*(1), 19–30.

Individuals with Disabilities Education Improvement Act of 2004, P.L. 108–466. *Federal Register, 70*(118), 31–162.

Kaufman, A. S. (1979). *Intelligent testing with the WISC-R.* New York, NY: Wiley.

Kaufman, A. S. (1994). *Intelligence testing with the WISC-III.* New York, NY: Wiley.

Kaufman, A. S., & Kaufman, N. L. (1983). *Kaufman Assessment Battery for Children*. Circle Pines, MN: American Guidance.

Kaufman, A. S., & Kaufman, N. L. (2004). *Kaufman Assessment Battery for Children* (2nd ed.). Circle Pines, MN: American Guidance.

Kavale, K. A., Kaufman, A. S., Naglieri, J. A., & Hale, J. B. (2005). Changing procedures for identifying learning disabilities: The danger or poorly supported ideas. *The School Psychologist, 59*, 16–25.

Lewandowski, L., & Scott, D. (2008). Introduction to neuropathology and brain-behavior relationships. In R. C. D'Amato & L. C. Hartlage (Eds.), *Essentials of neuropsychological assessment: Treatment planning for rehabilitation* (2nd ed.). New York, NY: Springer.

Lichtenberger, E. O., Sotelo-Dynega, M., & Kaufman, A. S. (2009). The Kaufman Assessment Battery for Children–Second Edition. In J. A. Naglieri & S. Goldstein (Eds.), *A practitioner's guide to assessment of intelligence and achievement* (pp. 61–94). New York, NY: Wiley.

Lohman, D. F., & Hagen, E. P. (2001). *Cognitive Abilities Test (form 6): Interpretive guide for teachers and counselors*. Itasca, IL: Riverside.

Luria, A. R. (1966). *Human brain and psychological processes*. New York, NY: Harper & Row.

Luria, A. R. (1973). *The working brain*. New York, NY: Basic Books.

Luria, A. R. (1980). *Higher cortical functions in man* (2nd ed.). New York, NY: Basic Books.

Naglieri, J. A. (1999). *Essentials of CAS assessment*. Hoboken, NJ: Wiley.

Naglieri, J. A. (2000). Can profile analysis of ability test scores work? An illustration using the PASS theory and CAS with an unselected cohort. *School Psychology Quarterly, 15*(4), 419.

Naglieri, J. A. (2005). The Cognitive Assessment System. In D. P. Flanagan & P. L. Harrison (Eds.), *Contemporary intellectual assessment* (2nd ed., pp. 441–460). New York, NY: Guilford.

Naglieri, J. A. (2008). Traditional IQ: 100 years of misconception and its relationship to minority representation in gifted programs. In J. VanTassel-Baska (Ed.), *Alternative assessments for identifying gifted and talented students* (pp. 67–88). Waco, TX: Prufrock Press.

Naglieri, J. A. (2011). The discrepancy/consistency approach to SLD identification using the PASS theory. In D. P. Flanagan & V. C. Alfonso (Eds.), *Essentials of specific learning disability identification* (pp. 145–172). Hoboken, NJ: Wiley.

Naglieri, J. A. (2015). One hundred years of intelligence testing: Moving from traditional IQ to second-generation intelligence tests. In S. Goldstein, D. Princiotta, & J. A. Naglieri (Eds.), *Handbook of intelligence: Evolutionary theory, historical perspective, and current concepts* (pp. 295–316). New York, NY: Springer.

Naglieri, J. A. (2016). Theoretical and practical considerations of the WISC-V. In A. S. Kaufman, D. Coalson, & S. Engi Raiford (Eds.), *Intelligent testing with the WISC-V* (pp. 663–668). Hoboken, NJ: Wiley.

Naglieri, J. A., & Bornstein, B. T. (2003). Intelligence and achievement: Just how correlated are they? *Journal of Psycheducational Assessment, 21*, 244–260.

Naglieri, J. A., & Conway, C. (2009). The Cognitive Assessment System. In J. A. Naglieri & S. Goldstein (Eds.), *A practitioner's guide to assessment of intelligence and achievement* (pp. 3–10). New York, NY: Wiley.

Naglieri, J. A., & Das, J. P. (1997). *Cognitive Assessment System*. Itasca, IL: Riverside.

Naglieri, J. A., & Das, J. P. (2005). Planning, attention, simultaneous, successive (PASS) theory: A revision of the concept of intelligence. In D. P. Flanagan and P. L. Harrison

(Eds.), *Contemporary intellectual assessment* (2nd ed., pp. 136–182). New York, NY: Guilford.

Naglieri, J. A., & Das, J. P. (2006). *Cognitive Assessment System—Adattamento italiano a cura di S. Taddei.* Firenze, Italy: OS.

Naglieri, J. A., Das, J. P., & Goldstein, S. (2014a). *Cognitive Assessment System* (2nd ed.). Austin, TX: PRO-ED.

Naglieri, J. A., Das, J. P., & Goldstein, S. (2014b). *Cognitive Assessment System* (2nd ed.): Brief. Austin, TX: PRO-ED.

Naglieri, J. A., Das, J. P., & Goldstein, S. (2014c). *Cognitive Assessment System* (2nd ed.): Rating scale. Austin, TX: PRO-ED.

Naglieri, J. A., & Feifer, S. (2017). Intervention. In J. A. Naglieri & T. Otero (Eds.), *Essentials of CAS-2 assessment* (pp. 147–179). New York, NY: Wiley.

Naglieri, J. A., & Otero, T. (2011). Cognitive Assessment System: Redefining intelligence from a neuropsychological perspective. In A. Davis (Ed.), *Handbook of pediatric neuropsychology* (pp. 227–234). New York, NY: Springer.

Naglieri, J. A., & Otero, T. M. (2017). *Essentials of CAS-2 assessment.* Hoboken, NJ: Wiley.

Naglieri, J. A., Otero, T., DeLauder, B., & Matto, H. (2007). Bilingual Hispanic children's performance on the English and Spanish versions of the Cognitive Assessment System. *School Psychology Quarterly, 22,* 432–448.

Naglieri, J. A., & Pickering, E. (2010). *Helping children learn: Intervention handouts for use in school and at home* (2nd ed.). Baltimore, MD: Brookes.

Naglieri, J. A., & Rojahn, J. R. (2004). Validity of the PASS theory and CAS: Correlations with achievement. *Journal of Educational Psychology, 96,* 174–181.

Naglieri, J. A., Rojahn, J., & Matto, H. C. (2007). Hispanic and non-Hispanic children's performance on PASS cognitive processes and achievement. *Intelligence, 35*(6), 568–579.

Naglieri, J. A., Rojahn, J. R., Matto, H. C., & Aquilino, S. A. (2005). Black white differences in intelligence: A study of the PASS theory and Cognitive Assessment System. *Journal of Psychoeducational Assessment, 23,* 146–160.

Naglieri, J. A., Taddei, S., & Williams, K. M. (2013). Multigroup confirmatory factor analysis of US and Italian children's performance on the PASS theory of intelligence as measured by the Cognitive Assessment System. *Psychological Assessment, 25*(1), 157.

Natur, N. H. (2009). An analysis of the validity and reliability of the Das-Naglieri Cognitive Assessment System (CAS) (Arabic ed.). Unpublished doctoral dissertation, Howard University. *Dissertation Abstract International, 70,* no. 01B.

O'Donnell, L. (2009). The Wechsler intelligence Scale for Children (4th ed.). In J. A. Naglieri & S. Goldstein (Eds.), *Practitioner's guide to assessing intelligence and achievement* (p. 153). Hoboken, NJ: Wiley.

Otero, T., Gonzalez, L., & Naglieri, J. A. (2012). The neurocognitive assessment of Hispanic English language learners with reading problems. *Archives of Clinical Neuropsychology,* 1–9.

Roid, G. (2003). *Stanford-Binet* (5th ed.). Itasca, IL: Riverside.

Rosselli, M., Matute, E., Pinto, N., & Ardila, A. (2006). Memory abilities in children with subtypes of dyscalculia. *Developmental Neuropsychology, 30*(3), 801–818.

Schrank, F. A., McGrew, K. S., & Mather, N. (2014). *Woodcock-Johnson IV Tests of Cognitive Abilities.* Rolling Meadows, IL: Riverside.

Shadmehr, R., Smith, M. A., & Krakauer, J. W. (2010). Error correction, sensory prediction, and adaptation in motor control. *Annual Review of Neuroscience, 33*, 89–108.

Silverstein, A. B. (1993). Type I, type II, and other types of errors in pattern analysis. *Psychological Assessment, 5*, 72–74.

Suzuki, L. A., & Valencia, R. R. (1997). Race ethnicity and measured intelligence. *American Psychologist, 52*, 1103–1114.

Taddei, S., & Venditti, F. (2010). The evaluation of cognitive processes in attention deficit hyperactivity disorder. *Psichiatria dell'infanzia e dell'adolescenza, 77*, 305–319.

Wasserman, J. D., & Becker, K. A. (2000). *Clinical application of the Woodcock-Johnson Tests of Cognitive Ability—revised with children diagnosed with attention-deficit/hyperactivity disorders.* Itasca, IL: Riverside.

Wechsler, D. (2003). *Wechsler Intelligence Scale for Children* (4th ed.). San Antonio, TX: The Psychological Corporation.

Wechsler, D. (2014). *Wechsler Intelligence Scale for Children* (5th ed.). San Antonio, TX: The Psychological Corporation.

Wendling, B. J., Mather, N., & Schrank, F. A. (2009). Woodcock-Johnson III Tests of Cognitive Abilities. In J. A. Naglieri & S. Goldstein (Eds.), *Practitioner's guide to assessing intelligence and achievement* (pp. 191–232). Hoboken, NJ: Wiley.

Woodcock, R. W., McGrew, K. S., & Mather, N. (2001). *Woodcock-Johnson III Tests of Cognitive Abilities* (pp. 371–401). Rolling Meadows, IL: Riverside.

Van Luit, J. E., Kroesbergen, E. H., & Naglieri, J. A. (2005). Utility of the PASS theory and Cognitive Assessment System for Dutch children with and without ADHD. *Journal of Learning Disabilities, 38*(5), 434–439.

Thirteen

CORE SELECTIVE EVALUATION PROCESS (C-SEP) AND DUAL DISCREPANCY/CONSISTENCY (DD/C) MODELS FOR SLD IDENTIFICATION

A Case Study Approach

Gail M. Cheramie
G. Thomas Schanding Jr.
Kristin Streich

INTRODUCTION

A specific learning disability (SLD) is defined by the Individuals with Disabilities Education Improvement Act (IDEIA, or IDEA 2004) as

a disorder in one or more of the basic psychological processes involved in understanding or in using language, spoken or written, that may manifest itself in the imperfect ability to listen, think, speak, read, write, spell, or to do mathematical calculations, including conditions such as perceptual disabilities, brain injury, minimal brain dysfunction, dyslexia, and developmental aphasia. (CFR 300.8(c)(10))

This definition emphasizes three major concepts: the presence of a psychological processing disorder, an inability to learn an academic skill, and, most important, the assumption that the learning deficit is the direct result of the processing disorder. This has been the federal definition of SLD for special

Essentials of Specific Learning Disability Identification, Second Edition.
Edited by Vincent C. Alfonso and Dawn P. Flanagan
© 2018 John Wiley & Sons, Inc. Published 2018 by John Wiley & Sons, Inc.

education since 1975 (P.L. 94-142 §620 (4)(A)). Although the definition has not changed, methods for identification have changed (see Chapter 1).

Under the current federal statute, states are given the authority to choose the methodology for the determination of a SLD. IDEA 2004 (300.8 (c)(10)) makes the following allowances for methodology: It must not require the use of severe discrepancy between intellectual ability and achievement; it must permit the use of a process based on the child's response to scientific, research-based intervention; and it may permit the use of other alternative research-based procedures. More specifically, according to §300.309 (a)(2)(i)) an SLD is determined when the child does not make sufficient progress to meet age- or state-approved grade-level standards in one or more of the areas identified in paragraph (a)(1) of this section when using a process based on the child's response to scientific, research-based intervention (known as the Response to Intervention [RTI] method) or the child exhibits a pattern of strengths and weaknesses (PSW) in performance, achievement, or both, relative to age, state-approved grade-level standards, or intellectual development, which is determined by the group to be relevant to the identification of a specific learning disability, using appropriate assessments, consistent with §§300.304 and 300.305 (PSW method). The RTI approach was discussed in Chapters 7 and 8. Additionally, various PSW models have been presented in Chapters 9 through 12.

Because states can designate the methodology used for SLD determination, there is no one uniform approach across the country. However, the two major models for identification are RTI and processing models referred to as PSWs. There are multiple approaches related to the PSW model, but they do have some commonalities in that they address the three major concepts for SLD: (1) identification of one or more cognitive processing deficits, (2) identification of one or more areas of academic deficit, and (3) a presumed causal relationship between the identified deficit areas.

DON'T FORGET

There are multiple approaches related to the PSW model, but they do have some commonalities in that they address the three major concepts for SLD: (1) identification of one or more cognitive processing deficits, (2) identification of one or more areas of academic deficit, and (3) a presumed causal relationship between the identified deficit areas.

The purpose of this chapter is to (1) describe a recent approach for determining a PSW, the Core Selective Evaluation Process (C-SEP; Schultz & Stephens, 2015; Schrank, Stephens-Pisecco, & Schultz, 2017); (2) compare this model to the Dual Discrepancy/Consistency (DD/C) model (first introduced by Flanagan, Ortiz, Alfonso, & Mascolo in 2002; see Chapter 11); and (3) present two case studies using these approaches.

CORE SELECTIVE EVALUATION PROCESS (C-SEP)

Schultz and Stephens (2015) proposed the C-SEP as an efficient method for identifying SLD. Based on CHC theory, the C-SEP approach incorporates the use of norm-referenced cognitive, achievement, and oral language tests in conjunction with data-analysis techniques and the incorporation of the evaluator's professional judgment to determine the presence of an SLD through the identification of a PSW (Schultz & Stephens, 2015). The C-SEP was developed primarily for use of the Woodcock-Johnson IV Tests of Cognitive Abilities (WJ IV COG; Schrank, McGrew, & Mather, 2014), Tests of Achievement (WJ IV ACH; Schrank, Mather, & McGrew, 2014a), and Tests of Oral Language (WJ IV OL) (Schrank, Mather, & McGrew, 2014b). The creators of the C-SEP indicate that the WJ IV tests were designed in such a way that when using the C-SEP model, they will "allow for more efficient, comprehensive, and diagnostic testing" (Schultz & Stephens, 2015, p. 5). They also report that the use of the WJ IV in the C-SEP model creates a more-accurate mirroring of the student's actual performance in the classroom in that the core battery of tests are considered to be more cognitively complex (as compared to other cognitive batteries) just like most classroom tasks. Schultz and Stephens (2015) note that the C-SEP approach is "compatible" with other methods of SLD identification and "is not a radical departure from current practice; rather it is a refinement of current practice" (p. 11).

According to Schultz and Stephens (2015), approaches in determining SLD based on cognitive processing models have advanced the field but also have led to increased testing time. This increased time is due to the number of cognitive tests needing to be administered to meet the requirements of these models. In addition to the cognitive testing, achievement testing also needs to be conducted to aid in the determination of the presence of an SLD. Schultz and Stephens report that, often, students are being administered achievement tests in areas other than that of the original referral question. As such, Schultz and Stephens propose that the C-SEP model will be able to "answer SLD referral questions in a comprehensive, time-efficient, precise, and legally defensible manner" (p. 5).

Recently, Schrank et al. (2017) published *Assessment Service Bulletin, 8 (ASB8)* explaining the C-SEP process applied to SLD identification. It is noted that in some cases, the core tests may be sufficient to rule in or rule out SLD identification, but that additional testing may be warranted

C A U T I O N

Similar to all PSW models presented in this book, the C-SEP process is designed to be data-driven and based on professional judgment, although the authors note that C-SEP requires more clinical judgment.

in other cases. Similar to all PSW models presented in this book, the process is designed to be data-driven and based on professional judgment, although the authors note that the C-SEP requires more clinical judgment. The steps of the C-SEP model are presented in the next sections.

Step 1: Cognitive Battery

The first step of the C-SEP model is to measure cognitive processes through administration of the WJ IV COG CORE 7 tests: Test 1: Oral Vocabulary; Test 2: Number Series; Test 3: Verbal Attention; Test 4: Letter-Pattern Matching; Test 5: Phonological Processing; Test 6: Story Recall; and Test 7: Visualization. These seven core tests measure a narrow aspect of seven broad CHC cognitive domains. After analyzing the results through the WJ IV score report, if there are no relative weaknesses and no scores below average, there would not be a need to conduct further testing because there is no evidence of a cognitive processing deficit. However, should a specific test reveal a probable processing weakness (score is below average), evaluators explore this further through the administration of another WJ IV COG test measuring that process. The evaluator is directed to use the selective testing table in the WJ IV COG easel or the tables provided in *ASB8* to select the test. In addition, should these test results appear non-cohesive, rather than conducting additional testing in that certain domain to engage "in the relentless pursuit of cohesiveness" (p. 8), the data should instead be analyzed at the task-demand level (Schultz & Stephens, 2015). If further testing appears to be needed, Schultz and Stephens state this would solely be to "improve precision and explain performance" (p. 9).

Step 2: Oral Language Battery

Second, the evaluator administers the WJ IV Oral Language CORE four tests and analyzes the results. These tests are: Test 1: Picture Vocabulary; Test 2: Oral Comprehension; Test 3: Segmentation; and Test 4: Rapid Picture Naming. As before, if all scores fall within the average range or above, no additional testing is necessary because the "results sufficiently measure oral language" (Schultz & Stevens, 2015, p. 9). However, should a score fall below the average range, further exploration would be needed (e.g., comparing the oral language scores with the WJ IV COG scores or through further selective testing in the area of difficulty) to ensure that the components of oral language associated with the referral are sufficiently measured. The evaluator then compares the results of these data with other ecological data and uses professional judgment to analyze the student's performance on the oral language

⚡ Rapid Reference 13.1

CHC Cognitive Processing Domains and Tests Administered in C-SEP Steps 1 and 2

WJ IV COG	WJ IV OL	CHC Broad Ability
Oral Vocabulary	Picture Vocabulary	Comprehension-
	Oral Comprehension	Knowledge (Gc)
Number Series		Fluid Reasoning (Gf)
Verbal Attention		Short-Term Working Memory (Gwm)
Letter-Pattern Matching		Processing Speed (Gs)
Phonological Processing	Segmentation	Auditory Processing (Ga)
Story Recall	Rapid Picture Naming	Long-Term Retrieval (Glr)
Visualization		Visual Processing (Gv)

tests. On all testing conducted so far, the evaluator is encouraged to analyze, interpret, and report all below-average or non-cohesive scores, because these scores also contain valid information about the student. See Rapid Reference 13.1.

Step 3: Achievement Battery

The third step involves an evaluation of the student's academic achievement in order to identify and confirm areas of deficit. According to the model, one can choose to administer the WJ IV ACH CORE six tests when the referral question is not specific, or solely, the WJ IV ACH tests that represent the area of concern listed in the initial referral question. The CORE six tests are Test 1: Letter-Word Identification; Test 2: Applied Problems; Test 3: Spelling; Test 4: Passage Comprehension; Test 5: Calculation; and Test 6: Writing Samples. If all six tests are administered, additional tests can be added to measure a specific area more comprehensively. If no concerns are reported in an academic area (e.g., passing grades in math, passed state assessment in math, meeting grade-level benchmarks), then norm-referenced assessment in this area would not be indicated. If concerns are reported or indicated in an academic area, then more focus would be placed on comprehensive measurement of that area. The referral question is used as a guide for test selection and focus would be placed on those skills that the student is not meeting based on age and grade-level expectations.

Step 4: Exclusionary Factors

Step 4 involves considering all exclusionary factors. The evaluator must rule out that the student's academic deficits are not primarily caused by any of the following exclusionary factors per IDEA 2004: vision, hearing, or motor difficulties; intellectual disability; emotional disturbance; environmental, cultural, or economic disadvantage; lack of appropriate instruction in reading and math; and limited English proficiency (34 CFR, §300.311(a)(6)). This can be done through health screening, a home language survey, a review of the student's previous records and data, investigating the student's life experiences, teacher quality, and report cards. One could also use the WJ IV Cognitive Academic Language Proficiency scores and Comparative Language Index score to determine the student's English and Spanish language proficiency.

Step 5: Data Analysis

The final step involves analyzing the data collected by conducting an "integrated data analysis" (Schultz & Stephens, 2015; p. 10; Schrank et al., 2017, pp. 36–37) to describe and investigate systematic relationships between all data to make the determination of a PSW. The C-SEP model is said to rely on a normative-developmental perspective, which "consists of a combination of the normative approaches (i.e., above or below average standard scores) with developmental perspectives characterized by intra- and inter-individual differences in meeting developmental milestones including academic milestones" (Schultz & Stephens, 2015, p. 10; Schrank et al., 2017, p. 37).

DUAL DISCREPANCY/CONSISTENCY MODEL (DD/C)

The DD/C model for the identification of a PSW was described comprehensively in Chapter 11; therefore, only the basic premises of the model are summarized here.

- **The presence of an academic weakness or deficit.** Based on the DD/C model, an academic deficit is reflected when multiple sources of data converge. Data sources may include norm-referenced assessment (scores on standardized achievement tests), criterion-referenced assessment (e.g., performance on benchmark assessments and state assessments), curriculum-based assessment (e.g., progress-monitoring data collected as part of repeated measurement in documented interventions), and informal assessment (e.g., work samples, classroom observations, reports from teachers and parents, grades).

- **The presence of a cognitive processing weakness or deficit.** Data from cognitive and neuropsychological testing are used to determine areas of processing weakness. The DD/C model requires that the individual is assessed in at least seven broad CHC ability and processing domains, including Fluid Reasoning (Gf), Crystallized Intelligence (Gc), Short-term Memory (Gsm), Long-Term Storage and Retrieval (Glr), Visual Processing (Gv), Auditory Processing (Ga), and Processing Speed (Gs). Measurement of these domains (often referred to simply as *G's*) require that more than one subtest be administered to confirm the presence of a deficit. This general rule is based on the fact that single subtest scores make for poor measurement (see Flanagan & Schneider, 2016). Measurement of the G's may result in a broad cognitive composite in which two distinctly different narrow abilities are assessed (e.g., a test of working memory [MW] and memory span [MS] combine to yield a Gsm composite) or may reflect a more specific impairment in which the scores from two subtests measuring the same narrow ability (e.g., MW) form a narrow ability composite (e.g., Gsm:MW). The premise here is that to draw inferences about an individual's performance in a latent construct (e.g., Gsm or Gsm:MW), more than one subtest is required. Because academic deficits are typically due to multiple processing deficits and not just one narrow processing deficit, in the DD/C model, an inhibiting cognitive composite (ICC) is created statistically to represent the aggregate of cognitive processing weaknesses. When determining the presence of a PSW (i.e., DD/C), the examiner may choose only one narrow or broad composite as a possible contributory factor to the academic deficit or the ICC may be chosen. Note that when organizing an assessment of the seven G's, the authors of the DD/C model encourage the examiner to ensure that the abilities and processes that are most important in understanding the academic area in question are represented in the evaluation (see Chapter 11 for details).
- **Empirical or ecologically valid relationship between the processing deficit(s) and academic deficit—Consistency.** There is a consistency between the cognitive and academic deficits because the academic deficit is presumed to be caused, at least in part, by the processing deficit (e.g., a Ga deficit in phonological processing is likely related to a deficit in basic

reading skills). This relationship is sometimes referred to as cognitive aptitude-achievement *consistency* (i.e., the *C* in the DD/C model). It is important to note that "causal" in this context is used in a probabilistic, not deterministic, sense. That is, the presence of cognitive processing weaknesses or deficits raises the risk of academic weaknesses or deficits, but they do not guarantee them (Flanagan & Schneider, 2016). This fact highlights the importance of a thorough examination of exclusionary factors, especially when known cognitive correlates to the academic area in question are within the average (or better) range of functioning.

- **The student displays adequate ability to learn.** Several cognitive processes and abilities for the student are intact (i.e., at least average) and cumulatively ought to facilitate learning, indicating that the student has generally adequate ability to think and reason. It is well-known that if a test is given that measures multiple processes, and if the student has significant deficits in some areas, the resulting overall IQ score will be lowered or attenuated by specific cognitive impairments. In the DD/C model, the psychometric calculation of a facilitating cognitive composite (FCC) addresses this. Specifically, the FCC is the aggregate of the student's intact abilities and processes (i.e., scores that reflect at least average ability). The calculation of the FCC is dependent on which G's are considered strengths for the student as well as how many are considered strengths. Because the FCC is an analog of *g* or general intelligence, which G's and how many G's are important considerations in determining whether the FCC will be calculated for the student. These determinations are made by the Cross-Battery Assessment Software System (X-BASS; Flanagan, Ortiz, & Alfonso, 2016), thereby ensuring that any time an FCC is calculated by the program, it represents a reliable and valid estimate of the student's ability to think and reason.

- **Domain-specific cognitive weakness—Discrepancy 1.** In the DD/C model, there is a discrepancy between the weak cognitive process (i.e., ICC, narrow ability or processing composite, broad ability or processing composite) and overall ability to think and reason as estimated by the FCC. Specifically, the FCC is used in a regression equation to calculate a "predicted" score. For a cognitive weakness to be considered domain-specific, two conditions must be met: (1) the difference between the FCC and actual (weakness) score must be statistically significant ($p < .05$) and (2) the difference between the predicted and actual scores must be considered unusual or rare in the general population. When both conditions are met, the processing deficit is indeed specific and not attributable to or consistent with generally low overall ability to think and reason—the latter of which would be more in line with general learning difficulty (or slow learner; see Chapter 11). All calculations are conducted automatically by X-BASS.

- **Unexpected underachievement—Discrepancy 2.** In the DD/C definition, an academic weakness represents *unexpected underachievement* when two conditions are met: (1) the difference between the FCC and actual (weakness) score is statistically significant ($p < .05$) and (2) the difference between the predicted and actual scores is unusual or rare in the general population. Again, all calculations are conducted automatically by X-BASS.

These six components are the main diagnostic markers that result in a PSW consistent with SLD in the DD/C model (Flanagan, Ortiz, & Alfonso, 2013). That is, SLD is indicated when the student is unable to learn an academic skill commensurate with age and grade expectations and the difficulty to learn is not attributable to exclusionary factors. Furthermore, the student has one or more specific cognitive processing deficits (as opposed to general low ability) that are related to the area of academic skill deficiency. The discrepancies in the DD/C model are determined using the most psychometrically defensible procedures for determining score differences for the purpose of SLD identification (e.g., Wright, 2002; see Chapter 11 for an in-depth discussion).

DON'T FORGET
. . . .
The discrepancies in the DD/C model are determined using the most psychometrically defensible procedures for determining score differences for the purpose of SLD identification.

CASE ILLUSTRATIONS

In order to illustrate the C-SEP and DD/C models in the determination of SLD, two case studies are presented. The first involves a disorder in basic reading and the second a disorder in math.

Case 1: Olivia, Reading

Olivia is a 10-year-old fourth-grade student. She attended school in another state from kindergarten through mid-fourth grade. There was no previous evaluation, but her mother reported that she struggled with reading. She was involved in interventions in her previous school district, but no specific information was received regarding the interventions. On transferring to the current school district in Texas, it was very evident that she lacked skills in reading. Benchmark assessments led to being placed in a reading intervention program, *Take Flight*, for 4 months during the second semester of fourth grade. She attended this program 30 minutes per day, four days per week with a reading specialist. Olivia made "some" progress in this program, but the intervention specialist reported that she remained well below grade-level expectations. In April, she failed the state assessment in reading (STAAR), but passed the math assessment. Olivia was referred for evaluation in May 2016. Results of her evaluation are found in Table 13.1.

Table 13.1 Olivia's Obtained and Analyzed Scores Based on the C-SEP and DD/C Models

C-SEP		DD/C		
WJ-IV CORE COG Tests	**SS**	**WJ-IV COG and OL Tests**	**SS**	**G**
Oral Vocabulary	100	Oral Vocabulary	100	Gc=96
		General Information	93	
Number Series	98	Number Series	98	Gf=101
		Concept Formation	104	
Verbal Attention	95	Verbal Attention	95	Gwm=94
		Numbers Reversed	95	
Letter-Pattern Matching	88	Letter-Pattern Matching	88	Gs=94
		Pair Cancellation	101	
Phonological Processing	78	Phonological Processing	78	Ga=76
		Segmentation	82	
Story Recall	104	Story Recall	104	Glr=99
		Rapid Picture Naming	95	
Visualization	106	Visualization	106	Gv=111
		Picture Recognition	113	
WJ IV OL Battery				
Picture Vocabulary	108			
Oral Comprehension	113			
Rapid Picture Naming	95			
Segmentation	82			

WJ IV ACH Tests		WJ IV ACH Tests	
Letter Word Identification	74	Letter Word Identification	74
Word Attack	77	Word Attack	77
Basic Reading Skills	74	Basic Reading Skills	74
Passage Comprehension	88	Passage Comprehension	88
Spelling	75	Spelling	75
Writing Samples	84	Writing Samples	84
Calculation	105	Calculation	105
Applied Problems	102	Applied Problems	102
GIA	91	FCC	99
Total tests administered	18	**Total tests administered**	21

C-SEP Model

Steps 1 and 2. Based on the WJ IV COG Intra-Cognitive analysis, the only weakness identified was Phonological Processing. Although the Nonword Repetition test could have been administered, the Segmentation test of the WJ IV OL Battery had been administered as part of the recommended C-SEP procedures. Therefore, consistent with the C-SEP model, an additional test was administered due to the weakness in Phonological Processing.

Step 3. The academic achievement profile shows significant weaknesses in Letter-Word Identification and Spelling. Olivia's Writing and Reading Comprehension scores were below average, but these tests were investigated through error analysis. It was determined that Olivia's difficulties in Reading Comprehension were due to her inability to read many of the words. Her errors in Written Expression were primarily due to difficulties in spelling because many words written were not understandable. Olivia was able to write sentences with appropriate syntax.

Step 4. No exclusionary factors were indicated. Olivia has adequate vision and hearing and no significant health history. Her overall GIA falls in the average range (91), which indicates no intellectual disability. Olivia comes from an English-speaking home and she has had adequate instruction. She moved to Texas in December (over the holidays), and there was no interruption in school attendance. No behavioral problems were indicated.

Step 5. The cognitive-achievement comparison procedure of the WJ IV indicates a significant difference between actual and predicted performance in Basic Reading Skills.

Note: The C-SEP model does not specify any statistical criterion markers for the determination of a PSW for SLD. The authors of this chapter chose to use the cognitive-achievement comparison on the WJ IV Compuscore for the discrepancy analysis.

DD/C Model

Step 1. Using X-BASS, all seven cognitive processes were evaluated by administering two tests per broad ability domain. All domains were cohesive; therefore, no additional testing was necessary. Note that when composites are not cohesive, there is not always a need to conduct additional testing in the DD/C model. Clinical judgment must be exercised in the case of non-cohesive composites (see Chapter 11 for guidance). The only deficit noted was in Ga. The WJ IV OL tests of Segmentation and Rapid Picture Naming were used in the X-BASS analysis.

Step 2. Olivia demonstrated a weakness in Basic Reading Skills. This was confirmed through other data sources, such as teacher reports, grades, benchmark assessment, and state assessment results. As noted, Olivia's low scores in Reading Comprehension and Writing Samples were due to her deficits in word reading and spelling.

Note: For C-SEP and DD/C, the Word Attack test was administered to generate the Basic Reading Cluster, but this is not required in either model.

Step 3: There is a strong relationship between Ga and Basic Reading Skills according to the X-BASS analysis, which is also consistent with the literature. A deficit in Phonological Processing is considered a core deficit in the ability to learn how to read and decode unfamiliar words.

Step 4. Olivia's profile reflects average learning ability or at least average ability to think and reason. The FCC, an aggregate of Olivia's cognitive assets, is 99.

Steps 5 and 6. Olivia's Ga performance is domain-specific and her weakness in Basic Reading is unexpected as revealed by the analyses conducted by X-BASS.

Figure 13.1 depicts the results of the X-BASS PSW analysis following the DD/C criteria.

In the case of Olivia, the C-SEP and DD/C models yield the same results, a domain-specific cognitive-processing deficit in phonological processing that is associated with an inability to decode words. The conclusion regarding the presence of a PSW consistent with SLD would be the same using either the C-SEP or DD/C models. Given the background data in math, the tests of Applied Problems and Calculation could have been eliminated in each of the models, making the evaluation even more efficient.

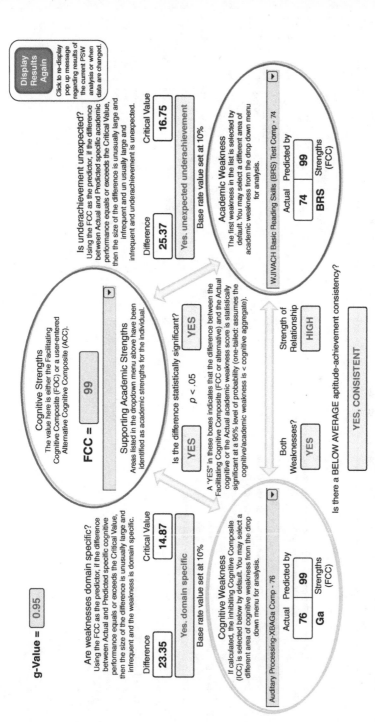

g-Value = 0.95

Are weaknesses domain specific?
Using the FCC as the predictor, if the difference between Actual and Predicted specific cognitive performance equals or exceeds the Critical Value, then the size of the difference is unusually large and infrequent and the weakness is domain specific.

Difference	Critical Value
23.35	14.87

Yes. domain specific

Base rate value set at 10%

Is underachievement unexpected?
Using the FCC as the predictor, if the difference between Actual and Predicted specific academic performance equals or exceeds the Critical Value, then the size of the difference is unusually large and infrequent and underachievement is unexpected.

Difference	Critical Value
25.37	16.75

Yes. unexpected underachievement

Base rate value set at 10%

Display Results Again
Click to re-display pop up message regarding results of the current PSW analysis or when data are changed.

Cognitive Strengths
The value here is either the Facilitating Cognitive Composite (FCC) or a user-entered Alternative Cognitive Composite (ACC).

FCC = 99

Supporting Academic Strengths
Areas listed in the dropdown menu above have been identified as academic strengths for the individual.

Academic Weakness
The first weakness in the list is selected by default. You may select a different area of academic weakness from the drop down menu for analysis.

WJ/ACH Basic Reading Skills (BRS) Test Comp - 74

Actual	Predicted by
74	99
BRS	Strengths (FCC)

Cognitive Weakness
If calculated, the Inhibiting Cognitive Composite (ICC) is selected below by default. You may select a different area of cognitive weakness from the drop down menu for analysis.

Auditary Processing-XBAGa Comp - 76

Actual	Predicted by
76	99
Ga	Strengths (FCC)

Is the difference statistically significant?

YES	p < .05	YES

A 'YES' in these boxes indicates that the difference between the Facilitating Cognitive Composite (FCC or alternative) and the Actual cognitive or the Actual academic weakness score is statistically significant at a 95% level of probability (one-tailed: assumes the cognitive/academic weakness is < cognitive aggregate).

Both Weaknesses?

YES

Strength of Relationship

HIGH

Is there a BELOW AVERAGE aptitude-achievement consistency?

YES, CONSISTENT

Figure 13.1. PSW Analyzer Results—X-BASS

Dual-Discrepancy/Consistency Model: Summary of PSW Analyses for SLD

Name: *Olivia* Age: *10 years 3 month (s)* Grade: *4* Date: *6/3/2016*

Did the individual's observed cognitive and academic performances meet criteria within the DD/C model consistent with PSW-based SLD identification?

g-Value = 0.95

General Intelligence

Aggregate of Cognitive Strengths
FCC = 99

Unexpected Underachievement?
YES

Academic Weakness
BRS = 74

Domain Specific Weakness?
YES

Cognitive Weakness
Ga = 76

Below Average Aptitude-Achievement Consistency?
YES

YES. Based on the data selected for use in the PSW Analyzer, specific criteria for establishing a PSW consistent with SLD have been met. However, this pattern of results does not automatically confirm the presence of SLD. This pattern must be considered within the context of the entire case history of the individual. In addition, other data gathered through multiple methods need to be considered (e.g., information regarding exclusionary factors) when identifying or diagnosing SLD (see chapter 4 in Essentials of Cross-Battery Assessment, 3rd Ed.).

Figure 13.1. (Continued)

Case 2: Alex, Mathematics

Alex is a 9-year-old male in the third grade. He was referred for a full and individual evaluation (FIE) by the school's RTI team due to concerns with his academic performance in math. Alex has attended school in the same school district since kindergarten. He comes from a monolingual English-speaking home and has no cultural or environmental factors that would affect his learning. No behavior problems have been reported, and Alex's vision and hearing are reported to be within normal limits unaided. His attendance is good with only eight absences his entire academic career.

Alex struggled academically in the second grade as reflected by failing grades in reading, writing, and math. His reading and writing skills greatly improved through the interventions he was provided, and he met all end-of-year benchmarks in these academic areas. However, he continues to display difficulty meeting grade-level expectations in math despite targeted interventions through RTI. According to his report card, Alex received a D− in math for his second-grade year and has consistently made grades of D to F in math during third grade. He did not meet the criterion performance for his end-of-year benchmark in second grade and has not met any benchmark criteria in third grade. In March of this year, Alex passed the state assessment for reading (writing is not administered until fourth grade), but he did not pass math. Given that he had focused intervention in math throughout third grade and did not pass the state assessment, Alex was referred for a FIE to investigate the possibility of a learning disability in math. Alex's evaluation results are found in Table 13.2.

C-SEP Model

Steps 1 and 2. Based on the WJ IV COG Intra-Cognitive analysis, there were no identified weaknesses related to cognitive processing; however, in the effort to be conservative and consistent with the C-SEP model, Number Series (88; Gf) was considered a potential area of weakness due to the referral concern of mathematics. The Concept Formation test was completed, and it was determined that Alex did not have a weakness in Fluid Reasoning. The WJ IV OL Battery had been administered as part of the recommended C-SEP procedures and no weaknesses were noted within these four subtests. Based on the data available, Alex does not exhibit a weakness in any cognitive process.

Step 3. The WJ IV ACH CORE six tests for academic achievement were administered to Alex. His profile shows low achievement in Calculation. Multiple sources of data (failing grades, prior intervention history, failure to make a passing score on the statewide assessment in mathematics) were consistent in showing this to be an area of weakness.

Table 13.2 Alex's Obtained and Analyzed Scores Based on the C-SEP and DD/C Models

C-SEP		DD/C		
WJ-IV CORE COG Tests	**SS**	**WJ-IV COG Tests**	**SS**	**G**
Oral Vocabulary	105	Oral Vocabulary	105	Gc=102
		General Information	98	
Number Series	88	Number Series	88	Gf=90
Concept Formation	94	Concept Formation	94	
Verbal Attention	96	Verbal Attention	96	Gwm=69
		Numbers Reversed	72	
		Letter-Number Sequencing (WISC-V)	75	
Letter-Pattern Matching	110	Letter-Pattern Matching	110	Gs=102
		Pair Cancellation	94	
Phonological Processing	95	Phonological Processing	95	Ga=97
		Segmentation	100	
Story Recall	95	Story Recall	95	Glr: MA=71
		Visual-Auditory Learning	74	
		Immediate Symbol Translation (WISC-V)	76	
Visualization	91	Visualization	91	Gv=92
		Picture Recognition	95	
WJ-IV OL Battery				
Picture Vocabulary	92			
Oral Comprehension	94			
Rapid Picture Naming	98			
Segmentation	100			
WJ-IV ACH Tests		**WJ-IV ACH Tests**		
Letter Word Identification	94	Letter Word Identification	94	
Passage Comprehension	98	Passage Comprehension	98	
Spelling	99	Spelling	99	

Writing Samples	100	Writing Samples	100
Calculation	78	Calculation	78
Applied Problems	93	Applied Problems	93
GIA	96	FCC	95
		ICC	65
Total Tests Administered	**18**	**Total Tests Administered**	24

Step 4. No exclusionary factors were indicated. Alex has adequate vision and hearing, no difficulties related to motor skills, and no significant health history. His overall GIA falls in the average range (96), which indicates no intellectual disability. Alex's native language is English (with no exposure to a second language). Alex has had adequate instruction and received targeted intervention related to math. He continues to fail to meet benchmark standards and did not pass the statewide assessment for mathematics. No behavioral problems have been indicated.

Step 5. Although Alex demonstrates a weakness in Calculation, he does not exhibit a cognitive processing PSW that would be indicative of an SLD.

Note: Consistent with C-SEP recommendations, it is possible that the evaluator would have conducted additional assessment because Alex clearly had a deficit in math calculation. This would be based on professional judgment.

DD/C Model

Step 1. Multiple sources of data converge to show that Alex has a weakness in mathematics (prior intervention history, failing grades in the classroom, and failure to make a passing score on the statewide assessment in mathematics). The WJ IV ACH CORE 6 tests for academic achievement were administered to Alex. His profile shows low achievement in Calculation, which is consistent with informal, criterion-referenced, and curriculum-based data.

Step 2. Using X-BASS, all seven cognitive processes were evaluated by administering a minimum of two tests per broad ability domain. Most domains were cohesive and within the average range; however, Gwm and Glr were not cohesive and further testing was conducted because the lower score in each composite was suggestive of a deficit. The Letter-Number Sequencing and Immediate Symbol Translation subtests from the WISC-V were administered and confirmed deficits in the areas of Gwm and Glr (i.e., Associative Memory).

Step 3. The ICC is based on Gwm and Glr and has a moderate relationship with Calculation according to the X-BASS analysis. A deficit in Working Memory (Gsm:MW) is consistent with difficulties in Math Calculation. Alex has difficulty maintaining information in short-term memory and reorganizing that information. This affects multistep problem-solving, remembering procedures, and memorizing math facts. The deficit in Glr is also consistent with difficulties in Calculation. This affects Alex's ability to store and retrieve associations. Overall, Gwm and Glr underlie procedural competence in math.

Step 4. Alex's cognitive profile reflects average learning ability. The FCC, an aggregate of Alex's cognitive assets, is 95.

Steps 5 and 6. The ICC, an aggregate of Alex's cognitive weaknesses, is domain-specific, and his weakness in Calculation is unexpected as revealed by the analyses conducted by X-BASS.

Figure 13.2 depicts the results of the X-BASS PSW analysis following the DD/C criteria.

In this case, the C-SEP and DD/C models yield different results in determining a PSW related to cognitive processing. Based on the C-SEP model, there was no PSW; however, two areas of cognitive processing weaknesses were identified following the DD/C model.

COMPARISON OF C-SEP AND DD/C

> **DON'T FORGET**
> ....
> As noted in the case illustrations, on some occasions the C-SEP and DD/C models will yield similar results, but on other occasions, they will yield different results.

As noted in the case illustrations, on some occasions the C-SEP and DD/C models will yield similar results, but on other occasions, they will yield different results. There are some nuanced differences between C-SEP and DD/C.

The C-SEP and DD/C models measure cognitive processes according to CHC theory. C-SEP recommends administering only one test to represent a processing dimension and DD/C requires two tests to form a cluster, whether that be a broad or narrow ability. In this regard, the DD/C model is more defensible psychometrically. The more qualitatively different indicators of a cognitive construct, the better the measurement of that construct (see Messick, 1995). Each model recommends follow-up testing when there is evidence of a processing weakness. In the original publications of the C-SEP, the first seven WJIV COG tests were recommended, but in the *ASB8* (Schrank et al., 2017)

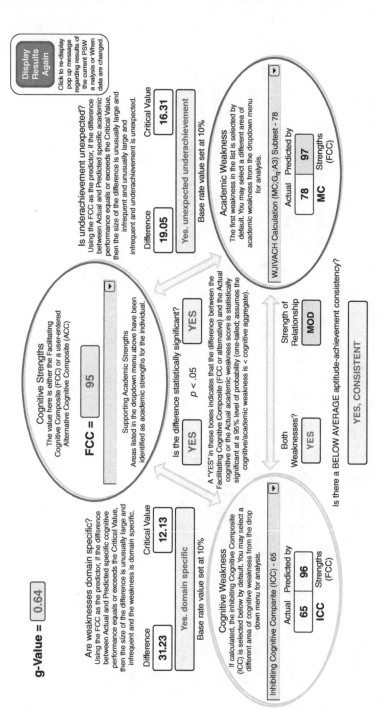

g-Value = 0.64

Are weaknesses domain specific?
Using the FCC as the predictor, if the difference between Actual and Predicted specific cognitive performance equals or exceeds the Critical Value, then the size of the difference is unusually large and infrequent and the weakness is domain specific.

Difference	Critical Value
31.23	12.13

Yes, domain specific

Base rate value set at 10%

Is underachievement unexpected?
Using the FCC as the predictor, if the difference between Actual and Predicted specific academic performance equals or exceeds the Critical Value, then the size of the difference is unusually large and infrequent and underachievement is unexpected.

Difference	Critical Value
19.05	16.31

Yes, unexpected underachievement

Base rate value set at 10%

Display Results Again
Click to re-display pop up message regarding results of the current PSW analysis or When data are changed.

Cognitive Strengths
The value here is either the Facilitating Cognitive Composite (FCC) or a user-entered Alternative Cognitive Composite (ACC)

FCC = 95

Supporting Academic Strengths
Areas listed in the dropdown menu above have been identified as academic strengths for the individual.

Academic Weakness
The first weakness in the list is selected by default. You may select a different area of academic weakness from the dropdown menu for analysis.

WJIVACH Calculation (MC;Gq;A3) Subtest - 78

	Actual	Predicted by
	78	97
	MC	Strengths (FCC)

Is the difference statistically significant?

YES	p <.05	YES

A "YES" in these boxes indicates that the difference between the Facilitating Cognitive Composite (FCC or alternative) and the Actual cognitive or the Actual academic weakness score is statistically significant at a 95% level of probability (one-tailed; assumes the cognitive/academic weakness is < cognitive aggregate).

Strength of Relationship

MOD

Cognitive Weakness
If calculated, the Inhibiting Cognitive Composite (ICC) is selected below by default. You may select a different area of cognitive weakness from the drop down menu for analysis.

Inhibiting Cognitive Comparite (ICC) - 65

	Actual	Predicted by
	65	96
	ICC	Strengths (FCC)

Both Weaknesses?

YES

Is there a BELOW AVERAGE aptitude-achievement consistency?

YES, CONSISTENT

Figure 13.2. PSW Analyzer results—X-BASS

Dual-Discrepancy/Consistency Model: Summary of PSW Analyses for SLD

Name: *Alex*   Age: *9 years 1 month (s)*   Grade: *3*   Date: *4/28/2016*

g-Value = 0.64

General Intelligence

Aggregate of Cognitive Strengths
FCC = 95

Unexpected Underachievement?
YES

Academic Weakness
MC = 78

Domain Specific Weakness?
YES

Cognitive Weakness
ICC = 65

Below Average Aptitude-Achievement consistency?
YES

Did the individual's observed cognitive and academic performances meet criteria within the DD/C model consistent with PSW-based SLD identification?

YES. Based on the data selected for use in the PSW Analyzer, specific criteria for establishing a PSW consistent with SLD have been met. However, this pattern of results does not automatically confirm the presence of SLD. This pattern must be considered within the context of the entire case history of the individual. In addition, other data gathered through multiple methods need to be considered (e.g., information regarding exclusionary factors) when identifying or diagnosing SLD (see chapter 4 in Essentials of Cross-Battery Assessment, 3rd Ed.).

Figure 13.2. (*Continued*)

the first 10 tests are considered the "standard WJ IV COG administration protocol" (p. 31). Thus, when the standard protocol of 10 tests is administered, there is no difference in the number of initial tests required in each model (i.e., C-SEP requires 10 WJ IV COG tests and four WJ IV OL tests (14) and DD/C requires 14 tests, two per each of the seven cognitive ability and processing domains). It should be noted that although both models recommend follow-up testing in the presence of a suspected cognitive processing weakness, the C-SEP model specifies that *any* WJ IV test that measures the same broad ability be administered, meaning that additional data about the processing area in question may not be obtained. Conversely, the DD/C model specifies that follow-up assessment be conducted *in the area of suspected processing weakness* via a test that purports to measure the processing area in question (as opposed to just any test that measures the broad ability that subsumes the processing area in question). Thus, the DD/C model places greater emphasis on examining the validity of lower score performances.

Subtest differences are important in addressing the issue of comprehensiveness regarding the measurement of cognitive processes. Keeping with the recommended administration of the first seven WJ IV COG tests, in C-SEP, Gc is measured through three tests (Oral Vocabulary, Picture Vocabulary, and Oral Comprehension) and in DD/C, Gc is measured through two tests (Oral Vocabulary and General Information). Interestingly, even when Oral Vocabulary is average or better, Picture Vocabulary *and* Oral Comprehension are administered (resulting in *three* measures of Gc), which is contradictory to the main purpose of the C-SEP (i.e., to avoid overtesting). In C-SEP and DD/C, two tests are given for Glr (Story Recall and Rapid Picture Naming in C-SEP; Story Recall and Visual-Auditory Learning in DD/C). Ga is usually measured through the same two tests in C-SEP and DD/C: Phonological Processing and Segmentation. However, in DD/C another instrument can be used for the additional measure of Ga or to replace the Phonological Processing test with cleaner measures of phonetic coding. Thus, in both models, multiple subtests are used to measure Gc, Glr, and Ga, although the DD/C model allows for inclusion of tests from more than one battery, whereas C-SEP does not.

If only seven tests are administered (along with the recommended tests from the WJ IV OL battery), then the cognitive areas of Gf, Gsm/Gwm, Gv, and Gs would be considered underrepresented from a DD/C perspective. However, if the additional three WJ IV core tests are administered (Test 8: General Information; Test 9: Concept Formation; and Test 10: Numbers Reversed), then Gf and Gwm would include two tests and the only underrepresented constructs would be Gv and Gs. According to Schrank et al. (2017), administering Tests 1 through 10 is advantageous for several reasons: All tests are used in the intra-cognitive analysis; the Gc-Gf composite is calculated; the Gc, Gf, Gwm, and Cognitive Efficiency clusters are calculated; and there is a comparison between cognitive efficiency and working memory clusters. These advantages are of course also available when the DD/C model is followed using WJ IV data.

The C-SEP and DD/C models allow for academic skills to be represented by individual subtest scores or composites, meaning that there are no differences between the models related to decisions about how many achievement tests should be administered and which ones. This is primarily because many other data sources can be used to support or refute findings from standardized tests of academic achievement.

DON'T FORGET

The DD/C model allows for the use of subtests from various batteries and therefore gives more flexibility with regard to selection and use of assessment measures.

Regarding test selection, C-SEP was developed for use with the WJ IV COG, ACH, and OL batteries. The DD/C model allows for the use of subtests from various batteries and therefore gives more flexibility with regard to selection and use of assessment measures.

The analyses in DD/C are conducted automatically by X-BASS and therefore are consistent across examiners. Professional judgment in DD/C is necessary throughout the evaluation process, such as in decisions about test selection and whether the individual's performance is suggestive of a strength or weakness. The C-SEP does not specify which analyses (i.e., variation and comparison procedures) are to be used in the determination of a PSW. This is based on the professional judgment of the evaluator. Because the WJ IV system allows for multiple possibilities, the evaluator could choose one of myriad comparisons (e.g., Gf-Gc—Achievement, GIA—Achievement, Aptitude-Achievement, Oral-Language—Achievement, for example). Because C-SEP does not specify which variation and comparison procedures are most useful for the purpose of PSW analysis, different results (and thus conclusions about SLD) are possible with the same evaluation data.

The C-SEP and DD/C models require ecological validity and emphasize that the determination of a PSW is based not only on test scores but also thorough analysis of all data gathered in the evaluation process. Each model is complex, technical, and requires training. Rapid Reference 13.2 presents a synopsis of the comparison between C-SEP and DD/C.

⟱ Rapid Reference 13.2

....

Synopsis of the Comparison Between C-SEP and DD/C

Domain	C-SEP	DD/C	Impressions
Comprehensiveness			
Measures cognitive processes	√	√	Each model measures cognitive processes. C-SEP recommends administering one subtest per cognitive process and DD/C requires two. If 10 subtests are administered in C-SEP, there is underrepresentation of Gv and Gs. Processes are not underrepresented in the DD/C model. A broader range of cognitive processing measures and a more in-depth assessment of cognitive processes are achieved with the DD/C model because it is not battery specific.
Measures language processes	√	√	In the C-SEP model, Gc is measured by three tests, one from the COG and two from the OL battery. DD/C requires two tests for Gc. If the 10 standard battery tests of the WJ IV COG are administered (along with the recommended tests from the WJ IV OL battery), then Gc is overrepresented in the C-SEP model (i.e., four Gc tests). The DD/C model guards against underrepresentation and overrepresentation of cognitive abilities and processes.
Measures achievement	√	√	The C-SEP and DD/C recommend testing in the referral area. Additional testing in other academic domains is based on the professional judgment of the evaluator, district guidelines, and

			so forth. Both models allow for administering the six CORE WJ IV achievement tests. Note however that the DD/C model allows for the administration of any achievement test; it is not restricted to the WJ IV ACH battery.
Relies on CHC theory for interpretation of data	√	√	Each method is based on CHC theory.
Efficiency			
Minimum number of cognitive tests or subtests required for administration	11 (7 COG and 4 OL) or 14 (10 COG and 4 OL)	14	If the first seven tests of the WJ IV COG (along with the four tests from the OL battery) are administered, then an initial evaluation following C-SEP contains three fewer subtests compared to DD/C. However, if the recommended 10 WJ IV COG (plus recommended OL tests) are administered, then there is no difference in number of tests that constitute an initial evaluation across models.
Test based	√		C-SEP is based on the WJ IV; DD/C allows for flexibility in assessment tools.
Individualization of test selection		√	DD/C allows for an individualized approach to test selection; C-SEP does not
Steps required for analyzing standard scores	One step	Two steps	C-SEP uses the WJ IV online score report. DD/C requires the extra step of inputting data into X-BASS.
Precision			
Accounts for attenuation of an overall ability score due to specific areas of processing weakness		√	DD/C allows for the use of the FCC, which provides an estimate of an individual's ability to think and reason without the attenuating influence of the processing areas of weakness. Although C-SEP allows for the use of a Gf-Gc composite as an alternative to the GIA (when the latter score is attenuated by

			processing areas of weakness), the Gf-Gc composite may also be attenuated (e.g., Number Series is often low for individuals suspected of an SLD in math, but it cannot be removed from the calculation of the Gf-Gc composite).
Incorporates triangulation of data including ecological data	√	√	The models require ecological validity for areas of processing weakness identified via standardized, norm-referenced tests.
Specific technique or specific analyses are evident		√	DD/C has a sophisticated method for analyzing all data through use of X-BASS. C-SEP does not identify which specific analyses are to be used in the determination of a PSW.
Complexity and need for training	√	√	The models are technical and require training.

CONCLUSION

This chapter used case study data to compare two models that assist in making SLD determination decisions. The first case showed that both models supported SLD. The second case showed that the DD/C model supported SLD whereas the C-SEP model did not. In the second case, the steps involved in the DD/C model led to the discovery of underlying processing weaknesses with established relationships to the area of academic skill deficit. The C-SEP model missed the processing weaknesses. However, a clinician following C-SEP may have chosen to ignore the "rules" and continue to assess processing areas more thoroughly based on professional judgment.

Ultimately, the evaluator who conducts the assessment for the determination of SLD must be well versed in multiple areas, not just tests and models for score analysis, but in theoretical and practical considerations, factors affecting test scores and general school performance indicators, and intervention techniques used before referral and those recommended as a result of the assessment. The evaluator must take all factors into consideration and choose the model that he or she believes is most comprehensive, most precise, and most likely to generate a true positive.

☙ TEST YOURSELF ☙

1. There are multiple approaches related to the PSW model, but they have some commonalities including all of the following *except:*
   (a) Identification of one or more cognitive processing deficits
   (b) Identification of one or more areas of academic deficit
   (c) A presumed causal relationship between the identified deficit areas
   (d) Identification of specific brain structures involved in the deficit areas

2. The first step of the C-SEP model is to measure cognitive processes through administration of the WJ IV COG Core 7 tests. True or false?

3. The FCC in the DD/C model reflects:
   (a) The aggregate of the student's intact abilities and processes (i.e., scores that reflect at least average ability)
   (b) The student's IQ
   (c) The student's fluid and crystallized abilities
   (d) None of the above

4. On some occasions the C-SEP and DD/C models will yield similar results, but on other occasions, they will yield different results. True or false?

5. The DD/C and C-SEP models differ in the following ways *except:*
   (a) They account for attenuation of an overall ability score due to specific areas of processing weakness
   (b) They are based on CHC theory
   (c) There is an individualization of test selection
   (d) Specific technique or specific analyses are evident

Answers: 1. d; 2. True; 3. a; 4. True; 5. b.

REFERENCES

Flanagan, D. P., Ortiz, S. O., & Alfonso, V. C. (2013). *Essentials of Cross-Battery Assessment* (3rd. ed.). New York, NY: Wiley.

Flanagan, D. P., Ortiz, S. O., & Alfonso, V. C. (2016). *Cross-Battery Assessment software system (X-BASS)* New York, NY: Wiley.

Flanagan, D. P., Ortiz, S. O., Alfonso, V. C., & Mascolo, J. (2002). *The achievement test desk reference (ATDR): Comprehensive assessment and learning disabilities.* Boston, MA: Allyn & Bacon.

Flanagan, D. P., & Schneider, W. J. (2016). Cross-Battery Assessment? XBA PSW? A case of mistaken identity: A commentary on Kranzler and colleagues' "Classification agreement analysis of Cross-Battery Assessment in the identification of specific learning disorders in children and youth." *International Journal of School & Educational Psychology, 4*(3), 137–145.

Messick, S. (1995). Validity of psychological assessment: Validation of inferences from persons' responses and performances as scientific inquiry into score meaning. *American Psychologist, 50*, 741–749.

Schrank, F. A., Mather, N., & McGrew, K. S. (2014a). *Woodcock-Johnson IV Tests of Achievement*. Rolling Meadows, IL: Riverside.

Schrank, F. A., Mather, N., & McGrew, K. S. (2014b). *Woodcock-Johnson IV Tests of Oral Language*. Rolling Meadows, IL: Riverside.

Schrank, F. A., McGrew, K. S., & Mather, N. (2014). *Woodcock-Johnson IV Tests of Cognitive Abilities*. Rolling Meadows, IL: Riverside.

Schrank, F. A., Stephens-Pisecco, T. L., & Schultz, E. K. (2017). The WJ IV core selective evaluation process applied to identification of a specific learning disability. *Woodcock-Johnson IV Assessment Service Bulletin, 8*. Itasca, IL: Houghton Mifflin Harcourt.

Schultz, E. K., & Stephens, T. L. (2015). Core-selective evaluation process: An efficient & comprehensive approach to identify students with SLD using the WJIV. *Journal of the Texas Educational Evaluators' Association, 44*, 5–12.

Wright, J. (2002). Best practices in calculating several discrepancies between expected and actual academic achievement scores: A step-by-step tutorial. Retrieved June 1, 2010, from www.kasp.org/Documents/discrepancies.pdf.

Part Three

SPECIAL CONSIDERATIONS IN SPECIFIC LEARNING DISABILITY IDENTIFICATION

Fourteen

DIFFERENCE OR DISORDER

Assessment of SLD with an English Learner

Samuel O. Ortiz
Kristan E. Melo
Meghan A. Terzulli

T
he recent revision of the *Standards for Educational and Psychological Testing* (American Educational Research Association [AERA], American Psychological Association [APA], & National Council on Measurement in Education [NCME], 2015) was reorganized and expanded so that its first section addresses the principal notion of "foundations" in which the ubiquitous chapters on validity and reliability are now accompanied by a conspicuously new one—fairness. This arrangement is not an arbitrary one and highlights recognition of the importance of the issue of fairness as a fundamental criterion on which tests and testing must be based. In fact, of the four clusters (or standards) contained in the chapter on fairness, three of them are specifically related to the concept of validity itself, including Cluster 1, which addresses attempts to minimize barriers to valid score interpretation; Cluster 2, which addresses validity of test score interpretations; and Cluster 3, which removes construct-irrelevant barriers to support valid interpretations of scores (AERA, APA, NCME, 2015). Of significant note is the manner in which fairness is being tied to notions of validity rather than the traditional view of test bias as related to issues of reliability. There is little

Essentials of Specific Learning Disability Identification, Second Edition.
Edited by Vincent C. Alfonso and Dawn P. Flanagan
© 2018 John Wiley & Sons, Inc. Published 2018 by John Wiley & Sons, Inc.

DON'T FORGET

....

The recent revision of the *Standards for Educational and Psychological Testing* (American Educational Research Association, American Psychological Association, & National Council on Measurement in Education, 2015) was reorganized and expanded so that its initial section addresses the principal notion of "foundations" in which the ubiquitous chapters on validity and reliability are now accompanied by one on the concept of fairness to emphasize its centrality in test development.

dispute these days that tests provide accurate and consistent measurement. But what they are actually measuring may not be what they intended to measure, particularly when tests are administered to a wide range of individuals or subgroups who differ in some important way that may well invalidate the typical meaning assigned to a given test score.

One of the more obvious characteristics that may define a subgroup and threaten the potential validity of test scores is language. The problems inherent in administering a test developed in English to an individual who is not a native-English speaker (i.e., an English learner or EL) have long been recognized as issues to be addressed. The early and historical structure of the Wechsler Scales (i.e., Verbal IQ tests versus Performance IQ tests) provided one of the first attempts to ameliorate the problem but has never shown to have much validity or success, particularly because of the lack of any significant relation to academic success (Cathers-Schiffman & Thompson, 2007; Lohman, Korb, & Lakin, 2008), but also because such efforts fail to address the developmental aspects of language acquisition and its interaction with test performance (Ortiz, 2014). Despite recognition of the threat to validity that such language differences may present, there remains an alarming lack of professional agreement regarding systematic methods or frameworks for guiding such evaluations (Ortiz, 2014). Including fairness as a foundational chapter represents at least one attempt to address language differences in testing, albeit it represents only the general of guidelines at this time and emphasizes the need to prevent discriminatory interpretation of test scores more so than what constitutes appropriate practices for generating them (AERA, APA, NCME, 2015). Likewise, the National Association of School Psychologists (NASP) recently published a position statement on "The Provision of School Psychological Services to Bilingual Students" (NASP, 2015), which does include a section on assessment, but which necessarily remains rather broad and vague so as to apply to all members in the association, including those who do not speak any language other than English. And finally, any likelihood of reaching consensus in establishing appropriate guidelines is often impeded by the lack of coherence and quality in research studies that struggle to appreciate the complexity of the issues and that promulgate further confusion and disarray regarding what might work best (Ortiz, 2014; Ortiz, Ortiz, & Devine, 2016; Rhodes, Ochoa, & Ortiz, 2005).

Despite the rather chaotic state of affairs regarding evaluation of ELs, the purpose of this chapter is to provide a systematic and defensible framework that addresses the core issue of fairness in assessment—test score validity. Any approach employed in evaluation of ELs must provide a mechanism by which direct evaluation of the validity of obtained test scores can take place so as to determine whether they were primarily affected by cultural or linguistic factors. Failure to specify the manner in which test scores have been deemed to be valid is a failure to adhere to the requirements in the standards and thus represents an indefensible approach. Simply attesting to the validity of test scores via hollow assertions such as "the scores have been deemed to be valid" in the absence of any exercise or process that illustrates the path to this conclusion has no more defensibility than simply guessing what the scores might mean. Moreover, other attempts to temper one's conclusions by stating that the "results should be interpreted with extreme caution" are likewise a failure to establish the validity of the scores and render any such conclusions as specious, whether or not accomplished with extreme caution.

> **C A U T I O N**
>
> Failure to specify the manner in which test scores have been deemed to be valid is a failure to adhere to the requirements in the standards and thus an indefensible approach.

TEST SCORE VALIDITY AND TRADITIONAL ASSESSMENT APPROACHES

Over the years, a number of approaches have been suggested as possible frameworks for conducting evaluations in a manner that is presumed to address the issue of test score validity (Ortiz, 2014; Ortiz, Ochoa, & Dynda, 2012). It has often been assumed that by employing one or more of these approaches, the result is a collection of scores in which the evaluator may have confidence in terms of validity and may, therefore, draw valid conclusions and diagnostic impressions. These methods will be reviewed in the next sections with a particular eye on the extent to which they actually and successfully address test score validity and the extent to which they represent viable and defensible methods for evaluation of ELs that produce valid results.

Modified Methods of Evaluation: Modified or Altered Assessment

One of the more common approaches to testing diverse individuals is simply to modify or alter the test in a manner that enables the examinee to demonstrate his or her true ability and reduce potential bias inherent in strict administration of the test. Such methods may include allowing the lengthening of or completely eliminating time limits, accepting responses in languages other than English, repeating instructions or translating instructions to the native language, pre-teaching task concepts, skipping inappropriate items, and use of a translator or interpreter for administration. The intention is, of course, noble in that the alterations should assist the individual by providing better opportunities to demonstrate his or her abilities. And although one can assume that some of these modifications (e.g., removal of time limits) would certainly improve performance (as they would even with non-ELs), all of these methods violate standardization procedures, and thus they render the test scores invalid by undermining the psychometric properties of the test. Violating standardization introduces new and unquantifiable amounts of error, which could have either helped or hindered performance and which can no longer be discerned by the examiner or the test's publisher due to the altered administration. This would be particularly problematic in the diagnosis of a specific learning disability (SLD), because accurate diagnosis of SLD requires a valid and nuanced profile of strengths and weaknesses across many domains. As such, modified assessment, although well intended, is not a sufficient approach to generating test scores that are valid and permit interpretation. This is not to say that modifications or alterations should never be used, however, because information derived from this method can yield important and valuable *qualitative* information. However, if the purpose of a standardized test is to yield valid *quantitative* representations of an individual's cognitive abilities, modified assessment by itself will not serve this purpose adequately. This suggests that when practitioners decide to employ standardized tests they should consider administering them in the specified standardized manner first and modify or alter the administration only later in follow-up efforts to derive qualitative data. In this way, it leaves the original scores from the original administration unaltered and potentially subject to examination regarding the influence of linguistic and cultural variables. Scores obtained from any nonstandardized administration of a test cannot ever be determined to be valid and will effectively preclude any interpretation.

> # C A U T I O N
> ....
> Scores obtained from any nonstandardized administration of a test cannot ever be determined to be valid and will effectively preclude any interpretation.

Nonverbal Methods of Evaluation: Language-Reduced Assessment

Perhaps the most common method for assessing children from diverse backgrounds involves the administration of a nonverbal test or battery. In a survey of

323 school psychologists, Sotelo-Dynega and Dixon (2014) found that 88.6% of school psychologists use a measure of nonverbal intelligence. This method has also been recommended by various researchers (Cathers-Schiffman & Thompson, 2007; Wechsler, Raiford, & Holdnack, 2014). Despite its widespread adoption in practice, nonverbal assessment does not appear to provide a satisfactory or complete solution to the issue of test score validity. It has long been standard clinical practice for clinicians to administer and interpret only the subtests that made up the old Performance IQ (PIQ) and to simply disregard use of the Verbal IQ (VIQ) subtests in the Wechsler Scales (Figueroa, 1990). Given that the PIQ and VIQ originally reflected the name and structure as drawn from the Army Mental Tests (Yerkes, 1921) and were considered initially by Wechsler to represent a range of interchangeable tests (Wechsler, 1944), it is not surprising that these indexes have been eliminated beginning with the Wechsler Intelligence Scale for Children–Fourth Edition (WISC-IV; Wechsler, 2003) and continuing in the WISC-V (Wechsler, 2014). Nevertheless, for the WISC-V, Wechsler and colleagues still recommend that the "NVI [Nonverbal Index] may provide a more appropriate estimate of intellectual ability for children who are English language learners but who can comprehend English subtest instructions" (2014, p. 141).

At face value, it stands to reason that a nonverbal measure of intellectual ability would be a fairer estimate of general intelligence for children from diverse backgrounds. For one, it seems logical that children who have limited English proficiency would perform better on subtests that either reduce or attempt to eliminate language demands. Of course, it is an erroneous assumption to believe that a nonverbal measure is wholly "nonverbal," because it is impossible to administer any test without any communication whatsoever. That the communication may well be gestural rather than verbal does not eliminate the purpose of language in testing that is based on communication and comprehension (Mpofu & Ortiz, 2009; Ortiz et al., 2012). And although many tests exist that permit administration solely through the use of gestures, none of them provides guidance on how the meaning of the gestures are to be conveyed to and learned by the examinee in the absence of any verbal communication. Moreover, the test content and stimuli, and even the very act of testing itself, is a cultural artifact that is not completely removed from the testing situation (Ortiz & Melo, 2015). For these reasons, nonverbal tests might be more accurately referred to as "language-reduced" tests. And whereas it has been demonstrated that performance of diverse individuals on such language-reduced tests is much closer to the normative mean than on language-embedded tests (Cathers-Schiffman & Thompson, 2007), the scores remain narrow in scope and of limited interpretive applicability. For example, research has demonstrated that nonverbal tests have relatively poor predictive validity for overall academic performance

(Lohman et al., 2008), which is likely due to the lack of measurement of abilities that are most relevant and pertinent to school success (i.e., language abilities such as Gc and Ga that are related to the acquisition and development of reading and writing skills). Given the ubiquitous nature of reading and writing difficulties as the presumptive concerns for evaluation referrals involving suspected SLD, the use of tests that do not provide any information in this regard will have little utility.

When these shortcomings are combined with the one problem that plagues all tests in general (i.e., lack of norm sample stratification by language proficiency), it must be seen that language-reduced tests are also an insufficient and incomplete solution to the problem of test score validity. Whereas such tests clearly reduce the attenuating effect of language proficiency on test performance, the resulting narrow focus on abilities, over-reliance on the validity of general estimates of intelligence, and lack of predictive value in academic achievement make them no different than the tests (of Gv, Gf, and Gs) that appear on more-comprehensive batteries that also include verbal tests. To be sure, nonverbal tests are good and useful tests for various purposes, but they do not differ in any meaningful way from nonverbal tests found on comprehensive batteries. Thus, clinicians looking for an assessment method that provides valid estimates of general intelligence or a broad range of specific cognitive abilities cannot rely on nonverbal tests exclusively.

DON'T FORGET
....
Nonverbal tests are good and useful tests for various purposes, but they do not differ in any meaningful way from nonverbal tests found on comprehensive batteries.

Dominant Language Evaluation: Native Language Assessment

Native language tests give the immediate appearance of being able to solve all the problems inherent in evaluation of children from diverse backgrounds, at least for those who are Spanish speakers. Generally speaking, the decision to use a native language test often comes after testing the individual's language dominance in English and the native language. When the individual is dominant in English, testing is done in English. When the individual is found to be dominant in the native language, in this case Spanish, the testing is done in the native language. One of the problems with this approach, however, is the assumption that if the individual is dominant in the native language, then the individual's level of proficiency in that language is comparable to other age- or grade-matched peers and thus scores obtained via the native language would be automatically valid (Esparza-Brown, 2007). The same problem holds if the individual is dominant in English. Dominance, however, is not an indicator of proficiency or development in a language. It merely indicates which language is better developed at that point. One can easily be dominant in a language and still lack significant proficiency in it as compared to another language. Dominance and proficiency are therefore not equivalent, and establishing dominance serves only to indicate in which language the individual is likely to perform better but not necessarily comparable to other children of the same age or grade. How well-developed specific skills and abilities are in a particular individual is not described by dominance and thus fail to provide valid information on whether that individual in fact possesses age- or grade-appropriate development in that language (Ortiz et al., 2016). Beyond this issue lies the fact that little research exists that may be used to guide and inform clinicians' interpretations of test scores obtained via native language administration (Ortiz, 2014; Ortiz et al., 2016). Even when an individual is tested in his or her native or dominant language, the type of educational programming the individual has received and for how long, as well as the parents' own literacy level in the native language and English, all play a role in the language development of the individual (Rhodes et al., 2005). Their impact is not altered by the presence or absence of dominance. Still other potentially problematic issues in the implementation of native-language tests is that they require clinicians to be qualified and competent to administer and score the test in the native language. Such "bilingual" clinicians, as noted previously, are relatively uncommon and become exceedingly scarce for languages other than Spanish.

One basic problem with native-language testing is the lack of adequate representation in the norm sample along the lines of developmental language proficiency for individuals who are bilingual, not monolingual. This may be due in part to the mistaken notion that language-related validity issues are overcome by a native-language test. Such an assumption, however, ignores the significant range of variability that may exist among ELs in the native language as well as in English, and, thus, test development has not paid much attention to controlling for these differences in language development, particularly for children here in the United States. For example, the type of education being received by ELs in the United States can vary from English immersion, to ESL services, to bilingual programs, to dual-language programs. These programs produce significant variability in native-language development and also produce varying proficiency in English. Because of the differences that may exist among ELs in their relative proficiency in both languages, use of norms that treat them as a monolithic entity are unlikely to serve as a fair or equitable standard for comparison of expected or average performance (Braden & Iribarren, 2007). Current norms that rely on typical variables for stratification (e.g., age, gender, geographic location, SES, and race-ethnicity) do not account for the nonlinear trajectory of language acquisition as well as the non-normative distribution of language proficiency that exists among ELs and is not tied strictly to age. That is, although three individuals could all be 12 years old and from the same country of origin, their relative language skills in English and Spanish could be vastly different. There seems to be an obvious recognition of the inherent problems in testing a native-English speaker in Spanish, yet there seems to be little recognition of the same problem when native-Spanish speakers are tested in English, as illustrated best by the recommendation by the publisher of the WISC that children who have been in the United States for more than 5 years should be tested in English. Such a recommendation implies the existence of a rather homogenous level of language proficiency across the equated sample, which cannot be true or even possible with the sampling techniques that were used. But it does restrict the variability in language proficiency and suggests that the norms are applicable only to children with fewer than 5 years of learning English. Thus, test performance for children of the same age is less likely to be based on intrinsic individual differences and more likely to be based on varying levels of formal education in the native language.

It should be noted that such problems in norm sample representation are not limited to any one native-language test. A truly adequate and representative EL norm sample would need to use only ELs, not native speakers in other countries, and would have to be stratified by the examinees' levels of English exposure across each age group. This is a complicated and difficult process that has not yet been accomplished in the development of any comprehensive test of intelligence or cognitive ability to date and therefore should not be construed as a technical deficiency as much as a practical limitation. However, it has been accomplished in a more narrowly focused test, the Ortiz Picture Vocabulary Acquisition Test (Ortiz PVAT; Ortiz, 2018), which incorporates native English as well as English learner norms and illustrates the feasibility and viability of a substantive improvement in test design and applicability with ELs.

Despite the presence of these issues, native-language evaluation problems could well be mitigated substantially if there were an established literature base regarding the manner in which ELs in the United States perform on tests given to them in their native languages. Unfortunately, this is an area that has been significantly overlooked, and there is precious little data on which to base expectations of performance for US bilinguals. What data do exist seem to suggest that the effects of linguistic proficiency continue to have a linear and predictable effect on test performance (Esparza-Brown, 2007). Not only does it appear that language proficiency moderates performance on tests as a function of the degree to which the tests require or rely on linguistic development but also the pattern is similar for children receiving native-language instruction as for those receiving English-only instruction, although the pattern of decline is less steep for the former (Esparza-Brown, 2007). Nevertheless, without a body of literature on which practice can be based, it must be concluded that native-language evaluation also remains an unsatisfactory solution for addressing issues of test score validity.

Dominant-Language Evaluation: English Language Assessment

A survey of members of NASP indicates that only 13.9% identified fluency in a language other than English (Klotz, 2016). Likewise, only 27 languages other than English are represented among these individuals compared to the over 400 languages spoken by families living in the United States (Klotz, 2016; US Census Bureau, 2015). Such statistics indicate that it is unavoidable that most ELs will invariably continue to be evaluated in English by English speakers (Ochoa, Powell, & Robles-Piña, 1996).

On the surface, this method appears rather counterintuitive considering the history of poor performance of ELs on tests administered to them in English as well as the fact that the three methods described in the preceding sections arose precisely because of the questionable validity of interpreting scores obtained via English language administration of tests. Research has consistently shown that ELs perform about 15–20 points lower on verbal tasks and about 3–5 points lower on language-reduced tasks when tests are administered in English (DiCerbo & Barona, 2000; Neisser et al., 1996; Ortiz & Melo, 2015; Valdes & Figueroa, 1994). Thus, suggesting that testing of ELs be conducted in English seems to perpetuate the inherent bias obvious in this approach. Yet many clinicians probably see themselves as having no other real option. For example, in a survey of school psychologists, only 11.6% identified themselves as "bilingual/multicultural school psychologists," but 87.2% of the sample reported that they routinely evaluated students who were culturally and linguistically diverse with significant reliance on "nonverbal" tests administered in English (Sotelo-Dynega & Dixon, 2014). Given the problems with validity that surround over-reliance on nonverbal tests of cognitive ability and intelligence, such a finding is rather alarming but not entirely surprising. Not only do recent statistics suggest that about 20% or more of the student population is composed of current and former ELs (O'Bryon & Rogers, 2010) but also the numbers are expected to increase rapidly, far outpacing the number of qualified bilingual professionals. Moreover, if a child is considered to be "fluent" in English according to state standards, and thus no longer receives ESL-type support services or instruction, IDEA (2004) permits testing solely in English and without any consideration regarding the child's native language, despite the fact that the child is not a native English speaker and never will be.

It cannot be overstated that a child who learns two languages (i.e., is bilingual) does not stop being bilingual simply because he or she has become dominant in

English. The child is still bilingual and still has varying and likely unequal levels of proficiency in English relative to his or her native language. Once a second language is introduced into a child's formal education as a part of core instruction (reading, writing, and math) the student is no longer a monolingual speaker of either language but rather a bilingual and is thus distinctly different from monolingual peers. Whereas an individual may reach "English proficiency" after a few years in an English educational environment, this does not mean that he or she has "caught up" to, from a developmental perspective, his or her monolingual peers in any meaningful way (Thomas & Collier, 2002).

Given this landscape, it is hard to see the merits of English language assessment, but there is an important practical advantage to this approach: The evaluator does not have to speak any other language than English. Moreover, even when an evaluator may be bilingual, it does not render one automatically qualified and competent as a bilingual evaluator. The process of nondiscriminatory assessment and the ability to interpret data fairly and drawing valid, defensible conclusions from test scores must be taught, learned, and practiced every bit as much as any other psychological skill regardless of the language or languages used in the evaluation. Professional knowledge regarding the various techniques necessary to discern the manner in which linguistic and cultural variables could be affecting test performance must be acquired and is a far more valuable type of competency than is merely being able to speak the examinee's native language. Another major advantage concerns the vast array of tests and instruments that may be drawn on for evaluation. Once testing shifts to a language other than English, the choices narrow severely and are almost completely absent when the other language is not Spanish. And finally, perhaps the most significant advantage that testing in English has that other methods do not lies in the fact that research describing the test performance of ELs now spans more than 100 years. This vast body of literature provides a useful and valuable context for practitioners who may be able to use it for the purposes of directly evaluating the validity of test scores obtained from testing in English. For this last reason alone, the ability to establish an evidence-based "norm group" by which to compare test performance of ELs fairly, testing in English represents the only viable method for at least initiating an evaluation that effectively addresses the problem of establishing test score validity.

A Recommended Best-Practice Approach for Testing ELs

An in-depth discussion of all aspects of nondiscriminatory assessment is beyond the scope of this chapter, and the reader is referred to other sources for information regarding the full extent of what constitutes equitable assessment (Ortiz, 2014).

The approach described in this section is primarily intended to focus on the use of tests and testing in evaluation of ELs. It cannot be stressed enough that use of tests by themselves or an over-reliance on them is not sufficient to constitute comprehensive assessment, let alone nondiscriminatory evaluation. Rather, the approach outlined in this section is intended only to serve as a best-practice guide for the use of tests and testing with ELs. Moreover, it is understood that the results and conclusions from this approach must be integrated with additional data, particularly pre-referral information and other contextual factors, so as to arrive at defensible and ecologically valid conclusions. Any attempt to follow the guidelines for testing described herein for diagnostic purposes in the absence of integration and corroboration by additional data would be clinically insufficient. But when test results generated by adherence to the following guidelines are combined with the type of information generally gathered during the pre-referral process (e.g., progress monitoring data, background and development, referral concerns, informal and authentic measures of academic skills, etc.), then a strong case is made regarding the validity of any diagnostic conclusions and inferences.

As noted at the beginning of this chapter, fairness in evaluation of students from diverse backgrounds using standardized tests rests on the degree to which validity of the scores can be established, specifically the construct validity of the obtained test scores. When an EL obtains a low score on a test administered in English (or even the native language), it becomes necessary to determine if the scores represent a difference in experiential background (because of language or opportunity for acculturative knowledge acquisition) or whether they constitute evidence of an intrinsic disorder. In terms of validity, one must decide if the test scores actually represent what they were intended to represent (the level of ability in the domain intended to be measured by the specific subtest) or if the test score might instead represent the extraneous and confounding influence of factors that were not intended to be measured (e.g., linguistic proficiency). If one can establish that the obtained test scores are valid and truly measure the intended areas of cognitive functioning (unencumbered by external influences), then one can make claims about the presence of a disorder. However, if the validity of test scores cannot be established (or is simply ignored), then one cannot make any such claims or provide any such interpretations. Clinicians must carefully consider and defend the validity of obtained test scores, particularly with respect to the

C A U T I O N

Attempts to interpret test scores without establishing their validity violates basic psychometric standards of practice and renders such conclusions drawn from those interpretations as at best useless and at worst harmful to the examinee.

presence and impact of factors that constitute a difference (e.g., limited English development) whenever an EL is being evaluated. Without such due consideration and defense, interpretation of test scores is specious and indefensible, regardless of hollow admonitions that the results were interpreted with "extreme caution." Attempts to interpret test scores without establishing their validity violates basic psychometric standards of practice and renders such conclusions drawn from those interpretations as at best useless and at worst harmful to the examinee.

General Considerations

One, if not perhaps the most important, consideration in evaluation of any kind involves the reason and purpose of testing being conducted. The use of standardized tests is often employed in evaluation as an efficient means of identifying deficits in cognitive abilities by comparing them to a normative standard. As such, the major focus of testing and interpretation typically rests on whether scores are normatively *low,* rather than being average or above average. It is easily understood that scores that reflect poor performance are relatively easy to obtain because there are myriad reasons having nothing to do with lack of ability that can readily explain why an individual may have underperformed on a standardized test. For example, being hungry, tired, emotionally upset, sick, nervous, angry, distracted, and so forth are all simple explanations regarding why someone managed to perform at a level below their actual or true ability. The same cannot be said, however, for scores that are *above* one's own ability, because it is extremely unlikely that one would manage to demonstrate a level of ability that they do not actually possess. This is especially true for cognitive ability tests when simple guessing is unlikely to have any effect on improving performance. Therefore, it can be assumed that if an examinee scores in the average range or above on a given test of ability, it must mean that his or her ability is at least in the average range—it could very well be higher, but it cannot be lower and, by definition, cannot be an indication of possible disability and does not, for the purposes of most evaluations, require any further validation. Conversely, if testing results in low scores, the need to consider and establish validity is essential in determining whether the scores are reflections of true deficits and the extent to which subsequent interpretations and conclusions can be drawn and defended. For this reason, standardized administration becomes a requirement because it assists in ensuring that many of the factors that could confound test results have been controlled or eliminated. In the case of ELs, standardization is insufficient, however, because it does not address the possibility that the presence of factors related to language proficiency and acculturative knowledge acquisition could potentially have attenuated test performance nonetheless—factors that are specifically identified as exclusionary variables in the identification of an SLD according to IDEA (2004).

Step 1. Evaluate Construct Validity in English

Because the fundamental goal of evaluation with ELs is to establish the validity of the obtained test scores, an approach that starts with standardized administration of tests in English takes on various advantages. As noted previously, evaluation in English represents the only current, evidence-based method for assessment because it can be guided by more than a century of research on the performance of ELs on such tests. This means that it is the only approach in which the possibility exists of being able to evaluate the validity of test scores for ELs by comparing them to that found in the literature. When organized within the structure of the Culture-Language Interpretive Matrix (C-LIM; Flanagan, Ortiz, & Alfonso, 2013; Ortiz, 2014; Ortiz & Melo, 2015; Ortiz, Melo, & Terzulli, 2017; Ortiz et al., 2016), results from research can serve as a sort of de facto and appropriate "norm" sample regarding expected and average performance. In other words, use of the C-LIM facilitates determination of whether scores obtained from testing an individual EL in English are somehow comparable to scores on the same tests generated by ELs via research. Note that if the evaluation process began with native language testing, the lack of any substantive body of research on the performance of ELs would preclude evaluation of the validity of such scores in this manner. Thus, it is only with an approach that begins with tests administered in English that the lack of adequate norm representation can be ameliorated by turning to the existing research evidence.

Beginning an evaluation in English also means that any evaluator, whether monolingual or bilingual, can conduct the initial testing without assistance. Furthermore, if the evaluation is conducted for the purposes of identifying a possible disability, and should all of the obtained test scores suggest average or higher functioning, it can then be reasonably concluded that, as far as the test data are concerned, the examinee has no cognitive deficits in the areas assessed. This means that no further testing is necessary and that, in the absence of other compelling evidence to the contrary, the evaluation could effectively end as having provided sufficient information that the individual does not possess any identifiable cognitive-based disability. This does not mean that no intervention or other action is required or that the examinee will simply return to the general education environment and suddenly start to succeed academically. Because the most-common purpose for an evaluation is linked to intervention, such a finding not only rules out the presence of a disability but also strongly suggests the need to examine instructional and other factors that are affecting school performance. It is more likely, however, that evaluation of one or more cognitive domains via testing in English first are likely to result in low scores. Such a result now requires direct evaluation of the validity of the test scores. Because the testing was conducted in English, clinicians may use research on the performance of ELs to assist in evaluating the extent to which linguistic and cultural factors may have affected and potentially invalidated the resulting test performance. This is the singular purpose of the C-LIM—a framework that systematically collates the research in a way that facilitates comparisons of individual performance to the collective research-based normative performance.

Using the C-LIM

The C-LIM (Flanagan et al., 2013; Ortiz & Melo, 2015; Ortiz, Flanagan, & Alfonso, 2015) is based on an aggregation of research on the test performance of ELs. By collating results from a wide variety of studies conducted on ELs who were tested in English, the C-LIM provides a simple, evidence-based method that facilitates analysis of the extent to which linguistic and cultural variables may have affected test performance. When that impact is reflected by a broad and systematic attenuation of scores, it suggests that the test scores are more likely to be reflections of linguistic-cultural variables rather than actual ability and thus likely invalid (Cormier, McGrew & Ysseldyke, 2014). When there is no observance of a general attenuating effect on test scores, it suggests that the results are more likely to be reflections of true ability (or lack thereof) than reflections of linguistic-cultural variables, and thus they are likely to be valid. Given the limited scope of this chapter, the C-LIM will be discussed primarily with respect to its use and application in the final case study example and under the assumption that its basic principles, guidelines, purpose, and rationale are already familiar to the reader via the original sources. It should be noted as well that the enhanced, full-featured C-LIM is no longer a separate software application and has instead been integrated with other cross-battery tools (i.e., Data Management and Interpretive Assistant [DMIA] and Pattern of Strengths and Weaknesses Analyzer [PSW-A]) to form the *Cross-Battery Assessment Software System* (X-BASS; Ortiz et al., 2015). However, a free "basic" version of the C-LIM is still available for download, which albeit a bit more cumbersome to use nevertheless can perform all of the same functions and analyses that are demonstrated in the case study.

The C-LIM is a two-dimensional matrix that consists of nine cells representing various degrees of linguistic demand and cultural loading. Originally, classifications of subtests were based on the test's characteristics regarding each dimension

(Flanagan & Ortiz, 2001). However, since 2007 classifications have been based on actual mean values aggregated across a wide range of research studies on EL test performance found in the literature (Cormier et al., 2014; Flanagan, Ortiz, & Alfonso, 2007; Flanagan et al., 2013; Sotelo-Dynega & Dixon, 2014). Because the C-LIM is concerned with basic construct validity, only subtests are classified as it makes no sense to determine the validity of composites if the validity of the subtests that comprise the composites has not been determined to be valid itself. As a point of reference, Figure 14.1 provides an example of the subtest classifications for the WISC-V. With the exception of the legacy tests carried over from the previous version, which have substantial empirical evidence, classifications of the new tests on the WISC-V are necessarily based on research with similar tests as well as on expert consensus. Such new classifications take into consideration the intended construct, task demands, and similarity to other current subtests on the same and on other batteries for which evidence already exists. Of particular note is that these classifications, as with all classifications in the C-LIM, are subject to modification pending the results of ongoing and future research. The C-LIM is dynamic in this regard, and it is intended to be molded on the basis of studies that administer tests in English to ELs who are not disabled and of generally average ability.

To use the C-LIM, practitioners simply enter the subtest scores into the appropriate cells and the program automatically generates an aggregate value for each cell as well as a series of graphs of the pattern of aggregate values for all cells in which data are entered. The aggregate values in the matrix, and more important the resulting bar graphs that are generated from the results, display the individual's pattern of performance and permit comparison to the "average" values culled from the literature. In general, if linguistic and cultural factors are broadly and systematically attenuating an EL's test scores, then the pattern of test scores should be relatively consistent with the expected pattern of decline (or attenuation) as depicted in the C-LIM. This pattern involves not only an overall pattern of decline but also aggregate scores for cells with data that are of the same or similar magnitude as that obtained by normal ELs according to the literature. The observance of such a pattern would then indicate that performance was likely subject to the systematic attenuating effect of limited English proficiency and lack of opportunity for the acquisition of acculturative knowledge. Furthermore, if this is the case, and if the primary purpose of the evaluation was to identify a potential disability, then it means that testing can now cease and the examiner may reasonably conclude that the test scores do not support the presence of any type of cognitive disability. That is, the individual's performance was commensurate with the performance of other ELs who are known to be nondisabled and of generally average ability.

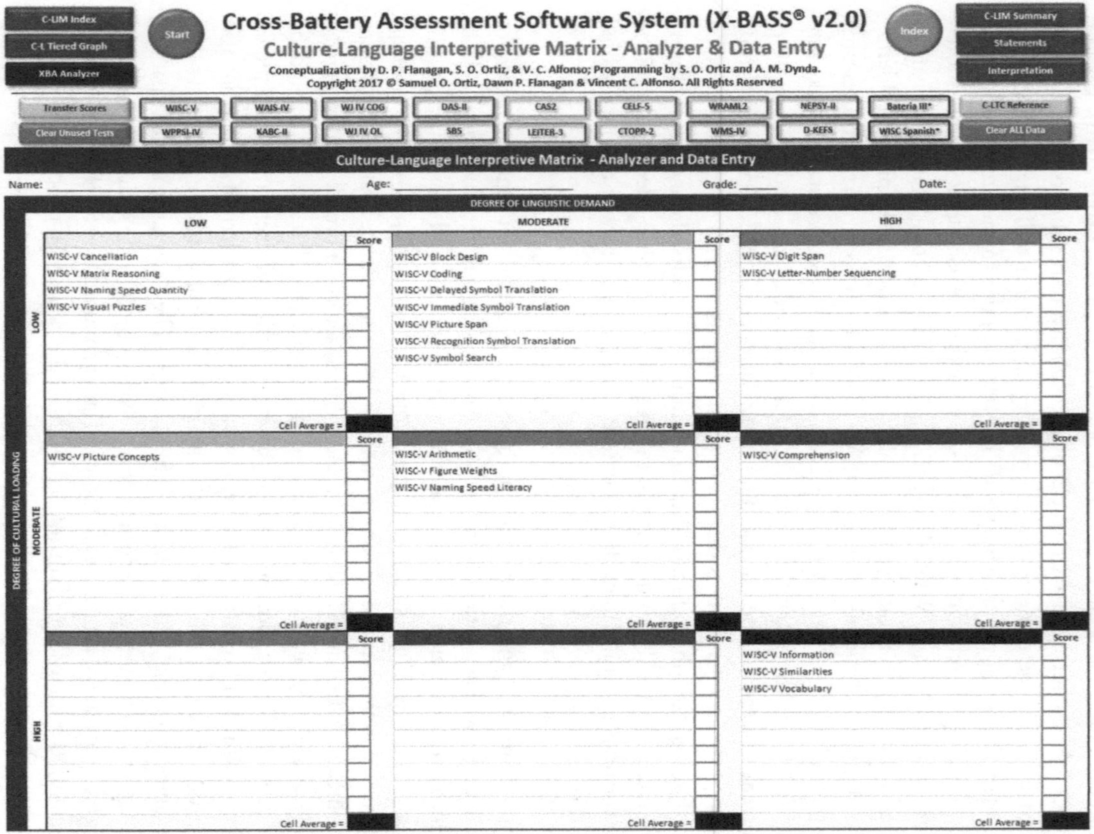

Cross-Battery Assessment Software System (X-BASS® v2.0)

Culture-Language Interpretive Matrix - Analyzer & Data Entry

Conceptualization by D. P. Flanagan, S. O. Ortiz, & V. C. Alfonso; Programming by S. O. Ortiz and A. M. Dynda.
Copyright 2017 © Samuel O. Ortiz, Dawn P. Flanagan & Vincent C. Alfonso. All Rights Reserved

Index

C-LIM Summary
Statements
Interpretation

C-LTC Reference
Clear All Data

C1 Tiered Graph
XBA Analyzer
Transfer Scores
Clear Unused Tests

WISC-V   WAIS-IV   WJ IV COG   DAS-II   CAS2   WRAML2   NEPSY-II   Batería III*
WPPSI-IV   KABC-II   WJ IV OL   SB5   LEITER-3   CTOPP-2   D-KEFS   WISC Spanish*

Culture-Language Interpretive Matrix - Analyzer and Data Entry

Name: _____ Age: _____ Grade: _____ Date: _____

DEGREE OF LINGUISTIC DEMAND

DEGREE OF CULTURAL LOADING	LOW	MODERATE	HIGH
LOW	WISC-V Cancellation WISC-V Matrix Reasoning WISC-V Naming Speed Quantity WISC-V Visual Puzzles	WISC-V Block Design WISC-V Coding WISC-V Delayed Symbol Translation WISC-V Immediate Symbol Translation WISC-V Picture Span WISC-V Recognition Symbol Translation WISC-V Symbol Search	WISC-V Digit Span WISC-V Letter-Number Sequencing
MODERATE	WISC-V Picture Concepts	WISC-V Arithmetic WISC-V Figure Weights WISC-V Naming Speed Literacy	WISC-V Comprehension
HIGH			WISC-V Information WISC-V Similarities WISC-V Vocabulary

Score / Cell Average = (for each cell)

Figure 14.1. Current WISC-V Subtest Classification in the C-LIM

However, when there is an absence of an overall pattern of decline, or when one or more of the cell aggregates is seen to be below the expected level of performance as established by normal ELs in the literature, then it suggests that the results are not primarily due to linguistic-cultural influences, and the results are possibly valid (pending further validation via native-language evaluation). In such cases, linguistic and cultural influences may well remain contributory in nature, but they have been determined not to be the primary reason for the low performance. This suggests that not only are the results possibly valid but also they cannot be explained by linguistic-cultural factors, and thus some other factor must be present to account for the observed scores—one possible explanation may well be a true deficit if cross-validated with native-language evaluation and other convergent data.

Step 2. Reevaluate Construct Validity in the Native Language

This evaluative process is not possible, however, if tests are first administered in the native language instead of English. This is primarily because there is a stunning lack of research on how ELs perform on tests given to them in their native language. Thus, if an evaluation begins by using native-language tests, there is no way to evaluate the extent to which cultural and linguistic factors may have affected performance (remember, the examinee is bilingual, not monolingual), and therefore test score validity cannot be established. Thus, for practical reasons, it makes sense to test in English first from which the scores can be evaluated for validity. It is important to understand the significance of the word *first* as used herein. The term *first* is not synonymous with the term *only* and it should never be thought that testing an EL in English only is sufficient to identify an individual with a disability. Rather, testing an EL in English only is sufficient to identify that an individual does not have a disability (i.e., all scores fall within the average range or higher). Thus, to determine that an individual actually has a disability must necessarily involve some type of native-language evaluation component. For example, whenever evaluation of test scores with the C-LIM suggests that the results are possibly or likely to be valid, additional evidence of their validity becomes necessary. The most appropriate and direct manner for providing this additional validation must come from follow-up administration of tests in areas of possible deficit as identified by testing in English but now via use of tests given in the native language (either directly by a bilingual evaluator or via the use of an interpreter or translator). The process of follow-up evaluation in this manner becomes relatively efficient because it is not necessary to reevaluate every domain but rather only those that were found to be below average (or suggestive of deficits in functioning). Test scores obtained in English that are found to be within the average range or higher need not be retested for reasons stated previously. Thus, follow-up evaluation in the native language will, in most cases, be quicker and more efficient than initial testing in English because the primary purpose of such is to provide cross-linguistic confirmation of the original test scores obtained in English. Cross-linguistic confirmation refers to the general consensus that cognitive deficits transcend language. That is, if there is a true cognitive deficit, the deficit will appear in *both* languages, not just one (Bialystok, 1991; Grosjean, 1989; Paradis, 2014). With respect to testing, if a low score is obtained via English language administration of a test, then that deficit in performance should appear in the same domain even when testing is conducted in the native language. Conversely, if the domain in which a deficit has been observed in testing conducted in English but is not observed when that domain is evaluated in the native language, it can be concluded that the original score was in fact invalid after all (for reasons that may or may not be due to language) and that the native language score represents a valid indicator of at least average ability in the domain that was measured.

Obviously, bilingual practitioners will have no difficulty using parallel native-language tests, when available, for follow-up evaluation, particularly with Spanish examinees. However, given the fraction of practitioners who are sufficiently competent to evaluate in a language other than English, combined with the dearth of tests and batteries for use in the United States in languages other than Spanish, follow-up testing in some cases will need to rely predominantly on the only feasible methods left available—direct translation by the examiner or the use of a translator or interpreter for administration of an English language test. Although it cannot be denied that psychometric problems are rampant when it comes to the use of translators or interpreters and informal translation of tests, this concern is often overridden by legal considerations, such as IDEA, which requires some sort of native-language evaluation for examinees who are still considered to be "limited English proficient." In addition, psychometric concerns may be further lessened to some degree because the point of follow-up testing is primarily to obtain *qualitative* information for cross-linguistic confirmation, not necessarily quantitatively valid scores. Furthermore, should performance improve significantly or rise to the average range for abilities tested in the native language (as compared to having been in the deficit range when tested in English), it should be construed as strong evidence of excellent learning potential on the part of the individual as well as ability that is likely to be at least average and possibly even higher. In such cases, practice effects would effectively provide diagnostic information and constitute considerable evidence that learning problems must reside in the classroom and not in the child. In addition, because scores in the average range obtained via cognitive testing are very unlikely to occur by chance or for spurious reasons, such patterns of performance must be viewed as evidence of abilities that are intact and not indicative of deficit or disability.

The Gc Caveat

Although the method for cross-linguistic confirmation described in the previous section can be employed to validate test scores in any cognitive domain, there is a notable exception for Gc. By its very definition, Gc comprises various aspects of language development as well as the amount of cultural knowledge one has acquired. It is, therefore, impossible to separate Gc from the influence of linguistic-cultural factors because Gc is itself nothing more than culture and language. The overwhelming majority of culture-bound information representative of Gc is acquired in formal educational settings as well as incidentally in social settings typical of a particular culture. This is one reason why Gc correlates so highly with formal education (Schrank, McGrew, & Mather, 2015). And because language and the acquisition of acculturative knowledge occur in a known developmental manner associated closely with and measurable by age, it would be unreasonable to expect an EL, irrespective of English language proficiency, to possess comparable knowledge or language skill as compared to same-age, native-English-speaking peers. By definition, ELs have been exposed to culture-specific and English language environments for a shorter period of time, in some cases considerably shorter, than their native-English-speaking peers. Such comparisons would be tantamount to comparing the vocabulary of a 5-year-old to that of a 10-year-old or expecting the general knowledge of a 10-year-old to be comparable to the knowledge of a 15-year-old.

Therefore, when interpreting abilities in the domain of Gc, scores for an EL should be evaluated only relative to the selected pattern of expected performance that corresponds to the degree of difference indicated in the C-LIM. Normative comparisons to batteries or tests in either English or the native language will always remain inherently discriminatory, and the only manner in which a fair and equitable assessment of Gc can be obtained is relative to other ELs. ELs generally score poorly on Gc tests because of the high reliance on age-appropriate development of language and acculturative knowledge. The attenuation can be as high as nearly two full standard deviations below the mean depending on their level of English proficiency (Sotelo-Dynega, Ortiz, Flanagan, & Chaplin, 2013). Thus, in many cases, ELs will present with a score for Gc that may be considerably below average (SS < 90) from a test's normative perspective. But when that same aggregate score is viewed within the context of the expected range in the C-LIM (a comparison that is made only to other ELs with similar experiential backgrounds), it may still fall within the range that is considered normal or average for an EL as specified by research. To avoid potentially discriminatory interpretation of test scores measuring Gc, clinicians should only examine the extent to which a Gc score (as indicated by the aggregate value for the "high-high" cell, because all Gc tests are invariably classified in this category) is within or above the specified range of performance generated via the accumulated research and as represented by the shaded region at the far right side of the C-LIM.

In addition, the magnitude of the aggregate value represents a good guide regarding the need for follow-up testing in the native language. If the magnitude of the Gc aggregate score is within or above the shaded range in the C-LIM, then Gc should be considered to be within the average range and no further testing in this area is necessary. Only when the aggregate value for Gc is below the shaded range in the C-LIM is follow-up testing in the native language determined to be appropriate and necessary. Note that it is even possible that a low English Gc score might result in a high-average native-language Gc score and that both can be simultaneously valid because each represents the degree of relative proficiency in each language. However, such contrasting results do not indicate the presence of a disability because language skills are not deficient in the native language. It merely indicates that the examinee's language abilities are better developed in one language than in the other, likely as a function of differences in experience and education in each one. Extremely low scores in Gc (below the shaded band), particularly if coupled with low native-language Gc scores (especially in the narrow ability areas related to listening ability [LS] or communication ability [CM]), may be a red flag for a speech and language impairment (SLI), as opposed to SLD. Appropriate bilingual speech-language referrals should be made if such is the case. Recent updates to X-BASS have largely automated consideration of these and other issues related to Gc in evaluation of ELs and will be illustrated in the case study that follows.

Step 3. Cross-Validate Test Scores with Pre-Referral Data

The main purpose of follow-up evaluation in the native language of low test scores originally obtained in English is to provide cross-linguistic confirmation or disconfirmation of those scores. As such, this process can result in two possible outcomes: (1) that the follow-up native-language test scores also suggest deficits in functioning because they are at the same or similar levels of performance (i.e., below-average range) and (2) that the follow up native-language test scores instead do not suggest deficits in functioning because they are at a higher level of performance than the scores originally obtained in English (i.e., average or above-average range).

In cases when follow-up native-language test scores are similar or within the same range of functioning

as the original English language test scores, it would be reasonable to conclude that the individual has a true and valid deficit in the domain that was measured as supported by the presence of cross-linguistic confirmatory evidence (i.e., the deficit appears in both languages, not just one). The original scores obtained from testing in English can then be considered to be likely valid, and further interpretations and conclusions can be drawn from the English score(s) if additional converging evidence supports them. Low scores in English and the native language may occur for reasons other than true deficits—for example, in cases when an EL has received all instruction in English. To avoid making interpretive errors or discriminatory judgments regarding the meaning of test scores, even when cross-linguistic support is present, requires consideration of additional ecological factors that includes the referral concerns, teacher and parent observations, work samples, progress monitoring data, and the degree to which the observed and suspected cognitive deficits provide reasonable and empirically associated explanations for the reported academic difficulties. Such contextual evaluation is part and parcel of a nondiscriminatory approach and is the final consideration necessary to definitively establish the validity of test scores and the subsequent clinical inferences and interpretations that may emanate from them.

In cases when follow-up native-language test scores are significantly higher than the English scores and when such scores are observed to be in the average or higher range, cross-linguistic validation and confirmation has not occurred. Because a disorder cannot exist in only one language, and because average or higher scores are unlikely to occur by chance (as compared to low scores that may well be spurious), average or higher scores in follow-up native-language testing effectively serve to invalidate the original test score obtained in English. It can thus be reasonably concluded that the original English test score is *invalid* (for reasons that may or may not be due to linguistic or cultural factors) and that the follow-up native-language test score is *valid* and better represents the individual's true ability in this domain. In essence, the follow-up native-language score replaces the original score from testing in English. As noted, average or better scores are highly unlikely to have occurred by chance and although the increase in performance may not be entirely explainable in all cases, it must nevertheless be accepted as evidence of at least average ability and in no way an indication of cognitive dysfunction. Note that the C-LIM is designed to investigate the effects of culture and language on test scores only and that there are an infinite number of other extraneous variables that could account for low test scores obtained in English. The absence of such factors in follow-up testing may therefore increase performance, not because of the use of the native language but merely because they were present in the original but not the follow-up testing situation. Whatever the case, whenever follow-up native language test results provide sufficient data to indicate that performance in a given domain has risen to the point that it denotes average or better performance, it stands to reason that it represents a better and more-valid estimate of the individual's true ability than does the original scores obtained from testing the same domain in English.

On a final note, native-language test scores should not be considered a definitive method for evaluating the validity of English-language test scores. Qualitative analysis can and should be used in the assessment of test score validity. In cases when there is no native-language version of the test, this type of analysis becomes critical because it is the only means by which to validate the test scores obtained via English-language administration. Moreover, low performance in English and the native language may occur for reasons other than a true deficit, for example, the typical absence of native language instruction. And as with any aspect of assessment, conclusions drawn from such data should be based on converging information from multiple sources of data as described previously and as related to referral concerns, progress monitoring data, parent and teacher observations, and the extent to which any presumed cognitive deficits provide logical or empirically driven explanations of reported academic deficits.

> ## CAUTION
> ....
> Native-language test scores should not be considered a definitive method for evaluating the validity of English-language test scores. Qualitative analysis can and should be used in the assessment of test score validity.

Summary of Best Practice Recommendations

It is important to emphasize the logical and rational aspects of this approach because they are integral to the development of the process. If testing begins in English and all scores are found to be in the average range or higher, then testing can cease because the examinee has demonstrated at least average ability in all areas measured. Thus, the *absence* of a disability can be confirmed via English-language administration alone and can save significant time and resources. Not only does it not require a bilingual evaluator but also it prevents needless native-language testing of children from diverse backgrounds. If any low scores are obtained via testing conducted via English-language administration, and after having been judged to be possibly or likely valid when examined within the C-LIM, then follow-up in the native language is necessary for cross-linguistic confirmation but not for all areas that were assessed. Instead, the evaluator only needs to follow-up with native-language tests that measure the same abilities in which low scores were obtained in English, thus streamlining the assessment process. This also means that *presence* of a disability can be confirmed only with a combination of English- and native-language evaluations.

A final consideration in this approach is the fact that native-language follow-up conducted on low scores obtained from testing initially in English need not and should not be concerned primarily with quantitative scores. For one, when testing outside of English and Spanish, native-language tests are few and far between, so the generation of quantitative normative scores is only possible via use of a translator or interpreter. Further, because the native-language tests lack proper sampling and linguistic stratification necessary to adequately represent ELs in the United States, the generation of scores from such tests is not likely to be valid anyway. This is also why clinicians need not be concerned about practice effects. Because the purpose of follow-up is to confirm or disconfirm the validity of scores obtained via testing English and not to generate valid measures of cognitive ability, evidence of improved performance via incidental exposure (i.e., a practice effect) becomes powerful evidence of learning and belies the very presence of a disability. Accordingly, when observation of performance or actual test scores from native language evaluation suggest or indicate an ability as likely being within the average range or higher, this implicates the original scores from testing in English as likely to be invalid for reasons that may or may not have anything to do with language. Therefore, the point of follow-up evaluation is to pay particular attention to the qualitative and quantitative information that can be readily gleaned from testing, which is then corroborated with test data from evaluation in English.

The following section provides a brief, illustrative case study that applies the three basic steps for assessment outlined in this section. The case study is meant to serve as a general guide for how the recommended approach can be applied in practice but is by no means intended as a comprehensive or exhaustive portrayal of all procedures. Nevertheless, it should provide a general but solid demonstration regarding the various considerations and decision points required for completing an assessment of an EL suspected of having a learning disability that employs best-practice methodology to create a systematic, defensible, and nondiscriminatory evaluation.

CASE STUDY: GABRIEL VEGA

Gabriel Vega is a 9-year-old fourth-grader of Bolivian heritage who was evaluated for suspected learning disability by the school's psychologist, a bilingual English-Spanish speaker. Gabriel's teacher reported that he was having significant difficulty in a variety of academic areas as compared to his classmates. The problems appeared to be related primarily to reading and writing, and no concerns regarding math skills were noted. Gabriel was born in a rural area of Bolivia and came to the United States at the age of 1 with his mother and father (including a brother 5 years older) and moved around the southwestern parts of the United States until finding a more-permanent residence near San Antonio, Texas. His parents have little formal education and both work daily to support the family as much as possible, with his father employed primarily in construction and his mother as a maid in the hotel industry. Gabriel and his family speak Spanish predominantly and although his parents can understand only rudimentary English, Gabriel's English is advanced enough that he no longer receives ESL services from his district. In fact, Gabriel's experiences from having been raised primarily in the United States and the fact that all of his education has been in English since kindergarten has led to substantial conversational proficiency in English, and he speaks without a trace of accent. The final testing conducted by the district's ESL department indicated that he had long been dominant in English and his recent score on the district's proficiency examination (i.e., IDEA Proficiency Test; IPT) was above the necessary cutoff and provided the impetus to withdraw his ESL services last year. Although his teacher and other educators involved in the case suggest that Gabriel's English abilities are now advanced enough to make language a negligible factor in explaining his academic difficulties, the psychologist assigned to the case recognized that a lack of an accent is not an indicator of developmental proficiency and that even after being declassified as a limited English speaker, his language development in English was unlikely to be commensurate with that of his same-age or -grade native-English-speaking peers. Nevertheless, the extent to which Gabriel's observed academic difficulties might be attributable to simple developmental differences in English language proficiency or the acquisition of acculturative knowledge rather than reflections of potential disability (e.g., manifestation of an SLD) was not clear given the available information and remained a question that could benefit from a comprehensive evaluation.

The psychologist chose to use the WISC-V as the core battery for evaluation because it provides adequate measures of Gc (VCI), Gf (FRI), Gv (VSI), Gsm (WMI), and Gs (PSI). Although Glr is now also measurable via the new Naming

Speed and Symbol Translation subtests, the psychologist's unfamiliarity with these tests led to the decision to measure Glr and Ga via Cross-Battery Assessment methods using the Woodcock-Johnson IV (WJ IV; Schrank, McGrew, & Mather, 2014a). In this manner, the psychologist would be able to begin the evaluation using tests to be administered in English and that cover the seven major CHC broad abilities necessary to implement the district's pattern of strengths and weaknesses (PSW) model for identification of SLD. Such a battery would provide a general idea regarding overall ability but, more important, it would provide a comprehensive examination of the full range of cognitive abilities, including those that might be most related to the reported reading and writing difficulties in the classroom. In addition, the WISC-V is co-normed with the Woodcock Individual Achievement Test (WIAT-III; Pearson, 2009), which would provide an ideal assessment of Gabriel's current levels of academic functioning.

Gabriel's teacher had reported that his problems were primarily in the area of reading comprehension and retention. Although he seemed to be able to decode words efficiently and sounded as if he were reading somewhat fluently, Gabriel was often observed to have trouble recalling the meaning of the paragraphs and passages he just read. His teacher also reported that Gabriel displayed inconsistent patterns in learning in which he often seemed unable to remember or recall things he had learned on a consistent basis whereas at other times his knowledge seemed solid. These problems in reading and retention were beginning to put Gabriel at a significant disadvantage given the increasing reading demands of the curriculum, and it was clear to his teacher that he was struggling more and more to keep up with the rest of the class and the assigned work. The teacher reported similar concerns with written language—inconsistent learning, trouble expressing his thoughts clearly, not remembering what his topic was when he was writing, and so on. Accordingly, the psychologist chose to evaluate distinct aspects of reading, including basic reading skills and reading comprehension, as well as written expression. Despite the lack of concern with mathematics, the psychologist included evaluation of math calculation and concepts as a way of highlighting Gabriel's strengths in these areas relative to the reported weaknesses in reading and writing. There were no strong indications of any behavioral problems reported by Gabriel's teacher, although she did mention that this year he did seem to be more distracted and disruptive than in the past. She is unsure whether this is simple frustration, evidence of some other type of dysfunction, or whether it constitutes some aspect of his language and cultural difference.

Results from administration of the core and supplemental batteries are presented in Rapid Reference 14.1 in a format that is typical of the way results are often presented in tabular form in reports. Such tables are invariably intimidating because the sheer number of tests and scores can easily overwhelm nonprofessionals. Still, even an experienced psychologist is unlikely to be able to examine results in this manner and make headway in evaluating the effect of cultural and linguistic influences on test performance. It is for this reason that the C-LIM exists. In accordance with the specified instructions and guidance gleaned from readings on use of the C-LIM, the psychologist used the C-LIM Analyzer tab in the Cross-Battery Assessment Software System (X-BASS v 2.0) and began by entering the obtained subtest scores from all batteries. The first step was to click the WISC-V button from the top menu bar to populate the matrix with the corresponding WISC-V subtests and their correct classifications. Once the scores for the subtests that were administered were entered, the psychologist clicked on the Woodcock-Johnson IV Tests of Cognitive Abilities (WJ IV COG; Schrank, McGrew, Mather, 2014b) button at the top and the subtests from that battery were now populated in the matrix and any WISC-V subtests for which no score had been entered were removed to make space for the WJ IV COG subtests. Once the scores for the WJ IV COG were entered, the psychologist use the Clear Unused Tests button to remove the names of subtests from the WJ IV COG that had not been administered and for which no score existed. The C-LIM automatically calculates cell aggregates and graphs the results for analysis that permitted the psychologist to examine the validity of the test scores from a perspective that accounts for the impact of cultural and linguistic differences on performance. The main matrix, tiered graph, and primary culture-language graph generated by the C-LIM with Gabriel Vega's subtest data are depicted in Figures 14.2, 14.3, and 14.4, respectively.

Prior to examining the pattern of scores, the psychologist obtained and confirmed information from the pre-referral team and the ESL department regarding Gabriel's language proficiency and development. As noted, Gabriel had recently taken and passed the federally mandated English proficiency testing required for assessing and demonstrating progress in English language acquisition for the district's EL population. Careful examination of the information contained in Gabriel's records revealed no unusual events or circumstances in his development. Gabriel was only a year old when he came to the United States, had learned and used Spanish at home almost exclusively and up until starting kindergarten. On entering school, Gabriel was instructed only in English and was given ESL support services (which are, of course, rendered in English). Overall, the psychologist concluded that Gabriel's developmental history and his experiences in language and educationally were rather typical of other ELs born in the United States or who come to the United States at an early age. Furthermore, the records available to the psychologist indicated that his parents were of very modest means and could be classified as low SES (Gabriel was enrolled in the school's free and

≡ Rapid Reference 14.1

Test Scores from WISC-V, WIAT-III, and WJ IV COG for Gabriel Vega

Wechsler Intelligence Scale for Children–Fifth Edition

Verbal Comprehension Index	76	Fluid Reasoning Index	82	Visual-Spatial Index	95
Similarities	5	Matrix Reasoning	7	Block Design	9
Vocabulary	6	Figure Weights	7	Visual Puzzles	9
Working Memory Index	**79**	**Processing Speed Index**	**94**		
Digit Span	5	Coding	9		
Picture Span	7	Symbol Search	8		

Wechsler Individual Achievement Test—Third Edition

Basic Reading	94	Reading Comprehension	76	Written Expression	92
Word Reading	92	Reading Comprehension	76	Spelling	100
Pseudoword Decoding	98	Oral Reading Fluency	80	Sentence Composition	86
				Essay Composition	93

Woodcock-Johnson IV Tests of Cognitive Ability

Auditory Processing	91	LT Storage/ Retrieval	77
Phonological Processing	99	Story Recall	79
Nonword Repetition	84	Visual-Auditory Learning	75

reduced lunch program). Again, Gabriel's background and experience appeared to be very comparable to other children who also first began to learn English on entering school at the age of 5 and who received ESL services but never any form of native-language instruction. Accordingly, the psychologist determined that the most-appropriate basis for evaluating Gabriel's test performance within the

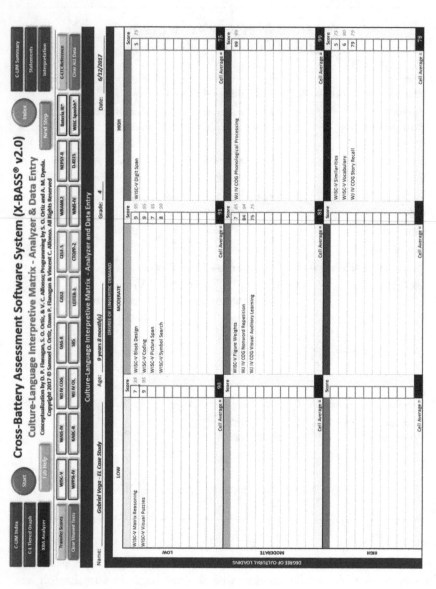

Figure 14.2. C-LIM with WISC-V Subtest Scores for Gabriel Vega Case Study

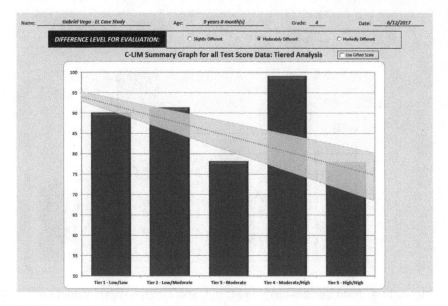

Figure 14.3. Tiered Graph of C-LIM Aggregate Values for Gabriel Vega Case Study

C-LIM was best represented by the category of "moderately different" and thus this level of difference was indicated by selection of the appropriate radio button visible at the top left of each graph in Figures 14.3 and 14.4.

On evaluation of the pattern of scores from the perspective regarding research that demonstrates an attenuation of performance because tests require increased developmental acculturative knowledge acquisition and English-language proficiency, the school psychologist concluded that there did not appear to be an overall or general pattern of decline across all scores and that there were some cell aggregates where the subtests that comprise them did not reach the expected range for ELs of average ability and similar "moderately different" backgrounds. This indicated that there did not appear to be a primary effect of these cultural and linguistic variables on Gabriel's test performance, and, consequently, the results were declared to be valid. The psychologist noted, however, that the impact of linguistic and cultural differences evaluated within the C-LIM did not simply disappear. Rather, these variables and their effect remain present and likely continue to exert some degree of contributory influence on Gabriel's test performance, albeit not to the extent that it is systematic across all test scores or powerful enough to constrain the test scores within or above the expected range.

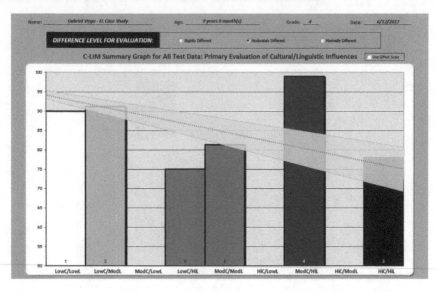

Figure 14.4. Main Culture-Language Graph of C-LIM Aggregate Values for Gabriel Vega Case Study

As such, the psychologist could not reasonably consider the alternative that the pattern of test scores suggested that they were likely to be invalid. To the contrary, evaluation within the C-LIM appeared to provide clear support that the results were possibly valid and that evaluation should therefore proceed.

Having declared the results possibly valid, the psychologist proceeded to consider the data using XBA principles to carefully evaluate and enhance the theoretical and psychometric validity of the obtained results. The DMIA module within X-BASS provided the functionality necessary to carry out these procedures. When the subtest data were transferred from the C-LIM and the composites entered into their respective cells on each test tab (including entry of all WIAT-III scores as well) in X-BASS, the only cluster that failed to demonstrate the requisite cohesion for which XBA follow-up was recommended was in the Auditory Processing (Ga) domain. Close inspection of the composition of the subtests that comprise the Ga cluster in the WJ IV COG reveals that of these two subtests (Phonological Processing and Nonword Repetition), the latter is classified as having a primary loading on Short-Term Memory (Gsm) and only a secondary loading on Ga. Further examination of the data also indicated that Gsm could not be determined reliably to be an area of strength or weakness given that the Phonological Processing score was average (SS = 99) but the Nonword Repetition score was low average and outside normal limits (SS = 84). The problem was resolved via supplemental testing using the Sound Blending subtest from the WJ IV OL battery. The resulting score (SS = 88) was combined via XBA methods to form an XBA Ga composite of 92, which suggested no real difficulties in this domain. Moreover, there had been no reported concerns with decoding difficulties in reading on Gabriel's part and his performance in the Basic Reading Skills (BRS) domain of the WIAT-III corroborated the lack of any problems with this aspect of reading (e.g., Word Reading SS = 92, Pseudoword Decoding SS = 98). As such, it was clear that Gabriel's auditory processing ability was in reality a strength, not a weakness, and that the presence of a low score on Nonword Repetition was likely attributable to deficits in Gsm as indicated by the low score on the WMI of the WISC-V (SS = 79).

In addition to a possible weakness in the area of Gsm, the psychologist noted potential deficits in Gf (FRI SS = 82), Glr (SS = 77), and Gc (VCI SS = 76). The psychologist then decided to conduct follow-up native-language evaluation of these areas to provide the necessary cross-linguistic confirmation that they are indeed domains that represent areas of true weaknesses. In recognition of the Gc caveat discussed previously, the psychologist first sought to determine whether this ability actually required reevaluation or not. This was accomplished by examining the magnitude of the aggregate value for Gc within the context of the C-LIM graphs as reflected by the high-high cell in the matrix (bottom right location) (see Figure 14.2) and the bars at the far right-hand side of the graphs (see Figure 14.3 and Figure 14.4). The psychologist noted that although the magnitude of the Gc cluster was low (SS = 76), performance in the high culture–high language (Tier 5) cell was well within the shaded and expected range. The psychologist recognized that this finding indicated that Gabriel's Gc abilities were in fact comparable to other ELs with comparable experiential and developmental backgrounds and that it should therefore be considered a "strength" within the context of assigning meaning and for the purposes of identifying SLD as well via the district's PSW model. This obviated the need for follow-up testing in the native language for Gc and instead, the psychologist conducted follow-up evaluation in the native language only for Gsm, Glr, and Gf. Because the psychologist was competent and qualified to evaluate in Spanish, it was not necessary to rely on the assistance of a bilingual evaluator or a translator or interpreter. Had this not been the case, the appropriate procedure would have been to either secure the assistance of a bilingual evaluator for the follow-up testing or to engage the services of a translator or interpreter for readministration of the tests via the native language. Also, because the original data were collected in a manner consistent with XBA procedures (using two batteries), the need to provide reasonably parallel testing meant that Gsm was evaluated using the WMI from the WISC-IV Spanish

(Wechsler, 2004), albeit only the Digit Span subtest, was the same for both domains. Likewise, Gf was also reevaluated using subtests from the WISC-IV Spanish, although only the Block Design subtest was common in both domains. As for Glr, it was reevaluated using the Glr cluster from *The Batería III Woodcock-Muñoz* (Batería III; Munoz-Sandoval, Woodcock, McGrew, & Mather, 2005) because it had originally been evaluated using the WJ IV COG. In these cases, the new clusters only use one of the two tests from the old clusters and the corresponding subtests from the old clusters were used to create composites that mirror the same domains but that did not use the exact same tests. Again, this is a concession to the fact that there is no current WISC-V Spanish or Batería IV. If and when such tests become available, and assuming that they retain the same structure, future applications of the WISC-V and WJ IV COG in testing with ELs will become more straightforward and strictly parallel. Results from follow-up evaluation are provided in Figure 14.5.

Although acknowledging the slight differences in subtest composition among the Gf, Gsm, and Glr clusters from the WISC-V/WISC-IV Spanish and WJ IV COG/Batería III, it was nevertheless clear that performance in the area of Gf increased significantly when evaluated in the native language (SS = 91) as compared to English (SS = 82). Because the native-language score was now within the average range, the psychologist concluded that the original score

WECHSLER INTELLIEGENCE SCALE FOR CHILDREN-V

Verbal Comprehension Index	76	*Fluid Reasoning Index*	82	*Visual-Spatial Index*	95
Similarities	5	Matrix Reasoning	7	Block Design	9
Vocabulary	6	Figure Weights	7	Visual Puzzles	9
Working Memory Index	79	*Processing Speed Index*	94	WISC IV Spanish (Gf subtests)	91
Digit Span	5	Coding	9	Matrix Reasoning	8
Picture Span	7	Symbol Search	8	Picture Concepts	9
WISC IV Spanish WMI	72				
Digit Span	5				
Letter-Number Sequencing	4				

WECHSLER INDIVIDUAL ACHIEVEMENT TEST-III

Basic Reading	94	*Reading Comprehension*	76	*Written Expression*	92
Word Reading	92	Reading Comprehension	76	Spelling	100
Pseudoword Decoding	98	Oral Reading Fluency	80	Sentence Composition	86
				Essay Composition	93

WOODCOCK JOHNSON-IV TESTS OF COGNITIVE ABILITY

Auditory Processing	91	*LT Storage/Retrieval*	77	*Follow Up Testing*	
Phonological Processing	99	Story Recall	79	WJ IV OL Sound Blending	88
Nonword Repetition	84	Visual-Auditory Learning	75		
		Bateria III LT Retrieval	79		
		Visual-Auditory Learning	81		
		Retrieval Fluency	78		

Figure 14.5. Results of Follow-up Evaluation in the Native Language for Gabriel Vega Case Study

must have been attenuated by factors other than cultural and linguistic difference. In fact, the psychologist was able to recall that the English administration of the two subtests from this cluster had been administered immediately preceding lunch and a recess break and that this may have caused Gabriel to rush through items and lose some concentration in an effort to ensure that he wouldn't miss being able to eat and play with his friends. Regardless of the reason, the native-language Gf cluster clearly represents a better and more-valid indication of his true ability in this domain, and it renders the original score from English testing invalid. Thus, the psychologist chose to use the new composite instead of the original cluster to ensure fair and equitable interpretation and for use in later PSW analysis as correctly representing an area of strength rather than one of weakness, as was implied by the original score. By contrast, Gabriel's performance in the area of Gsm on the WISC-IV Spanish was actually found to be slightly lower (WMI SS = 72) than what was originally found when evaluated in English (SS = 79). Similarly, Gabriel's performance in the area of Glr on the Batería III was only slightly higher (SS = 79) but still within the deficit range, as was his original score obtained from testing in English (SS = 77). In both cases, the psychologist properly concluded that these results served to provide cross-linguistic confirmation of the validity of the original scores obtained from testing in English. Therefore, in the absence of any other extraneous variables that might be recognized or identified, follow-up testing in the domains of Gsm and Glr strongly suggest that that the original scores are likely to be valid and true indicators of deficits in these domains.

To complete the assessment, the psychologist next conducted a PSW-based evaluation of SLD using the model and analyses operationalized in the X-BASS and which is based on a PSW approach known as the Dual-Discrepancy/ Consistency model of SLD identification (Flanagan et al., 2013). This included selection of the most-defensible and most-valid representations of ability in each domain and indication of each ability (cognitive and academic) as either a strength or weakness. A summary of the data as so indicated and organized for the purpose of this analysis is presented in Figure 14.6. Note that the summary indicates that Gabriel does not meet the criteria necessary for establishing an SLD within the framework of this model largely because the g-value (an indicator of overall general ability) is .38 and falls well below the necessary .51 lower limit for acceptable defense of generally average ability. The psychologist was at first a bit surprised but then rightly realized that Gc had been erroneously marked as a weakness rather than as a strength based on the Gc caveat that its evaluation is within the expected range in the C-LIM. The psychologist corrected this error in designation and the new results are presented in Figure 14.7, which now demonstrate that Gabriel

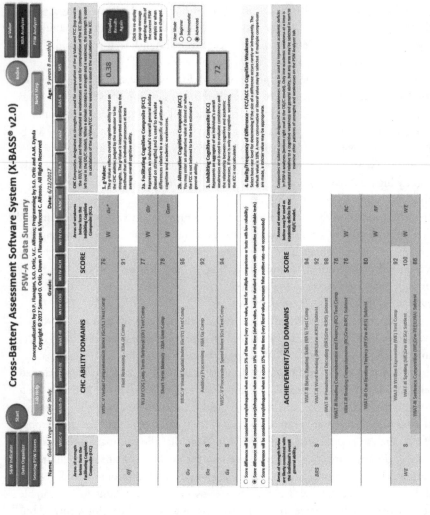

Figure 14.6. Initial PSW-A Data Summary and Results for Gabriel Vega Case Study

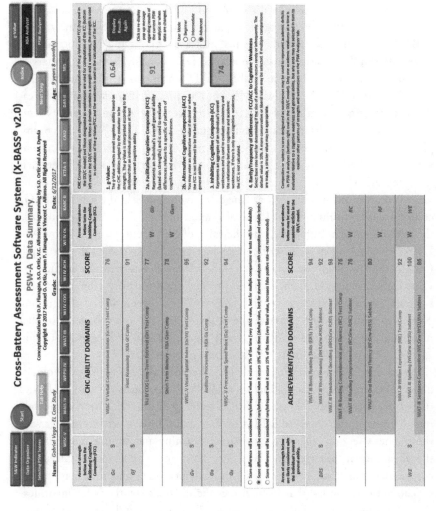

Figure 14.7 Corrected PSW-A Data Summary and Results for Gabriel Vega Case Study

does indeed have sufficient general ability to meet the criterion necessary for establishing overall general ability as required by most consensus definitions of SLD. In this case, the g-value is now a robust .64 and the Facilitating Cognitive Composite (FCC) (which was not calculated or displayed previously) is now shown to be SS = 91. The summary also correctly shows that the only areas of suspected weakness are seen in the Gsm and Glr domains.

The psychologist next examined the data within the PSW Analyzer in X-BASS and, in this case, the results indicated that the PSW for Gabriel were indeed fully consistent with probable SLD. This analysis and a summary of the operational criteria used to establish SLD are provided in Figure 14.8. It should be noted that this analysis does not require any alterations or modifications subject to evaluation of ELs. All such necessary accommodations have already been accomplished via automatic guidance within X-BASS. For example, although the psychologist "forgot" to mark Gc as a strength, the current version of X-BASS provides a pop-up message that reminds practitioners that the value should rightly be considered a strength, not a weakness, whenever the value meets certain specific criteria (the case involves an EL, the value of the Gc composite falls within or above the shaded range in the C-LIM corresponding to the selected range of difference, and the value of the Gc composite is below 90). Likewise, when all of these criteria are met and Gc is marked as a strength (despite the low magnitude of the score), X-BASS will automatically exclude the value from calculation of the FCC to prevent discriminatory attenuation that suggests less than average general ability. By incorporating these guiding principles within X-BASS, use of the WISC-V (or any other battery for that matter) in the evaluation of ELs is greatly simplified and adds extra protection against potentially discriminatory decisions or oversights.

Based on the information provided by the PSW Analyzer, the psychologist ultimately concluded that Gabriel's overall PSW was consistent with SLD and that all necessary criteria for establishing a learning disorder had been adequately met. Moreover, the observed deficits in Gsm and Glr were very consistent with the teacher's reports regarding inconsistent learning and trouble remembering the meaning of passages that had just been read by Gabriel. Given the consistency and further support of this ecological data and information, the psychologist concluded that Gabriel met the district's standards for identification as having an SLD within the requisite PSW model and that coupled with his observed educational needs in the areas of reading comprehension, oral reading fluency, and written expression (notably sentence composition), he was likely to be eligible for special education and related services. At the IEP

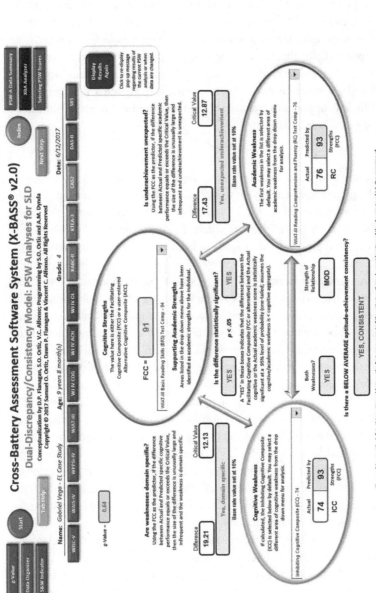

Figure 14.8. Results of PSW Analyses for SLD for Gabriel Vega Case Study

meeting, the psychologist advocated for culturally and linguistically appropriate goals and objectives as well as interventions within the general education setting for Gabriel to help him manage and ameliorate his deficits in Gsm and Glr, as well as his specific difficulties in reading comprehension and written language. By ensuring that Gabriel receives culturally and linguistically relevant support in the special and general education environments, it is expected that he will be afforded sufficient opportunity necessary to maximize his success in the class-room (Brown & Ortiz, 2014).

CONCLUSION

Although the preceding case study, to a large extent, tended to somewhat simplify the process of evaluation of ELs, care was taken to illustrate some of the more critical points and decisions that are likely to cause the most problems for clinicians. For example, had the evaluation been undertaken in a manner that did not follow the recommended best-practice framework, the psychologist would have been in problematic situations from which escape may not have been possible. Use of native-language tests at the beginning of the evaluation would have resulted in an inability to evaluate or assess the impact of linguistic-cultural variables on test performance—thereby wasting precious time and resources. Had the psychologist conducted follow-up evaluation of all areas of functioning that were initially assessed in English, more time and resources would have been spent unnecessarily in the evaluation of abilities that were already known to be strengths for the individual. Had the psychologist failed to consider the Gc caveat and maintained a strict normative interpretation for Gc, Gabriel would not have met criteria for SLD and may well have been thought, at best, not to be disabled, or at worst, possibly intellectually disabled. And had the psychologist not used the C-LIM to evaluate the impact of linguistic and cultural factors on test perform-ance, it would have been impossible to continue with any type of evaluation, because the test scores used in identifying SLD must be first established as being valid. The entire process of evaluation described by the case study sought to examine and ensure validity of the obtained results so as to permit valid and defensible interpretations and conclusions. Use of the recommended best-practice approach, along with XBA principles and procedures and use of the automated processes and analyses contained in X-BASS (e.g., C-LIM, PSW Analyzer, etc.) provided a comprehensive and systematic approach to evaluation that is easily defensible from a legal, theoretical, and psychometric standpoint. Had the psychologist not followed all of the procedures described in the case study, it is likely that the results would have been discriminatory. And without any attempt to establish validity, the obtained test scores could not have been given any meaning and attempts to do so would be no more valid than merely guessing. Clearly, the adherence to the proposed best-practice framework assisted greatly in preventing a wide range of potentially critical mistakes in the evaluation process—most of which would likely have had rather negative consequences for Gabriel.

It is worth mentioning that although SLD was the outcome in this case, it is entirely possible that the results from initial testing in English could have formed a pattern that was consistent with the levels of performance typical of ELs who are nondisabled and of average ability or higher. That is, when the results follow the type of systematic decline and the magnitude of the aggregate scores in each cell are within the range consistent with what has been found in the research, the only reasonable conclusion is that the obtained test scores are invalid because they reflect primarily the influence of linguistic and cultural variables rather than the individual's true level of ability. For reference purposes, an example of what such likely "invalid" results might look like in the C-LIM graphs is presented in Figure 14.9. But the determination of invalid test scores carries with it the benefit of being able to cease further testing because the resulting pattern is consistent

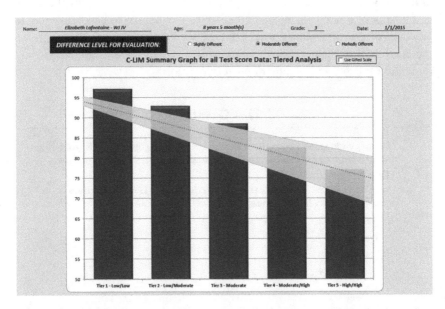

Figure 14.9. Example C-LIM Pattern of Results Suggesting Invalid Test Scores

with performance of other individuals with comparable backgrounds who are of average ability or higher and who are also not disabled. This significantly enhances the efficiency of the approach and again reduces the possibility of discriminatory conclusions and indefensible attempts to ascribe meaning to invalid data. This is not to say, however, that the presence of such a pattern means that the assessment is invalid—only that the test scores are invalid. In fact, by invalidating the test scores in this manner (should the pattern suggest it), the assessment maintains its validity because it provides a defensible position that the individual is, in fact, not disabled.

DON'T FORGET

It is worth mentioning that although SLD was the outcome in the case of Gabriel, it is entirely possible that the results from initial testing in English could have formed a pattern that was consistent with the levels of performance typical of ELs who are nondisabled and of average ability or higher.

In conclusion, the methods for nondiscriminatory evaluation of diverse individuals outlined in this chapter are not necessarily specific to use of the WISC-V. They do illustrate, however, that it can be used as an effective tool for evaluation of ELs, particularly when supplemented with tests from the WISC-IV Spanish. Even when the examinee's heritage language is something other than Spanish, the framework proposed herein can be used via the aid of a translator or interpreter. As such, the WISC-V continues to be a viable tool to evaluate diverse individuals when applied within the best-practice approach outlined in this chapter, which is arguably necessary to achieve fairness and promote equitable and nondiscriminatory practices.

🐟 TEST YOURSELF 🐟

1. There is widespread consensus in psychology regarding specific guidelines and procedures for evaluating English learners with standardized tests. True or false?

2. The most critical issue necessary for evaluation of English learners is rooted primarily in the concept of:
   (a) Reliability
   (b) Validity
   (c) Item bias
   (d) Racial differences

3. **Of the following variables, which one is typically not included in the stratification of norm samples of current tests?**
   (a) Race
   (b) Socioeconomic status
   (c) Geographic location
   (d) English exposure

4. **Test performance of English learners is influenced by the presence of differences relative to the norm sample primarily with regard to:**
   (a) Gender
   (b) Experience and development
   (c) Ethnicity
   (d) Geographical location

5. **The factor that is responsible for the observation that English learners score well below the normative mean on tests that measure verbal ability is:**
   (a) Limited English proficiency
   (b) Intelligence
   (c) Scoring errors
   (d) Genetics

6. **Which of the following methods of assessment, when used with English learners, automatically results in valid scores for comprehensive abilities that can be interpreted and defended?**
   (a) Modified or altered testing
   (b) Nonverbal testing
   (c) Native-language testing
   (d) None of the above

7. **Although testing in English seems counterintuitive, it is the only method in which scores may be evaluated and determined to be valid because:**
   (a) It can be conducted by any evaluator including those who are not bilingual.
   (b) English-language tests have norms that are entirely appropriate for English learners.
   (c) A large body of empirical research exists that can guide expectations of performance.
   (d) Language is not an important factor in the test performance of English learners.

8. **The primary purpose of the C-LIM is to:**
   (a) Reduce the psychometric bias found in tests
   (b) Evaluate the impact of cultural and linguistic differences on test performance so that a decision regarding the validity of the test results can be made systematically
   (c) Assist bilingual clinicians in performing evaluations in the native language
   (d) Eliminate the need for clinical judgment or collection of data regarding cultural, linguistic, and educational background

9. **When using the C-LIM, which of the following general interpretive statements is _incorrect_?**

   (a) When test performance increases diagonally across the cells from the upper left to the bottom right, scores should be deemed to be likely invalid and should not be interpreted.

   (b) When test performance increases diagonally across the cells from the lower left to the top right, scores should be deemed to be likely invalid and should not be interpreted.

   (c) When test performance decreases diagonally across the cells from the upper left to the bottom right, scores should be deemed to be likely invalid and should not be interpreted.

   (d) When test performance decreases diagonally across the cells from the lower left to the top right, scores should be deemed to be likely invalid and should not be interpreted.

10. **The validity of test scores obtained from administration of any test to English learners requires the accumulation of evidence that should include, at a minimum:**

   (a) Scores that have been found validated via use of the C-LIM

   (b) Cross-validation from native-language testing to confirm areas of deficit

   (c) Ecological information and data from converging sources

   (d) All of the above

Answers: 1. false; 2. b; 3. d; 4. b; 5. a; 6. d; 7. c; 8. b; 9. c; 10. d.

REFERENCES

American Educational Research Association, American Psychological Association, & National Council on Measurement in Education. (2015). _Standards for educational and psychological testing._ Washington, DC: Author.

Bialystok, E. (1991). _Language processing in bilingual children._ New York, NY: Cambridge University Press.

Braden, J. P., & Iribarren, J. A. (2007). Test review: Wechsler, D. (2005). Wechsler Intelligence Scale for Children–Fourth edition Spanish. _Journal of Psychoeducational Assessment, 25,_ 292–299.

Brown, J. E., & Ortiz, S. O. (2014). Interventions for English language learners with learning difficulties. In J. T. Mascolo, D. P. Flanagan, & V. C. Alfonso (Eds.), _Essentials of planning, selecting, and tailoring intervention_ (pp. 267–313). Hoboken, NJ: Wiley.

Cathers-Schiffman, T. A., & Thompson, M. S. (2007). Assessment of English- and Spanish-speaking students with the WISC-III and Leiter-R. _Journal of Psychoeducational Assessment, 25,_ 41–52.

Cormier, D. C., McGrew, K. S., & Ysseldyke, J. E. (2014). The influences of linguistic demand and cultural loading on cognitive test scores. _Journal of Psychoeducational Assessment, 32_(7), 610–623.

DiCerbo, K. E., & Barona, A. (2000). A convergent validity study on the Differential Ability Scales and the Wechsler Intelligence Scale for Children–Third Edition with Hispanic children. *Journal of Psychoeducational Assessment, 18,* 344–352.

Esparza-Brown, J. (2007). *The impact of cultural loading and linguistic demand on the performance of English/Spanish bilinguals on Spanish language cognitive tests.* Unpublished manuscript. Portland, OR: Portland State University.

Figueroa, R. A. (1990). Assessment of linguistic minority group children. In C. R. Reynolds & R. W. Kamphaus (Eds.), *Handbook of psychological and educational assessment of children: Intelligence and achievement* (Vol. 1). New York, NY: Guilford.

Flanagan, D. P., & Ortiz, S. O. (2001). *Essentials of cross-battery assessment.* New York, NY: Wiley.

Flanagan, D. P., Ortiz, S. O., & Alfonso, V.C. (2007). *Essentials of Cross-Battery Assessment* (2nd ed.). New York, NY: Wiley.

Flanagan, D. P., Ortiz, S. O., & Alfonso, V. C. (2013). *Essentials of Cross-Battery Assessment* (3rd ed.). New York, NY: Wiley.

Grosjean, F. (1989). Neurolinguists beware! The bilingual is not two monolinguals in one person. *Brain and Language, 36,* 3–15.

Klotz, M. (2016). *The provision of school psychological services to bilingual students.* New Orleans, LA: National Association of School Psychologists.

Lohman, D. F., Korb, K., & Lakin, J. (2008). Identifying academically gifted English language learners using nonverbal tests: A comparison of the Raven, NNAT, and CogAT. *Gifted Child Quarterly, 52,* 275–296.

Mpofu, E., & Ortiz, S. O. (2009). Equitable assessment practices in diverse contexts. In E. L. Grigorenko (Ed.), *Multicultural psychoeducational assessment* (pp. 41–76). New York, NY: Springer.

Muñoz-Sandoval, A. F., Woodcock, R. W., McGrew, K. S., & Mather, N. (2005). *Batería III Woodcock-Muñoz.* Itasca, IL: Riverside.

National Association of School Psychologists. (2015). *The provision of school psychological services to bilingual students* [Position statement]. Bethesda, MD: Author.

Neisser, U., Boodoo, G., Bouchard, T. J., Boykin, A. W., Brody, N., Ceci, et al. (1996). Intelligence: Knowns and unknowns. *American Psychologist, 51,* 77–101.

O'Bryon, E. C., & Rogers, M. R. (2010). Bilingual school psychologists' assessment practices with English language learners. *Psychology in the Schools, 47,* 1018–1034.

Ochoa, S. H., Powell, M. P., & Robles-Piña, R. (1996). School psychologists' assessment practices with bilingual and limited-English-proficient students. *Journal of Psychoeducational Assessment, 14,* 250–275.

Ortiz, S. O. (2014). Best practices in nondiscriminatory assessment. In A. Thomas & J. Grimes (Eds.), *Best practices in school psychology VI.* Washington, DC: National Association of School Psychologists.

Ortiz, S. O. (2018). *Ortiz Picture Vocabulary Acquisition Test (Ortiz PVAT).* Toronto, Canada: Multi-Health Systems.

Ortiz, S. O., Flanagan, D. P., & Alfonso, V. C. (2015). *Cross-Battery Assessment software system* (X-BASS v1.0 PC and Mac versions). Hoboken, NJ: Wiley.

Ortiz, S. O., & Melo, K. (2015). Evaluation of intelligence and learning disability with Hispanics. In K. Geisinger (Ed.), *Psychological testing of Hispanics* (pp. 109–134). Washington, DC: APA Books.

Ortiz, S. O., Melo, K., & Terzulli, M. (2017). Assessment of English learners with the WISC-V. In D. P. Flanagan & V. C. Alfonso (Eds.), *Essentials of WISC-V assessment* (pp. 539–590). Hoboken, NJ: Wiley.

Ortiz, S. O., Ochoa, S. H., & Dynda, A. M. (2012). Testing with culturally and linguistically diverse populations: Moving beyond the verbal-performance dichotomy into evidence-based practice. In D. P. Flanagan & P. L. Harrison (Eds.), *Contemporary intellectual assessment: Theories, tests, and issues* (3rd ed., pp. 526–552). New York, NY: Guilford.

Ortiz, S. O., Ortiz, J. A., & Devine, R. I. (2016). Use of the WJ IV with English language learners. In D. P. Flanagan & V. C. Alfonso (Eds.), *WJ IV clinical use and interpretation* (pp. 317–354). New York, NY: Elsevier.

Paradis, M. (2014). *The assessment of bilingual aphasia*. New York, NY: Psychology Press.

Pearson. (2009). *The Wechsler Individual Achievement Test* (3rd ed.). San Antonio, TX: Author.

Rhodes, R., Ochoa, S. H., & Ortiz, S. O. (2005). *Assessment of culturally and linguistically diverse students: A practical guide*. New York, NY: Guilford.

Schrank, F. A., McGrew, K. S., & Mather, N. (2014a). *Woodcock-Johnson IV*. Rolling Meadows, IL: Riverside.

Schrank, F. A., McGrew, K. S., & Mather, N. (2014b). *Woodcock-Johnson IV Tests of Cognitive Abilities*. Rolling Meadows, IL: Riverside.

Schrank, F. A., McGrew, K. S., & Mather, N. (2015). The WJ IV Gf-Gc composite and its use in the identification of specific learning disabilities. *Assessment Service Bulletin, 3.* Rolling Meadows, IL: Riverside.

Sotelo-Dynega, M., & Dixon, S. G. (2014). Cognitive assessment practices: A survey of school psychologists. *Psychology in the Schools*, *51*(10), 1031–1045.

Sotelo-Dynega, M., Ortiz, S. O., Flanagan, D. P., & Chaplin, W. (2013). English language proficiency and test performance: Evaluation of bilinguals with the Woodcock-Johnson III Tests of Cognitive Ability. *Psychology in the Schools*, *50*(8), 781–797.

Thomas, W. P., & Collier, V. P. (2002). *A national study of school effectiveness for language minority students' long-term academic achievement.* Retrieved from www.usc.edu/dept/education/CMMR/CollierThomasExReport.pdf

US Census Bureau. (2015). *Current population survey.* Retrieved October 22, 2015, from www.census.gov/cps/

Valdes, G., & Figueroa, R. A. (1994). *Bilingualism and testing: A special case of bias*. Norwood, NJ: Ablex.

Wechsler, D. (1944). *The measurement of adult intelligence* (3rd ed.). Baltimore, MD: Williams & Wilkens.

Wechsler, D. (2003). *Wechsler Intelligence Scale for Children–Fourth edition (WISC-IV)*. San Antonio, TX: Pearson.

Wechsler, D. (2004). *Wechsler Intelligence Scale for Children–Fourth edition Spanish (WISC-IV Spanish)*. San Antonio, TX: Pearson.

Wechsler, D. (2014). *Wechsler Intelligence Scale for Children–Fifth edition (WISC-V)*. San Antonio, TX: Pearson.

Wechsler, D., Raiford, S. E., & Holdnack, J. A. (2014). *WISC-V technical and interpretive manual*. Bloomington, MN: Pearson Psychological Corporation.

Yerkes, R. M. (1921). Psychological examining in the United States Army. *Memoirs of the National Academy of Sciences*, 15.

Fifteen

DIFFERENTIAL DIAGNOSIS OF SLD VERSUS OTHER DIFFICULTIES

Benjamin J. Lovett
David A. Kilpatrick

C onsider a boy named Noah, whose teacher refers him to a student study team because of her concerns regarding his reading skills. In first grade, his reading was unimpressive but not especially poor. Now, in October of second grade, his reading performance is the lowest in his class, other than that of students who have already been identified as having learning disabilities. Outside of school, Noah never reads, and even in school, he seems to avoid reading whenever possible. When given a norm-referenced test of academic skills, his overall reading score is at the 5th percentile for his age group. Does Noah have a specific learning disability (SLD) in reading?

Low levels of academic achievement are a central component of SLD, but not all cases of low achievement represent SLD. Instead, low achievement is common to many disabilities—indeed, the Individuals with Disabilities Education Act (IDEA, 2004) requires that a student be impaired in school before he or she can be served under any IDEA disability category, and school impairment most often means low academic achievement. Therefore, in the case described, Noah has deficits in reading that are *consistent with* SLD, but we lack sufficient information to identify his problem as SLD. The process of distinguishing between SLD and other problems is one of *differential diagnosis*. This chapter addresses that process by considering several causes of low achievement and how to distinguish among them. Regardless of the SLD-identification model endorsed (e.g., Response to

Essentials of Specific Learning Disability Identification, Second Edition.
Edited by Vincent C. Alfonso and Dawn P. Flanagan
© 2018 John Wiley & Sons, Inc. Published 2018 by John Wiley & Sons, Inc.

> **DON'T FORGET**
> ....
> The process of distinguishing between SLD and other learning difficulties is one of *differential diagnosis*—considering alternative explanations of low academic achievement.

Intervention [RTI], pattern of strengths and weaknesses [PSW]), all such models require that certain alternative explanations of low achievement be ruled out. Those alternative explanations are the focus of this chapter. We begin by considering the conceptual underpinnings of differential diagnosis and by providing a working definition of SLD; we then move on to discuss three specific alternative explanations of low achievement: low general ability, emotional-behavioral difficulties, and sensory impairments. Finally, we consider the case of students who have "low" achievement by local (or familial) standards but who do not have SLD (or any other disability, quite possibly). The one alternative explanation of low achievement that we do not cover in this chapter is cultural-linguistic difference (see Chapter 14 on this issue).

WHAT DIFFERENTIAL DIAGNOSIS OF SLD REALLY MEANS

Recall Noah, our second-grader with low reading skills. If the SLD diagnosis is being considered, would it matter if Noah's intelligence quotient (IQ) was 70? What if his first-grade teacher was on medical leave for most of the year and replaced by substitute teachers, each of whom never stayed for more than a few days? What if Noah has a significant vision problem that was just detected last month? To us, any of those pieces of information would matter a great deal and would influence our diagnostic judgments considerably, because they all suggest alternative ways of understanding Noah's low reading skills.

We view SLD, like all diagnostic categories, as a practical conceptual "bin" in which some students' learning difficulties are best placed. In reality, every student has a unique profile of abilities, skills, and other traits, but of course we cannot have as many diagnostic categories as there are students. One purpose of diagnostic categorization is to identify a student as a member of a group (e.g., SLD) with known characteristics, so that interventions that have been shown to work for that group can be applied. Therefore, we try to match each student's problem with the conceptual bin that makes the most sense.

> **DON'T FORGET**
> ....
> All diagnostic categories, including SLD, can be thought of as a conceptual "bin" in which some students' difficulties are best placed. In reality, every student has a unique profile of abilities, skills, and other traits. The goal is to match each student's difficulty with the conceptual bin that makes the most sense.

Some scholars would describe this process of differential diagnosis in terms of what disorder a student *really* has versus what disorders he or she *appears* to have. For some medical problems, such language makes sense; differential diagnosis in medicine involves distinguishing between multiple real, physical entities. For instance, when a child has anemia (insufficient oxygenation of the blood), there are a variety of different possible causes of the anemia; sickle cell disease (improperly shaped red blood cells) and iron deficiency are two different mechanisms of anemia that could really be physically present inside the child (Marieb & Hoehn, 2007). However, when we ask whether Noah has an SLD in reading or if instead he has not been given exposure to proper reading instruction, we are not talking about physical mechanisms. In fact, the only "mechanisms" of his inability to read (e.g., poor understanding of the sounds of language, etc.) might be the same regardless of the ultimate explanation. Therefore, rather than asking if Noah *really* has a learning disability, we prefer to ask whether SLD is the *most useful* label for Noah's low reading skills. We apply that pragmatic perspective throughout the chapter.

A WORKING DEFINITION OF SLD

Before covering alternative explanations of low achievement, it is important to specify what would make SLD the most useful label for a student's learning difficulties. In keeping with our emphasis on differential diagnosis, we offer a working definition of SLD that emphasizes *exclusionary criteria*—factors that should be ruled out before SLD is identified. Exclusionary definitions have often been criticized for telling us what SLD is *not* rather than what it *is* (e.g., Blair & Scott, 2002; Fletcher & Morris, 1986; Lyon, 1995). However, there is simply no way to go about the process of differential diagnosis without specifying exclusionary criteria; moreover, it is very important to know when *not* to apply the SLD classification, because the classification is often given to any student who is challenging to educate (see Senf, 1987, for a discussion). Of course, although exclusionary criteria play a large role in defining SLD, the classification also has "positive features"—factors that must be *present* (not just features that must be absent).

DON'T FORGET

Differential diagnosis typically requires consideration of positive features (the features needed to establish the presence of a given classification or disorder) and exclusionary criteria (the features that rule out alternative explanations of symptoms). Although the exclusionary criteria have been controversial in SLD diagnosis, there is simply no way to go about the process of differential diagnosis without such criteria.

Historically, SLD has been defined as a disorder in a "basic psychological process" causing a discrepancy between a student's *potential for achievement* (i.e., aptitude, most commonly evaluated via conventional IQ tests) and his or her *actual achievement.* Although the discrepancy aspect of this definition has not stood up to empirical investigation (e.g., Lovett & Gordon, 2005; Stanovich, 2005; Sternberg & Grigorenko, 2002), the "basic psychological process" aspect *has.* Research has uncovered a number of cognitive/linguistic skills that appear to be essential for the acquisition of reading, writing, and math skills. In addition, deficits in those cognitive/linguistic skills appear to contribute directly to SLD. Those skills include language comprehension, working memory, phonological awareness, rapid automatized naming, and executive functioning (Fletcher, Lyon, Fuchs, & Barnes, 2018; Hulme & Snowling, 2009; Kilpatrick, 2015; Vellutino, Fletcher, Snowling, & Scanlon, 2004).

The 2004 reauthorization of IDEA added two methods of defining SLD in addition to the aptitude-achievement discrepancy. One method focuses on a student's failure to respond to high-quality general educational instruction and high-quality remedial instruction (the RTI method). The other method involves examining a student's profile of cognitive and academic skills (the PSW method) while looking for a meaningful pattern that logically explains low achievement. The RTI method focuses on the environmental/instructional factors that affect underachievement whereas the PSW method focuses on the cognitive characteristics of SLD (see Chapters 7 through 13 for details on these methods).

With this as background, we propose a working definition of SLD that is consistent with all assessment approaches found in federal regulations. The premises on which this definition is based are listed in Exhibit 15.1 and are derived from more than 30 years of research regarding typical academic skill development and academic skill difficulties.

Based on the premises detailed in Exhibit 15.1, our definition of SLD is as follows:

A student with a specific learning disability is an individual who displays substantial underachievement in reading, writing, or math as a result of a deficit in one or more of the cognitive or linguistic skills empirically demonstrated as necessary for academic skill development. This underachievement persists despite adequate effort and learning opportunities, and it is not due to another type of disability such as a speech or language impairment, an intellectual disability, an emotional disturbance, autism, or deficits in vision or hearing.

To illustrate the application of this definition, consider the most researched area within the designation of SLD: word-level reading difficulties (Fletcher et al., 2018). This disability area is known in IDEA as an SLD in basic reading or reading

---

Exhibit 15.1
Assumptions Behind an Empirically Based Definition of SLD

- Researchers have identified several important cognitive and linguistic factors that directly or indirectly contribute to academic skill development in reading, writing, and math. These include, but are not limited to, language comprehension, working memory, phonological awareness, rapid automatized naming, and executive functioning.
- Along with appropriate learning opportunities and motivation, academic skills are based largely on a student's cognitive and linguistic skills.
- Students display differing degrees of competence in the previously mentioned cognitive and linguistic skills that affect learning.
- A substantial amount of research has demonstrated that learning disabilities do not differ *qualitatively* from milder learning difficulties. Rather, learning disabilities and milder learning difficulties differ *quantitatively*; that is, they differ in severity.
- If a deficit in one or more of the cognitive and linguistic skills critical for academic achievement is substantial enough, it can impair a student's academic skill development.

---

fluency. It is known to researchers as *dyslexia*. Dyslexia is thought to be caused by the *phonological core deficit* (Ahmed, Wagner, & Kantor, 2012; Fletcher et al., 2018; Vellutino et al., 2004).[1] Individuals with the phonological core deficit display difficulties in one or more of the following skills: nonsense word reading, phonemic awareness, phonological blending, rapid automatized naming, and phonological working memory. A substantial deficit in just one of these five skills can impair word-reading skill development. However, most students with dyslexia display substantial difficulties in more than one underlying skill and often show difficulties in all five skills. By contrast, it is rare to find any substantial difficulties in any of these five skills among students whose word-level reading is developing typically. Thus, as a general guideline, we would expect a deficit in one or more of the phonological core deficit "markers" in students who have an SLD in basic reading. Similarly, in a student who has an SLD in reading comprehension, math, or writing, we would expect to see deficits in cognitive-linguistic skills that have been empirically demonstrated to be critical for acquiring the related academic skills (Fletcher et al., 2018; Hulme & Snowling, 2009, Oakhill, Cain, & Elbro, 2015).

We should note two caveats regarding our working definition of SLD. First, students with other IDEA designations, such as speech-language impairment (SLI), emotional disturbance (ED), intellectual disability (ID), deafness, or autism spectrum disorder (ASD), sometimes display underachievement in specific academic areas due to deficits in the same cognitive/linguistic skills that impair students with SLD. However, based on our pragmatic approach to diagnostic categories, we believe that when full criteria for non-SLD categories are met, those other categories are more appropriate classifications for students' learning difficulties. With the defining characteristics of those other disabilities ruled out, SLD then becomes the appropriate classification for students with academic achievement deficits apparently caused by deficits in relevant cognitive/linguistic skills.

> **DON'T FORGET**
> ....
> Students with other IDEA designations, such as SLI, ED, ID, deafness, or ASD, sometimes display underachievement in specific academic areas due to deficits in the same cognitive/linguistic skills that impair students with SLD.

A second caveat: although our definition notes that SLD is presumed to be due to deficits in underlying cognitive/linguistic skills, this does not mean that the underlying cognitive/linguistic skills must be directly assessed to identify a student as having an SLD. Although research has established the basis for SLD in cognitive/linguistic skill deficits, particularly in the area of reading, we are mindful of the debate over whether such skills must be directly measured when assessing a student for possible SLD (e.g., Hale, Kaufman, Naglieri, & Kavale, 2006; Johnson, Humphrey, Mellard, Woods, & Swanson, 2010; Stuebing et al., 2015). We see benefits as well as limitations to requiring such direct measurement, but even in diagnostic models (such as some RTI models) in which cognitive processes are not assessed directly, our *working* definition holds; SLD is presumed to be based on deficits in cognitive/linguistic skills.

With our definition of SLD in mind, we now turn to the process of differentiating SLD from other specific causes of underachievement. We begin with low general ability.

SLD VERSUS LOW GENERAL ABILITY

Intelligence has a causal effect on academic achievement (Watkins, Lei, & Canivez, 2007), and one cause of low academic achievement is low intelligence. Well-known studies (Gresham, MacMillan, & Bocian, 1996; MacMillan, Gresham, & Bocian, 1998) have shown that the SLD label is often used for students with below-average intelligence. Is this appropriate?

Some students with low achievement meet the official criteria for ID: an IQ below 70 along with impairments in adaptive functioning. These criteria are from the current edition of *Diagnostic and Statistical Manual of Mental Disorders*

(5th ed.) (*DSM-5;* American Psychiatric Association [APA], 2013). State and federal regulations for identifying ID are generally quite similar. Students with ID often have low levels of academic skills (e.g., Koritsas & Iacono, 2011; Wei, Blackorby, & Schiller, 2011), and indeed, some academic skills (e.g., reading and writing) are often considered to be part of adaptive functioning (Tassé et al., 2012). It is not surprising, then, when a student with ID has low academic skills. The question of whether to diagnose SLD is rarely raised in students who meet the criteria for ID, because ID tends to take priority over other diagnostic labels (Jopp & Keys, 2001).

A more difficult case occurs when a student does *not* meet the criteria for ID, yet still has a below-average IQ. This range of IQ is typically called *borderline intellectual functioning* (*BIF;* APA, 2013) and has historically included Full Scale IQs from 71 to 84, or between one and two standard deviations below the mean. An earlier, somewhat pejorative, term for students with BIF was *slow learners* (Shaw, 2008). Regardless of the term used, this is a sizeable group of students, given that the mathematics of the normal distribution would predict that 14% of students have IQs between 70 and 85. These students are vulnerable to falling through the cracks in our general and special education support systems because they do not qualify for the ID label, and yet they are at high risk of struggling in school and beyond (Ferrari, 2009). Specifically, students with BIF usually obtain lower scores on standardized achievement tests than their typically developing peers (for a review, see Peltopuro, Ahonen, Kaartinen, Seppälä, & Närhi, 2014). It is common for students with BIF to have SLD-range achievement test scores. This is not a surprise, given that their IQ scores are between one and two standard deviations below the mean, and IQ and achievement are correlated.

Despite the academic skills deficits typically seen in students with BIF, we would generally recommend against categorizing these students as SLD. Instead, there are other ways of meeting their needs. First, many students with BIF have below-average language skills. As a result, it should be common practice to refer such students for a speech-language evaluation to determine if they could be considered as having SLI. Unfortunately, there is an assumption in some educational circles that if a student's below-average language skills are consistent with other low cognitive skills (e.g., nonverbal reasoning, working memory, processing speed), then the SLI label is contraindicated. However, this is not at all presumed in IDEA's definition of SLI, nor is it considered appropriate practice by the American Speech-Language-Hearing Association (ASHA):

> *Cognitive referencing* is the practice of comparing IQ scores and language scores as a factor for determining eligibility for speech-language intervention. It is based on the assumption that language functioning cannot surpass

[nonlinguistic] cognitive levels. However, according to research, some language abilities may in fact surpass cognitive levels. Therefore, ASHA does not support the use of cognitive referencing. (ASHA, n.d.)

Based on IDEA's definition of SLI, along with the policy of the professional organization charged with setting policy for assessing and treating language issues (i.e., ASHA), many students with BIF qualify for services under SLI. Indeed, without such a designation, it is possible that they will not receive the attention they need to address the language skill deficits that are infringing on their ability to make adequate progress in school, given that many of these students are not being identified at all. As a result, a fair number of students with BIF can be helped by designating them as SLI and providing them with language-related services in addition to addressing their academic concerns.

DON'T FORGET

Many students with borderline intellectual functioning can qualify for services under SLI. Unfortunately, the traditional and non-research-supported practice of cognitive referencing has been used to keep students from receiving much needed help.

A second way of addressing the needs of students with BIF involves the multitiered systems of support that make up the backbone of RTI service-delivery models. Academic skills, such as word-level reading, spelling, and basic math computation, can be increased substantially through the use of highly effective interventions. Such interventions have been validated for use with a wide variety of students, including students with lower cognitive levels (e.g., Denton, Fletcher, Anthony, & Francis, 2007). As students with these basic academic skill deficits are identified (through progress monitoring as part of Tier 1 of an RTI model), a Tier 2 intervention can be implemented.

Of course, we should note that the *potential* of an RTI-based service-delivery system does not mean that any district using RTI will naturally implement evidence-based interventions appropriate to the needs of students with BIF. Indeed, it is an unfortunate reality that the academic outcomes from the widespread implementation of RTI have not matched the impressive results from the studies that prompted the development of RTI in the first place. The actual instructional and remediation methods used in the studies that yielded highly successful outcomes (thus prompting RTI) were never adequately communicated (Kilpatrick, 2015). Instead, educators were merely told to use "research-based" teaching approaches and were never told what those were. As a result, some of the most-common teaching and remedial practices used for all tiers of RTI involve methods that were not used in the studies that prompted RTI. Unfortunately, some of these methods have been shown in study after study to produce minimal gains (Kilpatrick, 2015). This likely explains why a recent federal report found that RTI is having very limited impact (Balu et al., 2015). Yet there *are* highly effective approaches that have been shown to produce large gains, at least in word-reading skills (for reviews, see Foorman, 2003; Foorman & Al Otaiba, 2009; Kilpatrick, 2015; Torgesen, 2004, 2005; Torgesen, Rashotte, Alexander, Alexander, & MacPhee, 2003), and those approaches would make an important contribution to the academic achievement of students with BIF.

We conclude with a third method of improving the academic skills of students with BIF that is related to the two methods already described. There is now available a comprehensive and rather inexpensive Tier 1 language program that can boost vocabulary and language functioning for students with low-average and below-average language skills. It is based on the York Reading for Meaning Project in the United Kingdom. After publishing studies in scientific journals on the efficacy of this approach, the researchers provided the educational community with two slim volumes that provide all the details needed for implementing this effective program (Carroll, Bowyer-Crane, Duff, Hulme, & Snowling, 2011; Clarke, Truelove, Hulme, & Snowling, 2014). The Reading for Meaning project would help many students with BIF. Rapid Reference 15.1 summarizes how we can serve students with BIF.

≋ *Rapid Reference 15.1*

Serving Students with BIF

Students with BIF (IQs between 71 and 84) often have low academic skills, but there is often no need to label such students as SLD. The *S* in *SLD* argues against inclusion of students with low global learning ability, and instead there are other ways of serving such students:

- Many students with BIF will qualify as speech or language impaired due to deficits in expressive or receptive language skills. Including a comprehensive language assessment by a speech-language pathologist is often helpful in these cases.
- Students with BIF can often be detected and remediated by multitiered systems of academic support—systems that are part of RTI service-delivery models. Careful monitoring of progress during Tier 1 instruction will detect problems, and Tier 2 interventions can be used to improve basic academic skills (e.g., decoding) in these students.
- An effective general curriculum (perhaps serving as Tier 1 within an RTI model) can prevent deficits in academic skills in many students with BIF. We particularly recommend the Reading for Meaning curriculum as a way of preventing reading problems.

SLD VERSUS EMOTIONAL AND BEHAVIORAL PROBLEMS

Differential diagnosis of SLD versus emotional and behavioral problems can be very challenging. On the one hand, research has repeatedly found that students with SLD are more likely than their peers to have such problems. For instance, Mammarella et al. (2016) found that students with SLD had higher levels of anxiety and depression than their nondisabled peers, and Klassen, Tze, and Hannok (2013) found that even adults with SLD continued to have higher levels of such internalizing symptoms. Attention-deficit hyperactivity disorder (ADHD) is reportedly present in up to 40% of students with SLD (Weis, 2014), and ADHD appears to be at least part of the reason for increased risk of aggression and other conduct problems in students with SLD (Willcutt & Pennington, 2000). More generally, Sundheim and Voeller (2004) summarized their review of relevant literature by concluding that "learning disabilities carry a significant risk of comorbid psychiatric disorders" (p. 824).

On the other hand, definitions of SLD typically make clear that SLD should not be diagnosed if a student's academic skills deficits are *due to* emotional or behavioral difficulties. The current version of IDEA (2004) notes that SLD does not cover "a learning problem that is primarily the result of . . . emotional disturbance." If Noah, our second-grader with apparent reading problems, has extremely high levels of anxiety, and whenever he is asked to read, his anxiety severely interferes with his performance, it may be that he has an anxiety disorder rather than SLD. Similarly, if he has ADHD and is unable to pay attention during reading instruction, SLD may not be the most appropriate label for his difficulties.

At times, it is possible to try treating the emotional-behavioral symptoms (e.g., with medication for ADHD) to see if a student's measured academic skills improve. However, this process can take a long time while the student may be falling further and further behind academically. Therefore, several clinical strategies are helpful in differentiating SLD from low achievement that is due to emotional and behavioral problems. First, a careful history can determine whether academic skills deficits preceded other symptoms; if Noah was noticed to have poor reading skills long before his anxiety developed, the anxiety could not be the (sole) cause of the weak reading performance. Teachers and especially parents are often able to estimate when emotional and behavioral difficulties began. Of course, even if those problems began before the low academic skills were noticed, genuine comorbidity may still be present. In that case, SLD may be an appropriate label.

A second clinical strategy for differential diagnosis in this situation is direct behavioral observation in classroom and testing settings. With regard to classroom observation, students with some emotional and behavioral difficulties may simply not attend to instruction enough to profit from it. (Such inattention is not exclusively due to ADHD; anxiety and depression interfere with attention, and students with conduct problems will often *choose* to not pay attention to instruction, preferring other activities.) Classroom observation can establish whether a student is paying attention or is off task. With regard to test observation, students who exhibit certain symptoms during testing (e.g., anxiety) may not have academic skills as low as their resulting test scores suggest, putting them at risk for inappropriate (and unhelpful) SLD labels. Although unstructured classroom observations are useful at times, only structured observations can be used to compare a student's behaviors to normative levels; for instance, the *Achenbach System of Empirically Based Assessment* (ASEBA; see www.aseba.org) includes norm-referenced measures for behavioral observation in classroom and testing settings.

A third clinical strategy is to directly assess some of the key cognitive/linguistic skills that are known to be critical for the development of academic skills, as mentioned previously. For example, with word-level reading this might involve an assessment of nonsense word reading, phonological awareness, phonological blending, rapid automatized naming, and phonological working memory. Low levels of these skills are likely to be better accounted for by the phonological core deficit (and therefore by SLD) than by anxiety. This is because these skills are assessed using very simple and nonthreatening tasks that developing readers typically perform with ease. By contrast, students with reading disabilities almost invariably display great difficulty on one or more of these tasks.

Finally, if there is concern that a student has low motivation or even active resistance (whether due to depression, conduct problems, or some other condition), then diagnosticians should consider administering measures of effort and motivation. Sometimes called *performance validity tests* (*PVTs;* Kirkwood, 2015), these measures are easy enough that even students with severe disabilities will generally do well, but students who are not putting forth adequate effort (or who are *trying* to do poorly) will obtain low scores. Such measures are often used in neuropsychological evaluations (Martin, Schroeder, & Odland, 2015), but Harrison (2015) made an excellent case for incorporating them into routine psychoeducational evaluations. At the very least, they may be especially helpful in these kinds of differential diagnosis situations. Rapid Reference 15.2 lists several methods for distinguishing between SLD and emotional and behavioral problems.

SLD VERSUS SENSORY IMPAIRMENTS: RULE-OUTS OR COMORBIDITIES?

Difficulties with vision or hearing can have a substantial negative impact on the acquisition of reading, writing, and math skills (Kirk, Gallagher, & Coleman, 2015).

≡ Rapid Reference 15.2

Distinguishing Between SLD and Emotional and Behavioral Problems

There are several methods for differentiating between SLD and emotional and behavioral problems in students who have symptoms of both types of conditions:

- Use parent and teacher interviews, in conjunction with school records, to determine which type of problems (academic versus emotional and behavioral) started first.
- Conduct structured classroom observations to determine if students are attending to instruction sufficiently to have consistent exposure to academic material.
- Directly assess the cognitive/linguistic skills that have been found to underlie SLD as opposed to emotional and behavioral disorders.
- Try treating emotional/behavioral problems and assess for concomitant improvement in academic skills.
- Assess motivation and effort with performance validity tests to determine if students are putting forth adequate effort when completing academic tasks.

IDEA stipulates that SLD "does not include learning problems that are primarily the result of visual, hearing, or motor disabilities" (IDEA, 2004, §300.8(10)(ii)). At first glance, this seems to be a simple distinction to make. However, scholars have taken seriously the idea that a student could have comorbid visual impairments and learning disabilities (e.g., Jones, Smith, Hensley-Maloney, & Gansle, 2015) or comorbid hearing impairments and learning disabilities (Gilbertson & Ferre, 2008). Therefore, differential diagnosis is necessary here as well.

The issue of differential diagnosis is particularly interesting when one considers deaf students. This is because phonemic awareness is central to the development of skilled reading, and, due to their hearing impairment, it is extremely difficult for deaf students to develop phonemic awareness. On average, less than 15% of deaf students graduating from high school are able to read above a sixth-grade level, and most graduate reading at a third- to fourth-grade level (Goldin-Meadow & Mayberry, 2001; Lederberg, Schick, & Spencer, 2013). The ostensible reason is lack of phonemic awareness, which is also common in many students with SLD in reading. However, for most students who are deaf, their poor phonemic awareness is due to a problem in perceiving spoken phonemes. Presumably, most students who are deaf would have no difficulty in developing phonemic awareness were they not deaf. Thus, given that it is the deafness that prevents the development of phonemic awareness (and is thus responsible for the poor reading skills), we believe that deafness—not SLD—is the proper label for such students' problems.

Identifying students with genuine comorbid sensory impairments and SLD is beyond the scope of our chapter. Rather, our purpose is to attempt

> ## DON'T FORGET
> ....
> Students who are deaf often struggle tremendously with reading, likely due to inadequate access to the phonemic structure of spoken language. Such difficulties are a direct result of their sensory impairment and thus not best captured by the designation of SLD.

to differentiate between SLD and those other disabilities. It is likely that a subset of students with sensory disabilities also have SLD (i.e., these are students who would have struggled even if they had normal vision and hearing). However, if the judgment of the evaluation team is that vision or hearing issues are the primary source of poor reading, writing, or math skills, then deafness or visual impairment would generally be the most appropriate label. If, however, a student with a visual impairment is perfectly capable of perceiving printed text or numbers of a given font size yet still struggles in reading or math, SLD may be a more appropriate label. In such a case, it was not primarily the vision that was interfering with the reading because, even when the visual acuity issues were addressed via large enough print, the problems persisted. Similarly, if a student who is hearing impaired (not deaf) can distinguish all the phonemes of spoken English with hearing aids, yet continues to struggle in reading and displays characteristics of the phonological core deficit, then again, SLD may be a more appropriate designation.

SLD VERSUS THE AVERAGE-BUT-UNAPPRECIATED STUDENT

A final diagnostic alternative to consider in contrast to SLD is no diagnosis at all. Some students have academic skills that are in the average range or above, but fail to live up to the even-higher *expectations* for achievement in their family or school. Identifying such students as SLD was (and is) abetted by the use of ability-achievement discrepancy formulas because IQ is a common source of expectations for what a student's academic skill levels should be. Although the problems with these discrepancy formulas are well-known (e.g., Aaron, 1997; Sternberg & Grigorenko, 2002), many states continue to permit IQ-achievement discrepancies as the basis for SLD identification (Maki, Floyd, & Roberson, 2015). Similarly, even though the *DSM-5* has eliminated any requirement of a discrepancy in its diagnostic criteria for SLD (APA, 2013, pp. 66–67), in our experience, diagnosticians in private practice continue to use a discrepancy as the foundation of the diagnosis, especially in high-performing students.

Students with average achievement levels and high IQs are sometimes identified as intellectually gifted and SLD. This has been described as *dual exceptionality*, also known as *twice-exceptional* or *2/E* (e.g., Brody & Mills, 1997; Moon, Brighton, Callahan, & Jarvis, 2008). Scholars and practitioners who promote the use of these terms argue that giftedness and SLD are conditions that mask each other (the *masking hypothesis*; for further discussion, see Lovett, 2013; Lovett & Lewandowski, 2006). For example, Reis, Baum, and Burke (2014) assert that, in students with dual exceptionality, "their gifts may mask their disabilities and their disabilities may mask their gifts" (p. 222). In particular, proponents of the masking hypothesis have argued that, in gifted students with SLD, the giftedness enables the students to attain achievement test scores in the average range, thus "hiding" the learning disability.

As might be expected, such premises lead to a rejection of standard assessment approaches. For instance, van Viersen, Kroesbergen, Slot, and de Bree (2014) recently argued that, because gifted students with dyslexia have "high reading skills" (p. 189), they "require their own broader diagnostic criteria that take into account their high intelligence" (p. 197). Of course, students with high reading skills should not be identified as having dyslexia in the first place.[2] Similarly, students with SLD in written language should have below-average scores in that area, but in Assouline, Nicpon, and Whiteman's (2010) sample of twice-exceptional children with "SLD" in written language, the sample's mean scores on writing tests were in the average range. In samples like these, the students typically have high IQ scores and average achievement scores, and so the researchers use an ability-achievement discrepancy approach to define SLD, despite the problems of that approach. Other scholars and practitioners in the twice-exceptional area (e.g., Nielsen, 2002; Silverman, 2003) suggest looking at the scatter and profile of subtest scores on an IQ test to divine which students have giftedness and SLD. Unfortunately, there has been no agreement on what profile shows dual exceptionality, and scatter and profile analysis techniques lack reliability and validity evidence (Lovett & Lewandowski, 2006).

IQ is only one source of expectations for students' academic skills levels that leads students with average academic skills to be identified as SLD. Another source is students' family backgrounds. In high-achieving families, in which a student's parents and siblings have above-average academic skills, having only average skills can be mistaken for a disability. If the first child in a family was precocious and attained a certain level of reading skill by age 6, the second child may lag behind his or her sibling, prompting parental concern. We have worked with families in which exactly this happens. Admittedly, there are times when high-achieving families are unable to accept genuine disabilities, but, just as often, these families are worried about a child who is simply typical rather than superior to most of their same-age peers in the general population. Unfortunately, given the haphazard manner in which SLD is identified in schools and clinical settings, an SLD diagnosis is often made if parents are sufficiently concerned or put sufficient pressure on schools or private evaluators.

Parental concern, in turn, is influenced by another source of expectations for student achievement: local school standards. Schools vary widely in terms of their achievement levels. For instance, the 2015 average score on the SAT Mathematics section at Philadelphia's Masterman School was 678 (Pennsylvania Department of Education, n.d.), which is at the 90th percentile nationally (College Board, 2015). A student with only average mathematics skills would likely appear to be impaired at Masterman. By contrast, he or she might be a star pupil at another Philadelphia school, Fels High School, where the average 2015 SAT Mathematics score was 347 (a score at the 8th percentile nationally) and where most seniors did not even take the SAT. Masterman and Fels are public schools; the variability is even greater when one considers private schools, especially elite private schools where aptitude test scores are required for admission. We have seen students who were first diagnosed with learning disabilities when they failed to meet the achievement expectations of such schools. Rather than considering that the school placement was a poor match, an SLD identification was made, even when the student's academic skill levels were in the average range on standardized diagnostic achievement tests when compared against national norms.

A final, related group of students with average achievement levels being identified with SLD are young adults who are expected to perform in high-pressured settings such as elite colleges, graduate or professional schools, or who are trying to pass high-stakes exams for admission, certification, and licensure in high-achieving professions. Diagnosticians often use grade-based norms to score achievement tests for these clients, leading to much lower estimates of the clients' academic skills (Cressman & Liljequist, 2014; Giovingo, Proctor, & Prevatt, 2005). We have even seen Grade 18 norms used for the Woodcock-Johnson IV Tests of Achievement (Schrank, Mather, & McGrew, 2014) as the basis for SLD identification of medical students. Although grade norms may be clinically useful (i.e., in informing the individual about likely challenges in that educational setting), such norms should *not* be the basis of SLD identification. Indeed, a study of medical students and physicians referred for learning disability evaluations found that these individuals were typically in the average range on measures of achievement when compared to age norms and even when compared to college seniors (Banks, Guyer, & Guyer, 1995).

Similarly, at selective colleges, learning disability diagnoses appear to signify that students' skills are merely average, and perhaps below the level required to succeed without excessive effort at a rigorous school. Weis, Erickson, and Till (2017) found precisely that in the diagnostic evaluations of students at a selective liberal arts college who had been diagnosed with learning disabilities. Weis et al. (2017) concluded that

> although not disabled, they face the same hardships as the amateur photographer who wants to show her work in a professional gallery, the weekend golfer who tries for a spot on the Professional Golfers Association (PGA) Tour, or the small-town musician who auditions for the symphony of a major city. (p. 697)

To differentiate between SLD and cases such as the ones in this section, diagnosticians should require below-average achievement levels before SLD is even considered. By "below-average," we support the cutoff suggested in the *DSM-5* (APA, 2013): A student's skills in reading, mathematics, or writing should be at least one standard deviation below the mean for the student's age group. Students whose achievement is only low compared to excessive expectations may benefit from counseling or other supportive intervention, but an SLD label would not be appropriate.

C A U T I O N

Don't diagnose SLD in students with average or higher levels of academic skills relative to age norms. Sometimes students, their families, or their schools may be dissatisfied with merely average skills that are inadequate for performance in elite settings, but those skill levels are *not* indicative of a learning disability.

CONCLUSION

The boundaries of the SLD construct are often disputed. There are several reasons for this, including changes in our conceptualization of learning disabilities over the past century (Hallahan & Mock, 2003), the high prevalence of these disorders (compared, for example, to sensory impairments), and widely varying approaches to identification (see other chapters in this book). The disputed boundaries of SLD make differential diagnosis especially challenging. Differential diagnosis is nonetheless important; although all SLD involves low achievement, not all low achievement should lead to SLD identification.

In this chapter, we provided a definition of SLD before differentiating the construct from other difficulties that can cause low achievement. We concluded by considering students who do not even have low achievement, but who are increasingly identified with SLD. We encourage diagnosticians to take the exclusionary clauses of the SLD definition seriously and to engage in the type of assessment necessary to rule out other difficulties that could be causing academic concerns. Often this type of assessment requires collaboration between professionals in different disciplines, the recording of a thorough clinical history, or the use of assessment tools beyond measures of achievement. Proper identification of SLD is not simple, but it is often vital to the formulation of appropriate intervention strategies.

⚓ TEST YOURSELF ⚓

1. **The process of distinguishing between SLD and other IDEA diagnostic categories is called:**
   (a) SLD diagnosis
   (b) SLD determination
   (c) Differential diagnosis
   (d) Disability determination

2. **All the following represent assumptions behind the definition of an SLD presented in this chapter except:**
   (a) A discrepancy will be present between the low achievement and some other area of achievement or aptitude.
   (b) A deficit will typically be present in one or more cognitive/linguistic skills known to affect the acquisition of reading, writing, or math.
   (c) Students with learning difficulties differ from typically developing students quantitatively along any one of a number of continua of cognitive/linguistic or academic skills and do not differ qualitatively.
   (d) Academic skills are based largely on student-level factors (cognitive/linguistic skills and motivation) and environmental factors (learning opportunities).

3. **The most researched skill area within SLD is:**
   (a) Word-level reading skills
   (b) Reading comprehension
   (c) Math skills
   (d) Written expression

4. **Performance validity tests are designed to assess:**
   (a) Academic skills, especially mathematics
   (b) Internalizing disorders, such as anxiety and depression
   (c) A student's tendency toward extroversion versus introversion
   (d) The amount of effort being put forth during an evaluation

5. The kinds of cognitive-linguistic deficits that underlie **SLD** are unique to SLD and not typically found in students with other designations such as **SLI, ED, ID,** or **OHI** who struggle in reading. True or false?

6. Students with borderline intellectual functioning (IQs of 71 to 85) often fall through the cracks in terms of receiving additional services. However, what designation appropriately applies to a large proportion of these students?

   (a) Other health impaired (OHI)
   (b) Specific learning disability (SLD)
   (c) Intellectual disability (ID)
   (d) Speech or language impaired (SLI)

7. The unsupported practice of disqualifying students with borderline intellectual functioning from being considered as having an **SLI** because their other cognitive skills are consistent with or lower than their language skills is called:

   (a) Undifferentiating diagnosis
   (b) Following the aptitude-linguistic discrepancy requirement
   (c) Cognitive referencing
   (d) Implementing the IQ consistency clause

8. Which of the following is *not* one of the ways, suggested in the chapter, of determining whether emotional or behavioral issues are the primary source of academic skills deficiencies?

   (a) Directly testing for deficits in the cognitive and linguistic skills that may underlie the academic skill deficits
   (b) Directly asking the student to provide insight into why he or she struggles in reading and attempting to tie this back to emotional issues such as anxiety or depression
   (c) Doing direct classroom observation in a classroom setting
   (d) Doing a careful history based on parental or teacher input to determine which came first—the emotional or behavioral issues or the academic issues

9. The likely reason that students who are deaf struggle in reading is:

   (a) Inadequate access to the phonemic structure of spoken language
   (b) The phonological core deficit found in students with dyslexia
   (c) Low teacher expectations and related stigma
   (d) Shared genetic bases for deafness and SLD

10. Students with "dual exceptionality" or who are "twice-exceptional" are said to have:

    (a) SLD and an emotional disorder
    (b) SLD and intellectual disability
    (c) Learning disabilities but their achievement levels are average, purportedly being elevated by their giftedness

(d) Changed their disability category during development (e.g., from speech or language impaired to SLD)

Answers: 1. c; 2. a; 3. a; 4. d; 5. False; 6. d; 7. c; 8. b; 9. a; 10. c.

NOTES

1. Despite popular beliefs about dyslexia being based in visual-perceptual deficits, empirical research has failed to support those beliefs (Kilpatrick, 2015; Lewandowski & Lovett, 2014).
2. It is certainly possible, in theory, for a student with high general intelligence to use alternative strategies for reading or other academic tasks, but at present, the masking hypothesis has never been rigorously tested with empirical data. Moreover, in a student who has average or above-average levels of academic skills, the SLD label would be inappropriate, even if the student is using his or her high general intelligence to compensate for specific underlying cognitive/academic skill weaknesses.

REFERENCES

Aaron, P. G. (1997). The impending demise of the discrepancy formula. *Review of Educational Research, 67*(4), 461–502.

Ahmed, Y., Wagner, R. K., & Kantor, P. T. (2012). How visual word recognition is affected by developmental dyslexia. In J. S. Adelman (Ed.), *Visual word recognition: Meaning and context, individuals and development* (Vol. 2, pp. 196–215). New York, NY: Psychology Press.

American Psychiatric Association. (2013). *Diagnostic and statistical manual of mental disorders* (5th ed.). Arlington, VA: Author.

American Speech-Language-Hearing Association (ASHA). (n.d.). *Eligibility and dismissal in schools.* Retrieved from www.asha.org/slp/schools/prof-consult/eligibility

Assouline, S. G., Nicpon, M. F., & Whiteman, C. (2010). Cognitive and psychosocial characteristics of gifted students with written language disability. *Gifted Child Quarterly, 54*, 102–115.

Balu, R., Zhu, P., Doolittle, F., Schiller, E., Jenkins, J., & Gersten, R. (2015). *Evaluation of response to intervention practices for elementary school reading* (NCEE 2016–4000). Washington, DC: National Center for Education Evaluation and Regional Assistance, Institute of Education Sciences, US Department of Education.

Banks, S. R., Guyer, B. P., & Guyer, K. E. (1995). A study of medical students and physicians referred for learning disabilities. *Annals of Dyslexia, 45*(1), 233–245.

Blair, C., & Scott, K. G. (2002). Proportion of LD placements associated with low socioeconomic status: Evidence for a gradient? *The Journal of Special Education, 36*, 14–22.

Brody, L. E., & Mills, C. J. (1997). Gifted children with learning disabilities: A review of the issues. *Journal of Learning Disabilities, 30*, 282–296.

Carroll, J. M., Bowyer-Crane, C., Duff, F., Hulme, C., & Snowling, M. J. (2011). *Developing language and literacy: Effective interventions in the early years.* Chichester, UK: Wiley.

Clarke, P. J., Truelove, E., Hulme, C., & Snowling, M. J. (2014). *Developing reading comprehension*. Chichester, UK: Wiley.

College Board (2015). *2015 college-bound seniors: Critical reading, mathematics, and writing percentile ranks*. Retrieved from https://secure-media.collegeboard.org/digitalServices/pdf/sat/sat-percentile-ranks-crit-reading-math-writing-2014.pdf

Cressman, M. N., & Liljequist, L. (2014). The effect of grade norms in college students using the Woodcock-Johnson III Tests of Achievement. *Journal of Learning Disabilities, 47*(3), 271–278.

Denton, C. A., Fletcher, J. M., Anthony, J. L., & Francis, D. J. (2007). An evaluation of intensive intervention for students with persistent reading difficulties. *Journal of Learning Disabilities, 39*(5), 447–466.

Ferrari, M. (2009). Borderline intellectual functioning and the intellectual disability construct. *Intellectual and Developmental Disabilities, 47*(5), 386–389.

Fletcher, J. M., Lyon, G. R., Fuchs, L. S., & Barnes, M. A. (2018). *Learning disabilities: From identification to intervention* (2nd ed.). New York, NY: Guilford.

Fletcher, J. M., & Morris, R. (1986). Classification of disabled learners: Beyond exclusionary definitions. In S. J. Ceci (Ed.), *Handbook of cognitive, social, and neuropsychological aspects of learning disabilities* (Vol. 1, pp. 55–80). Hillsdale, NJ: Erlbaum.

Foorman, B. R. (Ed.). (2003). *Preventing and remediating reading difficulties: Bringing science to scale*. Baltimore, MD: York Press.

Foorman, B., & Al Otaiba, S. (2009). Reading remediation: State of the art. In K. Pugh & P. McCardle (Eds.), *How children learn to read: Current issues and new directions in the integration of cognition, neurobiology and genetics of reading and dyslexia research and practice* (pp. 257–274). New York, NY: Psychology Press.

Gilbertson, D., & Ferre, S. (2008). Considerations in the identification, assessment, and intervention process for deaf and hard of hearing students with reading difficulties. *Psychology in the Schools, 45*, 104–120. doi:10.1002/pits.20286

Giovingo, L. K., Proctor, B. E., & Prevatt, F. (2005). Use of grade-based norms versus age-based norms in psychoeducational assessment for a college population. *Journal of Learning Disabilities, 38*(1), 79–85.

Goldin-Meadow, S., & Mayberry, R. I. (2001). How do profoundly deaf children learn to read? *Learning Disabilities Research & Practice, 16*, 222–229. doi:10.1111/0938-8982.00022

Gresham, F. M., MacMillan, D. L., & Bocian, K. M. (1996). Learning disabilities, low achievement, and mild mental retardation: More alike than different? *Journal of Learning Disabilities, 29*(6), 570–581.

Hale, J. B., Kaufman, A., Naglieri, J. A., & Kavale, K. A. (2006). Implementation of IDEA: Integrating response to intervention and cognitive assessment methods. *Psychology in the Schools, 43*(7), 753–770.

Hallahan, D. P., & Mock, D. R. (2003). A brief history of the field of learning disabilities. In H. L. Swanson, K. R. Harris, & S. Graham (Eds.), *Handbook of learning disabilities* (pp. 16–29). New York, NY: Guilford.

Harrison, A. G. (2015). Child and adolescent psychoeducational evaluations. In M. W. Kirkwood (Ed.), *Validity testing in child and adolescent assessment: Evaluating exaggeration, feigning, and noncredible effort* (pp. 185–206). New York, NY: Guilford.

Hulme, C., & Snowling, M. J. (2009). *Developmental disorders of language learning and cognition*. Malden, MA: Wiley-Blackwell.

Johnson, E. S., Humphrey, M., Mellard, D. F., Woods, K., & Swanson, H. L. (2010). Cognitive processing deficits and students with specific learning disabilities: A selective meta-analysis of the literature. *Learning Disability Quarterly, 33*(1), 3–18.

Jones, B. A., Smith, H. H., Hensley-Maloney, L., & Gansle, K. A. (2015). Applying response to intervention to identify learning disabilities in students with visual impairments. *Intervention in School and Clinic, 51*, 28–36. doi:10.1177/1053451215577475

Jopp, D. A., & Keys, C. B. (2001). Diagnostic overshadowing reviewed and reconsidered. *American Journal on Mental Retardation, 106*(5), 416–433.

Kilpatrick, D. A. (2015). *Essentials of assessing, preventing, and overcoming reading difficulties*. Hoboken, NJ: Wiley.

Kirk, S. A., Gallagher, J. J., & Coleman, M. R. (2015). *Educating exceptional children* (14th ed.). Stamford, CT: Cengage Learning.

Kirkwood, M. W. (2015). Review of pediatric performance and symptom validity tests. In M. W. Kirkwood (Ed.), *Validity testing in child and adolescent assessment: Evaluating exaggeration, feigning, and noncredible effort* (pp. 79–106). New York, NY: Guilford.

Klassen, R. M., Tze, V. M., & Hannok, W. (2013). Internalizing problems of adults with learning disabilities: A meta-analysis. *Journal of Learning Disabilities, 46*(4), 317–327.

Koritsas, S., & Iacono, T. (2011). Secondary conditions in people with developmental disability. *American Journal of Intellectual and Developmental Disabilities, 116*(1), 36–47.

Lederberg, A. R., Schick, B., & Spencer, P. E. (2013). Language and literacy development of deaf and hard-of-hearing children: Successes and challenges. *Developmental Psychology, 49*(1), 15–30. doi:10.1037/a0029558

Lewandowski, L. J., & Lovett, B. J. (2014). Learning disabilities. In E. J. Mash & R. A. Barkley (Eds.), *Child psychopathology* (3rd ed., pp. 625–669). New York, NY: Guilford.

Lovett, B. J. (2013). The science and politics of gifted students with learning disabilities: A social inequality perspective. *Roeper Review, 35*(2), 136–143.

Lovett, B. J., & Gordon, M. (2005). Discrepancies as a basis for the assessment of learning disabilities and ADHD. *ADHD Report, 13*(3), 1–4.

Lovett, B. J., & Lewandowski, L. J. (2006). Gifted students with learning disabilities: Who are they? *Journal of Learning Disabilities, 39*(6), 515–527.

Lyon, G. R. (1995). Toward a definition of dyslexia. *Annals of Dyslexia, 45*(1), 1–27.

MacMillan, D. L., Gresham, F. M., & Bocian, K. M. (1998). Discrepancy between definitions of learning disabilities and school practices an empirical investigation. *Journal of Learning Disabilities, 31*(4), 314–326.

Maki, K. E., Floyd, R. G., & Roberson, T. (2015). State learning disability eligibility criteria: A comprehensive review. *School Psychology Quarterly, 30*(4), 457–469.

Mammarella, I. C., Ghisi, M., Bomba, M., Bottesi, G., Caviola, S., Broggi, F., & Nacinovich, R. (2016). Anxiety and depression in children with nonverbal learning disabilities, reading disabilities, or typical development. *Journal of Learning Disabilities, 49*, 130–139.

Marieb, E. N., & Hoehn, K. (2007). *Human anatomy and physiology* (7th ed.). San Francisco, CA: Pearson.

Martin, P. K., Schroeder, R. W., & Odland, A. P. (2015). Neuropsychologists' validity testing beliefs and practices: A survey of North American professionals. *The Clinical Neuropsychologist, 29*(6), 741–776.

Moon, T. R., Brighton, C. M., Callahan, C. M., & Jarvis, J. M. (2008). Twice-exceptional students: Being gifted and learning disabled—implications of IDEIA. In E. L. Grigorenko (Ed.), *Educating individuals with disabilities: IDEIA 2004 and beyond* (pp. 295–317). New York, NY: Springer.

Nielsen, M. E. (2002). Gifted students with learning disabilities: Recommendations for identification and programming. *Exceptionality, 10*, 93–111.

Oakhill, J., Cain, K., & Elbro, C. (2015). *Understanding and teaching reading comprehension: A handbook*. New York, NY: Routledge.

Peltopuro, M., Ahonen, T., Kaartinen, J., Seppälä, H., & Närhi, V. (2014). Borderline intellectual functioning: A systematic literature review. *Intellectual and Developmental Disabilities, 52*(6), 419–443.

Pennsylvania Department of Education. (n.d.). *SAT and ACT scores*. Retrieved from www.education.pa.gov/K-12/Assessment and Accountability/Pages/SAT-and-ACT.aspx

Reis, S. M., Baum, S. M., & Burke, E. (2014). An operational definition of twice-exceptional learners: Implications and applications. *Gifted Child Quarterly, 58*(3), 217–230.

Schrank, F. A., Mather, N., & McGrew, K. S. (2014). *Woodcock-Johnson IV Tests of Achievement*. Rolling Meadows, IL: Riverside.

Senf, G. (1987). Learning disabilities as sociologic sponge: Wiping up life's spills. In S. Vaughn & C. Bos (Eds.), *Research in learning disabilities: Issues and future directions* (pp. 87–101). Boston, MA: Little, Brown.

Shaw, S. R. (2008). An educational programming framework for a subset of students with diverse learning needs: Borderline intellectual functioning. *Intervention in School and Clinic, 43*(5), 291–299.

Silverman, L. K. (2003). Gifted children with learning disabilities. In N. A. Colangelo & G. A. Davis (Eds.), *Handbook of gifted education* (3rd ed., pp. 533–543). Boston, MA: Allyn & Bacon.

Stanovich, K. E. (2005). The future of a mistake: Will discrepancy measurement continue to make the learning disabilities field a pseudoscience? *Learning Disability Quarterly, 28*(2), 103–106.

Sternberg, R. J., & Grigorenko, E. L. (2002). Difference scores in the identification of children with learning disabilities: It's time to use a different method. *Journal of School Psychology, 40*(1), 65–83.

Stuebing, K. K., Barth, A. E., Trahan, L. H., Reddy, R. R., Miciak, J., & Fletcher, J. M. (2015). Are child cognitive characteristics strong predictors of responses to intervention? A meta-analysis. *Review of Educational Research, 85*, 395–429.

Sundheim, S. T., & Voeller, K. K. (2004). Psychiatric implications of language disorders and learning disabilities: Risks and management. *Journal of Child Neurology, 19*(10), 814–826.

Tassé, M. J., Schalock, R. L., Balboni, G., Bersani, H., Jr., Borthwick-Duffy, S. A., Spreat, S., . . . & Zhang, D. (2012). The construct of adaptive behavior: Its conceptualization, measurement, and use in the field of intellectual disability. *American Journal on Intellectual and Developmental Disabilities, 117*(4), 291–303.

Torgesen, J. K. (2004). Lessons learned from the last 20 years of research on interventions for students who experience difficulty learning to read. In P. McCardle & V. Chhabra (Eds.), *The voice of evidence in reading research* (pp. 355–382). Baltimore, MD: Brookes.

Torgesen, J. K. (2005). Recent discoveries on remedial interventions for children with dyslexia. In M. J. Snowling & C. Hulme (Eds.), *The science of reading: A handbook* (pp. 521–537). Malden, MA: Wiley-Blackwell.

Torgesen, J. K., Rashotte, C. A., Alexander, A., Alexander, J., & MacPhee, K. (2003). Progress toward understanding the instructional conditions necessary for remediating reading difficulties in older children. In B. R. Foorman (Ed.), *Preventing and remediating reading difficulties: Bringing science to scale* (pp. 275–297). Baltimore, MD: York Press.

van Viersen, S., Kroesbergen, E. H., Slot, E. M., & de Bree, E. H. (2014). High reading skills mask dyslexia in gifted children. *Journal of Learning Disabilities, 49*, 189–199.

Vellutino, F. R., Fletcher, J. M., Snowling, M. J., & Scanlon, D. M. (2004). Specific reading disability (dyslexia): What have we learned in the past four decades? *Journal of Child Psychology and Psychiatry, 45*(1), 2–40.

Watkins, M. W., Lei, P. W., & Canivez, G. L. (2007). Psychometric intelligence and achievement: A cross-lagged panel analysis. *Intelligence, 35*(1), 59–68.

Wei, X., Blackorby, J., & Schiller, E. (2011). Growth in reading achievement of students with disabilities, ages 7 to 17. *Exceptional Children, 78*(1), 89–106.

Weis, R. (2014). *Introduction to abnormal child and adolescent psychology* (2nd ed.). Los Angeles, CA: Sage.

Weis, R., Erickson, C. P., & Till, C. H. (2017). When average is not good enough: Students with learning disabilities at selective, private colleges. *Journal of Learning Disabilities, 50*, 684–700.

Willcutt, E. G., & Pennington, B. F. (2000). Psychiatric comorbidity in children and adolescents with reading disability. *Journal of Child Psychology and Psychiatry, 41*(8), 1039–1048.

ABOUT THE EDITORS

Vincent C. Alfonso, PhD, is the dean of the School of Education at Gonzaga University. He is past president of Division 16 (School Psychology) of the American Psychological Association (APA), fellow of Divisions 5, 16, and 43 of the APA, and a certified school psychologist and licensed psychologist. Most recently, Dr. Alfonso received the Jack Bardon Distinguished Service Award from Division 16. He has been providing psychoeducational services to individuals across the life span for more than 25 years and is the coeditor of *Essentials of Specific Learning Disability Identification*, 2nd edition, and coauthor of *Essentials of Cross-Battery Assessment*, 3rd edition.

Dawn P. Flanagan, PhD, is professor of psychology at St. John's University and affiliate clinical professor of psychology at Yale Child Study Center, Yale University School of Medicine. She serves as an expert witness, learning disabilities consultant, and psychoeducational test–measurement consultant and trainer for national and international organizations. Dr. Flanagan is an author and editor of numerous publications, including more than 20 books on assessment and learning disabilities. She is best known for her development of the Cross-Battery Assessment approach and the Dual Discrepancy/Consistency operational definition of specific learning disabilities.

Essentials of Specific Learning Disability Identification, Second Edition.
Edited by Vincent C. Alfonso and Dawn P. Flanagan
© 2018 John Wiley & Sons, Inc. Published 2018 by John Wiley & Sons, Inc.

ABOUT THE CONTRIBUTORS

Vincent C. Alfonso, PhD, School of Education, Gonzaga University, Spokane, WA

Nicole Lynne Alston-Abel, PhD, Federal Way Public Schools, Federal Way, WA

Virginia Berninger, PhD, Department of Educational Psychology, College of Education, University of Washington, Seattle, WA

Rachel M. Bridges, Department of Psychology, University of South Carolina, Columbia, SC

Matthew K. Burns, PhD, College of Education, University of Missouri, Columbia, MO

Gail M. Cheramie, PhD, University of Houston–Clear Lake, Houston, TX

Scott L. Decker, PhD, Department of Psychology, University of South Carolina, Columbia, SC

Steven G. Feifer, DEd, Monocacy Neurodevelopmental Center, Frederick, MD

Dawn P. Flanagan, PhD, Department of Psychology, St. John's University, Jamaica, NY, and Yale Child Study Center, Yale University, School of Medicine, New Haven, CT

Jack M. Fletcher, PhD, Department of Psychology, University of Houston, Houston, TX

David A. Kilpatrick, PhD, State University of New York at Cortland, Cortland, NY

Benjamin J. Lovett, PhD, State University of New York at Cortland, Cortland, NY

Kathrin E. Maki, Department of Educational Psychology, Ball State, Muncie, IN

Essentials of Specific Learning Disability Identification, Second Edition.
Edited by Vincent C. Alfonso and Dawn P. Flanagan
© 2018 John Wiley & Sons, Inc. Published 2018 by John Wiley & Sons, Inc.

Jennifer T. Mascolo, PsyD, Department of Psychology, St. John's University, Jamaica, NY

Nancy Mather, PhD, Department of Psychoeducational Studies, University of Arizona, Tucson, AZ

Michèle M. M. Mazzocco, PhD, Institute of Child Development, University of Minnesota, Minneapolis, MN

Erin M. McDonough, PhD, Graduate School of Applied and Professional Psychology, Rutgers University, Piscataway, NJ

Kristan E. Melo, Department of Psychology, St. John's University, Jamaica, NY

Jeremy Miciak, PhD, Department of Psychology, University of Houston, Houston, TX

Jack A. Naglieri, PhD, University of Virginia, Charlottesville, VA, and Devereux Center for Resilient Children, Villanova, PA

Nickola Wolf Nelson, PhD, Department of Speech Pathology and Audiology, Western Michigan University, Kalamazoo, MI

Samuel O. Ortiz, PhD, Department of Psychology, St. John's University, Jamaica, NY

June L. Preast, Department of Educational Psychology, University of Missouri, Columbia, MO

G. Thomas Schanding Jr., University of Houston–Clear Lake, Houston, TX

Margaret Semrud-Clikeman, PhD, Department of Pediatrics, the University of Minnesota Minneapolis Medical School, Minneapolis, MN

Marlene Sotelo-Dynega, PhD, Department of Psychology, St. John's University, Jamaica, NY

Kristin Streich, University of Houston–Clear Lake, Houston, TX

Megan C. Sy, Department of Psychology, St. John's University, Jamaica, NY

Meghan A. Terzulli, Department of Psychology, St. John's University, Jamaica, NY

Tayllor Vetter, Department of Psychology, University of South Carolina, Columbia, SC

Rose Vukovic, PhD, Department of Educational Psychology, University of Minnesota, Minneapolis, MN

Kristy Warmbold-Brann, Department of Educational Psychology, Miami University of Ohio

Barbara J. Wendling, MA, Consultant, Dallas, TX

Elizabeth H. Wiig, PhD, Professor Emerita, Boston University, Boston, MA

Author Index

Aaron, P. G., 14, 378, 561
Abbott, R. D., 114, 168, 294, 308, 309, 317–320
Abbott, S. P., 114
Abell, F., 198
Abrams, D. A., 43, 295, 456
Abu-Akel, A., 199
Adams, A. M., 170
Adams, G., 265
Adelstein, J. S., 297
Adlof, S. M., 146, 150
Adolphs, R., 199
Ahissar, M., 160
Ahmad, S. A., 195, 202
Ahmed, Y., 242, 308, 553
Ahonen, T., 555
Akbudak, E., 199
Alexander, A., 557
Alexander, J., 557
Alfonso, V. C., 115, 329–332, 335, 336, 338, 340, 342, 350, 351, 371, 385, 386, 460, 476, 482, 483, 517–519
Algina, J., 261
Algozzine, B., 270
Alibali, M. W., 71
Allen, E., 119
Allen, S. H., 262
Alloway, R. G., 79
Alloway, T. P., 79

Alonzo, C. N., 149, 178
Alston-Abel, N. L., 17, 310, 321
Amaral, D. G., 199
American Educational Research Association, 506
American Psychiatric Association, 35, 62, 104, 151, 555, 561, 564
American Psychological Association, 506
Andersen, M. N., 266
Anderson, D., 167
Anderson, L., 115
Anderson, M. A., 181
Anderson, P., 167
Anderson, V., 167
Andrade, C., 105
Ansari, D., 43, 62, 67–69, 83, 84, 89–91, 354
Anthony, H., 115
Anthony, J. L., 556
Anticevic, A., 297
Antshel, K., 205
Applebee, A. N., 123
Appleton, J. J., 268
Aquilino, S. A., 462, 463
Arañas, Y. A., 272
Araújo, S., 35
Archer, A. L., 265
Archibald, L., 83
Ardila, A., 443

Essentials of Specific Learning Disability Identification, Second Edition.
Edited by Vincent C. Alfonso and Dawn P. Flanagan
© 2018 John Wiley & Sons, Inc. Published 2018 by John Wiley & Sons, Inc.

Subject Index

Ability tests, 372
Ability-achievement discrepancy
  dual exceptionality and, 562
  IDEIA amendments on, 257, 267
  LDs and, 330
  reading disabilities identification
    and, 32–33
  RTI compared to, 271–273
  shortcomings of, 32, 257
  SLD identification with, 14–15, 20,
    226, 227, 330
Academic weaknesses, 18, 19,
  357–359
ACC. *See* Alternative Cognitive
  Composite; Anterior cingulate
  cortex
Achievement. *See also* Ability-
  achievement discrepancy; Low
  achievement
  actual compared to potential, 552
  CELF-5 measuring SLD areas of,
    339–341
  C-SEP and, 479–480
  C-SEP measurement of, 497–498
  DD/C measurement of, 497–498
  DD/C model level 1 analysis of,
    337–341
  factors that inhibit and facilitate,
    342

gifted student identification and,
  248–249
IQ, discrepancy in, 227, 249
KTEA measuring SLD areas of,
  339–341
math function etiology, CHC
  domains and math, 354–355
NLDs and, 202
PASS theory relationship to,
  465–467
reading function etiology, CHC
  domains and reading, 352–353
WIAT-III measuring SLD areas of,
  339–341
writing function etiology, CHC
  domains and writing, 356–357
Achievement score-cutoff approach,
  for MLD identification, 60–62
Adaptive functioning exclusionary
  factors, in SLD identification,
  345
ADHD. *See* Attention-deficit
  hyperactivity disorder
ADI-R. *See* Autism Diagnostic
  Interview–Revised
Age-equivalent scores, in
  norm-referenced testing, 177
Altered assessments, test score validity
  and, 507–508

Essentials of Specific Learning Disability Identification, Second Edition.
Edited by Vincent C. Alfonso and Dawn P. Flanagan
© 2018 John Wiley & Sons, Inc. Published 2018 by John Wiley & Sons, Inc.